3 -

Re D

"[*Word Finder*]* is an ingenious idea. . . . It shows you how to look up words you can't get even close to on your own."
—George Christian, "The Houston Chronicle"

". . .the cleverest method I have yet seen for showing the correct spelling of words that one cannot spell—even those to which you may not have a clue. . . . As a simple solution to a problem that besets many people, [*Word Finder*] stands out as a useful and elegant solution."
—Laurence Urdang, "VERBATIM, The Language Quarterly"
(Spring 1983)

". . .a valuable resource."
—Reprinted by permission of the American Library Association from *Booklist* (March, 1983), page 868; copyright 1983 by ALA.

"The book will help poor spellers find the correct spelling to words they do not know how to look up in a conventional dictionary. . . . [*Word Finder*] looks promising for poor spellers at virtually every level above the fifth or sixth grade.
—Reprinted with permission from the October 1983 issue of *Curriculum Review*, published by Curriculum Advisory Service, Chicago, Illinois.

"Morrison's invention is simple, and it works. . . . If you can say it, you can look it up. . . . Morrison's language tool is now as new as the thesaurus, also a language tool, once was. It is equally useful, and when the poor spellers of the world discover that deliverance from their misery is at hand, Morrison's name may become as illustrious as Roget's."
—Julie Jacoby, Editor, "The Workbook" - Vol. VIII, page 142 (July-October, 1983) Reprinted with permission from the Southwest Research and Information Center.

Word Finder is a revision of Word City: a new language tool, published in 1982.

Testimonials

"The book is a clever compendium. . . . It is designed for those whose visual memory may be poor or less than it once was. It is also for those dyslexics for whom spelling is difficult but who can recognize the word they are seeking. . . . In fact, word lovers of every description should be grateful to Mr. Morrison for the certainty this book gives to the unsure speller."
—Alice Ann Koontz, Adjunct Instructor
The Johns Hopkins University
Baltimore, Maryland

"I am a tutor of learning disabled elementary students and encourage all of my 4th- to 6th-grade students to own and use this book."
—Marjorie Lacey
Findlay, Ohio

"I have shared your book with my students as well as with many of my colleagues. The responses have been amazing and exciting. Almost everyone has wanted a copy, including students who want to pay for it out of their allowances! I even had one young girl recently refer to it as 'that awesome book'. . . . It is an extraordinary book."
—Cathryn C. Weiss, Speech/Language Pathologist
Downingtown, Pennsylvania

"It is exactly what I need to use with my learning disabled language students."
—Casey Zawacki, Teacher of LD students
Circleville, Ohio

"It just seems I can't stop telling people what a wonderful resource this book is."
—Becky A. Ritter, Speech and Language Therapist
West Grove, Pennsylvania

The Phonic Key To The Dictionary

WORD FINDER

WORD FINDER
The Phonic Key
to the
Dictionary

Originated and Compiled by
Marvin L. Morrison

Edited by
Penelope A. Kister and Marvin L. Morrison

Pilot Light
Stone Mountain, Georgia

To
Spencer and Chad
and
all of us
who have asked,

"How can I look it up if I can't spell it?"

Published in the United States of America by:

Pilot Light
Stone Mountain, GA 30086-0305

Cover Design by Parrish Communications, Norcross, GA

Word Finder: the Phonic Key to the Dictionary is a revision of
Word City: a new language tool published in 1982.

Library of Congress Catalog Card Number 86-61846

ISBN 0-9608376-1-2

First Printing

CONTENTS

INTRODUCTION to the REVISED EDITION ix

INTRODUCTION xi

PREFACE xiii

GUIDE to the USE of THIS BOOK xv

    Addresses xv

    Sound Symbols. xvi

    Guidelines xviii

    Hints xx

    Additional Information xx

    Abbreviations xx

KEY to SOUND SYMBOLS xxi

WORD FINDER 1

PUNCTUATION GUIDELINES 355

INTRODUCTION
to the
REVISED EDITION

Marvin Morrison may prove to be one of the best friends that dyslexics and poor spellers have ever had. His strikingly simple and effective book has the power to set poor spellers free from the embarrassment and reluctance to write that goes along with spelling difficulty. Morrison's book becomes a liberating tool for everyone who has trouble looking up those words they can't spell in the first place.

A copy of this book belongs on the desk of every teacher in America, and in the bookbag of many a student (not to mention those copies that could profitably be tucked away in the briefcases of professionals and executives). Marvin Morrison has rendered exemplary service to lexicography and orthography with this little book. It is my hope that this revised edition will receive the critical attention and the wide usage that it deserves.

Wood Smethurst, Ed. D.
Director
Emory University Reading Center
March, 1987

INTRODUCTION

English orthography, the system of rules and customs by which English words are spelled, represents a bewildering challenge to anyone learning to write or read the language. Not only is our spelling system difficult for the foreigner, it is difficult for the native born as well.

To be a good speller in English means, as a matter of practicality, that one must have an exceptional visual memory for word forms. Knowledge of rules does not help you much with words like *steak*, say or *bough*, or *their*. It is a melancholy fact that being able to speak a word does not offer the poor speller any assurance that she or he can find that word in a dictionary.

At least, such has been the case up until now. Marvin Morrison has come forward with a new system of word-finding which, I believe, has great power and simplicity. Indeed, the fact that the system is exceptionally easy to learn and to use is perhaps its strongest recommendation.

Using Mr. Morrison's materials, a poor speller can look up quickly and accurately such words as *chloroform, recondite, accommodate, gnomon,* and so on. With this system, the poor speller receives substantial help for the first time since speakers of English began to tinker with their alphabet centuries ago.

Wood Smethurst, Ed. D.
Director
Emory University Reading Center
August, 1982

PREFACE

Word Finder is a new threshold to information. This new language tool uses *sound*, not spelling, to identify a word's location. This means that you can quickly look up a word without having to know how it's spelled.

The problem of looking up a word you can't spell has been with us for a long time. For me, it was the hardest part of dictionary usage. This is how the problem came about:

In the late 1400's, England was in the midst of the Renaissance (the period of Western civilization's transition from the Middle Ages to modern times). At the same time, our language was changing from Middle English to Modern English. There were several varieties of English and no dictionaries. And since there was no general agreement about spelling among scholars, people who could write spelled words the way they pronounced them: phonetically. Because of this, there were variant spellings for almost all words.

The printing press and movable type had just arrived from Germany and the Netherlands. And when the early printers set their type, they too spelled words the way they pronounced them: phonetically. The new printing technology quickly made knowledge and learning available to larger and larger numbers of people. Before long, English spelling had become fixed on the printed page by the early printers.

In the 1600's and 1700's, when the first dictionaries appeared, English spelling became standardized and kept many of its earlier phonetic spellings.

What caused the differences between spelling and pronunciation that we have today? With the introduction of printing, spelling change slowed drastically while change in pronunciation continued to evolve. So, what we have today is our Modern English pronunciation with its heritage of Middle English spelling.

A major step in solving this problem occurred in the 1960's, when Joseph Krevisky and Jordan L. Linfield published *The Bad Speller's Dictionary* (now published by Random House). Their system places the word *phone* under the spelling *fone*. This method works well. Its drawback is that one's visual memory may adopt the misspelled words. (The number of words it contains is somewhat limited because of the many vowel combinations that would be required to include a large number of words.)

Word Finder takes the next logical step: it drops the vowel sounds and places the word *phone* under the *address* **FN**.

Our modern alphabet can be traced to the Phoenicians and other Semites of Syria and Palestine, who developed related syllabaries. (A syllabary is not an alphabet because it doesn't contain symbols for vowel sounds.) Later on, the Greeks adopted the Phoenician syllabary, modified it, developed symbols for vowel sounds and produced the world's first alphabet. Being a syllabary system, *Word Finder* is based on these early concepts of written language.

This book began as a project that was prompted by my inability to satisfactorily answer a question posed repeatedly by my sons, Spencer and Chad: "But Dad, how can I look it up if I can't spell it?"

My intent for this book is that it will save time and eliminate frustration when you want to find or check the spelling of English words.

Marvin L. Morrison
February, 1987

GUIDE to the USE of THIS BOOK

Word Finder uses *sound*, not spelling, to locate words. Being able to look up a word's sound lets you find words easily and quickly — no matter how they are spelled.

The best way to learn how to use this book is to:

- Read the following sections to make sure you know the basics and
- Practice looking up a few words.

Addresses

Just as you have an *address* that tells where your home is located, each word has an *address* that tells where it is is located in *Word Finder*.

- A word's address is made from the *consonant sounds* that you *hear* when the word is spoken.

  (Consonant sounds are made when your breath flow is blocked or partially blocked in some way. So, when you say a word *slowly* and bring your attention to what is happening to your *lips* and *tongue*, the consonant sounds stand out.)

- Vowel sounds are not used in making addresses.

An example:

- The word *phone* has two consonant sounds: the **F** sound and the **N** sound.
- When you put these two sounds together (leaving out the vowel sound on purpose), you have made the address for the word *phone*: **FN**.

So, if you wanted to find the word *phone*, you would look up the *address*: **FN**.

Sound Symbols

- Each of the twenty-four consonant sounds in English is linked with a SOUND SYMBOL that is *always* used for that sound.

The KEY to SOUND SYMBOLS (on page xxi) lists all of the SOUND SYMBOLS. The following sound-to-symbol linkages are the ones I feel will assist you most in making addresses:

- The address for the word *honest* is **NST**.
- The word *honest* has the *h* letter, but not the **H** sound. (Think sound.)

- The two sounds **G** and **J** can be confused if you are not careful because the letter *g* is often pronounced as a **J** sound as in the word *age* — **J**.

- The address for the word *human* includes the **Y** sound — **HYMN**.
- If you say the word *human* using only the **HMN** sounds, the error is easy to hear.
- This is also true for words like *beauty* — **BYT**, *cube* — **KYB** and *music* — **MYZK**.

- When we say the word *what*, we normally don't notice that the **H** sound comes before the **W** sound: *what* — **HWT**.
- The only difference in sound between the two words *what* and *watt* is the almost silent stream of air at the beginning.

- The address for the word *ink* includes the **NG** sound — **NGK**.
- The **NG** sound is also included in words like *uncle* — **NGKL**, *anchor* — **NGKR** and *think* — **THNGK**.

- The letters *x* and *q* are not used as SOUND SYMBOLS. The following examples show the sound-to-symbol linkages for words that have the letters *x* and *q*:
    quick — **KWK**
    explore — **KSPLR**
    exam — **GZM**
    (Think sound.)

- The letter *c* is used only in combination with the letter *h* to make the SOUND SYMBOL for the **CH** sound as in the word *each* — **CH**.

- The **TH** SOUND SYMBOL represents *two* sounds:
    (1) the voiceless **TH** as in the word *thin* — **THN** and
    (2) the voiced **TH** as in the word *these* — **THZ**.
    (Voiced sounds are made when your vocal cords vibrate.)

Guidelines

- Each address is in alphabetical order.
- Words are listed in alphabetical order under each address.
- Related words are indented.

FL
flea(insect)
flee(escape)
  fled

- SOUND SYMBOLS are repeated if there is a vowel sound between them.

BBL	**NSTTT**	**SS**
bubble	institute	cease
	NSTTYT	
	institute	

- You can use this book to find out if a word is a compound word, a hyphenated word or two separate words.

HDK	**PPSKWK**	**TBG**	**BGTP**
headache	pip-squeak	tea bag	big top

- Words that are made by the addition of suffixes will not be listed unless the original word's spelling is changed by the addition of a suffix.

Z	**SHRT**
easy	short
easier	

- Verb forms are given for irregular verbs. (Regular verb forms are made by adding the endings *ed, ing* and *s*.)
- Irregular verbs have their forms indented and placed under them.

BD	**SHV**	**STP**	**NSST**
bid	shove	stop	insist
bid	shoved	stopped	
bidding	shoving	stopping	

- Look for words in their singular form.
- If the plural of a word is formed in a way other than adding *s*, the plural form will be indented and placed under it.

ST	**RDS**	**VM**	**SS**
city	radius	ovum	oasis
cities	radiuses(or)	ova	oases
	radii		

- When a word has more than one pronunciation, each pronunciation will have its own address.

FN	**FTN**	**MTR**	**MCHR**	**MTYR**
often	often	mature	mature	mature

- Words that have no consonant sounds are listed first—on page one.

Hints

Word Finder often places several words at the same address. Many times, it is helpful to show a difference between these words.

- Hints are used to give you an idea of what a word is about. They are not intended to define words.
- Hints are placed in parentheses after the word.
- Even though a word may have several meanings, it will usually have only one hint.

KRNL
colonel(rank)
kernel(grain)

PR
peer(look, equal)
pier(structure)

RT
right(correct)
write(pen and ink)

Additional Information

- **HW, KS** and **KW** are indented in the KEY to SOUND SYMBOLS to show that they are not single consonant sounds. They are common combinations of separate sounds.

- Many alternate spellings and forms are included in *Word Finder*; however, no attempt has been made to include all alternate spellings and forms.

Abbreviations

(adj)	adjective
(adv)	adverb
(B)	British spelling
(conj)	conjunction
(f)	feminine
(interj)	interjection
(m)	masculine
(n)	noun
(pl)	plural
(prep)	preposition
(pron)	pronoun
(sing)	singular

KEY to SOUND SYMBOLS

SYMBOL . . . . WORD . . . . ADDRESS

B . . . . baby . . . . **BB**
                    bell . . . . **BL**
                    ability . . . . **BLT**
CH . . . . bench . . . . **BNCH**
                    church . . . . **CHRCH**
                    chief . . . . **CHF**
                    itch . . . . **CH**
D . . . . dog . . . . **DG**
                    dumb . . . . **DM**
                    admire . . . . **DMR**
                    medical . . . . **MDKL**
                    adage . . . . **DJ**
F . . . . fox . . . . **FKS**
                    five . . . . **FV**
                    graph . . . . **GRF**
                    phone . . . . **FN**
                    rough . . . . **RF**
G . . . . eggnog . . . . **GNG**
                    go . . . . **G**
                    bag . . . . **BG**
                    ugly . . . . **GL**
                    exam . . . . **GZM**
                    eagle . . . . **GL**
H . . . . who . . . . **H**
                    how . . . . **H**
                    enhance . . . . **NHNS**
                    hat . . . . **HT**
        HW . . . . . which . . . . **HWCH**
                    when . . . . **HWN**
J . . . . Egypt . . . . **JPT**(or)**JP**
                    age . . . . **J**
                    gentle . . . . **JNTL**
                    fudge . . . . **FJ**
                    judge . . . . **JJ**
                    marriage . . . . **MRJ**
                    gem . . . . **JM**

K		acre	**KR**
		king	**KNG**
		kick	**KK**
		cue	**KY**
		class	**KLS**
	KS	axle	**KSL**
		tax	**TKS**
		x-ray	**KSR**
		expense	**KSPNS**
	KW	quiz	**KWZ**
		quality	**KWLT**
		quick	**KWK**
		equal	**KWL**
L		alien	**LN**(or)**LYN**
		lily	**LL**
		oil	**L**(or)**YL**
		laugh	**LF**
M		image	**MJ**
		come	**KM**
		magic	**MJK**
		match	**MCH**
		machinery	**MSHNR**
N		knee	**N**
		no	**N**
		nature	**NCHR**
		nose	**NZ**
NG		singer	**SNGR**
		anger	**NGGR**
		jungle	**JNGGL**
		think	**THNGK**
P		opaque	**PK**
		pigeon	**PJN**
		ape	**P**
		proxy	**PRKS**
		keep	**KP**
R		area	**R**
		car	**KR**
		roar	**RR**
		righteous	**RCHS**
		earache	**RK**

S	ace	**S**
	place	**PLS**
	sauce	**SS**
	Sioux	**S**
	cynic	**SNK**
SH	shoe	**SH**
	should	**SHD**
	dish	**DSH**
T	tea bag	**TBG**
	list	**LST**
	tight	**TT**
	oatmeal	**TML**
	typhoid	**TFD**
TH	thin	**THN**
	this	**THS**
	both	**BTH**
	brother	**BRTHR**
V	vast	**VST**
	avow	**V**
	avoid	**VD**
	revolve	**RVLV**
	cave	**KV**
W	Iowa	**W**
	wash	**WSH**
	with	**WTH**
	wise	**WZ**
	bewitch	**BWCH**
	wage	**WJ**
Y	yes	**YS**
	yo-yo	**YY**
	use (v)	**YZ**
	annual	**NYL**(or)**NYWL**
	loyal	**LYL**
	unity	**YNT**
Z	ease	**Z**
	Xerox (trademark)	**ZRKS**
	czar	**ZR**
ZH	vision	**VZHN**
	corrosion	**KRZHN**
	Asia	**ZH**
	regime	**RZHM**

a(article)
agh(interj)
  agghhh
ah(interj)
  ah's
  aah(pleasure)
aw(interj)
awe(wonder)
  awed
  awing
aye(yes)
  aye-aye
eh(interj)
eye
  eyed
  eyeing
I(me)
i.e.(id est)
oh(interj)
  oh's
  ooh(realization)
owe(debt)
  owed
  owing

B

aba(fabric)
Abba(God)
abbe(title)
abbey(place)
baa(sound)
bah(interj)
bay(water,
  sound,color,
  opening)
be(exist)(v)
  am
  are
  is
  was
  were
  been
beau(sweetheart)
bee(insect)
bo(friend)
  bos
boa(snake)
boo(interj)
bough(tree branch)
bow(bend,boat)
boy(child)

buoy(float)
buy(purchase)
  bought
by(prep)
bye(side issue)
ebb(flow)
hautboy(oboe)
Ob
obey
oboe(music)

BB
babe(baby)
babu(Hindi)
baby(coddle)
  babied
  babies
BB(shot)
  BB gun
bib
  bibbed
  bibbing
  bibber
bibb(boat)
bob
  bobbed
  bobbing
bobby(policeman)
  bobbies
boob
booby(bird,dunce)
  boobies
boo-boo
bub(fellow)
bubby(breast)
  bubbies
bubo(swelling)
bye-bye(Good-by)
BBGN
  BB gun
BBHCH
  booby hatch
BBHWT
  bobwhite
BBKT
  bobcat
BBL
babble(talk)
  babbled
  babbler
  babbling
bauble(trinket)
bibelot(trinket)
Bible(book)
bible(guide)
bobble
  bobbled

bobbling
bubble
  bubbled
  bubbling
  bubbly
  buyable
BBLBLT
  Bible Belt
BBLFL
  bibliophile
BBLGRF
  bibliography
  bibliographies
BBLGRFR
  bibliographer
BBLKL
  Biblical
BBLN
  Babylon
BBLPL
  bibliopole
BBLR
  babbler
  bubbler
BBLTF
  bibliotaph
BBLTHK
  bibliotheca
BBN
  baboon
  bobbin(sewing)
BBNK
  bubonic
BBNKPLG
  bubonic plague
BBP
  bebop(music)
BBPN
  bobby pin
BBPRZ
  booby prize(award)
BBR
  bayberry
  bayberries
  bobber
BBSH
  babyish
BBSKS
  bobby socks
BBSKSR
  bobbysoxer
BBSLD
  bobsled
BBST
  baby-sit
  baby-sat

baby-sitting
bobstay(rope)
BBSTR
  babysitter
BBT
  babbitt(metal)
  Babbitt(person)
BBTL
  bobtail
BBTRP
  booby trap(n)
  booby-trap(v)
BBTST
  Baptist
BBTSTR
  baptistery
  baptisteries
BBTZ
  baptize
  baptized
  baptizing
BBTZM
  baptism
BBWZ
  booboisie
BBYLS
  bibulous
BBZ
  boobs
BCH
  bach(live alone)
  baches
  batch(amount)
  batches
  beach(sand)
  beaches
  beech(tree)
  beeches
  bitch(dog)
  bitches
  bitchy
  bitchier
  bitchiest
  bitchiness
  botch(ruin)
  botches
  botchy
  botchier
  botchiest
  botchily
  butch
  butches
BCHHD
  beachhead
BCHKMR
  beachcomber

BCHLN
botulin
BCHLR
bachelor
BCHLZM
botulism
BCHN
Batjan
BCHNT
beechnut
BCHR
butcher
butchery
butcheries
obituary
obituaries
BCHWR
obituary
obituaries
BD
abide(wait)
abided(or)abode
abiding
abode(place)
aubade(music)
bad
worse
worst
bade(bid)
batty
battier
battiest
battily
battiness
bawd(a madam)
bawdy(vulgar)
bawdier
bawdiest
bawdily
bawdiness
bead(ball)
beady(eyes)
beadier
beadiest
bed
bedded
bedding
bid(offer)
bid
bidding
bid(direct)
bade(or)bid
bidding
bidden
biddy(fowl,woman)
biddies

bide(stay)
bided(or)bode
biding
bidet(bathing)
bode(omen)
boded
boding
body
bodies
bodied
bodily
bodiless
bootee(shoe)
booty(loot)
booties
bud(grow)
budded
budding
Buddha
buddy
buddies
BDB
Abu Dhabi
BDBG
bedbug
BDBL
biddable
BDBLD
bad blood
BDFST
bedfast
BDG
bodega(store)
BDGRD
bodyguard
BDGRDBL
biodegradable
BDK
bedeck
buttock
BDKN
bodkin
BDKSHN
abdication
abduction(kidnap)
BDKT
abdicate
abdicated
abdicating
abduct
BDKTR
abdicator
abductor
BDL
battle(war)
battled

battling
beetle(insect)
bodily
bottle(glass)
bottled
bottling
BDLFL
bottleful
BDLFLD
battlefield
BDLKS
battle-ax
battle-axes
BDLM
bedlam
BDLNDZ
badlands
BDLNK
bottleneck
BDLNZ
badlands
BDLR
bottler
BDLRZ
bowdlerize
bowdlerized
bowdlerizing
bowdlerization
BDLS
bodiless
BDLSHP
battleship
BDLZ
Beatles, the
BDM
bottom
BDMN
abdomen
BDMNL
abdominal
BDMNS
abdominous
BDMTN
badminton
BDN
bedouin
bidden
BDNG
beating
bedding
boding(omen)
BDNS
abidance
obedience
BDNSK
buttinsky

buttinskies
BDNT
obedient
BDNZH
badinage
BDPN
bedpan
BDPST
bedpost
Budapest
BDR
abider
batter
battery
batteries
bawdry(language)
bayadere(fabric)
beater(hit)
bedder(bed)
better(quality)
bettor(person)
bidder
bitter(taste)
budder
butter(food)
BDRBL
butterball
BDRDN
bedridden
BDRGL
bedraggle
bedraggled
bedraggling
BDRK
bedrock
BDRL
bedroll
BDRS
obduracy
BDRST
bed rest
BDRSWT
bittersweet
BDRT
obdurate
BDS
bodice
BDSD
bedside
BDSHS
bodacious
BDSPRD
bedspread
BDSPRNG
bedspring
BDSR

B:by **CH**:each **D**:day **F**:if **G**:go **H**:he **HW**:why **J**:joy **K**:cow **KS**:ax **KWL**:equal **L**:all **M**:may **N**:in

bedsore
BDSTD
bedstead
BDSTV
bodhisattva
BDTD
beatitude
BDTM
bedtime
BDTMPRD
bad-tempered
BDTYD
beatitude
BDVL
bedevil, (B)-lled, - lling
BDWR
boudoir
BDWTNG
bed-wetting
BDYRS
obduracy
BDYRT
obdurate
BDZ
beads(jewelry)
BDZL
bedazzle
bedazzled
bedazzling
BDZM
Buddhism
BF
beef(meat)
beefs(or)
beeves
beef(complaint)
beefs
beefy
beefier
beefiest
beefiness
bouffe(opera)
buff
buffet(cabinet)
buffet(food)
BFBRGNYN
beef bourguignon
BFDBK
biofeedback
BFDL
befuddle
befuddled
befuddling
BFG
befog
befogged

befogging
BFKL
bifocal
BFL
baffle
baffled
baffling
befall
befell
befallen
befool
befoul(soil)
Buffalo
buffalo
buffaloes
BFLMNT
bafflement
BFLR
baffler
BFN
buffoon
BFNB
Baffin Bay
BFNR
buffoonery
buffooneries
BFNT
bouffant
BFR
before
buffer
BFRHND
beforehand
BFRKT
bifurcate
bifurcated
bifurcating
BFRND
befriend
boyfriend
BFRNT
bowfront
BFS
beefs(complaints)
BFSKT
obfuscate
obfuscated
obfuscating
BFSKWD
beef-squad
BFSTK
beefsteak
BFSTRGNF
beef stroganoff
BFT
abaft

befit
befitted
befitting
buffet
BFZKS
biophysics
BFZSST
biophysicist
BG
bag
bagged
bagging
baggy
baggier
baggiest
bagginess
beg
begged
begging
big
bigger
biggest
bog
bogged
bogging
bogey(golf)
boggy(bog)
boggier
boggiest
boggily
bogginess
bogy(evil spirit)
(or)boogie
boogie(dance)
boogied
boogies
boogying
bug
bugged
bugging
buggy(cart)
buggies
buggy(insects)
buggier,buggiest
bugginess
BGB
bugaboo
bugbear
BGBNG
big bang(theory)
BGBR
bugbear
BGBRD
Big Board
BGBRTHR
Big Brother

(government)
BGD
Big D(Dallas, TX)
bug-eyed(adj)
BGDD
Baghdad
BGFL
bagful
BGHD
bighead
BGHDD
bigheaded
BGHRTD
big-hearted
BGHWL
big wheel
BGJ
baggage
BGL
bagel(food)
beagle(dog)
beguile
beguiled
beguiling
boggle
boggled
boggling
BGLG
big league(n)
big-league(adj)
BGLGR
big leaguer
BGLMNT
beguilement
BGLR
beguiler
BGM
big game(n)
big-game(adj)
bigamy
BGMN
bagman
bagmen
bogyman(or)
boogieman
bogymen(or)
boogiemen
BGMS
bigamous
BGMST
bigamist
BGN
begin
began
beginning
begun

---

begone(interj)
beguine(dance)
bygone
BGNG
begging
bugging
BGNNG
beginning
BGNR
beginner
BGNVL
bougainvillea
BGNVLY
bougainvillea
BGNY
begonia
BGNZ
bygones
BGPL
Big Apple(New York)
BGPP
bagpipe
bagpiper
BGR
beggar
beggary
bigger
bugger
buggery
BGRF
biography
biographies
BGRFR
biographer
BGRJ
begrudge
begrudged
begrudging
BGRL
beggarly
beggarliness
BGRNG
beggaring
BGRZLS
beggar's-lice
BGS
bogus
BGSH
biggish
bugsha
BGSHT
big shot
BGT
Big Eight(sports)
beget
begot

begetting
begotten
begetter
bigot
bigotry
Bogota
BGTKT
big-ticket
BGTL
bagatelle
BGTM
big time(n)
big-time(adj)
BGTN
begotten
Big Ten(sports)
BGTP
big top
BGTR
bigotry
bigotries
BGVDGT
Bhagavad Gita
BGWG
bigwig
boogie-woogie
BH
Baja
bohea(tea)
boohoo
BHD
behead
BHF
behalf
BHLD
behold
beheld
BHLDN
beholden
BHMN
Bohemian
BHMTH
behemoth
BHMZ
Bahamas, The
BHND
behind
BHNDHND
behindhand
BHNGK
bohunk(slang)
BHVYR
behavior, (B)behaviour
BHR
abhor
abhorred

abhorring
BHRNS
abhorrence
BHRNT
abhorrent
BHRR
abhorrer
BHST
behest
BHV
beehive
behave
behaved
behaving
behoove
behooved
behooving
BJ
badge
badged
badging
beige(color)
budge(move)
budged
budging
BJKSHN
abjection
objection
BJKSHNBL
objectionable
objectionably
BJKT
abject
object
BJKTR
objector
BJKTV
objective
BJKTVT
objectivity
BJNSS
abiogenesis
BJR
abjure
abjured
abjuring
badger(animal,
pester)
BJRGSHN
objurgation
BJRGT
objurgate
objurgated
objurgating
BJRR
abjurer

BJRSHN
abjuration
BJST
beau geste
BJT
budget
BJTR
budgetary
budgeter
BJWL
bejewel
BK
abaca(plant)
Bach
back
bake(cook)
baked
baking
balk(stop)
balky
balkier
balkiest
balkiness
beak(bird)
bike
biked
biking
book
bookie
bouquet(flowers)
buck
buckeye(tree)
bucko
buckoes
BKBN
backbone
BKBR
bock beer
BKBRD
buckboard
BKBRKNG
backbreaking
BKBT
backbite
backbit
backbiting
backbiter
backbitten
BKDR
back door
BKDRP
backdrop
BKFLD
backfield
BKFR
backfire

B:by **CH**:each **D**:day **F**:if **G**:go **H**:he **HW**:why **J**:joy **K**:cow **KS**:ax **KWL**:equal **L**:all **M**:may **N**:in

backfired
backfiring
BKFVR
buck fever
BKGMN
backgammon
BKGRND
background
BKHND
backhand
BKJKT
book jacket
BKKS
bookcase
BKL
buccal(cheek)
buckle
buckled
buckling
buckler
BKLB
book club
BKLD
becloud
BKLG
backlog
backlogged
backlogging
BKLM
becalm
BKLR
buckler
BKLRD
bicolored
BKLRNNG
book learning
BKLRT
baccalaureate
BKLSH
backlash
backlashes
BKLT
booklet
BKM
becalm
become
became
becoming
BKMCH
book match
book matches
BKMKL
biochemical
BKMKR
bookmaker
BKMNG

becoming
BKMRL
bicameral
BKMST
biochemist
BKMSTR
biochemistry
BKN
bacon(meat)
beacon(light)
beckon
bikini
BKND
bookend
BKNG
backing
booking
BKNR
buccaneer
BKNT
bacchant
BKP
back-up(n)(adj)
BKPDL
backpedal
BKPK
backpack
BKPNG
bookkeeping
BKPR
beekeeper
bookkeeper
BKPSNG
buck-passing
BKPSR
buck-passer
BKR
baccarat(game)
backer(person)
baker
bakery
bakeries
beaker(glass)
bicker(fight)
buckaroo
BKRBNT
bicarbonate
BKRD
Bacardi
  (trademark)
back road
BKRDR
back order(n)
back-order(v)
BKRK
by cracky(interj)

BKRM
buckram
BKRST
Bucharest
BKRT
backcourt
BKRVY
book review
BKS
abacus
abaci(or)
abacuses
bookcase
box
boxes
boxy
boxier
boxiest
BKSD
backside
BKSFS
box office(n)
box-office(adj)
BKSH
bookish
buckshee
BKSHSH
baksheesh
BKSHT
buckshot
BKSKN
buckskin
BKSKR
boxcar
box score
BKSKT
box kite
BKSL
abaxial
BKSLNCH
box lunch
box lunches
BKSM
buxom
BKSNG
boxing
BKSPD
bicuspid
BKSPN
backspin
BKSPRNG
box spring
BKSPS
backspace
backspaced
backspacing

BKSR
boxer
BKST
backseat(car)
box seat
BKSTCH
backstitch
backstitches
BKSTDRVR
back-seat driver
BKSTJ
backstage
BKSTP
backstop
BKSTR
ab extra
BKSTRCH
backstretch
BKSTRK
backstroke
BKSTRZ
backstairs
BKT
becket(fastener)
boycott
bucket
BKTBK
back to back(adv)
back-to-back(adj)
BKTBRGD
bucket brigade
BKTFL
bucketful
BKTK
back talk(n)
back-talk(v)
BKTR
bacteria
boycotter
BKTRK
backtrack
BKTRM
bacterium
bacteria
BKTSHP
bucket shop
BKTST
bucket seat
BKVLY
book value
BKTTH
bucktooth
buckteeth
BKWDZ
backwoods
backwoodsman

NGK:ink P:pie R:air S:ice SH:show T:toy THN:thin TH:the V:of W:we Y:you Z:is VZHN:vision

BKWRD
backward
BKWSH
backwash
BKWST
bequest
BKWTH
bequeath
BKWTHL
bequeathal
BKYRD
back yard(n)
backyard(adj)
BKZ
because
BL
able
abler
ablest
ably
Baal(god)
bail(money,empty)
bailee(law)
bailey(wall)
bale(wrap)
baled
baling
balk
ball
ballet(dance)
bawl(cry)
bel(ratio)
belay(hold)
belie(lie)
belied
belying
bell
belle(girl)
bellow(roar)
belly(stomach)
bellies
below(under)
bile(liquid)
bill
billow(sail)
billy(club, pot)
billies
blah(nonsense)
blow(air, hit)
blew
blown
blowy(wind)
blowier
blowiest
blue(color)
blued

bluing
bluer
bluest
boil
bola(rope)
bole(color, tree
trunk)
boll(seed pod)
bowel(intestine)
bowl(dish,sport)
buhl(style)
bull
bully
bullies
bylaw
eyeball
BLB
balboa(money)
Balboa(city)
bellboy
bell buoy(water)
blab
blabbed
blabbing
blabber
blob
blobbed
blobbing
bulb
BLBB
blue baby
BLBBL
blow-by-blow
BLBDD
able-bodied
BLBK
blue book
BLBL
bailable
bilabial(lips)
billable
boilable
BLBLD
blue blood
BLBND
bellyband
BLBNT
bluebonnet
BLBR
belabor
blabber
blubber
blueberry
blueberries
bulbar
BLBRD

billboard
bluebird
BLBRMTH
blabbermouth
BLBRNG
ball bearing
BLBS
bulbous
BLBSTR
belly-buster
BLBTM
bell-bottom(adj)
BLCH
belch
belches
bleach
bleaches
blotch
blotches
BLCHP
blue chip(n)
blue-chip(adj)
BLCHR
bleacher
blucher(shoe)
BLCHZ
blue cheese(or)bleu
BLD
bald
ballad(song)
ballade(verse)
billet-doux
billets-doux
billed(bill)
blade
bleed
bled
blood
bloody
bloodied
bloodies
bloodier
bloodiest
bloodily
bloodiness
bold
build
built(or)
builded
building
BLDBNK
blood bank
BLDBRTHR
blood brother
BLDBTH
blood bath

BLDD
belated
BLDFS
boldface
boldfaced
boldfacing
BLDFST
bald-faced(adj)
bold-faced(adj)
BLDG
bulldog
BLDGL
bald eagle
BLDGRP
blood group
BLDHD
baldhead
BLDHND
bloodhound
BLDKNT
blood count
BLDKRDLNG
bloodcurdling
BLDL
belittle
belittled
belittling
BLDLTNG
bloodletting
BLDM
beldam
BLDMN
blood money
BLDMR
Bloody Mary
BLDN
belladonna
BLDNG
building
BLDNGHRT
bleeding-heart
BLDP
build-up(n)
BLDPRSHR
blood pressure
BLDPZNNG
blood poisoning
BLDR
balladeer(singer)
balladry
bladder
bleeder
blotter(ink)
bolder(daring)
Boulder(city)
boulder(rock)

B:by **CH**:each **D**:day **F**:if **G**:go **H**:he **HW**:why **J**:joy **K**:cow **KS**:ax **KWL**:equal **L**:all **M**:may **N**:in

builder
BLDRD
blood-red
BLDRL
bilateral
BLDSHD
bloodshed
BLDSHT
bloodshot
BLDSKR
bloodsucker
BLDSL
blood cell
BLDSTN
bloodstain
BLDSTRM
bloodstream
BLDTHRST
bloodthirsty
bloodthirstily
bloodthirstiness
BLDTP
blood type(n)
BLDTST
blood test
BLDZ
bulldoze
bulldozed
bulldozing
BLDZHR
bulldozer
BLDZR
bulldozer
BLF
bailiff
bay leaf
belief
blow off(v)
blowoff(n)
bluff
BLFL
baleful
bellyful
billfold
BLFLD
billfold
BLFR
belfry
belfries
BLFRG
bullfrog
BLFS
boldface
boldfaced
boldfacing
BLFSH

bluefish
BLFST
bald-faced(adj)
Belfast
bold-faced
BLFT
bullfight
BLG
bowleg
BLGD
bowlegged
BLGM
ball game
BLGN
blowgun
BLGR
beleaguer
Bulgaria
BLGRD
Belgrade
BLGRN
Bulgarian
BLGRS
bluegrass
BLGSHN
obligation
BLGT
obbligato
obbligati
obligate
obligated
obligating
BLGTR
obligatory
obligatories
BLGTZ
obbligatos
BLH
ballyhoo
BLHD
billhead
BLHDD
bullheaded
BLHP
bellhop
BLHR
ballyhooer
BLHRD
blowhard
BLHRN
bullhorn
BLHWP
bullwhip
bullwhipped
bullwhipping
BLJ

bilge(hull)
bilged
bilging
bilge(worthless)
biology
blue jay
bulge
bulged
bulging
bulgy
bulginess
oblige
obliged
obliging
BLJK
biologic
BLJKL
biological
BLJM
Belgium
BLJN
Belgian
bludgeon
BLJNS
blue jeans
BLJRNS
belligerence
belligerency
BLJRNT
belligerent
BLJST
biologist
BLK
balk
balky
balkier
balkiest
balkiness
bellyache
bellyached
bellyaching
bilk
black
black eye
bleak
bloc(alliance)
block
blocky
blockier
blockiness
bloke(man)
bulk
bulky
bulkier
bulkiest
bulkily

bulkiness
bullock(bull)
oblique
BLKBK
black book
BLKBL
blackball
BLKBR
blackberry
blackberries
BLKBRD
blackbird
blackboard
BLKBSTNG
blockbusting
BLKBSTR
blockbuster
BLKD
black-eyed(adj)
blockade
blockaded
blockading
blockader
BLKDRNR
blockade-runner
BLKFLG
black flag
BLKGRD
blackguard
BLKHD
blackhead
blockhead
bulkhead
BLKHS
blockhouse
BLKJ
blockage
bulkage
BLKJK
blackjack
BLKL
obliquely
BLKLB
ball club(team)
BLKLR
blue-collar(adj)
BLKLST
blacklist
BLKLTR
block letter
BLKMJK
black magic
BLKML
blackmail
BLKMRK
black mark

NGK:ink **P**:pie **R**:air **S**:ice **SH**:show **T**:toy **THN**:thin **TH**:the **V**:of **W**:we **Y**:you **Z**:is **VZHN**:vision

BLKMRKT
black market(n)
black-market(v)
BLKMRKTR
black marketeer
BLKMZLMZ
Black Muslims
BLKN
balcony
balconies
blacken
BLKNDBL
black-and-blue(adj)
BLKNDHWT
black-and-white(adj)
BLKNDWT
black-and-white(adj)
BLKNT
bel canto
BLKPWR
Black Power
BLKR
bellyacher
BLKS
bellicose
Biloxi
Black Sea
BLKSHN
by-election
BLKSHP
black sheep
BLKSMTH
blacksmith
BLKT
blackout(n)
black out(v)
black tie(n)
black-tie(adj)
BLKTP
blacktop
BLKW
obloquy
obloquies
BLKWD
black widow
BLKWT
obliquity
BLKWZ
obloquies
BLL
blue law
BLLF
belly laugh
BLLN
blue line
BLLND

belly-land(v)
BLLNDNG
belly landing(n)
BLM
abloom
blame
blamed
blaming
bloom
bulimia(disease)
bulimic(person)
BLMBL
blamable
BLMFL
blameful
BLMK
bulimic
bulimia
BLMNJ
blancmange
BLMP
blimp
BLMR
bloomer
BLMRZ
bloomers
BLMSH
blemish
blemishes
BLMSTF
bullmastiff
BLMWRTH
blameworthy
BLN
abalone
balloon
baloney(slang)
beeline
bland
blind
blown
blow
bologna(meat)
bowline
by-line
BLNCH
blanch
blanches
BLND
bland
blend
blind
blond(m,f)
blonde(f only)
BLNDFLD
blindfold

BLNDL
blind alley
BLNDMNZBF
blindman's buff
BLNDR
blinder
blunder
BLNDRBS
blunderbuss
BLNDSH
blandish
BLNDSHR
blandisher
BLNDSPT
blind spot
BLNDT
blind date
BLNFLD
blindfold
BLNG
belaying
(securing)
belong
belying
(show to be
false)
bluing
boiling(hot)
boweling
bowling(game)
oblong
BLNGGWL
bilingual
BLNGK
blank
blink
BLNGKR
blinker
BLNGKRD
blinkard
BLNGKT
blanket
BLNGL
bowling alley
BLNGNGZ
belongings
BLNGPNT
boiling point
BLNGWL
bilingual
BLNKCHK
blank check
BLNKT
bullnecked
BLNKRD
blinkard

BLNKT
bullnecked
BLNMN
blind man
BLNMNZBF
blindman's buff
BLNS
balance
balanced,-cing
BLNSBL
balanceable
BLNSHT
balance sheet
BLNSHWL
balance wheel
BLNSPT
blind spot
BLNSR
balancer
BLNSWL
balance wheel
BLNT
blatant
blunt
BLNZ
bluenose
bullnose
BLP
bleep
blip
blipped,-pping
bloop(sound)
blowup(n)
blow up(v)
BLPLR
ballplayer
BLPN
ball-peen(hammer)
bullpen
BLPNHMR
ball-peen hammer
BLPNSL
blue-pencil(v)
BLPNT
bluepoint
BLPNTPN
ball-point pen
BLPR
blooper
BLPRK
ball park(n)
ball-park(adj)
BLPRNT
blueprint
BLR
abler

B:by CH:each D:day F:if G:go H:he HW:why J:joy K:cow KS:ax KWL:equal L:all M:may N:in

ablest
bailer
bailor(law)
baler(machine)
belier(liar)
blare
  blared
  blaring
blear(blur)
bleary
  blearier
  bleariest
  blearily
  bleariness
blower(blow)
blur
  blurred
  blurring
blurry
  blurrier
  blurriest
  blurriness
boiler
bolero
BLRB
blurb
BLRBN
blue ribbon(n)
blue-ribbon(adj)
BLRD
bleary-eyed
bollard
BLRG
bullyrag
  bullyragged
  bullyragging
BLRM
ballroom
BLRMKR
boilermaker
BLRN
ballerina
blarney
BLRNG
bullring
BLRPLT
boiler plate
BLRRR
bullroarer
BLRSH
bulrush
  bulrushes
BLRT
blurt
BLS
balas

balsa(wood)
Belize
bless
  blessed(or)
  blest
  blesses
  blessing
bliss
blouse(shirt)
bolus(pill)
  boluses
BLSD
blessed(adj)
BLSFM
blaspheme
  blasphemed
  blaspheming
  blasphemer
  blasphemy
  blasphemies
BLSFMS
blasphemous
BLSH
abolish
  abolishes
bluish
blush
  blushes
bullish
BLSHN
ablation
  (carry away)
ablution(liquid)
abolition
ebullition(boil)
oblation(offer)
BLSHNR
abolitionary
BLSHNST
abolitionist
BLSHNZM
abolitionism
BLSHT
bullshit
BLSK
blue-sky(adj)
obelisk
BLSM
balsam
blossom
BLSNG
blessing
BLSSHN
bull session
BLST
ablest

ballast
ballista(warfare)
  ballistae
blast
blest(bless)
BLSTD
balustrade
BLSTF
blast off(v)
blast-off(n)
BLSTK
ballistic
  ballistics
  ballistically
BLSTKNG
bluestocking
BLSTR
baluster
blister
bluster
blustery
bolster
BLSTRD
balustrade
BLSTRR
blusterer
BLT
ability
  abilities
ablaut(sound)
ballot
belt(gird)
blat
  blatted
  blatting
bleat(cry)
billet
blight
bloat(swell)
blot(spot)
  blotted
  blotting
  blotter
blowout(n)
blow out(v)
bolt
built(build)
bullet
eyebolt
BLTBKS
ballot box
BLTD
belated
BLTH
blithe
BLTHR

blather
BLTHRNG
blithering
BLTHSM
blithesome
BLTKS
Baltic Sea
BLTL
belittle
  belittled
  belittling
BLTLMNT
belittlement
BLTLR
belittler
BLTMR
Baltimore
BLTN
built-in(adj)
bulletin
BLTNS
blatancy
  blatancies
BLTNT
blatant
BLTP
built-up(adj)
BLTPRF
bulletproof
BLTR
balloter(ballot)
belles-lettres
blotter
BLTRCH
blowtorch
  blowtorches
BLTRL
bilateral
BLTRR
bull terrier
BLTRSHN
obliteration
BLTRSTK
belletristic
BLTRT
obliterate
  obliterated
  obliterating
BLTRTR
obliterator
BLTS
blitz
  blitzes
BLTSKRG
blitzkrieg
BLTV

NGK:ink **P**:pie **R**:air **S**:ice **SH**:show **T**:toy **THN**:thin **TH**:the **V**:of **W**:we **Y**:you **Z**:is **VZHN**:vision

ablative
BLV
believe
  believed
  believing
  believer
bolivar(money)
Bolivia
BLVBL
believable
BLVFR
bill of fare
BLVGDZ
bill of goods
BLVHLTH
bill of health
BLVLDNG
bill of lading
BLVN
oblivion
BLVR
believer
bolivar(money)
BLVRD
boulevard
BLVRDR
boulevardier
BLVRTS
Bill of Rights
  (document)
BLVS
oblivious
BLVSL
bill of sale
BLWK
bailiwick
BLWP
bullwhip
  -pped,-pping
BLWRK
buhlwork
bulwark(protect)
BLWTHR
bellwether
BLWVL
boll weevil
BLYN
billion(number)
bouillon(soup)
bullion(metal)
BLYNR
billionaire
BLYNT
ebullient
BLYRD
billiard

BLYRDZ
billiards
BLYS
bilious
BLZ
ablaze
Belize
bellows(air)
blahs(mental)
blasé
blaze(fire)
  blazed
  blazing
blouse
blowzy(sloppy)
  blowzier
  blowziest
blues
bull's-eye
bylaws
BLZBB
Beelzebub
BLZN
blazon
BLZNR
blazoner
blazonry
BLZR
blazer
BLZRD
blizzard
BM
abeam
ABM
  anti-ballistic
  missile
A-bomb
balm
balmy
  balmier
  balmiest
  balmily
  balminess
beam
bomb
bombe(dessert)
boom
bum
  bummed
  bumming
BMB
bamboo
bimbo
Bombay
BMBDR
bombardier

BMBL
bumble
  bumbled
  bumbling
  bumbler
BMBLB
bumblebee
BMBLPP
bumblepuppy(cards)
  bumblepuppies
BMBN
bambino
BMBRD
bombard
BMBRDR
bombardier
BMBST
bombast
BMBSTK
bombastic
BMBZL
bamboozle
  bamboozled
  bamboozling
BMBZLR
bamboozler
BMD
bombed
BMDL
bimodal
BMKN
bumpkin
BMN
bemean
bemoan
BMNBL
abominable
BMND
beau monde
  beaux mondes
BMNSHN
abomination
BMNT
abominate
  abominated
  abominating
Beaumont
BMNTHL
bimonthly
  bimonthlies
BMNTR
abominator
BMP
bump
bumpy
  bumpier

bumpiest
  bumpily
  bumpiness
BMPKN
bumpkin
BMPR
abampere
bumper
BMPSHS
bumptious
BMR
bemire
  bemired
  bemiring
bomber
bummer
BMRNG
boomerang
BMSHL
bombshell
BMSTR
bum steer
BMTLK
bimetallic
BMTLZM
bimetallism
BMTN
boom town
BMTRKS
biometrics
BMYZ
bemuse
  bemused
  bemusing
BN
ban
  banned
  banning
bane(ruin)
bean(plant)
beanie(hat)
been(to be)
benny(tablet)
  bennies
bin(container)
  binned
  binning
bind(tie)
  bound
binny(pocket)
bone
  boned
  boning
bony
  bonier
  boniest

boniness
bonne(maid)
bonny(pleasing)
  bonnier
  bonniest
  bonnily
Bonn
boon(good)
bun
bunny(rabbit)
  bunnies
button
ebony
BNB
bombe(dessert)
by and by(later)
by-and-by(a place)
BNBKS
bandbox
bandboxes
BNBLK
boneblack
BNBN
bonbon
BNBNYR
bonbonniere
BNBRTH
B'nai B'rith
BNCH
bench
  benches
bunch
  bunches
BNCHMRK
bench mark
BNCHN
bone china
BNCHWRNT
bench warrant
BND
abound
band
bandeau(pl-deaux)
bandy
  bandied
  bandies
bend
  bent
beyond
bind(tie)bound
bond
bound(jump)
BNDB
by and by(adv)
by-and-by(n)
BNDBKS

bandbox
  bandboxes
BNDGL
boondoggle
BNDHLDR
bondholder
BNDJ
bandage(cover)
  bandaged
  bandaging
bondage
BNDKS
boondocks
(out-of-the-way
  area)
BNDKSHN
benediction
BNDKT
benedict
BNDKTR
benedictory
BNDL
bindle(bedroll)
bundle
  bundled
  bundling
BNDLR
bandoleer
BNDMSTR
bandmaster
BNDN
abandon
bandanna(or)-ana
BNDNG
binding
BNDNS
abundance
BNDNT
abundant
BNDPPR
bond paper
BNDR
banderilla(dart)
binder
bindery
  binderies
bone-dry
bounder
boundary
  boundaries
BNDRLY
banderilla(dart)
BNDRYLR
banderillero
BNDRYR
banderillero

BNDS
band saw
BNDSHL
band shell
BNDSTND
bandstand
BNDT
bandit
BNDWGN
bandwagon
BNDZMN
bondsman(pl-men)
BNF
bowie knife
BNFD
bona fide
BNFKTR
benefactor
BNFL
baneful
BNFM
bonne femme
  (simple)
BNFS
benefice
BNFSH
bonefish
BNFSHL
beneficial
BNFSHR
beneficiary
  beneficiaries
BNFSNS
beneficence
BNFSNT
beneficent
BNFT
benefit
BNG
bang
being
bhang(plant)
bhong(pipe)
bingo
bong
BNGG
bingo(game)
bongo(drum)
BNGGL
bangle
  bangled
BNGGLDSH
Bangladesh
BNGGR
Bangor
BNGHL

bunghole
BNGK
bank
banco(bet)
bunco
bunk
BNGKBK
bankbook
BNGKBL
bankable
BNGKHS
bunkhouse
BNGKK
bangkok(straw)
Bangkok
BNGKKNT
bank account
BNGKM
bunkum
BNGKNG
banking
BNGKNT
bank note
BNGKR
banker
bunker
BNGKRL
bankroll
BNGKRPS
bankruptcy
  bankruptcies
BNGKRPT
bankrupt
BNGKT
banquette(seat,
  platform)
BNGKRTST
bunco artist
BNGKWT
banquet(meal)
BNGKWTR
banqueter
BNGL
bangle
  bangled
Bengal
Bengali
bungalow
bungle(fail)
  bungled
  bungling
BNGLDSH
Bangladesh
BNGLR
bungler
BNGNNT

benignant
BNGNT
benignity
benignites
BNGP
bang-up
(first rate)
BNGR
Bangor
BNGSHN
abnegation
BNGT
abnegate
abnegated
abnegating
BNGZ
bangs(hair)
Benghazi
BNHD
bonehead(slang)
BNJ
banjo
binge
BNJM
benjamin
BNJST
banjoist
BNK
bionic
BNKK
Bangkok
bangkok(straw)
BNKL
binnacle
BNKLR
binocular
BNKS
bionics
bionic
BNKSHS
obnoxious
BNKWT
banquet
BNKWTR
banqueter
BNKYLR
binocular
BNL
banal
biennial
binal(double)
BNLS
boundless
BNM
bantam(fowl)
benumb

biennium
bonhomie(good)
bon mot(clever)
BNML
binomial
bone meal
BNMR
bain-marie
bains-marie
BNMZ
bons mots
BNN
banana
benign
Benin
BNNZ
bonanza
BNR
Abner
banner
binary
boner
boutonniere(flower)
BNRL
binaural
BNRML
abnormal
BNRMLT
abnormality
abnormalities
BNRT
banneret
BNRZH
Baton Rouge
BNS
abeyance
band saw
banns
banns
bonsai(tree)
bonus
bounce
bounced
bouncing
bouncer
bouncy
bouncier
bounciest
buoyancy
BNSH
ab initio
banish
banishes
banshee
BNSHL
band shell

BNSNBRNR
Bunson burner
(trademark)
BNSR
bouncer
BNSRZ
Buenos Aires
BNSTND
bandstand
BNSTR
banister
BNT
bayonet
bent(bend)
bonito
bonnet
bounty
bounties
bowknot
bunt
buoyant
BNTD
benighted
BNTFL
bountiful
BNTH
beneath
BNTLN
buntline
BNTM
bantam
BNTMWT
bantamweight
(113-118 lbs)
BNTNG
bunting
BNTR
ab intra
banter
BNTS
bounteous
BNTWD
bentwood
BNVLNS
benevolence
BNVLNT
benevolent
BNVVN
bon vivant
bons vivants
BNVYZH
bon voyage
BNWGN
bandwagon
BNYL
biannual

BNYN
banyan(tree)
bunion
BNZ
bands(music)
banns(words)
banns
banzai(cry)
bends(pain)
bonds(money,
fasteners)
bounds (limits)
BNZDRN
Benzedrine
(trademark)
BNZMN
bondsman
bondsmen
BNZN
benzene
BP
beep
bop
bopped
bopping
BPD
biped(or)
bipedal
bipod
tripod
BPL
byplay
BPLN
biplane
BPR
beeper
BPRDKT
by-product
BPRDZN
bipartisan
BPRS
biparous
BPRTSN
bipartisan
BPRTT
bipartite
BPRTZN
bipartisan
BPS
biopsy
biopsies
bypass
bypasses
bypassed(v)
BPST
bypast(bygone)

B:by **CH**:each **D**:day **F**:if **G**:go **H**:he **HW**:why **J**:joy **K**:cow **KS**:ax **KWL**:equal **L**:all **M**:may **N**:in

BPTH
bypath
BPTSTR
baptistery
baptisteries
BPTST
Baptist
BPTZ
baptize
baptized
baptizing
BPTZM
baptism
BR
bar(structure,
to block)
barred
barring
bare(reveal)
bared
baring
barer
barest
barrio
barrow(cart)
bear(support)
bore
borne
bear(animal)
beer(beverage)
beery(beer)
beerier
beeriest
beret(cap)
berry
berries
bier(platform)
birr(sound)
boar(pig)
boor(person)
bore(hole,dull,
wave)
bored
boring
borough(town)
borrow(loan)
bower
bowery(farm)
bra(brassiere)
bray(cry)
brew(cook)
brio(vigor)
brow(face)
bur(drill,pod)
burr(rough edge)
burro(donkey)

burrow(hole)
burry(bur)
burrier
burriest
bury(cover)
buried
buries
buyer
eyebrow
obeyer
BRB
barb
bribe
bribed
bribing
BRBBL
bribable
BRBDS
Barbados
BRBDWR
barbed wire
BRBK
bareback
BRBKN
barbican(tower)
BRBKY
barbecue
barbecued
barbecuing
BRBL
barbell
bearable
brabble(quarrel)
brabbled
brabbling
brabbler
burble
burbled
burbling
BRBN
bourbon
BRBR
barber
Berber
beriberi(disease)
briber
bribery
BRBRK
barbaric
BRBRN
barbarian
BRBRS
barbarous
BRBRSHP
barbershop
BRBRT

barbarity
barbarities
BRBRZ
barbarize
barbarized
barbarizing
BRBRZM
barbarism
BRBT
barbet(bird)
barbette(war)
browbeat
browbeaten
BRBWR
barbwire
BRCH
abroach(astir)(adj)
birch(tree)
birches
breach(gap,
violation)
breaches
breech(buttocks)
breeches
broach(tool)
broaches
brooch(pin,clasp)
brooches
BRCHBLK
breechblock(gun)
BRCHR
Bircher
Birchism
BRCHZ
britches(pants)
BRD
aboard(on)
abrade(erode)
abraded
abrading
abroad(away)
beard
bird
birdie(bird,golf)
biretta(cap)
board(wood)
bored(dull,drill)
bore
Bordeaux
brad(nail)
bradded
bradding
braid
bread(food)
breed
bride

broad(wide)
brood(animals,
ponder)
broody
broodier
broodiest
byroad
BRDBN
broad bean
BRDBRM
broadbrim
BRDBRN
birdbrain
BRDBSKT
breadbasket
BRDBTH
birdbath
BRDFT
board foot
BRDG
bird dog(n)
birddog(v)
BRDGJ
broad gauge
BRDGJD
broad-gauged(adj)
BRDGRM
bridegroom
BRDHS
birdhouse
BRDJMP
broad jump
BRDKL
birdcall
BRDKLTH
broadcloth
BRDKS
broadax
broadaxes
BRDKST
broadcast
broadcast
BRDKSTR
broadcaster
BRDL
bordello
bridal(wedding)
bridle(horse)
bridled
bridling
brittle(fragile)
brutal
BRDLF
broadleaf(n)
broadleaves
BRDLM

broadloom
BRDLPTH
bridle path
BRDLVD
broad-leaved(adj)
(or)broad-leaf
BRDLZ
brutalize
brutalized
brutalizing
BRDM
boredom
BRDMNDD
broad-minded
BRDN
broaden
burden
BRDNDBTR
bread and butter(n)
bread-and-butter
(adj)
BRDNGHS
boardinghouse
BRDNGSKL
boarding school
BRDNG
breeding
BRDNSM
burdensome
BRDR
barter
breeder
boarder(person)
border
brooder
BRDRLN
borderline
BRDRM
board room
BRDRR
barterer
BRDSD
birdseed
broadside
BRDSH
brutish
BRDSRD
broadsword
BRDTH
breadth
BRDVPRDS
bird-of-paradise
BRDW
Broadway
BRDWCHNG
bird watching

BRDWCHR
bird watcher(n)
BRDWK
boardwalk
BRDWNR
breadwinner
BRDZ
bird's-eye
Bordeaux
BRDZMD
bridesmaid
BRF
brief
BRFKS
briefcase
BRFL
barfly
barflies
BRFNG
briefing
BRFST
barefaced
BRFT
barefoot
bereft
BRG
berg(ice)
brag
bragged
bragging
brig(jail)
brogue
burg(town)
burgoo(food)
BRGD
brigade
BRGDR
brigadier
BRGDSH
braggadocio
BRGL
burgle(rob)
burgled
burgling
burglar
BRGLR
burglar
burglary
burglaries
BRGLRZ
burglarize
burglarized
burglarizing
BRGN
bargain
brogan

BRGND
brigand
Burgundy
BRGNDJ
brigandage
BRGNDZM
brigandism
BRGNR
bargainer
BRGNTN
brigantine(boat)
BRGNYN
bourguignon
BRGNZM
brigandism
BRGR
bragger
burger(food)
burgher(class)
BRGRD
Beauregard
BRGRF
bar graph
BRGRM
barogram
BRGRT
braggart
BRGT
abrogate
abrogated
abrogating
abrogation
BRGTR
abrogator
BRHDD
bareheaded
BRHH
brouhaha
BRHNDD
barehanded
BRJ
abridge
abridged
abridging
barge(boat,enter)
barged
barging
barrage(dam)
barrage(artillery)
barraged
barraging
borage(plant)
bridge
bridged
bridging
burgee(flag)

BRJBL
abridgable
bridgeable
BRJHD
bridgehead
BRJMNT
abridgment, (B)- ement
BRJN
aborigine
burgeon(grow)
BRJNG
bridging
BRJNL
aboriginal
BRJNT
beer joint
BRJR
abridger
BRJS
bourgeois(type)
burgess
BRJWRK
bridgework
BRK
bark(tree,sound,
ship)
baroque
barrack
brake(stop)
braked
braking
break(smash)
broke
broken
brick
broke(no $)
brook(water)
burke(murder)
burked
burking
BRKBL
breakable
BRKBRK
bric-a-brac
BRKBT
brickbat
BRKD
barracuda
barricade
barricaded
barricading
brocade
brocaded
brocading
BRKDBR
abracadabra

BRKDN
breakdown(n)
BRKFRNT
breakfront
BRKFST
breakfast
BRKJ
breakage
BRKL
broccoli
BRKLN
Brooklyn
BRKLR
bricklayer
BRKMLD
brick mold
BRKN
barracoon
break-in
broken
BRKNDN
broken-down
BRKNHRTD
brokenhearted
BRKNK
breakneck
BRKP
barkeep
breakup(n)
break up(v)
BRKPR
barkeeper
BRKR
barker
breaker
broker($)
BRKRD
brick red(n)
brick-red(adj)
BRKRJ
brokerage
BRKRL
barcarole
BRKS
barracks
borax
BRKSD
boric acid
BRKSH
brackish
BRKSHN
abreaction
BRKSHR
Berkshire
BRKSHRNT
bergschrund

BRKT
abreact
bearcat(fighter)
bracket
bract(plant part)
breakout(n)
briquette
briquetted
briquetting
BRKTHR
breakthrough(n)
BRKVN
break-even
BRKW
breakaway
BRKWRK
brickwork
BRKWTR
breakwater
BRKYRD
brickyard
BRL
aboral
barely(hardly)
barley
barrel
birl(v)(logs)
(noise)
boreal(north)
brail(sail)
Braille
brawl(fight)
broil
burial(bury)
burl(knot)
burley(tobacco)
burly(shape)
BRLCHSTD
barrel-chested
BRLDK
bar-le-duc(food)
BRLF
bas-relief
BRLFL
barrelful
BRLGD
barelegged
BRLHS
barrelhouse
BRLN
Berlin
berlin(wool,
carriage)
berline(car)
BRLNG
birling

BRLP
burlap
BRLR
broiler
BRLSK
burlesque
BRLT
briolette
BRLYNS
brilliance
brilliancy
BRLYNT
brilliant
BRM
barm(foam)
barmy
barmier
barmiest
barroom
berhyme
berhymed
berhyming
berm
bream(fish)
brim(rim)
brimmed
brimming
broom
brougham
brume(vapor)
Burma
BRMBL
bramble
brambly
BRMD
barmaid
Bermuda
bromide
BRMFL
brimful
BRMJM
brummagem
BRML
brumal
BRMN
barman
Brahman(caste)
Brahmin(person)
BRMNGHM
Birmingham
BRMSTK
broomstick
BRMSTN
brimstone
BRMTR
barometer

barometry
BRMTRK
barometric
BRMTSV
bar mitzvah
BRMYD
Bermuda
BRMZ
Brahms
Burmese
BRN
auburn
Bahrain
baron(person)
barony
baronies
barren(bare)
Bern
born(passive)
borne(active,
passive when
used with by)
Borneo
brain
brainy
brainier
brainiest
braininess
bran(food)
brand(name)
brand-new
brawn
brawny
brawnier
brawniest
brawnily
brawniness
brighten
brine(water)
briny
brinier
briniest
brininess
brown
brownie
bruin(bear)
Brunei
buran(wind)
burn
burnt(or)
burned
BRNBRD
brown bread
BRNBRNR
barnburner(slang)
BRNCH

branch
  branches
brunch
  brunches
BRNCHLD
  brainchild
BRND
  brand
  brandy
  brandies
BRNDL
  brindle(gray)
  brindled
BRNDN
  brand-new
BRNDNM
  brand name(n)
BRNDNY
  brand-new
BRNDSH
  brandish
  brandishes
BRNG
  barong(knife)
  bearing
  boring(dull)
  bring(brought)
BRNGK
  barranca
  brink
  bronc(horse)(slang)
  bronchia
  bronco
BRNGKL
  bronchial
BRNGKMNSHP
  brinkmanship
BRNGKS
  bronchus(pl-chi)
BRNGKTS
  bronchitis
BRNGN
  Bren gun
BRNGS
  Bering Sea
BRNGSTRT
  Bering Strait
BRNJ
  baronage
BRNK
  brink
  bronc(horse)
    (slang)
  bronco(horse)
BRNKL
  barnacle

BRNL
  baronial
  barn owl
BRNNG
  burning
BRNPR
  brainpower
BRNPWR
  brainpower
BRNR
  burner
BRNS
  aberrance
  aberrancy
  baroness(person)
    baronesses
  barrenness
  burnoose
BRNSH
  burnish
    burnishes
BRNSHGR
  brown sugar
BRNSTD
  brown study
BRNSTN
  brownstone
BRNSTRM
  barnstorm
  brainstorm
BRNSTRMR
  barnstormer
BRNT
  aberrant
  baronet(title)
  brownout(n)
  brunet(m&f)
  brunette(f only)
  burnout(n)
  brunt
  burnt(fire)
  burn
BRNTJ
  baronetage
BRNTRST
  braintrust
BRNTS
  baronetcy
BRNTSR
  brontosaur
    brontosaurus
BRNWSH
  brainwash
    brainwashes
BRNWSHNG
  brainwashing

BRNWV
  brain wave
BRNY
  brand-new
BRNYRD
  barnyard
BRNZ
  bronze
  bronzed
  bronzing
  bronzy
  brown-nose
  brown-nosed
  brown-nosing
  brown-noser
BRNZJ
  Bronze Age
BRP
  burp
BRPGN
  burp gun
BRPT
  abrupt
BRR
  barrier
  bearer
  brayer(roller)
  brewer
  brewery
    breweries
  briar(bush)
  brier(thorn)
BRRWD
  briarwood
BRS
  brace
  braced
  bracing
  brass
  brassie(golf)
  brassy
  brassier
  brassiest
  brassiness
  bursa
  bursae(or)
  bursas
BRSDS
  bursitis(joint)
BRSH
  barouche(carriage)
  bearish
  boarish(boar,
    brutish)
  boorish(rude)
  brash(rash)

  brioche(food)
  broche(sew)
  brush
    brushes
BRSHL
  biracial
BRSHN
  aberration
  abortion
BRSHNST
  abortionist
BRSHR
  brochure
BRSHT
  borscht(soup)
  brass hat
  brochette
BRSK
  brisk(fast)
  brusque
BRSKL
  brusquely
BRSKT
  brisket
BRSL
  Brasilia
  bristle
  bristled
  bristling
  bristly
  bristlier
  bristliest
  bristliness
BRSLN
  Barcelona
BRSLNG
  brisling(fish)
BRSLS
  Brussels
BRSLSPRTS
  Brussels sprouts
BRSLT
  bracelet
BRSLY
  Brasilia
BRSLZ
  Brussels
BRSNG
  bracing
BRSNKLS
  brass knuckles
BRSR
  bursar
  bursary
BRSRD
  brassard(arm band)

BRSRK
 berserk
BRSRT
 brassard(arm band)
BRST
 abreast
 breast
 burst
 burst
BRSTBN
 breastbone
BRSTFD
 breast-feed
 breast-fed
BRSTKS
 brass tacks
BRSTN
 buhrstone
BRSTR
 barrister
BRSTS
 bursitis
BRSTSTRK
 breaststroke
BRSTWRK
 breastwork
BRSV
 abrasive
BRSZ
 berceuse(song)
BRT
 abort
 barret(cap)
 barrette(clasp)
 Beirut
 berate
  berated
  berating
 biretta(cap)
  barret
 bort(diamond)
 brat
 bratty
  brattiness
  brattish
 bright
 brought
 bring
 bruit(repeat)
 brut(wine)
 Brut(history)
 brute(beast)
BRTFSHNT
 abortifacient
BRTH
 berth(place)

 bertha(collar)
 birth(event)
 breath(n)
 breathe(v)
  breathed
  breathing
 broth
BRTF
 brutify
  brutifies
  brutified
BRTHBL
 breathable
BRTHD
 birthday
BRTHL
 brothel
BRTHMRK
 birthmark
BRTHPLS
 birthplace
BRTHR
 brother
BRTHRHD
 brotherhood
BRTHRN
 brethren
BRTHRNL
 brother-in-law
BRTHRT
 birthrate
 birthright
BRTHRZNL
 brothers-in-law
BRTHSRTFKT
 birth certificate
BRTHSTN
 birthstone
BRTHTKNG
 breathtaking
BRTL
 brattle(sound)
  brattled
  brattling
 brittle
 brutal
BRTLZ
 brutalize
  brutalized
  brutalizing
  brutalization
BRTN
 baritone
 brighten
 Britain
 Britannia

 Briton(person)
 Brittany
BRTNDR
 bartender
BRTNY
 Britannia
BRTR
 barratry
 barter
BRTRR
 barterer
BRTS
 abortus
BRTSH
 brattish
 British
 brutish
BRTSHKLMB
 British Columbia
BRTSHVRJNLNZ
 British Virgin
  Islands
BRTV
 abortive
BRTWRST
 bratwurst
BRV
 bereave
  bereaved
  bereaving
 brave
  braved
  braving
 bravo
 breve(symbol)
BRVD
 bravado
BRVMNT
 bereavement
BRVR
 braver
  bravest
 bravery
  braveries
 breviary(book)
  breviaries
 brevier(type)
BRVSHN
 abbreviation
BRVSM
 bravissimo
BRVT
 abbreviate
  abbreviated
  abbreviating
 brevet

 brevetted
 brevetting
 brevity
  brevities
BRVTR
 abbreviator
BRVTS
 brevetcy
BRVYR
 bravura(style)
BRVZ
 bravoes(assassins)
 bravos(shouts)
BRZ
 braise(cook)
  braised
  braising
 braze(brass)
  brazed
  brazing
 breeze
  breezed
  breezing
 breezy
  breezier
  breeziest
  breezily
  breeziness
 browse
  browsed
  browsing
 bruise(hurt)
  bruised
  bruising
  bruiser
BRZH
 auberge
 barege(fabric)
 barrage
  barraged
  barraging
BRZHN
 aubergine
 abrasion
BRZHNF
 Brezhnev
  Leonid
BRZHR
 brazier
BRZHW
 bourgeois
BRZHWZ
 bourgeoisie
BRZL
 Brazil
BRZLNG

brisling(fish)
BRZLY
Brasilia
BRZN
brazen
BRZNS
brisance
BRZNT
brisant
BRZR
brassiere
bruiser(person)
BRZRK
berserk
BRZRKR
berserker
BS
abaci(abacus)
abase
abased
abasing
abbacy
abbacies
abbess
abbesses
abyss(pit)
base
based
basing
base(valueless)
baser
basest
bass(fish,voice)
bass(fish)
basses(voices)
basso(singer)
B.C.
(before Christ)
bias
biases
boss
bosses
bossy
bossier
bossily
bossiest
bossiness
bus
buses
bused
busing
buss(kiss)
busses
obese
BSB
bus boy

BSBL
baseball
bice blue
BSBRD
baseboard
BSCH
beseech
beseeches
BSCHL
bestial
BSCHLT
bestiality
bestialities
BSCHN
bastion
BSCHR
bestiary
BSD
beside
BSDN
obsidian
BSDR
abecedary
BSDRM
bass drum
BSDRN
abecedarian
BSDZ
besides
BSFDL
bass fiddle
BSFR
biosphere
BSH
abash
abashes
bash(hit, party)
bashes
boyish
bush
bushes
bushy
bushier
bushiest
bushily
bushiness
BSHFL
bashful
BSHL
bushel
BSHLBSKT
bushel basket
BSHLG
bush league(n)
bush-league(adj)
BSHLGR

bush leaguer
BSHMSTR
bushmaster
BSHNG
bushing
BSHP
bishop
BSHPRK
bishopric
BSHRN
basshorn
BSHT
base hit
bushed(tired)
BSHWK
bushwhack
BSHWKR
bushwhacker
BSJ
besiege
besieged
besieging
BSJR
besieger
BSK
basic
bask(warmth)
Basque(person)
basque(clothing)
bisque(food)
BSKL
basically
bicycle
bicycled
bicycling
BSKLF
bass clef
BSKLST
bicyclist
BSKN
buskin
BSKND
abscond
BSKNDR
absconder
BSKSHL
bisexual
BSKT
basket
biscuit
bisect
Boy Scout
BSKTBL
basketball
BSKTR
basketry

bisector
BSKTS
Boy Scouts
BSKTWV
basket weave
BSKWCHLSHN
absquatulation
BSKWCHLT
absquatulate
absquatulated
absquatulating
BSKWS
obsequious
BSKYL
bascule
BSKWZ
obsequies
BSKYR
obscure
obscured
obscuring
BSKYRT
obscurity
obscurities
BSL
abyssal
abyss
basal
bustle
bustled
bustling
BSLK
basilica
BSLN
base line
BSLS
baseless
obsolesce
BSLSHN
absolution
BSLSNS
obsolescence
BSLSNT
obsolescent
BSLT
absolute
basalt(rock)
obsolete
BSLTST
absolutist
BSLTSTK
absolutistic
BSLTZM
absolutism
obsoletism
BSMN

baseman
BSMNT
basement
BSMR
besmear
BSN
basin
bassoon
bison
boatswain(officer)
bo's'n
obscene
BSNS
absence
obeisance
BSNSCHR
boatswain's chair
BSNSMT
boatswain's mate
BSNT
absent
absentee
bassinet
obeisant
obscenity
obscenities
BSNTH
absinth
BSNTMNDD
absent-minded
BSNTNL
bicentennial
BSNTNR
bicentenary
BSNTZM
absenteeism
BSP
base pay
BSPK
bespeak
bespoke
bespoken
BSPNGL
bespangle
bespangled
bespangling
BSPS
biceps
BSRB
absorb
BSRBBL
absorbable
BSRBNS
absorbency
BSRBR
absorber

BSRD
absurd
BSRDT
absurdity
absurdities
BSRK
berserk
berserker
BSRNR
base runner
BSRPSHN
absorption
BSS
abscess(pus)
abscesses
abscissa(match)
abscissae(or)
abscissas
basis
bases
obsess
obsesses
BSSHN
obsession
BSSV
obsessive
BST
basset
baste
basted
basting
beast
beset
besetting
besot(muddle)
besotted
besotting
besought
beseech
best
good
better
bestow
boast(brag)
boost
bust(arrest,break)
bust(bosom)
busty
bustier
bustiest
obesity
oboist(music)
BSTD
busted(no $)
BSTFL

boastful
BSTKL
obstacle
BSTL
bastille
bestowal
BSTLT
bestiality
bestialities
BSTMN
best man
BSTMNT
besetment
BSTMS
abstemious
BSTN
abstain
bastion
(stronghold)
Boston
BSTND
bastinado
BSTNDR
bystander
BSTNG
basting(sew)
BSTNNS
abstinence
BSTNNT
abstinent
BSTNR
abstainer
BSTNS
abstinence
obstinacy
BSTNSHN
abstention
BSTNT
abstinent
obstinate
BSTR
bestir
bestirred
bestirring
bistro(café)
booster
BSTRD
bastard
BSTRDZ
bastardize
bastardized
bastardizing
bastardization
BSTRKSHN
abstraction
obstruction

BSTRKSHNST
abstractionist
obstructionist
BSTRKSHNZM
abstractionism
BSTRKT
abstract
obstruct
BSTRKTR
abstracter
obstructer
BSTRKTV
abstractive
obstructive
BSTRNG
bowstring
BSTRPRS
obstreperous
BSTRS
abstruse
boisterous
BSTRT
Bass Strait
bystreet
BSTSLNG
best-selling(adj)
BSTSLR
best seller
BSTTRK
obstetric
BSTTRKL
obstetrical
BSTTRSHN
obstetrician
BSTYL
bestial
bestiality
bestialities
BSVL
bass viol
BSWD
basswood
BSZ
abscise
abscised
abscising
besides
BSZHN
abscission
BT
abate(lessen)
abated
abating
abbot(title)
abet(incite)
abetted

---

abetting
about
abut(touch)
  abutted
  abutting
  abutter
bait(fish,torment)
bat(animal)
bat(club)
  batted,batting
  batter
bate(lessen)
  bated
  bating
bateau(boat)
  bateaux
batty(crazy)
  battier
  battiest
  battily
  battiness
beat
  beat
  beaten
beet(plant)
bet(wager)
  bet
  betting
  bettor
bight(loop,curve)
bit(unit,tool)
bit(horse)
  bitted
  biting
bite(teeth)
  bit
  biting
  bitten
bitt(post)
boat
boot
bootee(shoe)
booty(loot)
  booties
bought(buy)
bout(contest)
bowtie
but
butt(ram,end)
byte(computer)
  (group of bits)
BTBLK
  bootblack
BTD
  betide
  betided

betiding
  ebb tide
BTF
  beatify
  beatified
  beatifies
BTFK
  beatific
BTFS
  about-face
BTH
  bath(n)
  bathe(v)
  bathed
  bathing
  both(two)
  booth
BTHK
  boat hook
BTHL
  bethel
BTHNGK
  bethink
  bethought
BTHR
  bother
BTHRB
  bathrobe
BTHRM
  bathroom
BTHRSM
  bothersome
BTHS
  bathos
  boathouse
BTJK
  bootjack
BTK
  batik
  boutique
  buttock
BTKMP
  boot camp
BTKN
  betoken
BTL
  abuttal
  battle
  battled
  battling
  beetle
  betel(plant)
  bottle
  bottled
  bottling
BTLD

boatload
BTLFL
  bottleful
BTLFLD
  battlefield
BTLG
  bootleg
  bootlegged
  bootlegging
BTLGR
  bootlegger
BTLKS
  battle-ax
  battle-axes
BTLNK
  bottleneck
BTLR
  battler(war)
  bottler
  butler
BTLS
  Beatles,the
BTLSHP
  battleship
BTLYN
  battalion
BTLZ
  Beatles, the
BTM
  bottom
BTMN
  batman
  batmen
  bitumen
  boatman
  boatmen
BTMNS
  bituminous
BTMNT
  abatement
  abetment(incite)
  abutment
BTMTSV
  bat mitzvah
BTMZ
  betimes
BTN
  baton
  batten(thin strip)
  beaten
  beat
  Bhutan
  bitten
  botany
  button
  obtain

BTNDN
  button-down(adj)
BTNG
  beating
BTNHK
  buttonhook
BTNHL
  buttonhole
  buttonholed
  buttonholing
BTNK
  beatnik
BTNKL
  botanical
BTNR
  boutonniere
BTNSK
  buttinsky(slang)
  buttinskies
BTNST
  botanist
BTNZ
  botanize
  botanized
  botanizing
BTR
  abettor(incite)
  abutter(abut)
  batter
  battery
  batteries
  beater
  beat
  betray
  better(good)
  bettor(bet)
  bitter(taste)
  butter
  buttery
  butteriness
BTRBL
  butterball
BTRBN
  butter bean
BTRD
  obtrude
  obtruded
  obtruding
BTRDKT
  obiter dicta
BTRDKTM
  obiter dictum
BTRFL
  butterfly
  butterflies
BTRFNGRD

B:by CH:each D:day F:if G:go H:he HW:why J:joy K:cow KS:ax KWL:equal L:all M:may N:in

butterfingered
BTRFT
butterfat
BTRKP
buttercup
BTRL
betrayal
BTRMLK
buttermilk
BTRN
boat train
BTRND
bitter end
BTRNF
butter knife
BTRNG
battering
BTRNGRM
battering-ram
BTRNT
butternut
BTRR
betrayer
BTRS
abtruse
bitters
buttress   buttresses
BTRSKCH
butterscotch
BTRSV
obtrusive
BTRSWT
bittersweet
BTRT
bitterroot
BTRTH
betroth
BTRTHL
betrothal
BTRYR
betrayer
BTRZHN
obtrusion
BTS
obtuse
BTSWN
Botswana
BTTD
beatitude
BTTYD
beatitude
BTWKST
betwixt
BTWN
between
BTWNTMS

betweentimes
BTWR
abattoir
BTY
Btu
  Btu(pl)
  British thermal
  unit
BTYMN
bitumen
BTYMNS
bituminous
BTYS
obtuse
BTZ
bateaux(boats)
  bateau(sing)
BV
above
bevy(group)
  bevies
BVBNGL
Bay of Bengal
BVBRD
aboveboard
BVBSK
Bay of Biscay
BVDZ
beeveedees(or)
  B.V.D.'s
BVK
bivouac
  bivouacked
  bivouacking
BVL
bevel
BVLV
bivalve
BVMNSHND
above-mentioned
BVN
bovine
BVNMD
above-named
BVR
beaver
BVRJ
beverage
BVRS
obverse
  obversion
  obvert
BVRT
obvert
BVRZHN
obversion

BVS
obvious
BVT
obviate
  obviated
  obviating
BVWK
bivouac
  bivouacked
  bivouacking
BW
bow-wow(dog)
byway
BWCH
bewitch
  bewitches
BWDRZ
bois de rose
BWKL
biweekly
  biweeklies
BWL
bewail
bowel
BWLDR
bewilder
BWLDRD
bewildered
BWND
bay window
bow window
BWNF
bowie knife
BWNSRZ
Buenos Aires
BWR
beware
  bewared
  bewaring
BWRD
byword
BY
Bayeux(tapestry)
bayou
BYB
bubo(swelling)
BYBNK
bubonic
BYBNKPLG
bubonic plague
BYBS
bouillabaisse
BYGL
bugle
  bugled
  bugling

bugler
BYGLR
bugler
BYKLK
bucolic
BYLM
bulimia(disease)
  bulimic(person)
BYLMK
bulimic(person)
  bulimia(disease)
BYN
billion
bouillon(soup)
bullion(metal)
BYND
beyond
BYNS
abeyance
buoyancy
BYNT
buoyant
BYR
bureau
buyer
BYRKRS
bureaucracy
  bureaucracies
BYRKRT
bureaucrat
BYRL
biyearly
BYRN
burin(tool)
BYRT
burette
BYRZ
bureaus
BYS
abuse
BYSH
boyish
BYSV
abusive
BYT
beaut(slang)
beauty
  beauties
Butte
butte(hill)
BYTF
beautify(pretty)
  -fied,-fies
  beautification
beatify(happy)
  -fied,-fies

NGK:ink **P:**pie **R:**air **S:**ice **SH:**show **T:**toy **THN:**thin **TH:**the **V:**of **W:**we **Y:**you **Z:**is **VZHN:**vision

beatification
BYTFL
beautiful
BYTL
butyl
BYTN
butane
BYTRK
butyric
BYTRT
butyrate
BYTS
beauteous
BYTSHN
beautician
BYTSHP
beauty shop
BYZ
abuse
  abused
  abusing
  abuser
BYZV
abusive
BZ
baize(cloth)
biz(business)
Boise
booze
  boozed
  boozing
  boozer
  boozy
bouse(hoist)
  boused
  bousing
bozo(person)
busy
  busier
  busiest
  busily
  busyness
busy
  busied
  busies
buzz
  buzzes
BZB
busby(hat)
  busbies
BZBD
busybody
  busybodies
BZH
beige(color)
bijou

bijoux
bougie(candle)
BZHDR
objet d'art
  objets d'art
BZHST
beau geste
BZHZ
bijoux
BZK
bazooka
bezique(card game)
BZL
basil
bezel(bevel)
BZLV
absolve
  absolved
  absolving
BZLVBL
absolvable
BZLVR
absolver
BZM
abysm
besom(broom)
bosom
BZML
abysmal
BZMRK
Bismarck
BZMRKS
Bismarck Sea
BZN
bison
BZNBR
boysenberry
  boysenberries
BZNS
business
  businesses
BZNSHM
Byzantium
BZNSLK
businesslike
BZNSMN
businessman
  businessmen
BZNT
bezant
BZNTM
Byzantium
BZNTN
Byzantine
BZR
bazaar(sale)

bizarre(odd)
buzzer
BZRB
absorb
BZRBBL
absorbable
BZRBBLT
absorbability
BZRBNT
absorbent
BZRD
buzzard
BZRK
berserk(crazy)
  berserker
  (fighter)
BZRPSHN
absorption
BZRV
observe
  observed
  observing
  observer
BZRVBL
observable
BZRVBLT
observability
BZRVNS
observance
BZRVNT
observant
BZRVR
observer
BZRVSHN
observation
BZRVTR
observatory
  observatories
BZS
buzz saw
BZSGNL
busy signal
BZV
absolve
  absolved
  absolving
BZVBL
absolvable
BZVR
absolver
BZWRK
busy-work
BZWKS
beeswax

CH

aitch(letter *h*)
chaw(a chew)
chew
chow
each(every)
etch(engrave)
  etches
itch(scratch)
  itches
  itchy
  itchier
  itchiest
  itchiness
ouch(interj)
CHB
chubby
  chubbier
  chubbiest
  chubbiness
CHBL
chewable
CHBM
H-bomb
CHBN
aitchbone(cow)
CHCH
cha-cha
  cha-chaed
  cha-chaing
chow chow(dog)
chow-chow(relish)
CHD
Chad
chatty
  chattier
  chattiest
  chattily
  chattiness
cheetah(cat)
chide
  chided
  chiding
CHDR
chatter(talk)
cheater(cheat)
cheddar
chowder
CHDRBKS
chatter box
  chatter boxes
CHDRR

B:by **CH**:each **D**:day **F**:if **G**:go **H**:he **HW**:why **J**:joy **K**:cow **KS**:ax **KWL**:equal **L**:all **M**:may **N**:in

chatterer
CHF
chief
chafe(irritate)
chafed
chafing
chaff(husk)
chuff(boor)
CHFJSTS
chief justice
CHFNGDSH
chafing dish
CHFR
chaffer
CHFTN
chieftain
CHFVSTF
chief of staff
CHFVSTT
chief of state
CHG
chug
chugged
chugging
CHGLG
chug-a-lug(drink)
chug-a-lugged
chug-a-lugging
CHGR
chigger
CHK
chalk
check, (B)cheque
cheek
cheeky
cheekier
cheekiest
cheekiness
chick(chicken)
chick(girl)
chock
choke(strangle)
choked,choking
chuck
Czech
CHKBK
checkbook
CHKBN
cheekbone
CHKBRD
chalkboard
CHKD
chickadee
CHKF
checkoff(n)
Chekhov

CHKFL
chock-full
CHKFSK
Tchaikovsky
CHKHL
chuckhole
CHKL
chicle(gum)
chuckle
chuckled
chuckling
CHKLK
chuck-a-luck
CHKLST
check list
CHKLT
chocolate
CHKMRK
check mark
CHKMT
checkmate
CHKN
chicken
CHKNFD
chicken feed
CHKNHRTD
chicken-hearted
CHKNLVRD
chicken-livered
CHKNPKS
chicken pox
CHKNSHT
chicken shit
CHKNWR
chicken wire
CHKP
checkup(n)
CHKPNT
checkpoint
CHKR
checker, (B)chequer
chicory
choker(jewelry)
CHKRBRD
checkerboard
CHKRD
checkered
CHKRM
checkroom
CHKRN
checkrein
CHKRZ
checkers
CHKSLVK
Czechoslovakia
CHKT

checkout(n)
Choctaw
CHKTK
chalk talk
CHKWGN
chuck wagon
CHL
cello(music)
chela(pupil)
child
Chile
chili(food), (B)chilli
chilies
chill(cold)
chilly
chillier
chilliest
chilliness
choil(blade)
CHLBLN
chilblain
CHLD
child
children
CHLDBD
childbed
CHLDBRNG
childbearing
CHLDBRTH
childbirth
CHLDHD
childhood
CHLDLBR
child labor
CHLDLK
childlike
CHLDSH
childish
CHLDSPL
child's play
CHLKNKRN
chili con carne
CHLNJ
challenge
challenged
challenging
challenger
CHLNJBL
challengeable
CHLNJR
challenger
CHLR
chiller(thriller)
CHLRND
accelerando
CHLS

chalice
CHLSS
chili sauce
CHLST
cellist
CHM
chime
chimed
chiming
chum(friend)
chummed
chumming
chummy
chummier
chummiest
chummily
chumminess
CHMBL
cembalo(music)
CHMBR
chamber
CHMBRD
chambered
CHMBRLN
chamberlain
CHMBRMD
chambermaid
CHMBRMZK
chamber music
CHMN
chimney
chow mein
CHMNKRNR
chimney corner
CHMNPT
chimney pot
CHMNSWP
chimney sweep
CHMP
champ
chimp(ape)
chump
CHMPNZ
chimpanzee
CHMPRT
champerty
CHMPYN
champion
CHMPYNSHP
championship
CHN
chain
chin
chinned
chinning
China

china(chinaware)
chine(back)
CHNCHBG
chinch bug
CHNCHL
chinchilla
CHNDLR
chandler
chandlery
CHNG
Ching
etching
I Ching
CHNGK
Chink(slang)
chink(small bit)
chunk(hunk)
chunky
chunkier
chunkiest
chunkiness
CHNGM
chewing gum
CHNGNG
chain gang
CHNJ
change
changed
changing
CHNJBL
changeable
CHNJLNG
changeling
CHNJLS
changeless
CHNJP
change-up(n,adj)
CHNJVR
changeover
CHNL
channel
CHNLLNZ
Channel Islands
CHNLTR
chain letter
CHNLZ
channelize
channelized
channelizing
CHNMN
Chinaman
Chinamen
CHNRKSHN
chain reaction
CHNRKT
chain-react(v)

CHNS
chain saw
chance
chanced
chancing
chancy
chancier
chanciest
CHNSL
chancel
CHNSLR
chancellery
chancellor
CHNSMK
chain-smoke
chain-smoked
chain-smoking
CHNSMKR
chain smoker
CHNSR
chancery
chanceries
CHNSTCH
chain stitch
chain stitches
chain stitcher
CHNSTR
chain store
CHNT
chant
chantey
CHNTKLR
chanticleer
CHNTN
Chinatown
CHNTR
chanter(bagpipe)
chantry
chantries
CHNTS
chintz(cloth)
chintzy(gaudy)
chintzier
chintziest
CHNWR
chinaware
CHNZ
Chinese
CHNZLNTRN
Chinese lantern
CHP
chap
chapped
chapping
cheap(not costly)
cheep(sound)

chip
chipped
chipping
chipper
chop(cut)
chopped
chopping
choppy
choppier
choppiest
choppiness
CHPCHP
chop-chop(hurry)
CHPHS
chophouse
CHPL
chapel
CHPLJK
choplogic
CHPLN
chaplain
CHPMNGK
chipmunk
CHPN
cheapen
CHPR
chipper
chopper
CHPS
chaps
chops
chop suey
CHPSKT
cheapskate
CHPSTKS
chopsticks
CHPTR
chapter
CHR
chair
char
charred
charring
chary(careful)
cheer
cheerio(interj.)
cheery(emotion)
cheerier
cheeriest
cheerily
cheeriness
cherry(fruit)
cherries
chirr(sound)
chore
H-hour

CHRB
cherub
CHRCH
church
churches
CHRCHGNG
churchgoing
CHRCHGR
churchgoer
CHRCHMN
churchman
churchmen
CHRCHWRDN
churchwarden
CHRCHYRD
churchyard
CHRD
chard(beet)
CHRDR
charter
CHRDSH
czardas
CHRFL
cheerful
CHRJ
charge
charged
charging
charger
CHRJBL
chargeable
CHRJKNT
charge account
CHRJPLT
charge-a-plate
CHRK
Cherokee
Cherokee(or)
Cherokees
charqui(meat)
CHRKL
charcoal
CHRL
cerol(freeman)
churl
CHRLFT
chair lift
CHRLHRS
charley horse
CHRLSH
churlish
CHRLSTN
Charleston
CHRM
charm
CHRMN

---

chairman
  chairmanned
  chairmanning
  chairmen
CHRN
  churn
CHRNL
  charnel
CHRP
  chirp
  chirrup(chirp)
CHRSH
  cherish
  cherishes
CHRSTN
  cherrystone
CHRT
  chariot
  charity
  charities
  chart
CHRTBL
  charitable
CHRTL
  chortle
  chortled
  chortling
  chortler
CHRTLR
  chortler
CHRTR
  charioteer
  charter
CHRVL
  chervil
CHRWMN
  chairwoman
  (leader)
  chairwomen
  charwoman
  charwomen
CHRZ
  Cheers(interj)
  (a toast)
  chores(work)
CHS
  chase
  chased
  chasing
  chassis(frame)
  chassis(pl)
  chess
  choice
CHSBRD
  chessboard
CHSHRKT

Cheshire cat
CHSMN
  chessman
  chessmen
CHSN
  chasten
CHSNT
  chestnut
CHSPK
  Chesapeake
CHSR
  chaser
CHSS
  chassis
  chassis
CHST
  chaste(pure)
  chaster
  chastest
  chest
  chesty
  chestier
  chestiest
CHSTT
  chastity
CHSTZ
  chastise
  chastised
  chastising
  chastiser
CHSTZMNT
  chastisement
CHSTZR
  chastiser
CHSYBL
  chasuble(cloak)
CHSZ
  chassis
  chassis
CHT
  chat
  chatted
  chatting
  chatter
  chatty
  chattier
  chattiest
  chattily
  chattiness
  cheat
  cheetah
  chit(bill,child)
CHTCHT
  chitchat
CHTHR
  each other

CHTL
  chattel
CHTLNZ
  chitterlings
CHTN
  chutney
CHTNG
  Chattanooga
CHTR
  chatter
  cheater(person)
CHTRBKS
  chatter box
  chatter boxes
CHTRNG
  chattering
CHTRR
  chatterer
CHV
  achieve
  achieved
  achieving
  achiever
  chive(plant)
  chivvy(harass)
  chivvied
  chivvies
CHVBL
  achievable
CHVMNT
  achievement
CHVR
  achiever
CHZ
  cheese
  cheesy
  cheesier
  cheesiest
  cheesiness
  chews(mouth)
  choose
  chose
  choosing
  chosen
  chooser
  choosy
  choosier
  choosiest
  choosiness
CHZBRGR
  cheeseburger
CHZKK
  cheesecake
CHZKLTH
  cheesecloth
CHZL

chisel
CHZLR
  chiseler
CHZN
  chosen
  (choose)
  Chosen(Korea)
CHZYBL
  chasuble(cloak)

D

A.D.
  anno Domini
ad(advertise)
add(join)
adieu(farewell)
aid
  aided
  aiding
ado(fuss)
aide(helper)
awed
  awe
audio(sound)
dah(code,dash)
dit(dot)
daw(bird)
day
de(origin)
dew(water)
dhow(boat)
die
  died
  dying
die(cube)
  dice
do(tone)
do
  did
  done
  does
  doing
doe(deer)
dough(meal,
  money)
doughy
  doughier
  doughiest
  doughiness
due(payable)
duo(two)

---

dye(color)
  dyed
  dyeing
eddy(water)
  eddied
  eddies
eyed
  eye
I.D.
  identification
I'd
  I had
  I should
  I would
id(psyche)
idea
odd
ode(poem)
owed
  owe

DB
adobe
dab
  dabbed
  dabbing
daub(cover)
daube(meat)
dub
  dubbed
  dubbing
DBCH
debauch
  debauches
  debauchee
DBCHR
debaucher
debauchery
  debaucheries
DBD
daybed
DBDK
diabetic
DBDZ
diabetes
DBG
debug
  debugged
  debugging
DBK
daybook
dieback
DBKL
debacle
DBL
addable(or)
  addible

audible(sound)
dabble
  dabbled
  dabbling
dibble
  dibbled
  dibbling
  dibbler
doable(do)
double
  doubled
  doubling
  doubly
edible(or)
  eatable
oddball
DBLBRLD
double-barreled
DBLBRSTD
double-breasted
DBLCHK
double-check(v)
DBLD
doubled
double
  doubling
DBLDKR
double-decker
DBLDLNG
double-dealing
DBLDT
double-date(v)
  double-dated
  double-dating
DBLFST
double-faced
DBLHDR
double-header
DBLJ
double-edge
DBLJD
double-edged
DBLJNTD
double-jointed
DBLK
diabolic
DBLKRS
double-cross
  double-crosses
  double-crosser
DBLKWK
double-quick
DBLN
doubloon(gold)
Dublin
DBLNT

double-knit(adj)
DBLNTNDR
double-entendre
DBLPRK
double-park
DBLR
dabbler
doublure(lining)
DBLSPS
double-space
  double-spaced
  double-spacing
DBLT
debility
  debilities
doublet
edibility
DBLTNGD
double-tongued
DBLTRBL
double-trouble
DBLTT
debilitate
  debilitated
  debilitating
  debilitation
DBLY
double-u(*w*)
DBLYL
AWOL
  absent without
  leave
DBN
autobahn
dobbin
DBNCHR
debenture
DBNGK
debunk
DBNR
debonair
DBR
dabber
dauber
daubery
debar
  debarred
  debarring
debris(ruins)
dewberry
  dewberries
dibber(tool)
DBRF
debrief
DBRFNG
debriefing

DBRK
daybreak
debark
DBRMNPNSHR
Doberman pinscher
DBS
D-base(computer)
debase(cheapen)
  debasing debased
dubious
DBSH
debouch(v)debouches
débouché(n)
DBSHR
debouchure
DBT
debate
  debated
  debating
debit
dubiety
DBTBL
debatable
DBTK
diabetic
DBTR
debater
DBTS
diabetes
DBTZ
diabetes
DBY
debut
DBYK
Dubuque
DBYTNT
debutante
DBZ
dibs(claim)
DCH
dacha
ditch
  ditches
duchy
  duchies
Dutch
DCHDR
Dutch door
DCHMN
Dutchman
Dutchmen
DCHMRK
deutsche mark
DCHS
duchess
  duchesses

B:by **CH**:each **D**:day **F**:if **G**:go **H**:he **HW**:why **J**:joy **K**:cow **KS**:ax **KWL**:equal **L**:all **M**:may **N**:in

DCHTRT
  Dutch treat
DD
  dad
  daddy
    daddies
  dado
  data(information)
  D-day
  dead
    deaden
  deadeye
  deed
  dewy-eyed
  did(do)
  dido(antic)
  didy(diaper)
    didies
  diode
  dirty(soiled)
    dirtied
    dirties
    dirtier
    dirtiest
    dirtily
    dirtiness
  ditto(same)
  ditty(song)
    ditties
  dodo(bird,stupid)
  dowdy(shabby)
    dowdier
    dowdiest
    dowdily
    dowdiness
  duad(pair)
  dud(fail)
  dude(person)
  duty
    duties
  dyad(pair)
DDBT
  deadbeat
DDD
  doodad
DDFL
  deadfall
DDHD
  deadhead
DDHND
  dead hand
DDHT
  dead heat
DDK
  idiotic
DDKMP

aide-de-camp
  aides-de-camp
DDKSHN
  deduction
DDKT
  dedicate
    dedicated
    dedicating
    dedication
    dedicatee(person)
  deduct
DDKTBL
  deductible
DDKTK
  didactic
DDKTKS
  didactics
DDKTR
  dedicator
  dedicatory
DDKTV
  deductive
DDL
  dawdle
    dawdled
    dawdling
  deadly(killing)
    deadlier
    deadliest
    deadliness
  diddle
    diddled
    diddling
  doodle
    doodled
    doodling
  dottle(tobacco)
DDLFT
  dead lift
DDLK
  deadlock
DDLN
  deadline
DDLTR
  dead letter
DDM
  diadem
DDMRCH
  dead march
DDN
  deaden
  dead
  didn't
    did not
DDND
  dead end(n)

dead-end(adj)
DDNNG
  deadening
DDNS
  dedans
DDNTHWL
  dyed-in-the-wool
DDPN
  deadpan
DDR
  dodder
DDRKNNG
  dead reckoning
DDRM
  daydream
DDRMR
  daydreamer
DDRNT
  deodorant
DDRP
  dewdrop
DDRZ
  deodorize
    deodorized
    deodorizing
DDRZR
  deodorizer
DDS
  Dead Sea
  deduce
    deduced
    deducing
DDSBL
  deducible
DDSML
  duodecimal
DDSNTR
  dead center
DDST
  dead set
DDT
  DDT(insecticide)
DDWD
  deadwood
DDWT
  dead weight
DDYS
  deduce
    deduced
    deducing
    deducible
DDZ
  duds
DF
  daffy(silly)
    daffier

daffiest
  deaf(sound)
  defy(go against)
    defied
    defies
  deify(God)
    deified
    deifies
  doff(remove)
  duff(posterior)
  edify
    edified
    edifies
DFDL
  daffodil
DFDNS
  diffidence
DFDNT
  diffident
DFDST
  defeatist
DFDZM
  defeatism
DFK
  deific
DFKLT
  difficult
  difficulty
    difficulties
DFKSHN
  defecation(feces)
  defection(leave)
  deification(God)
  edification(improve)
DFKT
  de facto
  defecate
    defecated
    defecating
  defect
DFKTR
  defector
DFKTV
  defective
DFL
  audiophile
  defile
    defiled
    defiling
  dewfall
  duffel
DFLBG
  duffel bag
DFLD
  defilade
    defiladed

defilading
DFLGMTR
dephlegmator
DFLGRT
deflagrate
deflagrated
deflagrating
DFLKSHN
defalcation(misuse)
deflection(swerve)
(B)deflexion
DFLKT
defalcate(misuse)
-cated,-cating
deflect(swerve)
DFLKTR
defalcator
deflector
DFLNT
defoliant
DFLR
defiler
deflower
DFLRSHN
defloration
DFLSHN
deflation
defoliation
DFLSHNR
deflationary
DFLT
default
deflate
deflated
deflating
defoliate
defoliated
defoliating
DFLTR
defaulter
deflator
defoliator
DFM
defame
defamed
defaming
DFMR
defamer
DFMSHN
defamation
DFMT
deaf-mute
DFMTR
defamatory
DFMYT
deaf-mute

DFN
daphne
daphnia(fish)
deafen(ear)
define
defined
defining
DFNBL
definable
DFND
defend
DFNDBL
defendable
DFNDDM
deaf-and-dumb(adj)
DFNDNT
defendant
DFNDR
defender
DFNGKT
defunct
DFNNG
deafening
DFNR
definer
DFNS
defense, (B)defence
defensed
defensing
defiance(defy)
diaphanous
DFNSBL
defensible
DFNSHN
definition
DFNSTRSHN
defenestration
DFNSV
defensive
DFNT
defiant
definite
DFNTD
definitude
DFNTV
definitive
DFNTYD
definitude
DFR
defer(put off)
deferred
deferring
defier(defy)
defray
differ(unlike)
duffer(person)

DFRBL
deferrable
defrayable
DFRD
defraud
DFRK
defrock
DFRKSHN
diffraction
DFRKT
diffract
DFRL
deferral
defrayal
DFRM
deform
diaphragm
DFRMD
deformed
DFRMNT
deferment
DFRMSHN
deformation
DFRMT
deformity
deformities
DFRNCHL
differential
DFRNCHT
differentiate
differentiated
differentiating
differentiation
DFRNS
deference(manner)
difference
DFRNSH
differentia
differentiae
DFRNSHL
deferential
(respect)
differential
DFRNSHSHN
differentiation
DFRNSHT
differentiate
differentiated
differentiating
DFRNT
deferent(manner)
different
DFRST
deforest
defrost(ice)
defroster

DFRSTR
deforester
defroster
DFRSTSHN
deforestation
DFS
deface
defaced
defacing
defacer
edifice
DFSHNS
deficiency
deficiencies
DFSHNT
deficient
DFSMNT
defacement
DFST
deficit
DFT
daft
defeat
deft(skill)
DFTHNG
diphthong
DFTHR
diphtheria
DFTST
defeatist
DFTZM
defeatism
DFYSV
diffusive
DFYZ
defuse(fuse, calm)
defused
defusing
diffuse(spread)
diffused
diffusing
DFYZBL
diffusible
DFYZHN
diffusion
DFYZR
diffuser
DFZBL
defeasible
diffusible
DFZNS
defeasance
DG
dago(slang)
dig
dug

digging
dog
  dogged
  dogging
  dogie(calf)
  doggie(dog)
DGDL
  doggedly
DGDR
  do-gooder
DGFT
  dogfight
DGHS
  doghouse
DGKCHR
  dogcatcher
DGLG
  dogleg
  doglegged
DGM
  digamy
  digamous
DGMDK
  dogmatic
  dogma
DGMTK
  dogmatic
DGMTKL
  dogmatical
DGMTST
  dogmatist
DGMTZ
  dogmatize
  dogmatized
  dogmatizing
DGMTZM
  dogmatism
DGN
  doggone(slang)
DGNF
  dignify
  dignified
  dignifies
DGNGZ
  diggings
DGNL
  diagonal
DGNP
  dognap
DGNS
  diagnose
  diagnosed
  diagnosing
DGNSBL
  diagnosable
DGNSS

diagnosis
  diagnoses
DGNSTK
  diagnostic
DGNSTSHN
  diagnostician
DGNT
  dignity
  dignities
DGNTR
  dignitary
  dignitaries
DGNZ
  diagnose
  diagnosed
  diagnosing
DGR
  dagger
  degree
  digger
  dogear
DGRBRD
  daggerboard
DGRD
  degrade
  degraded
  degrading
  degree-day
  dog-eared
DGRDBL
  degradable
DGRDSHN
  degradation
DGRF
  ideograph
DGRFK
  ideographic
DGRFKL
  ideographical
DGRL
  doggerel
DGRM
  diagram
  ideogram
DGRMTK
  diagrammatic
DGRS
  degrease(oil)
  degreased
  degreasing
  degreaser
  digress
  digresses
DGRSHN
  degression(down)
  digression(stray)

DGRSV
  digressive
DGRTP
  daguerreotype
DGS
  degas(gas)
  degassed
  degassing
  degasses
  degasser
  degauss
  degausses
  degausser
DGSH
  doggish
DGSR
  degasser(gas)
  degausser
DGT
  dugout
DGTDG
  dog-eat-dog
DGTG
  dog tag
DGTRD
  dog-tired
DGTRT
  dogtrot
DGWCH
  dogwatch
DGWD
  dogwood
DGZH
  dégagé
DGZR
  degausser
DH
  Idaho
DHDRSHN
  dehydration
DHDRT
  dehydrate
  dehydrated
  dehydrating
DHK
  ad hoc
  doohickey
DHMNM
  ad hominem
DHRD
  die-hard
DHRNS
  adherence
DHRNT
  adherent
DHS

  dehisce
DHSV
  adhesive
DHYMDF
  dehumidify
  dehumidified
  dehumidifies
  dehumidification
DHYMDFR
  dehumidifier
DHYMNZ
  dehumanize
  dehumanized
  dehumanizing
  dehumanization
DHZHN
  adhesion
DHZV
  adhesive
DJ
  adage(saying)
  adagio
  DJ
  disc jockey
  dodge
  dodged
  dodging
  dodger
DJDL
  digital
DJKSHN
  dejection
DJKT
  deject
  dejecta(feces)
DJN
  dudgeon
  tuchun
DJNRS
  degeneracy
  degeneracies
DJNRSHN
  degeneration
DJNRT
  degenerate
  degenerated
  degenerating
DJNRTV
  degenerative
DJNT
  adjutant
DJR
  de jure
  dodger
  dodgery
  dowager

NGK:ink **P**:pie **R**:air **S**:ice **SH**:show **T**:toy **THN**:thin **TH**:the **V**:of **W**:we **Y**:you **Z**:is **VZHN**:vision

DJSCHN
digestion
DJST
digest
DJSTBL
digestible
DJSTR
digester
DJSTV
digestive
DJT
digit
DJTL
digital
DJTLS
digitalis
DK
addict(person)
attic(room)
Dacca
decay(rot)
deck(cards,porch)
decoy(imitation)
dhak(tree)
dick
dickey(collar)
dike(dam)
diked
diking
dock(boat,cut)
duck(bird,flinch)
ducky(fine)
duckier
duckiest
duke
Duke(title)
DKCHR
deck chair
DKD
decade(time)
decayed(dissolve)
decode
decoded
decoding
decoder
DKDM
dichotomy
dichotomies
DKDNS
decadence
DKDNT
decadent
DKHND
deckhand
DKHS
deckhouse

DKJ
dockage
DKL
decal(sign)
deckle
dewclaw
ducal(duke)
DKLG
Decalogue
DKLJD
deckle-edged
DKLM
declaim
DKLMR
declaimer
DKLMSHN
declamation
DKLMTR
declamatory
DKLN
decline
declined
declining
DKLNG
duckling
DKLNSHN
declension
DKLNTR
declinatory
DKLR
declare
declared
declaring
decolor
DKLRBL
declarable
DKLRNT
decolorant
DKLRR
declarer
DKLRSHN
declaration
DKLRTR
declaratory
DKLRTV
declarative
DKLSF
declassify
declassified
declassifies
declassification
DKLT
décolleté
DKLTZH
décolletage
DKLVT

declivity
declivitous
DKMBNT
decumbent
DKMP
aide-de-camp
aides-de-camp
decamp
DKMPRS
decompress
decompresses
DKMPRSHN
decompression
DKMPZ
decompose
decomposed
decomposing
DKMPZSHN
decomposition
DKMTR
decameter
DKN
deacon
DKNR
deaconry
deaconries
DKNS
deaconess
deaconesses
DKNT
decant
DKNTMNNT
decontaminant
DKNTMNT
decontaminate
(make safe)
-nated,-nating
decontamination
DKNTR
decanter
DKNTRL
decontrol
decontrolled
decontrolling
DKNZ
dickens(interj)
DKP
da capo
DKPD
decapod
DKPN
duckpin
DKPTT
decapitate
decapitated
decapitating

decapitation
decapitator
DKPZH
decoupage
DKR
daiquiri(drink)
day-care(adj)
decor
decree(announce)
decreed
decreer
decry
decried
decries
dicker
DKRDKL
diacritical
DKRL
decrial
DKRM
decorum
DKRMNT
decrement
DKRN
Dacron(trademark)
DKRPD
decrepit
DKRPT
decrepit
DKRPTYD
decrepitude
DKRR
decrier
DKRS
decorous
decrease
decreased
decreasing
DKRSHN
decoration
DKRSNTR
day-care center
DKRT
decorate
decorated
decorating
DKRTK
diacritic
DKRTKL
diacritical
DKRTL
decretal
DKRTR
decorator
DKRTV
decorative

DKS
Dixie
doxy
doxies
dukes(fists)
DKSD
dioxide
dockside
DKSDRN
Dexedrine
(trademark)
DKSHN
addiction
diction
DKSHND
dachshund
DKSHNR
dictionary
dictionaries
DKSHNT
dachshund
DKSLJ
doxology
doxologies
DKSLND
Dixieland
DKSN
dachshund
DKST
die cast
DKSTNG
die casting
DKSTR
dexter(right)
DKSTRL
dextral(right)
DKSTRS
dexterous
dextrose
DKSTRT
dexterity
dexterities
DKT
addict(drugs)
docket(court)
ducat
duct
edict
etiquette(manners)
DKTHLN
decathlon
DKTHLT
decathlete
DKTK
deictic
DKTL

dactyl(finger,
verse)
ductile(metal)
DKTLS
ductless(endocrine)
DKTLT
ductility(flexible)
DKTM
dichotomy
dichotomies
dictum
dicta
DKTR
doctor
DKTRL
doctoral
DKTRN
doctrine
DKTRNL
doctrinal
DKTRNR
doctrinaire
DKTRT
doctorate
DKTSHN
dictation
DKTT
dictate
dictated
dictating
DKTTR
dictator
DKTTRL
dictatorial
DKTTRSHP
dictatorship
DKTV
addictive
DKTVSHN
deactivation
DKTVT
deactivate
deactivated
deactivating
DKWS
adequacy
adequacies
DKWT
adequate
etiquette
DKYMNT
document
DKYMNTL
documental
DKYMNTR
documentary

documentaries
DKYMNTSHN
documentation
DKYPL
decuple
DKYRD
dockyard
DL
addle(spoil)
addled
addling
daily
dale(valley)
dally
dallied
dallies
deal
dealt
del(math)
delay
dele(symbol)
deled
Delhi
deli(food)
dell
(wooded valley)
dhole(animal)
dial
dill(herb)
dilly(slang)
dillies
do-all(person)
doily
doilies
dol(unit)
dole(give)
doled
doling
dole(grief)
doleful
doll
dolly
dollies
dowel(rod)
dual(two)
duel(fight)
dull
duly(due)
ideal
idle(not active)
idled
idling
idler
idly(idle)
idol(image)
idyll(poem)

DLB
ad lib(adv)
ad-lib(v,n,adj)
ad-libbed
ad-libbing
Dolby(trademark)
DLBR
ad-libber(n)
DLBRND
addlebrained
DLBRR
day laborer
DLBRT
deliberate
deliberated
deliberating
deliberation
DLBRTR
deliberator
DLBRTV
deliberative
DLBTM
ad libitum
DLCH
dolce
DLD
delude
deluded
deluding
deluder
dildo
DLDBL
deludable
DLDD
delighted
DLDKSHN
delayed-action
DLDL
dilly-dally
dilly-dallied
dilly-dallies
DLDR
deluder
DLDRM
doldrum
DLDRMZ
doldrums
DLF
delft(or)delf
DLFL
doleful
DLFN
dolphin
DLFT
delft(or)delf
DLG

dialogue
  dialogued
  dialoguing
DLGBL
  delegable
DLGS
  delegacy
DLGSHN
  delegation
DLGT
  delegate
  delegated
  delegating
DLJ
  deluge
  deluged
  deluging
  etiology
  ideology(ideas)
  ideologies
DLJKL
  ideological
DLJNS
  diligence
DLJNT
  diligent
DLJST
  ideologist
DLJZ
  ideologize
  ideologized
  ideologizing
DLK
  idyllic
DLKS
  delicacy
  delicacies
  deluxe
DLKT
  delicate
  delict(offense)
  dialect
DLKTBL
  delectable
DLKTK
  dialectic
  dialectical
DLKTSHN
  delectation
DLKTSN
  delicatessen
DLLM
  Dalai Lama(person)
  Dalai Lama(title)
DLM
  bdellium

dilemma
DLMN
  dolman(robe)
  dolmen(tomb)
DLMSHN
  Dalmatian
DLMT
  delimit
DLMTK
  dalmatic
DLN
  delaine(fabric)
DLNG
  daylong(adj,adv)
  dealing
  dealings
DLNGKWNS
  delinquency
  delinquencies
DLNGKWNT
  delinquent
DLNS
  dalliance
  dullness
  idleness
DLNSHN
  delineation
DLNT
  delineate
  delineated
  delineating
DLNTR
  delineator
DLP
  dewlap
  dollop
DLPDT
  dilapidate
  dilapidated
  dilapidating
  dilapidation
DLPDTR
  dilapidator
DLPRPS
  dual-purpose(adj)
DLR
  dallier
  dealer
  delayer(postpone)
  dialer
  dollar(money)
  dolor(grief), (B)dolour
  dueler
  idler
DLRD
  dullard

DLRM
  delirium
DLRMTRMNZ
  delirium tremens
DLRS
  delirious
  dolorous
DLRSHN
  deliration
DLS
  Dallas
  delouse
  deloused
  delousing
  dulse(seaweed)
DLSHN
  deletion
  dilation
  dilution(thin)
DLSHS
  delicious
DLSMR
  dulcimer
DLSNS
  adolescence
DLSNT
  adolescent
DLSNY
  dal segno
DLSR
  delusory
DLSS
  dialysis
  dialyses
DLST
  duelist(fighter)
  dulcet
  idealist
  idlest(lazy)
DLSTK
  dualistic(two)
  idealistic
DLSTKL
  idealistical
DLSV
  delusive
DLT
  adult
  daylight
  delete(remove)
  deleted
  deleting
  delight
  delta
  dilate(open)
  dilated

dilating
dilute
diluted
diluting
dolt
DLTBL
  dilatable
DLTD
  deltoid
DLTFL
  delightful
DLTH
  Duluth
DLTN
  dial tone
DLTNT
  dilettante
DLTNTSH
  dilettantish
DLTNTZM
  dilettantism
DLTR
  adultery
  adulteries
  day letter
  dilator
  dilatory
  idolater(pagan)
  idolatry
  idolatries
DLTRNT
  adulterant
DLTRR
  adulterer
DLTRS
  adulteress(woman)
  adulterous
  deleterious
  idolatrous
DLTRSHN
  adulteration
DLTRT
  adulterate
  adulterated
  adulterating
DLTRTR
  adulterator
DLTS
  daylights(slang)
DLTSH
  doltish
DLTSHN
  dilatation
DLTSVNGTM
  daylight-saving
  time

B:by **CH**:each **D**:day **F**:if **G**:go **H**:he **HW**:why **J**:joy **K**:cow **KS**:ax **KWL**:equal **L**:all **M**:may **N**:in

DLV
delve
  delved
  delving
DLVR
deliver
delivery
  deliveries
DLVRBL
deliverable
DLVRNS
deliverance
DLVRR
deliverer
DLVS
edelweiss
DLWR
Delaware
DLY
dahlia
DLYJ
deluge
  deluged
  deluging
DLZ
dailies(day)
dalles(valley)
idealize
  idealized
  idealizing
idolize
  idolized
  idolizing
oodles
DLZHN
delusion
DLZM
dualism
idealism
DLZSHN
idealization
idolization
DM
atom
autumn
dam
  dammed
  damming
dame(woman)
damn(ruin)
  damnation
deem
demy(paper)
  demies
dim
  dimmed

dimming
dimmer
dimmest
dime(money)
dome(top)
  domed
  doming
doom(fail)
dumb
dummy
  dummies
edema
idiom
item
odium
DMBL
dumbbell
DMBLZ
demobilize
  demobilized
  demobilizing
DMBLZSHN
demobilization
DMD
damned(ruin)
DMDK
automatic
idiomatic
DMDM
dumdum
DMDNS
admittance
DMDST
damnedest
DMFB
demophobia
  demophobic
DMFND
dumfound
DMFSS
de-emphasis
  de-emphases
DMFSZ
de-emphasize
  de-emphasized
  de-emphasizing
DMGD
demigod
DMGG
demagogue
DMGGR
demagoguery
  demagogueries
DMGJ
demagogy
DMGJK

demagogic
DMGNTZ
demagnetize
  demagnetized
  demagnetizing
  demagnetization
DMGRF
demography
  demographic
  demographical
DMGRFR
demographer
DMJ
damage
  damaged
  damaging
DMJBL
damageable
DMJLT
demodulate
  demodulated
  demodulating
  demodulation
  demodulator
DMJN
demijohn
DMKLK
dumb cluck
DMKRS
democracy
  democracies
DMKRT
democrat
DMKRTK
democratic
DMKRTZ
democratize
  democratized
  democratizing
DMKS
dumb ox
DML
dumbly
DMLJ
etymology
  etymologies
  etymological
DMLN
demilune
DMLSH
demolish
  demolishes
DMLSHN
demolition
DMLSHNST
demolitionist

DMLSNT
demulcent
DMLTRZ
demilitarize
  demilitarized
  demilitarizing
  demilitarization
DMN
adman
admen
demean
demesne(law)
demon
  demonic
Des Moines
diamond(stone)
domain
domino
  dominoes
ottoman
DMNBL
damnable
DMNCH
dementia
DMNCHN
dimension
DMND
demand
diamond
DMNDBL
demandable
DMNDNG
demanding
DMNDPL
demand-pull
DMNK
demoniac
demonic
Dominica
Dominique(fowl)
DMNKL
demoniacal
dominical
DMNKNRPBKL
Dominican
Republic
DMNLJ
demonology
DMNNS
dominance
DMNNT
dominant
DMNR
demeanor
domineer
DMNS

dimness
DMNSH
admonish
admonishes
dementia
diminish
diminishes
DMNSHBL
diminishable
DMNSHN
admonition
damnation(curse)
dimension
diminution(small)
domination
DMNSTR
administer
DMNSTRBL
administrable
demonstrable
DMNSTRSHN
administration
demonstration
DMNSTRT
administrate
administrated
administrating
demonstrate
demonstrated
demonstrating
DMNSTRTR
administrator
demonstrator
DMNSTRTV
administrative
demonstrative
DMNT
adamant
dement(mad)
demented
demount
dominate
dominated
dominating
DMNTBL
demountable
DMNTD
demented
DMNTN
Edmonton
DMNTR
admonitor
admonitory
damnatory
dominator
DMNTZ

demonetize
demonetized
demonetizing
DMNYN
dominion(rule,land)
DMNYND
diminuendo
DMNYTV
diminutive
DMNZ
Des Moines
diamonds
dominoes
domino
DMP
damp
dump
DMPDR
damp-dry
damp-dried
damp-dries
DMPF
damp off(v)
DMPK
demipique
DMPL
dimple
dimpled
dimpling
DMPLNG
dumpling
DMPN
dampen
DMPNGF
damping-off(n)
DMPNR
dampener
DMPR
damper
DMR
admire
admired
admiring
dammar(resin)
demur(object)
demurred
demurring
demurrer
demure(reserved)
demurer
demurest
dimmer
DMRBL
admirable
DMRJ
demiurge(deity)

demurrage
DMRJK
demiurgic
DMRKSHN
demarcation
DMRKT
demarcate
demarcated
demarcating
demarcator
DMRL
admiral
Demerol(trademark)
demurral
DMRLT
admiralty
DMRLZ
demoralize
demoralized
demoralizing
demoralization
demoralizer
DMRP
demirep
DMRR
admirer
demurrer
DMRSH
démarche
DMRT
demerit
demeritorious
DMSBL
admissible
DMSHN
admission
demission
DMSK
damask
DMSKS
Damascus
DMSL
damsel
domicile
domiciled
domiciling
DMSN
damascene
damascened
damascening
DMST
dimmest
DMSTF
demystify
demystified
demystifies

DMSTFKSHN
demystification
DMSTK
domestic
DMSTKSHN
domestication
DMSTKT
domesticate
domesticated
domesticating
DMSTST
domesticity
domesticities
DMT
admit
admitted
admitting
demit(resign)
demitted
demitting
demission
demote
demoted
demoting
demotion
dimity(fabric)
dimities
dimout
DMTBL
admittable
DMTK
idiomatic
DMTKL
idiomatically
DMTNS
admittance
DMTR
diameter
dimeter(verse)
odometer
DMTRK
diametric
DMTRKL
diametrical
DMTS
demitasse
DMVRT
duumvirate
DMVYRZH
demivierge
DMWT
dimwit
dimwitted
DMWTD
dimwitted
DMWTR

dumbwaiter
DMWZL
demoiselle
DMYR
demure
 demurer
 demurest
DMZ
demise(death)
 demised
 demising
 demisable
DMZ
 demilitarized
 zone
itemize
 itemized
 itemizing
 itemization
DMZD
doomsday
DMZL
damsel
DMZN
damson(plum)
DMZR
atomizer
DN
dawn
dean(college)
deign
den(place)
deny
 denied
 denies
din(noise)
 dinned
 dinning
dine(eat)
 dined
 dining
Don(or)
don(title)
don(put on)
 donned
 donning
done(do)
donee(recipient)
Donna(or)
donna(title)
down
downy
 downier
 downiest
 downiness
doyen(eldest)(m)

doyenne(f)
duenna(person)
dun(bill)
 dunned
 dunning
dyne(force)
iodine
DNBL
deniable
DNBRK
donnybrook
DNBT
downbeat
DNCHLS
dentulous
DNCHR
denature
 denatured
 denaturing
 denaturant
 denaturation
DNCHRLZ
denaturalize
 denaturalized
 denaturalizing
 denaturalization
DNCHRNT
denaturant
DND
addend(numbers)
addenda(additions)
adenoid
dandy
 dandies
 dandier
 dandiest
denude
 denuded
 denuding
 denudation
DNDF
dandify
 dandified
 dandifies
 dandification
DNDL
adenoidal
dandle
 dandled
 dandling
DNDLN
dandelion
DNDM
addendum
 addenda
DNDR

dander
DNDRF
dandruff
 dandruffy
DNDRLJ
dendrology
DNDZ
adenoids
DNF
identify
 identified
 identifies
DNFKSHN
identification
 I.D.
DNFL
downfall
DNFNTM
ad infinitum
DNG
dengue(disease)
ding(noise)
 dong
dinghy(boat)
dong(noise)
 ding
dung
dying(die)
DNGBT
dingbat
DNGDNG
ding-dong(bell)
DNGG
dengue(disease)
DNGGL
dangle
 dangled
 dangling
 dangler
DNGGR
dungaree
DNGGS
dingus(slang)
DNGHL
dunghill
DNGK
dank(damp)
dinkey(train)
dinky(small)
 dinkier
 dinkiest
donkey
dunk
DNGL
dangle
 dangled

dangling
dangler
DNGLNG
ding-a-ling
DNGLR
dangler
DNGR
dungaree
DNGRD
downgrade
 downgraded
 downgrading
DNGRSHN
denigration
DNGRT
denigrate
 denigrated
 denigrating
 denigrator
DNGSHN
denegation
DNHL
downhill
DNHRTD
downhearted
DNJ
dingy(dirty)
 dingier
 dingiest
 dinginess
dunnage
DNJN
dungeon
DNJR
danger
DNJRS
dangerous
DNKHT
Don Quixote
DNKST
downcast
DNKWKST
Don Quixote
DNL
denial
DNM
denim
dynamo
DNMK
dynamic
DNMKL
dynamically(force)
DNMN
denouement
DNMNSHN
denomination

DNMNTR
denominator
DNMNTV
denominative
DNMRK
Denmark
DNMT
dynamite
dynamited
dynamiting
DNMZM
dynamism
DNNDR
down under
DNNGKR
dining car
DNNS
denounce
denounced
denouncing
DNNSR
denouncer
DNNSSHN
denunciation
DNNST
denunciate
denunciated
denunciating
DNPR
downpour
DNR
deanery
deaneries
denier(deny)
denier(weave)
diner(person)
dinero(money)
dinner(meal)
donor
downer(slang)
DNRNJ
downrange
DNRSR
day nursery
day nurseries
DNRT
downright
DNS
audience
dance
danced
dancing
dancer
dense(thick)
denser
densest

dunce
DNSBL
danceable
DNSH
Danish
danish(pastry)
donnish
DNSHN
donation
DNSHNLZ
denationalize
denationalized
denationalizing
denationalization
DNSPT
downspout
DNSR
dancer
dinosaur
DNST
density
densities
dynasty
dynasties
DNSTJ
downstage
DNSTRM
downstream
DNSTRZ
downstairs
DNSTT
downstate
DNSWNG
downswing
DNT
dainty(delicate)
daintier
daintiest
daintily
daintiness
dainties
daunt
denote
denoted
denoting
dent
detonate(explode)
detonated
detonating
detonation
detonator
dinette(table)
dint(force)(n)
donate(give)
donated
donating

donation
don't
doughnut
identity
identities
DNTF
identify
identified
identifies
DNTFBL
identifiable
DNTFKSHN
identification
DNTFR
identifier
DNTFRS
dentifrice
DNTHNG
do-nothing
DNTHNGZM
do-nothingism
DNTK
identic
DNTKL
identical
DNTL
dental
DNTLJ
deontology
DNTLS
dauntless
DNTM
downtime
DNTN
dentine
dentinal
downtown
DNTRDN
downtrodden
DNTRM
ad interim
DNTRN
downturn
DNTRTH
down-to-earth
DNTSHN
denotation
dentation
DNTST
dentist
DNTSTR
dentistry
DNTT
identity
identities
DNWND

downwind
DNWRD
downward
DNWSH
downwash
DNY
denier
Doña(or)
doña(title)
DNYB
Danube
DNYD
denude
denuded
denuding
denudation
DNYR
denier
DNZHM
ad nauseam
DNZLST
dean's list
DNZM
ad nauseam
DNZN
denizen
DP
dap(fish)
dapped
dapping
deep
depot(station)
dip
dipped
dipping
dipper
dippy(foolish)
dippier
dippiest
dope
doped
doping
dopy(dazed)
dopier
dopiest
dupe(fool)
duped
duping
DPCHSTD
deep-chested
DPDD
deep-dyed
DPDSHP
deep-dish pie
DPFR
deep-fry

B:by **CH**:each **D**:day **F**:if **G**:go **H**:he **HW**:why **J**:joy **K**:cow **KS**:ax **KWL**:equal **L**:all **M**:may **N**:in

deep-fried
deep-fries
DPFRZ
  Deepfreeze
    (trademark)
DPFRZR
  deepfreezer
    (refrigerator)
DPKSHN
  depiction
DPKT
  depict
DPKTR
  depictor
DPL
  dapple
    dappled
    dappling
  deploy
  dipole(antenna)
  duple(two)
DPLD
  deep-laid
DPLJ
  deplegia
DPLKS
  duplex
    duplexes
    duplexity
DPLKSHN
  duplication
DPLKT
  duplicate
    duplicated
    duplicating
DPLKTR
  duplicator
DPLM
  deplume
    deplumed
    depluming
    deplumation
  diploma(school)
DPLMNT
  deployment
DPLMS
  diplomacy
    diplomacies
DPLMT
  diplomat(official)
  diplomate(medical)
DPLMTK
  diplomatic
DPLMTKL
  diplomatically
DPLN

deplane
deplaned
deplaning
DPLR
  deplore
    deplored
    deploring
  Doppler(physicist)
    Christian Johann
DPLRBL
  deplorable
DPLRFKT
  Doppler effect
DPLRZ
  depolarize
    depolarized
    depolarizing
    depolarization
DPLSHN
  depletion
DPLST
  duplicity
    duplicities
DPLT
  depilate
    depilated
    depilating
  deplete
    depleted
    depleting
DPLTBL
  depletable
DPLTR
  depilator
    depilatory
    depilatories
DPN
  deepen
DPND
  depend
DPNDBL
  dependable
DPNDNS
  dependence
  dependency
    dependencies
    dependents
DPNDNT
  dependent
DPNNT
  deponent
DPNT
  dew point
DPPYLT
  depopulate
    depopulated

depopulating
depopulation
DPR
  dapper(neat)
  diaper
  dipper(scoop)
DPRCHR
  departure
DPRDD
  departed
DPRDSHN
  depredation
DPRDT
  depredate
    depredated
    depredating
DPRFL
  dipperful
DPRGRM
  deprogram
    deprogrammed
    deprogramming
    deprogrammer
DPRKSHN
  deprecation
DPRKT
  deprecate
    deprecated
    deprecating
DPRKTR
  deprecator
  deprecatory
DPRS
  depress
    depresses
DPRSBL
  depressible
DPRSHBL
  depreciable
DPRSHN
  depression
DPRSHT
  depreciate
    depreciated
    depreciating
    depreciation
DPRSHTR
  depreciator
  depreciatory
DPRSNLZ
  depersonalize
    depersonalized
    depersonalizing
    depersonalization
DPRSNT
  depressant

DPRSR
  depressor
DPRT
  depart
  deport
  deportee
DPRTBL
  deportable
DPRTD
  deep-rooted
  departed
DPRTMNT
  department
  deportment
DPRTMNTLZ
  departmentalize
    departmentalized
    departmentalizing
DPRTMNTLZSHN
  departmentalization
DPRTSHN
  deportation
DPRV
  deprave
    depraved
    depraving
  deprive(deny)
    deprived
    depriving
DPRVSHN
  deprivation
DPRVT
  depravity
    depravities
DPS
  adipose
  deep-sea(adj)
  depths(deepest part)
DPSDDL
  dipsy-doodle
DPSHN
  adaption(or)
    adaptation
  adoption
DPSMN
  dipsomania
    dipsomaniac
DPSPS
  deep space
DPSTD
  deep-seated
DPSTK
  dipstick
DPT
  adapt(adjust)
  adept(skilled)

---

adopt(keep)
DPTBL
adaptable
adoptable
DPTH
depth
DPTHNG
diphthong
DPTHR
diphtheria
DPTR
adapter
adopter
diopter
DPTRKS
dioptrics
DPTSHN
adaptation
DPTV
adaptive
DPYD
deputy
deputies
DPYRT
depurate
depurated
depurating
depuration
DPYT
depute(delegate)
deputed
deputing
deputy
deputies
DPYTSHN
deputation
DPYTZ
deputize
deputized
deputizing
DPZ
depose
deposed
deposing
DPZHN
depositon
DPZL
deposal
DPZT
deposit
DPZTR
depositor
depository
depositories
DR
adder(snake)

adore
adored
adoring
dairy(cow)
dairies
dare
dared
daring
dear(loved)
deary(darling)
dearies
deer(animal)
derry(music)
derries
diarrhea
diary(record)
diaries
dire(dreadful)
doer(do)
door
dor(insect)
dory(water)
dories
dour(stern)
dower(estate)
dowry
dowries
draw
drew
drawn
drawee
dray(cart)
dry
dried
dries
durra(grain)
dyer(dye)
eider(duck)
odor(smell), (B)odour
otter
outer(out)
udder(milk)
utter(speak)
DRB
darb
derby(hat)
derbies
Derby(race)
drab(dull)
drabber
drabbest
drab(whore)
drabbed
drabbing
drub
drubbed

drubbing
DRBK
drawback
DRBL
adorable
doorbell
dribble(drip)
dribbled
dribbling
dribbler
durable
durably
DRBLT
driblet
durability
durabilities
DRBNKS
Outer Banks
DRBR
drabber
DRBRJ
drawbridge
DRBRN
Dearborn
DRBST
drabbest
DRD
deride
derided
deriding
do-or-die
dread(fear)
druid
dry-eyed
DRDFL
dreadful
DRDK
dry dock(n)
dry-dock(v)
DRDL
dartle(dart)
dartled
dartling
DRDN
eiderdown
DRDNT
dreadnought
DRDP
dried-up
DRDVL
daredevil
DRF
draff(days)
DRFL
direful
DRFRM

dairy farm
DRFRS
odoriferous
DRFT
adrift
draft, (B)draught
draftee
drafty
draftier
draftiest
draftiness
drift
drifty
DRFTR
drifter
DRFTSMN
draftsman (B)draughts-
draftsmen (B)draughts-
DRFTWD
driftwood
DRG
drag
dragged
dragging
draggy
draggier
draggiest
drug
drugged
drugging
DRGDZ
dry goods
DRGL
draggle
draggled
draggling
DRGLCH
drygulch(ambush)
drygulches
drygulcher
DRGMN
dragoman
DRGN
dragon(monster)
dragoon(soldier)
DRGNFL
dragonfly
dragonflies
DRGNT
dragnet
DRGR
de rigueur(fashion)
DRGSHN
derogation
DRGST
druggist

B:by **CH**:each **D**:day **F**:if **G**:go **H**:he **HW**:why **J**:joy **K**:cow **KS**:ax **KWL**:equal **L**:all **M**:may **N**:in

DRGSTR
dragster(car)
drugstore
DRGSTRP
drag strip
dragway
DRGT
derogate
derogated
derogating
drugget(fabric)
DRGTR
derogatory
derogatorily
DRGTV
derogative
DRGZ
dregs
drugs
DRJ
dirge(lament)
drayage
dredge(deepen)
dredged
dredging
drudge
drudged
drudging
DRJBL
dirigible
DRJLNG
Darjeeling
DRJM
doorjamb
DRJR
dredger
drudgery
drudgeries
DRK
dark
darky(slang)
darkies
derrick(crane)
dirk
dreck(trash)
duroc(hog)
DRKDL
dairy cattle
DRKHRS
dark horse
DRKJZ
Dark Ages
DRKLN
dry-clean
DRKLNG
darkling

DRKLNNG
dry cleaning
DRKLNR
dry cleaner
DRKLNTRN
dark lantern
DRKM
drachma
DRKN
darken
DRKNN
draconian
DRKNTNNT
Dark Continent
DRKPR
doorkeeper
DRKRM
darkroom
DRKSHN
direction
DRKT
direct
DRKTL
dairy cattle
DRKTR
director
directory
directories
DRKTRL
directorial
DRKTRT
directorate
DRKTV
directive
DRL
dariole(food)
derail
drawl(accent)
drill
droll(clown)
drolly
drool
dryly
DRLKSHN
dereliction
DRLKT
derelict
DRLMSTR
drillmaster
DRLNG
darling
DRLNS
drollness
DRLPRS
drill press
drill presses

DRLR
derailleur
drollery
drolleries
DRM
derma(skin)
dermal
dharma(law)
diorama
dirham
do-re-mi(slang-$)
dorm(dormitory)
dram(weight)
drama(theater)
dream
dreamy
dreamier
dreamiest
dreamily
dreaminess
drum
drummed
drumming
drummer
durum(wheat)
DRMBT
dreamboat
drumbeat
DRMD
dairymaid
DRMDK
dramatic
DRMDR
dromedary
dromedaries
DRMHD
drumhead
DRMJR
drum major
DRML
dermal
dreamily
DRMMN
Dramamine
(trademark)
DRMN
dairyman(milk)
dairymen
doorman
doormen
drayman
draymen
DRMNS
dormancy
dormancies
dreaminess

DRMNT
diriment(void)
dormant
DRMR
dormer
dreamer
dreamier
drummer
DRMS
dermis(skin)
dormouse
dormice
DRMST
dreamiest
DRMSTK
drumstick
DRMT
doormat
DRMTK
dramatic
DRMTKL
dramatically
DRMTLJ
dermatology
DRMTR
dormitory
dormitories
DRMTRJ
dramaturge
dramaturgy
DRMTSS
dermatosis
DRMTST
dramatist
DRMTTS
dermatitis
DRMTZ
dramatize
dramatized
dramatizing
DRMTZSHN
dramatization
DRN
adorn
darn
dourine(disease)
drain(pipe,empty)
drawn
drone(noise)
droned
droning
drone(bee)
drown(water)
DRNB
doorknob
DRNCH

drench
drenches
DRND
derring-do
DRNDK
Adirondack
DRNDL
dirndl
DRNF
drawknife
DRNG
drawing
during
DRNGK
drink
drank
drunk
DRNGKBL
drinkable
DRNGKN
drunken
DRNGKNG
drinking
DRNGKNS
drunkenness
DRNGKRD
drunkard
DRNJ
derange
deranged
deranging
drainage
DRNJMNT
derangement
DRNJR
derringer
DRNL
adrenal
diurnal
doornail
DRNPP
drainpipe
DRNS
dryness
durance
utterance
DRNVS
drawknives
DRNWRK
drawnwork
DRNYKR
dernier cri
DRP
drape
draped
draping

drip
dripped
dripping
drippy
drippier
drippiest
droop(bend)
droopy
droopier
droopiest
droopily
droopiness
drop
dropped
dropping
dropper
drupe(fruit)
drupelet
drupaceous
DRPDR
drip-dry
drip-dried
drip-dries
DRPFRJ
drop-forge
drop-forged
drop-forging
DRPKK
drop kick(n)
drop-kick(v)
DRPKLTH
drop cloth(cover)
DRPLT
doorplate
droplet
drupelet(berry)
DRPNGZ
drippings
droppings
DRPR
eyedropper
draper
drapery
draperies
dropper
DRPS
dropsy
DRPT
dropout(n)
drop out(v)
DRR
derrière(rear)
drawer
dreary
drearier
dreariest

drearily
dreariness
drier(dry)
dryer(machine)
DRS
address
addresses
addressee
dress(attire)
dresses
dressy
dressier
dressiest
dressily
dressiness
dross
drossy
drossiness
dry ice
duress(force)
odorous
DRSBL
derisible
DRSHN
adoration
duration
DRSJ
dressage
DRSL
doorsill
dorsal(rear)
DRSMKR
dressmaker
DRSNG
dressing
DRSNGDN
dressing-down
DRSR
addresser
derisory(or)
derisive
dresser
DRSS
dieresis
diereses
DRST
diarist
DRSTK
drastic
DRSTKL
drastically
DRSTP
doorstep
doorstop
DRSTRNG
drawstring

derisive
DRSZH
dressage
DRT
adroit
dart
dirt(soil)
dirty
dirtied
dirties
dirtier
dirtiest
dirtily
dirtiness
drat(interj)
draught(draft)
droit(right)
drought(scarcity)
(or)drouth
DRTCHP
dirt-cheap
DRTDR
door-to-door(adj)
DRTFRMR
dirt farmer
DRTH
dearth
DRTKS
Adriatic Sea
DRTL
dartle(dart)
dartled
dartling
DRTR
darter
DRTSMN
draughtsman
draughtsmen
DRV
derive
derived
deriving
drive(direct)
drove
driving
driven
DRVBL
derivable
drivable
DRVL
drivel
DRVN
drive-in(n)
driven
DRVNG

DRSV

B:by **CH**:each **D**:day **F**:if **G**:go **H**:he **HW**:why **J**:joy **K**:cow **KS**:ax **KWL**:equal **L**:all **M**:may **N**:in

driving(power)
DRVR
driver
drover
DRVSH
dervish
DRVSHN
derivation
DRVTV
derivative
DRVW
driveway
DRW
doorway
DRYR
dryer(machine)
DRZ
drowse
drowsed
drowsing
drowsy
drowsier
drowsiest
drowsily
drowiness
DRZH
dragée(candy)
DRZHN
derision
DRZL
drizzle
drizzled
drizzling
drizzly
drizzlier
drizzliest
drizzliness
DS
adduce(cite)
adduced
adducing
adios
dais(platform)
daises
deice
deiced
deicing
deicer
deuce
dice(cut)
diced
dicing
dice(game)
die
dose(quantity)
dosed

dosing
doss(bed)(slang)
dosses
dossier(file)
douse(water)
doused
dousing
douser
educe(deduce)
educed
educing
educible
idiocy
idiocies
odious
Odyssey(epic)
odyssey
DSB
disobey
DSBB
Addis Ababa
DSBDNS
disobedience
DSBDNT
disobedient
DSBL
adducible(cite)
educible(deduce)
decibel(sound)
disable
disabled
disabling
dishabille(dress)
DSBLF
disbelief
DSBLJ
disoblige
disobliged
disobliging
DSBLMNT
disablement
DSBLT
disability
disabilities
DSBLV
disbelieve
disbelieved
disbelieving
disbeliever
DSBR
disbar
disbarred
disbarring
DSBRMNT
disbarment
DSBRS

disburse
disbursed
disbursing
DSBRSBL
disbursable
DSBRSMNT
disbursement
DSBRSR
disburser
DSBYZ
disabuse
disabused
disabusing
DSCHRJ
discharge
discharged
discharging
discharger
DSD
decide
decided
deciding
DSDBL
decidable
DSDN
disdain
DSDNBL
disdainable
DSDNFL
disdainful
DSDNS
dissidence
dissidents
(people)
DSDNT
decedent
dissident
(disagree)
DSDRSHN
desideration
DSDVNTJ
disadvantage
disadvantaged
DSDVNTJS
disadvantageous
DSDVNTJT
disadvantaged
DSFGRMNT
disfigurement
DSFGYR
disfigure
disfigured
disfiguring
DSFGYRMNT
disfigurement
DSFJ

dysphagia
DSFKSHN
disaffection
DSFKT
disaffect
DSFLT
disaffiliate
disaffiliated
disaffiliating
DSFN
dysphonia
DSFNGSHN
dysfunction
DSFR
decipher
dysphoria
DSFRBL
decipherable
DSFRM
disaffirm
DSFRNCHZR
disfranchiser
DSFVR
disfavor
DSFZH
dysphasia
DSGR
disagree
disagreed
DSGRBL
disagreeable
DSGRGSHN
desegregation
DSGRGT
desegregate
desegregated
desegregating
DSGRJ
disgorge
disgorged
disgorging
DSGRM
decigram
DSGRMNT
disagreement
DSGRNTL
disgruntle
disgruntled
disgruntling
disgruntlement
DSGRS
disgrace
disgraced
disgracing
DSGRSFL
disgraceful

NGK:ink **P**:pie **R**:air **S**:ice **SH**:show **T**:toy **THN**:thin **TH**:the **V**:of **W**:we **Y**:you **Z**:is **VZHN**:vision

DSGRSHN
discretion
DSGRSHNR
discretionary
DSGST
disgust
DSGZ
disguise
disguised
disguising
DSH
dash
dashes
dish
dishes
douche
douched
douching
DSHBRD
dashboard
DSHN
audition
edition(book)
ideation
DSHNG
dashing
DSHNST
dishonest
dishonesty
dishonesties
DSHPN
dishpan
DSHR
dasher
DSHRG
dishrag
DSHRMN
disharmony
disharmonies
DSHRTN
dishearten
DSHS
audacious
DSHTL
dishtowel
DSHTWL
dishtowel
DSHVL
dishevel
DSHVLD
disheveled
DSHVLMNT
dishevelment
DSHWSHR
dishwasher
DSHWTR

dishwater
DSJ
dosage
DSJK
disc jockey
DJ
DSJKT
disject
DSJN
disjoin
DSJNGKSHN
disjunction
DSJNK
dysgenic
DSJNT
disjoint
DSJS
deciduous
DSK
desk
disc(record)
disco
disk(all but
record)
dusk
dusky
duskier
duskiest
duskily
duskiness
DSKGRF
discography
DSKGRFR
discographer
DSKHWL
disk wheel
DSKJK
disc jockey
DJ
DSKL
day school
DSKLM
disclaim
DSKLMR
disclaimer
DSKLR
discolor
DSKLSHN
de-escalation
DSKLT
de-escalate
de-escalated
de-escalating
DSKLZ
disclose
disclosed

disclosing
DSKLZHR
disclosure
DSKMBBYLT
discombobulate
discombobulated
discombobulating
DSKMD
discommode
discommoded
discommoding
DSKMFCHR
discomfiture
DSKMFT
discomfit
DSKN
doeskin
DSKNKSHN
disconnection
DSKNKT
disconnect
DSKNSLT
disconsolate
DSKNSRT
disconcert
DSKNT
descant
desiccant
discount
DSKNTN
discontinue
discontinued
discontinuing
DSKNTNNS
discontinuance
discountenance
DSKNTNS
discontinuous
DSKNTNT
discontent
DSKNTNY
discontinue
discontinued
discontinuing
discontinuance
discontinuation
DSKNTNYNS
discontinuance
DSKNTNYS
discontinuous
DSKR
descry
descried
descries
descrier
DSKRB

describe
described
describing
DSKRBBL
describable
DSKRD
disaccord
discard
discord
DSKRDNS
discordance
DSKRDNT
discordant
DSKRDT
discredit
DSKRDTBL
discreditable
DSKRJ
discourage
discouraged
discouraging
DSKRJMNT
discouragement
DSKRMNBL
discriminable
DSKRMNNT
discriminant
DSKRMNT
discriminate
discriminated
discriminating
discrimination
DSKRMNTR
discriminator
discriminatory
DSKRPNS
discrepancy
discrepancies
DSKRPNT
discrepant
DSKRPSHN
description
DSKRPTV
descriptive
DSKRR
descrier
descry
DSKRS
discourse
discoursed
discoursing
DSKRSHN
desecration
discretion
discreet
discursion

DSKRSHNR
discretionary
DSKRSV
discursive
DSKRT
desecrate
desecrated
desecrating
desecration
discreet(prudent)
discrete(separate)
DSKRTR
desecrater
DSKRTS
discourteous
discourtesy
discourtesies
DSKRZHN
discursion
DSKS
discus(sport)
discuss(talk)
discusses
DSKSBL
discussible
DSKSHN
discussion
dissection
DSKSNT
discussant
DSKT
desiccate(dry)
-ated,-ating
-ation,-ative
desiccator
diskette
dissect
DSKTK
discotheque
DSKTR
desiccator
dissector
DSKVR
discover
discovery
discoveries
DSKVRBL
discoverable
DSKVRR
discoverer
DSKWL
disk wheel
DSKWLF
disqualify
disqualified
disqualifies

disqualifier
DSKWLFKSHN
disqualification
DSKWT
disquiet
DSKWTYD
disquietude
DSKWZSHN
disquisition
DSKZ
disguise
disguised
disguising
DSL
diesel
disallow
docile
odiously
DSLJ
dislodge
dislodged
dislodging
DSLJMNT
dislodgment
DSLK
dislike
disliked
disliking
DSLKBL
dislikable
DSLKS
dyslexia
DSLKSHN
dislocation
DSLKT
dislocate
dislocated
dislocating
DSLL
disloyal
DSLLT
disloyalty
disloyalties
DSLRN
deceleron
DSLRSHN
deceleration
DSLRT
decelerate
decelerated
decelerating
deceleration
DSLRTR
decelerator
DSLSHN
disillusion

dissolution
desolation
DSLT
desolate(empty)
desolated
desolating
desolation
dissolute
docility
DSLTR
deciliter(measure)
desolater
desultory
desultorily
desultoriness
DSLV
dissolve
dissolved
dissolving
DSLYBL
dissoluble
DSLYL
disloyal
DSLYLT
disloyalty
disloyalties
DSLYN
decillion
DSM
dismay
DSMBD
disembody
disembodied
disembodies
DSMBL
disembowel
dissemble
dissembled
dissembling
DSMBLMNT
disembowelment
DSMBLNS
dissemblance
DSMBLR
dissembler
DSMBR
December
DSMBRK
disembark
DSMBRKSHN
disembarkation
DSMDR
decimator(destroy)
decimeter(length)
DSML
decimal

DSMLR
dissimilar
DSMLRT
dissimilarity
dissimilarities
DSMLSHN
dissimilation
DSMLTD
dissimilitude
DSMLTYD
dissimilitude
DSMLZ
decimalize
decimalized
decimalizing
DSMMBR
dismember
DSMNSHN
dissemination
DSMNT
dismount
disseminate
disseminated
disseminating
DSMNTL
dismantle
dismantled
dismantling
DSMNTR
disseminator
DSMS
dismiss
dismisses
DSMSBL
dismissible
DSMSL
dismissal
DSMT
decimate
decimated
decimating
decimation
DSMTR
decimator(destroy)
decimeter(length)
dissymmetry
dissymmetries
DSMYLT
dissimulate
dissimulated
dissimulating
dissimulation
DSMYLTR
dissimulator
DSN
disown

NGK:ink P:pie R:air S:ice SH:show T:toy THN:thin TH:the V:of W:we Y:you Z:is VZHN:vision

DSNCHN
dissension
DSNCHNT
disenchant
dissentient
DSNCHNTMNT
disenchantment
DSNCHS
dissentious
DSND
descend
DSNDBL
descendible
DSNDNT
descendant(n)
descendent(adj)
DSNDR
descender
DSNFKT
disinfect
DSNFKTNT
disinfectant
DSNFLSHN
disinflation
DSNFLT
disinflate
disinflated
disinflating
DSNFRNCHZ
disenfranchise
disenfranchised
disenfranchising
DSNFST
disinfest
DSNG
dousing
educing
DSNGKRS
idiosyncrasy
idiosyncrasies
DSNGKRTK
idiosyncratic
DSNGRSHN
disintegration
DSNGRT
disintegrate
disintegrated
disintegrating
disintegrator
disintegration
DSNHRT
disinherit
DSNHRTNS
disinheritance
DSNJNYS
disingenuous

DSNKLN
disincline
disinclined
disinclining
DSNKLNSHN
disinclination
DSNL
decennial
DSNM
decennium
DSNNS
desinence(ending)
dissonance(discord)
DSNNT
dissonant
DSNR
dishonor
DSNRBL
dishonorable
DSNS
decency
decencies
DSNSHN
dissension
DSNSHNT
dissentient
DSNSHS
dissentious
DSNSNTV
disincentive
DSNST
dishonest
dishonesty
dishonesties
DSNSTZ
desensitize
desensitized
desensitizing
DSNSTZR
desensitizer
DSNT
adducent
decent(passable)
descent(down)
dissent(disagree)
docent(teacher)
DSNTGRSHN
disintegration
DSNTGRT
disintegrate
disintegrated
disintegrating
DSNTGRTR
disintegrator
DSNTHRL
disenthrall

DSNTHRLMNT
disenthrallment
DSNTL
disentail
DSNTNGL
disentangle
disentangled
disentangling
DSNTR
disinter(dig up)
disinterred
disinterring
dissenter(disagree)
dysentery
DSNTRLZ
decentralize
decentralized
decentralizing
decentralization
DSNTRMNT
disinterment
DSNTRST
disinterest
DSPCH
dispatch
dispatches
DSPCHR
dispatcher
DSPKBL
despicable
DSPL
despoil
disciple(follower)
discipled
discipling
dispel
dispelled
dispelling
display
DSPLD
displode
disploded
disploding
DSPLN
discipline
disciplined
disciplining
DSPLNR
disciplinary
DSPLR
despoiler
dispeller
DSPLS
displace
displaced
displacing

DSPLSBL
displaceable
DSPLSHN
despoliation
DSPLSMNT
displacement
DSPLZ
displease
displeased
displeasing
DSPLZH
dysplasia
DSPLZHR
displeasure
displeasured
displeasuring
DSPN
dyspnea
DSPND
despond
DSPNDNS
despondence
despondency
despondencies
DSPNDNT
despondent
DSPNS
dispense
dispensed
dispensing
DSPNSBL
dispensable
DSPNSBLT
dispensability
DSPNSR
dispensary
dispensaries
dispenser
DSPNSSHN
dispensation
DSPNT
disappoint
DSPPS
dyspepsia
DSPPSH
dyspepsia
DSPPTK
dyspeptic
DSPR
despair
disappear
DSPRBSHN
disapprobation
DSPRD
desperado
DSPRF

B:by CH:each D:day F:if G:go H:he HW:why J:joy K:cow KS:ax KWL:equal L:all M:may N:in

disproof
DSPRJ
disparage
disparaged
disparaging
DSPRJMNT
disparagement
DSPRJR
disparager
DSPRNS
disappearance
DSPRPRSHN
disproportion
DSPRPRSHNL
disproportional
DSPRPRSHNT
disproportionate
DSPRS
disperse
dispersed
dispersing
DSPRSBL
dispersible
DSPRSHN
desperation
DSPRSL
dispersal
DSPRSV
dispersive
DSPRT
desperate
disparate(unlike)
disparity
disparities
dispirit
disport
DSPRV
disapprove
disapproved
disapproving
disprove
disproved
disproving
DSPRVBL
disprovable
DSPRVL
disapproval
disproval
DSPRZ
disprize
disprized
disprizing
DSPRZHN
dispersion
DSPSHN
deception

dissipation
dispassion
DSPSHNT
dispassionate
DSPT
despite
despot(ruler)
dissipate
dissipated
dissipating
DSPTR
dissipater
DSPTV
deceptive
DSPTZM
despotism
DSPYT
dispute
disputed
disputing
DSPYTBL
disputable
DSPYTNT
disputant
DSPYTR
disputer
DSPYTSHN
disputation
DSPYTSHS
disputatious
DSPZ
despise(hate)
despised
despising
dispose
disposed
disposing
DSPZBL
disposable
DSPZHR
disposure
DSPZL
disposal
DSPZR
disposer
DSPZS
dispossess
dispossesses
DSPZSHN
disposition
dispossession
DSPZSR
dispossessor
dispossessory
DSR
adducer

deicer(ice)
dicer(cut)
disarray
douceur(tip)
DSRB
adsorb
disrobe
disrobed
disrobing
DSRBBL
adsorbable
DSRBNT
adsorbent
DSRDR
disorder
DSRDRL
disorderly
DSRGNZ
disorganize
disorganized
disorganizing
DSRGNZSHN
disorganization
DSRGRD
disregard
DSRM
disarm
DSRMMNT
disarmament
DSRMNG
disarming
DSRN
discern
DSRNBL
discernible
DSRNJ
disarrange
disarranged
disarranging
DSRNR
discerner
DSRNT
disorient
disorientation
DSRPR
disrepair
DSRPSHN
disruption
DSRPT
disrupt
DSRPTR
disrupter
DSRPTV
disruptive
DSRPYT
disrepute

disreputed
disreputing
DSRPYTBL
disreputable
DSRSPKT
disrespect
DSRSPKTBL
disrespectable
DSRSPKTFL
disrespectful
DSRT
desert(dry,
abandon)
dessert(food)
disrate(demote)
disrated
disrating
DSRTR
deserter
DSRTSHN
dissertation
DSRTSPN
dessertspoon
DSRTT
dissertate
dissertated
dissertating
DSRTWN
dessert wine
DSRV
disserve
disserved
disserving
DSRVS
disservice
DSS
decease
deceased
deceasing
diesis(symbol)
dieses
diocese
diocesan
DSSHBL
dissociable
DSSHT
dissociate
dissociated
dissociating
dissociation
DSSMBL
disassemble
disassembled
disassembling
DSSSHN
dissociation

DSSSHT
  disassociate
    disassociated
    disassociating
    disassociation
DSST
  deceased(dead)
  desist
DSSTBLSH
  disestablish
    disestablishes
DSSTNS
  desistance
DSSTR
  disaster
DSSTRS
  disastrous
DSSV
  decisive
DST
  audacity
    audacities
  deceit
  doughiest
  dust
  dusty
    dustier
    dustiest
    dustiness
DSTF
  distaff
  dyestuff
DSTJKT
  dust jacket
DSTK
  distich
    distichs
DSTKS
  distichous
DSTL
  de Stijl(art)
  diastole(heart)
  distill, (B)distil
DSTLR
  distiller
  distillery
    distilleries
DSTLSHN
  distillation
DSTLT
  distillate
DSTMPR
  distemper
DSTN
  destine
    destined

    destining
  destiny
    destinies
DSTNCHN
  distention
DSTND
  distend
DSTNGKSHN
  distinction
DSTNGKT
  distinct
    distinction
    distinctive
DSTNGWSH
  distinguish
    distinguishes
DSTNGWSHBL
  distinguishable
DSTNKSHN
  distinction
DSTNKT
  distinct
DSTNS
  distance
    distanced
    distancing
DSTNSBL
  distensible
DSTNSHN
  destination
  distention
DSTNT
  distant
DSTPN
  dustpan
DSTR
  destroy
  duster
DSTRB
  disturb
DSTRBNS
  disturbance
DSTRBR
  disturber
DSTRBYSHN
  distribution
DSTRBYT
  distribute
    distributed
    distributing
DSTRBYTBL
  distributable
DSTRBYTR
  distributor
DSTRD
  dastard

DSTRDL
  dastardly
DSTRF
  dystrophy
    dystrophies
DSTRKSHN
  destruction
  distraction
DSTRKT
  destruct
  distract
  district(area)
DSTRKTBL
  destructible
  distractible
DSTRKTR
  destructor
  distracter
DSTRKTV
  destructive
  distractive
DSTRLZ
  desterilize
    desterilized
    desterilizing
    desterilization
DSTRN
  distrain
DSTRNR
  distrainor
DSTRNT
  distraint
DSTRR
  destroyer
DSTRS
  distress
    distresses
DSTRSHN
  distortion
DSTRST
  distrust
DSTRSTFL
  distrustful
DSTRT
  distort
  distraught
DSTRYR
  destroyer
DSTSF
  dissatisfy
    dissatisfied
    dissatisfies
DSTSFKSHN
  dissatisfaction
DSTSFKTR
  dissatisfactory

DSTSHS
  adscititious
DSTTYT
  destitute
  destitution
DSV
  deceive
  deceived
  deceiving
  deceiver
  disavow
DSVBL
  deceivable
DSVL
  disavowal
DSVR
  deceiver(trick)
  dissever
DSVRNS
  disseverance
DSWD
  dissuade
    dissuaded
    dissuading
    dissuasion
DSWDR
  dissuader
DSWSHN
  dissuasion
DSWSV
  dissuasive
DSWTD
  desuetude
DSWZHN
  dissuasion
DSY
  dossier
DSYNT
  disunite
    disunited
    disuniting
  disunity
    disunities
DSYNYN
  disunion
DSYR
  dysuria
DSYS
  disuse
DSZ
  disease(sick)
  diseased
  disseize
    disseized
    disseizing
DSZHN

---

decision
DT
audit
data
date(day,fruit)
date(take out)
  dated,dating
debt(money)
deity
  deities
dhoti(garment)
diet
dit(code)(dot)
  dah(dash)
ditto
  dittoed
  dittoing
ditty(song)
  ditties
dot(mark)
  dotted
  dotting
dote(lavish)
  doted
  doting
dotty(shaky)
  dottier
  dottiest
doubt
doughty(brave)
  doughtier
  doughtiest
  doughtily
duet
duty
  duties
edit
ideate(think)
  ideated
  ideating
idiot
iodate
  iodated
  iodating
oddity
  oddities
DTBL
datable
dutiable
DTCH
detach
  detaches
DTCHBL
detachable
DTCHMNT
detachment

DTCHT
detached
DTD
dated
  day-to-day(adj)
DTDKS
dietetics
DTFL
doubtful
  dutiful
DTFR
duty-free
DTH
death
DTHBD
deathbed
DTHBL
death bell
  deathblow
DTHCHMBR
death chamber
DTHL
deathly
  deathliness
DTHMSK
death mask
DTHR
dither
DTHRN
dethrone
  dethroned
  dethroning
DTHRT
death rate
DTHSHD
death's-head
DTHTRP
deathtrap
DTHWCH
deathwatch
  deathwatches
DTHWRNT
death warrant
DTJ
dotage
DTK
eidetic
idiotic
DTKL
idiotically
DTKSF
detoxify
  detoxified
  detoxifies
DTKSFKSHN
detoxification

DTKSHN
detection
DTKT
detect
DTKTBL
detectable
DTKTR
detector
DTKTV
detective
  detection
DTL
detail
  dottle(tobacco)
DTLN
dateline(print)
  datelined
  datelining
  date line(place)
DTLS
doubtless
DTM
datum
  data(or)
  datums
  daytime
DTN
Dayton
detain
dittany(plant)
  dittanies
duotone
DTNK
diatonic(music)
  diatonicism
DTNR
detainer
DTNSHN
detention
DTNT
detent(tool)
  pawl
detente
detonate
  detonated
  detonating
  detonation
DTNTR
detonator
DTNY
detinue
DTP
duotype
DTR .
auditor
auditory

daughter
debtor(money)
deter
  deterred
  deterring
detour(route)
dietary
dieter
editor
DTRB
diatribe
DTRD
dotard
DTRJ
deterge
DTRJNT
detergent
DTRKSHN
detraction
DTRKT
detract
DTRKTR
detractor
DTRL
editorial
DTRLZ
editorialize
  editorialized
  editorializing
DTRM
auditorium
DTRMN
determine
  determined
  determining
DTRMNBL
determinable
DTRMNNT
determinant
DTRMNR
determiner
DTRMNS
determinacy
  determinacies
DTRMNSHN
determination
DTRMNT
determent(deter)
determinate
  determinated
  determinating
  determinative
detriment
DTRMNTL
detrimental
DTRMNTR

determinator
DTRMNZM
determinism
DTRNL
daughter-in-law
daughters-in-law
DTRNS
deterrence
(hindrance)
deterrents(pl)
DTRNT
deterrent
(hindrance)
DTRRSHN
deterioration
DTRRT
deteriorate
deteriorated
deteriorating
DTRT
Detroit
DTRTL
detrital(adj)
detritus(n)
DTRTS
detritus(n)
detrital(adj)
DTS
deutzia(shrub)
ditsy
duteous
DTSHN
dietitian
DTST
detest
DTSTBL
detestable
DTTK
dietetic
DTTKS
dietetics
DTV
dative
DTYRSLF
do-it-yourself(adj)
DTZ
dittos
oddities
DV
diva
dive
dived(or)
dove
diving
dove(bird)
divvy(divide)

divvied
divvies
DVBM
dive-bomb
DVD
devoid
divide
divided
dividing
DVDBL
dividable
DVDND
dividend
DVDR
divider
DVGSHN
divagation
DVGT
divagate
divagated
divagating
DVKS
advocacy
advocacies
DVKT
advocate
advocated
advocating
dovecote
DVKTR
advocator
DVL
devalue
devalued
devaluing
devil
DVLJ
divulge
divulged
divulging
DVLJNS
divulgence
DVLMKR
devil-may-care(adj)
DVLP
develop
DVLPBL
developable
DVLPMNT
development
DVLPR
developer
DVLRM
ad valorem
DVLSFDKK
devil's-food cake

DVLSH
devilish
DVLSHN
devaluation
devolution
divulsion
(tear apart)
DVLTR
deviltry
deviltries
DVLV
devolve
devolved
devolving
DVLY
devalue
devalued
devaluing
devaluation
DVN
divan(sofa)
divine
divined
divining
DVNCH
da Vinci
DVNCHR
adventure
adventured
adventuring
DVNCHRR
adventurer
DVNCHRS
adventuress
adventurous
DVNCHRSM
adventuresome
DVNPRT
davenport
DVNR
diviner
DVNS
advance
advanced
advancing
deviance
DVNSHN
divination
DVNSMNT
advancement
DVNT
advent
deviant(odd)
divinity
divinities
DVNTJ

advantage
advantaged
DVNTJS
advantageous
DVNTJT
advantaged
DVNTSHS
adventitious
DVR
devour
diver
Dover
DVRB
adverb
DVRJ
diverge
diverged
diverging
DVRJNS
divergence
DVRJNT
divergent
DVRR
devourer
DVRS
adverse
diverse(many)
divorce
divorced
divorcing
divorcee(f)
DVRSF
diversify
diversified
diversifies
DVRSFKSHN
diversification
DVRSHNST
diversionist
DVRSR
adversary
adversaries
DVRST
adversity
adversities
diversity
diversities
DVRT
advert(refer)
divert
DVRTBL
divertible
DVRTR
diverter
DVRTSMN
divertissement

B:by **CH**:each **D**:day **F**:if **G**:go **H**:he **HW**:why **J**:joy **K**:cow **KS**:ax **KWL**:equal **L**:all **M**:may **N**:in

DVRTZ
advertise
advertised
advertising
DVRTZMNT
advertisement
DVRTZR
advertiser
DVRZ
divers(various)
DVRZHN
diversion
DVRZHNR
diversionary
diversionaries
DVRZHNST
diversionist
DVS
advice
device
devious(sly)
DVSHN
deviation
devotion
DVST
devest(law)
divest(strip)
DVSTCHR
divestiture
DVSTSHN
devastation
DVSTT
devastate
devastated
devastating
DVSTTR
devastator
DVSV
divisive
DVT
davit(bird,hoist)
deviate
deviated
deviating
devote
devoted
devoting
devotee(person)
devout(holy)
divot
DVTL
dovetail
DVTLZ
devitalize
devitalized
devitalizing

devitalization
DVTN
duvetyn(fabric)
DVTR
deviator
DVWR
devoir
DVY
debut
DVZ
advise
advised
advising
devise(invent)
devised
devising
devisee(law)
DVZBL
advisable
devisable(law)
divisible
DVZBLT
divisibility
DVZHL
audiovisual
DVZHN
division
DVZL
devisal
devise
DVZMNT
advisement
DVZR
adviser
advisory
advisories
devisor(law)
divisor(math)
DW
Ottawa
DWL
dowel(rod)
dual(two)
duel(fight)
dwell
DWLR
dweller
DWNDL
dwindle
dwindled
dwindling
DWRF
dwarf
dwarfs(or)
dwarves
DWRFZM

dwarfism
DWRKR
autoworker
DWRM
dew worm
DWRVZ
dwarves
DWYN
doyen(m)
doyenne(f)
DY
adieu
dew(water)
dewy(wet)
dewier
dewiest
dewiness
due(payable)
duo(two)
DYBR
dewberry
dewberries
DYBS
dubious
DYBT
dubiety
dubieties
DYD
dewy-eyed
duad(two)
dude(person)
duty
duties
DYDRP
dewdrop
DYDSML
duodecimal
DYDZ
duties
DYFL
dewfall
DYK
duke
Duke(title)
DYKL
dewclaw
DYKS
dukes(fists)
DYL
dual(two)
duel(fight)
duly(fit)
DYLP
dewlap
DYLPRPS
dual-purpose(adj)

DYLST
duelist(fighter)
dueler
DYLSTK
dualistic(two)
DYLT
duality
dualities
DYLZM
dualism
DYMVRT
duumvirate
DYN
duenna
DYP
dupe
duped
duping
DYPL
duple(two)
DYPLKS
duplex
duplexes
duplexity
DYPLKSHN
duplication
DYPLKT
duplicate
duplicated
duplicating
DYPLKTR
duplicator
DYPLST
duplicity
duplicities
DYPNT
dew point
DYR
de jure(by right)
DYRBL
durable
durably
DYRBLT
durability
durabilities
DYRK
duroc(hog)
DYRM
durum
DYRNG
during
DYRNS
durance
DYRS
duress
DYRSHN

duration
DYRTK
diuretic
DYS
  deuce(two)
  educe
    educed
    educing
  duos(duo)
DYSBL
  educible
DYSNT
  adducent
DYT
  duet
  duty
    duties
DYTBL
  dutiable
DYTFL
  dutiful
DYTFR
  duty-free
DYTN
  duotone
DYTP
  duotype
DYTS
  deutzia(shrub)
  duteous
DYTZ
  duties
DYVTN
  duvetyn(fabric)
DYWRM
  dew worm
DZ
  adz
  daisy(flower)
    daisies
  daze
    dazed
    dazing
  dizzy
    dizzied
    dizzies
    dizzier
    dizziest
    dizzily
    dizziness
  does(do)
  doozy(slang)
    doozies
  do's
    do's and don'ts
  dowse(water)

dowsed
dowsing
dowser
doze(sleep)
  dozed
  dozing
dozy(sleep)
  dozier
  doziest
  dozily
  doziness
duos(duo)
eddies(eddy)
odds(ratio)
  (3-2 or 3-to-2)
  odds-on
iodize
  iodized
  iodizing
DZD
  dos-a-dos
DZGN
  designee
DZGNSHN
  designation
  designatory
DZGNT
  designate
  designated
  designating
DZGNTR
  designator
  designatory
DZHV
  déjà vu
DZL
  dazzle
  dazzled
  dazzling
  diesel
DZLDRF
  Dusseldorf
DZLR
  dazzler
DZLV
  dissolve
  dissolved
  dissolving
DZLVBL
  dissolvable
DZLVNT
  dissolvent
DZM
  deism
  Taoism
DZMKR

oddsmaker
DZML
  dismal
DZN
  design
  diazine(compound)
  dizen
  dozen(twelve)
  odds-on
DZNR
  designer
DZNT
  does not
  doesn't
DZR
  desire
    desired
    desiring
  dowser
  dozer(bulldozer)
DZRBL
  desirable
DZRDR
  deserter
DZRS
  desirous
DZRSHN
  desertion
DZRT
  desert(dry,
    abandon)
  dessert(food)
DZRTR
  deserter
DZRV
  deserve
    deserved
    deserving
DZST
  desist
DZSTNS
  desistance
DZSTR
  disaster
DZZ
  daisies
  disease(sick)
    diseased
    diseasing
DZZD
  diseased

F

fa(tone)
fay(join)
  fayed
  faying
fee
foe(enemy)
if
iffy(doubtful)
oaf
ofay(slang)
off
phooey(interj)
FB
  fib
    fibbed
    fibbing
    fibber
  fob
    fobbed
    fobbing
  f.o.b.
    (free on board)
  phobia
  phoebe
FBDKP
  Phi Beta Kappa
FBK
  phobic
FBL
  affable
  fable(story)
    fabled
    fabling
  feeble
    feebler
    feeblest
    feebly
  foible
FBLD
  fabled
FBLMNDD
  feebleminded
FBLR
  feebler
FBLST
  feeblest
FBLT
  affability
FBR
  fibber(liar)
  fiber(material), (B)fibre

B:by **CH**:each **D**:day **F**:if **G**:go **H**:he **HW**:why **J**:joy **K**:cow **KS**:ax **KWL**:equal **L**:all **M**:may **N**:in

FBRBRD
fiberboard
FBRD
fibroid
FBRDW
off-Broadway
FBRFYJ
febrifuge
FBRGLS
Fiberglas
(trademark)
fiber glass
FBRK
fabric
FBRKD
Fabrikoid
(trademark)
FBRKSHN
fabrication
FBRKT
fabricate
fabricated
fabricating
FBRKTR
fabricator
FBRL
febrile(fever)
fibril(fiber)
FBRLSHN
fibrillation
FBRR
February
FBRS
fibrous
FBT
offbeat
FBTKP
Phi Beta Kappa
FBYL
fibula
fibulas(or)-lae
FBYLS
fabulous
FBYLST
fabulist
FBYLZ
fibulas(or)
fibulae
FBYR
February
FBYWR
February
FCH
fetch
fetches
FCHNG

fetching
FCHR
feature
featured
featuring
FCHRLNGTH
feature-length
FCHS
fatuous
FD
aphid(insect)
fad
fade
faded
fading
fatty
fattier
fattiest
fattiness
Fed(Federal
Reserve System)
feed
fed
feeding
food
FDBK
feedback
FDD
fatted
FDDD
fuddy-duddy
fuddy-duddies
FDL
fatal(death)
fetal(unborn)
fettle
fettled
fettling
fiddle
fiddled
fiddling
fiddler
fuddle
fuddled
fuddling
fuddler
FDLST
fatalist
FDLSTK
fatalistic
FDLSTKL
fatalistically
FDLT
fidelity(loyalty)
fidelities
FDLZM

fatalism
FDN
fade-in(n)
FDNG
feeding
FDR
fedora
feeder
fetter(binding)
fodder
FDRL
federal
FDRLZ
federalize
federalized
federalizing
FDRLZM
federalism
FDRLZSHN
federalization
FDRSHN
federation
FDRT
federate
federated
federating
FDS
fetus
FDSH
faddish(fad)
fattish(fat)
fetish(sex)
FDSHL
fiducial
FDSHR
fiduciary
fiduciaries
FDSHST
fetishist
fetishistic
FDSHZM
fetishism
FDSTF
foodstuff
FDSTT
Photostat
(trademark)
FDT
fade-out(n)
FDVD
affidavit
FDVT
affidavit
FDYSHL
fiducial
FDYSHR

fiduciary
fiduciaries
FDZM
faddism
FF
fief
fiefdom
fife(music)
fifed
fifing
FFDM
fiefdom
fief
FFT
fifty
fifties
FFTN
fifteen
FFTNTH
fifteenth
FFTTH
fiftieth
FFTZ
fifties
FG
fag(slang)
fag(tired)
fagged,fagging
fig
fog
fogged
fogging
fogger
fogey(old)
foggy
foggier
foggiest
foggily
fogginess
FGBND
fogbound
FGHRN
foghorn
FGMNT
figment
FGN
Afghan
afghani
Fagin(thief)
FGNSTN
Afghanistan
FGR
figure
figured
figuring
figurer

NGK:ink **P**:pie **R**:air **S**:ice **SH**:show **T**:toy **THN**:thin **TH**:the **V**:of **W**:we **Y**:you **Z**:is **VZHN**:vision

FGT
faggot(sex)
fagot(stick)
FGYR
figure
figured
figuring
figurer
FGYRHD
figurehead
FGYRN
figurine
FGYRSHN
figuration
FGYRTV
figurative
FGZ
fogeys(old)
FHND
offhand
FHNDD
offhanded
FHWT
off-white
FJ
aphagia
effigy(image)
effigies
Fiji
fudge
fudged
fudging
fudger
FJT
fidget
fidgety
fidgetiness
FJTV
fugitive
FK
fake
faked
faking
faker
folk(people)
fuck(vulgar)
fyke(net)
off-key
FKCHL
effectual
factual
FKCHR
facture
FKCHT
effectuate
effectuated

effectuating
FKL
faucal(sound)
fecal(waste)
fickle(changeable)
focal(light)
FKLNDLNZ
Falkland Islands
FKLNS
fickleness
FKLR
folklore
off-color
FKLS
feckless
FKLT
faculty
faculties
FKLZ
focalize
focalized
focalizing
FKND
fecund
FKNDT
fecundate
fecundated
fecundating
fecundity
fecundities
FKR
faker(fraud)
fakir(beggar)
FKS
affix
affixes
efficacy
efficacies
fix
fixes
focus
focuses(v)
foci(n)
fox
foxes
foxy
foxier
foxiest
foxily
foxiness
FKSCHR
fixture
FKSHL
foxhole
FKSHN
affection

faction
fiction
FKSHND
foxhound
FKSHNL
affectional
factional
fictional
FKSHNLZ
fictionalize
fictionalized
fictionalizing
fictionalization
FKSHS
efficacious
factious
FKSL
forecastle
FKSML
facsimile
facsimiled
facsimileing
FKSNG
folk song
folk singer
FKSSHN
fixation
FKST
affixed
fixate
fixated
fixating
fixation
fixed
FKSTRT
fox trot(n)
fox-trot(v)
FKSTV
fixative
FKSZ
focuses(v)
foci(n)
FKT
affect(influence,
feeling)
effect(result)
fact
FKTFNDNG
fact-finding
FKTR
factor
factory
factories
FKTRJ
factorage
FKTRL

factorial
FKTRZ
factorize
factorized
factorizing
FKTSHN
affectation
FKTSHS
factitious
(artificial)
fictitious
(imaginary)
FKTTM
factotum
FKTV
affective
(emotion)
effective
(result)
fictive(adj)
fiction
fictitious(adj)
FKYLNT
feculent
FL
afoul(conflict)
awful(bad)
eyeful
fail
fall
fell
fallen
fallow
feel
felt
feeling
fellow(person)
felly(rim)
fellies
file(order,scrape)
filed, filing
filet(n)(lace,beef)
fill(put into)
fillet(strip,band,
fish or beef)
filly(horse), -llies
flaw(mistake)
flea(insect)
flee(escape)
fled
fleeing
flew(fly)
floe(ice)
flow(glide)
flu(sickness)
flue(pipe)

B:by **CH**:each **D**:day **F**:if **G**:go **H**:he **HW**:why **J**:joy **K**:cow **KS**:ax **KWL**:equal **L**:all **M**:may **N**:in

fly
  flew
  flown
foal(horse)
  colt(m)
  filly(f)
foil
follow(go after)
folio
folly
  follies
fool
foul(filthy)
fowl(bird)
fuel
full
fully
offal(waste)
phalli
  phallus
phial(bottle)
phyle(clan)
phyllo(pastry)

FLB
flab
flabby
  flabbier
  flabbiest
  flabbiness
flub(error)(slang)
  flubbed
  flubbing
FLBDB
flubdub(slang)
FLBDD
full-bodied
FLBDS
phlebitis
FLBK
fullback
FLBL
fallible
flyable
FLBLDD
full-blooded
FLBLN
full-blown
FLBLT
fallibility
  fallibilities
FLBNT
fly-by-night
FLBRGST
flabbergast
FLBRGSTD
flabbergasted

FLBRT
filbert
FLBSTR
filibuster
FLBTN
flea-bitten
FLBTS
phlebitis
FLCH
filch(steal)
  filches
fletch
  fletches
FLCHLNS
flatulence
FLCHLNT
flatulent
FLD
field
flood
fluid(liquid)
fold
off-load
FLDGL
field goal
FLDGT
floodgate
FLDHS
field house
FLDK
phyletic(racial)
FLDLF
Philadelphia
FLDLFY
Philadelphia
FLDLT
floodlight
FLDNDRN
philodendron
FLDR
fielder
flatter(level)
  flattest
  flat
flatter(praise)
flattery
  flatteries
folder
FLDRL
folderol
FLDRS
full-dress
FLDS
felo de se
  felones de se(pl)
FLDT

fluidity
FLDTST
field-test(v)
FLDW
foldaway
FLDWDR
floodwater
  floodwaters
FLDWRK
field work(labor)
fieldwork(fort)
FLF
falloff
fluff
fluffy
  fluffier
  fluffiest
  fluffily
  fluffiness
FLFGRD
full-figured
FLFL
fulfill
FLFLD
fulfilled
FLFLJD
full-fledged
FLFLMNT
fulfillment
FLFLNG
fulfilling
FLFSHND
full-fashioned
FLG
flag
  flagged
  flagging
flog
  flogged
  flogging
  flogger
FLGL
field goal
FLGMTK
phlegmatic
FLGN
flagon
FLGPL
flagpole
FLGR
filigree
FLGRNS
flagrancy
  flagrancies
FLGRNT
flagrant

FLGSHP
flagship
FLGSTF
Flagstaff
FLGSTN
flagstone
FLGWVNG
flag-waving
FLHRD
foolhardy
  foolhardily
  foolhardiness
FLHRMNK
philharmonic
FLHS
full house
FLHWL
flywheel
FLJ
fledge
  fledged
  fledging
fledgy
  fledgier
  fledgiest
foliage
FLJL
flagella
FLJLM
flagellum
  flagellums(or)
  flagella
FLJLNG
fledgling
FLJLNT
flagellant
FLJLSHN
flagellation
FLJLT
flagellate
  flagellated
  flagellating
flageolet
FLJNS
effulgence
FLJNT
effulgent
FLK
felucca
flack(slang)
flak(gun fire)
flake
  flaked
  flaking
flaky
  flakier

flakiest
flakily
flakiness
flick
flock
fluke
folk
phallic
FLKCHNT
fluctuant
FLKCHR
flycatcher
FLKCHSHN
fluctuation
FLKCHT
fluctuate
fluctuated
fluctuating
FLKL
follicle
FLKLR
folklore
FLKM
flukum(slang)
FLKMZK
folk music
FLKN
falcon
FLKNR
falconer
falconry
FLKR
flicker
fulcra(pl)
fulcrum
FLKRM
fulcrum
fulcra
FLKS
flax(linen)
flex
flexes
flux
fluxes
fluxion
phlox
FLKSBL
flexible
FLKSBLT
flexibility
flexibilities
FLKSD
flaccid
flaxseed
FLKSDT
flaccidity

FLKSHN
affliction
flection,(B)-exion
flexuous
fluxion
FLKSN
flaxen
FLKT
afflict
falcate
falcated
FLKTR
phylactery
phylacteries
FLKW
folkway
FLKYLNT
flocculent
FLKYLT
flocculate
flocculated
flocculating
FLL
filial
flail
FLLF
flyleaf
FLLJ
philology
FLLJKL
philological
FLLJST
philologist
FLLNGKTH
full-length
FLLNGTH
full-length
FLLS
flawless
FLLVZ
flyleaves
flyleaf
FLM
film
filmy
filmier
filmiest
filminess
flam(drivel)
flammed
flamming
(trick)
flame(fire)
flamed,-ming
phlegm(mucus)
phylum(type)

FLMB
flambée(or)flambé
flambeau(torch)
-beaux(or)-beaus
FLMBL
flammable(fire)
FLMBLT
flammability
FLMBNS
flamboyance
FLMBNT
flamboyant
FLMBYNS
flamboyance
FLMBYNT
flamboyant
FLMFLM
flimflam
FLMKS
flummox(confuse)
flummoxes
FLMNGG
flamingo
FLMNGK
flamenco
(guitar)
FLMNNT
fulminant
FLMNT
filament
fulminate
fulminated
fulminating
fulmination
fulminator
FLMNYN
filet mignon
FLMPRF
flameproof
FLMSH
Flemish
FLMSTRP
filmstrip
FLMT
flameout
FLMTHD
foulmouthed
FLMTS
off-limits
FLMZ
flimsy
flimsier
flimsiest
flimsily
flimsiness
FLN

fallen
felon(criminal)
felony
felonies
feline(cat)
fill-in
flan(food,coin)
flown(fly)
off-line
FLNCH
flinch
flinches
FLNDR
flounder(fish)
philander
FLNDRR
philanderer
FLNG
falling
feeling
filing(file)
filling(fill)
fling(throw)
flung
flinging
flying
FLNGK
flank
flunk
flunky
flunkies
FLNGKR
flanker
FLNGKS
phalanx(army)
phalanxes(or)
phalanges
FLNGSSR
flying saucer
FLNGT
falling-out
FLNGZ
filings(file)
FLNJ
flange(edge)
flanged
flanging
phalange(bone)
phalangeal
phalanger
FLNL
flannel
FLNLT
flannelette
FLNS
affluence

B:by **CH**:each **D**:day **F**:if **G**:go **H**:he **HW**:why **J**:joy **K**:cow **KS**:ax **KWL**:equal **L**:all **M**:may **N**:in

effluence(flow)
felonious
flounce
  flounced
  flouncing
fluency
  fluencies
foulness
FLNT
affluent
effluent(flow)
flaunt(show)
flaunty
  flauntier
  flauntiest
  flauntily
  flauntiness
Flint
flint(fire)
flinty
  flintier
  flintiest
  flintily
  flintiness
fluent
FLNTHRP
philanthropy
  philanthropies
FLNTHRPK
philanthropic
FLNTHRPST
philanthropist
FLNTLK
flintlock
FLP
flap
  flapped
  flapping
  flapper
fillip(finger
  snap)
flip
  flipped
  flipping
  flipper
flop
  flopped
  flopping
follow-up(n,adj)
foul-up(n)
foul up(v)
FLPFLP
flip-flop(n)
FLPJK
flapjack
FLPN

Filipino(person)
Philippine(place)
FLPNS
flippancy
  flippancies
Philippine Sea
FLPNT
flippant
FLPNZ
Filipinos(people)
Philippines
  (place)
FLPPR
flypaper
FLPR
flapper
flipper
FLPRF
foolproof
FLR
feeler
filar
flair(knack)
flare
  flared
  flaring
fleer(sneer)
fleer(flee)
flier(pilot)
floor
flora
  floras(or)
  florae
flour(meal)
flower
  flowery
  flowerier
  floweriest
  floweriness
flurry
  flurried
  flurries
follower
foolery
fuller
FLRD
florid(blooming)
Florida
fluoride(chemical)
foulard
FLRDL
fleur-de-lis
  fleurs-de-lis
FLRDSHN
fluoridation
FLRDT

floridity
fluoridate
  fluoridated
  fluoridating
FLRKLCHR
floriculture
FLRL
floral
FLRMNK
philharmonic
FLRN
florin
FLRNG
flaring
flooring
FLRNT
fluorinate
  fluorinated
  fluorinating
  fluorination
FLRP
flare-up
FLRPT
flowerpot
FLRS
effloresce
  effloresced
  efflorescing
fluoresce(light)
  fluoresced
  fluorescing
FLRSH
flourish
  flourishes
FLRSKP
fluoroscope
fluoroscopy
FLRSNS
efflorescence
florescence(bloom)
fluorescence(light)
FLRSNT
florescent(bloom)
fluorescent(light)
FLRST
florist
FLRT
flirt
floret
FLRTSHN
flirtation
FLRTSHS
flirtatious
FLRWKR
floorwalker
FLRZ

floras
flora
FLRZRTH
fuller's earth
FLS
AFL-CIO
fallacy(false idea)
  fallacies
false
  falser
  falsest
falsie(false)
fleece(wool,cheat)
  fleeced
  fleecing
fleecy
  fleecier
  fleeciest
  fleeciness
floss
  flosses
flossy
  flossier
  flossiest
phallus(penis)
  phalli
FLSD
flaccid
FLSF
fail-safe
falsify
  falsified
  falsifies
philosophy
  philosophies
FLSFK
felicific
philosophic
FLSFKL
philosophical
FLSFKSHN
falsification
FLSFR
falsifier
philosopher
FLSFZ
philosophize
  philosophized
  philosophizing
FLSH
flash
flashy
  flashier
  flashiest
  flashily
  flashiness

flesh(skin)
  fleshes
fleshy
  fleshier
  fleshiest
  fleshily
  fleshiness
flush
  flushes
foolish

FLSHBK
  flashback
FLSHBLB
  flashbulb
FLSHD
  falsehood
FLSHKB
  flashcube
FLSHKLRD
  flesh-colored
FLSHKRD
  flash card
FLSHLT
  flashlight
FLSHN
  affiliation
  filiation
  foliation(leaf)
FLSHNS
  foolishness
FLSHP
  fellowship
FLSHPT
  fleshpot
FLSHPTS
  fleshpots
FLSHR
  flusher
FLSHRTD
  false-hearted
FLSHS
  fallacious
FLSK
  flask
FLSKL
  full-scale
  full-scaled
FLSL
  fuel cell
FLSM
  fulsome
FLSNG
  fleecing
FLSR
  falser
  falsest

FLST
  falsetto
  falsity(untruth)
  falsities
  felicity
  felicities
  foulest
FLSTR
  fluster
FLSTS
  felicitous
FLSTSHN
  felicitation
FLSTT
  felicitate
  felicitated
  felicitating
FLT
  affiliate
  affiliated
  affiliating
  affiliation
  fallout(nuclear)
  fault
  faulty
  faultier
  faultiest
  faultily
  faultiness
  fealty
  felt
  feel
  fillet(fish)
  flat
  flatter
  flattest
  fleet(fast,navy)
  flight(fly)
  flighty
  flightier
  flightiest
  flightily
  flightiness
  flit
  flitted
  flitting
  float(drift)
  flout
  flute(music,edge)
  fluted
  fluting
  foliate
  foliated
  foliating
  foliation
FLTBT

  flatboat
FLTDK
  flight deck
FLTFNDNG
  faultfinding
FLTFSH
  flatfish
FLTFTD
  flat-footed
FLTH
  filth
  filthy
  filthier
  filthiest
  filthily
  filthiness
FLTHR
  follow-through
FLTK
  phyletic(racial)
FLTKR
  flatcar
FLTL
  flotilla
  philately
FLTLK
  philatelic
FLTLS
  flightless
FLTLST
  philatelist
FLTM
  full-time(adj)
FLTN
  flatten
FLTNG
  flatting
  fleeting
FLTP
  flattop(crew cut)
FLTR
  Eiffel Tower
  falter
  filter(strain)
  flatter(level)
  flattest
  flat
  flatter(praise)
  flattery
  flatteries
  floater
  flutter
  philter(potion)
FLTRBL
  filterable
FLTRN

  flatiron
FLTRP
  flytrap
FLTRT
  filtrate
  filtrated
  filtrating
  filtration
FLTS
  afflatus
FLTSHN
  flotation
FLTSM
  flotsam
FLTST
  flautist(or)
  flutist
FLTWR
  Eiffel Tower
  flatware
FLTWRK
  flatwork
FLV
  effluvia
  effluvium
FLVL
  fluvial
FLVM
  effluvium
  effluvia(or)
  effluviums
FLVR
  flavor, (B)flavour
  flavored
  flavoring
FLVRFL
  flavorful
FLVRLS
  flavorless
FLVRNG
  flavoring
FLVSNT
  flavescent
FLW
  flyaway
FLWL
  flywheel
FLWR
  flour(meal)
  flower
  flowery
  flowerier,-iest
  flowerily,-iness
FLWRPT
  flowerpot
FLWT

B:by **CH**:each **D**:day **F**:if **G**:go **H**:he **HW**:why **J**:joy **K**:cow **KS**:ax **KWL**:equal **L**:all **M**:may **N**:in

flyweight
  (less than 112 lbs)
FLYR
  failure
FLZ
  floozy
    floozies
  folios
  follies
FLZKP
  foolscap
FM
  fame
    famed
    faming
  FM(radio)
  foam
  foamy
    foamier
    foamiest
    foamily
    foaminess
FMBL
  fumble
    fumbled
    fumbling
    fumbler
FMFTL
  femme fatale
    femmes fatales
FML
  family
    families
  female
FMLYL
  familial
FMLYR
  familiar
FMLYRT
  familiarity
    familiarities
FMLYRZ
  familiarize
    familiarized
    familiarizing
FMLYRZSHN
  familiarization
FMN
  famine
FMNN
  feminine
FMNNT
  femininity
    femininities
FMNS
  effeminacy

effeminacies
FMNT
  effeminate
  foment
FMNTSHN
  fomentation
FMNZ
  feminize
    feminized
    feminizing
FMNZM
  feminism
FMR
  ephemera
  femur
FMRL
  ephemeral
FMS
  famous
FMSD
  famaside
FMSH
  famish
    famishes
FMSHD
  famished
FN
  fan
    fanned
    fanning
  fanny
    fannies
  fatten
  faun(deity)
  fauna
    faunae
  fawn(deer,flatter)
  feign(trick)
  fen(marsh)
  fiend(monster)
  fin($5,fish)
  fine(fee)
    fined,fining
  fine(good)
    finer,finest
  finis(end)
  funny
    funnier,-iest
    funniness
  often(frequent)
  phone(telephone)
    phoned
    phoning
  phony
    phonier
    phoniest

phonily
  phoniness
FNBL
  finable(fine)
FNBLT
  fan belt
FNBRBTL
  phenobarbital
FNCH
  finch
    finches
FND
  feigned(adj)
  fiend(person)
  find
    found
  fond
  fondue
  found
  find
  fund
  offend
FNDK
  fanatic
    fanatical
    fanaticism
  phonetic
    phonetically
FNDL
  fondle
    fondled
    fondling
    fondler
FNDLNG
  foundling
FNDMNT
  fundament
FNDMNTL
  fundamental
FNDMNTLZM
  fundamentalism
FNDNGZ
  findings
FNDNS
  fondness
FNDNT
  fondant
FNDR
  fender
  finder
  founder
  foundry
    foundries
FNDRN
  fine-drawn
FNDRZNG

fund-raising(adj)
FNDRZR
  fund-raiser
FNDSH
  fiendish
FNDSHN
  foundation
FNFR
  fanfare
FNG
  fungo
  offing
FNGG
  fungo
FNGGL
  fungal
FNGGR
  finger
FNGGRBRD
  fingerboard
FNGGRNL
  fingernail
FNGGRPRNT
  fingerprint
FNGGRTP
  finger tip
FNGGS
  fungous(adj)
  fungus
    fungi(or)
    funguses
FNGK
  fink
  funky
    funkier
    funkiest
    funkily
    funkiness
FNGKSHN
  function
FNGKSHNL
  functional
FNGKSHNR
  functionary
    functionaries
FNGL
  finagle
    finagled
    finagling
    finagler
FNGR
  finger
FNGRBRD
  fingerboard
FNGRF
  phonograph

NGK:ink **P**:pie **R**:air **S**:ice **SH**:show **T**:toy **THN**:thin **TH**:the **V**:of **W**:we **Y**:you **Z**:is **VZHN**:vision

FNGRM
phonogram
FNGRND
fine-grained
FNGRNL
fingernail
FNGRPRNT
fingerprint
FNGRTP
finger tip
FNGS
fungous(adj)
fungus
fungi(or)
funguses
FNGSD
fungicide
FNGSDL
fungicidal
FNJ
fungi
fungus
FNJSD
fungicide
FNJSDL
fungicidal
FNK
aphonic
finicky
finickiness
fink
phonic
FNKL
finical
FNKR
funny car
FNKS
Phoenix
phoenix
phonics
FNKSHN
function
FNKT
fine-cut
FNL
fennel
final(end)
finale
(entertainment)
finely(well done)
finial
funnel
FNLJ
phonology
FNLN
Finland

FNLND
Finland
FNLST
finalist
FNLT
fanlight
finality
finalities
FNLZ
finalize
finalized
finalizing
FNM
Fannie Mae(money)
FNMA
Federal National
Mortgage
Association
phoneme
FNMN
phenomena
phenomenon
FNMNL
phenomenal
FNMNN
phenomenon
phenomena
FNMPN
Phnom Penh
FNNCHL
financial
FNNHD
finnan haddie
FNNS
finance
financed
financing
financier
FNNSHL
financial
FNNSNG
financing
FNNSR
financier
FNNT
fainéant
FNPNCHR
offenpenscher
FNR
finer(better)
finest
finery
fineries
FNRZNG
fund-raising(adj)
fund-raiser

FNS
affiance
fancy
fancied
fancies
fancier
fanciest
fantasy
fantasied
fantasies
fence
fenced
fencing
fiancé(m)
fiancée(f)
fineness
finesse
finessed
finessing
finis(end)
offense, (B)offence
FNSFL
fanciful
FNSFR
fancy-free
FNSH
finish
finishes
Finnish
FNSHN
Phoenician
FNSNG
fencing
FNSPN
finespun
FNST
finest
finer
fine
FNSTR
fenestra
FNSTRSHN
fenestration
FNSTRT
fenestrate
fenestrated
fenestrating
FNSV
offensive
FNSWRK
fancywork
FNZ
funds(money)
FNT
affinity
affinities

faint(weak)
feint(pretense)
finite
font(type), (B)fount
fount(water)
phonate
phonated
phonating
phonation
FNTCHN
fantoccine
FNTHRTD
fainthearted
FNTK
fanatic
phonetic
FNTKL
fanatical
phonetical
FNTL
fantail
FNTM
phantom
FNTMZ
oftentimes
FNTN
fan-tan
fountain
FNTNHD
fountainhead
FNTS
fantasy
fantasies
fantasied
FNTSHN
phonetician
FNTSTK
fantastic
FNTSTKL
fantastically
FNTSZ
fantasies
fantasize
fantasized
fantasizing
fantasizer
FNTSZM
fanaticism
FNTTHT
fine-toothed(adj)
FNTZ
fantasia
FNTZH
fantasia
FNTZM
phantasm

B:by **CH**:each **D**:day **F**:if **G**:go **H**:he **HW**:why **J**:joy **K**:cow **KS**:ax **KWL**:equal **L**:all **M**:may **N**:in

FNZ
faunas(or)
faunae
fauna
FP
faux pas
faux pas
fop(person)
FPRNT
offprint
FPSH
foppish
FPZ
faux pas
FR
afar(distance)
affair
Afro
fair(just,bazaar)
fairy(tiny person)
fairies
far
fare(fee)
fare(get by)
fared,faring
faro(game)
farrow
fear
ferry(boat)
ferries
fiery(fire)
fierier
fieriest
fierily
fieriness
fir(tree)
fire
fired
firing
for
fora
forum
foray
fore(front)
four(4)
foyer
fray
free
freer
freest
fry
fried
fries
fryer
fro(away)
to and fro

fur(hair)
furred
furring
furriery(business)
furrow
furry
furrier
furriest
furriness
offer
FRB
freebie
FRBD
forbid
forbade(or)
forbad
forbidding
forbidden
forebode
foreboded
foreboding
FRBG
fire bug(insect)
firebug(arsonist)
FRBJS
frabjous(splendid)
FRBKS
firebox
fireboxes
FRBL
fireball
friable
fribble(trifle)
-bbled,-bbling
furbelow
FRBLT
friability
FRBM
firebomb
FRBNGKS
Fairbanks
FRBR
forbear(abstain)
forbore
forborne
forebear(ancestor)
FRBRK
firebreak
firebrick
FRBRN
forborne(abstain)
forebrain
freeborn
FRBRND
firebrand
FRBRNS

forbearance
FRBSH
furbish
furbishes
FRBT
ferryboat
fireboat
FRBZ
freebies
FRCHKLB
Four-H club(or)
4-H club
FRCHN
fortune
FRCHNG
far-reaching
FRCHNT
fortunate
FRCHNTLR
fortuneteller
FRCHYN
fortune
FRCHYNT
fortunate
FRD
afeard(afraid)
afraid
afford
faraday
farad
ford(stream)
forty
forties
fraud(deceive)
Freud
Friday
FRDF
fortify
fortified
fortifies
fortification
FRDG
firedog
FRDK
foredeck
FRDLNS
fraudulence
FRDLNT
fraudulent
FRDM
foredoom
freedom
FRDMN
freedman
FRDMP
firedamp

FRDN
Freudian
FRDNR
affaire d'honneur
FRDR
fritter
FRDRNZ
fraternize
fraternized
fraternizing
fraternization
FRDTD
fortitude
FRDTYD
fortitude
FRDZ
forties
FRDZK
aphrodisiac
FRF
far-off(adj)
FRFCHR
forfeiture
FRFCHT
farfetched
FRFDR
firefighter
FRFL
fearful
firefly
fireflies
FRFLD
fourfold
FRFLNG
far-flung(adj)
FRFLSH
four-flush(v)
four flush(n)
FRFLSHR
four-flusher
FRFNGGR
forefinger
FRFNGR
forefinger
FRFRL
free-for-all
FRFRM
freeform
FRFRNT
forefront
FRFT
forfeit
forefoot
FRFTD
four-footed
FRFTHR

NGK:ink P:pie R:air S:ice SH:show T:toy THN:thin TH:the V:of W:we Y:you Z:is VZHN:vision

forefather
FRFTR
firefighter
FRG
farrago(mixture)
forego(precede)
foregoes
forewent
foregone
forgo(do without)
forwent
forgone
forgoes
frig
frigged
frigging
frog
frogeye
froggy
froggier
froggiest
frug(dance)
FRGHR
frog hair(golf)
FRGL
frugal
FRGLT
frugality
frugalities
FRGMN
frogman
frogmen
FRGMNT
fragment
FRGMNTL
fragmental
FRGMNTR
fragmentary
FRGRND
fairground
foreground
FRGRNS
fragrance
FRGRNT
fragrant
FRGT
forget
forgot
forgetting
forgotten
frigate(bird,boat)
FRGTBL
forgettable
FRGTFL
forgetful
FRGTMNT

forget-me-not
FRGTN
forgotten
FRGV
forgive
forgave
forgiving
forgiven
FRGVBL
forgivable
FRGVNS
forgiveness
FRHD
forehead
FRHND
forehand
freehand
FRHNDD
forehanded
FRHRD
fair-haired
FRHWL
four-wheel
FRHWLNG
freewheeling
FRJ
ferriage(toll)
forage(search)
foraged
foraging
forge
forged
forging
forger
FRJD
frigid
FRJDT
frigidity
FRJL
fragile
FRJLT
fragility
FRJR
forger
forgery
forgeries
FRK
Africa
fork
freak
frock
FRKCHR
fracture
fractured
fracturing
FRKCHS

fructuous
FRKD
forked
FRKL
fireclay
freckle
freckled
freckling
FRKLFT
fork lift
FRKLK
four-o'clock
FRKLR
four-color
FRKLZ
foreclose
foreclosed
foreclosing
FRKLZHR
foreclosure
FRKN
firkin
FRKNR
Afrikaner
FRKNS
Afrikaans
FRKRKR
firecracker
FRKRT
forecourt
FRKS
fracas
fricassee
fricasseed
FRKSH
freakish
FRKSHN
fraction
friction
FRKSHS
fractious
FRKSL
forecastle
FRKST
forecast
FRKTF
fructify
fructified
fructifies
FRKTS
fructose
FRKWNS
frequency
frequencies
FRKWNT
frequent

FRKWRTR
forequarter
FRKYR
fire-cure
fire-cured
fire-curing
FRL
fairly
feral
ferrule(metal
ring)
ferule(stick)
forel(slipcase)
frail
frill
frilly
frillier
frilliest
furl
furlough
FRLDR
freeloader
FRLDRWRD
four-letter word
FRLG
foreleg
FRLK
forelock
frolic
frolicked
frolicking
FRLKR
frolicker
FRLKSM
frolicsome
FRLND
fairyland
FRLNG
furlong
FRLNS
free-lance
FRLNZ
Faeroe Islands
FRLRN
forlorn
FRLS
fearless
FRLT
frailty
frailties
FRLTRWRD
four-letter word
FRLZ
frills
FRM
A-frame

affirm
farm
firm
form(shape)
forum
frame
  framed
  framing
from
FRMBL
  affirmable
FRMDBL
  formidable
  formidably
FRMHND
  farmhand
FRMHS
  farmhouse
FRMK
  Formica
  (trademark)
FRMKLJ
  pharmacology
FRMKP
  pharmacopoeia
FRML
  formal
FRMLDHD
  formaldehyde
FRMLS
  formless
FRMLT
  formality
  formalities
FRMLZ
  formalize
  formalized
  formalizing
FRMLZSHN
  formalization
FRMMNT
  firmament
FRMN
  fireman
  firemen
  foreman
  foremen
  freeman
  freemen
FRMNCHND
  aforementioned
FRMNDD
  fair-minded
FRMNSHND
  aforementioned
FRMNT

ferment
FRMNTSHN
  fermentation
FRMP
  frame-up
  frump
FRMPSH
  frumpish
FRMR
  affirmer
  farmer
  former
FRMRKN
  Afro-American
FRMS
  pharmacy
  pharmacies
FRMSDKL
  pharmaceutical
FRMSHN
  affirmation
  formation
FRMSN
  Freemason
FRMSST
  pharmacist
FRMST
  foremost
FRMSTD
  farmstead
FRMSTKL
  pharmaceutical
FRMT
  fermata
  format(layout)
  formatted,-tting
FRMTS
  fremitus
FRMTV
  affirmative
  formative
FRMWRK
  framework
FRMYL
  formula
  formulae(or)
  formulas
FRMYLSHN
  formulation
FRMYLT
  formulate
  formulated
  formulating
FRMYLWN
  Formula One
FRMYLZ

formulize
  formulized
  formulizing
FRMYLZSHN
  formulization
FRMYRD
  farmyard
FRN
  farina(cereal)
  fern(plant)
  foreign
  frown
FRNBRN
  foreign-born
FRNBWZ
  framboise
FRNCH
  French
FRNCHDRZ
  French doors
FRNCHFR
  French fry
  French fries
FRNCHGN
  French Guiana
FRNCHKF
  French cuff
FRNCHPLNZH
  French Polynesia
FRNCHR
  furniture
FRNCHTST
  French toast
FRNCHZ
  affranchise
  franchise
  franchised
  franchising
  franchiser
FRND
  friend
  frond
FRNDFT
  fore and aft
FRNDL
  friendly(nice)
  -lier,-liest
  friendliness
FRNDSHP
  friendship
FRNG
  offering
FRNGK
  franc(coin)
  frank(honest)
FRNGKFRDR

frankfurter
FRNGKFRT
  Frankfort(Ky)
  Frankfurt(Germany)
FRNGKFRTR
  frankfurter
FRNGKNS
  frankness
FRNGKNSNS
  frankincense
FRNGKS
  pharynx
FRNGNG
  far-ranging(adj)
FRNGPN
  frying pan
FRNHND
  four-in-hand
FRNHT
  Fahrenheit
FRNJ
  fringe
  fringed
  fringing
FRNJBL
  frangible
FRNJBLT
  frangibility
FRNJZ
  pharynges
FRNK
  franc(coin)
  frank
FRNKNG
  franking(mail)
FRNKNSNS
  frankincense
FRNKSHN
  fornication
FRNKSZ
  pharynxes
FRNKT
  fornicate
  fornicated
  fornicating
  fornicator
FRNKTR
  fornicator
FRNLJ
  foreknowledge
  phrenology
FRNMD
  forenamed
FRNN
  forenoon
FRNR

NGK:ink **P**:pie **R**:air **S**:ice **SH**:show **T**:toy **THN**:thin **TH**:the **V**:of **W**:we **Y**:you **Z**:is **VZHN**:vision

foreigner
forerunner
FRNS
France
furnace
FRNSH
furnish
furnishes
FRNSHNGZ
furnishings
FRNSHS
farinaceous
FRNSK
forensic
FRNSKL
forensical
FRNT
afferent(toward
the center)
affront
efferent(away from
the center)
front
FRNTJ
frontage
FRNTK
frantic
frenetic(or)
phrenetic
FRNTKL
frantically
frenetically
FRNTL
frontal
FRNTLN
front-line(adj)
FRNTLT
frontlet
FRNTN
fronton(jai alai)
FRNTPJ
front-page(adj)
FRNTR
effrontery
effronteries
frontier
FRNTRNR
front-runner
FRNTRZMN
frontiersman
frontiersmen
FRNTSPS
frontispiece
FRNZ
frenzy
frenzied

frenzies
FRNZK
forensic
FRNZKL
forensical
FRP
forepaw
frap
frapped
frapping
frappé
FRPL
foreplay
FRPLG
fireplug
FRPLS
fireplace
FRPR
frippery
fripperies
FRPRF
fireproof
FRPSTR
four-poster(bed)
FRPWR
firepower
FRR
freer
freest
free
friar(person)
friary
friaries
fryer(bird)
furrier(person)
furrier(fur)
furry
FRRDN
foreordain
FRRM
firearm
forearm
FRRN
fire iron
FRS
farce
ferrous(iron)
fierce
fiercer
fiercest
force
forced
forcing
foresee
foresaw
foreseen

foreseeing
pharisee
FRSBL
forcible(force)
forcibly
foreseeable
FRSD
aforesaid
fireside
FRSFL
forceful
FRSFLD
force field
FRSH
afresh(anew)
fairish
foreshow
foreshown
fresh
frosh
FRSHD
foreshadow
FRSHMN
freshman
freshmen
FRSHN
foreshown
freshen
fruition
FRSHR
a fortiori
FRSHRTN
foreshorten
FRSHS
ferocious
FRSHT
freshet
FRSHWL
Ferris wheel
FRSHWTR
freshwater
FRSK
forsake
forsook
forsaking
forsaken
fresco
frisk
frisky
friskier
friskiest
friskily
friskiness
pharisaic
FRSKL
farcical

FRSKN
forsaken
foreskin
FRSKP
fire escape
FRSKR
fourscore
FRSKT
frisket
FRSKWR
foursquare
FRSL
foresail
FRSLP
foreslope
FRSM
fearsome
foursome
FRSMZHR
force majeure
FRSN
foreseen
FRSPKN
fair-spoken
free-spoken
FRSPS
forceps
FRSR
farceur
fiercer
fiercest
fierce
foreseer
FRST
Far East
ferocity
ferocities
first
foresight
forest
frost
frosty
frostier
frostiest
frostily
frostiness
freest
freer
free
FRSTBRN
firstborn
FRSTBT
frostbite
frostbit
frostbiting
frostbitten

FRSTD
farsighted
FRSTDGR
first-degree(adj)
FRSTFML
first family
FRSTH
forsythia
FRSTHND
firsthand
FRSTK
aphoristic
aphoristical
FRSTKLS
first-class(adj)
FRSTL
forestall
FRSTLD
first lady
FRSTM
frustum
FRSTN
freestone
FRSTNDNG
free-standing
FRSTNG
frosting
FRSTR
forester
forestry
four-star
FRSTRSHN
frustration
FRSTRT
first-rate
frustrate(thwart)
frustrated,-ting
FRSTSHN
afforestation
forestation
FRSWL
Ferris wheel
FRSWR
forswear
forswore
forsworn
forswearing
FRT
affright
afreet(spirit)
effort
far-out
fart(vulgar)
ferret
fort(place)
forte(skill,music)

forty
forties
frat(fraternity)
fraught
freight
fret
fretted
fretting
fright(fear)
fruit
fruity
fruitier
fruitiest
fruitiness
FRTF
fortify
fortified
fortifies
FRTFKSHN
fortification
FRTFL
fretful
frightful
fruitful
FRTFR
fortifier
FRTH
firth
forth(forward)
fourth(4th)
froth
frothy
frothier
frothiest
frothily
frothiness
FRTHKLS
fourth-class
FRTHKMNG
forthcoming
FRTHNG
farthing
FRTHNGKR
freethinker
FRTHR
farther(distance)
further(degree,
time or quantity)
FRTHRMR
furthermore
FRTHRMST
farthermost(distant)
furthermost(remote)
FRTHRNS
furtherance
FRTHRT

forthright
FRTHST
farthest(distance)
furthest(degree,
time or quantity)
FRTHSTT
Fourth Estate
FRTHT
forethought
FRTHWTH
forthwith
FRTJ
freightage
FRTKK
fruitcake
FRTL
fertile
foretell
foretold
foretelling
foreteller
FRTLDRDL
Fort Lauderdale
FRTLS
effortless
fruitless
FRTLT
fertility
FRTLZ
fertilize
fertilized
fertilizing
FRTLZBL
fertilizable
FRTLZR
fertilizer
FRTLZSHN
fertilization
FRTN
fourteen
frighten
FRTNZ
fraternize
fraternized
fraternizing
FRTNZSHN
fraternization
FRTR
fire-eater
freighter
fritter
offertory
offertories
FRTRD
fair-trade
FRTRNL

fraternal
FRTRNT
fraternity
fraternities
FRTRNZ
fraternize
fraternized
fraternizing
fraternization
FRTRP
firetrap
FRTRS
fortress
fortresses
FRTRSD
fratricide
FRTSND
forzando
FRTST
foretaste
FRTT
fortuity
fortuities
FRTTD
fortitude
FRTTH
fortieth
FRTTS
fortuitous
FRTTYD
fortitude
FRTV
furtive
FRTWD
fruitwood
FRTWRK
fretwork
FRTWRTH
Fort Worth
FRTYT
fortuity
fortuities
FRTYTS
fortuitous
FRVD
fervid
FRVL
frivol
FRVLS
frivolous
FRVLT
frivolity
frivolities
FRVNT
fervent
FRVR

fervor, (B)fervour	froze	fustian	fishplate
forever	freeze	**FSD**	**FSHPND**
FRVS	phrase(words)	facade	fishpond
effervesce	phrased	offside	**FSHR**
effervesced	phrasing	**FSF**	fisher(fish)
effervescing	**FRZB**	face-off(n)	fishery
FRVSNS	Frisbee(trademark)	**FSFR**	fisheries
effervescence	**FRZBL**	phosphor	fissure
FRVSNT	freezable	**FSFRSNS**	fissured
effervescent	**FRZDR**	phosphorescence	fissuring
FRW	freeze-dry	**FSFRSNT**	offshore
fairway(golf)	freeze-dried	phosphorescent	**FSHRMN**
faraway	freeze-dries	**FSFT**	fisherman
four-way	**FRZHN**	phosphate	fishermen
freeway	Afro-Asian	**FSH**	**FSHS**
FRWD	**FRZHR**	fascia	officious
firewood	fourragére	fascial	**FSHSHN**
FRWL	**FRZL**	fichu(scarf)	fasciation
farewell	phrasal	fish	officiation
FRWRD	**FRZLJ**	fishy	**FSHST**
foreword(preface)	phraseology	fishier	fascist(fascism)
forward(front)	phraseologies	fishiest	**FSHT**
froward(obstinate)	**FRZM**	fishiness	fasciate
FRWRDNS	aphorism	oafish	officiate
forwardness	aphoristical	**FSHBL**	officiated
FRWRKS	**FRZMCHZ**	fishbowl	officiating
fireworks	forasmuch as	**FSHK**	offshoot
FRWRN	**FRZN**	fishhook	**FSHTL**
forewarn	frozen(freeze)	**FSHL**	fishtail
FRWST	**FRZR**	facial	**FSHTR**
Far West	freezer	official	officiator
FRWTHR	**FS**	**FSHLDR**	**FSHWF**
fair-weather(adj)	efface	officeholder	fishwife
FRWTR	effaced	**FSHLS**	**FSHZM**
firewater	effacing	officialese	fascism
FRYR	face	**FSHLZ**	**FSK**
furrier(person)	faced	officialese	fiasco
FRZ	facing	**FSHMNGR**	fossick
fraise(barrier)	fosse(ditch)	fishmonger	**FSKL**
freeze(ice)	fuss	**FSHN**	fascicle(bundle)
froze	fusses	fashion	fiscal
freezing	fussy	fission	**FSKY**
frozen	fussier	**FSHNBL**	fescue
frieze(cloth,	fussiest	fashionable	**FSL**
architecture)	fussily	fissionable	facile
frisé(fabric)	fussiness	**FSHNPLT**	fossil(remains)
frizz	office	fashion plate	**FSLJ**
frizzy	**FSBJT**	**FSHNS**	fuselage
frizzier	fuss-budget	efficiency	**FSLT**
frizziest	**FSBL**	efficiencies	facility
frizziness	effaceable	**FSHNT**	facilities
frowzy	feasible	efficient	**FSLTSHN**
frowzier	feasibly	**FSHNTS**	facilitation
frowziest	**FSCHLS**	efficiency	**FSLTT**
frowzily	fistulous	efficiencies	facilitate
frowziness	**FSCHN**	**FSHPLT**	facilitated

B:by **CH**:each **D**:day **F**:if **G**:go **H**:he **HW**:why **J**:joy **K**:cow **KS**:ax **KWL**:equal **L**:all **M**:may **N**:in

facilitating
FSLZ
fossilize
fossilized
fossilizing
FSLZH
fuselage
FSN
fasten
Pusan(Fusan)(city)
FSNG
facing
FSNR
fastener
FSNS
fastness
FSNSHN
fascination
FSNT
fascinate
fascinated
fascinating
FSNTR
fascinator
FSPLT
faceplate
FSPLTNG
fee splitting(pay)
FSPRNG
offspring
FSR
officer
FSSH
facetiae(pl,n)
FSSHS
facetious
FST
facet(part)
fast
faucet
feast
feisty(touchy)
feistier
feistiest
feistily
feistiness
fiesta
fist
foist
fusty
fustier
fustiest
fustily
fustiness
offset
offset

offsetting
FSTBK
fastback
FSTDS
fastidious
FSTFD
fast-food(adj)
FSTFS
face-to-face
FSTJ
offstage
FSTKFS
fisticuffs
FSTL
festal
FSTN
festoon
FSTNS
fastness
FSTP
f-stop
FSTR
fester
foster
FSTV
festive
FSTVL
festival
FSTVT
festivity
festivities
FSVL
face value
FSVLY
face value
FSVNG
face-saving
FSZ
fasces(emblem)
feces(dung)
FT
aft(nautical)
effete
fat
fatter
fattest
fate(destiny)
fated
fatty
fattier
fattiest
fattiness
feat(deed)
feet
foot
fete(feast)

feted
feting
fiat
fight
fought
fighting
fit
fitted(or)
fit
fitting
fitter
foot
feet
fought
fight
oft(often)
photo
photograph
FTBL
football
FTBRJ
footbridge
FTD
fated
fate
fatted
fat
fetid(stink)
FTFL
fateful
fitful
footfall
FTFLD
photoflood
FTFLSH
photoflash
photoflashes
FTFNSH
photo finish
FTFST
photo-offset
FTG
fatigue
fatigued
fatiguing
FTGBL
fatigable
FTGRF
photograph
FTGRFK
photographic
FTGRFKL
photographically
FTGRFR
photographer
FTGRVYR

photogravure
FTH
faith(believe)
fifth(number 5)
FTHFL
faithful
FTHLS
faithless
FTHLD
foothold
FTHLMLJ
ophthalmology
FTHLMLJST
ophthalmologist
FTHLMSKP
ophthalmoscope
FTHM
fathom
FTHMBL
fathomable
FTHMLS
fathomless
FTHR
father
feather
feathery
featheriness
FTHRBD
feather bed(n)
featherbed(v)
-bedded,-bedding
FTHRBRN
featherbrain
FTHRD
fathered(sired)
feathered
FTHRHD
fatherhood
FTHRL
fatherly
fatherliness
FTHRLND
fatherland
FTHRLNS
fatherliness
FTHRLS
fatherless
FTHRNL
father-in-law
fathers-in-law
FTHRNS
featheriness
FTHRSTCH
featherstitch
featherstitches
FTHRTM

NGK:ink P:pie R:air S:ice SH:show T:toy THN:thin TH:the V:of W:we Y:you Z:is VZHN:vision

Father Time
FTHRWT
  featherweight
    (119-126 lbs)
FTHRZNL
  fathers-in-law
FTJ
  footage
FTJNK
  photogenic
FTKNDL
  foot-candle
FTKP
  photocopy
    photocopies
    photocopied
FTKPR
  photocopier
FTKPZ
  photocopies
FTKRNGRF
  photochronograph
FTKTV
  photoactive
FTL
  fatal(death)
  fetal(unborn)
  fettle
    fettled
    fettling
FTLK
  fetlock
FTLKR
  footlocker
FTLKTRK
  photoelectric
FTLS
  footloose
FTLST
  fatalist
FTLSTK
  fatalistic
FTLSTKL
  fatalistically
FTLT
  fatality
    fatalities
FTLTHGRF
  photolithograph
  photolithography
FTLTS
  footlights
FTLZM
  fatalism
FTMNTZH
  photomontage

FTMP
  photomap
FTMST
  aftmost
FTMTR
  photometer
  photometry
FTMTRK
  photometric
FTMYRL
  photomural
FTN
  fatten
  foot-ton
  often(frequently)
  phaeton
  photon(particle)
  phyton(unit)
FTNG
  fighting
  footing
FTNGRV
  photoengrave
    photoengraved
    photoengraving
FTNS
  fitness
FTNT
  footnote
    footnoted
    footnoting
FTPD
  footpad
FTPK
  off-topic(debate)
FTPND
  foot-pound
FTPRNT
  footprint
FTPTH
  footpath
FTR
  after
  fatter
  fetter(restraint)
  fitter
  footer
FTRBRNR
  afterburner
FTRBRTH
  afterbirth
FTRDK
  afterdeck
FTRFKT
  aftereffect
FTRGL

  afterglow
FTRKLP
  afterclap
FTRKR
  aftercare
FTRMJ
  afterimage
FTRMST
  aftermost
FTRMTH
  aftermath
FTRNN
  afternoon
FTRPNZ
  afterpains
FTRPS
  afterpiece
FTRST
  footrest
FTRTHT
  afterthought
FTRTM
  aftertime
FTRTST
  aftertaste
FTRWRD
  afterward
FTRWRLD
  afterworld
FTS
  fetus
    fetuses
FTS
  footsie(game)
FTSD
  feticide
FTSH
  fattish(fat)
  fetish
FTSHST
  fetishist
    fetishistic
FTSHZM
  fetishism
FTSLYBL
  fat-soluble
FTSNSTV
  photosensitive
FTSNTHSS
  photosynthesis
FTSR
  footsore
FTST
  fattest
    fatter
    fat

  fittest
    fitter,fit
FTSTL
  footstool
FTSTN
  footstone
FTSTP
  footstep
FTSTT
  Photostat
    (trademark)
FTT
  fatuity
    fatuities
FTVLTK
  photovoltaic
FTWR
  footwear
FTWRK
  footwork
FTWRN
  footworn
FTWTD
  fat-witted
FTYT
  fatuity
    fatuities
FV
  five
FVFLD
  fivefold
FVR
  favor, (B)favour
  fever
FVRBL
  favorable
  favorably
FVRD
  favored
FVRSH
  feverish
FVRT
  favorite
FVRTZM
  favoritism
FWL
  foul
  fowl(bird)
FWT
  off-white(color)
FYCHR
  future
FYCHRSTK
  futuristic
    futuristical
FYD

B:by **CH**:each **D**:day **F**:if **G**:go **H**:he **HW**:why **J**:joy **K**:cow **KS**:ax **KWL**:equal **L**:all **M**:may **N**:in

feud
FYDL
feudal
futile(useless)
FYDLSTK
feudalistic
FYDLZM
feudalism
FYG
fugue(fugal)
FYGL
fugle(signal)
fugled
fugling
fugal(music)
FYGSHS
fugacious
FYJTV
fugitive
FYLD
fjeld(plateau)
FYLJNS
fuliginous
FYM
fume
fumed
fuming
FYMGNT
fumigant
FYMGSHN
fumigation
FYMGT
fumigate
fumigated
fumigating
FYMGTR
fumigator
FYMRL
fumarole
FYNKYLR
funicular
FYNRL
funeral(burial)
funereal
(mournful)
FYNRR
funerary
FYR
foyer
fury(rage)
furies
FYRD
fjord
FYRR
fuhrer(person)
furor, (B)furore

FYRS
furioso
furious
FYRZ
Furies
(mythology)
FYS
effuse
effused
effusing
FYSH
fuchsia(color)
FYSLD
fusillade
fusilladed
fusillading
FYSLZH
fuselage
FYSV
effusive
FYTL
futile
FYTLT
futility
futilities
FYTRT
futurity
futurities
FYZ
fuse
fused
fusing
fusee
FYZBL
fusible
FYZBLT
fusibility
FYZHN
effusion
fusion
FZ
faze(disturb)
fazed
fazing
fez(cap)
fezzes
fizz
fizzes
fuzz
fuzzes
fuzzy
fuzzier
fuzziest
fuzzily
fuzziness
phase(stage)
phased
phasing
phasic(adj)

phase in
phase out
FZBL
feasible
FZBLT
feasibility
feasibilities
FZGNM
physiognomy
FZGRF
physiography
FZH
aphasia
FZHN
fission
FZHR
fissure(cleft)
FZK
phasic(adj)
phase
physic(medicine)
physicked
physicking
physique(body)
FZKL
fiscal(money)
physical
FZKS
physics
FZL
fizzle
fizzled
fizzling
fizzler
foozle(slang)
foozled
foozling
FZLJ
fuselage
physiology
FZLJKL
physiological
FZLZH
fuselage
FZN
foison
FZNT
pheasant
FZSHN
physician
FZSST
physicist
FZTHRP
physiotherapy
physiotherapies
FZTHRPST

physiotherapist
FZZ
fezzes(caps)
fez

G

agh(interj)
agghhh
ago(time)
e.g.
exempli gratia
egg(new life)
ego(self)
gay(mirth)
gaily
gee (interj)
ghee(butter)
go (movement)
went
gone
goo
gooey(sticky)
gooier
gooiest
gooiness
guy(man, cable)
ugh(interj)
GB
gab(talk)
gabbed
gabbing
gabby
gabbier
gabbiest
gabbiness
gib(tool)
gob(lump)
gobbed
GBFST
gabfest
GBL
gabble(talk)
gabbled
gabbling
gable(roof)
gabled
gobble(eat)
gobbled
gobbling
GBLDGK
gobbledygook

GBLN
goblin
GBLT
goblet
GBN
Gabon
gibbon
GBR
goober
GBRD
gabbart
GBRDN
gabardine
GBRNTRL
gubernatorial
GBRT
gabbart
GBS
gibbous
GBST
gibbosity
gibbosities
GBTWN
go-between
GCH
Gaucho
GD
gad(tool)
gadded
gadding
gaud
gaudy(showy)
gaudier
gaudiest
gaudily
gaudiness
ghetto(slum)
gid(disease)
giddy(dizzy)
giddier
giddiest
giddily
giddiness
goad(prod)
God(Supreme Being)
good(okay)
better
best
goody(sweet)
goodies
guide(lead)
guided
guiding
guider
GDB
good-by

GDBK
guidebook
GDBL
guidable
GDBT
gadabout
GDCHLD
godchild
GDFL
gadfly
gadflies
godawful
GDFRNTHNG
good-for-nothing
GDFRSKN
godforsaken
GDFTHR
godfather
GDGD
goody-goody
GDGVN
God-given
GDHD
godhead
godhood
GDHMRD
good-humored
GDHRTD
good-hearted
GDL
godly
godlier
godliest
godliness
godling
goodly
goodlier
goodliest
goodliness
GDLKNG
good-looking
GDLN
guideline
GDLS
godless
GDMTHR
godmother
GDN
Ogden
GDNCHRD
good-natured
GDNS
guidance
GDNSK
Gdansk
GDNT

good night
GDPRNT
godparent
GDPST
guidepost
GDR
gaudery
gauderies
goiter
gutter(street)
GDRL
gutteral
GDRP
guide rope
GDRSNP
guttersnipe
GDS
goddess
goddesses
GDSN
godson
GDSND
godsend
GDSPD
Godspeed
GDSZD
good-sized
GDTMPRD
good-tempered
GDTR
goddaughter
GDWL
good will(n)
goodwill(adj)
GDZ
goodies
goody
GF
gaff(hook)
gaffe(error)
goof
goofy
goofier
goofiest
goofily
goofiness
guff(talk)
GFR
gaffer(old man)
gopher
GFRG
gaff rig
gaff rigged
GFT
gift
gifted

GFTD
gifted
GFTR
gaffer(old man)
GFTRP
gift-wrap(v)
gift-wrapped
gift-wrapping
GG
agog
à gogo(fast)
gag
gagged
gagging
gaga((crazy)
gig
gigged
gigging
go-go
GGL
gaggle
gaggled
gaggling
giggle(laugh)
giggled
giggling
giggler
giggly
gigglier
giggliest
goggle
goggled
goggling
googol(#)
GGLPLKS
googolplex
GGMN
gagman
gagmen
GGR
Geiger
gagger
GGTR
go-getter
GH
agh(interj)
agghhh
GHD
egghead
go-ahead
GJ
gage(pledge)
gaged
gaging
gauge(measure)
gauged

B:by **CH**:each **D**:day **F**:if **G**:go **H**:he **HW**:why **J**:joy **K**:cow **KS**:ax **KWL**:equal **L**:all **M**:may **N**:in

gauging
gouge
  gouged
  gouging
GJBL
gaugeable
GJN
gudgeon
GJR
gauger
GJT
gadget
GK
gawk(oaf,look)
gawky
  gawkier
  gawkiest
  gawkily
  gawkiness
geek(side show)
gook(slang)
GKRT
go-cart
GL
aglow
eagle
gaily
  gay
gal(girl)
gala
gale(wind)
gall(sore,vex)
galley(ship)
ghillie(shoe)
ghoul(demon)
gill(fish)
glee
glow(shine)
glue
  glued
  gluing
gluey
goal(purpose)
goalie(person)
gold(metal)
golly(interj)
guild(union)
guile(trick)
gull
gully
  gullies
igloo
ogle(look)
  ogled
  ogling

ugli(fruit)
uglis(or)
uglies
ugly
  uglier
  ugliest
  uglily
  ugliness
  uglies(slang)
GLB
glebe(soil)
glib
  glibber
  glibbest
glob(drop)
  globbed
globe(sphere)
GLBL
glibly
global
gullible
gullibly
GLBLT
gullibility
GLBRK
goldbrick
GLBRKR
goldbricker
GLBRTLNZ
Gilbert Islands
GLBTRTR
globe-trotter
GLBYL
globule
GLBYLR
globular
GLCH
gulch
  gulches
GLD
eagle-eyed
geld(castrate)
  gelding
gild(to coat
  with gold)
glad
  gladder
  gladdest
  gladded
  gladding
glade(open space)
glede(fowl)
glide(move)
  glided
  gliding
  glider

gold
  golden
guild(union)
GLDD
glutted
glut
GLDFLD
gold-filled
GLDFSH
goldfish
GLDGR
gold digger
GLDKLNG
ugly duckling
GLDL
gladiola
  gladioli(or)
  gladioluses
glottal
gluteal(muscle)
GLDLF
gold leaf
GLDLS
gladiolus
  gladioluses
GLDN
gladden
golden
GLDNG
gelding(animal)
gilding(gold)
GLDR
gladder
  gladdest
glad
glider
glitter(shine)
guilder
GLDS
glottis(throat)
  glottises(or)
  glottides
GLDSM
gladsome
GLDSMN
guildsman
guildsmen
GLDSMTH
goldsmith
GLDTR
gladiator
GLDZMN
guildsman
guildsmen
GLF
glyph(groove)

glyphic
golf
gulf
uglify
  uglified
  uglifies
GLFK
glyphic
glyph
GLFKRS
golf course
GLFKSHN
uglification
GLFKST
Gulf Coast
GLFL
gleeful
guileful
GLFR
golfer
GLFSTRM
Gulf Stream
Gulfstream
  (racetrack)
GLFVDN
Gulf of Aden
GLFVGN
Gulf of Guinea
GLFVKB
Gulf of Aqaba
GLFVLSK
Gulf of Alaska
GLFVMKSK
Gulf of Mexico
GLFVMN
Gulf of Oman
GLFVSZ
Gulf of Suez
GLFVTHLND
Gulf of Thailand
GLFVTLND
Gulf of Thailand
GLG
gulag
GLHD
Galahad
GLK
Gaelic
GLKJN
glycogen
GLKL
glycol(alcohol)
GLKM
glaucoma
GLKNSPL
glockenspiel

NGK:ink **P:**pie **R:**air **S:**ice **SH:**show **T:**toy **THN:**thin **TH:**the **V:**of **W:**we **Y:**you **Z:**is **VZHN:**vision

GLKPR
goalkeeper
GLKS
galaxy
galaxies
glucose
GLKTK
galactic
GLM
agleam
gleam(shine)
gloom
gloomy
gloomier
gloomiest
gloomily
gloominess
glum
glummer
glummest
GLMF
galumph
GLMNG
gloaming
GLMPS
glimpse
glimpsed
glimpsing
GLMR
aglimmer
glamour
glimmer
GLMRS
glamorous
GLMRT
agglomerate
agglomerated
agglomerating
glomerate
GLMRZ
glamorize
glamorized
glamorizing
glamorization
GLMSHS
galimatias
GLN
galleon(ship)
gallon(measure)
gland
glean
goal line(score)
GLND
gland
GLNJLR
glandular

GLNS
glance
glanced
glancing
GLNT
gallant
glint
GLNTR
gallantry
gallantries
GLNYLR
glandular
GLNZ
glans(sex)
glandes
GLP
gallop
glop(slang)(food)
gulp
GLPGZ
Galapagos
GLPST
goal post
GLPTK
glyptic(carved)
GLR
gallery
galleries
galleried
galore
glair(egg white)
glairy(egg white)
glairier
glairiest
glairily
glairiness
glare(bright)
glared
glaring
glary
glarier
glariest
glariness
gloria
glory
gloried
glories
glower(stare)
GLRD
galleried
GLRF
glorify
glorified
glorifies
GLRFKSHN
glorification

GLRS
glorious
GLS
eyeglass
eyeglasses
glacé
glacéed
glacéing
glacis(slope)
glass
glasses
glassy
glassier
glassiest
glassiness
gloss
glossy
glossies
glossier
glossiest
glossiness
guileless
GLSD
glissade
glissaded
glissading
GLSFL
glassful
GLSG
Glasgow
GLSH
galosh(overshoe)
galoshes
ghoulish(scary)
goulash(food)
GLSHL
glacial
GLSHLST
glacialist
GLSHR
glacier
GLSHS
galoshes
GLSHT
glaciate
glaciated
glaciating
GLSHZ
galoshes
GLSN
glassine
glisten(shiny)
glycin
(photography)
glycine
(amino acid)

GLSND
glissando
GLSR
glossary
glossaries
GLSRL
glycerol
glycerin
GLSRN
glycerin
GLSTN
gallstone
GLSWR
glassware
GLSZ
glossies
GLT
aglet
eaglet(eagle)
Galatea(myth)
gelt
gilt(gold)
gleet(discharge)
gloat
glut
glutted
glutting
guilt(blame)
guilty
guiltier
guiltiest
guiltily
guiltiness
gullet
GLTH
goliath (or)Goliath
GLTJD
gilt-edged
GLTL
glottal
gluteal(muscle)
GLTLS
guiltless
GLTN
gluten(proteins)
glutton(overeater)
gluttony
gluttonies
guillotine(chop)
guillotined
guillotining
GLTNDR
goaltender
GLTNS
glutenous(having
gluten)

B:by **CH**:each **D**:day **F**:if **G**:go **H**:he **HW**:why **J**:joy **K**:cow **KS**:ax **KWL**:equal **L**:all **M**:may **N**:in

glutinous(gluey)
gluttonous(greedy)
GLTNT
  agglutinate
    agglutinated
    agglutinating
GLTR
  aglitter
  glitter
  glittery
    glitterier
    glitteriest
GLTRN
  egalitarian
GLTS
  glitzy
  glottis
  gluteus(muscle)
GLV
  glaive(sword)
  glove
    gloved
    gloving
GLVNK
  galvanic
GLVNMTR
  galvanometer
GLVNT
  gallivant
GLVNZ
  galvanize
    galvanized
    galvanizing
GLVNZM
  galvanism
GLVNZSHN
  galvanization
GLWG
  golliwog
GLWR
  glower
GLWRM
  glowworm
GLYN
  galleon
GLZ
  igloos
  igloo
  gallows(hang)
  glaze
    glazed
    glazing
  gloze
    glozed
    glozing
GLZG

Glasgow
GM
gam(herd,visit)
  gammed
  gamming
game
  gamed
  gaming
gamin(boy)
gamma
gammon(victory)
gamy(flavor)
  gamier
  gamiest
  gaminess
Guam
gum
  gummed
  gumming
gummy(gum)
  gummier
  gummiest
  gumminess
GMB
Gambia, The
gumbo
GMBL
gamble(risk)
  gambled
  gambling
  gambler
gambol(frolic)
GMBLR
  gambler
GMBRL
  gambrel
GMBT
  gambit
GMDN
  gammadion
GMDRP
  gumdrop
GMK
  gimmick
  gimmicky
GMKK
  gamecock
GMKPR
  gamekeeper
GMLNG
  gambling
GMLR
  gambler
GMLT
  gimlet
GMN

egomania
GMNG
  gaming
GMNK
  egomaniac
GMNT
  augment
GMNTR
  augmenter
GMNTSHN
  augmentation
GMNY
  egomania
  egomaniac
GMP
  gamp
  gimp(cord)
  gimp(slang)
  guimpe(blouse)
GMSH
  gumshoe
GMSTR
  gamester
GMT
  gamut
GMZMNSHP
  gamesmanship
GN
  again
  agony
    agonies
    agonistic
    agonistical
  gain
    gainly
  Ghana
  gnu(animal)
  gone
  go
  goon
  gown(dress)
  Guinea
  guinea
  gun
    gunned
    gunning
    gunner
  gunny(fabric)
  Guyana
GNBL
  ignoble
    ignobled
    ignobling
GNBRD
  gooney bird(slang)
GNBS

egomania
  Guinea-Bissau
GNBT
  gunboat
GND
  gonad
  Uganda
GNDL
  gondola
GNDLR
  gondolier
GNDR
  gander
GNF
  ganef
GNFL
  gainful
GNFLN
  gonfalon
GNFR
  gunfire
GNG
  eggnog
  gang
  going
  go
  went
  gone
  gong
GNGH
  gung ho
GNGK
  gunk
GNGL
  ganglia
    ganglion
GNGLN
  ganglion
  ganglia
GNGLND
  gangland
GNGLNG
  gangling
GNGM
  gingham
GNGPLNGK
  gangplank
GNGRL
  gangrel
GNGRN
  gangrene
GNGRNS
  gangrenous
GNGSTR
  gangster
GNGW
  gangway

NGK:ink **P**:pie **R**:air **S**:ice **SH**:show **T**:toy **THN**:thin **TH**:the **V**:of **W**:we **Y**:you **Z**:is **VZHN**:vision

GNJZ
Ganges
GNK
agonic
GNKLJ
gynecology
GNKLJST
gynecologist
GNKTN
guncotton
GNL
agnail
gainly
gainlier
gainliest
gainliness
GNLK
gunlock
GNLS
gainless
GNMN
gunman
gunmen
ignominy
ignominies
GNMNS
ignominious
GNMNZ
ignominies
GNPDR
gunpowder
GNPG
guinea pig
GNPL
gunplay
GNPNT
gunpoint
GNR
gainer
goner(doomed)
gonorrhea
gunnery(guns)
ignore
ignored
ignoring
GNRMS
ignoramus
GNRNR
gunrunner
gunrunning
GNRNS
ignorance
GNRNT
ignorant
GNS
gainsay

gainsaid
igneous
GNSH
gun-shy
GNSHN
ignition
GNSHP
gunship
GNSHT
gunshot
GNSK
gunnysack
GNSLNGR
gunslinger
GNSMTH
gunsmith
GNSNG
gainsaying
GNST
against
GNSTK
agonistic(pain)
agonistical
agnostic
gunstock
GNSTSZM
agnosticism
GNT
agnate(male)
agnatic
agnatical
gannet(bird)
gaunt(thin)
ignite
ignited
igniting
igniter
GNTBL
ignitable
GNTLT
gauntlet
GNTR
gantry
gantries
GNY
gnu(animal)
GNZ
agonize
agonized
agonizing
GP
agape
gap(opening)
gapped
gapping
gapy

gape
gape(face)
gaped
gaping
goop(person)
goup(substance)
guppy
guppies
GPR
gaper
gape
GR
agree
agreed
auger(tool)
augur(predict)
augury
augural
eager
eagre(flood)
gear
gore(stab)
gored
goring
gory
gorier
goriest
goriness
gray(color)
(also)grey
grow
grew
grown
guru
ogre
GRB
garb(attire)
grab
grabbed
grabbing
grabber
grub
grubbed
grubbing
grubber
grubby
grubbier
grubbiest
grubbily
grubbiness
GRBJ
garbage
GRBKS
gearbox
gearboxes
GRBL

agreeable
agreeably
garble(mix up)
garbled
garbling
grabble(grope)
grabbled
grabbling
GRBLJ
agrobiology
GRBR
grubber
GRBSTK
grubstake
GRCH
grouch
grouchy
grouchier
grouchiest
grouchily
grouchiness
GRD
aggrade
aggraded
aggrading
aggradation
agreed
agree
gird
gourd(plant)
gourde(money)
grade
graded
grading
grader
greed
greedy
greedier
greediest
greedily
greediness
grid
gritty(grit)
grittier
grittiest
grittiness
grotto
guard
GRDHS
guardhouse
GRDL
girdle
girdled
girdling
griddle
griddled

griddling
GRDLKK
griddlecake
GRDLR
girdler
GRDN
garden
gradin(seat,step)
guardian
GRDNG
gardening
greeting
GRDNNG
gardening
GRDNR
gardener
GRDNT
gradient
GRDNY
gardenia
GRDR
garter(band)
girder
grader(grade)
grater(tool)
greater
great
GRDRL
guardrail
GRDRM
guardroom
GRDRN
gridiron
GRDS
gratis
GRDSHN
gradation
GRDSMN
guardsman
guardsmen
GRDT
gradate
gradated
gradating
GRDTD
gratitude
GRDZMN
guardsman
guardsmen
GRF
agraffe(tool)
agrapha(Jesus)
agraphia(mental
  disorder)
agraphic
graph

grief
gruff
gruffy(slang)
gruffier
gruffiest
gruffily
gruffiness
GRFB
agoraphobia
GRFD
graffiti(pl)
graffito
GRFK
graphic
GRFKL
graphical
GRFKS
graphics
GRFLJ
graphology
GRFM
grapheme
graphemic
GRFN
griffin
GRFSTRKN
grief-stricken
GRFT
graphite
graffiti
graffito
graft
graftage
GRFTR
grafter
GRG
grog
groggy
groggier
groggiest
groggily
grogginess
GRGL
gargle(throat)
gargled
gargling
gargoyle
gurgle
gurgled
gurgling
GRGNCHN
gargantuan
GRGRN
grosgrain
GRGRS
gregarious

GRGT
aggregate
aggregated
aggregating
aggregation
aggregator
GRHDD
gray-headed
GRHND
greyhound
GRJ
garage(car)
garaged
garaging
gorge
gorged
gorging
grudge
grudged
grudging
GRJL
gradual
GRJS
egregious
gorgeous
GRJSHN
graduation
GRJT
graduate
graduated
graduating
GRK
Gorky
Greek
GRKLTR
Greek letter
GRKN
gherkin
GRL
egg roll
girl
girlie(slang)
gorilla(ape)
grail
grill(v)
grille(n)
growl
gruel
guerrilla
  (soldier)
GRLJ
agriology(culture)
agrology(soil)
grillage
GRLK
garlic

garlicky
GRLND
garland
GRLNG
grueling
GRLR
growler
GRLRM
grillroom
GRLS
garrulous
GRLSH
girlish
GRLSKTS
Girl Scouts
GRLT
garrulity
GRM
gourmet
graham
gram, (B)gramme
grim(sad)
grimmer
grimmest
grime(dirt)
grimy
grimier
grimiest
grimily
griminess
groom
GRMBL
grumble
grumbled
grumbling
grumbler
grumbly
GRMBLR
grumbler
GRMDK
grammatic
GRMFN
gramophone
GRMLN
gremlin
GRMND
gourmand
GRMNDZ
gourmandise
GRMNT
agreement
garment
GRMP
grump
grumpy
grumpier

NGK:ink **P**:pie **R**:air **S**:ice **SH**:show **T**:toy **THN**:thin **TH**:the **V**:of **W**:we **Y**:you **Z**:is **VZHN**:vision

grumpiest
grumpily
grumpiness
GRMPS
  Gramps(or)
  gramps
GRMR
  grammar
GRMRN
  grammarian
GRMS
  grimace
  grimaced
  grimacing
GRMT
  grommet
GRMTK
  grammatic
GRMTKL
  grammatical
GRN
  grain
  grainy , grainier
    grainiest
    graininess
  grand
  green(color)
  grin
    grinned
    grinning
  groin
  groan(moan)
  ground(soil)
  grown(developed)
  gurney(stretcher)
GRNB
  Green Bay
GRNBK
  greenback
GRNCH
  Greenwich
GRNCHLD
  grandchild
    grandchildren
GRNCHR
  garniture
GRND
  aground
  grand
  green-eyed
  Grenada
  grenade
  grind
    ground
  ground(earth)
GRNDJR

grand jury
GRNDKNYN
  Grand Canyon
GRNDLKWNT
  grandiloquent
GRNDLS
  groundless
GRNDN
  grenadine
GRNDNFY
  grandnephew
GRNDNGKL
  granduncle
GRNDNS
  grandniece
GRNDNT
  grandaunt
GRNDPR
  Grand Prix
GRNDPRNT
  grandparent
GRNDR
  grenadier
GRNDS
  grandiose
  grandioso(music)
GRNDSKPR
  grounds keeper
GRNDSL
  groundsill
GRNDSN
  grandson
GRNDSPD
  groundspeed
GRNDSTN
  grindstone
GRNDSTND
  grandstand
GRNDSWL
  ground swell(rise)
GRNDTR
  granddaughter
GRNDWRK
  groundwork
GRNDZ
  aggrandize
    aggrandized
    aggrandizing
    aggrandizer
GRNFTHR
  grandfather
GRNGG
  gringo
GRNGJ
  greengage
GRNHRN

greenhorn
GRNHS
  greenhouse
GRNJ
  grange
  Greenwich
GRNJR
  grandeur
  grand jury
GRNKNYN
  Grand Canyon
GRNLND
  Greenland
GRNM
  agronomy
GRNMTHR
  grandmother
GRNP
  grown-up
GRNPR
  Grand Prix
GRNR
  garner
  granary
    granaries
  greenery
    greeneries
GRNRM
  greenroom
GRNSH
  garnish(adorn)
    garnishes
  garnishee
    garnisheed
GRNSHMNT
  garnishment
GRNSN
  grandson
GRNSTN
  grandstand
  grindstone
GRNSTND
  grandstand
GRNSTNDR
  grandstander
GRNSWL
  ground swell(rise)
GRNSWRD
  greensward
GRNT
  garnet
  granite(rock)
  grant
  grantee
    grantor
  grunt

guarantee
  (general
  responsibility)
  guaranteed
  guaranty(finance)
  guarantied
  guaranties
GRNTND
  grant-in-aid
GRNTR
  grantor(giver)
  guarantor
  (responsible one)
GRNTSND
  grants-in-aid
GRNTWR
  graniteware
GRNYL
  granule
GRNYLR
  granular
GRNYLSHN
  granulation
GRNYLT
  granulate
    granulated
    granulating
GRNYN
  grunion
GRNZ
  grains(harpoon)
  grounds
  Guernsey
  (island,cow)
  guernsey(shirt)
GRNZKPR
  grounds keeper
GRNZZ
  Guernseys(cows)
GRP
  grape
  grip(hold)
    gripped
    gripping
    gripper
  gripe(distress)
    griped
    griping
    griper
  grippe
  (influenza)
  grope(feel)
    groped
    groping
  group
  groupie

B:by **CH**:each **D**:day **F**:if **G**:go **H**:he **HW**:why **J**:joy **K**:cow **KS**:ax **KWL**:equal **L**:all **M**:may **N**:in

GRPFRT
grapefruit
GRPL
grapple
grappled
grappling
grappler
graupel(snow)
GRPLR
grappler
GRPNL
grapnel
GRPNT
gros point
GRPVN
grapevine
GRRN
agrarian
GRRNZM
agrarianism
GRS
aggress(quarrel)
aggresses
egress
egresses
grace
graced
gracing
grass(lawn)
grasses
grassy
grassier
grassiest
grassiness
grease(oil)
greased
greasing
greasy
greasier
greasiest
greasily
greasiness
Greece
gross
grosses
grouse(bird)
groused
grousing
grouser
(complain)
GRSCHL
agrestial(wild)
GRSFL
graceful
GRSH
garish

ogreish
GRSHFT
gearshift
GRSHN
aggression
GRSHPR
grasshopper
GRSHS
gracious
GRSL
gristle
gristly
gristlier
gristliest
gristliness
GRSM
gruesome
GRSMNGK
grease monkey
GRSN
garcon
garrison
GRSP
grasp
GRSPNT
greasepaint
GRSR
aggressor
grocer(food)
grocery
groceries
GRSSPN
greasy spoon
GRST
grist
GRSTK
agrestic(rural)
GRSTL
agrestal
GRSTLJ
agrostology
GRSTML
gristmill
GRSV
aggressive
GRT
aigrette(or)
aigret
egret(bird)
garret(loft)
garrote
garroted
garroting
girt(gird)
grate
grated

grating
great(large)
greet
grit
gritted
gritting
gritty
grittier
grittiest
grittiness
grotto(cave)
grout
GRTBRTN
Great Britain
GRTF
gratify
gratified
gratifies
GRTFKSHN
gratification
GRTFL
grateful
GRTGRNDCHLD
great-grandchild
GRTGRNDPRNT
great-grandparent
GRTH
girth
growth
GRTKT
greatcoat
GRTN
au gratin
GRTNF
great-nephew
GRTNG
greeting
grating
grate
GRTNGKL
great-uncle
GRTNS
greatness
great-niece
GRTNT
great-aunt
GRTPLNZ
Great Plains
GRTR
garter
grater(tool)
greater(great)
greeter(person)
GRTS
gratis
grits(food)

GRTSK
grotesque
GRTSTRLNBT
Great Australian
Bight
GRTT
gratuity
gratuities
GRTTD
gratitude
GRTTS
gratuitous
GRTTYD
gratitude
GRTYT
gratuity
gratuities
GRTYTS
gratuitous
GRV
aggrieve
aggrieved
aggrieving
grave(coffin)
grave(carve,clean)
graved,-ving,-ven
grave(serious)
graver
gravest
gravy
gravies
grieve(sorrow)
grieved
grieving
groove
grooved
grooving
groovy
groovier
grooviest
grove(trees)
GRVD
gravid
gravidity
GRVKLZ
graveclothes
GRVL
gravel(rock)
grovel
GRVN
graven
GRVNMJ
graven image
GRVNS
grievance
GRVR

NGK:ink **P**:pie **R**:air **S**:ice **SH**:show **T**:toy **THN**:thin **TH**:the **V**:of **W**:we **Y**:you **Z**:is **VZHN**:vision

graver(tool,
person)
GRVS
grievous
GRVSD
graveside
GRVSHN
aggravation
GRVSTN
gravestone
GRVT
aggravate
  aggravated
  aggravating
gravity
  gravities
GRVTR
aggravator
GRVTSHN
gravitation
GRVTT
gravitate
  gravitated
  gravitating
GRVYR
gravure
GRVYRD
graveyard
GRYR
Gruyère
GRZ
graze
  grazed
  grazing
greasy
  greasier
  greasiest
  greasily
  greasiness
GRZH
garage
  garaged
  garaging
GRZL
grisly(horrid)
  grislier
  grisliest
  grisliness
grizzly(bear,gray)
  grizzlies
  grizzlier
  grizzliest
GRZLBR
grizzly bear
GRZNG
grazing

GRZSPN
greasy spoon
GRZT
grisette
GS
gas
  gases
  gassed
  gassing
  gassy
  gassier
  gassiest
  geese
  goose
  goose
  geese
  guess
  guesses
GSH
gauche
  (lacking grace)
geisha
gosh(interj)
gouache(painting)
gush
  gushes
  gushy
  gushier
  gushiest
  gushiness
GSHK
goshawk
GSHL
eggshell
gasohol
GSHR
gaucherie
gusher
GSHS
gaseous
GSHTLT
gestalt(or)Gestalt
GSKND
gasconade
GSKT
gasket
GSL
ghastly
  ghastlier
  ghastliest
  ghastliness
GSLN
gasoline
GSLT
gaslight
GSMR

gossamer
GSMSK
gas mask
GSNK
gooseneck
GSNTRK
egocentric
GSNTRKL
egocentrical
GSP
gasp
gossip
GSPL
gospel
GSS
gaseous
GST
aghast
august(majestic)
August
Augusta
egoist
gast(scare)
ghost
guessed(guess)
guest
gusset
gust(air)
gusto
gusty
  gustier
  gustiest
  gustily
  gustiness
GSTL
ghastly
  ghastlier
  ghastliest
  ghastliness
ghostly
  ghostlier
  ghostliest
  ghostliness
GSTLT
gestalt(or)Gestalt
GSTP
goose-step
  goose-stepped
  goose-stepping
GSTRK
gastric
GSTRNM
gastronome
gastronomy
GSTRNMKL
gastronomical

GSTRT
ghostwrite
  ghostwriting
  ghostwrote
  ghostwritten
GSTRTR
ghostwriter
GSTSHN
gustation
GSTTR
gustatory
GSWRK
guesswork
GT
agate
gaiety
  gaieties
gait(walk)
gate(door)
get(receive)
  got
  getting
  gotten
  gettable
ghetto(place)
goat
goatee(beard)
gout
gut
  gutted
  gutting
  gutty
  guttier
  guttiest
  guttiness
GTGTHR
get-together
GTHK
Gothic
GTHR
gather
GTHRNG
gathering
GTKRSHR
gate-crasher
GTP
get-up(n)
GTPRCH
gutta-percha
GTR
gaiter
goiter
guitar
gutter
GTRL
guttural

B:by **CH**:each **D**:day **F**:if **G**:go **H**:he **HW**:why **J**:joy **K**:cow **KS**:ax **KWL**:equal **L**:all **M**:may **N**:in

GTRP	**GWL**	**GZD**	**GZLT**
ego trip	aiguille(point)	exude	exalt(praise)
GTRSNP	**GWLT**	exuded	exult(rejoice)
guttersnipe	aiguillette	exuding	**GZLTNT**
GTRST	**GWM**	**GZDK**	exultant
guitarist	Guam	exotic	**GZLTSHN**
GTST	**GWN**	exotica	exaltation(praise)
egotist	Guiana	**GZJRSHN**	exultation(rejoice)
GTSTK	· iguana	exaggeration	**GZLYR**
egotistic	**GWSH**	**GZJRT**	auxiliary
GTSTKL	gouache	exaggerate	auxiliaries
egotistical	**GWTML**	exaggerated	**GZM**
GTW	Guatemala	exaggerating	eczema(skin)
getaway	**GWTMLST**	**GZJRTR**	egoism
gateway	Guatemala City	exaggerator	exam
GTZ	**GWV**	**GZKL**	exhume
ghettoize	guava	exactly	exhumed
ghettoized	**GY**	**GZKT**	exhuming
ghettoizing	ague	exact	exhumation
ghettos	aguish	**GZKTL**	gismo
GTZM	**GYG**	exactly	**GZMN**
egotism	gewgaw	**GZKTNG**	examine
GV	**GYL**	exacting	examined
give	golly(interj)	**GZKTTD**	examining
gave	**GYR**	exactitude	examinee
giving	augury	**GZKTTYD**	**GZMNR**
given	auguries	exactitude	examiner
giver	**GZ**	**GZKYTR**	**GZMNSHN**
GVL	gauze(fabric)	executor	examination
gavel	gauzy	**GZKYTV**	**GZMPL**
GVN	gauzier	executive	example
given	gauziest	**GZL**	**GZMPLF**
give	gauzily	exile	exemplify
GVNG	gauziness	exiled	exemplified
giving	gaze(look)	exiling	exemplifies
GVR	gazed	gazelle(animal)	exemplifier
giver	gazing	guzzle	**GZMPLFKSHN**
GVRMNT	gazer	guzzled	exemplification
government	guise(dress)	guzzling	**GZMPLGRSH**
GVRN	guised	guzzler	exempli gratia
govern	guising	**GZLN**	e.g.
GVRNMNT	**GZB**	gasoline	**GZMPLR**
government	gazabo(fellow)	**GZLNG**	exemplar
GVRNMNTL	gazebo(pavilion)	gosling	exemplary
governmental	**GZBRNS**	**GZLR**	exemplarily
GVRNR	exuberance	auxiliary	exemplariness
governor	**GZBRNT**	auxiliaries	**GZMPSHN**
GVRNS	exuberant	guzzler	exemption
governess	**GZBRT**	**GZLRNT**	**GZMPT**
governesses	exuberate	exhilarant	exempt
GVW	exuberated	**GZLRSHN**	**GZMSHN**
giveaway	exuberating	exhilaration	exhumation
GWDLHR	**GZBT**	**GZLRT**	**GZNRSHN**
Guadalajara	exhibit	exhilarate	exoneration
GWDLP	**GZBTR**	exhilarated	**GZNRT**
Guadeloupe	exhibitor	exhilarating	exonerate

NGK:ink **P:**pie **R:**air **S:**ice **SH:**show **T:**toy **THN:**thin **TH:**the **V:**of **W:**we **Y:**you **Z:**is **VZHN:**vision

exonerated
exonerating
GZR
geezer(person)
geyser(water)
GZRB
exurb
exurbia
GZRBNT
exurbanite
GZRBTNS
exorbitance
GZRBTNT
exorbitant
GZRD
gizzard
GZRL
uxorial
GZRS
uxorious
GZRSHN
exertion
GZRST
Exocet(missile)
GZRT
exert
exhort
GZRTSHN
exhortation
GZSCHN
exhaustion
GZSPRSHN
exasperation
GZSPRT
exasperate
exasperated
exasperating
GZSRBSHN
exacerbation
GZSRBT
exacerbate
exacerbated
exacerbating
GZST
exhaust
exist
Exocet(missile)
GZSTBL
exhaustible
GZSTNCHL
existential
GZSTNCHLZM
existentialism
GZSTNS
existence
GZSTNSHL

existential
GZSTNSHLZM
existentialism
GZSTNT
existent
GZSTV
exhaustive
GZT
exit
gazette
GZTK
exotic
exotica
GZTKL
exotically
GZTR
gazetteer
GZVYR
Xavier
GZYD
exude
exuded
exuding
GZYM
exhume
exhumed
exhuming
GZYMSHN
exhumation

H

agh(interj)
agghhh
ah(interj)
aha(interj)
ahoy(interj)
eh(interj)
hay(plant)
haw
he
hey(interj)
hi(greeting)
hie(hurry)
hied
hieing
high
hoe(tool)
hooey(slang)
how
hoy(ship)
huh(interj)

Oahu
oh(interj)
oh's
Ohio
who
HB
hautboy(oboe)
highboy
hob(fireplace)
hobo
hobby
hobbies
hobbyist
hub
HBB
hubbub
HBCH
habitue
hibachi
HBCHL
habitual
HBCHT
habituate
habituated
habituating
HBGBLN
hobgoblin
HBHB
huba-huba(interj)
HBHRS
hobbyhorse
HBJBZ
heebie-jeebies
HBKP
hubcap
HBL
highball
hobble
hobbled
hobbling
hobbler
HBLTT
habilitate
habilitated
habilitating
habilitation
HBNB
hobnob
hobnobbed
hobnobbing
hobnobber
HBNL
hobnail
HBR
Hebrew
highbrow

HBRD
highbred
(highborn)
hybrid(mixed)
HBRDSHR
haberdasher
haberdashery
haberdasheries
HBRDZ
hybridize
hybridized
hybridizing
HBRK
Hebraic
HBRN
highborn
HBRNKL
hibernacle
HBRNSHN
hibernation
HBRNT
hibernate
hibernated
hibernating
HBRNTR
hibernator
HBSKRPS
habeas corpus
HBSKS
hibiscus
HBT
habit
HBTBL
habitable
HBTD
habitude
HBTFRMNG
habit-forming
HBTSHN
habitation
HBTT
habitat
HBZ
hobbies
hobby
hobos
hobo
HCH
hatch(egg)
hatches
hitch
hitches
hooch(liquor)
hotch(wiggle)
hotches
hutch

hutches
HCHHK
　hitchhike
　hitchhiked
　hitchhiking
　hitchhiker
HCHKCH
　hootchy-kootchy
HCHR
　hatchery
　hatcheries
　highchair
HCHT
　hatchet
HCHTMN
　hatchet-man
　hatchet-men
HCHW
　hatchway
HD
　ahead
　had
　have
　Haiti
　haughty
　haughtier
　haughtiest
　haughtily
　haughtiness
　head
　heady
　headier
　headiest
　headiness
　heed(take note)
　heyday
　hide
　hid
　hiding
　hidden
　hood
　howdah(seat)
　howdy(interj)
HDBN
　headband
HDBND
　headband
　hidebound
HDBRD
　headboard
HDCHZ
　headcheese
HDD
　heated
　hodad(slang)
HDDL

heatedly
HDFL
　headful
　heedful
HDFN
　headphone
HDFRST
　headfirst
HDGR
　headgear
HDHNTR
　headhunter
HDK
　haddock
　headache
HDKLD
　head cold
HDKWRTR
　headquarter
HDKWRTRZ
　headquarters
HDL
　huddle
　huddled
　huddling
HDLM
　hoodlum
HDLN
　headline
　headlined
　headlining
　headliner
HDLND
　headland
HDLNG
　headlong
HDLS
　headless
　heedless
HDLT
　headlight
HDMN
　headman
　headmen
HDMSTR
　headmaster
HDMSTRS
　headmistress
HDN
　head-on
　hidden
　hide
　hoedown(dance)
　Houdini
　hoyden
HDNDSK

hide-and-seek
HDNG
　heading
　hiding
　hide
HDNK
　hedonic
HDNSTK
　hedonistic
HDNT
　whodunit
HDNZM
　hedonism
HDPS
　headpiece
HDR
　header
　heater(hot)
　hydra(or)Hydra
HDRDNMK
　hydrodynamic
　hydrodynamics
HDRFB
　hydrophobia
HDRFBK
　hydrophobic
HDRFL
　hydrofoil
HDRFLK
　hydrophilic
HDRFLRK
　hydrofluoric
HDRFLS
　hydrophilous
HDRGRFK
　hydrographic
HDRJN
　hydrogen
HDRJNSHN
　hydrogenation
HDRJNT
　hydrogenate
　hydrogenated
　hydrogenating
HDRKLRK
　hydrochloric
HDRKNTK
　hydrokinetic
　hydrokinetics
HDRKRBN
　hydrocarbon
HDRLJ
　hydrology
HDRLK
　hydraulic
　hydraulics

HDRLKTRK
　hydroelectric
HDRLSS
　hydrolysis
HDRLTK
　hydrolytic
HDRM
　headroom
HDRMKNKS
　hydromechanics
HDRMTR
　hydrometer
HDRNJ
　hydrangea
HDRNM
　heteronym
　heteronomy
HDRNT
　hydrant
　hydronaut
HDRPLN
　hydroplane
　hydroplaned
　hydroplaning
HDRPNKS
　hydroponics
HDRS
　headdress
　headdresses
　hydrous
HDRSHN
　hydration
HDRST
　headrest
HDRSTTKS
　hydrostatics
HDRT
　hydrate
　hydrated
　hydrating
　hydration
HDRTHRP
　hydrotherapy
　hydrotherapies
HDRTR
　hydrator
HDS
　adios
　hiatus
　hiatuses
　hideous
HDSL
　headsail
HDSNB
　Hudson Bay
HDST

NGK:ink **P**:pie **R**:air **S**:ice **SH**:show **T**:toy **THN**:thin **TH**:the **V**:of **W**:we **Y**:you **Z**:is **VZHN**:vision

headset
HDSTK
headstock
HDSTND
headstand
HDSTRNG
headstrong
HDSTRT
head start
HDT
hide-out(n)
HDTD
hoity-toity
HDW
headway
hideaway
HDWDR
headwaiter
HDWND
headwind
HDWNGK
hoodwink
HDWTR
headwaiter
HDYD
how do you do
(greeting)
how-do-you-do
(situation)
HDZ
Hades
HF
half
hi-fi
hoof
huff
huffy
huffier
huffiest
huffily
huffiness
HFBK
halfback
HFBKT
half-baked
HFBRD
half-breed
HFBRTHR
half brother
HFBT
hoofbeat
HFDLT
high fidelity
high fidelities
HFHRTD
halfhearted

HFKKT
half-cocked
HFKST
half-caste
HFLD
hayfield
HFLN
highfalutin
high-flown
HFLNG
high-flying
HFLT
half-light(dim)
HFLTN
highfalutin
HFMN
half-moon
HFMST
half-mast
HFN
hyphen
HFNDHF
half-and-half
HFNDMTH
hoof-and-mouth
HFNSHN
hyphenation
HFNT
hyphenate
hyphenated
hyphenating
HFR
half-hour
heifer
HFSH
huffish
HFT
heft
hefty
heftier
heftiest
heftiness
HFTN
halftone
HFTRK
halftrack
HFTRTH
half-truth
HFVR
hay fever
HFW
halfway
HFWT
half-wit
half-witted
half-wittingly

HG
hag
hog
hogged
hogging
hug
hugged
hugging
hugger
HGFSH
hagfish
HGL
haggle
haggled
haggling
haggler
higgle
higgled
higgling
HGLDPGLD
higgledy-piggledy
HGLG
hawg leg(slang)
holster
HGRD
haggard
high-grade
HGRDN
hagridden
HGRK
hagiarchy
hagiarchies
HGRMTR
hygrometer
HGRSKP
hygroscope
HGSH
hoggish
HGT
hogtie
hogtied
hogtieing
HGWLD
hog wild
HGWSH
hogwash
HGZHD
hogshead
HH
ha-ha
he-he
ho-ho
HHM
ho-hum
HHNDD
high-handed

HJ
hedge
hedged
hedging
huge
huger
hugest
HJHP
hedgehop
hedgehopped
hedgehopping
hedgehopper
HJK
hijack
HJKNZDSZ
Hodgkin's disease
HJMN
hegemony
hegemonies
HJMNK
hegemonic
HJN
hygiene
HJNK
hygienic
hygienically
HJNST
hygienist
HJPJ
hodgepodge
HK
hack
haiku(poem)
hawk
hawkeye
heck
hick
hickey
hike(trail)
hiked
hiking
hiker
hock(pawn)
hockey(sport)
hook
hookah(water pipe)
hooky
HKBR
hackberry
hackberries
HKD
hawkeyed
high-keyed
HKK
hoecake
HKL

---

hackle
  hackled
  hackling
  heckle(harass)
  heckled
  heckling
  heckler
HKLBR
  huckleberry
  huckleberries
HKLR
  heckler
HKLS
  high-class
HKM
  hokum
HKMR
  hackamore
HKN
  hackney
  hook-and-eye
HKND
  hook-and-eye
HKP
  hiccough(or)
  hiccup
    hiccupped
    hiccupping
  hookup
HKR
  hawker
  hickory
    hickories
  hooker
HKS
  hacksaw
  hex
    hexes
  hoax
    hoaxes
HKSGN
  hexagon
HKSGNL
  hexagonal
HKSGRM
  hexagram
HKSH
  hawkish
HKSHDRN
  hexahedron
    hexahedrons(or)
    hexahedra
HKSHP
  hockshop
HKSPKS
  hocus-pocus

HKSTR
  huckster
HKTGRF
  hectograph
HKTK
  hectic
HKTKL
  hectically
HKTR
  hector
HL
  eyehole
  hail(ice)
  hale(healthy)
    haler
    halest
  hale(compel)
    haled
    haling
  hall
  hallow(holy)
  halo
  haul
  heal(cure)
  heel(foot,tilt)
  heil(greeting)
  hell
  he'll(he will)
  hello
    helloes
  Hialeah
  highly
  hill
  hilly
    hillier
    hilliest
    hilliness
  hole(opening)
    holed
    holing
  holey(hole)
  hollow(space)
  holly(tree)
    hollies
  holy(sacred)
    holier
    holiest
    holily
    holiness
  howl
  hula
  jai alai(game)
  whole(all parts)
  who'll(who will)
  wholly(entirely)
HLBL

hillbilly
  hillbillies
  hullabaloo
HLBLD
  whole blood
HLBNT
  hell-bent
HLBRD
  halberd
HLBRL
  hurly-burly
HLBRT
  halbert
HLBT
  halibut
HLD
  hallowed
  hold(grasp)
  held
  holiday
HLDNGZ
  holdings
HLDP
  holdup(n,adj)
HLDR
  holder
HLDT
  holdout(n)
HLDVR
  holdover(n)
HLFKS
  Halifax
HLFT
  hayloft
HLGN
  hooligan
HLGRF
  heliograph
  holograph
  holography
HLGRM
  hologram
HLHG
  whole hog
HLHK
  hollyhock
HLHL
  hellhole
HLHRTD
  wholehearted
HLHWT
  whole wheat
HLWT
  whole wheat
HLJN
  halogen

HLK
  hillock
  hulk
HLKL
  heliacal(sum)
  helical(helix)
HLKNG
  hulking
HLKPTR
  helicopter
HLKS
  helix
    helices
HLKST
  holocaust
HLLY
  hallelujah
HLM
  helium
  helm
  holm(island)
HLMLK
  whole milk
HLMNT
  helmet
HLMRK
  hallmark
HLMT
  helmet
HLMZMN
  helmsman
HLN
  Halloween
  Helena
  hyaline
HLNDR
  highlander
HLNDZ
  hollandaise
HLNMBR
  whole number
HLNS
  wholeness
HLP
  help
HLPD
  helipad
HLPFL
  helpful
HLPLS
  helpless
HLPMT
  helpmate(or)
  helpmeet
HLPRT
  heliport

NGK:ink **P**:pie **R**:air **S**:ice **SH**:show **T**:toy **THN**:thin **TH**:the **V**:of **W**:we **Y**:you **Z**:is **VZHN**:vision

HLR
healer(heal)
heeler(worker)
holler(yell)
hollow(place)
howler
HLRLR
Holy Roller
HLRS
hilarious
HLRT
hilarity
hilarities
HLS
Holy See
HLSD
hillside
HLSHN
halation
HLSL
wholesale
wholesaled
wholesaling
wholesaler
HLSLR
wholesaler
HLSM
wholesome
HLSN
halcyon
HLSNGK
Helsinki
HLSNJN
hallucinogen
HLSNSHN
hallucination
HLSNT
hallucinate
hallucinated
hallucinating
HLSNTR
hallucinatory
HLSTK
holistic
HLSTN
hailstone
Holstein
HLSTR
holster
HLSTRM
hailstorm
HLT
highlight
halt
hilt
HLTH

health
healthy
healthier
healthiest
healthily
healthiness
HLTHFL
healthful
HLTNGL
haltingly
HLTR
halter
HLTRP
heliotrope
HLTRSKLTR
helter-skelter
HLTSS
halitosis
HLV
helve
helved
helving
HLVL
high-level
HLW
hallway
HLWD
Hollywood
HLWK
Holy Week
HLWN
Halloween
HLWR
hollowware
HLYN
hellion
HLYRD
halyard
HM
ahem(interj)
ham(meat,act)
hammed
hamming
hem(cuff)
hemmed
hemming
hemmer
him
holm(island)
home
homed
homing
homey(cozy)
homier
homiest
homeyness

hum(sound)
hummed
humming
hummer
hymn(music)
whom
HMBD
homebody
homebodies
HMBG
humbug
HMBL
humble
humbled
humbling
humbler
humblest
humbly
HMBLP
humble pie
HMBLR
humbler
HMBLST
humblest
HMBR
home-brew
HMBRD
homebred
HMBRG
Hamburg
homburg
HMBRGR
hamburger
HMD
homemade
HMDNGR
humdinger
HMDRM
humdrum
HMFL
hemophilia
HMFN
homophone
HMGLBN
hemoglobin
HMGRF
homograph
HMGRN
home-grown
HMJ
homage
HMJNS
homogeneous
HMJNT
homogeneity
homogeneities

HMJNYS
homogeneous
HMJNZ
homogenize
homogenized
homogenizing
homogenizer
HMK
hammock
hummock(mound)
HMKMNG
homecoming
HMKR
haymaker(swing)
homemaker
HML
hiemal
homely(plain)
homelier
homeliest
homeliness
homily
homilies
HMLGS
homologous
HMLJZ
homologize
homologized
homologizing
HMLN
hemline
HMLND
homeland
HMLS
homeless
HMLT
hamlet
HMLTKS
homiletics
HMLYZ
Himalayas
HMLZ
Himalayas
HMN
he-man
he-men
hominy(food)
human
hymen(membrane)
HMND
hominid
HMNDD
high-minded
HMNG
hemming
HMNGBRD

B:by **CH**:each **D**:day **F**:if **G**:go **H**:he **HW**:why **J**:joy **K**:cow **KS**:ax **KWL**:equal **L**:all **M**:may **N**:in

hummingbird
HMNGKYLS
  homunculus
  homunculi
HMNL
  hymeneal(wedding)
  hymnal(book)
HMNLJ
  hymnology
HMNM
  homonym
HMNR
  homeowner
HMNS
  homeyness
HMP
  hemp
  hump
  humpy
   humpier
   humpiest
   humpiness
HMPBK
  humpback
HMPR
  hamper
HMR
  hammer
  homer
HMRD
  hemorrhoid
HMRHD
  hammerhead
HMRJ
  hemorrhage
   hemorrhaged
   hemorrhaging
HMRKTS
  Homo erectus
HMS
  ahimsa(doctrine)
HMSD
  homicide
HMSDL
  homicidal
HMSFR
  hemisphere
HMSFRK
  hemispheric
HMSFRKL
  hemispherical
HMSK
  homesick
HMSKCHL
  homosexual
HMSKSHL

homosexual
HMSKSHLT
  homosexuality
HMSLF
  himself
HMSNTRK
  homocentric
HMSPN
  homespun
  Homo sapien
   Homo sapiens
HMSTCH
  hemstitch
   hemstitches
HMSTD
  homestead
HMSTR
  hamster
HMSTRCH
  homestretch
   homestretches
HMSTRNG
  hamstring
HMSTSS
  hemostasis(blood)
  homeostasis
   (body balance)
HMSTT
  hemostat
HMSVR
  whomsoever
HMTLJ
  hematology
HMTN
  hometown
HMVR
  whomever
HMWRD
  homeward
HMWRK
  homework
HN
  hand
  handy
   handier
   handiest
   handiness
  Hanoi
  heinie(buttocks)
  hen
  henna
  hon(name)
  hone(sharpen)
   honed
   honing
   honer

honey(sweet)
  hound(dog)
  Hun(people)
  hyena(animal)
HNB
  honeybee
HNBG
  handbag
HNBK
  handbook
HNBL
  handball
  handbill
HNBR
  handbarrow
HNBRDTH
  handbreadth
HNCH
  haunch(leg)
   haunches
  honcho(boss)
  hunch
   hunches
HNCHBK
  hunchback
HNCHMN
  henchman
  henchmen
HND
  hand
  handy
   handier
   handiest
   handily
   handiness
  hind
  Hindi
  Hindu
   Hinduism
  Honda(trademark)
  honda(noose)
  honeydew
  hound
HNDBG
  handbag
HNDBK
  handbook
HNDBL
  handball
  handbill
HNDBR
  handbarrow
HNDBRDTH
  handbreadth
HNDFL
  handful

HNDGN
  handgun
HNDGRND
  hand grenade
HNDGRP
  handgrip
HNDKF
  handcuff
HNDKLSP
  handclasp
HNDKP
  handicap
   handicapped
   handicapping
   handicapper
HNDKRCHF
  handkerchief
HNDKRFT
  handicraft
HNDKWRTR
  hindquarter
HNDL
  handle
   handled
   handling
   handler
HNDLBR
  handlebar
HNDLR
  handler
HNDMD
  handmade
HNDMDN
  hand-me-down
  handmaiden
HNDMN
  handyman
  handymen
HNDMST
  hindmost
HNDPK
  hand-pick
HNDR
  hinder
HNDRD
  hundred
HNDRDFLD
  hundredfold
HNDRDTH
  hundredth
HNDRDWT
  hundredweight
HNDRL
  handrail
HNDRMST
  hindermost

HNDRNS
hindrance
HNDRS
Honduras
HNDRTNG
handwriting
handwritten
HNDS
handsaw
HNDSHK
handshake
HNDSL
handsel
HNDSPRNG
handspring
HNDST
handset
hindsight
HNDSTND
handstand
HNDT
handout
HNDTHND
hand-to-hand
HNDTMTH
hand-to-mouth
HNDWRK
handlwork
handwork
HNDYRS
Honduras
HNFL
handful
HNG
hang
hung(or)
hanged
HNGDG
hangdog
HNGGRND
hand grenade
HNGK
honky(slang)
honkies
hunk
HNGKDR
hunky-dory
HNGKNG
Hong Kong
HNGKPNGK
hanky-panky
HNGKR
hanker
hunker
HNGKRCHF
handkerchief

HNGKTNGK
honky-tonk
HNGMN
hangman
hangmen
HNGN
handgun
HNGNG
hanging
HNGNL
hangnail
HNGP
hang-up(n)
HNGR
hangar(aircraft)
hanger(clothes)
Hungary
hunger
hungry
hungrier
hungriest
hungrily
hungriness
HNGRN
hanger-on
Hungarian
HNGRND
hand grenade
HNGRP
handgrip
HNGRZN
hangers-on
HNGT
hangout(n)
hang out(v)
hung out
HNGVR
hangover(n)
hang over(v)
hung over
HNJ
hinge
hinged
hinging
HNK
Hanukkah(Jewish)
HNKF
handcuff
HNKLSP
handclasp
HNKM
honeycomb
HNKR
hunker
HNKRCHF
handkerchief

HNLL
Honolulu
HNLNG
handling
HNLR
handler
HNMD
handmade
HNMDN
hand-me-down
HNMN
honeymoon
HNPK
hand-pick
henpeck
HNPKT
hand-picked
henpecked
HNR
hennery(farm)
henneries
henry(unit)
henrys
hunter
HNRL
handrail
HNRTNG
handwriting
handwritten
HNS
hance(curved)
handsaw
heinous
hence
highness
HNSFRTH
henceforth
HNSHK
handshake
HNSKL
honeysuckle
HNSL
handsel
HNSM
handsome
hansom(cab)
HNSPRNG
handspring
HNST
handset
hindsight
HNSTND
handstand
HNT
haunt
hint

hunt
junta
HNTHN
hand-to-hand
HNTMTH
hand-to-mouth
HNTR
hunter
HNTRLND
hinterland
HNTRS
huntress
HNTSMN
huntsman
huntsmen
HNWRK
handwork
HNZ
hands
HNZBRDTH
hand's breadth
HNZF
hands-off
HNZTTH
hound's-tooth
HP
hap
happy
happier
happiest
happily
happiness
heap(pile)
hip
hippie
hippo(animal)
hoop
hop
hopped
hopping
hopper
hope(wish)
hoped
hoping
hype
hyped
hyping
hyper
whoop(yell)
HPBN
hipbone
HPCHT
high-pitched
HPDRM
hippodrome
HPDRMK

B:by CH:each D:day F:if G:go H:he HW:why J:joy K:cow KS:ax KWL:equal L:all M:may N:in

hypodermic
HPFJ
hippophagy
HPFL
hopeful
HPGLK
happy-go-lucky
HPHZRD
haphazard
HPKNDR
hypochondria
HPKNDRK '
hypochondriac
HPKNDRKL
hypochondriacal
HPKRS
hypocrisy
hypocrisies
HPKRT
hypocrite
HPKRTKL
hypocritical
HPKRTKTH
Hippocratic oath
HPKS
hypoxia
HPKT
hep cat(slang)
HPL
hoi polloi
hoopla
HPLS
hapless
hopeless
HPN
happen
HPNGKF
whooping cough
HPNNG
happening
HPNNLSS
hypnoanalysis
HPNS
happiness
HPNSS
hypnosis
hypnoses
HPNSTNS
happenstance
HPNSZ
hypnoses
HPNTHRP
hypnotherapy
hypnotherapies
HPNTK
hypnotic

HPNTKL
hypnotically
HPNTST
hypnotist
HPNTZ
hypnotize
hypnotized
hypnotizing
hypnotist
HPNTZBL
hypnotizable
HPNTZM
hypnotism
hypnotist
HPPTMS
hippopotamus
hippopotami(or)
hippopotamuses
HPR
hopper
hyper(slang)
whooper(yell)
HPRBL
hyperbola(curve)
hyperbole
(exaggeration)
HPRBLK
hyperbolic
HPRFL
high profile
HPRKR
hopper car
HPRKRTKL
hypercritical
HPRKTV
hyperactive
HPRSDT
hyperacidity
HPRSHR
high-pressure
high-pressured
high-pressuring
HPRSNK
hypersonic
HPRSNSTV
hypersensitive
HPRST
high-priced
HPRTNSHN
hypertension
HPRVNTLSHN
hyperventilation
HPRVNTLT
hyperventilate
hyperventilated
hyperventilating

HPSKCH
hopscotch
HPTD
heptad
HPTGN
heptagon
HPTHLMS
hypothalamus
HPTHKT
hypothecate
hypothecated
hypothecating
HPTHRM
hypothermia
HPTHSS
hypothesis
hypotheses
HPTHSZ
hypothesize
hypothesized
hypothesizing
HPTHTK
hypothetic
HPTHTKL
hypothetical
HPTK
hepatic
HPTNS
hypotenuse
HPTNYS
hypotenuse
HPTTS
hepatitis
HPWRD
high-powered
HR
hair
hairy
hairier
hairiest
hairiness
hare(rabbit)
harrow
harry(raid)
harried
harries
hear(ear)
heard
her
here(not there)
hero
heroes
higher
hire(work)
hired
hiring

hoary(gray)
hoarier
hoariest
hooray(interj)(or)
hurrah(interj)
rah
hurry
hurried
hurries
whore(person)
whored
whoring
HRB
herb
hereby
HRBL
herbal
hirable(hire)
horrible
horribly .
HRBNJR
harbinger
HRBR
harbor, (B)harbour
HRBRDTH
hairbreadth
HRBRND
harebrained
HRBSD
herbicide
HRBSHS
herbaceous
HRBT
hereabout
HRBVR
herbivore
HRBVRS
herbivorous
HRCH
huarache
HRD
hairdo
hard
hardy(tool)
hardies
hardy(strong)
hardier
hardiest
hardily
hardiness
harried
hayride
heard(sound)
hearty(vigorous,
food)
herd(group)

NGK:ink **P**:pie **R**:air **S**:ice **SH**:show **T**:toy **THN**:thin **TH**:the **V**:of **W**:we **Y**:you **Z**:is **VZHN**:vision

hoard(reserve)
horde(crowd)
horrid
HRDBK
hardback
HRDBL
hardball
HRDBLD
hard-boiled
HRDBND
hard-bound
HRDBTN
hard-bitten
HRDFSTD
hard-fisted
HRDGDS
hard goods
HRDGRD
hurdy-gurdy
HRDHD
hardhead
hardihood
HRDHDD
hardheaded
HRDHT
hard hat
HRDHRTD
hardhearted
HRDKL
heretical
HRDKR
hard-core
HRDKVR
hard-cover
HRDL
hardly(barely)
hurdle(barrier)
hurdled
hurdling
hurdler
HRDLKR
hard liquor
HRDN
harden
HRDNR
hardener
HRDNS
hardness
HRDNZD
hard-nosed
HRDPN
hardpan
HRDR
harder
hardest
HRDRSR

hairdresser
HRDSHL
hard-shell
HRDSHP
hardship
HRDSL
hard sell
HRDT
heredity
heredities
HRDTK
hardtack
HRDTP
hardtop
HRDTR
hereditary
HRDWD
hardwood
HRDWR
hardware
HRDZMN
herdsman
herdsmen
HRF
horrify
horrified
horrifies
HRFKSHN
horrification
HRFRST
hoarfrost
HRFTR
hereafter
HRGLFK
hieroglyphic
hieroglyphics
HRGRM
hierogram
HRHND
horehound
HRHS
whorehouse
HRK
hark(listen)
heroic
hierarch
hierarchy
hierarchies
HRKKL
hierarchical
HRKL
heroical
HRKN
hearken(heed)
hurricane
HRKR

hara-kiri(suicide)
HRKRS
hierocracy
hierocracies
HRKT
haircut
HRKYLN
herculean
HRKYLZ
Hercules
HRL
herald
herl(fly)
hurl(throw)
HRLBRL
hurly-burly
HRLD
herald
HRLDK
heraldic
HRLDR
heraldry
heraldries
HRLJ
horology
HRLKWN
harlequin
HRLN
hairline
HRLNG
hireling
HRLP
harelip
HRLR
hurler
HRM
harem
harm
HRMDK
hermetic
hermetically
HRMFL
harmful
HRMFRDT
hermaphrodite
HRMJST
Her Majesty
HRMLS
harmless
HRMN
harmony
harmonies
hormone
HRMNGR
whoremonger
HRMNK

harmonic
harmonica
HRMNL
hormonal
HRMNS
harmonious
HRMNTKS
hermeneutics
HRMNZ
harmonize
harmonized
harmonizing
harmonizer
HRMSKRM
harum-scarum
HRMT
hermit
HRMTK
hermetic
HRMTKL
hermetical
HRN
herein
heroin(narcotic)
heroine(hero)
heron(bird)
hernia
herniae(or)
hernias
horn
horny
hornier
horniest
horniness
HRND
horned
HRNDS
horrendous
HRNDTD
horned toad
HRNFTR
hereinafter
HRNG
harangue
harangued
haranguing
harrowing
hearing
herring(fish)
HRNGBN
herringbone
HRNGR
haranguer
HRNPP
hornpipe
HRNS

harness
HRNSWGL
hornswoggle
hornswoggled
hornswoggling
HRNT
hornet
herniate
herniated
herniating
herniation
HRP
harp
harpy
harpies
higher-up
HRPN
harpoon
HRPS
hairpiece
HRPSKRD
harpsichord
HRPST
harpist
HRPZ
herpes(disease)
HRR
horror
HRRK
hierarch
hierarchy
hierarchies
HRRKKL
hierarchical
HRS
harass
harasses
hearsay
hearse(death)
heresy(belief)
heresies
hoarse(voice)
horse(animal)
horsed
horsing
horsy
horsiness
HRSBK
horseback
HRSBRG
Harrisburg
HRSFL
horsefly
horseflies
HRSH
harsh

horseshoe
horseshoed
whorish
HRSHD
horsehide
HRSHM
Hiroshima
HRSHNS
harshness
HRSHR
horsehair
HRSHWP
horsewhip
-whipped,-whipping
HRSKP
horoscope
horoscopy
HRSKR
hurry-scurry
hurry-scurried
hurry-scurries
HRSLF
herself
horselaugh
HRSMN
horseman
horsemen
HRSPL
horseplay
HRSPLTNG
hairsplitting
HRSPR
horsepower
HRSPRNG
hairspring
HRSPWR
horsepower
HRSRDSH
horseradish
HRSSH
horseshoe
horseshoed
HRST
harassed
harass
hirsute(hairy)
horst
HRSTL
horsetail
HRSWMN
horsewoman
horsewomen
HRSWP
horsewhip
-whipped,-whipping
HRT

heart
hearty
heartier,-iest
hurt
HRTBL
heritable
HRTBRK
heartbreak
HRTBRKN
heartbroken
HRTBRKR
heartbreaker
HRTBRN
heartburn
HRTBST
hartebeest
HRTBT
heartbeat
HRTFL
hurtful
HRTFLT
heartfelt
HRTFR
heretofore
HRTFRD
Hartford
HRTH
hearth
HRTHRT
heart-to-heart
HRTHSTN
hearthstone
HRTJ
heritage
HRTK
heartache
heretic
HRTKL
heretical
HRTKLCHR
horticulture
HRTKLCHRST
horticulturist
HRTL
hurtle
hurtled
hurtling
hurtler
HRTLS
heartless
HRTN
hearten
HRTR
heritor
HRTRNDNG
heart-rending

HRTS
hertz(frequency)
hurts(pain)
HRTSK
heartsick
HRTSTRNGZ
heartstrings
HRTTHRT
heart-to-heart
HRTTK
heart attack
HRTWRM
heartworm
HRTWRMNG
heartwarming
HRVST
harvest
HRVSTR
harvester
HRWN
heroin(narcotic)
heroine(hero)
HRWTH
herewith
HRZ
here's(here is)
heroes
hers
high-rise
HRZM
heroism
HRZN
horizon
HRZNG
hair-raising
HRZNL
horizontal
HRZNTL
horizontal
HS
Hausa
hiss
hisses
hissy(anger)
hissies
house
housed
housing
hussy
hussies
HSBRK
housebreak
housebroke
housebroken
HSBT
houseboat

HSDRS
housedress
housedresses
HSFL
housefly
houseflies
houseful
HSG
hoosegow
HSH
hash
hashes
hush
hushes
HSHHSH
hush-hush
HSHLD
household
HSHMRK
hash mark
HSHPP
hushpuppy
hushpuppies
HSHSH
hashish
HSK
hassock
husk
husky
huskies
huskier
huskiest
huskily
huskiness
HSKLNNG
housecleaning
HSKPR
housekeeper
HSKT
housecoat
HSKZ
huskies
HSL
hassle
hassled
hassling
hassler
hustle
hustled
hustling
hustler
HSLR
hostler
hustler
HSLT
houselight

HSMD
housemaid
HSMN
houseman
housemen
HSMTHR
housemother
HSN
hasten(speed)
high sign
hyson
HSND
hacienda
HSNDNG
high-sounding
HSNFFR
hasenpfeffer
HSNG
hissing
HSNTH
hyacinth
HSP
hasp(tool)
hyssop
HSPRN
Hesperian
Hesperides
HSPRT
house party
house parties
HSPRTD
high-spirited
HSPS
hospice
HSPTBL
hospitable
HSPTL
hospital
HSPTLT
hospitality
hospitalities
HSPTLZ
hospitalize
hospitalized
hospitalizing
HSPTLZSHN
hospitalization
HSRGN
house organ
HSRZNG
house-raising
HST
haste
hasty
hastier
hastiest

hastily
hastiness
heist(rob)
hoist
host
HSTJ
hostage
HSTK
haystack
HSTL
hostel(inn)
hostile
(unfriendly)
HSTLJ
histology
HSTLL
hostilely
HSTLR
hostelry
hostelries
HSTLT
hostility
hostilities
HSTMN
histamine
HSTN
Houston
HSTR
history
histories
hysteria
HSTRK
historic
hysteric
HSTRKL
historical
hysterical
HSTRKTM
hysterectomy
hysterectomies
HSTRN
historian
HSTRNG
high-strung
HSTRNK
histrionic
HSTRNKL
histrionical
HSTRNKS
histrionics
HSTS
hostess
hostesses
HSVR
howsoever
whosoever

HSWF
housewife
housewives
HSWFR
housewifery
HSWRK
housework
HSWRMNG
housewarming
HSWVZ
housewives
HT
Haiti
hat(head)
hatted
hatting
hatter
hate(emotion)
hated
hating
haughty
haughtier
haughtiest
haughtily
haughtiness
hauteur
heat(hot)
height
hit
hit
hitting
hitter
hoot(owl)
hot
hotter
hottest
how-to(adj)
hut(shelter)
hutted,hutting
HTBD
hotbed(soil)
HTBKS
hotbox(axle)
hotboxes
HTBL
hatable(hate)
heatable(heat)
HTBLDD
hot-blooded(rash)
HTBND
hatband
HTDG
hot dog(food)
hot-dog(v)
hot-dogged
hot-dogging

B:by **CH**:each **D**:day **F**:if **G**:go **H**:he **HW**:why **J**:joy **K**:cow **KS**:ax **KWL**:equal **L**:all **M**:may **N**:in

hot-dogger
HTDL
heatedly
HTFL
hateful
HTFST
hitfest
HTFT
hotfoot
hotfoots
HTH
heath
HTHD
hothead
hotheaded
HTHN
heathen
HTHNSH
heathenish
HTHR
hither
HTHRT
hitherto
HTHS
hothouse
HTL
hightail
hotel
HTLN
hot line
HTMPRD
hot-tempered
HTN
heighten
HTND
high-toned
HTNDRN
hit-and-run
HTNN
hootenanny
hootenannies
HTNSHN
high-tension
HTR
hatter(hat)
hauteur(n)
  (arrogance)
heater
hotter
hottest
HTRD
hatred
HTRDKS
heterodox
heterodoxy
heterodoxies

HTRDN
heterodyne
heterodyned
heterodyning
HTRJNS
heterogeneous
HTRJNSS
heterogenesis
HTRJNT
heterogeneity
  heterogeneities
HTRK
hatrack
hat trick
HTRMS
hit-or-miss
HTRNM
heteronym
heteronomy
HTRSKSHL
heterosexual
HTS
hiatus
  hiatuses
hots(slang)
HTSH
hot shoe
HTSHT
hotshot
HTSP
hutzpa
HTSPR
hotspur
HTSR
howitzer
HTST
high-test
hottest
hotter
hot
HTSTRK
heat stroke
HTTT
hoity-toity
HV
halve(½)
halved
halving
have
had
has
having
heave(throw)
heaved
heaving
heavy

heavier
heaviest
heavily
heaviness
HVDT
heavy-duty
HVH
heave-ho
HVHNDD
heavy-handed
HVHRTD
heavy-hearted
HVK
havoc
HVL
hovel
HVLK
havelock
HVN
Havana
haven(safe place)
heaven(ideal
  place)
HVNT
have-not
HVNWRD
heavenward
HVR
hover
however
whoever(anyone)
HVRSK
haversack
HVST
heavyset
HVWT
heavyweight
  (176 or more lbs)
HVZ
heaves
hives
HW
Hawaii
highway
whoa(stop)
whew(interj)
whey(milk)
why(cause)
HWBTS
whereabouts
HWCH
which
HWCHMKLT
whatchamacallit
HWCHVR
whichever

HWD
whitey(slang)
whydah
HWDL
wheedle(persuade)
wheedled
wheedling
whittle(carve)
whittled
whittling
whittler
HWF
whiff
HWFL
whiffle
whiffled
whiffling
HWFLTR
whiffletree
HWH
Hawaii
HWK
wacky(crazy)
wackier
wackiest
wackily
wackiness
HWKNG
whacking
HWL
awhile(adv)
a while(n)
whale
whaled
whaling
whaler
wheal(pimple)
wheel(disk)
while(time)
whiled
whiling
HWLBN
whalebone
HWLBR
wheelbarrow
HWLBS
wheelbase
HWLBT
whaleboat
HWLCHR
wheelchair
HWLD
wheeled
HWLHS
wheel house
HWLM

NGK:ink **P**:pie **R**:air **S**:ice **SH**:show **T**:toy **THN**:thin **TH**:the **V**:of **W**:we **Y**:you **Z**:is **VZHN**:vision

whelm
HWLNG
whaling
HWLP
whelp
HWLR
whaler
wheeler
HWLRDLR
wheeler-dealer
HWLRT
wheelwright
HWM
wham
whammed
whamming
whammy
whammies
whim
HWMPR
whimper
HWMZ
whimsy
whimsies
HWMZKL
whimsical
HWMZKLT
whimsicality
whimsicalities
HWN
when
whine(complain)
whined
whining
whiner
whiny(whine)
whinier
whiniest
whininess
whinny(neigh)
whinnied
whinnies
HWNG
whang
HWNR
whiner
HWNS
whence
HWNVR
whenever
HWP
whip
whipped(or)
whipt
whipping
whoop(yell)

whoopee
whop(hit)
whopped
whopping
HWPDD
whoop-de-do
HWPKRD
whipcord
HWPLSH
whiplash
whiplashes
HWPNG
whipping
whopping
whopper
HWPNGB
whipping boy
HWPR
whooper(one that yells)
whopper(big)
whopping
HWPRSNPR
whippersnapper
HWPRWL
whippoorwill
HWPS
whipsaw
whoops(interj)
HWPSTCH
whipstitch
whipstitches
HWPSTK
whipstock
HWPSTL
whipstall
HWPT
whippet
whipt(whipped)
HWR
haywire
where(place)
wherry(boat)
wherries
whir
whirred
whirring
HWRB
whereby
HWRBTS
whereabouts
HWRF
wharf
wharfs(or)
wharves
HWRFJ

wharfage
HWRFNJR
wharfinger
HWRFR
wherefore
HWRFRT
wharf rat
HWRL
whirl(revolve)
whorl(flywheel)
HWRLBRD
whirlybird
HWRLGG
whirligig
HWRLPL
whirlpool
HWRLWND
whirlwind
HWRN
wherein
HWRPN
whereupon
HWRT
whereat
HWRV
whereof
HWRVR
wherever
HWRWTH
wherewith
HWRWTHL
wherewithal
HWRZ
whereas
HWSH
whoosh
whooshes
HWSK
whisk
whiskey(liquor)
Canadian
Irish
Scotch
HWSKBRM
whisk broom
HWSKR
whisker
HWSL
whistle
whistled
whistling
whistler
HWSLR
whistler
HWSLSTP
whistle stop(n)

whistle-stop(v)
whistle-stopped
whistle-stopping
HWSPR
whisper
HWST
whist
HWT
what
wheat
whet(sharpen)
whetted
whetting
whit
white(color)
whited
whiting
whiten
whiter
whitest
whitey(slang)
HWTFSH
whitefish
HWTFST
white-faced
HWTGLD
white gold
HWTHDD
white-headed
HWTHR
whether
whither
HWTHRD
white-haired
HWTHS
White House
HWTHT
white-hot
HWTKLR
white-collar
HWTKP
whitecap
HWTL
white lie
whitlow
whittle
whittled
whittling
whittler
HWTLDR
white-tailed deer
HWTLFNT
white elephant
HWTLNGZ
whittlings
HWTMT

B:by **CH**:each **D**:day **F**:if **G**:go **H**:he **HW**:why **J**:joy **K**:cow **KS**:ax **KWL**:equal **L**:all **M**:may **N**:in

white meat
HWTN
whiten
HWTNG
whiting
HWTNNG
whitening
HWTNR
whitener
HWTNS
whiteness
HWTNT
whatnot
HWTNZ
white noise
HWTPPR
white paper
HWTRM
white room
HWTRSH
white trash
HWTSH
whitish
HWTSR
howitzer
HWTSTN
whetstone
HWTSVR
whatsoever
HWTT
whiteout
white tie
HWTVR
whatever
HWTWL
whitewall
HWTWSH
whitewash
whitewashes
HWTWTR
white water
HWTZR
howitzer
HWY
Hawaii
whew(interj)
HWYN
Hawaiian
HWZ
wiz(skilled)
wizard
wheeze
wheezed
wheezing
wheezy
wheezier

wheeziest
wheezily
wheeziness
whiz(sound)
whizzes
whizzed
whizzing
HWZBNG
whizz-bang
HY
hew(chop)
hewn
hue(color)
hued
HYBRS
hubris
HYJ
huge
huger
hugest
HYJNS
hugeness
HYJR
huger
hugest
huge
HYJST
hugest
HYMD
humid
HYMDF
humidify
humidified
humidifies
humidifier
HYMDFKSHN
humidification
HYMDFR
humidifier
HYMDR
humidor
HYMDT
humidity
humidities
HYMKTNT
humectant
HYMLSHN
humiliation
HYMLT
humiliate
humiliated
humiliating
humility
humilities
HYMN
human(person)

humane(action)
HYMND
humanoid
HYMNGGS
humongous
HYMNGS
humongous
HYMNKND
humankind
HYMNL
humanely(action)
humanly(person)
HYMNS
humaneness
(quality)
humanness
(human)
HYMNSTK
humanistic
HYMNSTKL
humanistical
HYMNT
humanity
humanities
HYMNTRN
humanitarian
HYMNTZ
humanities
HYMNZ
humanize
humanized
humanizing
HYMNZM
humanism
HYMR
humeri
humerus(bone)
humor, (B)humour
HYMRL
humeral
HYMRS
humerus(bone)
humeri
humorous(funny)
HYMRSK
humoresque
HYMRST
humorist
HYMS
humus
HYN
hewn
hew
HYR
higher
hire

hired
hiring
HYRSTK
heuristic
HYRSTKL
heuristical
HYSTN
Houston
HZ
Hausa
hawse
has(have)
haze
hazed
hazing
hazer
hazy
hazier
haziest
hazily
haziness
his
hose
hosed
hosing
house(shelter)
housed
housing
hussy
hussies
who's(who is)
(who has)
whose
(possessive)
HZBN
has-been
HZBND
husband
HZBNDR
husbandry
husbandries
HZHL
hawsehole
HZHR
hosiery
hosieries
HZL
hazel
HZLNT
hazelnut
HZN
hosanna
HZNG
hazing
housing
HZR

hawser
hosiery
 hosieries
HZRD
 hazard
HZRDS
 hazardous
HZTNS
 hesitancy
 hesitancies
HZTNT
 hesitant
HZTSHN
 hesitation
HZTT
 hesitate
 hesitated
 hesitating
 hesitater
HZZ
 houses
 house

J

age
 aged
 aging, (B)ageing
agio(money)
edge
 edged
 edging
 edger
edgy
 edgier
 edgiest
 edginess
e.g.(for example)
 exempli gratia
gee
GI(soldier)
 GIs
jaw
jay(bird)
Jew
joy
 joyous
ogee(shape)
JB
 gibe(taunt)
 gibed
 gibing

jab
 jabbed
 jabbing
jib(stop short)
 jibbed
 jibbing
jibe(agree,
  nautical)
 jibed
 jibing
job
 jobbed
 jobbing
JBL
 jubilee
JBLNT
 jubilant
JBLSHN
 jubilation
JBLT
 jubilate
 jubilated
 jubilating
 giblet
JBN
 jawbone
 jawboned
 jawboning
 jawboner
JBR
 jabber
 jobber
 jobbery
 gibber(talk)
JBRKR
 jawbreaker
JBRLTR
 Gibraltar
JBRSH
 gibberish
JBT
 Djibouti
 jabot
 gibbet(gallows)
JD
 aged
 age
 jade
 jaded
 jading
 jetty(pier)
 jetties
 judo
JDD
 jaded
JDK

Judaic
JDKBL
 judicable
JDKCHR
 judicature
JDKT
 adjudicate
 adjudicated
 adjudicating
 adjudication
JDKTR
 adjudicator
 adjudicative
 judicator
 judicatory
 judicatories
JDKTV
 adjudicative
 judicative
JDNS
 adjutancy
JDNT
 adjutant
JDNTS
 adjutancy
JDPRZ
 jodhpurs
JDR
 jitter
 jittery
JDRBG
 jitterbug
 jitterbugged
 jitterbugging
 jitterbugger
JDSHL
 judicial
JDSHR
 judiciary
 judiciaries
JDSHS
 judicious
JDSK
 geodesic
JDSN
 jettison
JF
 jiffy
JFBG
 jiffy bag
JFL
 joyful
JFRSNST
 Jefferson City
JFZKL
 geophysical

JFZKS
 geophysics
JFZSST
 geophysicist
JG
 jag(spree)
 jag(tooth)
 jagged
 jagging
 jaggy
 jaggier
 jaggiest
 jagginess
 jig(dance)
 jigged
 jigging
 jig(fishing)
 jog(run)
 jogged
 jogging
 jogger
 jug
 jugged
 jugging
JGHD
 jughead
JGL
 gigolo(lover)
 jiggle
 jiggled
 jiggling
 joggle
 joggled
 joggling
 juggle(toss)
 juggled
 juggling
 juggler
JGNTK
 gigantic
JGNTKL
 gigantically
JGNTSK
 gigantesque
JGNTZM
 gigantism
JGR
 jigger
 jogger
JGRF
 geography
 geographies
JGRFK
 geographic
JGRFKL
 geographical

JGRFR
geographer
JGRNT
juggernaut
JGS
jigsaw
JGT
jugate
JGWR
jaguar
JGYLR
jugular
JGYR
jaguar
JHK
j-hook
JHKR
jayhawker
JHNSBRG
Johannesburg
JHV
Jehovah
JJ
adjudge
adjudged
adjudging
judge
judged
judging
juju
JJB
jujube
JJMNT
judgment
JJN
jejune
JJTS
jujitsu
JK
jack
jake
jock
jockey
joke(funny)
joked
joking
joker
JKBKS
jukebox
jukeboxes
JKBL
educable
JKBLT
educability
JKBSLDR
Jacob's ladder

JKBT
jackboot
JKD
jockeyed
JKFLTRDZ
jack-of-all-
trades
JKHMR
jackhammer
JKL
jackal
JKLNRN
jack-o-lantern
JKLNTRN
jack-o-lantern
JKND
jocund
JKNDT
jocundity
JKNF
jackknife
jackknifed
jackknifing
jackknives
JKNPS
jackanapes
JKNTHBKS
jack-in-the-box
-boxes
JKNVZ
jackknives
JKPSLDR
Jacob's ladder
JKPT
jackpot
JKR
joker
JKRBT
jack rabbit
JKRD
Jakarta
jacquard
JKRT
Jakarta
JKS
jackass
jackasses
jocose
JKSFLTRDZ
jacks-of-all-
trades
JKSHN
education
ejection
JKSKR
jackscrew

JKSN
Jackson
JKST
jocosity
jocosities
JKSTPZ
juxtapose
juxtaposed
juxtaposing
JKSTPZSHN
juxtaposition
JKSTR
jackstraw
JKSTRP
jockstrap
JKT
educate
educated
educating
eject
jacket
JKTR
educator
ejector
JKTTSHN
jactitation
JKTV
adjective
educative
JKWRT
jequirity
JKYLR
jocular
JKYLRT
jocularity
JKYLSHN
ejaculation
JKYLT
ejaculate
ejaculated
ejaculating
JKYLTR
ejaculator
JKZ
Jacuzzi(trademark)
JL
agile
gel(semisolid)
jail(prison), (B)gaol
jell(v)
Jell-O
(trademark)
jelly(ied)
jellies
jewel(gem)
jolly

jollies
jollier
jolliest
jolliness
joule(unit)
jowl(face)
July
Julies
JLBRD
jailbird
JLBT
jailbait
JLD
age-old
gelid
jellied
JLDT
gelidity
JLF
jellify
jellified
jellifies
jollify
jollified
jollifies
JLFKSHN
jollification
JLFRTH
July Fourth
JLFSH
jellyfish
JLJ
geology
geologies
JLJK
geologic
JLJKL
geological
JLJST
geologist
JLN
julienne
JLNG
agelong
JLP
jalopy
jalopies
julep
JLR
jailer
jeweler, (B)jeweller
jewelry, (B)jewellry
JLRL
jellyroll
JLS
ageless

jealous(envy)
jealousy
  jealousies
joyless
jalousie(window)
JLSHN
  adulation
  gelation
JLT
  adulate
    adulated
    adulating
  agility
    agilities
    agile
  jollity
    jollities
    jolt
JLTN
  gelatin
JLTNS
  gelatinous
JLTNZ
  gelatinize
    gelatinized
    gelatinizing
JLTR
  adulator
  adulatory
JM
  gem(stone)
  gym(sport)
  jam
    jammed
    jamming
  jamb(door)
  jimmy, (B)jemmy
    jimmied
    jimmies
JMB
  jumbo
JMBL
  jumble
    jumbled
    jumbling
JMBLY
  jambalaya
JMBLZ
  gimbals
JMBR
  jamboree
JMK
  Jamaica
JMKLP
  gem clip
JMKR

jim crow(or)J- C-
JMKRK
  gimcrack
JMN
  Gemini
JMNSPRM
  gymnosperm
JMNST
  gymnast
JMNSTKL
  gymnastically
JMNSTKS
  gymnastics
JMNT
  geminate
    geminated
    geminating
JMNZM
  gymnasium
    gymnasia(or)
    gymnasiums
JMP
  jam-up
  jump
  jumpy
    jumpier
    jumpiest
    jumpiness
JMPK
  jam-pack
JMPR
  jumper
JMPSTRT
  jump-start
JMRFK
  geomorphic
JMSSHN
  jam session
JMSTN
  gemstone
JMTR
  geometry
    geometries
JMTRK
  geometric
JMTRKL
  geometrical
JN
  adjoin
  Aegean
  gene
  genie(or)
    jinni(jinn)
  gin
  jean
  jenny(animal)

jennies
jinni(spirit)
  jinn
  genie
  john(slang)
  join
  June
  Juneau
JNCHL
  agential
JNCHR
  jointure
JND
  agenda
    agendum
    augend(math)
JNDK
  genetic
JNDM
  agendum
    agenda
JNDR
  gender
  joinder
JNDS
  jaundice
    jaundiced
    jaundicing
JNG
  aging, (B)ageing
  age
  jingo
    jingoes
JNGG
  jingo
    jingoes
    jingoism
    jingoist
    jingoistic
    jingoistically
JNGK
  jink
  junk
  junkie
JNGKCHR
  juncture
JNGKMN
  junkman
  junkmen
JNGKS
  jinx
    jinxes
JNGKSHN
  junction
JNGKT
  junket

JNGKWL
  jonquil
JNGL
  jangle
    jangled
    jangling
  jingle
    jingled
    jingling
  jungle
  jungly
    junglier
    jungliest
JNGST
  jingoist
JNGSTK
  jingoistic
JNGSTKL
  jingoistically
JNGT
  adjunct
JNGZ
  jingoes
JNGZM
  jingoism
JNJR
  ginger
  gingery
JNJRBRD
  gingerbread
JNJRL
  gingerly
JNHNKK
  John Hancock
JNKMLTL
  Johnny-come-
    -lately
JNKWL
  jonquil
JNL
  genial
  (friendly)
JNLJ
  genealogy
    genealogies
JNLJKL
  genealogical
JNLNZ
  Aegean Islands
JNLT
  geniality
    genialities
JNNTHSPT
  Johnny-on-the-
    -spot
JNP

GNP(gross
national product)
JNPR
  juniper
JNR
  genera(genus)
  genre(type)
  joiner
JNRK
  generic
JNRKL
  generically
JNRKSH
  jinrikisha
JNRL
  general
JNRLT
  generality
  generalities
JNRLZ
  generalize
  generalized
  generalizing
JNRLZSHN
  generalization
JNRS
  generous
JNRSHN
  generation
JNRST
  generosity
  generosities
JNRT
  generate
  generated
  generating
JNRTR
  generator
JNS
  Aegean Sea
  agency
  agencies
  genus
  genera
  jounce
  jounced
  jouncing
JNSD
  genocide
JNSFST
  Janus-faced
JNSHL
  agential
JNSNG
  ginseng
JNSS

Genesis(Bible)
  genesis
  geneses
JNSTNLND
  Johnston Island
JNSZ
  geneses
  genesis
JNT
  adjutant(rank)
  giant(huge)
  jaunt
  jaunty
  jauntier
  jauntiest
  jauntily
  jauntiness
  joint
  junta(government)
  junto(group)
JNTK
  genetic
JNTKL
  genetical
JNTL
  genital
  genitalia
  genteel(style)
  gentile(person)
  gentle(manner)
  gentler
  gentlest
  gently
  jointly
JNTLMN
  gentleman
  gentlemen
JNTLR
  gentler
  gentlest
JNTLST
  gentlest
  gentler
  gentle
JNTLT
  gentility
  gentilities
JNTLWMN
  gentlewoman
  gentlewomen
JNTLY
  genitalia
JNTP
  genotype
JNTR
  genitor

gentry
  gentries
  janitor
JNTRL
  janitorial
JNTV
  genitive
JNYFLKT
  genuflect
JNYL
  genial
JNYN
  genuine
JNYR
  junior
  Jr.
JNYRT
  juniority
JNYRVRST
  junior varsity
  varsities
JNYS
  genius
  geniuses
JNYWN
  genuine
JNYWR
  January
JNZTN
  Johnstown
JP
  Egypt
  GOP
  Grand Old Party
  gyp
  gypped
  gypping
  jeep
  Jeep(trademark)
JPJNT
  gyp joint
JPLTKL
  geopolitical
JPLTKS
  geopolitics
JPN
  Japan
  japan(paint)
  japanned
  japanning
JPNK
  geoponic
JPNKRNT
  Japan Current
JPNZ
  Japanese

JPRD
  jeopardy
  jeopardies
JPRDZ
  jeopardize
  jeopardized
  jeopardizing
JPS
  Gypsy
  Gypsies
JPSM
  gypsum
JPT
  Egypt
JPTR
  Jupiter
JR
  adjure
  adjured
  adjuring
  ajar
  gyre
  gyro
  jar(bottle)
  jar(jostle)
  jarred,-rring
  jeer
  Jewry
  Jewries
  jury(legal)
  juries
JRBKS
  jury box
JRBL
  gerbil
JRBLD
  jerrybuild
  jerrybuilt
JRD
  joy ride(n)
  joy-ride(v)
  joy-rode
  joy-riding
  joy-ridden
JRDK
  juridic
JRDKL
  juridical
JRDN
  Jordan
JRDNR
  jardiniere
JRF
  giraffe
JRFL
  jarful

NG K:ink **P:**pie **R:**air **S:**ice **SH:**show **T:**toy **THN:**thin **TH:**the **V:**of **W:**we **Y:**you **Z:**is **VZHN:**vision

JRGN
jargon
JRGNZ
jargonize
jargonized
jargonizing
JRJ
Georgia
JRK
jerk
jerky
jerkier
jerkiest
jerkily
jerkiness
JRKF
jerk-off(n)(slang)
JRKMPS
gyrocompass
gyrocompasses
JRKN
jerkin
JRKWTR
jerkwater
JRL
jural
JRM
germ
jorum
JRMD
jeremiad
JRMN
German
germane(pertinent)
Germany
juryman(jury)
jurymen
JRMNDR
gerrymander
JRMNL
germinal
JRMNSHN
germination
JRMNT
germinate
germinated
germinating
JRMSD
germicide
JRMSDL
germicidal
JRN
adjourn
journey
JRND
gerund

JRNL
journal
JRNLSTK
journalistic
JRNLSTKL
journalistically
JRNLZ
journalese
journalize
journalized
journalizing
JRNLZM
journalism
JRNM
geranium
Geronimo
geronimo(interj)
JRNMN
journeyman
journeymen
JRNTLJ
gerontology
JRR
adjurer
juror
JRRM
jury room
JRSDKSHN
jurisdiction
JRSHN
adjuration
gyration
JRSKP
gyroscope
JRSKPK
gyroscopic
JRSLM
Jerusalem
JRSPRDNS
jurisprudence
JRST
jurist
JRSTBLZR
gyrostabilizer
JRSTK
juristic
JRSTKL
juristically(law)
JRSTKSHN
jurisdiction
JRT
gyrate
gyrated
gyrating
JRTM
ageratum

JRTR
juratory
JRTRK
geriatric(adj)
JRTRKS
geriatrics
JRZ
Jersey(cow)
jersey(cloth)
juries
jury
JRZLM
Jerusalem
JS
aegis
gesso
Jaycee
jess
jesses
joyous
juice(sap)
juiced
juicing
juicer
juicy
juicier
juiciest
juicily
juiciness
JSCHR
gesture
gestured
gesturing
JSH
Jewish
josh
joshes
JSHRP
Jew's harp
JSL
jostle
jostled
jostling
JSMNT
adjustment
JSNS
adjacency
adjacencies
JSNT
adjacent
JSNTH
jacinth
JSNTRK
geocentric
JSNTRKL
geocentrically(adv)

JSPR
jasper
JSR
juicer
JST
agist(care for)
adjust
geste(notable
deed)
gist
G-suit
jest(joke)
joist
joust
just(only,fair)
JSTBL
adjustable
JSTF
justify
justified
justifies
JSTFBL
justifiable
JSTFKSHN
justification
JSTFR
justifier
JSTK
joy stick
JSTKYLSHN
gesticulation
JSTKYLT
gesticulate
gesticulated
gesticulating
JSTKYLTR
gesticulator
JSTL
justly
JSTMNT
adjustment
JSTR
adjuster
jester
JSTRFK
geostrophic
JSTRNG
G-string
JSTS
justice
JSTSHN
gestation
JSTT
gestate
gestated
gestating

JSTTKS
geostatics
JSZ
Jaycees
JT
jato(or)JATO
jet
jetted
jetting
jetty(pier)
jetties
jot
jotted
jotting
jut
jutted
jutting
jute(plant)
JTBKS
jukebox
jukeboxes
JTBLK
jet-black
JTHRML
geothermal
JTJ
agiotage
JTLG
jet lag
JTLNR
jetliner
JTN
jitney
JTNJN
jet engine
JTNS
adjutancy
adjutancies
JTNT
adjutant
JTPRPLD
jet-propelled
JTPRPLSHN
jet propulsion
JTPRT
jetport
JTR
jitter
jittery
JTRBG
jitterbug
jitterbugged
jitterbugging
JTRPZM
geotropism
JTRZ

jitters
JTSHN
agitation
JTSM
jetsam
JTSN
jettison
JTST
jet set
JTSTR
jet setter
JTSTRM
jet stream
JTT
agitate
agitated
agitating
agitato(music)
JTTR
agitator
JTV
adjective
JV
Java
jayvee
jive(music,talk)
jived
jiving
ogive
JVL
jovial
JVLN
javelin
JVLT
joviality
jovialities
JVNL
juvenile
JVNLDLNGKWNS
juvenile
delinquency
delinquent
JVNLT
juvenility
juvenilities
JVS
Java Sea
JWK
jaywalk
JWKR
jaywalker
JWL
jewel
JWSH
Jewish
JWZ

edgeways
edgewise
JYN
Aegean
JYS
joyous
JZ
jazz
jazzes
jazzy
jazzier
jazziest
jazzily
jazziness
JZBL
Jezebel
JZHRP
Jew's harp
JZHT
Jesuit
JZM
ageism
JZMN
jasmine
JZS
Jesus
JZYWT
Jesuit

K

ache(pain)
ached
aching
akee(tree)
A-OK
auk(bird)
auklet
caw(sound)
cey(islet)
coo(sound)
coup(successful
move)
cow(animal)
coy
cue
cued
cueing
echo
echoes
eek(interj)
eke(make do)

eked
eking
Kauai
kayo(knock out)
key(lock)
oak
OK
OK'd
OK's
OK'ing
okay(formal usage)
Okie(person)
quay(wharf)
KB
Aqaba(city)
cab
cabby(driver)
cabbies
cob(corn)
cowboy
cub
cubby(room)
cubbies
Cuba
cubé(shrub)
cube(solid)
cubed
cubing
KBB
kebab
KBDL
caboodle
KBDRVR
cabdriver
KBHL
cubbyhole
KBJ
cabbage
KBK
Kabuki(or)kabuki
Quebec
KBL
cabal(intrigue)
caballed
caballing
cabala
cable (metal rope,
cabled message)
cabling
cabrilla(fish)
cobble
cobbled
cobbling
cobbler
coble(boat)
Kabul

NGK:ink **P**:pie **R**:air **S**:ice **SH**:show **T**:toy **THN**:thin **TH**:the **V**:of **W**:we **Y**:you **Z**:is **VZHN**:vision

kibble	**KBSTND**	**KCHN**	kidding
KBLGRM	cabstand	keychain	kidder
cablegram	**KBTS**	kitchen	Ok'd(or)
KBLJRNT	kibbutz	**KCHNG**	okayed
cobelligerent	kibbutzim	couching	**KDD**
KBLKN	kibitz	**KCHNL**	coated(covered)
Kublai Khan	kibitzes	cochineal(dye)	coat
KBLR	**KBTSR**	**KCHNT**	coded(message)
caballero(cowboy)	kibitzer	couchant	code
cobbler	**KBTZH**	kitchenette	**KDF**
KBLST	cabotage	**KCHNWR**	codify
cabalist	**KBWB**	kitchenware	codified
KBLSTCH	cobweb	**KCHP**	codifies
cable stitch	cobwebbed	ketchup	cutoff(n,adj)
KBLSTN	cobwebbing	**KCHR**	Gadhafi(or)
cobblestone	cobwebby	actuary	Khadafy(or)
KBLT	**KBYR**	actuaries	Qadhafi
cobalt	caballero	catcher	**KDFKSHN**
KBLYR	**KBZN**	eye-catcher	codification
caballero	cabezon(fish)	**KCHRL**	**KDFNDNT**
KBN	**KCH**	actuarial	codefendant
cabana	catch	**KCHS**	**KDFR**
cabin	catches	Cochise(Indian)	codifier
KBNKLS	caught	**KCHT**	**KDFSH**
cabin class	catchy	actuate	codfish
KBNT	catchier	actuated	**KDGR**
cabinet	catchiest	actuating	coup de grace
KBNTMKR	catchiness	**KCHTR**	**KDGRS**
cabinetmaker	coach	actuator	coup de grace
KBNTWRK	coaches	**KCHWRD**	**KDK**
cabinetwork	couch(sofa)	catchword	chaotic
KBNY	couches	**KCHZ**	Kodiak
cabana	ketch(boat)	Cochise(Indian)	Kodak(trademark)
KBR	ketches	**KCHZKCHKN**	okey-doke
cabaret	kitsch	catch-as-catch-can	okey-dokey
caber(pole)	kitschy	**KD**	**KDKBR**
cobra	**KCHFRZ**	cad(person)	Kodiak bear
KBRD	catch phrase	caddish	**KDKM**
cowbird	**KCHK**	caddie(golf)	catacomb
cupboard	caoutchouc(rubber)	caddies	**KDKRNRD**
keyboard	**KCHL**	Caddy(car)(slang)	cater-cornered
KBRL	actual	caddy(container)	**KDKS**
cabriole(leg)	catchall	caddies	codex
cabriolet(vehicle)	**KCHLT**	cod	codices
KBRT	actuality	coda(end)	**KDL**
cabretta(leather)	actualities	code(system)	acaudal(no tail)
KBRY	**KCHLZ**	coded	cattle(cows)
cabrilla(fish)	actualize	coding	caudal(tail)
KBS	actualized	coed(female	caudle(beverage)
caboose	actualizing	student)(or)	coddle
KBSH	actualization	co-ed	coddled
cubbish	**KCHMN**	cootie(bug)	coddling
KBSHNS	coachman	cud	cuddle(snuggle)
cubbishness	coachmen	cuddy(space)	cuddled
KBSKTS	**KCHMNT**	kid	cuddling
Cub Scouts	catchment	kidded	cuddly

KDLDK
catalytic
KDLST
catalyst
KDLVRL
cod-liver oil
KDM
academe(n)
(scholarship)
academia
Academy
(specific society)
academy(school)
academies
KDMK
academic
KDMKLZ
academicals
(cap and gown)
KDMM
cadmium
KDMN
coup de main
KDMRN
catamaran
KDMSHN
academician
KDMSZM
academicism
KDMWRDS
Academy Awards
KDN
codeine
kidney
KDNG
coating(coat)
coding(code)
cutting(cut)
KDNP
kidnap
KDNPR
kidnaper
KDNS
cadence
KDNT
cadent(rhythm)
couldn't
could not
KDNZ
cadenza
KDPLT
catapult
KDPS
codpiece
KDR
cadre

coterie
cater
cotter(pin)
KDRK
cataract
KDRKRNRD
cater-cornered
KDRKT
cataract
KDRPLR
caterpillar
KDRR
caterer
KDS
caddis(fabric)
KDSL
codicil
KDSS
caduceus(symbol)
caducci(pl)
KDST
caducity
KDSTR
cadastre(record)
KDT
acaudate(no tail)
cadet
chaotic
chaos
chaotically
coup d'état
KDVR
cadaver
KDVRS
cadaverous
KDYSS
caduceus
caducei
KDYST
caducity
KDZ
kudzu
KF
cafe(restaurant)
calf
calves
coffee
coif(cap)
coiffed
coiffing
cough(throat)
cuff
kef(narcotic)
KFBRK
coffee break
KFDRP

cough drop
KFHS
coffeehouse
KFK
Kafka
Franz
KFKK
coffee cake(food)
KFKLCH
coffee klatch
KFL
coffle
coffled
coffling
KFLNKS
cuff links
KFML
coffee mill
KFN
caffeine
coffin
KFNM
ecphonema(cry)
KFNWR
café noir(black
KFPT   coffee)
coffeepot
KFR
coffer
KFRDM
cofferdam
KFSHNT
coefficient
KFSHP
coffee shop
KFSKN
calfskin
KFTBL
coffee table
KFTN
caftan
KFTR
cafeteria
KG
cog
cogged
cogging
keg(cask)
KGHWL
cogwheel
KGLR
kegler
KGNSHN
cognition
KGNT
cognate

KGNZBL
cognizable
KGNZNS
cognizance
KGNZNT
cognizant
KGR
cougar
KGRLW
cog railway
KGYLNT
coagulant
KGYLSHN
coagulation
KGYLT
coagulate
coagulated
coagulating
KGYLTR
coagulator
KGYLTV
coagulative
KGZKYTR
coexecutor
KGZST
coexist
KGZSTNS
coexistence
KGZSTNT
coexistent
KHBT
cohabit
KHBTNT
cohabitant
KHBTSHN
cohabitation
KHD
cowhide
KHL
keyhole
keyholed
keyholing
KHLTZ
halutz
KHLTZM
halutzim
KHN
cowhand
KHND
cowhand
KHR
cohere
cohered
cohering
KHRNS
coherence

NGK:ink **P**:pie **R**:air **S**:ice **SH**:show **T**:toy **THN**:thin **TH**:the **V**:of **W**:we **Y**:you **Z**:is **VZHN**:vision

KHRNT
coherent
KHRT
cohort(ally)
KHSV
cohesive(stick)
KHTS
cahoots
KHZHN
cohesion
KHZV
cohesive
KJ
cadge(beg)
cadged
cadging
cage
caged
caging
cagey
cagier
cagiest
cagily
caginess
EKG
electrocardiogram
electrocardiograph
kedge(anchor)
kedged
kedging
quayage
KJB
KGB
Committee for
State Security
KJKSHN
co-education
KJKSHNL
co-educational
KJL
cajole
cajoled
cajoling
cudgel(club)
KJLR
cajoler
cajolery
cajoleries
KJNS
cogency
cogencies
KJNT
coadunate
coadunated
coadunating
cogent

KJR
cadger(beggar)
codger(old man)
KJTNT
coadjutant
KJTR
coadjutor
KJTSHN
cogitation
KJTT
cogitate
cogitated
cogitating
KJTTR
cogitator
KK
ack-ack(gun)
cacao(tree)
caique(boat)
cake
caked
caking
calk(shoe)
caulk(stop up)
coca(shrub)
cocaine
cock
cockeye
cockeyed
cocky
cockier
cockiest
cockily
cockiness
coco(palm)
cocoa(chocolate)
coke
coked
coking
Coke(trademark)
coke(slang)
cocaine
coo-coo(crazy)
cook
cookie(food)(or)
cooky
cookies
cuckoo(bird)
echoic
kaka(parrot)
kayak(canoe)
keck
khaki(cloth)
kick
kook(person)
kooky

kookiness
kyack(packsack)
KKBK
cookbook
kickback(n)
kick back(v)
KKCHR
cowcatcher
KKD
cockade
cockeyed
KKDDLD
cock-a-doodle-doo
KKF
kickoff(n)
kick off(v)
KKFN
cacophony
cacophonies
KKFNS
cacophonous
KKFT
cockfight
KKHN
kuchen
KKHP
cock-a-hoop
KKKL
Coca Cola
(trademark)
KKKLK
cuckoo-clock
KKKS
cachexia
KKL
cackle
cackled
cackling
cochlea(ear)
cochleae
cochlear(adj)
cockle(wrinkle)
cockled
cockling
KKLB
key club
KKLBR
cocklebur
KKLD
cuckold
KKLKSKLN
Ku Klux Klan
KKLNZ
Cook Islands
KKLR
cochlear

KKLRM
cockalorum
KKLSHL
cockleshell
KKLT
cochleate(or)
cochleated
KKMM
cockamamie
KKMN
kakemono
KKN
cocaine
coke(slang)
coca(shrub)
kuchen(cake)
Cokaigne
(imaginary
island)
cockney
cocoon
KKNBL
cock-and-bull(adj)
KKNDBLSTR
cock-and-bull story
stories
KKNT
coconut
KKPT
cockpit
KKR
caulker
cocker(dog)
cooker(cook)
cookery
cookeries
kicker
KKRCH
cockroach
KKRL
cockerel
KKRSPNYL
cocker spaniel
KKS
caucus
caucuses
coax
coaxes
coccus(bacterium)
cocci
cox
coxes
coxa(hip)
coxae
KKSD
coccid(insect)

B:by **CH**:each **D**:day **F**:if **G**:go **H**:he **HW**:why **J**:joy **K**:cow **KS**:ax **KWL**:equal **L**:all **M**:may **N**:in

KKSDSS
coccidiosis
(disease)
KKSGZ
kok-saghyz(weed)
KKSHN
coaction
KKSHR
cocksure
KKSJZ
coccyges
coccyx
KKSKM
cockscomb
KKSKS
coccyx(bone)
coccyges
KKSL
coaxial
KKSLJ
coxalgia
coxalgic
KKSLNZ
Cocos Islands
KKSN
coxswain
KKSR
coaxer
KKSTNCHN
coextension
KKSTND
coextend
KKSTNSHN
coextension
KKSTNSV
coextensive
KKSTV
cookstove
KKT
cockatoo(parrot)
cocotte
(prostitute)
cookout
coquette(n)
coquet(v)
coquetted
coquetting
KKTHT
cocked hat
KKTL
cockatiel(parrot)
cocktail
KKTR
coquetry
coquetries
KKTS

cactus
cactuses(or)
cacti
KKTSH
coquettish
KKVN
coq au vin
KKWK
cakewalk
KKWL
coequal
KKWLT
coequality
coequalities
KKZ
khakis
khaki
KKZHN
Caucasian
KL
Cali
call
calla(plant)
callow
caul(membrane)
chela(claw)
claw
clay
clayish
clayey
clay
clew(thread)
cloy(too much)
clue(hint)
clued
cluing
coal
coil
cola(drink)
collie(dog)
cool
coolie(person)
coulee(stream)
cowl(hood)
coyly
cull
éclat(success)
kale
keel(boat)
kill(death)
kiln(heat)
kilo(unit)
kilogram
koala(animal)
kola(tree,nut)
KLB

callboy
club
clubbed
clubbing
clubby
clubbier
clubbiest
KLBBL
clubbable
KLBFT
clubfoot
KLBHS
clubhouse
KLBKR
club car
KLBL
callable
KLBR
caliber, (B)calibre
clabber
clobber(hit)
KLBRM
clubroom
KLBRSHN
calibration
collaboration
KLBRT
calibrate
calibrated
calibrating
collaborate
collaborated
collaborating
KLBRTR
calibrator
collaborator
KLBS
calaboose
KLBSD
club soda
KLBSH
calabash
KLBSMWCH
club sandwich
KLBSNWCH
club sandwich
KLBSTK
club steak
KLBWMN
clubwoman
clubwomen
KLCH
clutch
clutches
cultch(oyster)
KLCHR

cloture
clotured
cloturing
culture
cultured
culturing
KLCHRL
cultural
KLD
accolade
clad
clad
cladding
clod
cloddish
cloud(sky)
cloudy
cloudier
cloudiest
cloudily
cloudiness
cold
collide(hit)
collided
colliding
collision
colloid(suspension)
collude
colluded
colluding
keloid(scar)
occlude
occluded
occluding
KLDBLDD
cold-blooded
KLDBRST
cloudburst
KLDFRM
cold frame
KLDFRNT
cold front
KLDHPR
clodhopper
KLDHRTD
coldhearted
KLDKPT
cloud-capped
KLDKRM
cold cream
KLDKTS
cold cuts
KLDNG
cladding
KLDNN
cloud nine

KLDPK
cold pack
KLDR
caldera(crater)
clatter(noise)
clutter(mess)
collator
KLDRL
collateral
KLDRN
caldron
KLDSH
cloddish
KLDSHLDR
cold shoulder(n)
cold-shoulder(v)
KLDSK
cul-de-sac
cul-de-sacs
KLDSKP
kaleidoscope
KLDSKPK
kaleidoscopic
KLDSNP
cold snap
KLDSR
cold sore
KLDSTRJ
cold storage
KLDSWT
cold sweat
KLDTRK
cold turkey
KLDWR
Cold War
(US vs. USSR)
cold war
KLDWV
cold wave
KLDZDL
Clydesdale
KLF
caliph
clef(music)
cliff
KLFB
ochlophobia
KLFDWLR
cliff dweller
KLFHNGNG
cliffhanging
KLFHNGR
cliffhanger
KLFLD
coal field
KLFLR
cauliflower
KLFN
colophon
KLFPLT
cleft palate
KLFRNY
California
KLFT
cleft(split)
KLFTPLT
cleft palate
KLG
clog
clogged
clogging
clogger
colleague(person)
collogue(conspire)
collogued
colloguing
klieg(light)
KLGLT
klieg light
KLGR
clogger
KLGRF
calligraphy
calligrapher
KLGRL
call girl
KLGRM
kilogram
KLGS
coal gas
KLHDD
cool-headed
KLHL
keelhaul
KLHM
Oklahoma
KLHMST
Oklahoma City
KLHRTZ
kilohertz
KLJ
college
ecology
ecologies
killjoy
KLJKL
ecological
KLJM
collegium
KLJN
collegian
KLJST

ecologist
KLJT
collegiate
KLK
calico
calque(language)
calqued
calquing
clack(sound)
claque(group,paid)
click(sound)
clique(group)
cliqued,cliquing
cloaca
cloacae(pl)
cloacal
cloak
clock(time)
cluck
colic
colicky
cowlick(hair)
o'clock
KLKK
coldcock(hit)
KLKL
colloquial
KLKNDGR
cloak-and-dagger
(adj)
KLKRM
cloakroom
KLKRS
ochlocracy
(mob rule)
ochlocracies
KLKRT
ochlocrat
KLKS
calyx
calyxes(or)
calyces
KLKSH
cliquish
KLKSHN
collection
collocation
KLKSN
Klaxon
(trademark)
KLKST
chalcocite(copper)
KLKT
Calcutta
collect
collocate

collocated
collocating
KLKTBL
collectible
KLKTBLZ
collectibles
KLKTD
collected
KLKTK
eclectic
KLKTM
colectomy
KLKTR
collector
KLKTSZM
eclecticism
KLKTV
collective
KLKTVZ
collectivize
collectivized
collectivizing
KLKTVZM
collectivism
KLKW
colloquy
colloquies
KLKWL
colloquial
KLKWLZM
colloquialism
KLKWM
colloquium
KLKWRK
clockwork
KLKWZ
clockwise
KLKYLBL
calculable
KLKYLS
calculus
calculi
KLKYLT
calculate
calculated
calculating
calculation
KLKYLTR
calculator
KLL
echolalia
ukulele
KLLTR
kiloliter
KLM
acclaim

B:by **CH**:each **D**:day **F**:if **G**:go **H**:he **HW**:why **J**:joy **K**:cow **KS**:ax **KWL**:equal **L**:all **M**:may **N**:in

claim
clam
  clammed
  clamming
  clammy
  clammier
  clammiest
  clamminess
climb
clime(climate)
column
coulomb(unit)
KLMB
Columbia
KLMBK
  clambake
KLMBL
  claimable
  climbable
KLMBR
  clamber
KLMBRR
  clamberer
KLMBS
  Columbus
KLMKS
  climax
  climaxes
KLMKTK
  climactic
KLMKTRK
  climacteric
KLMN
  calamine
  calumny
  calumnies
KLMNGK
  calamanco
KLMNJR
  Kilimanjaro
KLMNNT
  culminant
KLMNR
  columnar
KLMNS
  calumnious
  clemency
  clemencies
KLMNSHN
  culmination
KLMNST
  columnist
KLMNT
  calumniate
  calumniated
  calumniating

clement
culminate
  culminated
  culminating
  culmination
KLMNTR
  calumniator
KLMP
  clamp
  clump
KLMPDN
  clampdown(n)
KLMR
  acclaimer
  claimer
  clamber(climb)
  clamor, (B)clamour
  climber
KLMRR
  clamberer
KLMRS
  clamorous, (B)- mourous
KLMSHL
  clamshell
KLMSHN
  acclamation
    (approval)
  acclimation
    (adjustment)
  collimation
KLMST
  columnist
KLMT
  acclimate
    acclimated
    acclimating
  calamity
  calamities
  climate(weather)
  collimate
    collimated
    collimating
KLMTK
  climatic
KLMTR
  kilometer
KLMTS
  calamitous
  clematis
KLMTZ
  acclimatize
    acclimatized
    acclimatizing
KLMTZSHN
  acclimatization
KLMZ

clumsy
  clumsier
  clumsiest
  clumsily
  clumsiness
  Kalamazoo
KLN
  call loan
  clan
    clannish
  clean(not dirty)
  clone
    cloned
    cloning
  clown(jester)
  Cologne(city)
  cologne(scent)
  Colón
  colon(money,
    intestine,verse)
  colons(or)
  cola
  colony
    colonies
  kaolin
  kiln
  Oakland
KLNBL
  cleanable
KLNCH
  clench(grasp)
    clenches
  clinch(secure)
    clinches
KLNCHR
  clincher
KLND
  calando(music)
  colonnade
  Oakland
KLNDR
  calendar(time)
  calender(pass
    between rollers)
  colander(tool)
KLNDSTN
  clandestine
KLNG
  calling
  clang(sound)
  cling
    clung
  cowling(cover)
KLNGGR
  clangor, (B)clangour
    clangorous

KLNGK
  clank
  clink
KLNGKR
  clinker
KLNGLNZ
  Keeling Islands
KLNGR
  clangor, (B)clangour
KLNGRS
  clangorous, (B)-
KLNHNDD   gourous
  cleanhanded
KLNK
  clank
  clinic
  clonic
    clonus
KLNKL
  clinical
KLNKR
  clinker
KLNKS
  Kleenex
    (trademark)
KLNKT
  clean-cut
KLNL
  cleanly
    cleanlier
    cleanliest
    cleanliness
  colonial
KLNLMD
  clean-limbed
KLNLNS
  cleanliness
KLNMTR
  clinometer
KLNP
  cleanup(n,adj)
KLNR
  culinary
KLNS
  clonus
    clonuses
    clonic
KLNSH
  clannish
KLNSHN
  clinician
KLNSHVN
  clean-shaven
KLNST
  colonist
KLNT

NGK:ink **P**:pie **R**:air **S**:ice **SH**:show **T**:toy **THN**:thin **TH**:the **V**:of **W**:we **Y**:you **Z**:is **VZHN**:vision

client
coolant
KLNTL
clientele
KLNZ
cleanse
cleansed
cleansing
cleanser
colonize
colonized
colonizing
KLNZMN
clansman(clan)
clansmen
Klansman
Klansmen
KLNZR
cleanser
colonizer
KLNZSHN
colonization
KLP
calliope
call-up(n,adj)
clap
clapped
clapping
clapper
clip
clipped
clipping
clipper
clop
clopped
clopping
collop
kelp
KLPBL
culpable
KLPBRD
clapboard
clipboard
KLPJNT
clip joint
KLPNG
clapping
clipping
KLPR
caliper
clapper
clipper
klupper
KLPRDR
colporteur(sales)
KLPRT

culprit
KLPRTJ
colportage
KLPRTR
colporteur(sales)
KLPS
collapse
collapsed
collapsing
eclipse
eclipsed
eclipsing
KLPSBL
collapsible
KLPSHT
clipsheet
KLPT
klepto(slang)
kleptomaniac
KLPTK
ecliptic
KLPTMN
kleptomania
KLPTMNK
kleptomaniac
KLPTRP
claptrap
KLPTS
colpitis
KLR
caller
calorie
choler(anger)
cholera(disease)
clear
collar
color, (B)colour
cooler
éclair(pastry)
killer
KLRB
kohlrabi
kohlrabies
KLRBL
colorable
KLRBLND
colorblind
KLRBN
collarbone
KLRBTN
collar button
KLRD
chloride
clear-eyed
collard(food)
Colorado

colored, (B)coloured
KLRF
clarify
clarified
clarifies
KLRFK
colorific
KLRFKSHN
clarification
KLRFL
chlorophyll
colorful, (B)colourful
KLRFRM
chloroform
KLRFST
colorfast
KLRHDD
clearheaded
KLRJ
clergy
clergies
KLRJMN
clergyman
clergymen
KLRK
caloric
choleric(bad
  tempered)
cleric
clerk
KLRKL
clerical
clericalist
KLRKLKLR
clerical collar
KLRKS
Clorox(trademark)
KLRKST
colorcast
KLRKT
clear-cut(adj)
KLRL
chloral
clearly
KLRLS
colorless, (B)colourless
KLRMTR
colorimeter
KLRN
chlorine
clarion
KLRNG
clearing
coloring
KLRNGHS
clearing house

KLRNS
clearance
KLRNT
chlorinate
chlorinated
chlorinating
chlorination
clarinet
colorant
KLRNTST
clarinetist
KLRS
clerisy
KLRSHN
coloration
KLRSS
chlorosis(disease)
KLRST
colorist
KLRSTD
clear-sighted
KLRSTR
clerestory
KLRT
claret
clarity
KLRTR
coloratura
KLRVNS
clairvoyance
KLRVNT
clairvoyant
KLRVYNS
clairvoyance
KLRVYNT
clairvoyant
KLS
callous(hardened)
callouses
callosity
callus(skin)
calluses
class
classes
classy
classier
classiest
close(nearby)
closer
closest
coalesce
coalesced
coalescing
coulisse(theater)
cullis(gutter)
cullis

KLSDN
chalcedony
chalcedonies
KLSF
calcify
calcified
calcifying
classify
-fied,-fies
KLSFBL
classifiable
KLSFKSHN
calcification(bone)
classification
KLSFR
classifier
KLSFSTD
close-fisted
KLSFTNG
close-fitting
KLSGRND
close-grained
KLSH
clash
clashes
clayish
cliché
cloche(hat)
KLSHN
coalition
collation
KLSK
calcic
classic
KLSKL
classical
KLSKNCHS
class-conscious
KLSKWRTRZ
close quarters
KLSL
coleslaw
colossal
KLSM
calcium
coliseum
KLSMN
calcimine
KLSMT
classmate
KLSMTHT
closemouthed
KLSN
keelson
KLSNS
coalescence

KLSNT
calescent(warm)
coalescent
KLSP
clasp
close-up(n)
KLSRDR
close order(n)
close-order(adj)
KLSRM
classroom
KLSS
colossus
KLSSST
classicist
KLST
calcite
calcium
callosity
callosities
callous
KLSTHNKS
calisthenics
KLSTM
colostomy
colostomies
KLSTR
cloister
cluster
clyster(enema)
KLSTRFB
claustrophobia
KLSTRL
cholesterol
cloistral
KLSV
collusive
occlusive
KLT
acolyte(person)
calotte(cap)
cleat
clot(blood)
clotted
clotting
clout(power)
collate(sort)
collated
collating
collet
colt(horse)
coltish
culotte(or)
culottes
cult
kilt

occult
KLTH
cloth(fabric)
cloths
clothe
clothed(or)
clad
clothing
KLTHNG
clothing
KLTHR
clothier
KLTHS
cloths(fabric)
KLTHYR
clothier
KLTHZ
clothes
KLTK
Celtic
KLTN
kiloton
kilotonnage
KLTR
clatter
clutter
coal tar
collator(sorter)
colter
kilter
KLTRL
collateral
KLTRS
call letters
clitoris
KLTS
colitis
culottes(clothing)
klutz
KLTSH
coltish
KLTSHN
occultation
KLTV
collative
KLTVBL
cultivable
KLTVSHN
cultivation
KLTVT
cultivate
cultivated
cultivating
KLTVTR
cultivator
cultivation

KLTZ
halutz(or)chalutz
halutzim(or)chalutzim
KLTZM
occultism
KLV
cleave
cleaved(or)
cleft(or)
clove
cleaving
cleaver
cloven
clove(tree,spice)
KLVBL
cleavable
KLVJ
cleavage
KLVKL
clavicle
KLVKRD
clavichord
KLVLND
Cleveland
KLVLT
kilovolt
KLVN
Kelvin(scale)
kelvin(unit)
KLVNZM
Calvinism
KLVR
calvary(sculpture)
calvaries
clavier(keyboard)
cleaver(tool)
clever(smart)
clover(plant)
KLVRLF
cloverleaf
KLVRN
klavern
KLVRT
culvert
KLVS
clevis(plow)
KLVT
acclivity
acclivities
KLWR
couloir(gully)
KLWT
kilowatt
KLWTR
kilowatt-hour
KLYML

NGK:ink P:pie R:air S:ice SH:show T:toy THN:thin TH:the V:of W:we Y:you Z:is VZHN:vision

columella	acne(disease)	cumbersome	**KMFLJ**
columellae	cam	**KMBSCHN**	camouflage
KLYNT	calm(peaceful)	combustion	**KMFLZH**
client	came(lead bar)	**KMBST**	camouflage
KLYR	came	cambist(money)	**KMFR**
collier	come	combust	camphor
colliery	cameo	**KMBSTBL**	**KMFRT**
KLZ	coma(sleep)	combustible	comfort
Achilles	comb(hair)	**KMBSTR**	**KMFRTBL**
clause	come	combustor	comfortable
close(shut)	came	**KMBT**	**KMFRTR**
closed	coming	combat	comforter
closing	comer	**KMBTNT**	**KMFT**
clothes(v)	comma(,)	combatant	comfit
clothes(n)(apparel)	commie(slang)	**KMBTV**	**KMHTHR**
cloths(fabric)	Communist	combative	come-hither(adj)
KLZDN	cum(prep)(with)	**KMD**	**KMJN**
close down	oakum	comedy	curmudgeon
KLZDND	Yquem(wine)	comedies	**KMK**
closed-end	**KMB**	committee(group)	comic
KLZDSRKT	akimbo	commode	**KMKBK**
closed circuit(n)	combo	**KMDD**	comic book
closed-circuit(adj)	**KMBD**	committed	**KMKL**
KLZH	Cambodia	**KMDK**	chemical
collage	**KMBDN**	comedic	comical
KLZHN	Cambodian	**KMDL**	**KMKR**
collision(hit)	**KMBDNG**	committal	comaker
collusion(plot)	combating(or)-tting	**KMDN**	**KMKS**
occlusion(omit)	**KMBK**	Camden	commix
KLZHR	comeback(n)	comedian(m)	commixes
closure	**KMBN**	comedienne(f)	**KMKSCHR**
KLZHRS	combine	comedown(n)	commixture
clotheshorse	combined	**KMDNG**	**KMKSTRP**
KLZL	combining	commanding	comic strip
clausal	**KMBNBL**	**KMDR**	**KMKWT**
KLZLN	combinable	commodore	kumquat
clothesline	**KMBNSHN**	**KMDS**	**KMKZ**
KLZN	combination	commodious	kamikaze(pilot)
cloisonné	**KMBNT**	**KMDSHN**	**KML**
KLZPN	accumbent	accommodation	camel
clothespin	**KMBNTV**	**KMDT**	comely
KLZPRS	combinative	accommodate	comelier
clothespress	**KMBR**	accommodated	comeliest
KLZSTK	camber	accommodating	comeliness
ecclesiastic	cumber	commodity	kummel(liqueur)
KLZSTKL	**KMBRJ**	commodities	**KMLD**
ecclesiastical	Cambridge	**KMDTR**	cum laude
KLZT	**KMBRK**	accommodator	**KMLF**
close-out(n)	cambric	**KMDTV**	comme il faut
closet	**KMBRN**	accommodative	**KMLFLJ**
KLZTNDN	Cambrian	**KMF**	camouflage
Achilles' tendon	**KMBRNS**	comfy	camouflaged
KLZV	cumbrance	comfier	camouflaging
occlusive	**KMBRS**	comfiest	**KMLFLZH**
KM	cumbrous	comfily	camouflage
acme(peak)	**KMBRSM**	comfiness	camouflaged

B:by **CH**:each **D**:day **F**:if **G**:go **H**:he **HW**:why **J**:joy **K**:cow **KS**:ax **KWL**:equal **L**:all **M**:may **N**:in

camouflaging
KMLT
Camelot
KMLY
camellia
KMLYN
chameleon
KMLZHR
camel's hair(n)
camel's-hair(adj)
KMMRSHN
commemoration
KMMRT
commemorate
commemorated
commemorating
commemoration
KMMRTR
commemorator
commemoratory
KMMRTV
commemorative
KMN
come-on(n)
common
kimono
KMNCH
Comanche
KMND
command(order)
commando(person)
commend(praise)
KMNDBL
commandable
commendable
KMNDMNT
commandment
KMNDNT
commandant
KMNDPST
command post
KMNDR
commandeer(take)
commander(chief)
commandery
KMNDRNCHF
commander in chief
KMNDSHN
commendation
KMNDTR
commendatory
KMNG
coaming(curb)
coming
KMNGGL
commingle

commingled
commingling
KMNGT
coming-out
KMNGZ
combings
KMNL
common law(n)
common-law(adj)
KMNLNZ
Cayman Islands
KMNLT
commonalty
commonalties
KMNMRKT
Common Market
KMNPLS
commonplace
KMNR
commoner
KMNRBND
cummerbund
KMNS
commence
commenced
commencing
comments(remarks)
KMNSL
commensal
KMNSMNT
commencement
KMNSNS
common sense
KMNSRBL
commensurable
KMNSRT
commensurate(equal)
commensurated
commensurating
KMNT
comment
KMNTDR
commentator
KMNTR
commentary
commentaries
KMNTT
commentate
commentated
commentating
KMNTTR
commentator
KMNWL
commonweal
KMNWLTH
commonwealth

KMNZ
commons
kimonos
KMP
camp
campo(field)
compo(mixture)
KMPDBL
compatible
KMPDR
compadre
KMPDTR
competitor
KMPDTV
competitive
KMPFR
campfire
KMPGRND
campground
KMPKSHN
compaction
KMPKT
compact
KMPKTR
compactor
KMPL
compel(force)
compelled
compelling
compile
compiled
compiling
compiler
comply
complied
complies
Kampala
KMPLBL
compellable
compliable
KMPLKS
complex
complexes
complicacy
complicacies
KMPLKSHN
complexion
complication
KMPLKSHND
complexioned
KMPLKST
complexity
complexities
KMPLKT
complect
complicate

complicated
complicating
KMPLKTD
complected
KMPLMNT
complement
(n-addition, v-add to)
compliment
(express esteem)
KMPLMNTL
complemental
KMPLMNTR
complementary
(completing)
complimentary
(praise)
KMPLN
complain
KMPLNNT
complainant
KMPLNS
compliance
KMPLNT
complaint
(dissatisfaction)
compliant
(yielding)
KMPLR
compiler
KMPLS
accomplice
complice
KMPLSH
accomplish
accomplishes
KMPLSHBL
accomplishable
KMPLSHN
compilation
completion
compulsion(urge)
KMPLSNS
complacence
complacency
complacencies
(contented)
complaisance
(obliging)
KMPLSNT
complacent
(content)
complaisant
(obliging)
KMPLSR
compulsory
compulsories

KMPLST
complicity
complicities
KMPLSV
compulsive
KMPLT
complete
completed
completing
completion
KMPLYNT
compliant
KMPLZNS
complaisance
KMPLZNT
complaisant
KMPMTNG
camp meeting
KMPN
accompany
accompanied
accompanies
campaign
company
companies
compound
KMPND
compend
compendium
compound
KMPNDBL
compoundable
KMPNDM
compendium
compendia(or)
compendiums
KMPNDS
compendious
KMPNGKSHN
compunction
KMPNL
campanile
campanili(or)
campaniles
KMPNLJ
campanology
KMPNMNT
accompaniment
KMPNNT
component
KMPNR
campaigner
KMPNS
comeuppance
KMPNSBL
compensable

KMPNSSHN
compensation
KMPNST
accompanist
compensate
compensated
compensating
KMPNSTR
compensator
compensatory
KMPNYN
companion
KMPNYNBL
companionable
KMPNYNSHP
companionship
KMPNYNW
companionway
KMPR
camper
compare(judge)
compared
comparing
compeer(equal)
KMPRBL
comparable
KMPRGSHN
compurgation
KMPRGTR
compurgator
KMPRHNCHN
comprehension
KMPRHND
comprehend
KMPRHNDBL
comprehendible
KMPRHNSBL
comprehensible
KMPRHNSHN
comprehension
KMPRHNSV
comprehensive
KMPRMZ
compromise
compromised
compromising
KMPRMZR
compromiser
KMPRS
compress
compresses
KMPRSBL
compressible
KMPRSHN
compression
KMPRSN

comparison
KMPRSR
compressor
KMPRT
compart(divide)
comport(behave)
KMPRTMNT
compartment
(section)
comportment(act)
KMPRTMNTL
compartmental
KMPRTMNTLZ
compartmentalize
-ized,-izing
KMPRTR
comparator
KMPRTST
comparatist
KMPRTV
comparative
KMPRZ
comprise
comprised
comprising
KMPS
campus(school)
campuses
compass(tool)
compasses
KMPSHN
compassion
KMPSHNT
compassionate
KMPSMNTS
compos mentis
KMPST
campsite
compost
KMPT
compete
competed
competing
compote
kempt
KMPTBL
compatible
computable
KMPTNS
competence
competency
competencies
KMPTNT
competent
KMPTRT
compatriot

KMPTSHN
competition
computation
KMPTTR
competitor
KMPTTV
competitive
KMPYDR
computer
KMPYT
compute
computed
computing
computer
KMPYTBL
computable
KMPYTR
computer
KMPYTRZ
computerize
computerized
computerizing
computerization
KMPYTSHN
computation
KMPZ
compose
composed
composing
composer
KMPZHR
composure
KMPZR
composer
KMPZSHN
composition
KMPZT
composite
KMPZTR
compositor
KMR
camera(photo)
chimera
comber
comb
comer
come
Cymry(people)
KMRBND
cummerbund
KMRD
comrade
KMRDR
camaraderie
KMRDSHP
comradeship

B:by CH:each D:day F:if G:go H:he HW:why J:joy K:cow KS:ax KWL:equal L:all M:may N:in

KMRK
Cymric
KMRKL
chimerical
KMRL
cameral
KMRLNZ
Comoro Islands
KMRMN
cameraman
cameramen
KMRN
Cameroon
KMRS
commerce
KMRSH
camera-shy
KMRSHL
commercial
KMRSHLZ
commercialize
commercialized
commercializing
commercialization
KMRSHLZM
commercialism
KMS
camise(shirt)
KMSH
cumshaw(a tip)
KMSHFT
camshaft
KMSHN
commission
(agency,order)
commotion
(agitation)
KMSHNR
commissionaire
(doorman)
commissioner
KMSL
camisole
KMSN
kham sin
KMSR
commissar
commissary
commissaries
KMSRT
commensurate(equal)
commiserate(grief)
commiserated
commiserating
commiseration
commissariat

KMST
chemist
KMSTBL
comestible
KMSTR
chemistry
chemistries
Kama Sutra(book)
KMT
comet
comity
comities
commit
committed
committing
committee
KMTBL
committable
KMTL
committal
KMTMN
committeeman
committeemen
KMTMNT
commitment
KMTS
comatose
KMTV
calmative
KMV
commove
commoved
commoving
commotion
KMYDR
commuter
KMYN
commune
communed
communing
KMYNK
communiqué
KMYNKBL
communicable
KMYNKNT
communicant
KMYNKSHN
communication
KMYNKT
communicate
communicated
communicating
KMYNKTR
communicator
KMYNKTV
communicative

KMYNL
communal
KMYNLZ
communalize
communalized
communalizing
KMYNST
communist(or)C-
KMYNT
community
communities
KMYNYN
communion
KMYNZ
communize
communized
communizing
KMYNZM
communism
KMYT
commute
commuted
commuting
commuter
KMYTBL
commutable
KMYTR
commuter
KMYTSHN
commutation
KMYTT
commutate
commutated
commutating
KMYTTR
commutator
KMZ
camise(shirt)
KMZRT
commiserate(grief)
commiserated
commiserating
commiseration
commiserator
KN
achene(fruit)
acme(peak)
acne(disease)
akin
can(able)
could
can(metal)
canned
canning
canner
cane(sugar)

caned
caning
cane(stick)
caned
caning
canine(dog)
canny(shrewd)
cannier
canniest
cannily
canniness
canoe(boat)
canoed
cayenne
coin(money)
con
conned
conning
con(against)
cone
coned
coning
coney
(rabbit)
coon(raccoon)
icon
keen
ken(know)
kenned(or)kent
kenning
keno(game)
khan(title)
kin(family)
koan(zen)
koine(language)
oaken
quoin(wedge)
KNBL
cannibal
connubial
KNBLZ
cannibalize
cannibalized
cannibalizing
KNBR
Canberra
con brio
KNBS
cannabis
KNCH
conch
KNCHNCHS
conscientious
KNCHNS
conscience
KNCHNSHS

---

conscientious
KNCHNSTRKN
conscience-striken
KNCHRT
concerto
KNCHRTN
concertino
KNCHS
conscious
KND
Canada
candy
candied
candies
kind
kindly
kindlier
kindliest
kindliness
KNDD
candid
candied
candy
KNDDS
candidacy
candidacies
KNDDT
candidate
KNDGRDN
kindergarten
KNDHRTD
kindhearted
KNDK
kinetic
KNDKSHN
conduction
KNDKT
conduct
Connecticut
KNDKTBL
conductible
KNDKTNS
conductance
KNDKTR
conductor
KNDKTV
conductive
KNDL
candle(wax)
condole
condoled
condoling
kindle(fire)
kindled
kindling
kindly

kindlier
kindliest
kindliness
KNDLBR
candelabra
candelabra(or)
candelabras
KNDLBRM
candelabrum
candelabra(or)
candelabrums
KNDLFT
candle-foot
KNDLLT
candlelight
KNDLNG
kindling
KNDLNS
condolence
KNDLPNZ
candlepins
KNDLPR
candlepower
KNDLR
con dolore(sadly)
KNDLSTK
candlestick
KNDLTR
condolatory
KNDM
condemn
condom
KNDMNBL
condemnable
KNDMNM
condominium
KNDMNSHN
condemnation
KNDMNT
condiment
KNDMNTR
condemnatory
KNDMR
condemner
KNDN
condign
condone
condoned
condoning
KNDNS
condense
condensed
condensing
condenser
KNDNSBL
condensable

KNDNSR
condenser
KNDNSSHN
condensation
KNDNST
condensate
condensated
condensating
KNDR
candor, (B)candour
condor
KNDRD
kindred
KNDRGRTN
kindergarten
KNDRGRTNR
kindergartner
KNDS
candidacy
candidacies
conduce
conduced
conducing
KNDSHN
condition
conditioned
conditioner
KNDSHNL
conditional
KNDSHNNG
conditioning
KNDSHNR
conditioner
KNDSND
condescend
KNDSNDNS
condescendence
KNDSNS
candescence
KNDSNSHN
condescension
KNDSV
conducive
KNDT
candidate
conduit
KNDYS
conduce
conduced
conducing
KNDYSV
conducive
KNFB
confab
KNFBYLT
confabulate

confabulated
confabulating
KNFD
confetti(paper)
confide
confided
confiding
KNFDNCHL
confidential
KNFDNS
confidence
KNFDNSHL
confidential
KNFDNT
confidant(m)
confidante(f)
confident(sure)
KNFDRS
confederacy
confederacies
KNFDRSHN
confederation
KNFDRT
confederate
confederated
confederating
KNFGYR
configure
configured
configuring
KNFGYRSHN
configuration
KNFK
kinfolk
KNFKSHN
confection
KNFKSHNR
confectioner
confectionery
confectioneries
KNFKT
confect
KNFLGRNT
conflagrant
KNFLGRSHN
conflagration
KNFLKT
conflict
KNFLNS
confluence
KNFLNT
confluent
KNFN
confine
confined
confining

B:by **CH**:each **D**:day **F**:if **G**:go **H**:he **HW**:why **J**:joy **K**:cow **KS**:ax **KWL**:equal **L**:all **M**:may **N**:in

KNFNBL
confinable
KNFND
confound
KNFNMNT
confinement
KNFR
confer
  conferred
  conferring
  conferee
  conifer
KNFRBL
conferrable
KNFRL
conferral
KNFRM
confirm
  conform
KNFRMBL
confirmable
  conformable
KNFRML
conformal
KNFRMNS
conformance
KNFRMNT
conferment
KNFRMR
conformer
KNFRMSHN
confirmation(sure)
conformation(same)
KNFRMST
conformist
KNFRMT
conformity
  conformities
KNFRMTR
confirmatory
KNFRNS
conference
KNFRNT
confront
KNFRR
conferrer
  confrere(colleague)
KNFS
confess
  confesses
KNFSDL
confessedly
KNFSHN
confession
KNFSHNL
confessional

KNFSKSHN
confiscation
KNFSKT
confiscate
  confiscated
  confiscating
KNFSKTR
confiscator
  confiscatory
KNFSR
confessor
KNFT
confetti
KNFYSHS
Confucius
KNFYT
confute
  confuted
  confuting
KNFYTR
confuter
KNFYTSHN
confutation
KNFYZ
confuse
  confused
  confusing
KNFYZHN
confusion
KNG
cangue(pillory)
Congo
okaying(or)
OK'ing
king
KNGBLT
kingbolt
KNGDM
kingdom
KNGG
Congo
congou(tea)
KNGGRNS
congruence
KNGGRNT
congruent
KNGGRS
Congress(law)
congress
  congresses
  congruous
KNGGRSHNL
Congressional
  congressional
KNGGRSMN
congressman

Congressman(title)
  congressmen
KNGGRSWMN
congresswoman
Congresswoman(title)
  congresswomen
KNGF
kung fu
KNGFSH
kingfish
KNGK
conch
conk(hit,tire)
kink
kinky
  kinkier
  kinkiest
  kinkily
  kinkiness
KNGKR
canker(sore)
conquer
KNGKRR
conqueror
KNGKRS
cankerous
KNGKRWRM
cankerworm
KNGKT
conk out(stop)
KNGKYBN
concubine
KNGL
kingly
  kinglier
  kingliest
  kingliness
KNGLMRSHN
conglomeration
KNGLMRT
conglomerate
  conglomerated
  conglomerating
KNGM
con game
KNGPN
kingpin
KNGPST
kingpost
KNGR
kangaroo
KNGRCHLSHN
congratulation
KNGRCHLT
congratulate
  congratulated

congratulating
KNGRCHLTR
congratulator
  congratulatory
KNGRFK
iconographic
KNGRGSHN
congregation
KNGRGT
congregate
  congregated
  congregating
KNGRGTR
congregator
KNGRNS
congruence
KNGRNT
congruent
KNGRS
Congress(law)
congress
  congresses
  congruous
KNGRSHNL
Congressional(law)
  congressional
KNGRSMN
congressman
Congressman(title)
  congressmen
KNGRSWMN
congresswoman
Congresswoman(title)
  congresswomen
KNGRT
congruity
  congruities
KNGSZ
king-size
  king-sized
KNHND
coonhound
KNJ
coinage
congee
  congeed
  congeeing
KNJGL
conjugal
KNJGSHN
conjugation
KNJGT
conjugate
  conjugated
  conjugating
KNJGTR

NGK:ink **P**:pie **R**:air **S**:ice **SH**:show **T**:toy **THN**:thin **TH**:the **V**:of **W**:we **Y**:you **Z**:is **VZHN**:vision

conjugator
KNJKCHR
 conjecture
  conjectured
  conjecturing
KNJKCHRBL
 conjecturable
KNJKCHRL
 conjectural
KNJKCHRR
 conjecturer
KNJL
 congeal
KNJLBL
 congealable
KNJNGKSHN
 conjunction
KNJNGKT
 conjunct
KNJNGKTV
 conjunctiva(eye
  mucous membrane)
 conjunctive
KNJNL
 congenial
KNJNTL
 congenital
KNJNYL
 congenial
KNJR
 conjure
  conjured
  conjuring
KNJRR
 conjurer
KNJRSHN
 conjuration
KNJRZ
 congeries
KNJSCHN
 congestion
KNJST
 congest
KNJSTV
 congestive
KNK
 Canuck(slang)
 conic
 iconic
KNKDNT
 concatenate
  concatenated
  concatenating
  concatenation
KNKKSHN
 concoction

KNKKT
 concoct(make)
 concocter
KNKL
 conical
KNKLD
 conclude
  concluded
  concluding
KNKLJ
 conchology
KNKLST
 iconoclast
KNKLSV
 conclusive
KNKLV
 conclave
KNKLZHN
 conclusion
KNKLZV
 conclusive
KNKMTNS
 concomitance
KNKMTNT
 concomitant
KNKN
 cancan
 Cancun
KNKR
 concur
  concurred
  concurring
 conquer
KNKRD
 Concord
 concord
KNKRDNS
 concordance
KNKRDNT
 concordant
KNKRDT
 concordat
KNKRNS
 concurrence
KNKRNT
 concurrent
KNKRS
 concourse
KNKRSHN
 concretion
KNKRT
 concrete
  concreted
  concreting
KNKS
 concuss(brain)

concusses
 concussive
KNKSHN
 concussion
 connection, (B)-
KNKSV nexion
 concussive
KNKT
 concoct
 connect
KNKTBL
 connectable
KNKTNSHN
 concatenation
KNKTNT
 concatenate
  concatenated
  concatenating
KNKTR
 concocter
 connector
KNKTV
 connective
KNKV
 concave
  concaved
  concaving
KNKVT
 concavity
  concavities
KNKWBN
 concubine
KNKWST
 conquest
KNKWSTDR
 conquistador
KNKYBN
 concubine
KNKYPSNS
 concupiscence
KNKYPSNT
 concupiscent
KNL
 achenial
 canal(waterway)
 kennel
KNLBT
 canalboat
KNLJ
 acknowledge
  acknowledged
  acknowledging
KNLJBL
 acknowledgeable
KNLJMNT
 acknowledgment

KNLKL
 cannel coal
KNLNGS
 cunnilingus
KNLZ
 canalize
  canalized
  canalizing
KNM
 economy
  economies
KNMK
 economic
KNMKL
 economical
KNMN
 con man
 con men
KNMR
 con amore(music)
KNMST
 economist
KNMTK
 kinematic
KNMTKS
 kinematics
KNMZ
 economize
  economized
  economizing
  economizer
KNN
 canine(dog)
 cannon(weapon)
 canon(standard)
KNNBL
 cannonball
KNND
 cannonade
  cannonaded
  cannonading
KNNDRM
 conundrum
KNNG
 canning(can)
 cunning
KNNKL
 canonical
KNNL
 canon law
KNNR
 cannoneer
KNNZ
 canonize
  canonized
  canonizing

B:by **CH**:each **D**:day **F**:if **G**:go **H**:he **HW**:why **J**:joy **K**:cow **KS**:ax **KWL**:equal **L**:all **M**:may **N**:in

canonization
conenose(bug)
KNP
canapé(food)
canopy
canopies
KNPRS
coin purse
KNPSHN
conniption
KNR
canary(bird)
canaries
canner(can)
cannery, -ries(pl)
counter
Kohinoor(diamond)
KNRL
Conrail
KNRD
canard(lie)
KNRFT
counterfeit
KNS
keenness
KNSBSTNSHSHN
consubstantiation
KNSD
coincide
coincided
coinciding
concede
conceded
conceding
KNSDD
conceited
conceit
KNSDNS
coincidence
KNSDNT
coincident
KNSDNTL
coincidental
KNSDR
consider
KNSDRBL
considerable
KNSDRD
considered
KNSDRNG
considering
KNSDRSHN
consideration
KNSDRT
considerate
KNSHN

conation
KNSHNBL
conscionable
KNSHNCHS
conscientious
KNSHNS
conscience
KNSHNSHS
conscientious
KNSHNSTRKN
conscience-stricken
KNSHP
kinship
KNSHR
coinsure
coinsured
coinsuring
KNSHRNS
coinsurance
KNSHRR
coinsurer
KNSHS
conscious
Kinshasa
KNSHSNS
consciousness
KNSKN
coonskin
KNSKP
kinescope
KNSKRPSHN
conscription
KNSKRPT
conscript
KNSKRSHN
consecration
KNSKRT
consecrate
consecrated
consecrating
KNSKRTR
consecrator
KNSKTV
consecutive
KNSKWNCHL
consequential
KNSKWNS
consequence
KNSKWNSHL
consequential
KNSKWNT
consequent
KNSKYTV
consecutive
KNSL
cancel(void)

conceal
console(furniture)
console(cheer)
consoled
consoling
consoler
consul(government)
council(group)
counsel(idea)
KNSLBL
cancelable
consolable
KNSLDSHN
consolidation
KNSLDT
consolidate
consolidated
consolidating
KNSLDTR
consolidator
KNSLMN
councilman
councilmen
KNSLR
canceler(void)
conciliar
consoler
(comfort)
consular(official)
councilor(person,
member of a
council)
counselor(advisor)
KNSLSGNRL
consuls general
KNSLSHN
cancellation(void)
conciliation
consolation
(comfort)
KNSLT
conciliate
(reconcile)
conciliated
conciliating
consulate(office)
consult
KNSLTNG
consulting
KNSLTNT
consultant
KNSLTR
conciliator
conciliatory
(reconcile)
consolatory

(comfort)
consulter
KNSLTSHN
consultation
KNSLTTV
consultative
KNSM
consommé
consume
consumed
consuming
consumer
KNSMBL
consumable
KNSMPSHN
consumption
KNSMPTV
consumptive
KNSMR
consumer
KNSMRZM
consumerism
KNSMSHN
consummation
KNSMT
consummate
consummated
consummating
KNSMTR
consummator
consummatory
KNSN
consign
consignee
KNSNBL
consignable
KNSNGWN
consanguine
KNSNGWNS
consanguineous
KNSNGWNT
consanguinity
KNSNMNT
consignment
KNSNNS
consonance
KNSNNT
consonant
KNSNNTL
consonantal
KNSNR
consignor
KNSNSHL
consensual
KNSNSS
consensus

KNSNT
concinnity
consent
KNSNTR
concenter(center)
consenter(consent)
KNSNTRK
concentric
KNSNTRSHN
concentration
KNSNTRT
concentrate
concentrated
concentrating
KNSNTRTR
concentrator
KNSPCHL
conceptual
KNSPCHLZ
conceptualize
conceptualized
conceptualizing
KNSPCHLZSHN
conceptualization
KNSPKTS
conspectus
KNSPKYS
conspicuous
KNSPR
conspire
conspired
conspiring
KNSPRS
conspiracy
conspiracies
KNSPRTR
conspirator
KNSPSHN
conception
KNSPT
concept
KNSR
Cancer
cancer
connoisseur
KNSRJ
concierge
KNSRN
concern
KNSRS
cancerous
KNSRSHM
consortium
KNSRT
concert
consort

NSRTM
consortium
KNSRTMSTR
concertmaster
KNSRTN
concertina
KNSRV
conserve
conserved
conserving
KNSRVNS
conservancy
conservancies
KNSRVSHN
conservation
KNSRVTR
conservator
conservatory
conservatories
KNSRVTV
conservative
KNSRZH
concierge
KNSS
concise
KNSSHN
concession
(grant)
concision
(brevity)
KNSSHNR
concessionaire
concessionary
KNSST
consist
KNSSTNS
consistence
consistency
consistencies
KNSSTNT
consistent
KNSSTR
consistory
consistories
KNST
canasta
canoeist
conceit(vanity)
Knesset
KNSTBL
constable
KNSTBYLR
constabular
constabulary
constabularies
KNSTCHNS

constituency
constituencies
KNSTCHNT
constituent
KNSTD
conceited
KNSTHK
kinesthetic
KNSTHZH
kinesthesia
KNSTLSHN
constellation
KNSTLT
constellate
constellated
constellating
constellatory
KNSTNS
constancy
constancies
KNSTNT
constant
KNSTNTNPL
Constantinople
KNSTPSHN
constipation
KNSTPT
constipate
constipated
constipating
KNSTR
canister
construe
construed
construing
KNSTRBL
construable
KNSTRKSHN
constriction
construction(build)
KNSTRKT
constrict
construct
KNSTRKTR
constrictor
constructor
KNSTRKTV
constrictive
constructive
KNSTRN
constrain
constrainable
constrainer
KNSTRNSHN
consternation
KNSTRNT

consternate
consternated
consternating
constraint
KNSTTSHN
constitution
KNSTTSHNL
constitutional
KNSTTT
constitute
constituted
constituting
KNSTTYSHN
constitution
KNSTTYSHNL
constitutional
KNSTTYT
constitute
constituted
constituting
KNSV
conceive
conceived
conceiving
KNSVBL
conceivable
KNSVR
conceiver
KNSYM
consume
consumed
consuming
consumer
consumable
KNSYMRZM
consumerism
KNSYRZH
concierge
KNSZHN
concision
KNT
account
cannot
cant(direction)
cant(noise)
can't(cannot)
canto(music,
poetry)
Comte, August
connate(from birth)
connote
connoted
connoting
conte(story)
contes
count

B:by **CH**:each **D**:day **F**:if **G**:go **H**:he **HW**:why **J**:joy **K**:cow **KS**:ax **KWL**:equal **L**:all **M**:may **N**:in

county
  counties
cunt(vulgar)
keynote
  keynoted
  keynoting
KNTBL
  accountable
  countable
KNTD
  cantata
KNTDN
  countdown
KNTGYS
  contiguous
KNTGYT
  contiguity
  contiguities
KNTHD
  acanthoid
KNTHS
  acanthus
  acanthuses(or)
  acanthi
KNTJM
  contagium(direct
  cause)
KNTJN
  contagion
  (influence)
KNTJS
  contagious
KNTK
  Kentucky
  kinetic
KNTKCHL
  contactual
KNTKDRB
  Kentucky Derby
  The Derby
KNTKL
  canticle(hymn)
KNTKS
  context
  kinetics
KNTKSCHL
  contextual
KNTKSHL
  contextual
KNTKST
  context
KNTKT
  Connecticut
  contact
KNTKTR
  contactor

KNTL
  cantle
KNTLP
  cantaloupe
KNTLS
  countless
KNTLVR
  cantilever
KNTM
  contemn
KNTMCHS
  contemptuous
KNTML
  contumely
KNTMLS
  contumelious
KNTMNNT
  contaminant
KNTMNSHN
  contamination
KNTMNT
  contaminate
  contaminated
  contaminating
KNTMNTR
  contaminator
KNTMPCHS
  contemptuous
KNTMPLSHN
  contemplation
KNTMPLT
  contemplate
  contemplated
  contemplating
KNTMPLTR
  contemplator
KNTMPLTV
  contemplative
KNTMPRNS
  contemporaneous
KNTMPRNT
  contemporaneity
KNTMPRR
  contemporary
  contemporaries
KNTMPT
  contempt
KNTMPTBL
  contemptible
KNTMPTCHWS
  contemptous
KNTMR
  contemner
KNTMS
  contumacy
  contumacies

KNTMSHS
  contemptuous
  contumacious
KNTMT
  contempt
KNTN
  canteen(water)
  cantina(bar)
  Canton(city)
  canton(area)
  contain(hold)
  contend
KNTNBL
  containable
KNTNCHN
  contention
KNTNCHS
  contentious
KNTND
  contend
  contented(rest)
KNTNDR
  contender
KNTNGKRS
  cantankerous
KNTNJNS
  contingence
  contingency
  contingencies
KNTNJNT
  contingent
KNTNKRS
  cantankerous
KNTNNS
  continence(or)
  continency
  (moderation)
  countenance
  (appearance)
  continents(pl)
KNTNNT
  continent
KNTNNTL
  continental
KNTNR
  container
KNTNRZ
  containerize
  containerized
  containerizing
KNTNS
  accountancy
KNTNSHN
  contention
KNTNSHS
  contentious

KNTNT
  accountant
  content
  continuity
  continuities
KNTNTD
  contented
KNTNTMNT
  contentment
KNTNY
  continue
  continued
  continuing
KNTNYL
  continual
KNTNYM
  continuum
KNTNYNS
  continuance
KNTNYNT
  continuant
KNTNYS
  continuous
KNTNYSHN
  continuation
KNTNYT
  continuity
  continuities
KNTNYTR
  continuator
KNTNYWSHN
  continuation
KNTR
  canter(pace)
  cantor(singer)
  counter
  contour(shape)
  country
  countries
  keynoter
KNTRBLNS
  counterbalance
  counterbalanced
  counterbalancing
KNTRBND
  contraband
KNTRBYSHN
  contribution
KNTRBYT
  contribute
  contributed
  contributing
KNTRBYTR
  contributor
  contributory
KNTRDKT

contradict
KNTRDKTBL
contradictable
KNTRDKTR
contradictor
contradictory
KNTRDSTNGKSHN
contradistinction
KNTRDSTNGWSH
contradistinguish
KNTRF
countrify
countrified
countrifies
KNTRFT
counterfeit
KNTRKCHL
contractual
KNTRKLB
country club
KNTRKLM
counterclaim
KNTRKSHN
contraction
KNTRKT
contract
counteract
KNTRKTBL
contractible
KNTRKTL
contractile
KNTRKTR
contractor
KNTRKLKWZ
counterclockwise
KNTRL
contrail(trail)
control
controlled
controlling
KNTRLBL
controllable
KNTRLBLT
controllability
KNTRLR
comptroller
(auditor)
controller
KNTRLT
contralto
KNTRMND
countermand
KNTRMNS
conterminous
KNTRMV
countermove

countermoved
countermoving
KNTRMYZK
country music
KNTRNTLJNS
counter-
intelligence
KNTRPN
counterpane
KNTRPNT
counterpoint
KNTRPRDKTV
counterproductive
KNTRPRT
counterpart
KNTRPSHN
contraption
KNTRR
contrary
contraries
contrarily
contrariness
KNTRRT
contrariety
contrarieties
KNTRRWZ
contrariwise
KNTRSD
countryside
KNTRSHN
contortion
contrition
KNTRSHNST
contortionist
KNTRSN
countersign
KNTRSNGK
countersink
countersunk
KNTRSP
counterspy
KNTRSPNZH
counterespionage
KNTRSPSHN
contraception
KNTRSPTV
contraceptive
KNTRST
contrast
contrasty
KNTRSTBL
contrastable
KNTRT
contort
contrite
KNTRTK

counterattack
KNTRTN
contretemps
KNTRV
contrive
contrived
contriving
KNTRVBL
contrivable
KNTRVN
contravene
contravened
contravening
contravener
contravention
KNTRVNS
contrivance
KNTRVR
contriver
KNTRVRS
controversy
controversies
KNTRVRSHL
controversial
KNTRVRT
controvert
KNTRVRTBL
controvertible
KNTRVRTR
controverter
KNTRWT
counterweight
KNTS
conatus
countess
countesses
KNTSHN
connotation
KNTST
contest
KNTSTBL
contestable
KNTSTNT
contestant
KNTT
cantata
KNTV
conative
KNTYZ
contuse
contused
contusing
contusion
KNTZ
contuse
contused

contusing
KNTZHN
contusion
KNV
connive
connived
conniving
conniver
convey
convoy
KNVBL
conveyable
KNVK
convict
convoke
convoked
convoking
KNVKS
convex
KNVKSHN
convection
(motion)
conviction
(belief)
convocation
KNVKST
convexity
convexities
KNVKT
convict
KNVKTR
convector
KNVKTV
convective
KNVLS
convalesce
(recover)
convalesced
convalescing
convulse
(shake)
convulsed
convulsing
KNVLSHN
convolution
convulsion
KNVLSNS
convalescence
KNVLSNT
convalescent
KNVLSV
convulsive
KNVLT
convolute
convoluted
convoluting

B:by **CH**:each **D**:day **F**:if **G**:go **H**:he **HW**:why **J**:joy **K**:cow **KS**:ax **KWL**:equal **L**:all **M**:may **N**:in

KNVN
convene
convened
convening
KNVNCHN
convention
KNVNNT
convenient
KNVNR
convener
KNVNS
connivance
conveyance
convince
convinced
convincing
KNVNSBL
convincible
KNVNSHN
convention
KNVNSHNL
conventional
KNVNSHNR
conventioneer
KNVNSNG
convincing
KNVNSR
convincer
KNVNT
convent
KNVNYNS
convenience
KNVNYNT
convenient
KNVR
conniver
conveyer(person)
conveyor(machine)
KNVRJ
converge
converged
converging
KNVRJNS
convergence
convergency
KNVRJNT
convergent
KNVRS
converse
conversed
conversing
KNVRSBL
conversable
KNVRSNS
conversance
conversancy

KNVRSNT
conversant
KNVRSSHN
conversation
KNVRSSHNLST
conversationalist
KNVRSSHNST
conversationist
KNVRT
convert
KNVRTBL
convertible
KNVRTR
converter
KNVRZHN
conversion
KNVS
canvas(cloth)
canvases
canvass(poll)
canvasses
KNVSR
canvasser
KNVVL
convivial
KNVVLT
conviviality
convivialities
KNW
Okinawa
KNY
Kenya
KNYK
cognac
KNYL
cannula
cannulae(or)
cannulas
KNYN
canyon
KNYSHNT
cognoscente
cognoscenti
KNZ
cons
pros and cons
KNZH
congé
KNZJ
coon's age
KNZMN
kinsman
kinsmen
KNZN
Keynesian
(economics)

John Keynes
KNZS
Kansas
KNZST
Kansas City
KP
cap(hat,top)
capped
capping
cape(cloth)
caped
caping
capo(music)
coop(cage)
co-op
cop(slang)
copped
copping
cope(contend)
coped
coping
copy
copied
copies
copier
coup(successful
move)
coupe(auto)
cup
cupped
cupping
keep
kept
KPBK
copybook
KPBL
capable(ability)
capably
culpable(guilty)
KPBLT
capability,-ties
KPBRR
cupbearer
KPCHLSHN
capitulation
KPCHLT
capitulate
capitulated
capitulating
KPCHN
cappuccino
KPCHR
capture
captured
capturing
KPDSK

copy desk
KPFL
cupful
KPK
cowpoke
kapok
KPKD
Cape Cod
KPKK
cupcake
KPKT
copycat
KPL
a cappella
couple
coupled
coupling
KPLK
Acapulco
KPLNG
coupling
KPLR
capillary
capillaries
coupler
KPLT
copilot
couplet(verse)
KPN
capon
coupon
cow pony
cow ponies
KPNCH
key punch
KPNCHR
cowpuncher
KPNGS
coping saw
KPNHGN
Copenhagen
KPNZ
caponize
caponized
caponizing
KPR
caper(plant,
adventure)
capper(cap)
cooper(barrel)
copier(copy)
copper(metal)
coppery
copra(coconut)
keeper
KPRHD

copperhead
KPRKRN
 Capricorn
KPRLJ
 coprology
KPRNKS
 Copernicus
 Copernican
KPRS
 caprice
KPRSHN
 cooperation
KPRSHS
 capricious
KPRSN
 caparison(finery)
KPRSNR
 coparcenary
KPRT
 cooperate
 cooperated
 cooperating
 copyright
KPRTBL
 copyrightable
KPRTCH
 a capriccio
KPRTNR
 copartner(or)
 co-partner
KPRTR
 copyrighter(law)
 copywriter(writer)
KPRTV
 cooperative
KPS
 capias(law)
 copious
KPSDK
 copacetic
KPSH
 capuche(hood)
KPSHN
 caption
 co-option
KPSHS
 capacious(roomy)
 captious
KPSK
 keepsake
KPSL
 capsule
KPSLR
 capsular
KPSLZ
 capsulize

capsulized
 capsulizing
KPST
 capacity
 capacities
 copyist
KPSTK
 copacetic
KPSTN
 capstan
 capstone(or)
 copestone
KPSTR
 capacitor
KPSTT
 capacitate
 capacitated
 capacitating
KPSZ
 capsize
 capsized
 capsizing
KPT
 co-opt
 cop out(v)
 cop-out(n)
 kaput
 kept(keep)
KPTL
 capital
 capitol(building)
KPTLST
 capitalist
KPTLZ
 capitalize
 capitalized
 capitalizing
KPTLZM
 capitalism
KPTN
 Capetown
 captain
KPTNS
 captaincy
KPTR
 captor
KPTSHN
 co-optation
KPTVT
 captivate
 captivated
 captivating
 captivity
 captivities
KPTVTR
 captivator

KPVRD
 Cape Verde
KPYLSHN
 copulation
KPYLT
 copulate
 copulated
 copulating
KR
 Accra
 accrue
 accrued
 accruing
 acre(area)
 acreage
 Cairo
 car
 CARE(needy)
 care
 cared
 caring
 carry
 carried
 carries
 carrier
 Chi-Rho(symbol)
 choir(music)
 chorea(disease)
 coheir
 coir(fiber)
 core(center)
 cored
 coring
 corps(group)
 cower(fear)
 craw
 crew(people)
 crow(animal)
 cry
 cried
 cries
 cur(dog)
 currish
 curry
 curried
 curries
 ecru(color)
 Korea
 Korean
 ocher
 ochery
 occur(happen)
 occurred
 occurring
KRB
 carabao

caribou(elk)
 crab
 crabbed
 crabbing
 crabby
 crabbier
 crabbiest
 crabbily
 crabbiness
 crib
 cribbed
 cribbing
 curb, (B)(or)kerb
KRBB
 crybaby
 crybabies
KRBD
 crabbed
 crabbing
 crab
KRBGRS
 crabgrass
 crabgrasses
KRBJ
 cribbage
KRBKK
 crab cake(food)
KRBL
 corbel
KRBLJ
 cryobiology
KRBLNG
 corbeling
KRBMT
 crab meat
KRBN
 carbine(firearm)
 carbon(element)
 Caribbean
KRBNBLK
 carbon black
KRBNG
 crabbing
 cribbing
KRBNGKL
 carbuncle
KRBNKP
 carbon copy
 carbon copies
KRBNL
 carbinol
KRBNPPR
 carbon paper
KRBNR
 carbineer
KRBNS

Caribbean Sea
KRBNT
carbonate
carbonated
carbonating
carbonation
KRBNZ
carbonize
carbonized
carbonizing
carbonization
KRBPL
crab apple
KRBR
crabber
cribber
crowbar
KRBRSHN
corroboration
KRBRT
corroborate
corroborated
corroborating
KRBRTR
carburetor
corroborator
corroboratory
KRBRTV
corroborative
KRBSTN
curbstone
KRBT
acrobat
KRBYRTR
carburetor
KRCH
caroche(carriage)
crotch
crotches
crouch
crouches
crutch
crutches
Karachi
KRCHF
kerchief
KRCHLR
cartulary
cartularies
KRCHR
creature
KRCHT
crotchet
crotchety
crotchetiness
KRD

acarid(mite or
  tick)
accord
acrid
caird(handyman)
card
chord(music)
cord(rope,wood)
corrade(erode)
  corraded
  corrading
corrode(erode by
  chemical action)
  corroded
  corroding
coward
credo
creed
crowd
crud(filth)
cruddy
crude(unrefined)
curd
KRDB
Cordoba(city)
cordoba(money)
KRDBL
corrodible
credible
creditable(praise)
KRDBRD
cardboard
KRDGN
cardigan
KRDGRM
cardiogram
KRDJ
cartage
  (transportation)
cordage(rope)
KRDK
cardiac
critic
KRDKL
critical
KRDL
creedal
cradle(crib)
  cradled
  cradling
curdle
  curdled
  curdling
KRDLGST
cardiologist
KRDLSNG

cradlesong
KRDLT
credulity
  credulities
KRDN
accordion
cordon
KRDNCHL
credential
KRDNL
cardinal
KRDNS
credence
accordance
KRDNSHL
credential
KRDNSHN
coordination
KRDNT
accordant
coordinate
  coordinated
  coordinating
  coordinator
corrodent
corrode
KRDNTR
coordinator
KRDNZ
credenza
KRDR
corduroy
corridor
cotter(pin)
crater(pit)
creator(maker)
critter(animal)
KRDS
cards
courteous
courtesy
  courtesies
cowardice
KRDSHRP
cardsharp
KRDT
accredit
acridity
credit
creditor
crudity
  crudities
crude
KRDTBL
creditable
KRDTBYR

credit bureau
KRDTR
creditor
KRDTSHN
accreditation
KRDTYNYN
credit union
KRDV
creative
KRDVN
cordovan
KRDWD
cordwood
KRDYLT
credulity
  credulities
KRF
carafe
corf(truck)
corves
kerf(groove)
KRFB
acrophobia
KRFL
careful
KRFR
carefree
KRFSH
craw-fish(v)
crawfish(n)(or)
crayfish
KRFT
craft(skill)
crafty
  craftier
  craftiest
  craftily
  craftiness
kraft(paper)
KRFTSMNSHP
craftsmanship
KRFTYNYN
craft union
KRFY
curfew
KRG
crag
craggy
  craggier
  craggiest
  cragginess
cargo
  cargoes
corgi(dog)
KRGRF
choreography

---

choreographies
KRGRFR
choreographer
KRGSHN
corrugation
KRGT
corrugate
corrugated
corrugating
KRJ
acreage
carriage
courage
KRJBL
corrigible
KRJL
cordial
KRJLS
credulous
KRJLT
cordiality
cordialities
KRJN
acrogen(plant)
cryogen
KRJNDM
corrigendum
corrigenda
KRJNKS
cryogenics
cryogenic
KRJS
courageous
KRK
cork
corky
corkier
corkiness
crack
cracky
by cracky
crake(bird)
creak(sound)
creek(stream)
crick(muscle
cramp)
croak
crock(pot)
crook(outlaw)
croquet(game)
Krakow
KRKBND
carrick bend
KRKBRN
crackbrain
KRKCHR

caricature
caricatured
caricaturing
KRKCHRST
caricaturist
KRKDL
crocodile
KRKDN
crackdown(n)
crack down(v)
KRKF
Kharkov
KRKL
caracul(fur)
coracle(boat)
crackle(sound)
crackled,-ling
karakul
KRKM
currycomb
KRKP
crack-up(n)
KRKPT
crackpot
KRKR
corker
cracker
crockery
crockeries
KRKRBRL
cracker-barrel
KRKRJK
crackerjack
KRKS
Caracas
carcass
carcasses
crocus
crux
cruces(or)
cruxes
KRKSHN
correction
KRKSKR
corkscrew
KRKT
corked
correct
crew cut
cricket
croquette(food)
KRKTBL
correctable
KRKTR
caricature
caricatured

caricaturing
character
corrector
KRKTRSTK
characteristic
KRKTRSTKL
characteristically
KRKTRZ
characterize
characterized
characterizing
characterization
KRKTTD
correctitude
KRKTTYD
correctitude
KRKTYR
caricature
caricatured
caricaturing
KRKV
Kharkov
KRKYL
curricula
curriculum
KRKYLM
curriculum
curricula
KRKYLMVT
curriculum vitae
KRKYLR
curricular
KRL
accrual
cariole(carriage)
carol, (B)-lled, -lling
carrel(place)
carryall
choral(chorus)
chorale(musical
piece)
coral(reef)
corolla(flower)
corral(enclosure)
corralled
corralling
crawl
creel(basket)
Creole(person)
crewel(yarn)
cruel(manner)
curl
curly
curlier
curliest
curliness

krill(marine
animal)
KRLD
carload
coralloid(coral)
KRLK
acrylic
KRLKY
curlicue
KRLN
carillon
KRLNG
caroling
curling(game)
KRLR
caroler(singer)
corollary
corollaries
crueler
cruel(pain)
cruelest
cruller(cake)
curler(hair)
KRLRF
coral reef
KRLS
careless
Coral Sea
KRLSHN
correlation
KRLSNK
coral snake
KRLT
correlate, (B)corelate
correlated
correlating
cruelty
cruelties
cryolite(ice stone)
KRLTV
correlative
KRLWRK
crewelwork
KRLYN
carillon
KRM
carom
chrome(metal)
chromed
chroming
cram
crammed
cramming
cream(milk)
creamy
creamier

---

creamiest
creaminess
crime
crumb
crummy
crummier
crummiest
karma
KRMB
corymb(flower)
KRMBL
crumble
crumbled
crumbling
crumbly
crumblier
crumbliest
crumbliness
KRMCHZ
cream cheese
KRMDLKRM
crème de la crème
KRMDMNT
crème de menthe
KRMJN
curmudgeon
KRMK
achromic
chromic
KRMKLRD
cream-colored
KRML
caramel
KRMLK
cromlech
KRMLZ
caramelize
caramelized
caramelizing
KRMM
chromium
KRMN
corpsman
corpsmen
acrimony
carman
carmine(color)
KRMNL
criminal
KRMNLJ
criminology
KRMNLZ
criminalize
criminalized
criminalizing
KRMNS

acrimonious
KRMNSHN
crimination
KRMNT
accruement
criminate
criminated
criminating
KRMP
cramp
crimp
crimpy
crimpier
crimpiest
crump
KRMPF
cream puff
KRMPL
crumple
crumpled
crumpling
KRMPN
crampon
KRMPT
crumpet(bread)
KRMR
crammer
creamer
creamery
creameries
krimmer(fur)
KRMRNT
cormorant
KRMS
kermis
KRMSHN
cremation
KRMSM
chromosome
KRMSN
crimson
KRMSS
cream sauce
KRMSTL
chrome steel
KRMT
cremate
cremated
cremating
cremation
KRMTK
achromatic
chromatic(color)
KRMTKL
achromatical
chromatical

KRMTR
cremator
crematory
crematories
cryometer(cold)
KRMTRM
crematorium
crematoria
KRMTS
achromatous
chromatous
KRMTZ
achromatize
achromatized
achromatizing
chromatize
chromatized
chromatizing
KRMZN
crimson
KRN
acorn
Akron
au courant
cairn(stones)
careen
carny(carnival)
carnies
carrion
carrion
corn
corny
cornier
corniest
cornea(eye)
corona(halo)
crane
craned
craning
cranny
crannies
crannied
crayon
crone(woman)
crony(friend)
cronies
croon(sing)
crown
kern
Koran
Korean
koruna
krona(Sweden)
krone(Denmark)
ocarina
KRNB

carnauba(palm)
KRNBL
cornball
KRNBLT
Corn Belt
KRNBR
cranberry
cranberries
KRNBRD
corn bread
KRNCH
crunch
crunches
KRNCHR
crenature
KRNDJR
corndodger
KRNFD
corn-fed
KRNFLD
cornfield
KRNFLKS
cornflakes
KRNFLR
cornflower
KRNG
crying
KRNGK
crank
cranky
crankier
crankiest
crankily
crankiness
KRNGKL
caruncle(a growth)
crinkle
crinkled
crinkling
crinkly
KRNGKPN
crankpin(part)
KRNGKS
crankcase
KRNGKSHFT
crankshaft
KRNGL
cringle
KRNGRM
cairngorm(gem)
KRNGZN
carryings-on
KRNHSKNG
cornhusking
KRNHWSK
corn whiskey

NGK:ink **P**:pie **R**:air **S**:ice **SH**:show **T**:toy **THN**:thin **TH**:the **V**:of **W**:we **Y**:you **Z**:is **VZHN**:vision

KRNJ
carnage
cringe
  cringed
  cringing
KRNJR
cringer
KRNK
chronic
crew neck
KRNKB
corncob
KRNKL
chronicle(record)
  chronicled
  chronicling
  chronical(long-
  term)
KRNKP
cornucopia
KRNKRB
corncrib
KRNKS
cryonics(bodies)
KRNL
carnal
colonel(rank)
cornel(shrub)
cranial
crenel(notch)
  crenelate
kernel(grain)
KRNLJ
chronology
  chronologies
craniology(skull)
KRNLJKL
chronological
KRNLN
crinoline
KRNLS
colonelcy
KRNLSHN
crenelation, (B)- llation
KRNLT
crenelate, (B)-llate
  crenelated
  crenelating
KRNLYN
carnelian(color)
KRNM
acronym
cranium
KRNML
cornmeal
KRNMTR

chronometer
KRNN
Ukrainian
KRNPN
corn pone
KRNR
coronary
  coronaries
corner
coroner(death)
crooner(singer)
KRNRBK
cornerback
KRNRSTN
cornerstone
KRNRWZ
cornerwise
KRNS
cornice
currency
  currencies
occurrence
KRNSH
Cornish
KRNSHHN
Cornish hen
KRNSHN
carnation
coronation
crenation
KRNSLK
corn silk
KRNSRP
corn syrup
KRNSTK
cornstalk
KRNSTRCH
cornstarch
  cornstarches
KRNT
cornet(horn)
crenate
  crenated
  crenating
  crenation
currant(fruit)
current(flow)
KRNTH
Corinth
KRNTHN
Corinthian
KRNTST
cornetist
KRNVL
carnival
KRNVR

carnivore
KRNVRS
carnivorous
KRNWSK
corn whiskey
KRNYLT
crenulate(notch)
  crenulated,-ting
KRNZM
cronyism
KRP
carp
crap
crappie(also pl)(fish)
crappy(slang, vulgar)
  crappier
  crappiest
  crappiness
creep
  crept
  creeper
creepy(scary)
  creepier,-iest
  creepiness
crepe(material)
crop
  cropped
  cropping
  cropper
croup(sickness,
  rump)
croupier(person)
crypt(grave)
KRPD
chiropody
KRPDR
curry powder
KRPDST
chiropodist
KRPL
car pool(n)
carpool(v)
carpul(wrist)
  carpus
cripple
  crippled
  crippling
KRPLS
acropolis
KRPMRTL
crape myrtle
KRPNDR
carpenter
carpentry
KRPNG
carping

KRPNTR
carpenter
carpentry
KRPPPR
crepe paper
KRPR
creeper
cropper
croupier(gamble)
crupper(strap)
KRPRBR
crepe rubber
KRPRD
crop-eared
KRPRKTK
chiropractic
KRPRKTR
chiropractor
KRPRL
corporal(body,
  rank)
corporeal(physical)
KRPRSHN
corporation
KRPRT
carport
corporate
KRPS
carpus(wrist)
carpul
craps(game)
corpse(dead body)
corpus
KRPSDLKT
corpus delicti
KRPSHN
corruption
KRPSHTR
crapshooter
KRPSJRS
corpus juris
KRPSKRST
Corpus Christi
KRPSKYL
crepuscule
KRPSKYLR
crepuscular
KRPSL
corpuscle
KRPSNT
corposant
KRPSZT
crepe suzette
KRPT
carpet
corrupt

B:by CH:each D:day F:if G:go H:he HW:why J:joy K:cow KS:ax KWL:equal L:all M:may N:in

crypt	course	cursed(adj)	**KRSHL**
KRPTBG	coursed	curst(v)	crucial
carpetbag	coursing	**KRSF**	**KRSHLMT**
KRPTBGR	crass	crucify	crash helmet
carpetbagger	crease	crucified	**KRSHLND**
KRPTBL	creased	crucifies	crash-land(v)
corruptible	creasing	crucifier	**KRSHLNDNG**
KRPTGRF	creosote(tar)	**KRSFKS**	crash-landing(n)
cryptography	cress(plant)	crucifix	**KRSHN**
KRPTGRM	cross	**KRSFKSHN**	accretion(growth)
cryptogram	crosses	crucifixion	coercion
KRPTJNK	crosse(game)	**KRSFL**	corrosion(rust)
cryptogenic	crus(leg)	cross-file	creation
KRPTK	crura(pl)	cross-filed	Croatian
cryptic	crural	cross-filing	Krishna
KRPTN	curse	**KRSFR**	**KRSHND**
krypton	cursed	crossfire	crescendo
KRPTNM	cursing	crossfired	**KRSHNG**
cryptonym	curser	crossfiring	crocheting
KRPTR	Icarus	crucifier	**KRSHR**
corrupter	**KRSB**	crucify(punish)	crocheter
KRPYLNS	crossbow	**KRSFRM**	cross hair
corpulence(fat)	**KRSBK**	cruciform	**KRSHT**
crapulence(sick)	crossbeak(bird)	**KRSFRTLZ**	cruciate
KRPYLNT	**KRSBL**	cross-fertilize	**KRSJ**
corpulent(fat)	coercible	cross-fertilized	corsage
crapulent(sick)	corrosible(adj)	cross-fertilizing	**KRSK**
KRPYLS	corrode	cross-	carsick
crapulous	crossable	fertilization	**KRSKNT**
KRR	crucible	**KRSGRND**	coruscant
career(work)	**KRSBM**	coarse-grained	**KRSKNTR**
carrier(carry)	crossbeam	cross-grained	cross-country
corer(tool)	**KRSBNZ**	**KRSGZMN**	**KRSKP**
courier(person)	crossbones	cross-examine	cryoscopy
crier(cry)	**KRSBR**	cross-examined	**KRSKRNGGL**
curare(resin)	crossbar	cross-examining	Kriss Kringle
currier(curry)	**KRSBRD**	cross-examiner	**KRSKRNT**
KRRL	crossbreed	**KRSGZMNSHN**	crosscurrent
crural	crossbred	cross-examination	**KRSKRS**
crus	**KRSCHN**	**KRSH**	crisscross
KRRST	Christian	caroche(carriage)	crisscrosses
careerist	**KRSCHNSNS**	crash	**KRSKSHN**
KRRZM	Christian Science	crashes	coruscation
careerism	**KRSCHNT**	crochet(knit)	cross section
KRS	Christianity	currish	**KRSKT**
acarus(mite)	**KRSCHNZ**	cur	coruscate
across(crossed)	Christianize	crush	coruscated
caress, (pl)-sses	Christianized	crushes	coruscating
chorus(music)	Christianizing	**KRSHCH**	crosscut
choruses	**KRSD**	crosshatch	**KRSKWSCHN**
coarse(rough)	acaricide	crosshatches	cross-question
coarser	cross-eyed	**KRSHDV**	**KRSKYR**
coarsest	crusade	crash dive(n)	chiaroscuro
coerce	crusaded	crash-dive(v)	**KRSL**
coerced	crusading	crash-dived	carousel
coercing	crusader	crash-diving	creosol

KRSLGD
cross-legged
KRSLS
chrysalis
KRSLT
corselet
KRSMS
Christmas
Xmas
KRSMSLND
Christmas Island
KRSMSV
Christmas Eve
KRSN
christen
coarsen(rough)
croissant(pastry)
kerosene
KRSNDKS
cross-index
KRSNDM
Christendom
KRSNG
crossing
coursing(sport)
KRSNJN
carcinogen
KRSNM
carcinoma
KRSNS
crassness
KRSNST
Carson City
KRSNT
crescent
KRSNTHMM
chrysanthemum
KRSP
crisp
crispy
crispier
crispiest
crispiness
KRSPCH
crosspatch
crosspatches
KRSPLNT
cross-pollinate
cross-pollinated
cross-pollinating
cross-pollination
KRSPND
correspond
KRSPNDNG
corresponding
KRSPNDNS

corespondents
(divorce)
correspondence
correspondents
(writers)
KRSPNDNT
corespondent
(divorce case)
correspondent
(writer)
KRSPNSV
corresponsive
KRSPRPS
cross-purpose
KRSPRZ
chrysoprase
KRSR
coarser
coarse
coercer
corsair
courser(dog,horse)
curser(curse)
cursor(sliding
part)
cursory
cursorily
cursoriness
KRSRD
crossroad
KRSRF
crossruff
KRSRFR
cross-refer
cross-referred
cross-referring
KRSRFRNS
cross-reference
KRSRJR
cryosurgery
KRSRL
cursorily
KRSS
crisis
crises
KRST
accursed
Christ
christy(turn)
christies
corset
creosote
crest
crosstie
crust
crusty

crustier
crustiest
crustily
crustiness
curst(or)
cursed
curse
KRSTCH
cross-stitch
cross-stitches
KRSTFLN
crestfallen
KRSTHBRD
across-the-
-board(adj)
KRSTK
acrostic
KRSTL
crustal(crust)
crystal
KRSTLGZR
crystal gazer
KRSTLKLR
crystal clear
KRSTLN
crystalline
KRSTLZ
crystallize
crystallized
crystallizing
crystallizer
KRSTN
cross-town(adj)
KRSTNG
cresting
KRSTR
chorister
KRSTSHN
crustacean
KRSTSHS
crustaceous
KRSTYR
corsetiere
KRSV
coercive
corrosive
corrode
cursive
KRSVR
crossover
KRSW
crossway
KRSWK
crosswalk
KRSWND
crosswind

KRSWRDPZL
crossword puzzle
KRSWZ
crosswise
KRSZ
cruces(pl)
crux
KRSZH
corsage
KRT
accurate
carat(diamond)
karat(gold)
caret(symbol)
carrot(vegetable)
cart
court
crate(box)
crated
crating
crater
create(make)
created
creating
creator
creation
cruet
curt(rude)
karat(gold)
carat(diamond)
caret(symbol)
karate(defense)
kraut
quart(cards)
quarte(fencing)
KRTBLNSH
carte blanche
KRTD
carotid
KRTGRF
cartography
KRTGRFR
cartographer
KRTHS
courthouse
KRTHWL
cartwheel
KRTK
critic(person)
critique
KRTKL
cortical
critical
KRTKR
caretaker
KRTKS

cortex
  cortices(or)
  cortexes
KRTKSTR
  criticaster
KRTL
  cartel
  courtly
    courtlier
    courtliest
    courtliness
  curtail
KRTLJ
  cartilage
KRTM
  Khartoum
KRTMRSHL
  court-martial
KRTN
  carotene(pigment)
  carton(box)
  cartoon(drawing)
  cretin(idiot)
  cretonne(cloth)
  crouton
  curtain
  keratin(protein)
KRTNKL
  curtain call
KRTNRZR
  curtain raiser
KRTNZM
  cretinism
KRTP
  carrot-top(hair)
KRTR
  cotter(pin)
  courtier
  crater
  creator(maker)
  criteria
  critter
KRTRJ
  cartridge
KRTRM
  courtroom
KRTRN
  criterion
  criteria
KRTS
  courteous
  courtesy
    courtesies
  curtsy
    curtsied
    curtsies

KRTSH
  cartouche
KRTSHP
  courtship
KRTSN
  cortisone
KRTSZ
  cortices
  criticize
    criticized
    criticizing
KRTSZBL
  criticizable
KRTSZM
  criticism
KRTV
  creative
KRTWL
  cartwheel(flip)
KRTYR
  courtier
KRTYRD
  courtyard
KRTZH
  cortege
KRTZN
  cortisone(heal)
  courtesan
KRV
  carve(cut up)
    carved,carving
    carver
  corvee
  crave(desire)
    craved,craving
  curve
    curved
    curving
  curvy
    curvier
    curviest
    curviness
KRVCHR
  curvature
KRVL
  caravel
  corrival(rival)
KRVLNR
  curvilinear
KRVN
  caravan
  craven
KRVNG
  carving
  craving
KRVNSR

caravansary
KRVR
  carry-over(n)
KRVS
  crevasse(dike,
    glacier)
  crevice(narrow
    opening)
KRVSHS
  curvaceous
KRVT
  corvette
  cravat
KRW
  caraway
KRWRN
  careworn
KRWSH
  car wash
  car washes
KRWSN
  croissant
KRYGSHN
  corrugation
KRYGT
  corrugate
  corrugated
  corrugating
KRZ
  caries(tooth
    decay)
  carouse
  caroused
  carousing
  carouser
  coryza(nose)
  craze
  crazed
  crazing
  crazy
    crazier
    craziest
    crazily
    craziness
  croze(tool)
  cruise
    cruised
    cruising
    cruiser
  cruse(jar)
  kersey
KRZBN
  crazy bone
    (olecranon)
KRZFT
  crow's-foot

crow's-feet
KRZHN
  coercion
  corrosion
KRZHR
  crosier
KRZKWLT
  crazy quilt
KRZL
  carousal(party)
KRZM
  charisma
  charismata
KRZMTK
  charismatic
KRZNST
  crow's-nest
KRZR
  cruiser
  cruzeiro
KRZV
  coercive
  corrosive
  cursive
KS
  ax
    axes
  case
    cased
    casing
  chaos
  cos(lettuce)
  cuss(old person)
    cusses
  cuss(curse)
    cusses
  echoes
  kiss
    kisses
  ox
    oxen
  x(v)
    x'd
    x'ing
    x's
KSB
  oxbow
KSBK
  casebook
KSBLD
  oxblood
KSBLNGK
  Casablanca
KSBSHN
  exhibition
KSBSHNZM

NGK:ink **P**:pie **R**:air **S**:ice **SH**:show **T**:toy **THN**:thin **TH**:the **V**:of **W**:we **Y**:you **Z**:is **VZHN**:vision

exhibitionism
KSCHKR
  exchequer
KSCHNJ
  exchange
    exchanged
    exchanging
    exchanger
KSCHNJBL
  exchangeable
KSCHNJBLT
  exchangeability
    exchangeabilities
KSD
  accede(agree)
    acceded
    acceding
  acedia(apathy)
  exceed(surpass)
KSDNGL
  exceedingly
KSDNS
  accedence(agree)
  accidence(basic
    elements)
KSDNT
  accident(mishap)
  occident(west)
KSDNTL
  accidental
  occidental
KSDR
  acceder
  accede
KSDS
  Exodus(Bible)
  exodus
KSDSHN
  oxidation
KSDZ
  oxidize
    oxidized
    oxidizing
    oxidizer
KSF
  kiss-off(n)
  kiss off(v)
KSFRD
  Oxford
  oxford
KSFSH
  ex officio
KSGM
  exogamy
KSGNTR
  cosignatory

cosignatories
KSH
  acacia(tree)
  cache(hiding
    place)
  cachet(seal)
  cachou(astringent)
  cash
    cashes
  cashew(nut)
  cosh(blackjack)
  cushy
    cushier
    cushiest
  kasha
  quiche(food)
KSHBK
  cashbook
KSHBKS
  cash box(safe)
  cash boxes
KSHL
  exhale
    exhaled
    exhaling
KSHLSHN
  exhalation
KSHLZ
  actualize
    actualized
    actualizing
    actualization
KSHN
  action
  auction(sale)
  caution
  coition(sex)
    coitus
    coital(adj)
  cushion
KSHNBL
  actionable
KSHNDKR
  cash-and-carry
KSHNR
  auctioneer
  cautionary
KSHP
  cachepot
KSHPT
  cachepot
KSHR
  cashier(person)
  cosher(pamper)
  kosher(dietary
    law)

KSHRDN
  caseharden
KSHRJSTR
  cash register
KSHS
  cautious
KSHSTR
  case history
    case histories
KSHY
  cashew(nut)
KSHYM
  exhume
    exhumed
    exhuming
KSHYMSHN
  exhumation
KSJN
  oxygen
KSJNS
  exigency
    exigencies
KSJNSHN
  oxygenation
KSJNT
  exigent
  oxygenate
    oxygenated
    oxygenating
KSJSS
  exegesis
KSK
  cask
  casque(helmet)
  cassock
  kiosk
KSKBL
  cascabel
KSKD
  cascade
    cascaded
    cascading
KSKLD
  exclude
    excluded
    excluding
KSKLDBL
  excludable
KSKLM
  exclaim
KSKLMSHN
  exclamation
KSKLMTR
  exclamatory
KSKLPSHN
  exculpation

KSKLPT
  exculpate
    exculpated
    exculpating
KSKLSV
  exclusive
KSKLSVT
  exclusivity
    exclusivities
KSKLV
  exclave
KSKLZHN
  exclusion
KSKMNKSHN
  excommunication
KSKMNKT
  excommunicate
    excommunicated
    excommunicating
KSKRBL
  execrable
KSKRMNT
  excrement
KSKRMSM
  X-chromosome
KSKRSHN
  excoriation
  excretion
  excursion(trip)
  execration
KSKRSHSHN
  excruciation
KSKRSHT
  excruciate
    excruciated
    excruciating
KSKRSNS
  excrescence
KSKRT
  excoriate(skin)
    excoriated
    excoriating
  excrete
    excreted
    excreting
  execrate
    execrated
    execrating
KSKRTR
  excretory
KSKRZHN
  excursion
KSKS
  couscous
KSKT
  casket

KSKTHDR
ex cathedra
KSKVSHN
excavation
KSKVT
excavate
excavated
excavating
KSKVTR
excavator
KSKWZT
exquisite
KSKYS
excuse
excused
excusing
KSKYSHN
execution
KSKYSHNR
executioner
KSKYT
execute
executed
executing
KSKYZBL
excusable
excusably
KSL
axial(adj)(axis)
axle(rod, bar)
case law
castle
excel
excelled
excelling
exile(banish)
exiled
exiling
KSLD
caseload
KSLN
coastline
KSLNS
excellence
excellency
excellencies
KSLNT
excellent
KSLRMTR
accelerometer
KSLRND
accelerando(music)
KSLRSHN
acceleration
KSLRT
accelerate

accelerated
accelerating
KSLRTR
accelerator
KSLSR
excelsior
KSM
axiom
eczema
KSMDK
axiomatic
KSMNT
casement
cosmonaut
KSMPLTN
cosmopolitan
KSMR
oxymora
KSMRN
oxymoron
oxymora
KSMT
kismet
KSMTK
axiomatic
KSMTSHN
cosmetician
KSN
axon(nerve)
caisson
casino(building)
cassino(game)
cosign
cosine(arc)
oxen
ox
KSNCHL
accentual
KSNCHT
accentuate
accentuated
accentuating
KSNDR
Cassandra
KSNF
case knife
KSNG
casing
x'ing
KSNR
cosigner
KSNSTR
Cosa Nostra
KSNT
accent
exeunt

KSNTRK
eccentric
KSNTRKL
eccentrical
KSNTRST
eccentricity
eccentricities
KSNV
Casanova
KSP
cusp
KSPBL
expiable
KSPDDR
expediter
KSPDNS
expedience
expediency
expediencies
KSPDNT
expedient
KSPDR
cuspidor
expiator
KSPDSHN
expedition
KSPDSHNR
expeditionary
KSPDSHS
expeditious
KSPDT
expedite
expedited
expediting
KSPDTR
expediter
KSPKT
expect
KSPKTNS
expectancy
expectancies
KSPKTNT
expectant
KSPKTRNT
expectorant
KSPKTRSHN
expectoration
KSPKTRT
expectorate
expectorated
expectorating
KSPKTSHN
expectation
KSPL
expel
expelled

expelling
expellee
KSPLBL
expellable
KSPLD
explode
exploded
exploding
KSPLDBL
explodable
KSPLKBL
explicable
KSPLKSHN
explication
KSPLKT
explicate
explicated
explicating
KSPLN
explain
KSPLNBL
explainable
KSPLNSHN
explanation
KSPLNT
expellant(adj)
KSPLNTR
explanatory
KSPLR
explore
explored
exploring
KSPLRR
explorer
KSPLRSHN
exploration
KSPLRTR
exploratory
KSPLSHN
expulsion
KSPLST
explicit
KSPLSV
explosive
KSPLT
exploit
KSPLTSHN
exploitation
KSPLTV
expletive
KSPLZHN
explosion
KSPLZV
explosive
KSPND
expand(get bigger)

NGK:ink **P**:pie **R**:air **S**:ice **SH**:show **T**:toy **THN**:thin **TH**:the **V**:of **W**:we **Y**:you **Z**:is **VZHN**:vision

expend(spend)
expound
KSPNDBL
expendable
KSPNDBLT
expendability
KSPNDCHR
expenditure
KSPNJ
expunge
expunged
expunging
KSPNNSHL
exponential
KSPNNT
exponent
KSPNS
Caspian Sea
expanse
expense(cost)
expensed
expensing
KSPNSBL
expansible
KSPNSHN
expansion
KSPNSV
expansive
expensive
KSPR
expire
expired
expiring
KSPRGSHN
expurgation
KSPRGT
expurgate
expurgated
expurgating
KSPRMNT
experiment
KSPRMNTL
experimental
KSPRMNTSHN
experimentation
KSPRNCHL
experiential
KSPRNS
experience
experienced
experiencing
KSPRNSHL
experiential
KSPRPRSHN
expropriation
KSPRPRT

expropriate
expropriated
expropriating
KSPRS
espresso
express
expresses
KSPRSBL
expressible
KSPRSHN
expiration
expression
KSPRSHNSTK
expressionistic
KSPRSHNZM
expressionism
KSPRSJ
expressage
KSPRSMN
expressman
expressmen
KSPRSV
expressive
KSPRSW
expressway
KSPRT
expert
export
KSPRTR
expiratory
KSPRTS
expertise
KSPRTSHN
exportation
KSPRTZ
expertise
KSPSCHLSHN
expostulation
KSPSCHLT
expostulate
expostulated
expostulating
KSPSCHLTR
expostulator
KSPSHN
exception
expiation
KSPSHNBL
exceptionable
KSPSHNL
exceptional
KSPSHSHN
expatiation
KSPSHT
expatiate
expatiated

expatiating
KSPSTFKT
ex post facto
KSPT
accept(receive)
except(omit)
expiate
expiated
expiating
KSPTBL
acceptable
KSPTBLT
acceptability
KSPTD
accepted(approved)
excepted(left out)
KSPTL
occipital
KSPTNG
accepting(receiving)
excepting(excluding)
KSPTNS
acceptance
KSPTNT
acceptant
KSPTR
accepter(receiver)
acceptor(finance)
accipter(hawk)
expiator
KSPTRSHN
expatriation
KSPTRT
expatriate
expatriated
expatriating
KSPTSHN
acceptation
KSPZ
expose
exposed
exposing
exposé
KSPZHR
exposure
KSPZSHN
exposition
KSPZTR
expositor
expository
KSR
kisser
x-ray(v)
x ray(n)
KSRB
exurbia

KSRBL
exorable
KSRBNT
exurbanite
KSRL
casserole
uxorial
KSRPT
excerpt
KSRS
uxorious
KSRST
Exocet(missile)
KSRSZ
exercise(use)
exercised
exercising
exerciser
exorcise(expel)
exorcised
exorcising
KSRSZBL
exercisable
KSRSZM
exorcism
KSRSZR
exerciser
KSRTD
X-rated
KSS
access(admittance)
accesses
axis
axes
excess(surplus)
excesses
KSSBL
accessible
KSSBLT
accessibility
KSSHN
accession
KSSR
accessory
accessories
KSSRBSHN
exacerbation
KSSRBT
exacerbate
exacerbated
exacerbating
KSST
Exocet(missile)
KSSTM
ecosystem
KSSTNCHL

existential
KSSTNCHLZM
existentialism
KSSTNSHL
existential
KSSTNSHLZM
existentialism
KSSV
excessive
KST
accost
cassette(tape)
cast
caste(social
  class)
coast
cosset(pamper)
  cosseted
  cossetting
cost(expense)
excite
  excited
  exciting
  excitation
x'd
x out
  x'd out
  x'ing out
KSTBL
excitable
excitably
KSTBLT
excitability
KSTD
case study
  case studies
custody
  custodies
KSTDL
custodial
KSTDN
custodian
KSTF
castoff(n)
cast-off(adj)
KSTGRD
coast guard(or)
Coast Guard
KSTGRDZMN
coastguardsman(or)
Coast Guardsman
coastguardsmen(or)
Coast Guardsmen
KSTGSHN
castigation
KSTGT

castigate
  -gated,-gating
KSTGTR
castigator
KSTK
acoustic(sound)
caustic
ekistic(design)
KSTKL
acoustical
ekistical
KSTKS
acoustics(sound)
ekistics(design)
KSTL
coastal
costly
  costlier
  costliest
  costliness
extol
  extolled
  extolling
oxtail
KSTLN
coastline
KSTM
accustom
costume
  costumed
  costuming
  costumer
custom(practice)
KSTMBLT
custom-built
KSTMD
custom-made
custom-make
KSTMHS
customhouse
KSTMNT
excitement
KSTMPR
extempore
KSTMPRNS
extemporaneous
KSTMPRZ
extemporize
  extemporized
  extemporizing
KSTMR
costumer
customary
customer
KSTMRL
customarily

KSTMZ
customize
  customized
  customizing
customs
  U.S. Customs
KSTN
keystone
KSTNCHN
extension
KSTND
extend
KSTNG
casting
exciting
KSTNGGWSH
extinguish
  extinguishes
  extinguisher
KSTNGKSHN
extinction
KSTNGKT
extinct
KSTNGT
extinct
extinction
KSTNGWSH
extinguish
  extinguishes
  extinguisher
KSTNKPS
Keystone Kops
KSTNSBL
extensible
KSTNSHN
extension
KSTNSV
extensive
KSTNT
castanet
extant(existing)
extent(scope)
extinct(not
  existing)
KSTNTS
castanets
KSTNYSHN
extenuation
KSTNYT
extenuate
  extenuated
  extenuating
KSTPLS
cost-plus
KSTR
caster(n,v)

castor(beaver,oil)
coaster
costar
extra
keister(buttocks)
KSTRD
costard(apple)
custard
extrude
  extruded
  extruding
extrusion
KSTRDSHN
extradition
KSTRDT
extradite
  extradited
  extraditing
KSTRDTBL
extraditable
KSTRK
Costa Rica
exoteric
KSTRKRKYLR
extracurricular
KSTRKSHN
extraction
extrication
KSTRKT
extract
extricate
  extricated
  extricating
KSTRKTBL
extractable
KSTRKTR
extractor
KSTRL
castor oil
KSTRM
extreme
KSTRMNGGR
costermonger
KSTRMNSHN
extermination
KSTRMNT
exterminate
  exterminated
  exterminating
  exterminator
  exterminatory
KSTRMRTL
extramarital
KSTRMST
extremist
KSTRMT

extremity
extremities
KSTRMYRL
extramural
KSTRMZM
extremism
KSTRN
cast iron(n)
cast-iron(adj)
KSTRNL
external
KSTRNLZ
externalize
externalized
externalizing
KSTRNS
extraneous
KSTRNSK
extrinsic
KSTRNSKL
extrinsical
KSTRPLSHN
extrapolation
KSTRPLT
extrapolate
extrapolated
extrapolating
extrapolative
KSTRPSHN
extirpation
KSTRPT
extirpate
extirpated
extirpating
KSTRR
exterior
KSTRRDNR
extraordinary
KSTRRDNRL
extraordinarily
KSTRSHN
extortion
KSTRSHNR
extortioner
KSTRSHNST
extortionist
KSTRSNSR
extrasensory
KSTRT
extort
KSTRTRSTRL
extraterrestrial
KSTRTRTRL
extraterritorial
KSTRVGNS
extravagance

KSTRVGNT
extravagant
KSTRVGNZ
extravaganza
KSTRVHKYLR
extravehicular
KSTRVRZHN
extroversion
KSTRVT
extrovert
KSTRZHN
extrusion
KSTS
ecstasy
ecstasies
KSTSHN
excitation
KSTTK
ecstatic
KSTTKL
ecstatically
KSTTRSKLN
oxytetracycline
KSTV
costive
KSTW
castaway
KSTWRD
coastward
KSTYM
costume
costumed
costuming
costumer
KSVYR
Xavier
KSWRK
casework
KSYDSHN
exudation
KSZ
excise
excised
excising
kisses
x's
KSZBL
excisable
KSZHN
excision
KSZML
coseismal(map)
KT
act
cat(kitty)
catty

cattier
cattiest
cattily
cattiness
coat
coot(bird,person)
cootie(bug)
cot(bed)
coyote
cut (divide)
cut
cutting, cutter
K^2 (or) K2 (mountain)
kit
kite(flyer)
kitty
kitties
kowtow
kyat
Kyoto(Japan)
Quito
quoit
KTBK
cutback(n,adj)
KTBR
October
KTBRD
catbird
KTBT
catboat
KTD
coated
KTDD
katydid
KTF
cutoff(n,adj)
KTFK
catafalque
KTFLK
catafalque
KTFSH
catfish
KTGLS
cut glass(n)
cut-glass(adj)
KTGN
octagon
KTGNL
octagonal
KTGR
category
categories
KTGRKL
categorical
KTGRZ
categorize

categorized
categorizing
KTGT
catgut
KTH
couth
uncouth
KTHD
cathode
cathode ray
cathode-ray tube
KTHDRL
cathedral
KTHDRN
octahedron
KTHKSS
cathexis
KTHL
cat-haul
KTHLJ
ichthyology
KTHLK
catholic(universal)
Catholic(church)
KTHLSZM
Catholicism
KTHR
coauthor
KTHRSS
catharsis
KTHRT
cutthroat
KTHRTK
cathartic
KTHS
cathouse
KTHTR
catheter
KTHTRZ
catheterize
catheterized
catheterizing
KTJ
cottage
KTJCHZ
cottage cheese
KTJNRN
octogenarian
KTJR
cottager
KTK
chaotic
KTKL
catcall
KTKLZM
cataclysm

B:by **CH**:each **D**:day **F**:if **G**:go **H**:he **HW**:why **J**:joy **K**:cow **KS**:ax **KWL**:equal **L**:all **M**:may **N**:in

KTKLZMK
cataclysmic
KTKM
catacomb
KTKRNRD
kitty-cornered
KTKWN
cotquean
KTKZM
catechism
KTL
cattail
cattle
coattail
kettle
kittle(touchy)
KTLDRM
kettledrum
KTLG
catalog
KTLGR
cataloger
KTLMN
cattleman
cattlemen
KTLN
Catalan
KTLPS
catalepsy
KTLR
cutler(person)
cutlery
KTLS
cutlass
cutlasses
KTLST
catalyst
KTLTK
catalytic
KTLYN
cotillion
KTLZ
catalyze
catalyzed
catalyzing
KTMRN
catamaran
KTN
cotton
cottony
cut-in(n,adj)
ecotone(ecology)
ketone
kitten(cat)
octane(gas)
KTNBLT

Cotton Belt
KTNBTNG
cotton batting
KTNDRD
cut-and-dried
KTNFLNL
cotton flannel
KTNG
acting
coating
cutting
KTNGYLR
octangular
KTNJN
cotton gin
KTNKND
cotton candy
KTNMTH
cottonmouth
KTNNS
cotenancy
KTNNT
cotenant
KTNNTLZ
cat-o'-nine-tails
KTNP
catnap
catnapped
catnapping
catnip(plant)
KTNPKR
cotton picker
KTNSD
cottonseed
KTNTL
cottontail
KTNWD
cottonwood
KTP
cutup(n)
KTPDZ
octopodes
octopus
KTPL
octuple
octupled
octupling
KTPLT
catapult
KTPRS
cutpurse
KTPS
octopus
octopuses(or)
octopi(or)
octopodes

KTR
accouter, (B)-tre
actor(theater)(m)
actress(f)
catarrh
cater
cautery
coterie(group)
cotter(pin)
couture(style)
cutter(cut)
Qatar
KTRK
cataract
KTRKRNRD
cater-cornered
KTRKT
cataract
KTRMNT
accouterment,(B)-
tre-
KTRPLR
caterpillar
KTRPN
cotter pin
KTRR
caterer
KTRT
cut-rate
KTRWL
caterwaul
KTRY
courturier(m)
KTRYR
courturiere(f)
KTRZ
cauterize
cauterized
cauterizing
KTRZSHN
cauterization
KTS
cat's eye(marble)
coitus
ictus
KTSK
Okhotsk(Sea of)
KTSKRDL
cat's cradle
KTSL
quetzal
KTSNJMR
katzenjammer
KTSNTRPTS
coitus interruptus
KTSP
cat's-paw

KTSTRF
catastrophe
KTT
cutout(n)
octet
KTTHRT
cutthroat
KTV
active
octave
octavo
KTVGD
act of God
KTVR
cutover
KTVRMS
coat of arms
KTVSHN
activation
KTVST
activist
KTVT
activate
activated
activating
activity
activities
KTVTR
activator
KTVWR
act of war
KTVZM
activism
KTW
cutaway
KTWK
catwalk
KTWRK
cutwork(n)
KTWRM
cutworm
KTYPL
octuple
octupled
octupling
KV
cave(hole)
caved
caving
calve(birth)
calved
calving
cove
covey
kava(shrub)
Kiev

NGK:ink **P**:pie **R**:air **S**:ice **SH**:show **T**:toy **THN**:thin **TH**:the **V**:of **W**:we **Y**:you **Z**:is **VZHN**:vision

KVDWLR
cave dweller
KVL
cavil
coeval
KVLKD
cavalcade
KVLR
cavalier
cavalry
cavalries
caviler(quibbler)
KVMN
cave man
cave men
KVN
cave-in(n,adj)
KVNNT
covenant
covenantee
KVNNTR
covenanter(maker)
covenantor(doer)
KVR
caviar
cover
KVRCHRJ
cover charge
KVRGRL
cover girl
KVRJ
coverage
KVRL
coverall
KVRLZ
coveralls
KVRN
cavern
KVRNG
covering
KVRNS
cavernous
covariance
KVRNT
covariant
KVRP
cover-up
KVRSHP
cover shop
KVRT
cavort(action)
covert(hidden)
KVT
caveat
cavity
cavities

covet(desire)
KVTMPTR
caveat emptor
KVTS
covetous
KVV
qui vive
KVZ
calves
calf
KW
aqua(water)
Kauai
keyway
kiwi
KWBK
Quebec
KWBL
equable
equably
quibble
quibbled
quibbling
quibbler
KWBLT
equability
equabilities
KWCH
kwacha
KWD
quad
quid
quota
KWDK
aquatic
aqueduct
KWDKT
aqueduct
KWDNNGK
quidnunc
KWDPRKW
quid pro quo
KWDR
Ecuador
quitter
KWDRL
quadrille
KWDRLTRL
quadrilateral
KWDRLYN
quadrillion
KWDRNGL
quadrangle
KWDRNGLR
quadrangular
KWDRPL

quadruple
quadrupled
quadrupling
KWDRPLJ
quadriplegia
KWDRPLJK
quadriplegic
KWDRPLKT
quadruplicate
quadruplicated
quadruplicating
quadruplication
KWDRPLT
quadruplet
KWDRNL
quadrennial
KWDRNT
quadrant
KWDRT
quadrate
quadrated
quadrating
KWDRTK
quadratic
KWDSTNT
equidistant
KWF
quaff(drink)
quiff(slang)
KWFR
coiffeur
(hairdresser)
KWFYR
coiffure(hair
style)
KWFZ
coiffeuse(female
hairdresser)
KWGMR
quagmire
KWK
quack
quake(shake)
quaked
quaking
quick
quickie(n)
KWKD
aquacade
KWKFRZ
quick-freeze
quick-froze
quick-freezing
quick-frozen
KWKN
quicken

KWKR
quackery
quackeries
Quaker
Religious Society
of Friends
KWKSLVR
quicksilver
KWKSND
quicksand
KWKSTK
quixotic
KWKSTKL
quixotical
KWKTMPRD
quick-tempered
KWKWTD
quick-witted
KWL
equal
quail(bird)
quell(stop)
quill
KWLBR
equilibria
KWLBRM
equilibrium
equilibria
KWLBRNT
equilibrant
KWLBRT
equilibrate
equilibrated
equilibrating
KWLD
Quaalude
(trademark)
KWLF
qualify
qualified
qualifies
KWLFKSHN
qualification
KWLFR
qualifier
KWLLMPR
Kuala Lumpur
KWLLPS
Kuala Lipis
KWLN
aquiline
KWLNG
equaling
KWLT
equality
equalities

B:by **CH**:each **D**:day **F**:if **G**:go **H**:he **HW**:why **J**:joy **K**:cow **KS**:ax **KWL**:equal **L**:all **M**:may **N**:in

quality
  qualities
quilt
KWLTNG
  quilting
KWLTRL
  equilateral
KWLTRN
  equalitarian
KWLTTV
  qualitative
KWLZ
  equalize
    equalized
    equalizing
    equalizer
KWLZR
  equalizer
KWLZSHN
  equalization
KWM
  qualm
KWMNTNG
  Kuomintang
KWMRN
  aquamarine
KWMSH
  qualmish
KWN
  equine
  queen
  quoin(wedge,
    corner)
KWNCH
  quench
  quenches
KWNCHBL
  quenchable
KWNDM
  quondam
KWNDR
  quandary
  quandaries
KWNG
  cowing
KWNGYLR
  equiangular
KWNKS
  equinox
KWNKSHL
  equinoctial
KWNKWNL
  quinquennial
KWNL
  queenly
    queenlier

queenliest
  queenliness
  quinella
KWNMT
  equanimity
  equanimities
KWNN
  Kiwanian
  quinine
KWNS
  Kiwanis
  quince
KWNSTHT
  Quonset hut
    (trademark)
KWNSZ
  queen-size
  queen-sized
KWNT
  acquaint(meet)
  aquanaut
  quaint
  quanta
KWNTLYN
  quintillion
KWNTM
  quantum
  quanta
KWNTNS
  acquaintance
KWNTPL
  quintuple
    quintupled
    quintupling
KWNTPLKT
  quintuplicate
  quintuplicated
  quintuplicating
KWNTPLT
  quintuplet
KWNTSNCHL
  quintessential
KWNTSNS
  quintessence
KWNTSNSHL
  quintessential
KWNTT
  quantity
  quantities
  quintet
KWNTTTV
  quantitative
KWNTYPL
  quintuple
    quintupled
    quintupling

KWNTYPLKT
  quintuplicate
  quintuplicated
  quintuplicating
KWNTYPLT
  quintuplet
KWP
  equip
    equipped
    equipping
  quip
    quipped
    quipping
KWPJ
  equipage
KWPLN
  aquaplane
  aquaplaned
  aquaplaning
KWPLNT
  equipollent
KWPMNT
  equipment
KWPZ
  equipoise
KWR
  acquire
    acquired
    acquiring
  choir(singing)
  cower
  equerry
    equerries
  quarry(stone)
    quarried
    quarries
  queer(odd)
  query(question)
    queried
    queries
  quire(paper)
KWRB
  choirboy
KWRBL
  acquirable
KWRD
  awkward
  coward
KWRDR
  quarter
KWRDRDK
  quarter-deck
KWRDS
  cowardice
KWRK
  quirk

KWRKR
  co-worker
KWRL
  quarrel
KWRLFT
  choir loft
KWRLS
  querulous
KWRLSM
  quarrelsome
KWRM
  aquarium
  quorum
KWRMNT
  acquirement
KWRMSTR
  choirmaster
KWRNTN
  quarantine
    quarantined
    quarantining
KWRNTNBL
  quarantinable
KWRS
  Aquarius
  cuirass(armor)
    cuirasses
KWRST
  aquarist
KWRT
  quart
  quarto
KWRTL
  quartile
KWRTN
  quartan
KWRTR
  quarter
KWRTRBK
  quarterback
KWRTRDK
  quarter-deck
KWRTRFNL
  quarterfinal
KWRTRL
  quarterly
    quarterlies
KWRTRMSTR
  quartermaster
KWRTRS
  quartersaw
    quartersawn
KWRTS
  quartz
  quartz
KWRTT

NGK:ink **P**:pie **R**:air **S**:ice **SH**:show **T**:toy **THN**:thin **TH**:the **V**:of **W**:we **Y**:you **Z**:is **VZHN**:vision

quartet
KWRYLS
querulous
KWS
aqueous
acquiesce(agree)
acquiesced
acquiescing
cuisse(armor)
quasi
KWSCHN
question
KWSCHNBL
questionable
KWSCHNR
questionnaire
KWSH
quash
quashes
KWSHN
equation
KWSHNT
quotient
KWSHRKR
kwashiorkor
KWSNS
acquiescence
quiescence
KWSNT
acquiescent
quiescent
KWSR
quasar
KWST
cuesta(land)
quest
KWSTRN
equestrian
equestrienne
KWT
acquit
acquitted
acquitting
equate(equal)
equated
equating
equity
equities
Kuwait
quiet(still)
quit(end)
quit(or)
quitted
quitting
quite(fully)
quoit

quota(amount)
quote
quoted
quoting
KWTBL
equitable
equitably
quotable
KWTD
quietude
KWTDN
quotidian
KWTK
aquatic(adj)
KWTKLM
quitclaim
KWTKS
aquatics(n)
KWTL
acquittal
KWTNS
acquittance
quittance
KWTNT
aquatint
KWTR
equator
quitter
KWTRL
equatorial
KWTRLGN
Equatorial Guinea
KWTRN
quatrain
KWTRNR
quaternary
quaternaries
KWTS
quietus
quits(n)(quit)
KWTSHN
quotation
KWTYD
quietude
KWVKL
equivocal
KWVKSHN
equivocation
KWVKT
equivocate
equivocated
equivocating
KWVKTR
equivocator
KWVLNS
equivalence

KWVLNT
equivalent
KWVR
quaver
quiver
KWVT
aqua vitae
KWZ
quasi
queasy
queasier
queasiest
queasiness
quiz
quizzed
quizzes
quizzing
quizzer
KWZHN
equation
KWZKL
quizzical
KWZLNG
quisling
KWZN
cuisine
KWZR
quasar
KWZSHN
acquisition
KWZTV
acquisitive
KY
cahier(pages)
cue(hint,stick)
cued
cuing
IQ(intelligence
   quotient)
kayo
kue(the letter *Q*)
queue(line)
queued
queuing
KYB
Cuba
cube
cubed
cubing
cubé(shrub)
KYBD
cuboid
cuboidal
KYBFRM
cubiform
KYBKL

cubical(cube)
cubicle(space)
KYBT
cubit
KYBZM
cubism
KYD
cutie
cute
KYDKL
cuticle
KYDP
cutie-pie
KYDS
kudos
KYK
kayak
KYKLKSKLN
Ku Klux Klan
KYKMBR
cucumber
KYLNR
culinary
KYLR
ocular
KYLS
oculus
oculi
KYLST
oculist
KYLT
culet
KYLTS
culottes
KYMN
acumen
KYMNKL
ecumenical
KYMYLS
cumulous(adj)
cumulus((n)
KYMYLSHN
accumulation
cumulation
KYMYLT
accumulate
accumulated
accumulating
cumulate
cumulated
cumulating
KYMYLTR
accumulator
KYMYLTV
accumulative
cumulative

B:by **CH**:each **D**:day **F**:if **G**:go **H**:he **HW**:why **J**:joy **K**:cow **KS**:ax **KWL**:equal **L**:all **M**:may **N**:in

KYNFRM
cuneiform
KYNL
cuneal
KYP
occupy
occupied
occupies
KYPD
cupid
KYPDT
cupidity
cupidities
KYPL
cupel(vessel)
cupola(roof)
cupula(anatomy)
KYPN
coupon
KYPNGKCHR
acupuncture
KYPNS
occupancy
occupancies
KYPNT
occupant
KYPSHN
occupation
KYPSHNL
occupational
KYPYL
cupula(anatomy)
cupule(biology)
KYR
cure
cured
curing
curia(people)
curie(unit)
curio(thing)
KYRBL
curable
KYRL
cure-all
KYRNT
currant(fruit)
KYRR
curare
KYRS
accuracy
accuracies
curacao(liqueur)
Curacao(island)
curious
KYRST
curiosity

curiosities
KYRT
accurate
curate
KYRTR
curator
KYRTV
curative
KYSK
cusec(unit)
KYT
acuate(pointed)
acuity
acuities
acute(sharp)
coyote
cute(pretty)
cuter
cutest
cutie
kyat
Kyoto
KYTKL
cuticle
KYTNS
cutaneous
KYTP
cutie-pie
Q-Tip(trademark)
KYZ
accuse
accused
accusing
accuser
KYZD
accused
KYZL
accusal
KYZR
accuser
KYZSHN
accusation
KYZTR
accusatory
KYZTRL
accusatorial
KZ
cause
caused
causing
coups(successful
moves)
coup
cozy
cozier
coziest

cozily
coziness
echoes
echo
kazoo
Ok's
KZB
Casbah
KZBL
causable
causably
KZH
acajou(wood)
KZHL
casual
KZHLT
casualty
casualties
KZHMR
cashmere
KZHN
occasion
KZHNL
occasional
KZHST
casuist
KZHSTR
casuistry
KZL
causal
KZLT
causality
causalities
KZM
chasm
eczema
KZMDK
cosmetic(make-up)
cosmetically
KZMGN
cosmogony
KZMK
cosmic
KZMLJ
cosmology
KZMPLTN
cosmopolitan
KZMS
chiasmus
cosmos
KZMT
kismet
KZMTK
cosmetic
KZMTKL
cosmetically

KZMTLJST
cosmetologist
KZMTSHN
cosmetician
KZN
cousin(relative)
cozen(cheat)
KZNJ
cozenage
KZNST
Quezon City
KZR
causer
Kaiser
KZRN
casern
KZSHN
causation
KZTV
causative
KZW
causeway

L

ail(ill)
aisle(walk)
à la(style)
ala(winglike)
alae
ale(beer)
alee(leeward)
all(total)
Allah(God)
allay(lessen)
alley(street)
allow
alloy(metal)
ally(friend)
allies
aloe(plant)
awl(tool)
eel(animal)
el(or)ell
(the letter *L*)
ell(measure)
ell(structure)
ill(sick)
isle(island)
la(interj)
la(tone)
law

lay(put)	**LBDNG**	lawbreaker	liberties
laid	ill-boding	**LBRKSHN**	libretto
lays	law-abiding	lubrication	librettos(or)
lei(flowers)	**LBDNS**	**LBRKT**	libretti
Leo	libidinous	lubricate	librettist
lie(rest)	**LBGRS**	lubricated	**LBRTL**
lay	elbow grease	lubricating	elaborately
lying	**LBJB**	**LBRKTR**	**LBRTN**
lain	lube job	lubricator	libertine
lies	**LBKR**	**LBRL**	**LBRTR**
lie(false)	albacore(fish)	illiberal	elaborator
lied	**LBKRK**	liberal	laboratory
lies	Albuquerque	**LBRLT**	laboratories
lying	**LBL**	liberality	liberator
lieu(in place	allowable	liberalities	**LBRTRN**
of)	label(tag)	**LBRLZ**	libertarian
lo(interj)	labial(lip)	liberalize	**LBRTST**
low	labile(unstable)	liberalized	librettist
luau(feast)	liable(likely,	liberalizing	**LBRV**
lye(chemical)	law)	**LBRLZR**	alla breve(music)
oil	libel(defame)	liberalizer	**LBSHN**
oily	**LBLS**	**LBRM**	libation
oilier	libelous	elbowroom	**LBSNT**
oiliest	**LBLT**	Librium	albescent
oiliness	liability	**LBRN**	**LBST**
old(time)	liabilities	librarian	lobbyist
olé(interj)	**LBM**	**LBRNTH**	**LBSTR**
oleo(butter)	Alabama	labyrinth	alabaster
olio(mixture)	album	**LBRNTHN**	lobster
olla(pot)	**LBN**	labyrinthine	**LBT**
olla podrida	Albania	**LBRR**	albeit
owl(bird)	Albany	laborer, (B)labourer	**LBTM**
LB	albino	library	lobotomy
alb(robe)	**LBNG**	libraries	lobotomies
alibi(story)	ill-being	**LBRRN**	**LBTRS**
Elba	**LBNN**	librarian	albatross
elbow	Albanian	**LBRS**	albatrosses
lab(laboratory)	Lebanon	laborious	**LBYMN**
Libya	**LBNY**	**LBRSHN**	albumen(egg white)
lob	Albania	elaboration	albumin
lobbed	**LBNZM**	liberation	(biochemistry)
lobbing	albinism	**LBRST**	**LBYMNS**
lobe(ear)	**LBR**	lubricity	albuminous
lobby	labor, (B)labour	**LBRSVNG**	**LCH**
lobbied	Liberia	labor-saving	latch
lobbies	Libra	**LBRT**	latches
looby(person)	library(books)	Alberta	leach(filter)
lowboy	libraries	elaborate	leaches
lube(lubrication)	lowbrow	elaborated	leech(worm)
lubed	**LBRD**	elaborating	leeches
lubing	ill-bred	liberate	**LCHK**
LBD	Labor Day, (B)Labour	liberated	latchkey
libido	lowbred	liberating	**LCHNT**
LBDM	**LBRKNT**	liberation	litchi nut
lobotomy	lubricant	liberator	**LCHR**
lobotomies	**LBRKR**	liberty	lecher

B:by **CH**:each **D**:day **F**:if **G**:go **H**:he **HW**:why **J**:joy **K**:cow **KS**:ax **KWL**:equal **L**:all **M**:may **N**:in

lechery
lecheries
LCHRS
lecherous
LCHSTRNG
latchstring
LCHZ
laches(delay)
LD
allowed(permit)
allow
allude(refer)
alluded
alluding
aloud(sound)
elide(leave out)
elided
eliding
elude(escape)
eluded
eluding
eyelid
Iliad(poem)
lad(boy)
lade(load)
laded
lading
laden
lady
ladies
laud(praise)
lead(metal)
lead(go before)
led
leader
lewd
lid
lidded
load(burden)
lode(ore)
loud(sound)
old
LDBG
ladybug
LDBL
laudable
laudably
LDD
alidade
loaded
LDF
leadoff(adj)
lead off(v)
LDFNGR
ladyfinger
LDFSHND

old-fashioned
LDG
Ladoga
LDK
lotic
LDKRS
ludicrous
LDL
ladle
ladled
ladling
little(small)
littler
littlest
LDLK
ladylike
LDLN
old-line
LDLNGZN
auld lang syne
LDLS
lidless
LDMTH
loudmouth
LDMTHT
loudmouthed
LDN
laden(loaded)
leaden(metal)
lead-in
low-down
louden(loud)
LDNG
lading(cargo)
leading
LDNGZN
auld lang syne
LDNS
lewdness
LDP
letup(n,adj)
LDR
elder
ladder(tool)
later(late)
latest
latter(last)
leader
letter(write)
liter(unit)
litter(trash,
birth)
older
LDRBG
litterbug
LDRHD

letterhead
LDRL
elderly
lateral
literal(exact)
LDRMN
alderman
LDRS
illiteracy
LDRSHN
alliteration
LDRSHP
leadership
LDRSHS
lateritious
LDRT
illiterate
LDS
lattice(design)
lettuce(food)
lotus
LDSH
oldish
LDSHP
ladyship
LDSPKR
loud speaker
LDSPZD
ill-disposed
LDST
eldest
oldest
LDSTH
Old South
LDSTN
lodestone
LDSTR
oldster
LDTMR
old-timer
LDTR
laudatory
LDTSTMNT
Old Testament
LDVZD
ill-advised
LDWRLD
old-world(adj)
Old World
LDZ
Leeds
LDZMN
lady's man
LDZRM
ladies' room
LF

aloof
elf(tiny helper)
elves
laugh
lay off(v)
layoff(n)
leaf(plant)
leaves
leafy
leafier
leafiest
leafiness
lev
leva
life
lives
loaf
loaves
luff(sail)
LFB
lifebuoy
LFBL
laughable
laughably
LFBLD
lifeblood
LFBLT
lifebelt
LFBT
alphabet
lifeboat
LFBTK
alphabetic
LFBTKL
alphabetical
LFBTZ
alphabetize
alphabetized
alphabetizing
LFGRD
lifeguard
LFGVNG
life-giving
LFKD
Alfa code
LFKSHN
olfaction
LFKTR
olfactory
olfactories
LFL
lawful
LFLF
alfalfa
LFLK
lifelike

LFLN
lifeline
LFLNG
lifelong
LFLS
lifeless
LFLSD
All Fools' Day
LFLT
leaflet
LFN
allophone
elfin
LFNDD
ill-founded
LFNG
laughing
LFNGSTK
laughingstock
LFNL
aleph-null
LFNMRK
alphanumeric
LFNT
elephant
LFNTN
elephantine
LFNTSS
elephantiasis
LFNYMRK
alphanumeric
LFR
lifer(prisoner)
loafer
LFRD
all-fired
LFRFT
life raft
LFRS
all fours
LFRSK
alfresco
LFSH
elfish
LFSNTR
Alpha Centauri
LFSTL
lifestyle
LFSVR
lifesaver
LFSZ
life-size
life-sized
LFT
left
lefty

lefties
lift
loft
lofty
loftier
loftiest
loftily
loftiness
LFTD
ill-fated
LFTF
liftoff
LFTHNDD
left-handed
LFTHNDR
left-hander
LFTM
lifetime
LFTR
laughter
LFTST
leftist
LFTVR
leftover
LFTWNG
left wing(n)
left-wing(adj)
LFTWNGR
left-winger
LFTZ
lifties(shoes)
LFVRD
ill-favored
LFWRK
lifework
LG
alga
algae
lag
lagged
lagging
league
leagued
leaguing
leaguer
leg(limb)
legged
legging
leggy
leggier
leggiest
legginess
log(wood)
logged
logging
logger

logo
logy(sluggish)
logier
logiest
lug
lugged
lugging
LGBRS
lugubrious
LGCHR
ligature
ligatured
ligaturing
LGFB
algophobia(pain)
LGGRF
logograph
LGGRM
logogram
logogrammatic
LGJ
luggage
LGJM
logjam
LGL
illegal
legal
LGLJ
legal age
LGLSTK
legalistic
LGLSTKL
legalistically
LGLT
illegality
illegalities
legality
legalities
LGLTNDR
legal tender
LGLZ
legalese
legalize
legalized
legalizing
LGLZM
legalism
LGLZSHN
legalization
LGMN
legman
legmen
LGMNT
ligament
LGN
Allegheny

Alleghenies
lagoon
LGNS
elegance
ligneous
LGNT
elegant
lignite
LGPDKS
logopedics
LGPL
oligopoly
oligopolies
LGPSN
oligopsony
oligopsonies
oligopsonistic
LGR
alegar(vinegar)
allegory
allegories
allegro
lager(beer)
leaguer
logger
logorrhea
Luger(gun)
lugger(boat)
LGRBR
lager beer
LGRD
laggard
low-grade
LGRHD
loggerhead
LGRK
allegoric
oligarch
oligarchy
oligarchies
LGRKL
allegorical
LGRM
legroom
LGRST
allegorist
LGRT
allegretto(music)
LGRTHM
algorithm
logarithm
LGRTHMK
algorithmic
logarithmic
LGRZ
allegorize

B:by **CH**:each **D**:day **F**:if **G**:go **H**:he **HW**:why **J**:joy **K**:cow **KS**:ax **KWL**:equal **L**:all **M**:may **N**:in

allegorized
allegorizing
LGS
Lagos
legacy
legacies
LGSHN
allegation
legation(trip)
ligation(binding)
LGT
legatee
(inheritor)
legato
ligate
ligated
ligating
ligation
LGTMS
illegitimacy
illegitimacies
legitimacy
legitimacies
LGTMT
illegitimate
legitimate
LGTN
ill-gotten
LGTR
alligator
LGVR
lawgiver
LGYBRS
lugubrious
LGYM
legume
LGZHR
luxury
luxuries
LGZHRNS
luxuriance
LGZHRNT
luxuriant
LGZHRS
luxurious
LGZHRT
luxuriate
luxuriated
luxuriating
LGZNDR
Alexander
Alexandria
LHR
Lahore
LHYMRD
ill-humored

LJ
algae(plants)
alga(sing)
algal
allege(say)
alleged
alleging
elegy
elegies
ledge
lodge(house)
lodged
lodging
lodger
loggia
ullage(liquid)
LJBL
allegeable(excuse)
eligible(fit)
eligibly
illegible
illegibly
legible(clear)
legibly
LJBLT
eligibility(fit)
eligibilities
illegibility
illegibilities
legibility
legibilities
LJBR
algebra
LJBRK
algebraic
LJD
algid
algidity
LJK
elegiac
elegy
logic
LJKL
illogical
logical
LJMNT
lodgment
LJN
legend
legion(many,army)
LJND
legend
LJNDR
legendary
LJNG
lodging(house)

LJNR
legionnaire
LJNS
allegiance
LJR
Algeria
ledger
lodger
LJRDMN
legerdemain
LJRZ
Algiers
LJSHN
logician
LJSLCHR
legislature
LJSLSHN
legislation
LJSLT
legislate
legislated
legislating
LJSLTR
legislator
LJSLTV
legislative
LJSTK
logistic
LJSTKL
logistical
LJSTKS
logistics
LJT
legit
LJTMS
illegitimacy
illigitimacies
legitimacy
legitimacies
LJTMST
legitimist
LJTMT
illegitimate
legitimate
LJTMZ
legitimize
legitimized
legitimizing
LJTMZM
legitimism
LJZ
elegize
elegized
elegizing
LK
alky(alcoholic)

alkies
ilk
lack
laic(adj)
laity
lake(water)
lackey
leak(escape)
leaky
leakier
leakiest
leakiness
leek(vegetable)
lick
like(prefer)
liked
liking
liken
lock(key)
loco(plant,crazy)
locus
loci
look
low-key
luck
lucky
luckier
luckiest
luckily
luckiness
LKBL
allocable
likable
LKCHR
lecture
lectured
lecturing
lecturer
LKD
alcaide
LKDSPLT
lickety-split
LKDZKL
lackadaisical
LKHL
alcohol
LKHLK
alcoholic
alcoholicity
alcoholism
LKHLZM
alcoholism
LKHYRN
Lake Huron
LKJ
leakage

lockjaw
LKL
  alkali
    alkalis
  likely
    likelier
    likeliest
  local(near)
  locale(area)
LKLD
  alcalde
LKLHD
  likelihood
LKLN
  alkaline
LKLNT
  alkalinity
LKLR
  all clear(n)
LKLS
  luckless
LKLSTR
  lackluster, (B)-tre
LKLT
  locality
    localities
LKLTH
  oilcloth
LKLZ
  localize
    localized
    localizing
LKLZM
  localism
LKLZSHN
  localization
LKM
  alchemy
    alchemies
  leukemia
LKMDV
  locomotive
LKMNDD
  like-minded
LKMSHN
  locomotion
LKMST
  alchemist
LKMSTK
  alchemistic
LKMTV
  locomotive
LKN
  lichen(plant)
  liken
LKNG

à la king
LKNK
  laconic
LKNKL
  laconically
LKNS
  likeness
LKNSDRD
  ill-considered
LKR
  lacquer(paint)
  Lake Erie
  liqueur(alcohol-
    sweet)
  liquor(alcohol)
  locker
  looker
  lucre(money)
LKRM
  locker room
LKRML
  lachrymal
LKRMS
  lachrymose
LKRMSHN
  lacrimation
LKRN
  looker-on
    lookers-on
  onlooker
LKRS
  lacrosse(game)
  licorice, (B)liquorice
LKRSH
  lickerish
    (lecherous)
  licorice, (B)liquorice
LKRT
  à la carte
  alacrity
    alacritous
LKRTS
  alacritous
    alacrity
LKRTV
  lucrative
LKRZN
  lookers-on
LKS
  alexia
  lax
  locus(place)
    loci
  locust(grasshopper)
    locust
  locks(hair)

look-see(a look)
lox(food,oxygen)
lux(lumen)
  luxes(or)
  luces
LKSDZKL
  lackadaisical
LKSHN
  allocation
  election
  location
LKSHNR
  electioneer
LKSKGRF
  lexicography
LKSKGRFR
  lexicographer
LKSKL
  lexical
LKSKLJ
  lexicology
LKSKLSKS
  locus classicus
    loci classici
LKSKN
  lexicon
LKSMBRG
  Luxembourg
LKSMTH
  locksmith
LKSN
  alexin(blood)
LKSNDR
  Alexander
  Alexandria
LKSNGTN
  Lexington
LKSPRR
  Lake Superior
LKSR
  elixir
LKSS
  lexis
LKST
  laxity
    laxities
  lockset
  locust(grasshopper)
    locust
  low-cost
LKSTV
  laxative
LKT
  alley cat
  allocate
    allocated

    allocating
  elect
  locate
    located
    locating
  locket(necklace)
  lockout(n)
  lookout
LKTK
  lactic
LKTL
  lacteal
LKTNSHTN
  Liechtenstein
LKTR
  elector
  locator
LKTRD
  electrode
LKTRF
  electrify
    electrified
    electrifies
LKTRFKSHN
  electrification
LKTRK
  electric
LKTRKL
  electrical
LKTRKYSHN
  electrocution
LKTRKYT
  electrocute
    electrocuted
    electrocuting
LKTRL
  electoral
LKTRLSS
  electrolysis
LKTRLT
  electrolyte
LKTRLTK
  electrolytic
LKTRLZ
  electrolyze
    electrolyzed
    electrolyzing
LKTRMGNT
  electromagnet
LKTRMTR
  electrometer
LKTRMTV
  electromotive
LKTRN
  electron
  lectern

B:by **CH**:each **D**:day **F**:if **G**:go **H**:he **HW**:why **J**:joy **K**:cow **KS**:ax **KWL**:equal **L**:all **M**:may **N**:in

LKTRNGTV
electronegative
LKTRNK
electronic
LKTRPLT
electroplate
electroplated
electroplating
LKTRSHN
electrician
LKTRSKP
electroscope
LKTRST
electricity
electricities
LKTRSTTK
electrostatic
LKTRSTTKS
electrostatics
LKTRT
electorate
LKTRTHRP
electrotherapy
electrotherapies
LKTRTP
electrotype
LKTS
lactose
LKTSHN
lactation
LKTSPLT
lickety-split
LKTT
lactate
lactated
lactating
LKTV
elective
LKV
alcove
LKWD
liquid
locoweed
LKWDSHN
liquidation
LKWDT
liquidate
liquidated
liquidating
liquidity
liquidities
LKWDTR
liquidator
LKWF
liquefy
liquefied

liquefies
LKWFBL
liquefiable
LKWFKSHN
liquefaction
LKWFR
liquefier
LKWNS
eloquence
LKWNT
eloquent
LKWRM
lukewarm
LKWSHS
loquacious
LKWSNT
liquescent
LKWST
loquacity
loquacities
LKWZ
likewise
LKYBRSHN
lucubration
LKYLNT
luculent
LKYN
lacuna
lacunae(or)
lacunas
LKYR
liqueur
LKYSHN
allocution(formal
  speech)
elocution(art of
  speaking)
locution(style of
  word spoken)
LKZNDR
Alexandria
LL
lily
  lilies
lisle
loll(movement)
lowly
  lowlier
  lowliest
  lowliness
loyal
lull(soothe)
lulu
LLB
lullaby
  lullabies

LLHWT
lily-white
LLK
lilac
LLLVRD
lily-livered
LLNGZN
auld lang syne
LLPP
lollipop
LLPYSHN
Lilliputian
LLS
lawless
LLSHN
lalation
LLST
loyalist
LLT
loyalty
  loyalties
LLVL
low-level
LLWT
lily-white(pure)
LLY
alleluia(interj)(or)
hallelujah
LM
alamo(tree)
Alamo(the)
elm
ileum(intestine)
ilium(bone)
lam(escape)
  lammed
  lamming
lama(monk)
lamb(animal)
lame(crippled)
lamé(fabric)
Lima
lima(bean)
limb(branch)
lime(fruit,mineral)
  limed,liming
limey(British
  seaman)
limo(slang)
  limousine
limmy(tool)(slang)
limn(draw)
llama(animal)
loam(soil)
loamy(soil)
loamier,-iest

loaminess
ulema
  ulema(or)
  ulemas
LMB
limbo
LMBG
lumbago
LMBK
alembic
LMBLST
lambaste
  lambasted
  lambasting
LMBN
lima bean
LMBNT
lambent
LMBR
limber(flexible)
lumbar(back)
lumber(wood)
LMBRJK
lumberjack
KMBRKN
lambrequin
LMBRN
lamebrain
LMBRYRD
lumberyard
LMBST
lambaste
  lambasted
  lambasting
LMD
alameda
à la mode(style)
alamode(silk)
LMDK
lame duck
LMF
lymph
LMFND
lymph node
LMFTK
lymphatic
LMKLS
limicolous
LMKN
lambkin
LMKR
lawmaker
LMKS
lummox
  lummoxes
LML

NG**K**:ink **P**:pie **R**:air **S**:ice **SH**:show **T**:toy **THN**:thin **TH**:the **V**:of **W**:we **Y**:you **Z**:is **VZHN**:vision

lamella
lamellae(or)
lamellas
LMLT
limelight
LMMDR
alma mater
LMMR
almemar
LMMTR
alma mater
LMN
alimony
alimonies
almond(nut)
alumna(f)
alumnae
layman
laymen
lemon(fruit)
lemony
lumen
lumina(or)
lumens
LMND
allemande
almond
lemonade
LMNDD
low-minded
LMNG
lemming
LMNK
Alemannic
almanac
LMNM
aluminum, (B)-nium
LMNR
almoner
luminary
luminaries
LMNRD
ill-mannered
LMNS
alumnus
alumni
luminous
LMNSHN
elimination
illumination
lumination
lamination
LMNSNS
luminescence
LMNSNT
luminescent

LMNST
luminosity
luminosities
LMNT
ailment(hurt)
aliment(food)
element
eliminate(remove)
eliminated
eliminating
elimination
illuminate
illuminated
illuminating
illumination
lament(sorry)
laminate
laminated
laminating
lamination
LMNTBL
lamentable
LMNTL
elemental
LMNTR
alimentary(food)
elementary(basic)
illuminator
LMNTRNS
elementariness
LMNTSHN
lamentation
LMNZ
lumens
LMP
lamp
limp
lump
lumpy
lumpier
lumpiest
lumpiness
Olympia
LMPBLK
lampblack
LMPD
limpid
olympiad
LMPK
olympic
LMPKS
Olympics
(international)
LMPN
lampoon
LMPR

lamprey(fish)
lamper(eel)
lempira
LMPRTNT
all-important
LMPSH
lumpish
LMPST
lamppost
LMRF
allomorph
LMRJRN
oleomargarine
LMRK
limerick
LMRKN
All-American(n)
all-American(adj)
LMSKN
lambskin
LMSNR
eleemosynary
LMSR
lamasery
lamaseries
LMST
almost(nearly)
lamest(lame)
loamiest(loamy)
LMSTN
limestone
LMT
Almighty(God)
almighty
almightiness
limit
LMTBL
illimitable
illimitably
limitable
LMTD
Ltd.(name)
limited
Ltd.(or)ltd.
LMTNS
almightiness
LMTR
limiter
LMTS
limits
LMTSHN
limitation
LMTTV
limitative
LMZ
alms

LMZN
limousine
LN
alien
align
alone(solitary)
élan(spirit)
Illinois
island
lain(resting)
lane(way)
Latin
lawn(grass)
lean(thin,slant)
lien(claim)
line
lined
lining
lion(animal)
llano(plain)
loan(lend)
loin(body area)
lone(solitary)
loon(bird,person)
loony(person)
loonies
loonier
looniest
loonily
looniness
lune(sphere)
luna(moon,silver)
Lyon
uhlan(cavalry)
ulna
LNBKR
linebacker
LNBL
alienable
LNBRN
lamebrain
LNCH
lunch
lunches
lynch
lynches
LNCHN
luncheon
LNCHNG
lynching
LNCHNT
luncheonette
LNCHPN
linchpin
LNCHRD
ill-natured

B:by **CH**:each **D**:day **F**:if **G**:go **H**:he **HW**:why **J**:joy **K**:cow **KS**:ax **KWL**:equal **L**:all **M**:may **N**:in

LND
island
land
landau
lend
lent
Luanda
LNDFL
landfill
LNDHLDR
landholder
LNDLBR
landlubber
LNDLD
landlady
landladies
LNDLKT
landlocked
LNDLRD
landlord
LNDMN
land mine
LNDMRK
landmark
LNDN
linden
London
LNDNG
landing
LNDNR
landowner
LNDR
launder
laundry
laundries
oleander
LNDRMN
laundryman
laundrymen
LNDRMT
Laundromat
(trademark)
LNDRS
laundress
LNDRVR
Land-Rover
(trademark)
LNDSKP
landscape
landscaped
landscaping
landscapist
LNDSLD
landslide (B)landslip
LNG
ailing

ail
along
lingo
lingoes
long
lung
oolong(tea)
LNGB
longbow
LNGDRN
long-drawn(adj)
long-drawn-out
LNGDSTNS
long-distance
(adj,adv)
LNGG
lingo
lingoes
LNGGWD
languid
LNGGWJ
language
LNGGWL
lingual
LNGGWN
linguini
LNGGWSH
languish
languishes
LNGGWST
linguist
LNGGWSTK
linguistic
linguistical
linguistics
LNGHND
longhand
LNGHR
longhair(person)
LNGHRN
longhorn
LNGK
lank
lanky
lankier
lankiest
lankiness
link
LNGKJ
linkage
LNGKN
Lincoln
LNGKNS
lankness(n)
Lincoln Sea
LNGKS

links(golf)
lynx(animal)
LNGLNG
ylang-ylang
LNGLVD
long-lived
LNGN
lying-in
LNGNG
longing
LNGPLNG
long-playing
LNGR
languor
linger(wait)
LNGRN
long run
LNGRNJ
long-range
LNGRS
languorous
LNGSD
alongside
LNGSFRNG
long-suffering
LNGSHN
elongation
LNGSHR
alongshore
LNGSHRMN
longshoreman
longshoremen
LNGSTNDNG
long-standing
LNGT
elongate
elongated
elongating
LNGTH
length
lengthy
lengthier
lengthiest
lengthily
lengthiness
LNGTHN
lengthen
LNGTHWZ
lengthwise
LNGTM
long time(n)
longtime(adj)
LNGTN
long ton
LNGTRM
long-term(adj)

LNGWD
languid
LNGWJ
language
LNGWL
lingual
LNGWN
linguini
LNGWNDD
long-winded
LNGWSH
languish
languishes
LNGWST
linguist
LNGWSTK
linguistic
LNGWSTKL
linguistically
LNGWSTKS
linguistics
LNGWZ
longwise
LNGZ
lingoes
LNGZN
auld lang syne
LNHRTD
lionhearted
LNJ
linage(number
of lines)
lineage(ancestry)
lounge(rest)
lounged
lounging
lounger
lunge(move)
lunged
lunging
lunger
LNJR
lingerie(attire)
lunger
LNJRN
longeron
LNJTD
longitude
LNJTDNL
longitudinal
LNJVT
longevity
LNKLSV
all-inclusive
LNKLTH
loincloth

NGK:ink **P**:pie **R**:air **S**:ice **SH**:show **T**:toy **THN**:thin **TH**:the **V**:of **W**:we **Y**:you **Z**:is **VZHN**:vision

LNKT
low-necked
LNL
lineal
lonely
lonelier
loneliest
loneliness
LNLM
linoleum
LNLN
lanolin
LNM
allonym
LNMN
lineman
linemen
LNMNT
alignment
lineament(feature)
liniment
(medication)
LNMR
lawn mower
LNMRK
Latin America
LNN
linen
LNNG
leaning
lining
LNNGRD
Leningrad
LNNS
leniency
leniencies
LNNT
lenient
LNP
line up(v)
line-up(n)
LNR
alienor(person)
eye liner
lanner(falcon)
linear(line,math)
liner(line)
loner(lone)
lunar(moon)
LNRDDVNCH
Leonardo da Vinci
LNRN
lantern
LNRT
lanneret
LNRVR

Land-Rover
(trademark)
LNS
alliance
allowance
illness
illnesses
lance(pole)
lanced
lancing
lancer
leanness
lenis(phonics)
lioness
lionesses
lunacy
lunacies
LNSD
linseed
LNSHN
alienation
lination
lunation
LNSHRK
loan shark
LNSM
lonesome
LNSNG
Lansing
LNSR
lancer
LNST
lancet
LNT
alienate
alienated
alienating
alienator
alienation
lanate(wool)
lean-to
lenity
lenities
Lent
lent(lend)
lento(music)
lineate(line)
lineated,-ting
lint(material)
lunette(shape)
lunt(smoke)
LNTK
lunatic
LNTKYLR
lenticular(lens)
LNTL

lentil(pea)
lintel(beam)
LNTP
linotype
LNTR
alienator
LNTRN
lantern
LNTSL
lenticel
LNTV
lenitive
LNYNS
leniency
leniencies
LNYNT
lenient
LNYP
lagniappe
LNYRD
lanyard
LNZ
Illinois
lens
lenses(or)
lens
lionize
lionized
lionizing
lionizer
lyonnaise
LNZHR
lingerie
LNZMN
landsman
landsmen
linesman
linesmen
LNZR
lionizer
LNZSHN
lionization
LNZWLZ
linsey-woolsey
LP
alp(mountain)
elope
eloped
eloping
lap
lapped
lapping
leap(jump)
leaped(or)
leapt
lip

lipped
lipping
loop(circle)
lop(cut off)
lopped
lopping
lope(run)
loped
loping
loupe(eye glass)
LPCHT
low-pitched
LPD
lipid
LPDR
lapidary
lapidaries
LPFL
lapful
LPFRG
leapfrog
leapfrogged
leapfrogging
LPGRF
lipography
LPHL
loophole
LPK
alpaca
LPL
aeolipile
lapel
LPLND
Lapland
LPMNT
elopement
LPN
alpine
lapin
lupine
LPNGL
alpenglow
LPNHRN
alpenhorn
LPNSTK
alpenstock
LPPR
oilpaper
LPR
leaper(jumper)
leper(sick one)
loper(runner)
LPRD
leopard
lip-read
lip-read

B:by **CH**:each **D**:day **F**:if **G**:go **H**:he **HW**:why **J**:joy **K**:cow **KS**:ax **KWL**:equal **L**:all **M**:may **N**:in

LPRDNG
lip-reading
LPRKN
leprechaun
LPRPS
all-purpose
LPRS
leprosy
leprosies
leprous
LPRSHR
low-pressure
low-pressured
low-pressuring
LPS
Alps
elapse
elapsed
elapsing
ellipse(shape)
El Paso
lapse
lapsed
lapsing
lupus
LPSD
ellipsoid
LPSDD
lopsided
LPSH
Lappish
LPSLZYL
lapis lazuli
LPSNGK
lip-sync
LPSS
ellipsis
ellipses
LPSTK
lipstick
LPSTRN
alpestrine
LPT
eelpout(fish)
eelpout(or)
eelpouts
lappet(fold)
LPTKL
elliptical
LPYR
leap year
LPZ
La Paz
LR
alar(adj)(wings)
(or)alary

allure
allured
alluring
lair(den)
layer(stratum)
leer(look)
leery
leerier
leeriest
leerily
leeriness
liar(lie)
lira(money)
lore(tradition)
lorry
lorries
lower
lure
lured
luring
lyre(harp)
LRCH
lurch
lurches
LRD
already(previously)
all ready(all
   prepared)
lard
Laredo
leeward
Lord(title)
lord
lurid
LRDL
lordly
lordlier
lordliest
lordliness
LRDR
larder
LRDSHP
lordship
LRDSS
lordosis
LRG
largo
LRGT
larghetto
LRJ
allergy
allergies
large
larger
largest
LRJK

allergic
LRJS
largess
LRJSH
largish
LRJSKL
large-scale
LRJST
allergist
LRK
lark
lurk(hide)
lyric
LRKL
lyrical
LRKLS
lower-class(adj)
lower class(n)
LRKLSMN
lower classman
lower classmen
LRKNG
lurking
LRKS
lyrics
LRL
laurel
LRM
alarm
LRMKLK
alarm clock
LRMNT
allurement
LRMST
alarmist
LRN
aileron
learn
learned(or)
learnt
LRND
all-around(or)
all-round
LRNGKS
larynx
larynxes
LRNJL
laryngeal
LRNJTS
laryngitis
LRNJZ
larynges
LRNKS
larynx
larynxes(or)
larynges

LRNNG
learning
LRNT
learnt
learn
LRNYN
lorgnon
LRNYT
lorgnette
LRSN
larceny
larcenies
LRSNS
larcenous
LRSST
lyricist
LRST
lyrist
LRSZM
lyricism
LRT
alert
all right
lariat(rope)
laureate(person)
LRV
larva
larvae(or)
larvas
LS
alas(interj)
alias
aliases
also
aweless
else
lace
laced
lacing
lacy
lacier
laciest
laciness
Laos
lass
lasso(rope)
lease
leased
leasing
less(not more)
lessee(lease)
lice
louse
loose(free)
loosed
loosing

NGK:ink P:pie R:air S:ice SH:show T:toy THN:thin TH:the V:of W:we Y:you Z:is VZHN:vision

looser
loosest
loosen
loss(thing lost)
losses
louse
lice(or)
louses
louse(slang)
loused
lousing
LSBK
lease-back
LSBL
leasable
LSD
LCD
liquid crystal
display
LSD
lysergic acid
diethylamide
lucid
LSDSHN
elucidation
LSDT
elucidate
elucidated
elucidating
lucidity
lucidities
LSFR
laissez faire
Lucifer
LSFRS
luciferous
LSH
eyelash
eyelashes
lash(tie,whip)
lashes
leash
leashes
lush
lushes
owlish
LSHLDR
leaseholder
LSHN
Aleutian
elation(emotion)
illation
(inference)
Laotian
lotion
LSHNG

lashing
LSHNS
lushness
LSHS
luscious
LSHWR
elsewhere
LSJNTD
loose-jointed
LSK
Alaska
LSKN
oilskin
LSL
loosely
LSLF
loose-leaf
LSLS
listless
LSLSD
All Souls' Day
LSLVDR
El Salvador
LSM
lissome(supple)
lyceum
LSN
lessen(less)
lesson
(instruction)
listen(ear)
loosen(free)
LSNCHS
licentious
LSNGGLS
Los Angeles
LSNJLS
Los Angeles
LSNN
Eleusinian
LSNR
listener
LSNS
license, (B)-ce(n)
licensed
licensing
LSNSBL
licensable
LSNSHS
licentious
LSNSR
licenser
LSNT
lucent
LSNTSD
All Saints' Day

LSP
lisp
LSPNT
ill-spent
LSPR
lisper
LSPRTD
low-spirited
LSPS
allspice
LSR
illusory
illusorily
illusoriness
lesser(smaller)
lessor(lease)
looser
ulcer
LSRL
illusorily
LSRN
also-ran(n)
LSRNS
illusoriness
LSRS
ulcerous
LSRSHN
laceration
ulceration
LSRT
lacerate
lacerated
lacerating
ulcerate
ulcerated
ulcerating
LSRTD
ill-sorted
LSRTV
ulcerative
LST
elicit(draw forth)
illicit(unlawful)
last
lawsuit
leased(contract)
least(smallest)
Lesotho
licit(legal)
list
lost
lowest
lust(desire)
lusty
lustier
lustiest

lustily
lustiness
LSTD
ill-suited
lassitude
LSTDCH
last-ditch
LSTFL
lustful
LSTH
Old South
LSTHN
lecithin
LSTK
elastic
LSTL
lastly
LSTLS
listless
LSTN
oilstone
LSTNG
lasting
LSTNGD
loose-tongued
LSTR
all-star(adj)
leister(spear)
luster, (B)lustre
ulster
Ulster(Ireland)
LSTRD
ill-starred
LSTRS
illustrious
lustrous
LSTRSHN
illustration
LSTRT
illustrate
illustrated
illustrating
illustrator
LSTRTR
illustrator
LSTRTV
illustrative
LSTSPR
Last Supper
LSTST
elasticity
elasticities
LSTSZ
elasticize
elasticized
elasticizing

LSTSZR
elasticizer
LSTYD
lassitude
LSV
allusive
(suggestive)
elusive(evade)
illusive(deceive)
LSVGS
Las Vegas
LSVL
Louisville
LSVS
lascivious
LSWR
elsewhere
LSWRK
lacework
LT
alight
alighted(or)
alit
allot
allotted
allotting
allottee(person)
allot
all out(adv)
all-out(adj)
a lot(many)
alto(stop)
elate
elated
elating
elite
eyelet(hole)
islet(island)
laity
laities
late
later
latest
layette(baby)
layout
let
let
letting
light
lit
lot
lout(oaf)
LTD
alated(winged)
elated(happy)
LTDN

letdown
LTFNGRD
light-fingered
LTFS
lightface
LTFTD
light-footed
LTGBL
litigable
LTGNT
litigant
LTGSHN
litigation
LTGT
litigate
litigated
litigating
LTGTHR
altogether
(entirely)
all together
(group)
LTH
althea(shrub)
although
eolith
lath(wood strip)
lathe(machine)
lathed
lathing
lithe(supple)
loath
(unwilling)
loathe(detest)
loathed
loathing
LTHDD
lightheaded
LTHGRF
lithograph
lithography
LTHGRFR
lithographer
LTHK
Eolithic
lithic
LTHL
lethal
LTHM
lithium
LTHNDD
light-handed
LTHNN
Lithuanian
LTHR
lather(soap)

leather(hide)
leathery
leatheriness
Lothario
LTHRJ
lethargy
lethargies
LTHRJK
lethargic
LTHRJKL
lethargical
LTHRJZ
lethargize
lethargized
lethargizing
LTHRNK
leatherneck
LTHRNS
leatheriness
LTHRT
leatherette
LTHRTD
lighthearted
LTHS
lighthouse
LTHSFR
lithosphere
LTHSM
loathsome
LTHVWT
light heavyweight
(161-175 lbs)
LTHWNN
Lithuanian
LTJS
litigious
LTK
lotic
LTKS
latex
latexes
LTKYLR
lenticular
LTL
all told
lightly
little
littler
littlest
LTLD
all told
LTLRK
Little Rock
LTM
all-time(adj)
ultima

LTMD
ill-timed
LTMDM
ultimatum
ultimatums(or)
ultimata
LTMNDD
light-minded
LTMNT
allotment
LTMPRD
ill-tempered
LTMS
litmus
LTMT
ultimate
LTMTM
ultimatum
ultimata(or)
ultimatums
LTMTR
altimeter
LTN
lateen(sail)
Latin
lighten
litany
litanies
LTND
lightened
LTNG
lighting
LTNMRK
Latin America
LTNNG
lightening
(less heavy)
lightning(flash
of light)
LTNNS
lieutenancy
LTNNT
lieutenant
LTNS
latency
latencies
LTNT
latent
LTP
let up(v)
letup(n)
LTR
aleatory(chance)
altar(worship)
alter(change)
later(time)

latter(place)
letter(paper)
lighter
liter(volume), (B)-tre
litter (rubbish)
loiter
lottery
lotteries
ultra
LTRB
altar boy
LTRBL
alterable
LTRBG
litterbug
LTRCHR
literature
LTRD
latter-day
leotard
lettered
LTRG
alter ego
LTRHD
letterhead
LTRHFRKWNS
ultrahigh
frequency
UHF
LTRJ
liturgy
liturgies
LTRJKL
liturgical
LTRKNSRVTV
ultraconservative
LTRKSHN
altercation
LTRKT
altercate
altercated
altercating
LTRL
altar rail
Laetrile
(trademark)
lateral
literal(exact)
littoral(shore)
LTRLZ
literalize
literalized
literalizing
LTRLZM
literalism
LTRMDRN

ultramodern
LTRMKRSKP
ultramicroscope
LTRMNDN
ultramundane
LTRMRN
ultramarine
LTRN
latrine
LTRNSHN
alternation
LTRNSHNLZM
ultranationalism
LTRNT
alternate
alternated
alternating
LTRNTR
alternator
LTRPRFKT
letter-perfect
LTRPRS
letterpress
letterpresses
LTRPS
altar piece
LTRR
literary
ulterior
LTRS
illiteracy
literacy
LTRSHL
altricial
LTRSHN
alliteration
alteration
LTRSHS
lateritious
LTRSND
ultrasound
LTRSNK
ultrasonic
LTRST
altruist
altruistic
LTRT
alliterate
alliterated
alliterating
illiterate
ill-treat
literate(read)
literati
LTRTV
alliterative

LTRVLT
ultraviolet
LTRVRS
ultravirus
LTRZM
altruism
ultraism
LTRZPTNT
letters patent
LTS
lattice(design)
latticed
latticing
lettuce(food)
lotus
LTSH
latish(late)
loutish
LTSNG
latticing
LTST
latest
lightest
lutist
LTSWRK
latticework
LTTD
altitude
latitude
LTTYD
altitude
latitude
LTTZ
litotes
LTV
illative
(inference)
LTWT
lightweight
(127-135 lbs)
LTYR
light-year
LTZ
altos
LTZM
elitism
LTZMTH
altazimuth
LV
alive
lava(hot rock)
lave(wash)
laved
laving
leave(let stay)
left

leaving
leave(foliage)
leaved
leaving
levee
(embankment)
levy(tax)
levied
levies
live
lived
living
Louvre(art)
love
loved
loving
lover
olive
LVB
lavabo
lavaboes
LVBL
leviable(tax)
livable(live)
lovable(love)
LVBRD
lovebird
LVD
livid
LVDV
lovey-dovey
LVL
alluvial
alluvium
level
lively(active)
livelier
liveliest
liveliness
Louisville
lovely
lovelier
loveliest
loveliness
LVLHD
livelihood
LVLHDD
levelheaded
LVLK
lovelock
LVLNG
livelong
LVLNS
levelness
liveliness
loveliness

LVLR
alveolar
lavaliere
LVLRN
lovelorn
LVLV
lava-lava
LVLYR
lavaliere
LVM
alluvium
alluvia(or)
alluviums
alluvial
LVMN
Isle of Man
LVN
eleven(number)
elevon
leaven(yeast)
liven
LVNDR
lavender
LVNG
living
loving
LVNGKNS
loving-kindness
LVNGZ
leavings
LVNT
levant
LVNTH
eleventh
LVR
allover(adj)
all over(adv)
laver(basin)
lay over(v)
layover(n)
lever(handle)
levier(levy)
liver(meat)
livery
liveries
louver, (B)louvre
lover(love)
LVRB
lover-boy
LVRJ
leverage
leveraged
leveraging
LVRPL
Liverpool
LVRT

levirate
LVRWRST
liverwurst
LVSH
lavish
lavishes
LVSHN
alleviation
elevation
lavation
LVSTK
livestock
LVT
alleviate
alleviated
alleviating
elevate
elevated
elevating
levity
levities
olivette(light)
LVTKNG
leave-taking
LVTR
elevator
lavatory
lavatories
LVTSHN
levitation
LVTT
levitate
levitated
levitating
LVZ
elves
elf
leaves
leaf(and)
leave
Levi's(trademark)
LW
alleyway
leeway
LWF
alewife
LWRD
leeward
LWRLD
Old World
LWZ
always(time)
all ways(methods)
LYL
loyal
LYLSHN

ululation
LYLST
loyalist
LYLT
loyalty
loyalties
ululate
ululated
ululating
LYN
alien
LYNBL
alienable
LYNG
allaying
LYNR
alienor(legal)
LYNSHN
alienation
LYNT
alienate
alienated
alienating
alienator
LYNTR
alienator
LYR
allayer
lawyer
LYS
alias
aliases
LYSJ
ill-usage
LYZD
ill-used
LYZJ
ill-usage
LYZNG
ill-using
LZ
allies(friends)
lase(light)
lased
lasing
laser
laze(loaf)
lazed
lazing
lazy
lazier
laziest
lazily
laziness
lose(mislay)
lost

losing
loser
lousy
lousier
lousiest
lousiness
LZBN
lesbian
Lisbon
LZBNZM
lesbianism
LZBTHN
Elizabethan
LZD
lased(light)
lazed
LZH
loge
(theater box)
luge(sled)
LZHM
Elysium(n)
Elysian(adj)
LZHN
allusion
(reference)
elision
(omission)
elusion(escape)
Elysian(adj)
Elysium(n)
illusion
(false idea)
lesion(skin)
LZHR
leisure
leisured
LZN
liaison
Louisiana
LZNJ
lozenge
LZNY
lasagna
LZR
laser(light)
loser
LZRD
lizard
LZRDSK
LaserDisc
(trademark)

M

aim
am
  to be
AM(radio)
A.M.(or)A.M.(or)a.m.
  ante meridiem
Emmy(award)
I'm(I am)
immie(marble)
ma
  mother
  mom
  maw(slang)
  mama
Maui
maw(mouth)
May
may
me
meow(cat)
mho(unit)
  ohm
mi(tone)
mow(cut)
  mown
my
ohm
  mho
MB
amoeba
embow
maybe
mob
  mobbed
  mobbing
MBB
imbibe
  imbibed
  imbibing
MBBR
imbiber
MBD
embed
  embedded
  embedding
embody
  embodied
  embodies
MBDKSTR
ambidexter
MBDKSTRS

ambidextrous
MBDMNT
embodiment
MBDZMN
ombudsman
ombudsmen
MBGYS
ambiguous
MBGYT
ambiguity
ambiguities
MBK
iambic
MBKRS
mobocracy
mobocracies
MBL
amble
  ambled
  ambling
amiable
amiably
emboli
  embolus
immobile
Mobile
mobile
MBLDN
embolden
MBLKL
umbilical
MBLKS
umbilicus
umbilici
MBLM
embalm(burial)
emblem(symbol)
MBLMTK
emblematic
MBLNS
ambulance
imbalance
  imbalanced,-cing
MBLNT
ambulant
MBLR
ambler
MBLS
embolus
  emboli
MBLSH
embellish
  embellishes
MBLSHMNT
embellishment
MBLT

immobility
  immobilities
mobility
  mobilities
MBLTR
ambulatory
MBLZ
emblaze
  emblazed
  emblazing
immobilize
  immobilized
  immobilizing
mobilize
  mobilized
  mobilizing
MBLZM
embolism
MBLZN
emblazon
MBLZSHN
immobilization
mobilization
MBM
embalm
MBNGKMNT
embankment
MBNS
ambiance
MBNT
ambient
MBR
amber(resin,
  color)
ambry(cupboard)
  ambries
ember(fire)
embryo
imbrue
  imbrued
  imbruing
hombre
umber(color)
umbra(shadow)
  umbrae(or)
  umbras
MBRDR
embroider
embroidery
  embroideries
MBRG
embargo
  embargoes
MBRGRS
ambergris
MBRJ

umbrage
MBRJS
umbrageous
MBRK
embark
MBRKSHN
embarkation
imbrication
MBRKT
embrocate(rub)
  embrocated
  embrocating
imbricate(overlap)
  imbricated
  imbricating
  imbrication
MBRL
embroil
umbrella
MBRLJ
embryology
MBRLY
imbroglio
MBRNK
embryonic
MBRS
embarrass
  embarrasses
embrace(hug)
  embraced
  embracing
MBRSBL
embraceable
MBRSMNT
embarrassment
MBRT
imbrute
  imbruted
  imbruting
MBRZH
ambrosia
MBRZHR
embrasure
MBS
embassy
  embassies
emboss
  embosses
MBSDR
ambassador
MBSDRL
ambassadorial
MBSH
ambush
  ambushes
  ambusher

MBSHN
ambition
MBSHR
embouchure
MBSHS
ambitious
MBSK
embusqué(shirk)
MBSKD
ambuscade
  ambuscaded
  ambuscading
MBSL
imbecile
MBSLK
imbecilic
MBSLT
imbecility
  imbecilities
MBSTR
mobster
MBT
ambit
MBTL
embattle
  embattled
  embattling
MBTR
embitter
MBVLNS
ambivalence
MBVLNT
ambivalent
MBY
imbue
  imbued
  imbuing
MBYLNS
ambulance
MBYLNT
ambulant
MBYLTR
ambulatory
MBZL
embezzle
  embezzled
  embezzling
MBZLR
embezzler
MBZM
embosom
MCH
macho
match
  matches
mooch

mooches
much
MCHBKS
matchbox
  matchboxes
MCHKLSHN
machicolation
MCHLK
matchlock
MCHLS
matchless
MCHMKR
matchmaker
MCHR
amateur
immature(young)
mature
  matured
  maturing
moocher
MCHRSHN
maturation
MCHRT
immaturity
  immaturities
maturate
  maturated
  maturating
maturity
  maturities
MCHT
machete
MCHZM
machismo
MD
amid
  amidst
mad
  madder
  maddest
made(create)
make
maid(person)
Mayday(distress)
May Day(holiday)
mead(meadow)
meadow
media
midday
middy(sailor)
middies
mode(manner)
mood
moody
  moodier
  moodiest

moodily
moodiness
motto(words)
mud
muddy
  muddier
  muddiest
  muddiness
MDBD
Ahmadabad
MDBRN
midbrain
MDD
matted(mat)
MDF
modify
  modified
  modifies
MDFKSHN
modification
MDFR
modifier
MDGSKR
Madagascar
MDHS
madhouse
MDK
medic(doctor)
MDKBL
medicable
MDKD
medicaid
MDKL
medical
MDKM
modicum
MDKP
madcap
MDKR
medicare(program)
mediocre(poor)
MDKRS
mediocracy
MDKRT
mediocrity
  mediocrities
MDKSHN
medication
MDKT
medicate
-cated, -cating
MDL
medal(award)
meddle(interfere)
meddled, -ddling
meddler

medial
medley
metal(iron)
middle(center)
modal(mode)
model(copy)
muddle
  muddled
  muddling
MDLBR
middlebrow
MDLJD
middle-aged
MDLJZ
Middle Ages
MDLKLS
middle-class(adj)
middle class(n)
  middle classes
MDLMN
middleman
  middlemen
MDLN
maudlin
Medellin
MDLND
midland
MDLNG
middling
MDLR
meddler
muddler
MDLSM
meddlesome
mettlesome
  (spirited)
MDLST
medalist, (B)-llist
MDLSZD
middle-sized
MDLVTHRD
middle-of-the-
  road
MDLWRK
metalwork
MDLWT
middleweight
  (148-160 lbs)
MDLYN
medallion
MDM
Madam(title)
  Mesdames
madam(person)
  mesdames
Madame(French)

Mesdames
Mrs.(English)
Mmes.(pl)
Ms.(sing)
Mses.(pl)
madame(married)
medium
mesdames(French)
modem(computer)
MDMN
madman
MDMZ
mediums
MDMZL
mademoiselle
mesdemoiselles
MDN
madden
madonna(and)M-
maiden
median
MDNHD
maidenhead
MDNHR
maidenhair
MDNM
maiden name
MDNNG
maddening
MDNS
madness
MDNT
midnight
MDP
made-up(adj)
MDPNT
midpoint
MDR
madder
mad
maddest
Madeira
matter
meteor(rock)
midair
motor(power)
mudder
mudra(dance)
mutter(speak)
MDRBK
motorbike
MDRD
Madrid
MDRF
midriff
MDRGL

madrigal
MDRLJST
meteorologist
MDRN
midiron
modern
MDRNSTK
modernistic
MDRNT
modernity
MDRNZ
modernize
modernized
modernizing
MDRNZM
modernism
MDRNZSHN
modernization
MDRS
Madras
madras
MDRSHN
immoderation
moderation
MDRT
immoderate
immoderated
immoderating
moderate
moderated
moderating
MDRTR
moderator
MDRZ
motorize
motorized
motorizing
motorization
MDS
immediacy
immediacies
medusa
medusas(or)
medusae
medusan(adj)
Medusa
(mythology)
MDSH
modish
MDSHN
mediation
MDSHPMN
midshipman
midshipmen
MDSLNGNG
mudslinging

MDSLNGR
mudslinger
MDSMR
midsummer
MDSN
Madison
medicine
medusan
medusa
MDSNL
medicinal
MDSNVNY
Madison Avenue
MDSPRND
modus operandi
MDSRVNT
maidservant
MDST
amidst
amid
immodest
immodesty
immodesties
maddest
midst
modest(shy)
modesty
modesties
modiste
MDSTRM
midstream
MDT
immediate
mediate
mediated
mediating
MDTDR
meditator
MDTR
mediator
MDTRDR
made-to-order
MDTRM
midterm
MDTRNN
Mediterranean
MDTRNNS
Mediterranean Sea
MDTSHN
meditation
MDTT
meditate
meditated
meditating
MDTTR
meditator

MDTTV
meditative
MDV
motive
motivate
motivation
motivator
MDVL
medieval
MDW
midway
MDWF
midwife
midwives
MDWFR
midwifery
MDWK
midweek
MDWLNZ
Midway Islands
MDWMN
madwoman
MDWNTR
midwinter
MDWST
Midwest
MDWSTRN
Midwestern
MDWSTRNR
Midwesterner
MDYL
module
MDYLR
modular
MDYLS
modulus(number)
MDYLSHN
modulation
MDYLT
modulate
modulated
modulating
MDYLTR
modulator
MDYR
midyear
MDYS
Medusa
(mythology)
medusa
medusas(or)
medusae
medusan(adj)
MDYZ
Medusa
medusa

B:by CH:each D:day F:if G:go H:he HW:why J:joy K:cow KS:ax KWL:equal L:all M:may N:in

MDZ
mezzo
MDZTNT
mezzotint
MF
Mafia
miff
muff
oomph(interj)
MFBN
amphibian
MFBS
amphibious
MFDMN
amphetamine
MFL
muffle
muffled
muffling
MFLR
muffler
MFN
muffin
MFR
amphora
MFRK
amphoric
MFRTN
M-14(weapon)
MFSM
emphysema
MFSS
emphasis
emphases
MFSZ
emphases
emphasis
emphasize
emphasized
emphasizing
MFT
mufti
MFTHTR
amphitheater, (B)- tre
MFTK
emphatic
mephitic
MFTKL
emphatically
mephitical
MFTMN
amphetamine
MFTS
mephitis
MFZM
emphysema

MG
amigo
MiG(aircraft)
MiG-19
MiG-21
mug(cup)
mug(accost)
mugged,-gging
mugger
muggy
muggier
muggiest
mugginess
omega
MGBK
megabuck
MGFN
megaphone
MGGPN
moo goo gai pan
MGHRTS
megahertz
MGL
mogul
MGLMN
megalomania
MGLPLS
megalopolis
MGLTH
megalith
MGM
megohm
MGND
magneto
MGNF
magnify
magnified
magnifies
MGNFKSHN
magnification
MGNFR
magnifier
MGNFSNS
magnificence
MGNFSNT
magnificent
MGNG
mugging
MGNKMLD
magna cum laude
MGNKRT
Magna Carta
MGNLKWNT
magniloquent
MGNLY
magnolia

MGNM
magnum
MGNNMS
magnanimous
MGNNMT
magnanimity
MGNSH
magnesia
MGNSHM
magnesium
MGNT
magnate(person)
magnet(metal)
magneto
MGNTD
magnitude
MGNTK
magnetic
MGNTKL
magnetically
MGNTMTR
magnetometer
MGNTYD
magnitude
MGNTZ
magnetize
magnetized
magnetizing
MGNTZM
magnetism
MGNZH
magnesia
MGNZM
magnesium
MGP
magpie
MGR
émigré(emigrant)
meager
mugger
MGRM
megrim
MGRN
migraine
MGRNT
emigrant(left
native land)
immigrant
(settler)
migrant
MGRSHN
emigration
(leaving)
immigration
(settling)
migration

(moving on)
MGRT
emigrate(leave)
emigrated
emigrating
immigrate(settle)
immigrated
immigrating
migrate(move on)
migrated
migrating
MGRTR
migratory
MGSHT
mug shot
MGSKL
megacycle
MGSKPK
megascopic
MGT
maggot
MGTN
megaton
MGWMP
mugwump
MGZN
magazine
MH
Omaha
MHGN
mahogany
MHM
mayhem
MHMD
Mohammed
MHR
mohair
MHRJ
maharajah
MHRN
maharani
MHRZH
maharajah
MHT
mahout
MHTM
mahatma
MHV
Mojave
MJ
image
imaged
imaging
MJK
magic
MJKL

magical
MJL
module
MJLK
majolica
MJLL
mogilalia
MJLR
modular
MJLS
modulus
MJLSHN
modulation
MJLT
modulate
modulated
modulating
MJLTR
modulator
MJN
imagine
imagined
imagining
MJNBL
imaginable
MJNG
imaging
MJNR
imaginary
imaginariness
MJNSHN
imagination
MJNT
magenta
MJNTV
imaginative
MJR
imagery
imageries
major
MJRDM
major-domo
MJRLG
major-league(adj)
MJRT
majority
majorities
MJSHN
magician
MJSKYL
majuscule
MJST
majesty
majesties
MJSTK
majestic

MJSTKL
majestical
MJSTRL
magisterial
MJSTRT
magistrate
MJT
midget
MJZM
imagism
MK
amuck
Macau
macaw(parrot)
Mach(speed of
sound)
Mach 1
Mach 2
(and so on)
make
made
making
maker
maquis(zone, fighter)
Mecca
meek
mica
Micah(Bible)
mike(microphone)
mocha
mock(deride)
muck
umiak
MKBL
amicable
amicably
MKBLV
make believe(v)
make-believe(n)
MKBR
macabre
micawber
MKCHRT
micturate
micturated
micturating
MKD
mikado
MKDM
macadam
MKDMNT
macadamia nut
MKDMZ
macadamize
macadamized
macadamizing

MKFL
mycophile(fungus)
MKFN
Mickey Finn
MKHRK
mock-heroic
MKLJ
mycology
MKLK
mukluk
MKLT
miquelet(soldier)
MKN
mackinaw
MKNGBRD
mockingbird
MKNGL
mockingly
MKNGZ
makings
MKNK
mechanic
MKNKL
mechanical
MKNKS
mechanics
MKNS
meekness
MKNSHN
mechanician
machination
MKNT
machinate
machinated
machinating
MKNTR
machinator
MKNTSH
mackintosh(coat)
McIntosh(apple)
MKNZ
mechanize
mechanized
mechanizing
MKNZM
mechanism
MKNZSHN
mechanization
MKP
makeup(n,adj)
make up(v)
mock-up
MKR
maker
meeker
mockery

mockeries
MKRB
microbe
MKRBK
microbic
MKRBLJ
microbiology
MKRBR
microbar
MKRBTKS
macrobiotics
MKRDT
microdot
MKRFLM
microflim
MKRFN
microphone
MKRFSH
microfiche
MKRGRV
microgroove
MKRKMSTR
microchemistry
MKRK
muckrake
muckraked
muckraking
MKRKP
microcopy
microcopies
MKRKR
muckraker
MKRKZM
macrocosm
microcosm
MKRL
mackeral
mercurial
MKRLKTRNKS
microelectronics
MKRM
macramé
microhm
MKRMTR
micrometer
MKRN
macaroni
macaroon(coconut)
macron(mark)
micron
microns(or)
micra
MKRNZH
Micronesia
MKRPRNT
microprint

B:by **CH**:each **D**:day **F**:if **G**:go **H**:he **HW**:why **J**:joy **K**:cow **KS**:ax **KWL**:equal **L**:all **M**:may **N**:in

MKRRDR	**MKSN**	mailbox	melodramatic
microreader	moccasin	mailboxes	**MLDRMTKL**
MKRRGNZM	**MKSNG**	**MLBL**	melodramatically
microorganism	mixing	malleable	**MLDRS**
MKRSKP	**MKSP**	**MLBLT**	malodorous
microscope	mix up(v)	malleability	**MLDRT**
MKRSKPK	mix-up(n,adj)	**MLBR**	maladroit
macroscopic	**MKSR**	millibar	**MLDS**
microscopic	mixer	mulberry	melodious
MKRSKPKL	**MKST**	mulberries	**MLDVLNZ**
microscopical	mixed	**MLBRN**	Maldive Islands
MKRSRKT	**MKTRT**	Melbourne	**MLDVZ**
microcircuit	micturate	**MLCH**	Maldives
MKRTHZM	micturated	milch(milk)	**MLDY**
McCarthyism	micturating	mulch	mildew
MKRWV	**MKVLN**	mulches	**MLF**
microwave	Machiavellian	**MLD**	mollify
MKS	Machiavellianism	malady(sickness)	mollified
Amex	**MKYL**	maladies	mollifies
American Stock	macula	meld	**MLFK**
Exchange	maculae	melody	malefic
max(slang)	**MKYLSHN**	melodies	**MLFKSHN**
maximum	maculation	milady	malefaction
maxi(skirt)	**MKYLT**	miladies	**MLFKTR**
mix	immaculate	mild	malefactor
mixes	maculate	mildew(fungus)	**MLFLS**
mixer	maculated	mold, (B)mould	mellifluous
moxie	maculating	moldy, (B)mouldy	**MLFN**
MKSCHR	**MKYRL**	moldier	mellophone
mixture	mercurial	moldiest	**MLFNGKSHN**
MKSH	**ML**	moldiness	malfunction
mawkish	mail	mulatto	**MLFRMD**
MKSHFT	Malay	**MLDBRD**	malformed
makeshift	male(gender)	moldboard	**MLFRMSHN**
MKSK	Mali	**MLDK**	malformation
Mexico	mall(area)	melodic	**MLFSNS**
Mexican(adj)	maul(injure)	**MLDKSHN**	maleficence
Mexico City	meal	malediction	**MLFSNT**
MKSL	mealy	maledictory	maleficent
maxilla	mealier	**MLDM**	**MLFZNS**
MKSLR	mealiest	milldam	malfeasance
maxillary	mealiness	**MLDMNSTR**	**MLGM**
MKSM	melee(fighting)	maladminister	amalgam
maxim	mellow	**MLDN**	**MLGMSHN**
maxima	mile	melodeon	amalgamation
maximum	mill	**MLDNG**	**MLGMTR**
MKSML	moil(toil)	molding, (B)moulding	amalgamator
maximal	mold(plant)	**MLDNS**	**MLGN**
MKSMM	mole(animal)	mildness	mulligan
maximum	moll(girl)	**MLDPTD**	**MLGNNS**
maxima(or)	moola(money)	maladapted	malignancy
maximums	mull	**MLDR**	malignancies
MKSMZ	mullah(title)	molder	**MLGNNT**
maximize	**MLBDNM**	**MLDRM**	malignant
maximized	molybdenum	melodrama	**MLGNT**
maximizing	**MLBKS**	**MLDRMTK**	malignity

NGK:ink P:pie R:air S:ice SH:show T:toy THN:thin TH:the V:of W:we Y:you Z:is VZHN:vision

malignities
MLGNY
malagueña
MLGRM
Mailgram(trademark)
milligram(unit)
myelogram(test)
MLGTN
mulligatawny
MLGWNY
malagueña
MLHL
molehill
MLHWL
mill wheel
MLJ
mileage(distance)
millage(tax)
MLJSTD
maladjusted
MLJSTMNT
maladjustment
MLK
milk
milky
milkier
milkiest
milkiness
MLKDL
mollycoddle
mollycoddled
mollycoddling
MLKLJ
malacology
MLKLZHN
malocclusion
MLKMD
milkmaid
MLKMN
milkman
milkmen
MLKNTNT
malcontent
MLKSHD
milk shed(barn)
MLKSHK
milk shake(drink)
MLKSP
milksop
MLKT
mulct
MLKTST
milk toast(food)
milquetoast
(timid person)
MLKW

Milky Way
MLKWD
milkweed
MLKYL
molecule
MLKYLR
molecular
MLLTR
milliliter
MLM
myeloma
MLMN
mailman
mailmen
MLMRKR
mile marker
MLMTHT
mealy-mouthed
MLMTR
millimeter
MLMYT
malamute
MLN
malign
malines(fabric)
melon
Milan
millennia(or)
millenniums
milline(copy)
moline(symbol)
MLNG
milling
MLNGGR
malinger
MLNGGRR
malingerer
MLNGR
malinger
MLNGRR
malingerer
MLNKL
melancholia
melancholy
melancholily
melancholiness
MLNKLK
melancholic
MLNM
millennium
millennia(or)
millenniums
MLNN
melanin
MLNR
millenary(l000)

milliner(hat maker)
millinery(cloth,
hats,etc)
MLNRSHT
malnourished
MLNS
maleness
mildness
MLNTRSHN
malnutrition
MLNYTRSHN
malnutrition
MLNZH
Melanesia
mélange(or)
melange
(mixture)
MLPD
millipede
MLPND
millpond
MLPRKTS
malpractice
malpracticed
malpracticing
MLPRP
malapropos
MLPRPZM
malapropism
MLPST
milepost
MLR
mailer
malaria
miler(mile)
miller(mill)
molar
muller(tool)
mylar
MLRD
mallard
MLRK
malarkey
MLRS
millrace
MLRSHN
amelioration
melioration
MLRT
ameliorate(make
better)
ameliorated
ameliorating
meliorate(grow
better)
meliorated

meliorating
millwright
MLRZM
meliorism
MLS
aimless
malice
MLSF
emulsify
emulsified
emulsifies
emulsifier
MLSFKSHN
emulsification
MLSFR
emulsifier
MLSH
militia
MLSHN
emulation(copy)
emulsion(coating)
immolation(kill)
MLSHS
malicious
MLSK
mollusk
MLSKN
moleskin
MLSM
melisma(music)
melismas(or)
melismata
melismatic
MLSML
millesimal
MLSS
molasses
molasses
MLST
molest
MLSTN
milestone
(achievement)
millstone(rock)
MLSTRM
maelstrom
(whirlpool)
millstream
MLSTSHN
molestation
MLSZ
molasses
molasses
MLT
amulet
emulate(copy)

B:by **CH**:each **D**:day **F**:if **G**:go **H**:he **HW**:why **J**:joy **K**:cow **KS**:ax **KW**L:equal **L**:all **M**:may **N**:in

emulated
emulating
immolate(kill)
immolated
immolating
mallet(hammer)
malt(grain)
Malta
melt(dissolve)
millet(grass)
milt(fish sperm)
molt(shed), (B)moult
mulatto
mullet(fish)
omelet(egg)
umlaut
MLTBL
meltable
MLTDN
meltdown
MLTFKKTL
Molotov cocktail
MLTFRM
multiform
MLTFRS
multifarious
MLTGRF
Multigraph
(trademark)
MLTKLR
multicolor
MLTKLRD
multicolored
MLTLDRL
multilateral
MLTLTH
Multilith
(trademark)
MLTLTRL
multilateral
MLTM
mealtime
MLTN
melton(cloth)
molten(hot)
MLTNGPNT
melting point
MLTNS
militancy
MLTNSHNL
multinational
MLTNT
militant
MLTPL
multiple
multiply

multiplied
multiplies
multiplier
MLTPLBL
multipliable
MLTPLKND
multiplicand
MLTPLKS
multiplex
MLTPLKSHN
multiplication
MLTPLR
multiplier
MLTPLST
multiplicity
multiplicities
MLTR
military
militaries
MLTRL
militarily
MLTRSTK
militaristic
MLTRT
maltreat
MLTRZ
militarize
militarized
militarizing
MLTRZM
militarism
MLTRZSHN
militarization
MLTS
Maltese
maltose
myelitis
MLTT
militate
militated
militating
MLTTD
multitude
MLTTDNS
multitudinous
MLTVRST
multiversity
multiversities
MLTZ
Maltese
MLVLNS
malevolence
MLVLNT
malevolent
MLW
Malawi

MLWK
Milwaukee
MLWL
mill wheel
MLWRK
millwork
MLY
milieu
MLYMNT
emolument
MLYN
million(number)
mullion(window)
MLYNR
millionaire
MLYNT
emollient
(skin softener)
MLYNTH
millionth
MLYRD
milliard
MLYRSHN
amelioration
melioration
MLYRT
ameliorate
(make better)
-rated,-rating
meliorate
(grow better)
-rated,-rating
MLYRTR
ameliorator
MLYRZM
meliorism
MLZ
malaise
MLZH
Malaysia
moulage
MLZM
melisma(music)
melismas(or)
melismata
melismatic
MLZPRGLN
miles per gallon
(m.p.g.)
MLZPRR
miles per hour
(m.p.h.)
MM
Ma'am
Madam
maim

malm(limestone)
mama
mom
mother
ma
mayhem
Miami
mime(mimic)
mimed
miming
mom(mother)
mommy
ma
mama
mum
mummy(death)
mummies
mummy(mother)
mummies
muumuu(dress)
myoma(tumor)
myomata(or)
myomas
MMB
mambo
MMBJMB
mumbo jumbo
MMBL
mumble
mumbled
mumbling
mumbler
MMBR
member
MMBRN
membrane
MMBRNS
membranous
MMBRSHP
membership
MMF
mummify
mummified
mummifies
mummification
MMFS
Memphis
MMGRF
mimeograph
MMK
mimic
mimicked
mimicking
MMKR
mimicker
mimicry

NGK:ink **P**:pie **R**:air **S**:ice **SH**:show **T**:toy **THN**:thin **TH**:the **V**:of **W**:we **Y**:you **Z**:is **VZHN**:vision

MML
mammal
MMLN
mammalian
MMLYN
mammalian
MMN
mammon
MMNT
memento
(souvenir)
moment(time)
momenta
momentum
MMNTM
momentum
momenta(or)
momentums
MMNTR
momentary
MMNTRL
momentarily
MMNTS
momentous
MMR
mammary(breast)
mammaries
memory(mind)
memories
mimer(mime)
mummer(actor)
mummery(show)
MMRBL
memorabilia
memorable
memorably
MMRBLNS
memorableness
MMRBLY
memorabilia
MMRL
immemorial
memorial
MMRLZ
memorialize
memorialized
memorializing
MMRLZSHN
memorialization
MMRND
memoranda
MMRNDM
memorandum
memoranda(or)
memorandums
MMRZ

memorize
memorized
memorizing
MMRZSHN
memorization
MMS
mimosa(tree)
momus
MMTH
mammoth
MMTK
mimetic
MMWR
memoir
MMZ
malmsey(wine)
mumsy(mother)
MN
almond(nut,tree)
amen(prayer)
amino(acid)
ammonia(gas)
main(major,
water)
Maine
man
men
manned
manning
mane(hair)
mania(craze)
manna(food)
many
more
most
men
man
mean(denote)
meant
mean(cruel,
middle)
meany(mean person)
meanies
mien(manner)
mini(small)
mind(brain)
mine(not yours)
mine(dig)
mined
mining
mine(bomb)
mined
mining
minnow(fish)
moan(sound)
money

moneys(or)
monies
moon(lunar)
moon(slang)
moonie(person)
moony(moon like)
moonier
mooniest
mown
mow
myna(bird)
Oman
omen(sign)
omni(all)
MNBG
moneybag
MNBL
amenable
MNBM
moonbeam
MNBRD
myna bird
MNBS
minibus
omnibus
MNCH
munch
munches
munchy(slang)
munchies
MNCHLD
man-child
MNCHLDRN
men-children
MNCHN
mention
MNCHNJR
moneychanger
MNCHR
miniature
MNCHRZ
miniaturize
miniaturized
miniaturizing
MNCHRZSHN
miniaturization
MNCHSTR
Manchester
MNCHT
manchette
MND
almond(tree,nut)
amend(change)
emend(correct)
maenad(woman)
maenads(or)

maenades
mend(repair)
mind(brain)
monad
Monday
moneyed
mooned(slang)
mound
MNDBL
amendable
mandible
mendable(fix)
MNDFL
mindful
MNDKNT
mendicant
MNDL
mandala
MNDLN
mandolin
Mendelian
MNDLS
mindless
MNDMS
mandamus
MNDN
mundane
MNDR
amender(changer)
maunder(talk)
meander(wander)
mender(fixer)
MNDRDR
mind reader
MNDRK
mandrake
MNDRL
mandrel(spindle)
mandrill(baboon)
MNDRM
monodrama
MNDRN
mandarin(fruit)
MNDSHN
emendation
MNDSHS
mendacious
MNDST
mendacity
MNDT
emendate(edit)
-dated,-dating
mandate(order)
mandated
mandating
MNDTR

amendatory
mandatory
MNF
  minify
    minified
    minifies
MNFKCHR
  manufacture
MNFKSHN
  minification
MNFL
  manful
  mindful
MNFLD
  manifold
MNFNK
  monophonic
MNFRS
  omnifarious
MNFST
  manifest
  manifesto
    manifestoes
  moon-faced
MNFSTSHN
  manifestation
MNG
  among
  mango
MNGG
  mango
MNGGL
  mangle
    mangled
    mangling
    mangler
  mingle
    mingled
    mingling
    mingler
MNGGLD
  Mongoloid
  Mongolism
MNGGR
  monger
MNGGRL
  mongrel
MNGGRLZ
  mongrelize
    mongrelized
    mongrelizing
MNGGRV
  mangrove
MNGGS
  mongoose
MNGK

mink(animal)
monk
monkey
MNGKR
  monkery
MNGKS
  minx
    minxes
MNGKSKLTH
  monk's cloth
MNGL
  mangle
    mangled
    mangling
    mangler
  mingle
    mingled
    mingling
    mingler
  Mongolia
MNGLD
  Mongoloid
MNGLZM
  Mongolism
MNGM
  monogamy
MNGMS
  monogamous
MNGMST
  monogamist
MNGNZ
  manganese
MNGR
  monger
MNGRBR
  moneygrubber
MNGRF
  monograph
MNGRL
  mongrel
MNGRLZ
  mongrelize
    mongrelized
    mongrelizing
MNGRM
  monogram
    monogrammed
    monogramming
MNGRV
  mangrove
MNGS
  mongoose
MNGW
  Managua
MNHD
  manhood

MNHL
  manhole
MNHN
  Manhattan
MNHNDL
  manhandle
    manhandled
    manhandling
MNHNT
  manhunt
MNHTN
  Manhattan
MNHWL
  meanwhile
MNJ
  manage
    managed
    managing
    manager
  mange
  mangy
    mangier
    mangiest
    mangily
    manginess
MNJBL
  manageable
MNJMNT
  management
MNJN
  monogyny
MNJNS
  monogynous
MNJR
  manger
  menagerie
MNJRL
  managerial
MNK
  maniac
  manic
  Monaco
MNKB
  minicab
MNKD
  manicotti
MNKDPRSV
  manic-depressive
MNKK
  monocoque
MNKL
  manacle
    manacled
    manacling
  maniacal
  monocle

MNKN
  manikin
    (model,
    dwarf size)
  mankind
  mannequin(life
    size dummy)
  minikin(small
    creature)
MNKND
  mankind
MNKR
  moniker(name)
MNKRD
  monochord
MNKRM
  monochrome
MNKRMTK
  monochromatic
MNKRS
  monocracy
    monocracies
MNKRT
  monocrat
MNKSD
  monoxide
MNKT
  manicotti
MNKYLR
  monocular
MNKYR
  manicure
    manicured
    manicuring
MNKYRST
  manicurist
MNL
  mainly
  main
  Manila
  manly
    manlier
    manliest
    manliness
  mantel(fireplace)
    mantelpiece
  mantle(coat,light)
    mantled
    mantling
  menial
  mental
MNLG
  monologue
MNLJST
  monologist
MNLN

main line(n)
mainline(v)
-lined,-lining
MNLND
mainland
MNLNDR
moneylender
MNLR
minelayer
MNLS
mindless
Mona Lisa
MNLT
moonlight
moonlit
moonlighting
MNLTH
monolith
MNLTNG
moonlighting
MNLTR
moonlighter
MNLZ
Mona Lisa
MNM
minim(fluid unit)
minima
minimum
MNMD
man-made
MNMKR
moneymaker
MNML
minimal
MNMM
minimum
minima(or)
minimums
MNMN
monomania
MNMTLZM
monometallism
MNMTR
manometer
MNMZ
minimize
minimized
minimizing
MNNDR
monandry
MNNDRS
monandrous
MNNG
meaning
mining(ore)
MNNJTS

meningitis
MNNKLSS
mononucleosis
MNNS
eminence(high
position)
immanence(within)
imminence(soon)
MNNT
eminent
(prominent)
immanent
(inherent)
imminent(soon)
Mennonite
MNNYKLSS
mononucleosis
MNPL
monopoly
monopolies
MNPLN
monoplane
MNPLS
Minneapolis
MNPLST
monopolist
MNPLSTK
monopolistic
MNPLSTKL
monopolistically
MNPLZ
monopolize
monopolized
monopolizing
MNPLZSHN
monopolization
MNPR
manpower
MNPRT
moon port
MNPRZNS
omnipresence
MNPRZNT
omnipresent
MNPTNS
omnipotence
MNPTNT
omnipotent
MNPYLR
manipular
MNPYLSHN
manipulation
MNPYLT
manipulate
manipulated
manipulating

MNPYLTR
manipulator
MNPYLTV
manipulative
MNPZ
menopause
MNR
man-hour
manner(way)
manor(residence)
manure
manured
manuring
menorah(candle)
miner(coal)
minor(lesser,
underage)
Monterey(Cal.)
Monterrey(Mex.)
MNRDR
money order
MNRFKCHR
manufacture
MNRK
monarch(royal)
monarchic
monarchy
monarchies
moon rock
MNRKL
monarchal
MNRKZM
monarchism
MNRL
mineral
monaural
monorail(train)
MNRLG
minor-league(adj)
minor league(n)
MNRLJ
mineralogy
MNRLJST
mineralogist
MNRLZ
mineralize
mineralized
mineralizing
MNRLZSHN
mineralization
MNRNJ
omnirange
MNRT
minaret
minority
minorities

MNRZ
moonrise
MNRZM
mannerism
MNS
immense(large)
manse(house)
meanness(cruel)
menace(threat)
menaced
menacing
mince(chop)
minced
mincing
mincer
minus(less)
ominous
MNSD
Minnesota
MNSDD
many-sided
MNSH
mannish
minutia
minutiae
MNSHN
emanation
mansion(house)
mention(talk)
monition(warning)
moonshine
MNSHNS
omniscience
MNSHNT
omniscient
MNSHRBL
mensurable
MNSHRSHN
mensuration
MNSHS
minacious
MNSHT
moon shot(flight)
MNSK
Minsk
MNSKP
moonscape
MNSKRT
miniskirt
MNSKS
meniscus
menisci(or)
meniscuses
MNSKYL
minuscule
MNSL

mainsail
MNSLBK
monosyllabic
MNSLBL
monosyllable
MNSLTR
manslaughter
MNSMT
mincemeat
MNSN
monsoon
MNSNGR
minnesinger
MNSNYR
monseigneur
(royal title)
messeigneurs
monsignor(church
official)
MNSPRNG
mainspring
MNSPSHN
emancipation
MNSPT
emancipate
emancipated
emancipating
MNSPTR
emancipator
MNSRBL
mensurable
MNSRD
mansard
MNSRSHN
mensuration
MNSRVNT
manservant
MNST
amnesty
amnesties
immensity
immensities
Minnesota
moonset
MNSTK
monastic(church)
monistic(unity,
monism)
MNSTKL
monastical
MNSTN
moonstone
MNSTR
minister(person)
ministry
ministries

minster(a church)
monastery
monasteries
monster
Muenster(cheese)
MNSTRK
moonstruck
MNSTRL
ministerial
(serving)
minstrel(music)
menstrual(blood
discharge)
MNSTRM
mainstream
MNSTRN
minestrone(soup)
MNSTRNT
ministrant
MNSTRS
monstrous
MNSTRSHN
ministration(aid)
menstruation(blood)
MNSTRST
monstrosity
monstrosities
MNSTRT
menstruate
menstruated
menstruating
MNSTSZM
monasticism
MNSWTD
mansuetude
MNSZ
menses
MNSZD
man-sized
MNT
amenity
amenities
emanate
emanated
emanating
manta(cloth)
manteau(cloak)
manteaus(or)
manteaux
meant
mean
mint(money,
plant)
minuet(dance)
minute(time,
small)

monte(game)
mount
Mounty(person)
Mounties
MNTB
Manitoba
MNTBNGK
mountebank
MNTGLFR
Montgolfier(balloon)
MNTGMR
Montgomery
MNTH
month
MNTHL
menthol
monthly
monthlies
MNTHLNG
monthlong(adj)
MNTHLTD
mentholated
MNTHSTK
monotheistic
MNTHZM
monotheism
MNTJ
mintage
MNTK
mantic
MNTKYL
monticule
MNTL
mantel
(fireplace)
mantilla
mantle(cloak)
mantled
mantling
mental(brain)
MNTLNG
mantling
MNTLPS
mantelpiece
MNTLT
mantelet
mentality
mentalities
MNTM
meantime
MNTMKNL
Mt. McKinley
MNTMN
minuteman
minutemen
MNTN

maintain
monotone
monotony
monotonies
Montana
mountain
MNTNNS
maintenance
MNTNR
mountaineer
MNTNS
monotonous
mountainous
MNTNSTTS
Mountain States
MNTP
monotype
MNTPLYR
Montpelier
MNTR
mantra
man-eater
mentor
minatory (threatening)
Minotaur(monster)
monetary(money)
monitor(checker)
monitory(check)
Monterey(Cal.)
Monterrey(Mex.)
MNTRK
minitrack
MNTRL
minatorial
(threatening)
Montreal
MNTS
mantis(insect)
-tises(or)-tes
MNTSNTHLNZ
Mount St. Helens
MNTSR
Montessori
(Maria)
MNTSRT
Montserrat
MNTVD
Montevideo
MNTVRST
Mount Everest
MNTY
mantilla
MNTZ
monetize
monetized
monetizing

MNTZH
montage(picture)
-taged,-taging
MNVLNZ
manavalins
MNVR
maneuver
(B)-oeuvre
-oeuvred,-oeuvring
miniver(fur)
MNVRBL
maneuverable
MNVRBLT
maneuverability
MNVRS
omnivorous
MNVWR
man-of-war(ship)
men-of-war
MNWL
meanwhile
MNY
ammonia
menu(food)
MNYDKSHN
manuduction
MNYFKCHR
manufacture(make)
-tured,-turing
MNYFKCHRR
manufacturer
MNYFKTR
manufactory
manufactories
MNYL
manual(hand)
MNYMNT
monument
MNYMNTL
monumental
MNYN
mañana
mignon(small)
minion(helper)
minyan(quorum)
manure(feces)
MNYNT
mignonette
(plant)
MNYR
manure
manured
manuring
MNYSH
minutia
minutiae

MNYSKRPT
manuscript
MNYT
minuet(dance)
minute(small)
MNYVR
maneuver,
(B)manoeuvre
MNYVRBL
maneuverable,
(B)manoeuvrable
MNYVRBLT
maneuverability,
(B)manoeuvrability
MNZ
amends
mayonnaise
mons
MNZH
amnesia
manège
(horsemanship)
ménage(group)
MNZHR
menagerie
MNZHTRW
ménage à trois
(threesome)
MNZM
monism
MNZNGR
minnesinger
MNZWR
menswear
MP
map(route)
mapped,mapping
mop(clean)
mopped,mopping
mope(sulk)
moped,moping
moper
mopish
myopia(eye)
myope(person)
MPCH
impeach
impeaches
MPCHBL
impeachable
MPCHS
impetuous
MPCHST
impetuosity
impetuosities
MPD

impede
impeded
impeding
moped(cycle)
moped(sulk)
mope
MPDMNT
impediment
impedimenta
MPDNS
impedance
MPJ
mpg(miles per gallon)
MPK
myopic
MPKBL
impeccable
impeccably
MPKBLT
impeccability
MPKSHN
impaction
MPKT
impact
MPKTD
impacted
MPKYNS
impecunious
MPKYNST
impecuniosity
MPL
ample
amply
ampoule(or)ampul
(or)ampule
employ(job)
employee(worker)
impale(pierce)
-paled,-paling
impel(force)
impelled
impelling
imply(suggest)
implied
implies
maple
Maypole
MPLBL
employable
MPLD
implode
imploded
imploding
MPLF
amplify
amplified

amplifies
amplifier
amplification
amplificatory
MPLKBL
implacable
MPLKSHN
implication
MPLKT
implicate
implicated
implicating
implication
MPLKTNT
amplectant
MPLKTV
implicative
MPLMNT
employment
implement
MPLMNTL
implemental
MPLMNTSHN
implementation
MPLNT
impellent
implant
MPLNTSHN
implantation
MPLPBL
impalpable
MPLPBLT
impalpability
MPLR
employer
impeller
implore
implored
imploring
MPLS
emplace
emplaced
emplacing
impulse
MPLSHN
impulsion
MPLSMNT
emplacement
MPLST
implicit
MPLSV
impulsive
MPLT
impolite
MPLTD
amplitude

MPLTHTR
amphitheater
MPLTK
impolitic
MPLZBL
implausible
MPLZHN
implosion
MPN
impone
imponed
imponing
MPND
impend
impound
MPNDNG
impending
MPNDRBL
imponderable
MPNJ
empennage
(tail)
impinge
impinged
impinging
MPNJMNT
impingement
MPNL
impanel, (B)empanel
MPNTNS
impenitence
MPNTNT
impenitent
MPNTRBL
impenetrable
MPNTRBLT
impenetrability
MPP
mop-up(n,adj)
mop up
mopped up
mopping up
MPR
ampere(volt)
empire
(kingdom)
emporia
empower
impair
umpire(referee)
umpired
umpiring
MPRBBL
improbable
improbably
MPRBBLT

improbability
improbabilities
MPRBMT
meprobamate
MPRCHN
importune
importuned
importuning
MPRCHNT
importunate
MPRDNS
imprudence
MPRDNT
imprudent
MPRDR
importer
MPRFKSHN
imperfection
MPRFKT
imperfect
MPRFRT
imperforate
MPRGNBL
impregnable
MPRGNBLT
impregnability
impregnabilities
MPRGNSHN
impregnation
MPRGNT
impregnate
impregnated
impregnating
MPRJ
amperage
MPRKL
empirical
MPRKSHN
imprecation
MPRKT
imprecate
imprecated
imprecating
MPRKTKBL
impracticable
MPRKTKBLT
impracticability
impracticabili-
ties
MPRKTKL
impractical
MPRL
imperial
(empire)
imperil
(endanger)

MPRLSTK
imperialistic
MPRLSTKL
imperialistically
MPRLZM
imperialism
MPRM
emporium
emporia(or)
emporiums
MPRMBL
impermeable
MPRMNNT
impermanent
MPRMPT
impromptu
MPRMSBL
impermissable
MPRMT
impromptu
MPRMTR
imprimatur
MPRN
Empirin(trademark)
MPRNT
imprint
MPRPR
improper
MPRPRT
impropriety
improprieties
MPRR
emperor
MPRS
empress(person)
empresses
imperious
(overbearing)
impress
impresses
MPRSBL
impressible
impressibly
MPRSHBL
imperishable
MPRSHL
impartial
MPRSHLT
impartiality
impartialities
MPRSHN
impression
MPRSHNBL
impressionable
impressionably
MPRSHNZM

impressionism
MPRSKRPTBL
imprescriptible
MPRSND
ampersand(&)
MPRSNL
impersonal
MPRSNLT
impersonality
MPRSNLZ
impersonalize
impersonalized
impersonalizing
MPRSNLZSHN
impersonalization
MPRSNSHN
impersonation
MPRSNT
impersonate
impersonated
impersonating
MPRSNTR
impersonator
MPRSPTBL
imperceptible
imperceptibly
MPRSPTBLT
imperceptibility
MPRSPTV
imperceptive
MPRSR
impresario
MPRSS
imprecise
MPRSV
impressive
MPRSZM
empiricism
MPRT
impart(make known)
import(bring in)
MPRTBL
impartable
(make known)
impartible
(indivisible)
importable
(bring in)
MPRTN
importune(ask)
importuned
importuning
MPRTNNS
impertinence
MPRTNNT
impertinent

NGK:ink **P**:pie **R**:air **S**:ice **SH**:show **T**:toy **THN**:thin **TH**:the **V**:of **W**:we **Y**:you **Z**:is **VZHN**:vision

MPRTNS
importance
MPRTNT
important
(great value)
importunity
importunities
MPRTR
importer
MPRTRBBL
imperturbable
imperturbably
MPRTRBBLT
imperturbability
MPRTSHN
importation
MPRTV
imperative
MPRTYN
importune(ask)
importuned
importuning
MPRTYNT
importunity
importunities
MPRV
improve
improved
improving
MPRVBL
improvable
MPRVDNT
improvident
MPRVMNT
improvement
MPRVS
impervious
MPRVZ
improvise
improvised
improvising
improviser
MPRVZSHN
improvisation
MPRZN
imprison
MPS
impasse
impious
MPSBL
impassable(pass)
impassible
(unfeeling)
impossible(not
able to happen)
MPSBLT

impassability
(pass)
impassibility
(unfeeling)
impossibility(not
able to happen)
MPSCHR
imposture
MPSH
impish
MPSHN
impassion
MPSHND
impassioned
MPSHNS
impatience
MPSHNT
impatient
MPST
impost
MPSTR
impostor
MPSV
impassive
MPSVT
impassivity
MPT
empty
emptied
empties
emptier
emptiest
emptily
emptiness
impiety
impieties
moppet
Muppet
(trademark)
MPTG
impetigo
MPTH
empathy
MPTHDD
empty-headed
MPTHK
empathic, empathetic
MPTHNDD
empty-handed
MPTHZ
empathize
empathized
empathizing
MPTN
umpteen
umpteenth

MPTNS
impotence
MPTNT
impotent
MPTNTH
umpteenth
umpteen
MPTS
impetus
MPVRSH
impoverish
impoverishes
MPWR
empower
MPWSNS
impuissance
MPYDNS
impudence
MPYDNT
impudent
MPYL
ampoule(or)ampul
(or)ampule
MPYN
impugn
MPYNBL
impugnable
MPYNT
impunity
impunities
MPYR
impure
MPYRT
impurity
impurities
MPYSNS
impuissance
MPYSNT
impuissant
MPYT
amputee
impute(fault)
imputed,-ting
MPYTBL
imputable
MPYTBLT
imputability
MPYTSHN
amputation(cut off)
imputation
MPYTT
amputate
amputated
amputating
MPYTTR
amputator

MPYTTV
imputative
MPZ
impose
imposed
imposing
MPZSHN
imposition
MR
amour(love)
emery
emir(ruler)
mar
marred
marring
mare(horse)
marrow(bone)
marry
married
marries
marriage
mayor(person)
mere
merest
merry(happy)
merrier
merriest
merrily
merriness
mire(stuck)
mired
miring
mirror
miry
mirier
miriest
miriness
moiré(grid, cloth,
design)
moor(make secure)
Moor(person)
mora(verse)
morae(or)moras
moray(eel)
more(not less)
morrow(time)
myrrh(aromatic)
MRB
marabou
MRBD
morbid
MRBDT
morbidity
MRBFK
morbific
MRBL

marble
marbled
marbling
MRBLZ
marbleize
marbleized
marbleizing
MRBN
marrowbone
MRBND
moribund
MRBNDT
moribundity
MRCH
March
march
marches
MRCHN
maraschino
MRCHNDS
merchandise(n)
MRCHNDZ
merchandise(v)
merchandised
merchandising
MRCHNDZR
merchandiser
MRCHNT
merchant
MRCHWR
mortuary
mortuaries
MRD
maraud
myriad(many)
MRDF
mortify
mortified
mortifies
mortification
MRDGR
Mardi Gras
MRDL
immortal
mortal
myrtle
MRDN
meridian
MRDNT
mordant(sarcastic)
mordent(musical)
MRDR
martyr(person)
mortar
murder
MRDRR

murderer
MRDRS
murderous
MRFLJ
morphology
MRFN
morphine
MRFS
amorphous
MRFZL
Murphy's law
MRG
morgue
MRGJ
mortgage
mortgaged
mortgaging
mortgagee
MRGJR
mortgagor(or)-ger
MRGLD
marigold
MRGNTK
morganatic
MRGRND
merry-go-round
MRGRT
margarita
MRGRV
margrave
MRJ
emerge(appear)
emerged
emerging
immerge(plunge)
immerged
immerging
marriage
merge(go
together)
merged
merging
moorage
MRJBL
marriageable
MRJN
margin
MRJNL
marginal
MRJNS
emergence
emergency
emergencies
immergence
(plunging)
MRJR

merger
MRJRM
marjoram
MRJRN
margarine
MRK
America
maraca
mark(spot,money)
markka(money)
markkaa(pl)
(Finland)
marquee(tent,
sign)
Marquis(title)
marquis(person)
marquis(or)
marquises
Morocco
morocco
murk
murky
murkier
murkiest
murkily
murkiness
MRKDL
markedly
MRKDN
markdown
MRKL
miracle
MRKN
American
Americana
MRKNG
marking
MRKNSM
American Samoa
MRKNTL
mercantile
MRKNTLZM
mercantilism
MRKNZ
Americanize
-ized,-izing
Americanization
MRKP
markup(n)(profit)
mark up(v)
MRKR
marker
MRKSH
Marrakesh
MRKSKP
Americas Cup

MRKSMN
marksman
marksmen
MRKSN
Marxian
MRKSST
Marxist
MRKST
marcasite
MRKSZM
Marxism
MRKT
market
MRKTBL
marketable
MRKTBLT
marketability
MRKTPLS
marketplace
MRKTR
marquetry
marquetries
MRKWS
Marquis(title)
marquis(person)
marquis(or)
marquises
MRKWZT
marquisette
MRKYLS
miraculous
MRKYR
Mercury
mercury
MRKYRKRM
Mercurochrome
(trademark)
MRKYRL
mercurial
MRKZ
marchesa(woman)
marchese
(nobleman)
marquise(ring)
MRKZKP
Americas Cup
MRKZT
marcasite
marquisette(fabric)
MRL
Amarillo
amoral(not judging)
emerald
immoral(bad)
marl
mayoral

moral(judgment)
morale(feeling)
MRLD
emerald
MRLN
marlin(fish)
marline(card)
Merlin(magician)
merlon(wall)
MRLND
Maryland
MRLNSPK
marlinespike
MRLS
amaryllis
MRLST
moralist
MRLSTK
moralistic
MRLSTKL
moralistically
MRLT
immorality
immoralities
mayoralty
mayoralties
morality
moralities
MRLZ
moralize
moralized
moralizing
moralizer
MRMB
marimba
MRMD
mermaid
MRMDN
myrmidon
MRMKNG
merrymaking
MRMLD
marmalade
MRMN
Mormon
MRMNT
merriment
MRMR
murmer
MRMRR
murmerer
MRMST
marmoset
MRMT
marmot
MRN

marina(dock)
marine
Marine(soldier)
maroon
merino
moraine
morn(morning)
moron
mourn(grieve)
MRND
marinade
MRNDR
merry-andrew
MRNFL
mournful
MRNG
meringue(pie
topping)
mooring
MRNK
moronic
MRNKR
Marine Corps
MRNNG
morning(time)
mourning(feel)
MRNR
mariner
MRNT
marinate
marinated
marinating
marionette
MRNZ
Marines
the Marine Corps
MRPD
myriapod
MRR
mirror
MRS
amerce(punish)
amerced
amercing
amorous(love)
immerse
immersed
immersing
Marseille
mercy
mercies
merciful
merciless
morass
morose(sad)
MRSBL

immersible
MRSFL
merciful
MRSH
marsh
marshes
marshy
marshier
marshiest
marshiness
MRSHL
marshal(enlist,
rank)
martial(war)
MRSHML
marshmallow
MRSHN
immersion
maraschino
Martian
MRSHNS
marchioness
marchionesses
MRSHS
Mauritius
MRSL
marcel
marcelled
marcelling
Marsala
morsel(food)
MRSLS
merciless
MRSNR
mercenary
mercenaries
MRSPL
marsupial
MRSPM
marsupium
marsupia
MRSRZ
mercerize
mercerized
mercerizing
MRSSNT
marcescent
MRST
merest
mere
MRT
mart
merit
MRTF
mortify
mortified

mortifies
MRTFKSHN
mortification
MRTH
mirth
MRTHLT
Merthiolate
(trademark)
MRTHN
marathon
MRTL
immortal
marital(marriage)
mortal
myrtle(tree)
MRTLT
immortality
mortality
MRTLZ
immortalize
immortalized
immortalizing
MRTLZSHN
immortalization
MRTM
maritime
MRTMPRVNSS
Maritime
Provinces
MRTN
marten(animal)
martin(bird)
martini
Mauritania
MRTNGL
martingale
MRTNK
Martinique
MRTNT
martinet
MRTR
martyr
moratoria
moratorium
mortar
MRTRBRD
mortarboard
MRTRDM
martyrdom
MRTRM
moratorium
moratoria(or)
moratoriums
MRTRS
meritorious
MRTRSHS

B:by CH:each D:day F:if G:go H:he HW:why J:joy K:cow KS:ax KWL:equal L:all M:may N:in

meretricious
MRTRZ
  martyrize
    martyrized
    martyrizing
MRTS
  emeritus
  mortise
    mortised
    mortising
MRTSHN
  mortician
MRTSPN
  marzipan
MRTZ
  amortize
    amortized
    amortizing
MRTZBL
  amortizable
MRTZSHN
  amortization
MRV
  MIRV(missile)
    MIRVs
MRVL
  marvel
MRVLS
  marvelous
MRVR
  moreover
MRWN
  marijuana(or)
  marihuana
MRZ
  Mars
  Moors(people)
  mores(customs)
MRZH
  mirage
MRZHN
  emersion
   (come forth)
  immersion(plunge)
MRZMS
  marasmus
MRZNST
  mare's-nest
MRZPN
  marzipan
MRZTL
  mare's-tail
MS
  amass
    amasses
  amiss

emcee
  emceed
mace
Mace(trademark)
  tear gas
maize(corn)
Mass(ceremony)
mass
  masses
massé(billiards)
mesa(area)
mess
  messes
messy
  messier
  messiest
messily
messiness
Messiah
  (religious)
messiah(liberator)
mice
  mouse
Miss
  Misses
miss
  misses
missy
  missies
moose(mammal)
  moose
moss(plant)
  mosses
mossy
  mossier
  mossiest
  mossiness
mouse(rodent)
  mice
mousy
  mousier
  mousiest
  mousiness
mousse(dessert)
muss(messy)
  musses
mussy
  mussily
MSBGTN
  misbegotten
MSBHV
  misbehave
    misbehaved
    misbehaving
MSBHVR
  misbehavior, (B)- viour

MSBK
  mossback
MSBL
  immiscible
  miscible
  miscibly
  omissible
MSBLF
  misbelief
MSBLT
  miscibility
MSBLV
  misbelieve
    misbelieved
    misbelieving
MSCHF
  mischief
MSCHFMKR
  mischief-maker
MSCHNS
  mischance
MSCHR
  moisture
MSCHRZ
  moisturize
    moisturized
    moisturizing
    moisturizer
MSCHSTS
  Massachusetts
MSCHVS
  mischievous
MSCHZTS
  Massachusetts
MSDD
  misdeed
MSDGNS
  misdiagnose
    misdiagnosed
    misdiagnosing
MSDGNSS
  misdiagnosis
    misdiagnoses
MSDL
  misdeal
  misdealt
MSDMNR
  misdemeanor, (B)-
MSDNN   nour
  Macedonian
MSDRKSHN
  misdirection
MSDRKT
  misdirect
MSDT
  misdate

  misdated
  misdating
MSDVNCHR
  misadventure
MSDVZ
  misadvise
    misadvised
    misadvising
MSF
  massif
MSFL
  misfile
    misfiled
    misfiling
MSFR
  misfire
    misfired
    misfiring
MSFRCHN
  misfortune
MSFRCHNT
  misfortunate
MSFT
  misfit
    misfitted
    misfitting
MSFZNS
  misfeasance
MSGD
  misguide
    misguided
    misguiding
MSGDNS
  misguidance
MSGM
  misogamy
MSGMST
  misogamist
MSGN
  misogyny
MSGVNG
  misgiving
MSGVNGZ
  misgivings
MSGVRN
  misgovern
MSH
  Amish
  mash
    mashes
  mashie(golf)
  mesh
    meshes
  meshy
  mush
    mushes

NGK:ink **P**:pie **R**:air **S**:ice **SH**:show **T**:toy **THN**:thin **TH**:the **V**:of **W**:we **Y**:you **Z**:is **VZHN**:vision

mushy
mushier
mushiest
mushily
mushiness
MSHD
machete
MSHG
mishugah
MSHGN
Michigan
MSHMSH
mishmash
mishmashes
MSHN
emission
emotion
machine
machined
machining
mission
motion(move)
omission
MSHNDL
mishandle
mishandled
mishandling
MSHNGN
machine gun(n)
machine-gun(v,adj)
machine-gunned
machine-gunning
MSHNL
emotional
MSHNLZ
emotionalize
emotionalized
emotionalizing
emotionalization
MSHNR
machinery
machineries
missionary
missionaries
MSHNSHN
machination
MSHNST
machinist
MSHNT
machinate
machinated
machinating
MSHP
mishap
misshape
misshaped

misshaping
misshapen
MSHR
masher
MSHRM
mushroom
MSHSH
maxixe
MSHSHN
emaciation
MSHT
emaciate
emaciated
emaciating
machete
MSHWRK
meshwork
MSJ
massage(rub)
massaged
massaging
message(note)
MSJJ
misjudge
misjudged
misjudging
MSJJMNT
misjudgment
MSJN
misogyny
MSJNSHN
miscegenation
MSJNST
misogynist
MSJNSTK
misogynistic
MSK
mask(cover)
masque(drama)
Moscow
mosque(church)
musk
musky
muskier
muskiest
muskiness
MSKD
mosquito
MSKDN
muscadine
MSKL
mescal
MSKLKYLSHN
miscalculation
MSKLKYLT
miscalculate

miscalculated
miscalculating
MSKLN
mescaline
MSKLNJ
muskellunge
MSKMLN
muskmelon
MSKN
misocainea
MSKNDKT
misconduct
MSKNSPSHN
misconception
MSKNSTR
misconstrue
misconstrued
misconstruing
MSKNSTRKSHN
misconstruction
MSKNSV
misconceive
misconceived
misconceiving
MSKNT
miscount
MSKR
mascara(make-up)
masker
massacre(kill)
massacred
massacring
miscarry
miscarried
miscarries
MSKRD
masquerade
masqueraded
masquerading
masquerader
MSKRJ
miscarriage
MSKRNS
miscreance
MSKRNT
miscreant
MSKRT
muskrat
MSKST
masochist
miscast
MSKSTK
masochistic
MSKSTKL
masochistically
MSKSTN

M-16(weapon)
MSKT
mascot(pet)
mosquito
Muscat(Oman)
muscat(grape)
musket(gun)
MSKTL
muscatel
MSKWT
misquote
misquoted
misquoting
MSKWTSHN
misquotation
MSKY
miscue
miscued
miscuing
MSKYLCHR
musculature
MSKYLN
masculine
MSKYLNT
masculinity
MSKYLR
muscular
MSKYLRDSTRF
muscular
dystrophy
MSKYLSHN
emasculation
MSKYLT
emasculate
emasculated
emasculating
MSKYLTR
emasculator
MSKZM
masochism
MSL
micelle(molecule)
micelles(or)
micellae
micellar(adj)
misally
misallied
misallies
mislay(misplace)
mislaid
missal(book)
missile(weapon)
muscle(power)
mussel(shellfish)
MSLBND
muscle-bound

B:by CH:each D:day F:if G:go H:he HW:why J:joy K:cow KS:ax KWL:equal L:all M:may N:in

MSLD
mislead
misled
MSLDNG
misleading
MSLF
myself
MSLM
mausoleum
mausolea(or)
mausoleums
Muslim
MSLN
messaline(cloth)
miscellany
miscellanea(or)
miscellanies
mousseline(cotton fabric)
MSLNS
misalliance
miscellaneous
MSLT
mistletoe
MSMCH
mismatch
mismatches
MSMNJ
mismanage
mismanaged
mismanaging
MSMNJMNT
mismanagement
MSMPL
misemploy
MSMRF
mesomorph
MSMT
mismate
mismated
mismating
MSN
mason(person)
Mason(Freemason)
meson(particle)
moisten(wet)
MSNDRSTND
misunderstand
misunderstood
MSNDRSTNDNG
misunderstanding
MSNFRM
misinform
MSNFRMSHN
misinformation
MSNJR

messenger
MSNK
Masonic
messianic
MSNM
misname
misnamed
misnaming
MSNMR
misnomer
MSNR
masonry
MSNS
moistness
MSNT
Masonite (trademark)
MSNTHRP
misanthrope
misanthropy
MSNTHRPK
misanthropic
MSNTHRPST
misanthropist
MSNTRPRT
misinterpret
MSNYR
Messeigneurs
MSPK
misspeak
misspoke
misspoken
MSPL
misapply
misapplied
misapplies
misspell
misspelt(or)
misspelled
MSPLKSHN
misapplication
MSPLNG
misspelling
MSPLS
misplace
misplaced
misplacing
misplacement
MSPND
misspend
misspent
MSPRHND
misapprehend
MSPRHNSHN
misapprehension
MSPRNNS

mispronounce
mispronounced
mispronouncing
MSPRNNSSHN
mispronunciation
MSPRNT
misprint
MSPRPRT
misappropriate
misappropriated
misappropriating
misappropriation
MSPRZHN
misprision
MSR
amasser
emissary
emissaries
masseur
MSRD
misread
misread
MSRL
misrule
misruled
misruling
MSRPRZNT
misrepresent
MSRPRZNTSHN
misrepresentation
MSRT
macerate
macerated
macerating
miswrite
miswrote
miswriting
miswritten
MSRZ
Messieurs(or)
Messrs.
MSS
emesis
emetic(adj)
masseuse
missis(wife)(or)
missus
tmesis
MSSP
Mississippi
MSSTMT
misestimate
misestimated
misestimating
misestimation
MST

Maoist
Maoism
mast(boat)
missed(miss)
mist
misty
mistier
mistiest
mistily
mistiness
most
must
musty
mustier
mustiest
mustiness
MSTD
mastoid
MSTDN
mastodon
MSTF
mastiff(dog)
mystify
mystified
mystifies
MSTFKSHN
mystification
MSTGRS
mistigris
MSTHD
masthead
MSTK
mastic(resin)
mistake
mistook
mistaking
mistaken
mystic(religious)
mystique(status)
MSTKL
mystical
MSTKSHN
mastication
MSTKT
masticate
masticated
masticating
MSTKTM
mastectomy
mastectomies
MSTNG
mustang
MSTP
misstep
misstepped
misstepping

MSTR
maestro
  maestri(or)
  maestros
master
mastery
  masteries
mister(slang)
Mister(or)
Mr.
  Messrs.
muster
mystery
  mysteries
MSTRBSHN
masturbation
MSTRBT
masturbate
  masturbated
  masturbating
MSTRBTR
masturbator
masturbatory
MSTRD
mustard
MSTRDM
Amsterdam
MSTRFL
masterful
MSTRL
mistral(wind)
mistrial(law)
MSTRMND
mastermind
MSTRP
mousetrap
MSTRPS
masterpiece
MSTRS
mistress
  mistresses
mysterious
MSTRST
mistrust
MSTRT
mistreat
MSTRTMNT
mistreatment
MSTSH
mustache, (B)mous-
MSTSZM
mysticism
MSTT
misstate
  misstated
  misstating

MSTTMNT
misstatement
MSV
massive(big)
missive(letter)
MSVL
misvalue
  misvalued
  misvaluing
MSVNCHR
misventure
MSY
Messiah(religious)
messiah(liberator)
Monsieur
MSYS
misuse(n)
MSYSJ
misusage
MSYZ
misuse(v)
  misused
  misusing
MSZ
masseuse(f)
Misses
Miss
missis(wife)
MSZH
massage(rub)
  massaged
  massaging
MT
amity
  amities
emit(give off)
  emitted
  emitting
empty
  emptied
  empties
  emptier
  emptiest
  emptily
  emptiness
mat(fabric)
  matted
  matting
mate(spouse)
  mated
  mating
meat(flesh)
  meaty
  meatier
  meatiest
  meatiness

meet(come upon)
  met
mete(deal out)
  meted
  meting
might
  may
might(power)
  mighty
  mightier
  mightiest
  mightily
  mightiness
mite(tiny,
  parasite)
mitt(glove)
moat(ditch)
moiety(half)
  moieties
moit(wool)
moot(debatable)
mote(speck)
motto(words)
mutt(dog)
omit
  omitted
  omitting
  omission
MTBL
imitable
MTBLK
metabolic
MTBLZ
metabolize
  metabolized
  metabolizing
MTBLZM
metabolism
MTD
matted(mat)
MTDR
matador
MTF
motif
MTFR
metaphor
MTFRK
metaphoric
MTFRKL
metaphorical
MTFZK
metaphysic
MTFZKL
metaphysical
MTFZKS
metaphysics

MTGBL
immitigable
mitigable
MTGSHN
mitigation
MTGT
mitigate
  mitigated
  mitigating
MTGTR
mitigator
MTH
math
moth(insect)
mouth
mouthy
  mouthier
  mouthiest
  mouthily
  mouthiness
myth
MTHBL
mothball
MTHD
method
MTHDK
methodic
MTHDKL
methodical
MTHDLJ
methodology
  methodologies
MTHDN
methadone
MTHDRN
methedrine
MTHDST
Methodist
MTHDZ
methodize
  methodized
  methodizing
MTHFL
mouthful
MTHK
mythic
MTHKL
mythical
MTHKWLN
methaqualone
  Quaalude
  (trademark)
MTHLJ
mythology
  mythologies
MTHLJKL

mythological
MTHLJZ
mythologize
 mythologized
 mythologizing
MTHMDK
 mathematic
MTHMTK
 mathematic
MTHMTKL
 mathematical
MTHMTKS
 mathematics
MTHMTSHN
 mathematician
MTHN
 methane
MTHNDD
 empty-handed
MTHNL
 methanol
MTHPK
 mythopoeic
MTHPRF
 mothproof
MTHPS
 mouthpiece
MTHR
 mother
MTHRHD
 motherhood
MTHRL
 motherly
 motherliness
MTHRLND
 motherland
MTHRNCHR
 Mother Nature
MTHRNL
 mother-in-law
 mothers-in-law
MTHRVL
 mother-of-all(tool)
MTHRVPRL
 mother-of-pearl
MTHRZNL
 mothers-in-law
MTHS
 mythos
MTHST
 amethyst
MTHTMTH
 mouth-to-mouth
MTHTN
 moth-eaten
MTHWSH

mouthwash
 mouthwashes
MTHWTRNG
 mouth watering
MTHYN
 Medellin
MTK
 emetic
 mattock
MTKYLS
 meticulous
MTL
 metal(alloy)
 mettle(courage)
 motel(lodge)
 motile(motion)
 motley(variety)
 mottle(spotted)
 mottled
 mottling
MTLF
 meat loaf
MTLK
 metallic
MTLRJ
 metallurgy
MTLRJKL
 metallurgical
MTLRJST
 metallurgist
MTLS
 matelassé
MTLSM
 mettlesome
 (spirited)
MTLT
 motility(motion)
MTLWRK
 metalwork
MTMRFK
 metamorphic
MTMRFS
 metamorphose
 metamorphosed
 metamorphosing
MTMRFSS
 metamorphosis
MTMRFZ
 metamorphose
 metamorphosed
 metamorphosing
MTMRFZM
 metamorphism
MTN
 matinee
 mitten(glove)

mouton(fur)
 mutton(meat)
 umpteen
 umpteenth
MTNCHP
 muttonchop(beard)
MTNG
 mating(sex)
 matting(material)
 meeting
MTNM
 metonymy
MTNTH
 umpteenth
 umpteen
MTR
 amateur
 amatory(love)(or)
 amatorial
 matter
 mature
 matured
 maturing
 meteor(space)
 meter(measure),(B)-tre
 miter(hat, join)(B)- tre
 motor(engine)
 mutter(sound)
 ohmmeter
MTRBK
 motorbike
MTRBKS
 miter box
 miter boxes
MTRBT
 motorboat
MTRD
 meteoroid
MTRDRM
 motordrome
MTRDTL
 maitre d'hotel
MTRK
 amtrac
 Amtrak(train)
 (trademark)
 meteoric
 metric
MTRKD
 motorcade
MTRKL
 metrical
MTRKS
 matrix
 matrices(or)
 matrixes

MTRKYLNT
 matriculant
MTRKYLSHN
 matriculation
MTRKYLT
 matriculate
 matriculated
 matriculating
MTRL
 immaterial
 material(matter)
 materiel(equipment)
 mitral(miter)
MTRLJ
 meteorology
MTRLJKL
 meteorological
MTRLJST
 meteorologist
MTRLSTK
 materialistic
MTRLZ
 immaterialize
 immaterialized
 immaterializing
 materialize
 materialized
 materializing
 materialization
 materializer
MTRLZM
 materialism
MTRMN
 matrimony
 motorman
 motormen
MTRMNL
 matrimonial
MTRN
 matron
MTRNL
 maternal
MTRNLNS
 matronliness
MTRNLSTK
 maternalistic
MTRNM
 metronome
MTRNT
 maternity
MTRPLS
 metropolis
MTRPLTN
 metropolitan
MTRRJ
 metrorrhagia

NGK:ink **P**:pie **R**:air **S**:ice **SH**:show **T**:toy **THN**:thin **TH**:the **V**:of **W**:we **Y**:you **Z**:is **VZHN**:vision

MTRRK
matriarch
matriarchy
matriarchies
MTRRKL
matriarchal
MTRS
mattress
mattresses
MTRSD
matricide
MTRSKL
motorcycle
motorcycled
motorcycling
motorcyclist
MTRST
motorist
MTRT
maturity
maturities
meteorite
MTRVFKT
matter-of-fact
MTRZ
motorize
motorized
motorizing
motorization
MTS
matzo(bread)
matzoth(or)
matzos
meatus(body canal)
mezzo(singer)
MTSHN
imitation
MTSRL
mozzarella
MTSRT
Mozart
MTSS
matzos
matzoth
MTSSPRN
mezzo-soprano
MTSTH
matzoth(food)
matzo
MTSTNT
mezzotint
MTSV
mitzvah
mitzvahs(or)
mitzvoth
MTT

imitate
imitated
imitating
imitation
MTTHSS
metathesis
metatheses
MTTR
imitator
MTTRSL
metatarsal
MTTV
imitative
MTV
motive
MTVSHN
motivation
MTVT
motivate
motivated
motivating
MTVTR
motivator
MTY
metier(a trade)
MTYR
amateur
immature
mature
matured
maturing
MTYRT
immaturity
immaturities
maturity
maturities
MV
mauve(color)
move
moved
moving
mover
movie
MVBL
immovable
immovably
movable
movably
MVBLT
immovability
movability
MVGR
moviegoer
MVHS
movie house
MVMNT

movement
MVNG
moving
MVRK
maverick
MW
Maui
MWN
M-1(weapon)
MWR
moire(silk)
MY
meow, mew(cat)
MYCHL
mutual
MYCHLT
mutuality
mutualities
MYCHLZ
mutualize
mutualized
mutualizing
MYDLT
mutilate
mutilated
mutilating
mutilation
MYKS
mucus(n)
mucous(adj)
MYL
mule
mulish
MYLD
mulatto
MYLK
majolica
MYLS
emulous
MYLSH
mulish
mule
MYLSHN
emulation
MYLSKNR
muleskinner
MYLT
amulet
emulate
emulated
emulating
emulator
mulatto
MYN
immune
MYNFSNS

munificence
MYNFSNT
munificent
MYNK
Munich
MYNLJ
immunology
MYNSHN
ammunition
munition
MYNSK
Minsk
MYNSPL
municipal
MYNSPLT
municipality
municipalities
MYNSPLZ
municipalize
municipalized
municipalizing
MYNT
immunity
immunities
MYNZ
immunize
immunized
immunizing
MYNZSHN
immunization
MYR
immure
immured
immuring
mayor
mure
mured
muring
MYRL
mayoral
mural
MYSLJ
mucilage
MYSLJNS
mucilaginous
MYT
mayotte
mute
muted
muting
muter
mutest
MYTBL
immutable
immutably
mutable

B:by CH:each D:day F:if G:go H:he HW:why J:joy K:cow KS:ax KWL:equal L:all M:may N:in

mutably
MYTBLT
immutability
mutability
MYTLSHN
mutilation
MYTLT
mutilate
mutilated
mutilating
mulilator
MYTN
mutiny
mutinied
mutinies
MYTNR
mutineer
MYTNS
mutinous
MYTNT
mutant
MYTSHN
mutation
MYTT
mutate
mutated
mutating
mutative
MYZ
amuse
amused
amusing
Muse(Zeus)
muse
mused
musing
MYZK
music
Muzak
(trademark)
MYZKL
musical(adj,n)
musicale(n)
MYZKLJ
musicology
MYZKLJST
musicologist
MYZM
museum
MYZMNT
amusement
MYZN
muezzin
MYZNG
amusing
MYZR

amuser
MYZSHN
musician
MYZT
musette
MZ
alms(money)
amaze
amazed
amazing
maize(corn)
maze(labyrinth)
mezzo(music)
mosey(walk)
mouse
moused
mousing
Ms.(title)
Mses.(or)Mss.
MZHN
maginot
Maginot Line
MZHNG
mahjong(game)
MZHNG
mahjong(or)
Mah-Jongg(game)
MZHNLN
Maginot Line
MZHR
measure
measured
measuring
MZHRBL
immeasurable
immeasurably
measurable
measurably
MZHRBLT
measurability
MZHRD
measured
MZHRMNT
measurement
MZHRR
measurer
MZK
mosaic
mosaicked
mosaicking
MZL
measly
measlier
measliest
mizzle(rain)
mizzled

mizzling
muzzle
muzzled
muzzling
MZLM
mausoleum
mausolea(or)
mausoleums
Muslim
MZLN
muslin(cloth)
MZLNS
mésalliance
MZLTF
mazel tov
MZLYNS
mésalliance
MZLZ
measles
MZM
Maoism
Maoist
miasma
miasmas(or)
miasmata
MZMBK
Mozambique
MZMNT
amazement
MZMRF
mesomorph
MZMRZ
mesmerize
mesmerized
mesmerizing
mesmerizer
MZMRZM
mesmerism
MZN
Amazon
meson(particle)
mizzen(sail)
muezzin(crier)
MZNG
amazing
MZNMST
mizzenmast
MZNN
mezzanine
MZNSN
mise en scène
MZNTHRP
misanthrope
misanthropy
MZNTHRPK
misanthropic

MZR
maser(device)
miser(person)
misery(suffer)
miseries
Missouri
mouser(animal)
MZRBL
miserable
miserably
MZRK
mazurka
MZTNT
mezzotint
MZZ
mezuzah
mezuzoth(or)
mezuzahs
Moses
Mrs.
Mmes.

N

an(article)
and
ampersand(&)
anew
ani(bird)
annoy
ante(money)
anted
anteing
any(one,every)
awn(botany)
eon(time)
ion(atom)
gnaw(bite)
gnawn
gnu(animal)
in(prep)
"in" (in vogue)
knee(joint)
know(perceive)
knew
known
nay(no)
neigh(whinny)
new
no(negative)
now
on(over)

own(belong)	**NBLNST**	newborn	**NCHN**
NB	unbalanced	unborn	enchain
knob(lump)	**NBLPRZ**	**NBRNSWK**	**NCHNJ**
knobby	Nobel Prize	New Brunswick	unchange
knobbier	**NBLT**	**NBRNT**	unchanged
knobbiest	inability	inebriant	unchanging
knobbiness	inabilities	**NBRSHN**	**NCHNJBL**
nab(catch)	nobility	inebriation	unchangeable
nabbed	nobilities	**NBRSK**	unchangeably
nabbing	unbolt	Nebraska	**NCHNT**
neb(beak,snout)	**NBLVBL**	**NBRT**	ancient
nib(point)	unbelievable	inebriate	enchant
nub(knob,gist)	unbelievably	inebriated	**NCHNTMNT**
nubby	**NBLVR**	inebriating	enchantment
nubbier	unbeliever	inebriety	**NCHNTR**
nubbiest	**NBN**	**NBSH**	enchanter
nubbiness	nubbin	nebbish	**NCHNTRS**
NBD	**NBND**	**NBSHT**	enchantress
anybody(general)	unbend	unabashed	enchantresses
any body(specific)	unbent(or)	**NBSNSH**	**NCHR**
nobody	unbended	in absentia	nature
nobodies	unbending	**NBSS**	**NCHRL**
NBDN	unbound	anabasis	natural
unbidden	**NBNN**	**NBST**	neutral
NBKL	unbeknown	unbiased	unnatural
unbuckle	**NBNNST**	**NBTBL**	**NCHRLST**
unbuckled	unbeknownst	unbeatable	naturalist
unbuckling	**NBR**	unbeatably	**NCHRLSTK**
NBKMNG	neighbor, (B)-bour	**NBTD**	naturalistic
unbecoming	neighborly	unabated	**NCHRLSTKL**
NBL	neighborliness	**NBTN**	naturalistical
enable	**NBRBL**	unbeaten	**NCHRLZ**
enabled	unbearable	unbutton	naturalize
enabling	unbearably	**NBTRSV**	naturalized
ennoble	**NBRD**	unobtrusive	naturalizing
ennobled	inbreed	**NBYL**	**NCHRLZM**
ennobling	inbred	nebula	naturalism
knowable	inboard	nebulae(or)	**NCHRLZSHN**
nibble	on board	nebulas	naturalization
nibbled	**NBRDL**	**NBYLR**	**NCHRTBL**
nibbling	unbridle	nebular	uncharitable
noble	unbridled	**NBYLS**	uncharitably
nobler	unbridling	nebulous	**NCHST**
noblest	**NBRDN**	**NBYLST**	unchaste
nobly	unburden	nebulosity	**NCHT**
nubile	**NBRHD**	nebulosities	notched
unable(not able)	neighborhood	**NBZM**	**NCHV**
NBLF	**NBRJD**	unbosom	anchovy
unbelief	unabridged	**NCH**	anchovies(or)
NBLK	**NBRKN**	niche(recess)	anchovy
niblick	unbroken	niched	**ND**
NBLMN	**NBRL**	niching	Aeneid(poem,Virgil)
nobleman	neighborly	notch	and(&)
noblemen	neighborliness	notches	end
NBLNGKNG	**NBRN**	**NCHLD**	endow(provide)
unblinking	inborn	enchilada	endue(clothe)

B:by **CH**:each **D**:day **F**:if **G**:go **H**:he **HW**:why **J**:joy **K**:cow **KS**:ax **KWL**:equal **L**:all **M**:may **N**:in

endued	indifference	indicated	undulant
enduing	**NDFRNT**	indicating	**NDLPNT**
ennead(nine)	indifferent	induct	needlepoint
India	**NDFTGBL**	inductee	**NDLR**
knead(press)	indefatigable	**NDKTL**	needler
naughty(bad)	indefatigably	inductile	**NDLS**
naughtier	**NDFZBL**	**NDKTNS**	endless
naughtiest	indefeasible	inductance	needless
naughtily	indefeasibly	**NDKTR**	**NDLSHN**
naughtiness	**NDG**	indicator	undulation
need(require)	indigo	inductor	**NDLT**
needy	**NDGM**	**NDKTRNSHN**	indult
needier	endogamy	indoctrination	undulate
neediest	**NDGNNT**	**NDKTRNT**	undulated
neediness	indignant	indoctrinate	undulating
nod	**NDGNSHN**	indoctrinated	**NDLTRTD**
nodded	indignation	indoctrinating	unadulterated
nodding	**NDGNT**	**NDKTRNTR**	**NDLWRK**
node(knob)	indignity	indoctrinator	needlework
nude	indignities	**NDKTV**	**NDM**
nudist	**NDGRD**	indicative	anatomy
nudism	nitty-gritty	inductive	anatomies
nudity	**NDJNS**	**NDKWS**	indium
undo	endogenous	inadequacy	**NDMK**
undid	(from within)	inadequacies	endemic
undoing	indigence(needy)	**NDKWT**	**NDMN**
undone	indigenous(native)	inadequate	anno Domini
undue(excessive)	**NDJNT**	**NDL**	A.D.
unduly	indigent(needy)	needle	**NDMNF**
NDBL	**NDJSCHN**	needled	indemnify
inaudible(ear)	indigestion	needling	indemnified
inedible(mouth)	**NDJSTBL**	New Delhi	indemnifies
NDBTBL	indigestible	nodal	**NDMNFKSHN**
indubitable	**NDJSTD**	node	indemnification
indubitably	indigested(or) undi-	noodle(food)	**NDMNSTRTV**
NDD	**NDKL**	unduly	undemonstrative
indeed	nautical	**NDLBL**	**NDMNT**
NDF	**NDKLNBL**	indelible	endowment
notify	indeclinable	indelibly	indemnity
notified	**NDKNT**	**NDLJ**	indemnities
notifies	indicant	indulge	**NDMSBL**
notification	**NDKRM**	indulged	inadmissible
NDFKTBL	indecorum	indulging	inadmissibly
indefectible	**NDKRN**	**NDLJNS**	**NDMST**
indefectibly	endocrine	indulgence	anatomist
NDFL	**NDKRS**	**NDLJNT**	endmost
needful	indecorous	indulgent	**NDMTBL**
NDFNBL	**NDKS**	**NDLKS**	indomitable
indefinable	index	indelicacy	indomitably
indefinably	indexes(or)	indelicacies	**NDMTRM**
NDFNSBL	indeces	**NDLKT**	endometrium
indefensible	**NDKSHN**	indelicate	**NDN**
indefensibly	indication	**NDLNS**	anodyne
NDFNT	induction	indolence	Indian
indefinite	**NDKT**	**NDLNT**	Indiana
NDFRNS	indicate	indolent	indign

NGK:ink **P**:pie **R**:air **S**:ice **SH**:show **T**:toy **THN**:thin **TH**:the **V**:of **W**:we **Y**:you **Z**:is **VZHN**:vision

undone
NDNBL
undeniable
undeniably
NDNCHN
indention
NDNCHR
indenture
  indentured
  indenturing
NDNG
ending
undoing
undying
NDNJR
endanger
NDNK
nudnik
NDNPLS
Indianapolis
NDNSHN
indention
Indian Ocean
NDNT
andante
indent
needn't
need not
NDNTD
undaunted
NDNTFD
unidentified
NDNTN
andantino
NDNTSHN
indentation
NDNZH
Indonesia
NDNZHN
Indonesian
NDP
knee-deep
NDPNDNS
independence
NDPNDNT
independent
NDPPR
endpaper
NDPTH
in-depth
NDR
and/or
Andorra
endear(love)
endure
  endured

enduring
indoor
nadir(low point)
neuter
under
NDRB
underbuy
  underbought
NDRBD
underbid
  underbid
  underbidding
NDRBL
endurable
endurably
NDRBRSH
underbrush
NDRCHRJ
undercharge
  undercharged
  undercharging
NDRCHV
underachieve
  underachieved
  underachieving
  underachiever
NDRD
android
underdo
  underdid
  underdone
NDRDG
underdog
NDRDRS
underdress
  underdresses
NDRDVLP
underdevelop
NDRDVLPD
underdeveloped
NDRFT
underfoot
NDRG
undergo
  undergoes
  underwent
  undergone
  undergoing
NDRGLZ
underglaze
NDRGRJT
undergraduate
NDRGRMNT
undergarment
NDRGRND
underground

NDRGRTH
undergrowth
NDRHNDD
underhanded
NDRHNG
underhung
NDRJ
underage
NDRJN
androgen
NDRJNS
androgenous(male)
androgynous(m,f)
androgyny(n)
NDRKLSMN
underclassman
underclassmen
NDRKLTHS
underclothes
NDRKLZ
underclothes
NDRKRJ
undercarriage
NDRKRNT
undercurrent
NDRKSHN
indirection
NDRKSPZ
underexpose
  underexposed
  underexposing
NDRKSPZHR
underexposure
NDRKT
indirect
undercoat
undercut
NDRKVR
undercover
NDRL
underlay
  underlaid
  underlaying
underlie
  underlay
  underlain
  underlying
NDRLN
underline
  underlined
  underlining
NDRLNG
underling
  (person)
underlying
NDRMD

andromeda(shrub)
Andromeda
  (constellation)
NDRMN
undermine
  undermined
  undermining
NDRMNT
endearment
NDRMPLD
underemployed
NDRN
andiron
NDRNRSH
undernourish
undernourishes
NDRNS
endurance
NDRNTH
underneath
NDRP
underpay
underpaid
NDRPL
underplay
NDRPN
underpin
  underpinned
  underpinning
NDRPNTS
underpants
NDRPRF
underproof
NDRPRS
underprice
  underpriced
  underpricing
NDRPRT
underpart
NDRPRVLJD
underprivileged
NDRPS
underpass
  underpasses
NDRRM
underarm
NDRRT
underwrite
  underwrote
  underwriting
  underwritten
NDRRTR
underwriter
NDRS
endorse
  endorsed

B:by CH:each D:day F:if G:go H:he HW:why J:joy K:cow KS:ax KWL:equal L:all M:may N:in

endorsing
endorser
endorsee
undersea
undress
undresses
NDRSD
underside
NDRSHN
induration
NDRSHRT
undershirt
NDRSHT
undershoot
undershot
NDRSKR
underscore
underscored
underscoring
NDRSKRT
underskirt
NDRSKRTR
undersecretary
undersecretaries
NDRSKST
undersexed
NDRSL
undersell
undersold
NDRSMNT
endorsement
NDRSND
undersigned
NDRSR
endorser
NDRSTD
understood
understudy
understudies
understudied
understudying
NDRSTFT
understaffed
NDRSTMSHN
underestimation
NDRSTMT
underestimate
underestimated
underestimating
NDRSTND
understand
understood
understanding
NDRSTNDBL
understandable
understandably

NDRSTT
understate
understated
understating
NDRSTTMNT
understatement
NDRSZ
undersize
undersized
undersizing
NDRT
indurate(harden)
indurated
indurating
underrate
underrated
underrating
undertow
NDRTHKNTR
under-the-counter
DNRTHTBL
under-the-table
NDRTK
undertake
undertook
undertaking
undertaken
NDRTKR
undertaker
NDRTN
undertone
NDRVLY
undervalue
undervalued
undervaluing
NDRW
under way
NDRWR
underwear
NDRWRLD
underworld
NDRWT
underweight
NDRWTR
underwater
NDRZ
indoors
NDS
induce
induced
inducing
Indus
NDSDD
undecided
NDSFR
indecipher

NDSFRBL
indecipherable
NDSH
indicia
NDSKRBBL
indescribable
indescribably
NDSKRMNT
indiscriminate
NDSKRSHN
indiscretion
NDSKRT
indiscreet
(no prudence)
indiscrete
(not separated)
NDSL
indocile
NDSLYBL
indissoluble
NDSMNT
inducement
NDSNS
indecency
indecencies
NDSNT
indecent
NDSPNSBL
indispensable
indispensably
NDSPNSBLT
indispensability
NDSPYTBL
indisputable
indisputably
NDSPZ
indispose
indisposed
indisposing
NDSPZD
indisposed(ill,
unwilling)
undisposed
(not settled)
NDSPZSHN
indisposition
NDSRNBL
indiscernible
indiscernibly
NDSSV
indecisive
NDST
nudist
NDSTNGKSHN
indistinction
NDSTNGKT

indistinct
NDSTNGKTV
indistinctive
NDSTNGWSHBL
indistinguishable
indistinguishably
NDSTR
industry
industries
NDSTRKTBL
indestructible
indestructibly
NDSTRL
industrial
NDSTRLST
industrialist
NDSTRLZ
industrialize
industrialized
industrializing
NDSTRLZM
industrialism
NDSTRLZSHN
industrialization
NDSTRS
industrious
NDSVD
undeceived
NDSZ
indeces
index
NDSZHN
indecision
NDT
indict(accuse
formally)
indite(write)
indited
inditing
nudity
nudities
NDTBL
indictable
NDTD
indebted
NDTDL
undoubtedly
NDTMNT
indictment
NDTRMNBL
indeterminable
indeterminably
NDTRMND
undetermined
NDTRMNS
indeterminacy

NGK:ink **P**:pie **R**:air **S**:ice **SH**:show **T**:toy **THN**:thin **TH**:the **V**:of **W**:we **Y**:you **Z**:is **VZHN**:vision

NDTRMNSHN
indetermination
NDTRMNT
indeterminate
NDV
endive
native
NDVJL
individual
NDVJLST
individualist
NDVJLSTK
individualistic
NDVJLT
individuality
NDVJLZ
individualize
individualized
individualizing
individualization
NDVJLZM
individualism
NDVJSHN
individuation
NDVJT
individuate
individuated
individuating
NDVR
endeavor, (B)-vour
NDVRTNS
inadvertence
NDVRTNT
inadvertent
NDVZBL
inadvisable
inadvisably
indivisible
indivisibly
NDVZBLT
inadvisability
indivisibility
NDWL
indwell
NDWZ
endways
endwise
NDY
endue(put on)
endued
enduing
undue
unduly
NDYL
unduly
NDYLNT

undulant
NDYLSHN
undulation
NDYLT
undulate
undulated
undulating
NDYR
endure
endured
enduring
endurance
endurable
endurably
NDYRNS
endurance
NDYRSHN
induration
NDYRT
indurate
indurated
indurating
NDYS
induce
induced
inducing
NDYSMNT
inducement
NDZ
Andes
anodize
anodized
anodizing
nowadays
undies
NDZM
nudism
NDZRBL
undesirable
undesirably
NDZRV
undeserve
undeserved
undeserving
NF
enough
knife(cutter)
knifed
knifing
NFBL
enfeeble
enfeebled
enfeebling
ineffable
ineffably
NFCHSHN

infatuation
NFCHT
infatuate
infatuated
infatuating
NFCHWSHN
infatuation
NFCHWT
infatuate
infatuated
infatuating
NFDL
infidel
NFDLT
infidelity
infidelities
NFDNG
unfitting
NFJ
knife-edge
knife-edged
NFKCHL
ineffectual
NFKS
inefficacy
inefficacies
infix
infixes
NFKSHN
infection
NFKSHS
inefficacious
infectious
NFKT
infect
unaffect(no
change)
NFKTR
infector
NFKTV
ineffective
(not having effect)
infective
(able to infect)
NFL
inflow
NFLBL
infallible
infallibly
NFLBLT
infallibility
NFLD
enfilade
enfiladed
enfilading
enfold(cover)

infield
unfold(open)
NFLDR
infielder
NFLKS
influx
influxes
NFLKSBL
inflexible
inflexibly
NFLKSHN
inflection, (B)inflexion
infliction
(impose)
NFLKSS
anaphylaxis
NFLKT
inflect(bend)
inflict(impose)
NFLM
inflame
inflamed
inflaming
NFLMBL
inflammable
NFLMSHN
inflammation
NFLMTR
inflammatory
NFLNCHL
influential
NFLNCHNG
unflinching
NFLNG
unfailing
unfeeling
NFLNS
influence
influenced
influencing
NFLNSHL
influential
NFLNZ
influenza
NFLPBL
unflappable
unflappably
NFLPBLT
unflappability
NFLSHN
inflation
NFLSHNR
inflationary
NFLST
infelicity
infelicities

NFLSTS
infelicitous
NFLT
inflate
inflated
inflating
in-flight(adj)
NFLTBL
inflatable
inflatably
NFLTRSHN
infiltration
NFLTRT
infiltrate
infiltrated
infiltrating
NFLTRTR
infiltrator
NFLZ
anopheles
(mosquito)
NFM
infamy
infamies
NFMLYR
unfamiliar
NFMLYRT
unfamiliarity
unfamiliarities
NFMS
infamous
NFND
unfeigned
NFNDD
unfounded
NFNDLN
Newfoundland
NFNDLND
Newfoundland
NFNG
knifing
NFNGLD
newfangled
NFNS
infancy
infancies
NFNSHT
unfinished
NFNSV
inoffensive
NFNT
infant(baby)
infinite
infinity
infinities
NFNTL

infantile
NFNTLZM
infantilism
NFNTR
infantry
infantries
NFNTRMN
infantryman
infantrymen
NFNTSD
infanticide
NFNTSML
infinitesimal
NFNTV
infinitive
NFR
anaphora
infer(deduce)
inferred
inferring
unfair
NFRBL
inferable
NFRCHNT
unfortunate
NFRDZ
anaphrodisia
NFRGTBL
unforgettable
unforgettably
NFRK
unfrock
NFRKCHS
anfractuous
NFRKSHN
infraction
NFRKT
infract
NFRKWNTD
unfrequented
NFRL
unfurl
NFRM
infirm
inform
NFRML
informal
NFRMLT
informality
informalities
NFRMNT
informant
NFRMR
infirmary
infirmaries
informer

NFRMSHN
information
NFRMT
infirmity
infirmities
NFRMTV
informative
NFRN
inferno
NFRNCHL
inferential
NFRNCHZ
enfranchise
enfranchised
enfranchising
NFRNJ
infringe
infringed
infringing
NFRNJBL
infrangible
infrangibly
NFRNJMNT
infringement
NFRNL
infernal
NFRNS
inference
NFRNSHL
inferential
NFRR
inferior
NFRRD
infrared
NFRRT
inferiority
inferiorities
NFRS
enforce
enforced
enforcing
enforcer
nefarious
NFRSBL
enforceable
enforceably
NFRSNK
infrasonic
NFRSTRKCHR
infrastructure
NFRTFL
unfruitful
NFRTL
infertile
NFRTS
nephritis

NFRMSHN
information
NFSBL
ineffaceable
NFSHL
unofficial
NFSHND
new-fashioned
NFSHNS
inefficiency
inefficiencies
NFSHNT
inefficient
NFSHS
inofficious
NFSN
unfasten
NFST
infest
NFT
neophyte
unfit
unfitted
unfitting
NFTH
naphtha
NFTHFL
unfaithful
NFTHLN
naphthalene
NFTNG
infighting
NFTR
infighter
NFVRBL
unfavorable
unfavorably
NFY
nephew
NFYRSHN
infuriation
NFYRT
infuriate
infuriated
infuriating
NFYZ
infuse
infused
infusing
NFYZHN
infusion
NFYZHNZM
infusionism
NFZ
inphase(adj)
NFZBL
infeasible
NG

nag
nagged
nagging
nagger
Nagoya
owing(owe)
NGDL
ungodly
ungodlier
ungodliest
ungodliness
NGDTD
ingratitude
NGGL
angle
angled
angling
angler(fish)
angular
Angola
NGGLFL
Anglophile
NGGLKN
Anglican
NGGLND
England
NGGLNG
angling
NGGLR
angler(fish)
angular(direction)
NGGLRN
angle iron
NGGLRT
angularity
angularities
NGGLSH
English
NGGLSKSN
Anglo-Saxon
NGGLSZ
Anglicize
Anglicized
Anglicizing
NGGR
anger
Angora(or)
angora
angry
angrier
angriest
angrily
angriness
NGGSH
anguish
NGGT

ingot
NGGWL
ungual
NGGWN
anguine
NGGWNT
unguent(salve)
NGGWS
unguis
ungues
NGGWSHT
anguished
NGGYLR
angular
NGGYLRT
angularity
angularities
NGGYLSHN
angulation
NGGYLT
angulate
angulated
angulating
NGHD
naugahyde
NGJ
engage
engaged
engaging
NGJMNT
engagement
NGK
ankh(symbol)
ink
inky
inkier
inkiest
inkiness
NGKBLT
inkblot
NGKCHS
unctuous
NGKHRN
inkhorn
NGKL
ankle
uncle
NGKLBN
anklebone
NGKLNG
inkling
NGKLSM
Uncle Sam
NGKLT
anklet
NGKLTM

Uncle Tom
NGKR
anchor(ship)
Ankara
encore
NGKRJ
Anchorage
NGKRMN
anchorman
anchormen
NGKRT
anchorite
NGKSHN
unction
NGKSHS
anxious
unctuous
NGKYBS
incubus
NGKYBT
incubate
incubated
incubating
incubation
incubator
NGL
angle
angled
angling
Angola
NGLD
unglued
NGLF
engulf
NGLFB
Anglophobe
NGLFL
Anglophile
NGLJBL
negligible
negligibly
NGLJNS
negligence
NGLJNT
negligent
NGLKT
neglect
NGLKTFL
neglectful
NGLKTHLK
Anglo-Catholic
NGLMRKN
Anglo-American
NGLND
England
NGLNG

angling
niggling
NGLR
angler
NGLRN
angle iron
NGLRS
inglorious
NGLSH
English
NGLSKSN
Anglo-Saxon
NGLSZ
Anglicize
Anglicized
Anglicizing
NGLSZM
Anglicism
NGLT
anklet
NGLZH
negligee
NGM
enigma
NGMTK
enigmatic
NGMTKL
enigmatical
NGN
New Guinea
noggin
NGNG
ongoing
NGNL
ungainly
ungainlier
ungainliest
ungainliness
NGR
anger
angry
angrier
angriest
angrily
angriness
Negro
NGRD
en garde
Negroid
niggard
NGRDD
unguarded
NGRDNT
ingredient
NGRDTD
ingratitude

B:by **CH**:each **D**:day **F**:if **G**:go **H**:he **HW**:why **J**:joy **K**:cow **KS**:ax **KWL**:equal **L**:all **M**:may **N**:in

NGRJ
engorge
engorged
engorging
NGRJTSHN
ingurgitation
NGRJTT
ingurgitate
ingurgitated
ingurgitating
NGRM
anagram
NGRMTK
anagrammatic
NGRN
ingrown
ingrain
NGRND
ingrained
NGRP
in-group
NGRS
engross
engrosses
ingress
ingresses
NGRSHS
ungracious
NGRSHT
ingratiate
ingratiated
ingratiating
ingratiation
ingratiatory
NGRT
ingrate
NGRTFL
ungrateful
NGRTTD
ingratitude
NGRTTYD
ingratitude
NGRV
engrave
engraved
engraving
NGRVR
engraver
NGS
negus
NGSHBL
negotiable
negotiably
NGSHBLT
negotiability
NGSHN

negation
NGSHS
unctuous
NGSHSHN
negotiation
NGSHT
negotiate
negotiated
negotiating
NGSHTR
negotiator
NGSHTRKS
negotiatrix
NGSK
Nagasaki
NGST
angst
NGSTRM
Angstrom
NGT
ingot
negate
negated
negating
nougat(candy)
nugget(rock)
NGTR
negator
negatory
nugatory
(no value)
NGTV
negative
NGTVZM
negativism
negativist
negativistic
negativity
NGVRNBL
ungovernable
ungovernably
NGWL
Anguilla
ungual
NGWN
anguine
NGWNL
inguinal
NGWNT
unguent
NGWS
unguis
NGWSH
anguish
anguishes
NGYLR

angular
ungular(hoof)
NGYLT
Ungulata
ungulate(hoof)
ungula
ungulous
NGYRL
inaugural
NGYRSHN
inauguration
NGYRT
inaugurate
inaugurated
inaugurating
NGZKT
inexact
NGZSTBL
inexhaustible
inexhaustibly
NGZSTNT
inexistent
NGZT
anxiety
anxieties
NH
anyhow
knee-high
know-how
NHBRDZ
New Hebrides
NHBSHN
inhibition
NHBT
inhabit(live)
inhibit(stop)
NHBTBL
inhabitable
NHBTNT
inhabitant
NHBTR
inhibitor
NHBTV
inhibitive
NHCH
unhitch
unhitches
NHL
inhale
inhaled
inhaling
inhaler
kneehole
unholy
unholier
unholiest

unholily
unholiness
NHLNT
inhalant
NHLR
inhaler
NHLSHN
inhalation
NHLSM
unwholesome
NHLTH
unhealthy
unhealthier
unhealthiest
unhealthily
unhealthiness
NHM
Anaheim
NHMPSHR
New Hampshire
NHMSHR
New Hampshire
NHND
unhand
unhandy
unhandier
unhandiest
unhandily
unhandiness
NHNJ
unhinge
unhinged
unhinging
NHNS
enhance
enhanced
enhancing
enhancement
NHP
unhappy
unhappier
unhappiest
unhappily
unhappiness
NHPTF
unhoped-for
NHR
inhere
inhered
inhering
NHRD
unheard
NHRDV
unheard-of
NHRMNK
inharmonic

NGK:ink **P**:pie **R**:air **S**:ice **SH**:show **T**:toy **THN**:thin **TH**:the **V**:of **W**:we **Y**:you **Z**:is **VZHN**:vision

NHRMNS
 inharmonious
NHRNS
 inherence
 unharness
 unharnesses
NHRNT
 inherent
NHRS
 unhorse
 unhorsed
 unhorsing
NHRT
 inherit
NHRTBL
 inheritable
NHRTNS
 inheritance
NHRTR
 inheritor
NHS
 in-house
NHSPTBL
 inhospitable
NHSPTLT
 inhospitality
NHT
 no-hit
NHTR
 no-hitter
NHWR
 anywhere
 nowhere
NHYM
 inhume(bury)
 inhumed
 inhuming
NHYMN
 inhuman(person)
 inhumane(style)
NHYMNT
 inhumanity
 inhumanities
NHYMSHN
 inhumation
NHZTTNG
 unhesitating
NJ
 enjoy
 nudge
 nudged
 nudging
NJBL
 enjoyable
 enjoyably
NJDSHS

 injudicious
NJKBL
 ineducable
NJKSHN
 injection
NJKT
 inject
NJKTR
 injector
NJL
 angel
 nodule
NJLK
 angelic
NJLNT
 undulant
NJLR
 nodular
NJLSHN
 undulation
NJLT
 undulate
 undulated
 undulating
NJMNT
 enjoyment
NJN
 angina(heart)
 engine(motor)
 enjoin
 injun(slang)
 Indian
NJNDR
 engender
NJNKSHN
 injunction
NJNKTV
 injunctive
NJNR
 engineer
NJNT
 ingenuity
NJNYS
 ingenious(clever)
 ingenuous(artless)
NJNYT
 ingenuity
 ingenuities
NJR
 injure(hurt)
 injured
 injuring
 injury
 injuries
 Niger
 Nigeria

NJRS
 injurious
NJRZ
 New Jersey
NJSCHN
 ingestion
NJST
 ingest(eat)
 unjust(not fair)
NJSTS
 injustice
NJZK
 analgesic
NK
 antic
 ionic
 knack
 knock(hit)
 neck
 nick(notch)
 nock(bow)
 nook
NKBLT
 inkblot
NKBT
 knockabout
NKCHD
 noctuid(moth)
NKD
 encode
 -coded,-coding
 naked(nude)
NKDN
 knockdown(n,adj)
 knock down(v)
NKDNS
 nakedness
NKDT
 anecdote
NKDTL
 anecdotal
NKGND
 incognito
NKGNT
 incognito
NKGNZNS
 incognizance
NKGNZNT
 incognizant
NKHRNS
 incoherence
NKHRNT
 incoherent
NKJTNT
 incogitant
NKK

 anechoic
NKL
 knuckle
 knuckled
 knuckling
 knuckler
 nickel
 nuclei(atom)
 nucleus
 uncoil
NKLD
 include
 included
 including
 unclad
NKLDFR
 uncalled-for
NKLDN
 New Caledonia
 nickelodeon
NKLHD
 knucklehead
NKLKSHN
 inculcation
NKLKT
 inculcate
 inculcated
 inculcating
NKLKYLBL
 incalculable
 incalculably
NKLMNS
 inclemency
NKLMNT
 inclement
NKLN
 incline(slant)
 inclined
 inclining
 neckline
 unclean
NKLNBL
 inclinable
NKLNCH
 unclench
 unclenches
NKLNDR
 knuckle under
NKLNK
 nucleonic
NKLNKS
 nucleonics
NKLNL
 uncleanly
NKLNLNS
 uncleanliness

NKLNMTR
inclinometer
NKLNSHN
inclination
NKLPBL
inculpable
NKLPSHN
inculpation
NKLPT
inculpate
inculpated
inculpating
NKLR
knuckler
nuclear(atomic)
unclear
NKLS
necklace
nucleus
nuclei(or)
nucleuses
NKLSF
unclassify
unclassified
unclassifies
NKLSK
neoclassic
NKLSKL
neoclassical
NKLSP
unclasp
NKLSV
inclusive
NKLT
nucleate
nucleated
nucleating
NKLTH
unclothe
unclothed
unclothing
NKLV
enclave
NKLZ
enclose
enclosed
enclosing
NKLZHN
inclusion
NKLZHR
enclosure
NKM
income
NKMBNS
incumbency
incumbencies

NKMBNT
incumbent
NKMBR
encumber
NKMBRNS
encumbrance
NKMBSTBL
incombustible
NKMD
incommode
incommoded
incommoding
NKMDS
incommodious
NKMFRTBL
uncomfortable
uncomfortably
NKMM
encomium
encomia(or)
encomiums
NKMN
uncommon
NKMNG
incoming
oncoming
NKMNSHRBL
incommensurable
NKMNSHRT
incommensurate
NKMNSRBL
incommensurable
NKMNSRT
incommensurate
NKMP
encamp
NKMPLMNTR
uncomplimentary
NKMPLNT
incompliant
NKMPLSHN
incompletion
NKMPLT
incomplete
incompleted
incompleting
incompletion
NKMPMNT
encampment
NKMPRBL
incomparable
incomparably
NKMPRHNSBL
incomprehensible
NKMPRMZNG
uncompromising

NKMPRSBL
incompressible
NKMPS
encompass
encompasses
NKMPT
unkempt
NKMPTBL
incompatible
incompatibly
NKMPTBLT
incompatibility
incompatibilities
NKMPTNS
incompetence
NKMPTNT
incompetent
NKMPYTBL
incomputable
NKMR
newcomer
NKMST
encomiast
NKMTD
uncommitted
NKMYNKBL
incommunicable
NKMYNKD
incommunicado
NKMYNKTV
uncommunicative
NKMYTBL
incommutable
NKN
uncanny
uncannier
uncanniest
uncannily
uncanniness
unkind
NKND
anaconda
knock-kneed
unkind
NKNDL
enkindle
enkindled
enkindling
NKNDSHNL
unconditional
NKNDSNS
incandescence
NKNDSNT
incandescent
NKNDT
incondite

NKNFRMT
inconformity
inconformities
NKNG
necking
NKNGRNT
incongruent
NKNGRS
incongruous
NKNGRT
incongruity
incongruities
NKNK
knickknack
NKNKLSV
inconclusive
NKNKTD
unconnected
NKNM
nickname
NKNSDRBL
inconsiderable
NKNSDRSHN
inconsideration
NKNSDRT
inconsiderate
NKNSHNBL
unconscionable
unconscionably
NKNSHS
unconscious
NKNSKWNS
inconsequence
NKNSKWNSHL
inconsequential
NKNSKWNT
inconsequent
NKNSLBL
inconsolable
NKNSMBL
inconsumable
NKNSNNT
inconsonant
NKNSPKYS
inconspicuous
NKNSRND
unconcerned
NKNSSTNS
inconsistency
inconsistencies
NKNSSTNT
inconsistent
NKNSTNS
inconstancy
NKNSTNT
inconstant

NKNSTTSHNL
unconstitutional
NKNSVBL
inconceivable
inconceivably
NKNT
no-account
NKNTBL
unaccountable
unaccountably
NKNTD
uncounted
NKNTDFR
unaccounted-for
NKNTNNT
incontinent
NKNTR
encounter
NKNTRLBL
incontrollable(or)
uncontrollable
uncontrollably
NKNTRLBLT
uncontrollability
NKNTRVRTBL
incontrovertible
NKNTSHN
incantation
NKNTSTBL
incontestable
NKNVNSBL
inconvincible
NKNVNSHNL
unconventional
NKNVNYNS
inconvenience
NKNVNYNT
inconvenient
NKNVRTBL
inconvertible
NKP
kneecap
uncap
uncapped
uncapping
NKPBL
incapable
incapably
NKPBLT
incapability
incapabilities
NKPL
uncouple
uncoupled
uncoupling
NKPR

innkeeper
NKPS
neckpiece
NKPSLSHN
encapsulation
NKPSLT
encapsulate
encapsulated
encapsulating
NKPST
incapacity
incapacities
NKPSTSHN
incapacitation
NKPSTT
incapacitate
incapacitated
incapacitating
NKR
encore(demand)
incur
incurred
incurring
knacker(person)
knocker(door)
nacre(shell)
NKRBKR
Knickerbocker
NKRBKRZ
knickerbockers
(pants)
NKRBLT
incurability
NKRCH
encroach
encroaches
NKRCHF
neckerchief
NKRCHMNT
encroachment
NKRD
una corda
NKRDBL
incredible
incredibly
NKRDBLT
incredibility
NKRDFR
uncared-for
NKRDJLS
incredulous
NKRDLT
incredulity
NKRDN
enchiridion
NKRDNSHN

incoordination
incoordinate
NKRDNTD
uncoordinated
(clumsy)
NKRDYLT
incredulity
NKRGW
Nicaragua
NKRJ
encourage
-raged, -raging
NKRJBL
incorrigible, -bly
NKRJBLT
incorrigibility
NKRJLS
incredulous
NKRJMNT
encouragement
NKRK
uncork
NKRKT
incorrect
NKRLJ
necrology
NKRMNS
necromancy
NKRMNSHN
incrimination
NKRMNT
increment
incriminate
incriminated
incriminating
NKRMNTL
incremental
NKRMNTR
incriminatory
NKRNSHN
incarnation
NKRNT
incarnate
incarnated
incarnating
NKRNZM
anachronism
NKRPRL
incorporeal
NKRPRSHN
incorporation
NKRPRT
incorporate
incorporated
incorporating
NKRPRTR

incorporator
NKRPSHN
encryption
NKRPT
encrypt
incorrupt
NKRPTBL
incorruptible
incorruptibly
NKRS
increase(add to)
-sed, -sing
knickers(pants)
nacreous(adj)(shell)
NKRSBL
incoercible
increasable
NKRSCHN
unchristian
NKRSRSHN
incarceration
NKRSRT
incarcerate
incarcerated
incarcerating
NKRST
Antichrist(person)
anti-christ
(attitude)
incrust
NKRSTSHN
incrustation
NKRVT
incurvate
incurvated
incurvating
NKRZ
knickers
NKRZHN
incursion
NKRZM
anachronism
NKS
annex
annexes
encase(cover)
-cased,-casing
knucks(slang)
Nicosia
nix(no,veto)
nixes
nixie(mail)
nukes(nuclear)
onyx
NKSDR
next-door(adj)

NKSHN
inaction
inchoation
NKSHS
noxious
NKSKYZBL
inexcusable
NKSPBL
inexpiable
NKSPDNT
inexpedient
NKSPGNBL
inexpugnable
NKSPKTD
unexpected
NKSPLKBL
inexplicable
inexplicably
NKSPLNBL
inexplainable
NKSPNSV
inexpensive
NKSPRNS
inexperience
NKSPRNST
inexperienced
NKSPRSBL
inexpressible
inexpressibly
NKSPRSV
inexpressive
NKSPRT
inexpert
NKSPSHNBL
unexceptionable
unexceptionably
NKSPSHNL
unexceptional
NKSRBL
inexorable
inexorably
NKSS
nexus
nexuses
NKSSBL
inaccessible
inaccessibly
NKSSHN
annexation
NKSTDR
next door(adv)
NKSTK
encaustic
NKSTMD
unaccustomed
NKSTNGWSHBL

inextinguishable
NKSTNS
in extenso
NKSTNSBL
inextensible
NKSTRKBL
inextricable
inextricably
NKSTRPBL
inextirpable
NKSVL
Knoxville
NKT
enact
inchoate
knockout(n)
knock out(v)
necktie
NKTH
uncouth
NKTMNT
enactment
NKTN
nicotine
NKTNZM
nicotinism
NKTR
nectar
NKTRN
nectarine
nocturn(matins)
nocturne(art)
NKTRNL
nocturnal
NKTTT
nictitate(wink)
-tated,-tating
NKTV
inactive
inchoative
NKTVSHN
inactivation
NKTVT
inactivate
inactivated
inactivating
inactivity
inactivities
NKVR
uncover
NKWL
unequal
NKWLD
unequaled
NKWLF
unqualify

unqualified
unqualifies
NKWLT
inequality
inequalities
NKWR
inquire
inquired
inquiring
inquirer
inquiry
inquiries
neckwear
NKWRR
inquirer
NKWRST
knackwurst
NKWSCHNBL
unquestionable
unquestionably
NKWSCHND
unquestioned
NKWSCHNNG
unquestioning
NKWST
inquest
NKWT
inequity
inequities
iniquity
(wickedness)
iniquities
unquote
unquoted
unquoting
NKWTBL
inequitable
inequitably
NKWTD
inquietude
NKWTS
iniquitous
NKWTYD
inquietude
NKWVKL
unequivocal
NKWZSHN
inquisition
NKWZTR
inquisitor
NKWZTRL
inquisitorial
NKWZTV
inquisitive
NKYBS
incubus

NKYBSHN
incubation
NKYBT
incubate
incubated
incubating
NKYBTR
incubator
NKYLM
inoculum
NKYLNT
inoculant
NKYLSHN
inoculation
NKYLT
inoculate
inoculated
inoculating
NKYNBYLM
incunabulum
NKYPD
unoccupied
(vacant,
at leisure)
NKYRBL
incurable
incurably
NKYRS
inaccuracy
inaccuracies
incurious
NKYRT
inaccurate
NKYS
innocuous
nocuous
NKYZ
incuse
incused
incusing
NL
anal(body)
anele(anoint)
aneled
aneling
annal(history)
anneal(tempered)
annul(cancel)
annulled
annulling
in-law
inlay
inlaid
inlays
inlaying
kneel(knee)

knelt(or)
kneeled
knell(ringing)
knoll(hill)
nail(hammer)
newel
Nile
noel
noil(fiber)
null
only
NLCH
unlatch
unlatches
NLD
inlaid
inlay
unlade
unladed
unlading
unladen
unload
NLDBL
ineludible
NLDK
analytic
NLF
nullify
nullified
nullifies
NLFKSHN
nullification
NLFL
unlawful
NLG
analogue(or)
analog
NLGHD
naugahyde
NLGNS
inelegance
NLGNT
inelegant
NLGS
analogous
NLHD
nailhead
NLJ
analogy
analogies
knowledge
neology
NLJBL
ineligible
ineligibility
knowledgeable

knowledgeably
NLJBLT
ineligibility
ineligibilities
NLJS
analogous
NLJZ
analogize
analogized
analogizing
NLJZK
analgesic
NLJZM
neologism
NLK
unlike
unlock
unlucky
unluckier
unluckiest
unluckily
unluckiness
NLKL
unlikely
unlikelier
unlikeliest
unlikeliness
NLKLHD
unlikelihood
NLKNTNDR
nolo contendere
NLKR
onlooker
NLKTBL
ineluctable
NLKTFR
unlooked-for
NLMNT
annulment
NLMTD
unlimited
NLN
aniline
inland
nylon
on-line
NLND
inland
Niue Island
NLNDS
Inland Sea
NLRJ
enlarge
enlarged
enlarging
enlarger

NLRJMNT
enlargement
NLRJR
enlarger
NLRND
unlearned
NLS
anlace(dagger)
enlace(entangle)
enlaced, enlacing
unlace, -ced, -cing
unless
unloose
unloosed
unloosing
unloosen
NLSH
unleash
unleashes
NLSHN
annihilation
NLSN
unloosen
NLSNST
unlicensed
NLSS
analysis
analyses
NLST
analyst(analysis)
annalist
(chronicler)
enlist
NLSTD
unlisted
NLSTK
inelastic
nihilistic
NLSTMNT
enlistment
NLSTST
inelasticity
NLT
annihilate
annihilated
annihilating
annihilation
inlet
knelt
kneel
NLTHK
neolithic
NLTK
analytic
NLTN
enlighten

NLTNMNT
enlightenment
NLTR
annihilator
NLTRBL
inalterable
inalterably
NLTRD
unlettered
NLV
in lieu of
NLVL
unlovely
NLVN
enliven
NLVND
unleavened
NLWD
newlywed
NLYNBL
inalienable
NLZ
analyze
analyzed
analyzing
analyzer
analyzation
analyzable
annals(records)
inlays
NLZM
nihilism
NLZR
analyzer
NM
anemia(weakness)
anima(soul)
anomie(without law)
enema(cure)
enemy
enemies
gnome(dwarflike)
Nam(Vietnam)
name
named
naming
nameable
namely
numb
pneuma
NMBL
nameable
name
nimble
nimbly
NMBLR

nimbler	enamel	nominating	numerating
nimblest	namely	nomination	**NMRTR**
NMBLST	numbly	**NMNTR**	enumerator
nimblest	**NMLS**	nominator	numerator
nimbler	anomalous	**NMNTV**	**NMS**
NMBPMB	nameless	nominative	animus
namby-pamby	**NMLWR**	**NMNY**	en masse
namby-pambies	enamelware	pneumonia	**NMSH**
NMBR	**NMMRM**	**NMNZLND**	enmesh
number	in memoriam	no man's land	enmeshes
NMBS	**NMN**	**NMPCHBL**	**NMSHN**
nimbus	anemone	unimpeachable	animation
nimbi(or)	gnomon	unimpeachably	**NMSK**
nimbuses	gnomonical	**NMPLBL**	namesake
NMD	nominee	unemployable	**NMSKL**
nomad	unman	**NMPLD**	numskull
NMDK	unmanned	unemployed	**NMSMTK**
nomadic	unmanning	**NMPLT**	numismatic
pneumatic	**NMNCHNBL**	nameplate	**NMSMTST**
NMDP	unmentionable	**NMPN**	numismatist
onomatopoeia	**NMND**	Phnom Penh	**NMSN**
NMDPLM	unmanned	**NMPRSHNZM**	neomycin
nom de plume	**NMNDFL**	neoimpressionism	**NMSS**
noms de plume	unmindful	**NMR**	nemesis
NMDRPR	**NMNFL**	anymore	nemeses
name-dropper	unmindful	enamor(love)	**NMST**
NMDVRT	**NMNK**	**NMRBL**	animosity
animadvert	mnemonic	innumerable	animosities
NMDVRZHN	**NMNKL**	numerable	endmost
animadversion	mnemonical	**NMRD**	inmost
NMF	**NMNKLCHR**	enamored	(innermost)
nymph	nomenclature	**NMRKL**	**NMSTKBL**
NMFL	**NMNKS**	numerical	unmistakable
unmuffle	mnemonics	**NMRKN**	unmistakably
unmuffled	**NMNL**	un-American	**NMT**
unmuffling	nominal(name)	**NMRKT**	animate
NMFMNK	nominally	unmarked	animated
nymphomaniac	unmanly	**NMRL**	animating
NMFT	unmanlier	numeral	animation
nymphet	unmanliest	**NMRLJ**	animator
NMK	unmanliness	numerology	enmity
anemic	**NMNNGL**	**NMRS**	enmities
gnomic	unmeaningly	numerous	inmate(jail)
unmake	**NMNRL**	**NMRSFL**	**NMTBL**
unmade	unmannerly	unmerciful	inimitable
unmaking	unmannerliness	**NMRSHN**	**NMTD**
NMKL	**NMNS**	enumeration	nematode
inimical	numbness	numeration	**NMTGTD**
NMKMPP	**NMNSHN**	**NMRT**	unmitigated
nincompoop	nomination	enumerate	**NMTK**
NMKSK	**NMNSHNBL**	enumerated	pneumatic
New Mexico	unmentionable	enumerating	**NMTP**
NML	unmentionably	inamorata	onomatopoeia
animal	**NMNT**	inamorato	**NMTR**
anomaly	nominate	numerate	animator
anomalies	nominated	numerated	**NMZDPLM**

NGK:ink **P**:pie **R**:air **S**:ice **SH**:show **T**:toy **THN**:thin **TH**:the **V**:of **W**:we **Y**:you **Z**:is **VZHN**:vision

noms de plume
NMZMTK
numismatic
NMZMTST
numismatist
NN
anon(soon,again)
gnawn(chew)
  gnaw
inane
Ionian
known
  know
nana(nurse)(slang)
nanny(nurse)
  nannies
neon(light)
nine
ninny
  ninnies
none
noon(time)
noun(word)
nun(person)
NNBJKTV
nonobjective
NNBL
unknowable
unknowably
NND
noonday
NNDL
neonatal(adj)
neonate(n)
NNDNMNSHNL
nondenominational
NNDRTHL
Neanderthal
NNDSHN
inundation
NNDSKRPT
nondescript
NNDT
inundate
  inundated
  inundating
NNFKSHN
nonfiction
NNFLD
ninefold
NNFZNS
nonfeasance
NNG
annoying
awning
gnawing(chew)

inning
NNGGLND
New England
NNGKSHN
inunction
NNGZSTNS
nonexistence
NNGZSTNT
nonexistent
NNHBTD
uninhibited
NNJ
nonage
NNJNRN
nonagenarian
NNKLR
nonnuclear
NNKMBTNT
noncombatant
NNKMPLNS
noncompliance
NNKMPP
nincompoop
NNKMPSMNTS
non compos mentis
NNKMSHND
noncommissioned
NNKMTL
noncommittal
NNKN
nankeen
NNKNFRMST
nonconformist
NNKPRSHN
noncooperation
NNLND
nonaligned
NNM
anonym
NNMS
anonymous
NNMT
anonymity
inanimate
NNN
ninon
unknown
NNNG
unknowing
NNNSNS
no-nonsense
NNNTRVNSHN
nonintervention
NNNTT
nonentity
nonentities

NNPLS
nonplus
NNPLST
nonplused, (B)-ssed
NNPNZ
ninepins
NNPRDKTV
nonproductive
NNPRFT
nonprofit
NNPRL
nonpareil
NNPRS
nonpros(law)
NNPRSKWTR
non prosequitur
NNPRTSPTNG
nonparticipating
NNPRTZN
nonpartisan
NNR
nunnery
  nunneries
NNRJD
nonrigid
NNRPRZNTSHNL
nonrepresentational
NNRSTRKTV
nonrestrictive
NNRZSTNT
nonresistant
NNS
announce
  announced
  announcing
  announcer
annoyance
Ionian Sea
nonce(time)
nuance
NNSCH
nonesuch
NNSHLNS
nonchalance
NNSHLNT
nonchalant
NNSHSHN
enunciation
NNSHT
enunciate
  enunciated
  enunciating
NNSHTR
enunciator
NNSK
nainsook

NNSKD
nonskid
NNSKJLD
nonscheduled
NNSKTRN
nonsectarian
NNSKWTR
non sequitur
NNSMNT
announcement
NNSNCHL
nonessential
NNSNS
nonsense
NNSNSKL
nonsensical
NNSPR
uninspire
uninspired
uninspiring
NNSPRT
nonsupport
NNSR
announcer
NNSSHN
annunciation
  (proclaim)
enunciation
  (clarity)
NNST
annunciate
  (proclaim)
  annunciated
  annunciating
enunciate(clarity)
  enunciated
  enunciating
NNSTP
nonstop
NNSTR
annunciator
  (announcer)
enunciator
  (clarity)
NNSWRD
nonce word
NNT
anoint
inanity(empty)
  inanities
ninety
  nineties
NNTD
noontide
NNTH
ninth

B:by **CH**:each **D**:day **F**:if **G**:go **H**:he **HW**:why **J**:joy **K**:cow **KS**:ax **KWL**:equal **L**:all **M**:may **N**:in

NNTHLS
nonetheless
NNTHNG
know-nothing
NNTL
neonatal(adj)
neonate(n)
NNTLJBL
unintelligible
unintelligibly
NNTLJNT
unintelligent
NNTM
noontime
NNTN
nineteen
NNTNTH
nineteenth
NNTR
anointer
NNTRSTD
uninterested
NNTRSTNG
uninteresting
NNTTH
ninetieth
NNVLNS
nonviolence
NNYKLR
nonnuclear
NNYNYN
nonunion
NNZ
nones
NP
knap(hit,bite)
knapped
knapping
nap(sleep,surface)
napped
napping
nape(neck)
nappe(water)
nappy(dish)
nappies
nappy(fuzzy)
nappier
nappiest
nip
nipped
nipping
nippy
nippier
nippiest
nippiness
NPCHL

nuptial
NPD
kneepad
unpaid
NPDFR
unpaid-for
NPK
unpack
NPKN
napkin
NPL
Nepal
nipple
NPLG
unplug
unplugged
unplugging
NPLKBL
inapplicable
NPLN
enplane
Napoleon
napoleon
NPLS
Annapolis
anyplace
NPLST
anaplasty
NPLSTK
anaplastic
NPLZ
Naples
NPLZH
anaplasia
NPLZM
neoplasm
NPLZNT
unpleasant
NPM
napalm
NPN
unpin
unpinned
unpinning
NPNG
napping
NPNTH
nepenthe
NPPYLR
unpopular
NPR
napery(linen)
napper
nipper
no-par
NPRBL

inoperable
NPRCHBL
inapproachable
NPRDKTBL
unpredictable
unpredictably
NPRDKTV
unproductive
NPRFSHNL
unprofessional
NPRFTBL
unprofitable
unprofitably
NPRJDST
unprejudiced
NPRLLD
unparalleled
NPRN
neoprene
NPRNSPLD
unprincipled
NPRNTBL
unprintable
NPRPRD
unprepared
NPRPRT
inappropriate
NPRSDNTD
unprecedented
NPRSHBL
inappreciable
NPRSHTV
inappreciative
NPRST
unpriced
NPRTN
inopportune
NPRTNCHS
unpretentious
NPRTNSHS
unpretentious
NPRTNZ
Newport News
NPRTYN
inopportune
NPRTV
inoperative
NPRVDD
unprovided
NPRVKT
unprovoked
NPS
anopsy(or)
anopsia
NPSHL
nuptial

NPSHNT
inpatient
outpatient
NPSK
knapsack
NPT
inept
in petto
input
output
unapt
NPTD
neap tide
NPTH
naphtha
NPTHLN
naphthalene
NPTN
Neptune
NPTTD
ineptitude
NPTTYD
ineptitude
NPTYN
Neptune
NPTZM
nepotism
NPZBL
inappeasable
NPZT
inapposite
NR
enter(go into)
inner(inside)
inter-(between)
honor, (B)honour
knur(knob)
narrow
nary(not one)
Nauru(island)
near
owner
NRB
Nairobi
nearby
NRBL
honorable
honorably
NRBN
inurbane
NRCH
enrich
enriches
NRCHR
nurture
nurtured

nurturing
NRCHS
unrighteous
NRD
aneroid
inroad
nerd(slang)
unread
unready
unreadily
unreadiness
NRDK
Antarctic
Antarctica
NRDKBL
ineradicable
NRDKSHN
interdiction
NRDKT
interdict
NRDNT
inordinate
NRDWL
ne'er-do-well
NRDZ
innards
NRFK
honorific
Norfolk
NRFKLND
Norfolk Island
NRFL
unruffle
unruffled
unruffling
NRGNK
inorganic
NRGNZ
unorganize
unorganized
unorganizing
NRGYMN
energumen
NRHRST
unrehearsed
NRHWL
narwhal
NRJ
energy
energies
enrage
enraged
enraging
NRJDK
energetic
NRJNL

unoriginal
NRJNRT
unregenerate
NRJTK
energetic
NRJTKL
energetically
NRJZ
energize
energized
energizing
NRJZR
energizer
NRK
anarch
anarchy
anarchies
nark(or)narc
Newark
oneiric(dreams)
NRKDK
narcotic
NRKK
anarchic
anarchy
NRKLPS
narcolepsy
NRKS
anorexia(or)
anorexy
NRKSHS
anorectous
anorexia
anorectic
NRKSS
narcosis
NRKST
anarchist
NRKTK
Antarctic
narcotic
NRKTZM
narcotism
NRKZM
anarchism
NRL
enroll
enrollee
gnarl(knot)
knurl(knob,knot,
ridge)
neural
unreal(not real)
unreel(unwind)
unruly
unrulier

unruliest
unruliness
NRLBL
unreliable
unreliably
NRLD
knurled
NRLJ
neuralgia
neurology
NRLJKL
neurological
NRLJST
neurologist
NRLMNT
enrollment
NRLNNG
interlining
NRLNTNG
unrelenting
NRLNZ
New Orleans
NRLSTK
unrealistic
NRLSTKL
unrealistically
NRM
norm
unarm
unarmed
unarming
NRML
normal
NRMLS
normalcy
NRMLT
normality
normalities
NRMLZ
normalize
normalized
normalizing
normalization
NRMNDD
narrow-minded
NRMS
enormous
NRMST
innermost
NRMT
enormity
enormities
NRMTV
normative
NRMYRL
intramural

NRND
unearned
NRNG
unerring
NRNS
inerrancy
NRNT
inerrant
NRPCHR
enrapture
enraptured
enrapturing
NRPL
Interpol
NRR
honorary
NRRM
honorarium
honoraria(or)
honorariums
NRS
nurse
nursed
nursing
onerous
NRSD
inner city
inner cities
inner-city(adj)
NRSH
inertia
inrush
inrushes
nourish
nourishes
onrush
onrushes
NRSHL
inertial
NRSHMNT
nourishment
NRSHN
narration
NRSHP
ownership
NRSMD
nursemaid
NRSNG
nursing
NRSPNSV
unresponsive
NRSPRNG
innerspring
NRSR
nursery
nurseries

NRSS
neurosis
neuroses
NRSSS
narcissus
NRSSSTK
narcissistic
NRSSZM
narcissism
NRST
inner city
inner cities
inner-city(adj)
Near East
unrest
NRSTD
nearsighted
NRSTHN
neurasthenia
NRSTRND
unrestrained
NRSZ
Inner Seas
NRT
en route
inert
inwrought
narrate
narrated
narrating
narration
NRTH
North(region)
north
unearth
NRTHBND
northbound
NRTHDKS
unorthodox
neoorthodoxy
NRTHDKT
North Dakota
NRTHKR
North Korea
NRTHKRLN
North Carolina
NRTHKS
narthex
NRTHL
unearthly
unearthlier
unearthliest
unearthliness
NRTHMRK
North America
NRTHRL

northerly
NRTHRN
northern
NRTHS
North Sea
NRTHSLP
North Slope
NRTHST
northeast
NRTHSTRL
northeasterly
NRTHSTRN
northeastern
NRTHWRD
northward
NRTHWST
northwest
NRTHWSTRL
northwesterly
NRTHWSTRN
northwestern
NRTHWSTTRTRZ
Northwest
Territories
NRTK
anorectic(starve)
anorexia(n)
Antarctic
Antarctica
neurotic
NRTKYLT
inarticulate
NRTR
narrator
NRTS
neuritis
NRTSTK
inartistic
NRTV
narrative
NRV
innerve
(stimulate)
innerved
innerving
nerve
nerved
nerving
nervy
nervier
nerviest
unnerve(take
energy)
unnerved
unnerving
NRVL

unravel(solve)
NRVLD
unrivaled
NRVN
nirvana
NRVRKNG
nerve-racking
NRVS
nervous
NRVT
enervate(weaken)
enervated
enervating
enervation
enervator
innervate
(stimulate)
innervated
innervating
innervation
NRW
Norway
NRWJN
Norwegian
NRWL
narwhal
NRZ
nares(nostrils)
naris(sing)
narial(adj)
naric(adj)
narine(adj)
NRZNBL
unreasonable
unreasonably
NS
anise(plant)
anus(buttocks)
anuses
ensue
ensued
ensuing
gneiss(rock)
NASA
National
Aeronautics
and Space
Administration
Nassau
niece(person)
nice(pleasing)
nicer
nicest
Nisei
noose(loop)
noosed

noosing
nous(reason)
onus(stigma)
ounce(weight)
NSBRDNSHN
insubordination
NSBRDNT
insubordinate
NSBRT
insobriety
NSBSTNSHL
insubstantial
NSCHRTD
unsaturated
NSD
antacid
inside
onside
unsaid
NSDNS
antecedence
(priority)
antecedents
(preceding)
incidence
incidents
(happenings)
NSDNT
antecedent
incident
NSDNTL
incidental
NSDR
insider
NSDS
insides
insidious
onsides
offsides
NSDV
nose-dive(v)
nose-dived(or)
nose-dove
nose-diving
nose dive(n)
NSFLTS
encephalitis
NSFR
encipher
insofar
ionosphere
NSFRBL
insufferable
NSFSHNS
insufficiency
insufficiencies

NSFSHNT
insufficient
NSFSTKTD
unsophisticated
NSGN
insignia
NSGNFKNS
insignificance
NSGNFKNT
insignificant
NSH
gnash
gnashes
niche
no-show
NSHD
unshod
NSHKL
unshackle
unshackled
unshackling
NSHL
initial
uncial(writing)
NSHN
nation
notion
NSHNL
national
NSHNLGRD
National Guard
(Guardsman)
NSHNLSTK
nationalistic
NSHNLSTKL
nationalistically
NSHNLT
nationality
nationalities
NSHNLZ
nationalize
nationalized
nationalizing
NSHNLZSHN
nationalization
NSHNLZM
nationalism
NSHNS
nescience
NSHNT
ancient
nescient
NSHNWD
nationwide
NSHR
ensure(make certain)

ensured
ensuring
insure(buy or sell)
insured
insuring
insurable
insurability
onshore
NSHRN
enshrine
enshrined
enshrining
NSHRNS
insurance
NSHRNT
insurant
NSHS
nauseous
NSHSHN
initiation
NSHT
initiate
initiated
initiating
initiator
nauseate
nauseated
nauseating
NSHTH
unsheathe
unsheathed
unsheathing
NSHTL
Neufchatel(cheese)
NSHTR
initiator
initiatory
NSHTV
initiative
NSHVL
Nashville
NSKLD
unschooled
unskilled
NSKLKL
encyclical
NSKLPD
encyclopedia(or)
encyclopaedia
NSKNS
ensconce
ensconced
ensconcing
NSKPBL
inescapable
inescapably

NSKR
unscrew
NSKRB
inscribe
inscribed
inscribing
NSKRMBL
unscramble
unscrambled
unscrambling
NSKRPSHN
inscription
NSKRPYLS
unscrupulous
NSKRTBL
inscrutable
NSKRTBLT
inscrutability
NSKSSFL
unsuccessful
NSKT
insect
NSKTHD
unscathed
NSKTSD
insecticide
NSKYLT
inosculate
inosculated
inosculating
NSKYR
insecure
NSKYRT
insecurity
insecurities
NSL
insole
nacelle
(aircraft)
nestle
nestled
nestling
NSLBL
unassailable
unassailably
NSLBRS
insalubrious
NSLFSH
unselfish
NSLN
insulin
NSLNS
insolence
NSLNT
insolent
NSLR

ancillary
ancillaries
insular
NSLSHN
insulation
NSLSTD
unsolicited
NSLT
insulate
insulated
insulating
insulator
insult
onslaught
NSLTR
insulator
NSLV
enslave
enslaved
enslaving
NSLVNS
insolvency
insolvencies
NSLVNT
insolvent
NSLYBL
insoluble
NSM
inseam
noisome
NSMBL
ensemble
NSMCH
insomuch
NSML
unseemly
unseemlier
unseemliest
unseemliness
NSMN
insomnia
NSMNG
unassuming
NSMNK
insomniac
NSMNSHN
insemination
NSMNT
inseminate
-nated,-nating
NSN
ensign(navy)
insane(crazy)
niacin(vitamin)
Nicene(creed)
unseen

B:by **CH**:each **D**:day **F**:if **G**:go **H**:he **HW**:why **J**:joy **K**:cow **KS**:ax **KWL**:equal **L**:all **M**:may **N**:in

unsound	insensitive	unsparing	**NSRTNT**
NSNCHL	**NSNSTVT**	**NSPRSBL**	uncertainty
inessential(or)	insensitivity	insuppressible	uncertainties
unessential	insensitivities	**NSPRSHN**	**NSRTTD**
NSND	**NSNT**	inspiration	incertitude
unsound	innocent	**NSPRSHNL**	**NSRVS**
NSNDR	insanity	inspirational	in-service
incendiary	insanities	**NSPRT**	**NSS**
incendiaries	nascent	inspirit	gnosis
NSNG	(emerging)	**NSPRTBL**	**NSSCHS**
unsung	nescient	insupportable	incestuous
NSNP	(ignorance)	**NSPSHN**	**NSSHBL**
unsnap	**NSNTFK**	inception	insatiable
unsnapped	unscientific	**NSPSHS**	**NSSNG**
unsnapping	**NSNTR**	inauspicious	unceasing
NSNR	insanitary	**NSPST**	**NSSNS**
ensnare	**NSNTV**	inspissate	insouciance
ensnared	incentive	inspissated	insouciant
ensnaring	**NSNYSHN**	inspissating	**NSSNT**
NSNRL	insinuation	**NSPTK**	incessant
ensnarl	**NSNYT**	antiseptic	insouciant
NSNRSHN	insinuate	**NSPTL**	**NSSPTBL**
incineration	insinuated	ancipital	insusceptible
NSNRT	insinuating	**NSPTV**	**NSSR**
incinerate	**NSPD**	inceptive	necessary
incinerated	insipid	**NSR**	necessarily
incinerating	**NSPDT**	answer	necessaries
NSNRTR	insipidity	nicer	unnecessary
incinerator	**NSPKBL**	nice	unnecessarily
NSNS	unspeakable	**NSRBL**	unnecessariness
incense	unspeakably	answerable	**NSST**
incensed	**NSPKSHN**	**NSRJNS**	incest(sex)
incensing	inspection	insurgence	insist(demand)
innocence(no guilt)	**NSPKT**	insurgency	necessity
nascence(emerging)	inspect	**NSRJNT**	necessities
nescience	**NSPKTR**	insurgent	nicest
(ignorance)	inspector	**NSRKL**	nice
nuisance	**NSPKTV**	encircle	**NSSTD**
NSNSBL	inspective	encircled	unassisted
insensible	**NSPNS**	encircling	**NSSTNS**
NSNSBLT	incipience	**NSRKMSZD**	insistence
insensibility	**NSPNT**	uncircumcised	**NSSTNT**
insensibilities	incipient	**NSRKMSZHN**	insistent
NSNSHL	**NSPR**	uncircumcision	**NSSTR**
inessential(or)	inspire	**NSRKSHN**	ancestor
unessential	inspired	insurrection	ancestry
NSNSHNT	inspiring	**NSRMNS**	**NSSTRL**
insentient	**NSPRBL**	unceremonious	ancestral
NSNSR	inseparable	**NSRMNTBL**	**NSSTS**
insincere	inseparably	insurmountable	necessitous
NSNSRT	insuperable	**NSRSHN**	**NSSTSHN**
insincerity	**NSPRBLT**	insertion	necessitation
insincerities	inseparability	**NSRT**	**NSSTT**
NSNST	insuperability	insert	necessitate
insensate	**NSPRNG**	**NSRTN**	necessitated
NSNSTV	inspiring	uncertain	necessitating

NSSTTV
  necessitative
NSSV
  incisive
NST
  honest
  honesty
  incite(provoke)
    incited
    inciting
  inset
  insight(discern)
  nasty
    nastier
    nastiest
    nastily
    nastiness
  nauseate
    nauseated
    nauseating
  nest
  nicety
    niceties
  onset
  unseat
NSTBL
  unstable
  unstably
  unsuitable
  unsuitably
NSTBLT
  instability
    instabilities
  unsuitability
NSTD
  instead
  unsteady
    unsteadier
    unsteadiest
    unsteadily
    unsteadiness
NSTG
  nest egg
NSTGSHN
  instigation
NSTGT
  instigate
    instigated
    instigating
NSTGTR
  instigator
NSTH
  New South
NSTHTK
  anesthetic
NSTHTST

anesthetist
NSTHTZ
  anesthetize
    anesthetized
    anesthetizing
NSTHZ
  anesthesia
NSTHZH
  anesthesia
NSTK
  gnostic
NSTL
  install
  instill, (B)instil
  unsettle
    unsettled
    unsettling
  unsightly
    unsightlier
    unsightliest
    unsightliness
NSTLJ
  nostalgia
NSTLJK
  nostalgic
NSTLMNT
  installment
NSTLNS
  unsightliness
NSTLSHN
  installation
NSTMBL
  inestimable
NSTNGKT
  instinct
NSTNGKTV
  instinctive
NSTNS
  instance(example)
  instants(time)
NSTNT
  instant
NSTNTNS
  instantaneous
NSTNTR
  instanter
NSTP
  instep
  unstop
    unstopped
    unstopping
NSTR
  ancestor
  inciter
  nester
NSTRF

anastrophe
NSTRKCHRD
  unstructured
NSTRKSHN
  instruction
NSTRKT
  instruct
NSTRKTR
  instructor
NSTRKTV
  instructive
NSTRL
  nostril
NSTRM
  nostrum
NSTRMNT
  instrument
NSTRMNTL
  instrumental
NSTRMNTLST
  instrumentalist
NSTRMNTLT
  instrumentality
NSTRMNTSHN
  instrumentation
NSTRNG
  unstring
    unstrung
NSTRSHM
  nasturtium
NSTRST
  unstressed
NSTSHN
  incitation
NSTT
  instate
    instated
    instating
NSTTSHN
  institution
NSTTSHNL
  institutional
NSTTSHNLZ
  institutionalize
    institutionalized
    institutionalizing
NSTTT
  institute
    instituted
    instituting
NSTTYSHN
  institution
NSTTYSHNL
  institutional
NSTTYSHNLZ
  institutionalize

institutionalized
  institutionalizing
NSTTYT
  institute
    instituted
    instituting
NSVD
  unsaved
NSVL
  uncivil
NSVLT
  incivility
    incivilities
NSVLZD
  uncivilized
NSVR
  unsavory
    unsavorily
    unsavoriness
NSYLR
  insular(island)
NSYSHNT
  insouciant
    insouciance
NSZ
  incise(cut)
    -cised,-cising
  Niseis(Nisei)
  nisus(connive)
NSZHN
  incision
NSZNBL
  unseasonable
  unseasonably
NSZND
  unseasoned
NSZR
  incisor
NT
  ain't
  isn't
  is not
  are not
  annuity(money)
    annuities
  anoint
    anointer
  ante(front,money)
    anted
    anteing
  anti-(against)
  ant(insect)
  aunt(person)
    auntie
  enate(relative)
  enatic

gnat(insect)
innate(inborn)
into
knight(rank)
knit
  knitted
  knitting
knot
  knotted
  knotting
knotty
  knottier
  knottiest
  knottiness
NATO
  North Atlantic
  Treaty
  Organization
natty
  nattier
  nattiest
  nattily
  nattiness
naught(nothing)
naughty(bad)
  naughtier
  naughtiest
  naughtily
  naughtiness
neat(orderly,clean)
net
  netted
  netting
newt(salamander)
night(darkness)
nighty(clothing)
  nighties
not(no)
note(music)
note(notice)
  noted,noting
nut(food,screw)
  nutted,nutting
nutty(crazy)
  nuttier
  nuttiest
  nuttily
  nuttiness
onto
untie
  untied
  untying(or)
  untieing
unto
NTBD
antibody

antibodies
NTBK
notebook
NTBL
notable(note)
notably
NTBLM
ante-bellum
NTBLSTK
antiballistic
NTBTK
antibiotic
NTCH
unattach
unattaches
NTCHBL
untouchable
NTCHMBR
antechamber
NTCHT
unattached
NTD
nitid(bright)
untidy
untidier
untidiest
untidily
untidiness
NTDLVN
antediluvian
NTDRS
nightdress
NTDT
antedate
antedated
antedating
antidote
NTF
notify
notified
notifies
NTFBL
notifiable
NTFKSHN
notification
NTFL
nightfall
NTFN
antiphony
antiphonies
NTFNL
antiphonal
NTFRZ
antifreeze
NTG
Antigua

NTGL
nutgall
NTGN
nightgown
NTGNST
antagonist
NTGNZ
antagonize
antagonized
antagonizing
antagonist
NTGNZM
antagonism
NTGRBL
integrable
NTGRL
integral
NTGRSHN
integration
NTGRT
integrate
integrated
integrating
integrity
integrities
nitty-gritty
NTGRTR
integrator
NTGW
Antigua
NTGYMNT
integument
NTHD
knighthood
NTHK
gnathic(jaw)
NTHL
anthill
knothole
NTHLJ
anthology
anthologies
NTHLJST
anthologist
NTHLJZ
anthologize
anthologized
anthologizing
NTHM
anthem(song)
anathema
NTHMTZ
anathematize
anathematized
anathematizing
NTHMTZSHN

anathematization
NTHNG
anything
nothing
NTHNGKBL
unthinkable
NTHNGKFL
unthankful
NTHR
another
anther
antihero
neither
nether(lower)
NTHRKS
anthrax(disease)
anthraces
NTHRL
enthrall
NTHRLNZ
Netherlands,The
NTHRLNZNTLZ
Netherlands
Antilles
NTHRN
enthrone
enthroned
enthroning
NTHRPD
anthropoid
NTHRPFJ
anthropophagi
NTHRPK
anthropic
NTHRPLJ
anthropology
NTHRPMRFZM
anthropomorphism
NTHRST
anthracite
NTHSTMN
antihistamine
NTHTV
unthought-of
NTHZ
enthuse
enthused
enthusing
NTHZSTK
enthusiastic
NTHZSTKL
enthusiastically
NTHZZM
enthusiasm
NTJN
antigen

NGK:ink **P**:pie **R**:air **S**:ice **SH**:show **T**:toy **THN**:thin **TH**:the **V**:of **W**:we **Y**:you **Z**:is **VZHN**:vision

antigenic
antigenicity
NTJR
integer
NTK
antic(act)
antique(old)
enatic(enate)
intake
NTKL
nautical
NTKLB
nightclub
NTKLMKS
anticlimax
NTKLMKTK
anticlimactic
NTKP
nightcap
NTKR
antiquer
NTKRKR
nutcracker
NTKRLR
night crawler
NTKRST
anti-christ
(attitude)
Antichrist
(predicted
person)
NTKSKNT
intoxicant
NTKSKSHN
intoxication
NTKSKT
intoxicate
intoxicated
intoxicating
NTKSKTR
intoxicator
NTKSKTV
intoxicative
NTKT
intact
NTKWR
antiquary
antiquaries
NTKWT
antiquate
antiquated
antiquating
antiquation
antiquity
antiquities
NTL

entail
know-it-all
natal(birth)
nettle
nettled
nettling
until
NTLD
untold
NTLJ
ontology
NTLJBL
intelligible
intelligibly
NTLJBLT
intelligibility
intelligibilities
NTLJKL
ontological
NTLJNS
intelligence
NTLJNT
intelligent
NTLJNTS
intelligentsia
NTLKCHL
intellectual
NTLKCHLZ
intellectualize
intellectualized
intellectualizing
NTLKCHWL
intellectual
NTLKSHN
intellection
NTLKT
intellect
NTLNG
nightlong
NTLP
antelope
NTLR
antler
NTLRBL
intolerable
NTLRNS
intolerance
NTLRNT
intolerant
NTLS
nautilus
nautili(or)
nautiluses
NTLY
intaglio
NTM

anatomy
anatomies
entomb
nighttime
NTMDR
antimatter
NTMDSHN
intimidation
NTMDT
intimidate
intimidated
intimidating
intimidator
NTMG
nutmeg
NTMK
anatomic
NTMKL
anatomical
NTMKSR
antimacassar
NTML
untimely
untimelier
untimeliest
untimeliness
NTMLJ
entomology
NTMLJST
entomologist
NTMNT
ointment
NTMPRNS
intemperance
NTMPRT
intemperate
NTMR
nightmare
nightmarish
NTMRDM
ante meridiem(A.M.)
NTMRDN
antemeridian
(morning)
NTMRSH
nightmarish
NTMS
intimacy
intimacies
NTMSHN
intimation
NTMST
anatomist
NTMT
intimate(n,v)
(close,hint)

intimated
intimating
nutmeat
NTMTR
antimatter
NTMZ
anatomize
anatomized
anatomizing
anatomization
NTN
antenna
antennas(radio)
antennae
(biology)
intone
intoned
intoning
NTNBL
untenable
untenably
NTNCHN
inattention
intention
NTND
intend
NTNDNT
intendant
NTNGL
entangle
entangled
entangling
nightingale
untangle(undo)
untangled
untangling
NTNJBL
intangible
NTNM
antinomy
antinomies
antonym(word)
NTNS
intense
intents(aims)
NTNSF
intensify
intensified
intensifies
NTNSFKSHN
intensification
NTNSHN
inattention
intention
(purpose)
intonation

NTNSHNL
  intentional
NTNST
  intensity
  intensities
NTNSV
  intensive
NTNT
  annuitant
  entente(agree)
  intent(purpose)
  natant
NTNTLKCHL
  anti-intellectual
NTNTV
  inattentive
NTPK
  nit-pick
  on-topic(debate)
  nutpick
NTPKNG
  nit-picking
NTPKR
  nit-picker
NTPNLT
  antepenult
NTPNLTMT
  antepenultimate
NTPST
  antipasto
  antipasti(or)
  antipastos
NTPTH
  antipathy
  antipathies
NTPTHTK
  antipathetic
NTR
  enter(go into)
  entire(whole)
  entrée(food,enter)
  entry(act,item)
  entries
  inter-(between)
  inter(bury)
  interred
  interring
  knitter
  neuter
  nutria(rodent)
  Ontario
  untrue
NTRBRD
  interbreed
  interbred
NTRBRDNG

  interbreeding
NTRCHNJ
  interchange
  interchanged
  interchanging
NTRCHNJBL
  interchangeable
  interchangeably
NTRD
  intrude
  intruded
  intruding
  intruder
  untoward
  untried
NTRDKSHN
  interdiction
    (prohibit)
  introduction
NTRDKT
  interdict
    (prohibit)
NTRDKTR
  introductory
NTRDNMNSHNL
  interdenominational
NTRDNTL
  interdental
NTRDPNDNS
  interdependence
NTRDPNDNT
  interdependent
NTRDPRTMNTL
  interdepartmental
NTRDR
  intruder
NTRDS
  introduce
  introduced
  introducing
  introduction
NTRDSPLNR
  interdisciplinary
NTRFN
  interphone
NTRFR
  interfere
  interfered
  interfering
NTRFRN
  interferon
NTRFRNS
  interference
NTRFS
  interface
  interfacial

  interoffice
NTRFSHL
  interfacial
NTRFTH
  interfaith
NTRG
  intrigue
  intrigued
  intriguing
NTRGLKTK
  intergalactic
NTRGLSRN
  nitroglycerin
NTRGSHN
  interrogation
NTRGT
  interrogate
  interrogated
  interrogating
NTRGTR
  interrogator
  interrogatory
  interrogatories
NTRGTV
  interrogative
NTRJKSHN
  interjection
    (exclamatory)
  introjection
NTRJKT
  interject
    (interpose)
NTRJN
  nitrogen
NTRKM
  intercom
NTRKMYNKSHN
  intercommunication
NTRKMYNKT
  intercommunicate
  intercommunicated
  intercommunicating
NTRKNKT
  interconnect
NTRKNTNNTL
  intercontinental
NTRKRFT
  antiaircraft
NTRKRP
  intercrop
NTRKRS
  intercourse
NTRKS
  intricacy
  intricacies
NTRKSHN

  interaction
NTRKT
  entr'acte(time)
  interact
  intricate
NTRKTBL
  intractable
NTRKTK
  Antarctic
  Antarctica
NTRKTV
  interactive
NTRL
  inter alia(among)
  neutral
NTRLD
  interlude
NTRLF
  interleaf
  interleaves
NTRLK
  interlock
NTRLKYSHN
  interlocution
NTRLKYTR
  interlocutor
  interlocutory
NTRLN
  interline
  interlined
  interlining
NTRLNNG
  interlining
NTRLNR
  interlinear
  interlunar
NTRLP
  interlope
  interloped
  interloping
NTRLPR
  interloper
NTRLRD
  interlard
NTRLS
  entrails
  interlace
  interlaced
  interlacing
NTRLSHN
  interrelation
NTRLT
  interrelate
  interrelated
  interrelating
  neutrality

NGK:ink **P**:pie **R**:air **S**:ice **SH**:show **T**:toy **THN**:thin **TH**:the **V**:of **W**:we **Y**:you **Z**:is **VZHN**:vision

neutralities

NTRLV
interleave
interleaved
interleaving
NTRLVZ
interleaves
NTRLZ
entrails
neutralize
neutralized
neutralizing
NTRLZR
neutralizer
NTRLZSHN
neutralization
NTRM
anteroom
interim
NTRMDR
intermediary
intermediaries
NTRMDT
intermediate
NTRMDZ
intermezzo
intermezzi(or)
intermezzos
NTRMKS
intermix
intermixes
NTRMKSCHR
intermixture
NTRMNBL
interminable
interminably
NTRMNGL
intermingle
intermingled
intermingling
NTRMNT
interment
nutriment
NTRMP
no-trump
NTRMR
intermarry
intermarried
intermarries
NTRMRJ
intermarriage
NTRMSHN
intermission
NTRMSKYLR
intramuscular
NTRMT

intermit
intermitted
intermitting
NTRMTNT
intermittent
NTRMTS
intermezzo
intermezzi(or)
intermezzos
NTRMYRL
intramural
NTRN
entrain
entre nous
intern(doctor,
    detain)
internee
neutrino
neutron
NTRNCH
entrench
entrenches
NTRNCHMNT
entrenchment
NTRNKLR
intranuclear
NTRNL
internal
NTRNLZ
internalize
internalized
internalizing
internalization
NTRNMNT
internment
NTRNS
entrance
entranced
entrancing
NTRNSHNL
international
internationale
    (song)
NTRNSHNLZ
internationalize
internationalized
internationalizing
NTRNSHNLZM
internationalism
NTRNSHNLZSHN
internation-
    alization
NTRNSHP
internship
NTRNSJNS
intransigence

intransigency
NTRNSJNT
intransigent
NTRNSK
intrinsic
NTRNSN
internecine
NTRNST
internist
NTRNSTV
intransitive
NTRNT
entrant
nutrient
NTRNZK
intrinsic
NTRP
entrap
entrapped
entrapping
entropy
NTRPBLK
notary public
notaries public
NTRPD
intrepid
NTRPDT
intrepidity
NTRPL
interplay
Interpol
International
    Criminal
    Police
    Organization
NTRPLD
interplead
NTRPLNTR
interplanetary
NTRPLSHN
interpolation
NTRPLT
interpellate
    (question)
interpellated
interpolate(insert)
interpolated
interpolating
NTRPMNT
entrapment
NTRPNR
entrepreneur
NTRPNTRT
interpenetrate
interpenetrated

interpenetrating
NTRPRNR
entrepreneur
NTRPRSNL
interpersonal
NTRPRT
interpret
NTRPRTR
interpreter
NTRPRTSHN
interpretation
NTRPRTV
interpretive
NTRPRZ
enterprise
enterprising
NTRPRZNG
enterprising
NTRPRZR
enterpriser
NTRPSHN
interruption
NTRPT
interrupt
NTRPZ
interpose
interposed
interposing
NTRR
anterior(front)
interior(inside)
NTRRBN
interurban
NTRS
inter se
notorious
NTRSD
intercede
interceded
interceding
NTRSHL
interracial
NTRSHN
nutrition
NTRSHS
nutritious
NTRSKLSTK
interscholastic
NTRSKLSTKL
interscholastical
NTRSKSHL
intersexual
NTRSKSHN
intersection
NTRSKT
intersect

NTRSPKSHN
introspection
NTRSPKT
introspect
NTRSPKTV
introspective
NTRSPRS
intersperse
interspersed
interspersing
NTRSPRZHN
interspersion
NTRSPS
interspace
interspaced
interspacing
NTRSPSHL
interspatial
NTRSPSHN
interception
NTRSPT
intercept
NTRSPTR
interceptor
NTRSSHN
intercession
(prayer)
intersession
(time)
NTRST
entrust
interest
NTRSTLR
interstellar
NTRSTNG
interesting
NTRSTRTF
interstratify
interstratified
interstratifies
interstratifi-
cation
NTRSTS
interstice
NTRSTT
interstate
(between states)
intrastate
(inside a state)
NTRSV
intrusive
NTRT
entirety(all)
entireties
entreat
entreaty

entreaties
nitrate
notoriety
NTRTDL
intertidal
NTRTHFL
untruthful
NTRTKSCHR
intertexture
NTRTN
entertain
NTRTRBL
intertribal
NTRTRPKL
intertropical
NTRTV
nutritive
NTRTWN
intertwine
intertwined
intertwining
NTRVL
interval
NTRVLD
untraveled
NTRVN
intervene
intervened
intervening
NTRVNCHN
intervention
NTRVNCHNZM
interventionism
NTRVNS
intravenous
NTRVNSHN
intervention
NTRVNSHNZM
interventionism
NTRVRT
introvert
NTRVRZHN
introversion
NTRVY
interview
NTRVYR
interviewer
NTRWV
interweave
interwove
interweaving
interwoven
NTRYDRN
intrauterine
NTRYTRN
intrauterine

NTRZ
notarize
notarized
notarizing
notarization
NTRZH
entourage
NTRZHN
intrusion
NTRZPBLK
notaries public
NTRZSHN
notarization
NTS
entice
enticed
enticing
enticer
Nazi
notice
noticed
noticing
NTSBL
noticeable
noticeably
NTSD
antacid
antecede
anteceded
anteceding
NTSDNS
antecedence
antecedents(pl)
(preceding)
NTSDNT
antecedent
NTSHL
nutshell
NTSHN
annotation
intuition
notation
NTSHRT
nightshirt
NTSMNT
enticement
NTSMTK
anti-Semitic
NTSPSHN
anticipation
NTSPT
anticipate
anticipated
anticipating
anticipation
NTSPTK

antiseptic
NTSPTR
anticipator
anticipatory
NTSRM
antiserum
NTSTMNT
New Testament
NTSTN
intestine
NTSTNL
intestinal
NTSTT
intestate
NTSZM
Nazism
NTT
annotate
annotated
annotating
annotation
annotator
annotative
entity
entities
in toto
intuit
untaught
NTTHSS
antithesis
antitheses
NTTHTK
antithetic
NTTKSK
antitoxic
NTTKSN
antitoxin
NTTL
entitle
entitled
entitling
NTTLD
untitled
NTTLMNT
entitlement
NTTR
annotator
natatory
natatories
NTTRD
untutored
NTTRL
natatorial
NTTRM
natatorium
NTTRST

NGK:ink **P**:pie **R**:air **S**:ice **SH**:show **T**:toy **THN**:thin **TH**:the **V**:of **W**:we **Y**:you **Z**:is **VZHN**:vision

antitrust	U.S.N.(or)USN	invoking	involuted
NTTV	nouveau(new)	**NVKN**	novelette
annotative	nova	Novocain	novelty
intuitive	novae(or)	(trademark)	novelties
NTTYL	novas	procaine	**NVLV**
entitule	**NVBL**	**NVKSHN**	involve
NTV	enviable	invocation	involved
native	enviably	**NVKT**	involving
NTVBRN	**NVD**	invocate	involver
native-born	invade	invocated	involvement
NTVT	invaded	invocating	**NVLYBL**
nativity	invading	**NVKTR**	invaluable
nativities	Nevada	invocatory	invaluably
NTWN	**NVDBL**	**NVKTV**	**NVMBR**
entwine	inevitable	invective	November
entwined	inevitably	**NVL**	**NVN**
entwining	unavoidable	anvil	uneven
NTWRK	unavoidably	naval(navy)	**NVNM**
network	**NVDR**	navel(body)	envenom
NTWRTH	invader	novel(book,new)	**NVNSBL**
noteworthy	**NVDS**	novella	invincible
noteworthier	invidious	unveil	invincibly
noteworthiest	**NVGBL**	**NVLBL**	**NVNSBLT**
noteworthiness	navigable	inviolable	invincibility
NTWTHSTNDNG	navigate	inviolate	**NVNSHN**
notwithstanding	**NVGL**	**NVLD**	invention
NTYSHN	inveigle	invalid(null,	**NVNT**
intuition	inveigled	crippled)	invent
NTYT	inveigling	**NVLDSHN**	**NVNTFL**
intuit	**NVGRSHN**	invalidation	uneventful
NTYTRD	invigoration	**NVLDT**	**NVNTR**
untutored	**NVGRT**	invalidate	inventor
NTYTV	invigorate	invalidated	inventory
intuitive	invigorated	invalidating	inventoried
NTYZ	invigorating	invalidity	inventories
intaglios	**NVGRTR**	invalidities	**NVNTV**
NTZ	invigorator	**NVLNRBL**	inventive
Nazi	**NVGRTV**	invulnerable	**NVR**
Nazism	invigorative	invulnerably	knavery
NV	**NVGSHN**	**NVLNRBLT**	never
envoi(verse)	navigation	invulnerability	**NVRBL**
envoy(person)	**NVGT**	invulnerabilities	invariable
envy(emotion)	navigate	**NVLNTR**	invariably
envied	navigated	involuntary	**NVRMNT**
envies	navigating	involuntarily	environment
inveigh	**NVGTR**	**NVLP**	**NVRMNTL**
knave(rogue)	navigator	envelop(v)	environmental
knavish	**NVJNSHN**	envelope(n)	**NVRMR**
knavery	invagination	**NVLSHN**	nevermore
naive(simple)	**NVJNT**	involution	**NVRN**
naiveté	invaginate	**NVLST**	environ
naiveties	invaginated	novelist	**NVRNMNT**
nave(church)	invaginating	**NVLT**	environment
navy	**NVK**	inviolate	**NVRNMNTL**
navies	invoke	inviolable	environmental
Navy, the	invoked	involute(or)	**NVRS**

B:by CH:each D:day F:if G:go H:he HW:why J:joy K:cow KS:ax KWL:equal L:all M:may N:in

inverse
NVRSH
nouveau riche
nouveaux riches
NVRSR
anniversary
anniversaries
NVRST
inveracity
NVRT
invert
inversion
NVRTBL
invertible
NVRTBRT
invertebrate(or)
invertebrated
NVRTHLS
nevertheless
NVRTR
inverter
NVRZHN
inversion
NVS
envious(envy)
invoice
invoiced
invoicing
nevus(birthmark)
nevi(or)
naevus
novice
NVSH
knavish
NVSHN
envision
innovation
NVSHT
novitiate
NVSKSH
Nova Scotia
NVST
invest
NVSTCHR
investiture
NVSTGSHN
investigation
NVSTGT
investigate
investigated
investigating
NVSTGTR
investigator
NVSTGTV
investigative
NVSTMNT

investment
NVSTR
investor
NVSV
invasive
NVT
innovate
innovated
innovating
invite
invited
inviting
naiveté
naiveties
NVTBL
inevitable
inevitably
NVTBLT
inevitability
inevitabilities
NVTR
innovator
in vitro
NVTRT
inveterate
NVTSHN
invitation
NVTV
innovative
NVV
in vivo
NVZ
knives
NVZBL
invisible
invisibly
NVZBLT
invisibility
NVZHN
envision(foresee)
invasion
NVZJ
envisage
envisaged
envisaging
NW
anyway(anyhow)
any way(course,
direction)
ennui
NWDZ
nowadays
NWLD
unwieldy
unwieldier
unwieldiest

unwieldiness
NWLNG
unwilling
NWN
anyone(person)
any one(of a group)
no one
NWND
unwind
unwound
NWNGL
knowingly
NWNTD
unwanted
(not wanted)
unwonted
(not usual)
NWR
anywhere
nowhere
unaware(asleep)
unwary
-warier,-wariest
-warily,-wariness
NWRD
inward
onward
unwearied
NWRLD
New World
NWRLDL
unworldly
unworldlier
unworldliest
unworldliness
NWRNTBL
unwarrantable
unwarrantably
NWRNTD
unwarranted
NWRTH
unworthy
unworthier
unworthiest
unworthily
unworthiness
NWRZ
unawares
NWTNGL
unwittingly
NWV
new wave
NWZ
anyways
anywise
nowise

unwise
NY
anew
gnu(animal)
knew(perceived)
know
new(recent)
NYBL
nubile
NYBRN
newborn
NYBRNSWK
New Brunswick
NYD
nude
NYDL
New Delhi
NYDR
neuter
NYDST
nudist
NYDT
nudity
nudities
NYFNDLND
Newfoundland
NYFNGLD
newfangled
NYFSHND
new-fashioned
NYGN
New Guinea
NYGTR
nugatory
NYHBRDZ
New Hebrides
NYHMSHR
New Hampshire
NYJRZ
New Jersey
NYK
gnocchi(food)
NYKLDN
New Caledonia
NYKLNK
nucleonic
NYKLNKS
nucleonics
NYKLR
nuclear
NYKLS
nucleus
nuclei(or)
nucleuses
NYKLT
nucleate

NGK:ink **P**:pie **R**:air **S**:ice **SH**:show **T**:toy **THN**:thin **TH**:the **V**:of **W**:we **Y**:you **Z**:is **VZHN**:vision

nucleated
nucleating
NYKMR
newcomer
NYL
annual(yearly)
newel
NYLN
inulin
NYLR
annular
NYLSHN
annulation
NYLWD
newlywed
NYMKSK
New Mexico
NYMNY
pneumonia
NYMRBL
innumerable
numerable
NYMRKL
numerical
NYMRL
numeral
NYMRLJ
numerology
NYMRS
numerous
NYMRSHN
enumeration
numeration
NYMRT
enumerate
enumerated
enumerating
numerate
numerated
numerating
NYMRTR
enumerator
numerator
NYMSMTK
numismatic
NYMSMTST
numismatist
NYMZMTK
numismatic
NYMZMTST
numismatist
NYN
onion
NYND
innuendo
innuendoes

NYNGGLND
New England
NYNS
annoyance
nuance
NYNSKN
onionskin
NYPRTNZ
Newport News
NYR
anuria
inure
inured
inuring
NYRK
Newark
New York
NYRL
neural
NYRLJ
neuralgia
neurology
NYRLJKL
neurological
NYRLJST
neurologist
NYRLNZ
New Orleans
NYRSS
anuresis
neurosis
neuroses
NYRSTHN
neurasthenia
NYRTK
neurotic
NYRTS
neuritis
NYRZM
aneurysm
NYSNS
nuisance
NYST
unused(not
   accustomed to)
NYSTH
New South
NYT
annuity
annuities
newt(salamander)
nyet(no)
NYTL
inutile
NYTNT
annuitant

NYTR
neuter
nutria
NYTRL
neutral
NYTRLT
neutrality
neutralities
NYTRLZ
neutralize
neutralized
neutralizing
neutralizer
NYTRLZR
neutralizer
NYTRLZSHN
neutralization
NYTRMNT
nutriment
NYTRN
neutrino
neutron
NYTRNT
nutrient
NYTRSHN
nutrition
NYTRSHS
nutritious
NYTRTV
nutritive
NYTSPTS
annuit coeptis
NYTSTMNT
New Testament
NYV
nouveau(new)
NYWRLD
New World
NYWV
new wave
NYYRK
New York
NYZ
news
NYZB
newsboy
NYZD
unused(not used)
NYZDLR
newsdealer
NYZHL
unusual
NYZKST
newscast
NYZLN
New Zealand

NYZLND
New Zealand
NYZLTR
newsletter
NYZMN
newsman
newsmen
NYZPPR
newspaper
NYZPRNT
newsprint
NYZRL
newsreel
NYZSTND
newsstand
NYZWRTH
newsworthy
   newsworthiness
NZ
ionize
ionized
ionizing
nausea
news
noise(sound)
noisy(sound)
noisier
noisiest
noisily
noisiness
nose(smell)
nosed
nosing
nosy
nosier
nosiest
nosily
nosiness
uneasy
uneasier
uneasiest
uneasily
uneasiness
NZB
newsboy
NZBLD
nosebleed
NZDLR
newsdealer
NZDV
nose-dive(v)
   nose-dived(or)
nose-dove
nose-diving
nose dive(n)
NZG

B:by **CH:**each **D:**day **F:**if **G:**go **H:**he **HW:**why **J:**joy **K:**cow **KS:**ax **KWL:**equal **L:**all **M:**may **N:**in

nosegay
NZH
nausea
NZHN
ingénue
NZHNY
ingénue
NZHS
nauseous
NZHT
nauseate
nauseated
nauseating
NZKN
nose cone
NZKST
newscast
NZL
nasal
nozzle
nuzzle
nuzzled
nuzzling
NZLN
New Zealand
NZLND
New Zealand
NZLT
nasality
NZLTR
newsletter
NZLZ
nasalize
nasalized
nasalizing
NZM
anosmia
enzyme
NZMCHZ
inasmuch as
NZMKR
noisemaker
NZMN
newsman
newsmen
NZP
unzip
unzipped
unzipping
NZPPR
newspaper
NZPRNT
newsprint
NZPS
nosepiece
NZRL

newsreel
NZS
nauseous
NZSHN
ionization
ionize
NZSM
noisome
NZSTND
newsstand
NZT
nauseate
nauseated
nauseating
NZWRTH
newsworthy
newsworthiness

P

AP(the AP)
The Associated
Press
ape(animal)
aped
aping
epee(sword)(or)
épée
pas(dance)
pas(pl)
paw(foot)
pay
paid
payee
pea(food)
pee(urinate)
peed
pi(Greek)
pie(food)
poi(food)
up
PB
up-bow
PBL
payable
pebble
pebbled
pebbling
pebbly
pebblier
pebbliest
PBLD

piebald
PBLK
public
PBLKSHN
publication
PBLM
Pablum(trademark)
pablum
PBLSH
publish
publishes
PBLSHR
publisher
PBLSST
publicist
PBLST
publicity
PBLSZ
publicize
publicized
publicizing
PBRD
upbraid
PBRNGNG
upbringing
PBRT
puberty
PBT
upbeat
PBYLM
pabulum
PCH
Apache
Apache(or)
Apaches
patch
patches
patchy
patchier
patchiest
patchiness
peach(fruit)
peaches
pitch
pitches
poach
poaches
pooch(dog)
pooches
pouch(bag)
pouches
pouchy
pouchiness
PCHBLK
pitch-black
PCHBLND

pitchblende
PCHDRK
pitch-dark
PCHFRK
pitchfork
PCHK
paycheck
upchuck
PCHLNS
petulance
PCHLNT
petulant
PCHPP
pitch pipe
PCHR
picture(photo)
pictured
picturing
pitcher
poacher
PCHRFL
pitcherful
PCHT
pitchout
PCHWRK
patchwork
PD
pad
padded
padding
paddy(rice)
paddies
paid
pay
patty(cake)
patties
payday
petty(trivial)
pettier
pettiest
pettily
pettiness
pied(splotched)
pity(sorrow)
pitied
pities
POed(slang)
pod
podia
podium
putty(clay)
uppity
PDD
pitted
pit
PDFL

pitiful(pity)
PDFSR
petty officer
PDGG
pedagogue
PDGJ
pedagogy
PDGJK
pedagogic
PDGR
pedigree
PDGRD
pedigreed
PDK
paddock
poetic
PDKL
pedicle
PDKYR
pedicure
PDL
paddle(boat)
paddled
paddling
pedal(foot)
peddle(sell)
peddled
peddling
peddler
petal(flower)
piddle(squander)
piddled
piddling
poodle(dog)
puddle(water)
puddled
puddling
PDLFR
pedalfer(soil)
PDLK
padlock
PDLR
peddler
PDM
epitome
podium
podia(or)
podiums
PDMK
epidemic
PDMNT
pediment
piedmont
PDMTR
pedometer
PDMZ

epitomize
epitomized
epitomizing
PDNG
padding
petting
pet
pudding(food)
PDNS
pittance
PDNT
pedant
PDNTK
pedantic
PDNTKL
pedantical
PDNTR
pedantry
pedantries
PDR
padre
powder
powdery
powderier
powderiest
powderiness
PDRDT
petered out
PDRFT
updraft
PDRMS
epidermis
PDRN
pattern
PDSL
pedicel
PDSTL
pedestal
PDSTRN
pedestrian
PDT
update
updated
updating
PDTR
podiatry
PDTRKS
pediatrics
PDTRSHN
pediatrician
PDTRST
podiatrist
PDWGN
paddy wagon
PDY
POW

prisoner of war
PF
payoff
pouf(style,tool,
   puffy)
puff
puffy
puffier
puffiest
puffiness
PFDR
puff adder
PFN
epiphany
PFR
puffer
puffery
PG
peg(wood)
pegged
pegging
pig(swine)
pigged
pigging
piggish
piggy
piggies
pogo
pogy(fish)
pogy(or)
pogies
pug
PGBK
piggyback
PGBRD
pegboard
PGD
pagoda
PGHDD
pigheaded
PGLT
piglet
PGLTS
epiglotis
PGM
pygmy
pygmies
PGMNT
pigment
PGMNTSHN
pigmentation
PGN
pagan
piggin(bucket)
pogonia
PGNSHS

pugnacious
PGNST
pugnacity
PGNY
pogonia
PGNZM
paganism
PGPG
Pago Pago
PGPN
pigpen
PGRD
upgrade
upgraded
upgrading
PGRF
epigraph
PGRFK
epigraphic
PGRFKL
epigraphical
PGRM
epigram
pogrom
PGRMTK
epigrammatic
PGRMTKL
epigrammatical
PGRN
pig iron
PGSH
piggish
PGSKN
pigskin
PGST
pigsty
pigsties
PGSTK
pogo stick
PGTL
pigtail
PHL
uphill
PHLD
uphold
upheld
upholding
PHLSTR
upholster
upholstery
upholsteries
PHLSTRR
upholsterer
PHVL
upheavel
PJ

B:by **CH**:each **D**:day **F**:if **G**:go **H**:he **HW**:why **J**:joy **K**:cow **KS**:ax **KWL**:equal **L**:all **M**:may **N**:in

apogee
page
  paged
  paging
pudgy
  pudgier
  pudgiest
  pudginess
PJB
pageboy
PJKT
pea jacket
PJMZ
pajamas, (B)pyjamas
PJN
pidgin(language)
pigeon
PJNHL
pigeonhole
  pigeonholed
  pigeonholing
PJNNGGLSH
Pidgin English
PJNSHN
pagination
PJNT
pageant
paginate
  paginated
  paginating
PJNTD
pigeon-toed
PJNTR
pageantry
  pageantries
PJR
progeria(age)
PJRSHN
pejoration
PJRTV
pejorative
PK
apeak(vertical)
epic(poem)
epoch(period)
opaque
OPEC(oil)
pack
peak(highest
  point)
peck
peek(look)
pekoe(tea)
pica(type)
pick
picot

pike
piqué(fabric)
pique(offend)
  piqued
  piquing
piquet(game)
poco
poke (prod)
  poked,poking
pokey(jail)
poky(slow)
  pokier
  pokiest
  pokiness
polka(music)
puck
pukka(genuine)
PKB
peekaboo
PKBL
peccable
PKBLT
peccability
PKCHR
picture
  pictured
  picturing
PKCHRSK
picturesque
PKD
peaked(adj)
PKDFNS
picket fence
PKDL
peccadillo
Piccadilly
PKDR
picador
PKDRM
pachyderm
PKDT
polka dot
  polka dotted
  polka dotting
PKJ
package
  packaged
  packaging
PKJNG
packaging
PKK
ipecac
peacock
  peahen(f)
  peafowl(m,f)
PKKS

pickax
  pickaxes
PKKYN
ipecacuanha
PKL
epochal
piccolo
pickle
  pickled
  pickling
PKLDR
peculator
PKLL
piccalilli
PKLPS
apocalypse
PKLPTK
apocalyptic
PKMNG
upcoming
PKMP
pick-me-up(n)
PKMRK
pockmark
PKMRKT
pockmarked
PKN
pecan
PKNG
packing
pecking(strike)
peeking(look)
Peking
picking(pluck)
PKNGRDR
pecking order
PKNK
picnic
  picnicked
  picnicking
PKNKR
picnicker
PKNS
Pekingese
piquancy
PKNT
peccant(faulty)
piquant(spicy)
PKNTR
upcountry
PKNZ
Pekingese
PKP
apocape
pick up(v)
pickup(n)

upkeep
PKPKT
pickpocket
PKR
packer
picker(pick)
piker(stingy)
poker
pucker
PKRF
Apocrypha
PKRFL
apocryphal
PKRL
pickerel(fish)
PKRSK
picaresque
PKRT
pack rat
PKS
apex
  apexes(or)
  apices
epoxy
  epoxies
Pecos
Picasso
pixy
  pixies
pox(disease)
pyx(container)
pyxie(shrub)
PKSDL
packsaddle
PKSK
packsack
PKSL
pixel
PKSNDR
pachysandra
PKSPK
Pikes Peak
PKSTN
Pakistan
PKT
packed(pack)
packet
  (package)
pact(agreement)
pea coat
peaked(pointed)
picket(stake)
pocket(pouch)
PKTBK
pocketbook(purse)
pocket book(book)

NGK:ink **P**:pie **R**:air **S**:ice **SH**:show **T**:toy **THN**:thin **TH**:the **V**:of **W**:we **Y**:you **Z**:is **VZHN**:vision

PKTFL
pocketful
PKTGRF
pictograph
pictography
pictographic
PKTHRD
packthread
PKTN
pectin
PKTNF
pocketknife
pocketknives
PKTRL
pectoral(body)
pictorial
PKTSZD
pocket-sized
PKYLDR
peculator
PKYLFRM
poculiform
PKYLRT
peculiarity
peculiarities
PKYLSHN
peculation
PKYLT
peculate
peculated
peculating
PKYLTR
peculator
PKYLYR
peculiar
PKYN
picayune
PKYNR
pecuniary
PKYR
epicure
PKYRN
Epicurean
PL
Apollo
apollo
appall
appeal
appel(feint)
appellee
apple(fruit)
apply
applied
applies
aptly(suitable)
pail(bucket)

pal(friend)
palled
palling
pale(white)
paled
paling
paler
palest
pall(coffin)
pawl(tool)
detent
payola
peal(sound)
peel(skin)
pile
piled
piling
pill
pillow
play
plea(request)
plow, (B)plough
ply(use,join)
plied
plies
Pole(person)
pole(rod)
poled
poling
polio(disease)
poliomyelitis
poll(vote)
pollee(person)
polo(game)
pool(game,water)
pull(tug)
pully(tool)
pullies
opal(stone)
PLB
playboy
plebe
PLBK
playback
pullback(n)
PLBKS
pillbox
pillboxes
PLBL
appealable
playbill
pliable
PLBLT
pliability
PLBN
plebeian

PLBPL
play-by-play
PLBRR
pallbearer
PLBST
plebiscite
PLBZ
plebes(pl)
PLCH
Appalachia
PLCHB
placebo
(religious)
PLCHN
Appalachian
PLD
applaud(clap)
pallid(dull)
payload
plaid(design)
plead(beg)
plod(pace)
plodded
plodding
plodder
PLDKL
political
PLDL
paludal
PLDM
palladium
PLDR
applauder
platter(plate)
plodder
PLDT
plaudit
PLF
pilaf
play-off(n)
PLFL
pailful
playful
PLFR
palfrey
pilfer
PLFRJ
pilferage
PLFRR
pilferer
PLFS
paleface
PLFT
uplift
PLG
epilogue

plague
plagued
plaguing
plug
plugged
plugging
PLGLT
polyglot
PLGM
polygamy
PLGMS
polygamous
PLGN
polygon
PLGR
pellagra
plaguer(plague)
playgoer
PLGRF
paleography, (B)palaeo-
polygraph
PLGRM
pilgrim
PLGRMJ
pilgrimage
PLGRND
playground
PLHS
playhouse
PLJ
apology
apologies
pillage
pillaged
pillaging
pillager
pledge
pledged
pledging
pledgee(person)
pledger
pledgor(law)
PLJDK
apologetic
PLJK
applejack
PLJN
polygyny
PLJR
plagiary
plagiaries
PLJRZ
plagiarize(copy)
plagiarized
PLJRZM
plagiarism

B:by CH:each D:day F:if G:go H:he HW:why J:joy K:cow KS:ax KWL:equal L:all M:may N:in

plagiarizing
PLJST
apologist
PLJTK
apologetic
PLJZ
apologize
  apologized
  apologizing
PLK
appliqué
  appliquéd
  appliquéing
  appliqués
palooka
plaque(teeth,
  award)
pluck(pick)
plucky
  pluckier
  pluckiest
  pluckiness
Polack(person)
polka(music)
pollock(fish)
  pollock(or)
  pollocks
pulque(drink)
PLKBL
applicable
placable(soothe)
placably
PLKBLT
placability
PLKDT
polka dot
PLKLNK
policlinic
  (outpatient)
polyclinic
  (hospital)
PLKN
pelican
PLKNT
applicant
PLKRD
placard
PLKRM
polychrome
PLKRMTK
polychromatic
PLKRT
apple cart
PLKRTD
pulchritude
PLKRTDNS

pulchritudinous
PLKRTYD
pulchritude
PLKRTYDNS
pulchritudinous
PLKS
pillowcase
poleax
  poleaxes
PLKSGLS
Plexiglas
  (trademark)
plexiglass
  (synthetic)
PLKSHN
application
placation
PLKT
placate(soothe)
  placated
  placating
  placater
  placation
placket
polecat
PLKTR
applicator
placater
PLKTRM
plectrum
  plectra(or)
  plectrums
PLKTV
applicative
PLLTHK
paleolithic, (B)palaeo-
PLM
aplomb
plum(fruit)
plumb(lead weight)
plume(feather)
  plumed
  pluming
PLMBB
plumb bob
PLMD
palmetto
PLMJ
plumage
PLMK
polemic
PLMKL
polemical
PLML
pall-mall(game)
pell-mell

(without order)
PLMLTS
poliomyelitis
polio
PLMN
palomino
PLMNG
plumbing
PLMNK
pulmonic
PLMNR
pulmonary
PLMP
plump
PLMR
palmyra
plumber
polymer
PLMS
plumose
PLMSST
polemicist
PLMT
palmetto
playmate
plummet
PLMTH
polymath
PLN
plain(clear,
  simple)
plan(scheme)
  planned
  planning
  planner
plane(air,level)
  planed
  planing
plena
Poland
pollen
Pollyanna
pylon(structure)
PLNCHT
planchet
PLND
Poland
upland
PLNDR
plunder
polyandry
PLNDRM
palindrome
PLNDRS
polyandrous
PLNF

plaintiff
PLNG
appalling(bad)
appealing(nice)
paling(fence)
piling(structure)
pile
PLNGK
plank
plunk
PLNGKNG
planking
PLNGKTN
plankton
PLNJ
plunge
  plunged
  plunging
PLNJR
plunger
PLNKN
palanquin
PLNM
plenum
  plena(or)
  plenums
PLNNG
planning
PLNPTNSHR
plenipotentiary
PLNR
planner
plenary
PLNS
appliance
pliancy
PLNSCHRTD
polyunsaturated
PLNSH
Polynesia
PLNSHN
pollination
Polynesian
PLNSHT
planchette
PLNSNG
plainsong
PLNSPKN
plain-spoken
PLNT
appellant
plaint(complaint)
planet(world)
plant
plenty
pliant(bend)

NGK:ink **P**:pie **R**:air **S**:ice **SH**:show **T**:toy **THN**:thin **TH**:the **V**:of **W**:we **Y**:you **Z**:is **VZHN**:vision

pollinate
pollinated
pollinating
pollinator
PLNTD
planetoid
plenitude
PLNTF
plaintiff
PLNTFL
plentiful
PLNTGRD
plantigrade
PLNTH
plinth(base)
PLNTLJ
paleontology, (B)-
PLNTLJKL laeo-
paleontological, (B)-
PLNTLJST laeo-
paleontologist, (B)
PLNTN -laeo-
plantain
PLNTR
planetary
plantar(foot)
planter(plant)
PLNTRM
planetarium
planetaria(or)
planetariums
PLNTS
plenteous
PLNTSHN
plantation
PLNTSML
planetesimal
PLNTV
plaintive
PLNTYD
plenitude
PLNV
plaintive
PLNZ
pollinize
pollinized
pollinizing
PLNZH
Polynesia
PLNZHN
Polynesian
PLNZM
pleonasm
PLNZMN
plainsman
plainsmen

PLP
pileup
plop
plopped
plopping
pulp
pulpy
pulpier
pulpiest
pulpiness
PLPBL
palpable
palpably
PLPN
pilipino
playpen
PLPRFKT
pluperfect
PLPS
epilepsy
PLPT
palpate
palpated
palpating
palpation
palpator
pulpit
PLPTK
epileptic
PLPTSHN
palpitation
PLPTT
palpitate
palpitated
palpitating
PLPWD
pulpwood
PLR
applier
paler(pale)
pallor(pale)
parlor(room)
pillar(support)
pillory
-ried,-ries
polar
PLRD
Polaroid
(trademark)
PLRL
pleural
pleura
plural(more
than one)
PLRLSTK
pluralistic

PLRLSTKL
pluralistically
PLRLT
plurality
pluralities
PLRLZ
pluralize
pluralized
pluralizing
pluralization
PLRLZM
pluralism
PLRM
playroom
poolroom
PLRS
pleurisy
PLRT
playwright
polarity
polarities
PLRZ
pliers(tool)
polarize
polarized
polarizing
PLRZSHN
polarization
PLS
appaloosa
palace(house)
pelisse(cloak)
pilose(hair)
place(location)
placed
placing
plissé(texture)
plus(add)
police(lawmen)
policed
policing
policy(plan)
policies
pulse(throb)
pulsed
pulsing
PLSB
placebo
PLSD
palisade(fence)
palisaded
palisading
pellucid(clear)
placid(calm)
PLSDT
placidity

PLSH
plush
plushy
plushier
plushiest
plushiness
Polish
polish(make shiny)
polishes
PLSHL
palatial
PLSHLDR
policyholder
PLSHN
appellation
pollution
PLSHR
plowshare
PLSLBK
polysyllabic
PLSLBL
polysyllable
PLSMKR
policy-maker
PLSMN
policeman
policemen
PLSMNT
placement
PLSNT
opalescent
placenta
placentae(or)
placentas
PLSR
placer
pulsar(star)
PLSS
applesauce
PLSSHN
pulsation
PLST
pulsate
pulsated
pulsating
PLSTK
plastic
PLSTKL
plastically
PLSTR
pilaster(motif)
plaster(coating)
polestar(star)
pollster(person)
polyester(material)
PLSTRBRD

B:by **CH**:each **D**:day **F**:if **G**:go **H**:he **HW**:why **J**:joy **K**:cow **KS**:ax **KWL**:equal **L**:all **M**:may **N**:in

plasterboard
PLSTRN
plastron
polystyrene
PLSTRR
plasterer
PLSTST
plasticity
PLSTSZ
plasticize
plasticized
plasticizing
PLSWMN
policewoman
policewomen
PLT
appellate(court)
epaulet(ornament)
palate(mouth)
palette(board)
pallet(tool,bed)
palliate(excuse)
palliated
palliating
pelt(fur,assail)
pellet(bullet)
pilot(guide)
plait(pleat,
braid)
plat(map)
platted
platting
plate(dish,cover)
plated
plating
plateau(level)
pleat(fold in
material)
plight
(adversity)
plot(plan)
plotted
plotting
Pluto(planet)
polite(nice)
politer
politest
polity(political
form)
polities
pollute(dirty)
polluted
polluting
pollution
pullet(fowl)
pullout(n)

PLTBL
palatable
palatably
PLTBYR
Politburo
PLTFL
plateful
PLTFRM
platform
PLTHLN
polyethylene, (B)
PLTHNG polythene
plaything
PLTHR
plethora
PLTHS
pilothouse
PLTHZM
polytheism
PLTJ
pilotage
PLTK
politic
politicked
politicking
politico
PLTKL
apolitical
political
PLTKNK
polytechnic
PLTKRS
plutocracy
plutocracies
PLTKRT
plutocrat
PLTKRTK
plutocratic
PLTKS
politics
poll tax
poll taxes
PLTL
palatal
PLTLT
pilot light
PLTN
palatine(cape)
platen(roller)
platoon
(soldiers)
PLTNG
plating(cover)
PLTNK
Platonic(or)platonic
PLTNKL

platonically
PLTNM
platinum
plutonium
PLTNT
pollutant
PLTPS
platypus
PLTR
palter(trickery)
paltry(trifling)
paltrier
paltriest
paltriness
platter(plate)
poultry(fowls)
PLTRGST
poltergeist
PLTRN
poltroon(coward)
PLTRNR
poltroonery
PLTS
poultice
PLTSHN
politician
PLTSRPRZ
Pulitzer Prize
PLTTD
platitude
PLTTDNS
platitudinous
PLTTYD
platitude
PLTTYDNS
platitudinous
PLTV
palliative
PLV
pahlavi(money)
Pahlavi(person)
PLVK
pelvic
PLVL
pluvial
PLVLT
pole vault(n)
pole-vault(v)
PLVNL
polyvinyl
PLVR
palaver
pullover
PLVRZ
pulverize
-ized,-izing

PLVRZBL
pulverizable
PLVRZSHN
pulverization
PLVS
pelvis
pluvious
PLWD
plywood
PLWG
polliwog
PLYLT
pullulate
pullulated
pullulating
pullulation
pullulative
PLYN
pillion
PLYRTHN
polyurethane
PLZ
applause
palsy(paralysis)
palsied
palsies
piles(ailment)
plaza
pleas(plea)
please
pleased
pleasing
pleaser
PLZBL
plausible
plausibly
PLZBLT
plausibility
PLZHN
plosion
PLZHR
pleasure
pleasured
pleasuring
PLZHRBL
pleasurable
pleasurably
PLZM
plasm
plasma
PLZNT
pleasant
PLZNTR
pleasantry
pleasantries
PLZV

plosive
PLZWLZ
palsy-walsy(slang)
PM
  opium
  palm(hand, tree)
  palmy
    palmier
    palmiest
  pam(card)
  Pima(tribe)
  pima(cotton)
  P.M.(or)P.M.(or)p.m.
    post meridiem
  poem
  puma(animal)
PMD
  pomade
PMFLT
  pamphlet
PMFLTR
  pamphleteer
PMGRNT
  pomegranate
PMKN
  pemmican
PMKTN
  pima cotton
PML
  pommel(beat,knob)
  (or)pummel, (B)- lled,
PMN   -lling
  ape-man
  ape-men
PMNT
  payment
  pimento
PMP
  pimp
  pomp(display)
  Pompeii
  pump
PMPDR
  pompadour
PMPKN
  pumpkin
PMPL
  pimple
    pimpled
  pimply
PMPM
  pom-pom(cannon)
  pompon(or)
  pompom
    (decoration)
PMPN

pompano
pompon
PMPR
  pamper
PMPRNKL
  pumpernickel
PMPS
  pompous
PMPST
  pomposity
PMPZ
  pampas
PMS
  pomace(pulp)
  pumice(rock)
PMSHS
  pomaceous
PMST
  palmist
PMSTR
  palmistry
  paymaster
PN
  apian(bees)
    apiarian
    apiarist
    apiary
  apnea(breath)
    apneic
  open
  paean(song)
  pain(hurt)
  pan(metal dish)
    panned
    panning
  pane(glass)
  panne(cloth)
  pawn(chess,loan)
  peen(hammer)
  pen(ink)
    penned
    penning
  pen(enclosure)
    pent(or)
    penned
    penning
  penny(money)
    pennies
  peon(person)
  peony(plant)
    peonies
  piano(music)
  pin(sharp wire)
    pinned
    pinning
  pine(tree,

    emotion)
    pined
    pining
  pony(horse)
    ponies
  pun(joke)
    punned
    punning
    punster
  upon
PNBL
  pinball
PNBRKR
  pawnbroker
PNCH
  paunch(belly)
    paunches
    paunchy
    paunchier
    paunchiest
    paunchiness
  penuche(candy)
  pinch(squeeze)
    pinches
  poncho
    (clothing)
  punch(hit)
    punches
    punchy
    punchier
    punchiest
    punchiness
PNCHBK
  pinchbeck
PNCHKRD
  punch card
PNCHN
  pension(money)
    pensioner
  puncheon
PNCHNT
  penchant
PNCHR
  pinscher
  puncher
PNCHT
  pinch hit(n)
  pinch-hit(v)
    pinch-hit
    -hitting,-hitter
PND
  append
  open-eyed
  panda
  pond(water)
  pound(weight)

  upend
PNDD
  pandowdy
    pandowdies
PNDFLSH
  pound-foolish
    penny-wise
PNDJ
  appendage
PNDKMNG
  up-and-coming
PNDKS
  appendix
    appendixes(or)
    appendices
PNDKT
  pandect
PNDKTM
  appendectomy
PNDLM
  pendulum
PNDMK
  pandemic
PNDMNM
  pandemonium
PNDN
  up-and-down(adj)
PNDNG
  pending
PNDNT
  appendant
  pendant(n)
  pendent(adj)
PNDR
  pander
  Pandora
  ponder(think)
PNDRBL
  ponderable
PNDRS
  ponderous
PNDSTRLNG
  pound sterling
PNDSTS
  appendicitis
PNDT
  pundit
PNDYLM
  pendulum
PNDYLS
  pendulous
PNF
  penknife
    penknives
  pontiff
PNFL

B:by **CH**:each **D**:day **F**:if **G**:go **H**:he **HW**:why **J**:joy **K**:cow **KS**:ax **KWL**:equal **L**:all **M**:may **N**:in

painful
PNFLSH
pound-foolish
  penny-wise
PNFR
pan-fry
  pan-fried
  pan-fries
pinafore
PNFTHR
pinfeather
PNG
painting
pang(feeling)
ping(sound)
pong
PNGGLN
pangolin
PNGGWD
pinguid
PNGGWN
penguin
PNGJ
Pangaea
PNGK
pink(color)
pinkeye
pinkie(or
pinky
  pinkies
punk
PNGKCHL
punctual
PNGKCHLT
punctuality
PNGKCHR
puncture
  punctured
  puncturing
PNGKCHRBL
puncturable
PNGKCHSHN
punctuation
PNGKCHT
punctuate
  punctuated
  punctuating
PNGKCHTR
punctuator
PNGKRS
pancreas
PNGKTL
punctilio
PNGKTLS
punctilious
PNGLN

pangolin
PNGPNG
ping-pong
PNGWN
penguin
PNHD
pinhead
PNHL
pinhole
PNHLDR
penholder
PNHNDD
openhanded
PNHNDL
panhandle
  panhandled
  panhandling
  panhandler
PNHNLR
panhandler
PNHRTD
openhearted
PNHRTH
open-hearth
PNHWL
pinwheel
PNHZ
pantyhose
PNJ
appanage
Pangaea
peonage
pongee
PNJLM
pendulum
PNJLS
pendulous
PNJNS
pungency
PNJNT
pungent
PNJRK
panegyric
PNJRKL
panegyrical
PNK
apneic(breath)
apnea
panic
  panicked
  panicking
  panicky
PNKK
pancake
PNKL
pentacle(star)

pinnacle(top)
  pinnacled
  pinnacling
pinochle(game)
PNKLR
painkiller
PNKRMTK
panchromatic
PNKRS
pancreas
PNKRTK
pancreatic
PNKSHN
pincushion
PNKST
Pentecost
PNKSTRKN
panic-stricken
PNL
panel
penal(law)
pianola
PNLJ
penology
PNLJKL
penological
PNLJST
penologist
PNLST
panelist
PNLT
penalty
  penalties
penult
PNLTMT
penultimate
PNLZ
penalize
  penalized
  penalizing
PNLZSHN
penalization
PNM
eponym
Panama
pen name
PNMBR
penumbra
  penumbrae(or)
  penumbras
PNMKNLZN
Panama Canal Zone
PNMN
penman
PNMNDD
open-minded

PNMNN
Panamanian
PNMNSHP
penmanship
PNMRKN
Pan-American
PNMST
Panama City
PNMTHT
open-mouthed
PNN
pennon
PNNCHL
peninsula
PNND
open-end
PNNDD
open-ended
PNNG
painting
PNNS
penance
PNNSHL
peninsula
PNNSHT
open-and-shut
PNNSL
peninsula
PNNSLR
peninsular
PNNT
opponent
pennant(flag)
penny ante(n)
penny-ante(adj)
poignant
PNP
pinup
PNPL
panoply
  panoplies
pineapple
PNPNT
pinpoint
PNPTK
panoptic(or)
  panoptical
PNR
eye-opener
opener
pannier
  (basket)
pioneer
PNRM
panorama
PNRMK

panoramic
PNRMKL
panoramically
PNRS
penurious
PNS
openness
panacea
pants
penis
  penes(or)
  penises
pounce
  pounced
  pouncing
PNSD
poinsettia
PNSH
panache
punish
  punishes
PNSHBL
punishable
PNSHD
Upanishad
PNSHMNT
punishment
PNSHN
pension
  pensioner
PNSHNR
pensionary
  pensionaries
PNSHP
pawnshop
PNSHR
pinscher(dog)
PNSL
pencil (B)-lled, - lling
PNSLN
penicillin
PNSLVN
Pennsylvania
PNSLVNY
Pennsylvania
PNSM
pianissimo
PNSN
pince-nez
PNSR
pincer
pinscher(dog)
pouncer(pounce)
PNSSM
open sesame
PNST

pianist
poinsettia
PNSTK
open stock
penstock(gate)
PNSTR
punster
PNSTRP
pinstripe
PNSV
pensive
PNT
appoint
appointee
paint
pant(breathe)
panty
  panties
peanut
pent(or)penned
pen
pennate(feather)
pint(volume)
pinto(horse)
point(tip,
  direction)
punt(kick)
PNTBLNGK
point-blank
PNTBRSH
paintbrush
  paintbrushes
PNTD
pentad
Pentateuch
PNTF
pontiff
PNTFKL
pontifical
PNTFKT
pontificate
  pontificated
  pontificating
  pontification
PNTGN
pentagon
PNTGNL
pentagonal
PNTGRF
pantograph
PNTHDRL
pentahedral
PNTHDRN
pentahedron
  pentahedra(or)
  pentahedrons

PNTHN
pantheon
PNTHR
panther
PNTHS
penthouse
PNTHSTK
pantheistic
PNTHZ
pantyhose
PNTHZM
pantheism
PNTK
Pontiac
PNTKL
pentacle
PNTKST
Pentecost
PNTL
panatela
pintle(pin)
ponytail
PNTLNZ
pantaloons
PNTLS
pointless
PNTMM
pantomime
  pantomimed
  pantomiming
PNTMMK
pantomimic
PNTMMST
pantomimist
PNTMNT
appointment
PNTMTR
pentameter
PNTN
pontoon
PNTNG
painting
PNTNS
penitence
PNTNSHL
penitential
PNTNSHR
penitentiary
  penitentiaries
PNTNT
penitent
PNTP
pent-up
PNTR
appointer
appointor(law)

painter
pantry
  pantries
pointer
PNTRBL
penetrable
penetrably
PNTRBLT
penetrability
PNTRL
penetralia
PNTRMTR
penetrometer
PNTRSHN
penetration
PNTRT
penetrate
  -trated,-trating
PNTS
pants
PNTST
pantsuit
PNTSZ
pint-size
  pint-sized
PNTTHLN
pentathlon
PNTTK
Pentateuch
PNTTYK
Pentateuch
PNTV
appointive
PNTWST
pantywaist
PNTZ
pontes
PNVS
penknives
PNWL
pinwale
pinwheel(toy)
PNWR
peignoir
PNWRK
openwork
PNWRM
pinworm
PNWRTH
pennyworth
PNWT
pennyweight
PNWZ
penny-wise
PNYN
opinion

---

pinion
PNYNS
poignancy
PNYNT
poignant
PNYNTD
opinionated
PNYNTV
opinionative
PNYR
pannier
penury
PNYRD
poniard
PNYRS
penurious
PNYT
piñata
PNZ
pansy(plant)
　pansies
panties
panty
pons
pontes
PNZR
panzer
PNZTKNG
painstaking
PP
pap
papa(dad)
papaw
peep(look)
pep(energy)
peppy
　peppier
　peppiest
　peppily
　peppiness
pip
　pipped
　pipping
pipe(tube)
　piped
　piping
　piper
pooh-pooh
poop(deck,fatigue)
poop(slang)
　(information)
pop(dad,music)
pop(burst)
　popped
　popping
pope(or)

Pope(title)
poppy(flower)
　poppies
pup
puppy
　puppies
PPD
popeyed
PPDK
poop deck
PPFL
pipeful
PPHL
peephole
PPKN
pipkin
PPKRN
popcorn
PPL
papal
papilla
　papillae
people
　peopled
　peopling
PPLKS
apoplexy
PPLKTK
apoplectic
PPLM
peplum
　pepla
PPLN
pipeline
poplin
PPLNNS
papal nuncio
PPLR
poplar(tree)
PPLT
papillote
PPN
pippin
PPNGTM
peeping Tom
PPR
paper
papery
pauper(poor)
pepper(spice)
peppery
　pepperier
　pepperiest
　pepperiness
peeper(looker)
piper(pipe)

popper(pop)
potpourri
　(collection)
PPRBK
paperback
PPRBND
paperbound
PPRHNGR
paperhanger
PPRK
paprika
PPRKRN
peppercorn
PPRL
pep rally
　pep rallies
PPRMNT
peppermint
PPRMSH
papier-maché
PPRN
pepperoni
PPRS
papyrus
　papyri(or)
　papyruses
PPRTS
paparazzo
　paparazzi
PPRWRK
paperwork
PPRWT
paperweight
PPS
papacy,-cies
papoose
PPSH
peep show
PPSKL
Pepsi-Cola
　(trademark)
Popsicle (trademark)
PPSKWK
pipsqueak
PPSMR
Pap smear
　Pap test
PPSN
pepsin
PPST
papist
peep sight
PPSTM
pipestem
PPT
pipette(tube)

pipetted
pipetting
pooped(fatigued)
poppet(oar,beam)
puppet(toy)
PPTK
pep talk
peptic
PPTNT
pup tent
PPTR
puppeteer
puppetry
PPTST
Pap test
　Pap smear
PPVR
popover
PPVRN
papaverine
PPY
papaya
Papua
PPYL
papule
PPYLR
popular(liked)
PPYLRT
popularity
PPYLRZ
popularize
　popularized
　popularizing
　popularizer
PPYLRZSHN
popularization
PPYLS
populace(masses)
populous(full
　of people)
PPYLSHN
population
PPYLT
populate
　populated
　populating
PPYMSH
papier-maché
PPYNGN
Papua New Guinea
PPYT
papillote
PR
apiary(bees)
appear
opera

pair(two)
par(average)
  parred
  parring
pare(trim)
  pared
  paring
pariah(outcast)
parry(ward off)
  parried
  parries
pear(fruit)
peer(look,equal)
per(prep)
Peru
pier(structure)
Pierre
poor(not rich)
pore(tiny
  opening)
pore(ponder)
  pored
  poring
pour(flow)
power(ability)
pray(implore)
prey(victim)
pro(favor)
  professional
prow(ship's bow)
pry(snoop,force)
  pried
  pries
purr(sound)
pyorrhea(disease)
pyre(fire)
upper(top half)

PRB
probe
  probed
  probing
PRBBL
probable
probably
PRBBLT
probability
  probabilities
PRBKL
parbuckle
  parbuckled
  parbuckling
PRBL
operable
parable
parabola
parboil

PRBLK
parabolic
PRBLKL
parabolical
PRBLM
problem
PRBLMTK
problematic
PRBLMTKL
problematical
PRBND
prebend
PRBRM
opprobrium
PRBRS
opprobrious
PRBSHN
approbation
probation
PRBSHNR
probationary(adj)
probationer
  (person)
PRBSKS
proboscis
  proboscises(or)
  proboscides
PRBSS
proboscis
  proboscises(or)
  proboscides
PRBT
probate
  probated
  probating
probity
PRBTR
approbatory
PRBTV
probative
PRCH
approach
  approaches
parch(dry)
  parches
perch
  perches
porch
  porches
preach
  preaches
PRCHBL
approachable
PRCHGL
Portugal
PRCHGZ

Portuguese
PRCHLK
portulaca
PRCHMNT
parchment
PRCHNS
perchance
PRCHR
aperture
preacher
PRCHRN
Percheron
PRCHS
purchase
  purchased
  purchasing
  purchaser
PRCHSBL
purchasable
PRCHSR
purchaser
PRCHZ
Parcheesi
PRD
operetta(music)
parade(display)
  paraded
  parading
parody
  parodied
  parodies
party(fun,person)
  parties
perdu
period
pretty(beautiful)
pride
  prided
  priding
prod
  prodded
  prodding
proud(pride)
prude
  prudish
PRDBL
portable
PRDGL
prodigal
PRDGLT
prodigality
  prodigalities
PRDJ
prodigy
  prodigies
PRDJS

prodigious
PRDJSCHN
predigestion
PRDJST
predigest
PRDK
periodic
portico
PRDKBL
predicable
predicably
PRDKBLT
predicability
PRDKL
particle
periodical
PRDKMNT
predicament
PRDKS
paradox
  paradoxes
PRDKSHN
predication
prediction
production
PRDKSKL
paradoxical
PRDKT
predicate
  predicated
  predicating
predict
product
PRDKTBL
predictable
predictably
PRDKTR
predictor
PRDKTV
predictive
productive
PRDKTVT
productivity
  productivities
PRDL
portal
PRDLKSHN
predilection
PRDM
paradigm
per diem
PRDMNNT
predominant
PRDMNT
predominate
  predominated

B:by **CH**:each **D**:day **F**:if **G**:go **H**:he **HW**:why **J**:joy **K**:cow **KS**:ax **KWL**:equal **L**:all **M**:may **N**:in

predominating
predomination
PRDN
pardon
PRDNBL
pardonable
pardonably
PRDNCHL
prudential
PRDNR
partner
PRDNRSHP
partnership
PRDNS
prudence
PRDNSHL
prudential
PRDNT
prudent
PRDR
operator
prudery
pruderies
prouder
PRDRBL
perdurable
PRDS
apparatus
paradise
produce
produced
producing
PRDSBL
producible
PRDSH
prudish
PRDSHN
perdition
predation
PRDSHS
predacious
PRDSPZ
predispose
predisposed
predisposing
PRDSPZSHN
predisposition
PRDSR
producer
PRDSS
predecease
predeceased
predeceasing
PRDSSR
predecessor
PRDST

parodist
periodicity
periodicities
proudest
PRDSTN
predestine
predestined
predestining
PRDSTNSHN
predestination
PRDT
predate
predated
predating
PRDTP
prototype
PRDTR
predator
predatory
PRDTRMN
predetermine
predetermined
predetermining
PRDVNCHR
peradventure
PRDY
perdu
PRDYRBL
perdurable
PRDYS
produce
produced
producing
producer
PRDYSBL
producible
PRDYSR
producer
PRDZ
paradise
PRDZN
partisan
PRF
paraph(mark)
parfait(food)
PRFB
prefab
PRFBRKSHN
prefabrication
PRFBRKT
prefabricate
prefabricated
prefabricating
PRFD
perfidy
perfidies

PRFDK
prophetic
PRFDS
perfidious
PRFGYR
prefigure
prefigured
prefiguring
PRFGYRSHN
prefiguration
PRFGYRTV
prefigurative
PRFKCHR
prefecture
PRFKS
prefix
prefixes
PRFKSHN
perfection
PRFKSHNZM
perfectionism
PRFKT
perfect(flawless)
perfecto
prefect(official)
PRFKTBL
perfectible
PRFKTBLT
perfectibility
perfectibilities
PRFL
powerful
profile(face)
profiled
profiling
purfle
purfled
purfling
PRFLGS
profligacy
profligacies
PRFLGT
profligate
PRFLKSS
prophylaxis
prophylaxes
PRFLKTK
prophylactic
PRFLNG
purfling(edging)
PRFLT
preflight
PRFN
paraffin
profane
profaned

profaning
PRFND
profound
PRFNDT
profundity
profundities
PRFNGKTR
perfunctory
perfunctorily
PRFNLY
paraphernalia
PRFNSHN
profanation
PRFNT
profanity
profanities
PRFR
periphery
peripheries
porphyry
porphyries
prefer
preferred
preferring
proffer
PRFRBL
preferable
preferably
PRFRD
proofread
proofread
proofreading
PRFRDR
proofreader
PRFRL
peripheral
PRFRM
perform
PRFRMNS
performance
PRFRMNT
preferment
PRFRNCHL
preferential
PRFRNLY
paraphernalia
PRFRNS
preference
PRFRNSHL
preferential
PRFRS
perforce
poriferous
PRFRSHN
perforation
PRFRSS

periphrasis
  periphrases
PRFRSTK
  paraphrastic
  (restate)
  periphrastic
  (around)
PRFRT
  perforate
  perforated
  perforating
PRFRTR
  perforator
PRFRZ
  paraphrase
  paraphrased
  paraphrasing
PRFS
  preface
  prefaced
  prefacing
  profess
  professes
  prophecy(n)
  prophecies
  prophesy(v)
  prophesied
  prophesies
PRFSHN
  profession
PRFSHNL
  professional
PRFSHNS
  proficiency
  proficiencies
PRFSHNT
  proficient
PRFSR
  professor
PRFSRL
  professorial
PRFT
  profit(gain)
  prophet(predictor)
PRFTBL
  profitable
  profitably
PRFTK
  prophetic
PRFTKL
  prophetical
PRFTKNG
  profit-taking
  (n,adj)
PRFTR
  prefatory

profiteer
PRFTS
  prophetess
PRFYM
  perfume
  perfumed
  perfuming
PRFYMR
  perfumer
PRFYS
  profuse
PRFYZ
  perfuse
  perfused
  perfusing
PRFYZHN
  perfusion
  (injection)
  profusion
  (abundance)
PRG
  Prague
  prig
  prigged
  prigging
  priggish
  priggery
PRGL
  pergola
PRGMTK
  pragmatic
PRGMTKL
  pragmatical
PRGMTST
  pragmatist
PRGMTZM
  pragmatism
PRGN
  paragon
PRGNBL
  pregnable
PRGNNS
  pregnancy
  pregnancies
PRGNNT
  pregnant
PRGNSS
  prognosis
  prognoses
PRGNSTK
  prognostic
PRGNSTKSHN
  prognostication
PRGNSTKT
  prognosticate
  prognosticated

prognosticating
PRGNSTKTR
  prognosticator
PRGNSZ
  prognoses
  prognosis
PRGNTHS
  prognathous
PRGRF
  paragraph
  pyrography
PRGRK
  paregoric
PRGRM
  program,(B)- gramme
  programmed
  programming
  programmer
PRGRMNG
  programming
PRGRMR
  programmer
PRGRMTK
  programmatic
PRGRN
  peregrine
PRGRNSHN
  peregrination
PRGRNT
  peregrinate
  peregrinated
  peregrinating
PRGRP
  peer group
PRGRS
  progress
  progresses
PRGRSHN
  progression
PRGRSV
  progressive
PRGRSV
  progressive
PRGRSVZM
  progressivism
PRGSH
  priggish
PRGSHN
  purgation(wash)
PRGTR
  purgatory
PRGTV
  purgative
PRGW
  Paraguay
PRGZST

preexist
PRGZSTNS
  preexistence
PRH
  aparejo
PRHBSHN
  prohibition
PRHBT
  prohibit
PRHBTR
  prohibitor
  prohibitory
PRHBTV
  prohibitive
PRHLN
  parhelion(spot)
  parhelia
  perihelion
  (near point)
  perihelia
PRHLYN
  parhelion(spot)
  parhelia
  perihelion
  (near point)
  perihelia
PRHND
  apprehend
PRHNSBL
  apprehensible
PRHNSHN
  apprehension
PRHNSL
  prehensile
PRHNSV
  apprehensive
PRHPS
  perhaps
PRHS
  poorhouse
  powerhouse
PRHSTRK
  prehistoric
PRJ
  perigee
  porridge
  purge
  purged
  purging
  purger
PRJDS
  prejudice
  prejudicing
  prejudiced
PRJDSHL
  prejudicial

B:by **CH**:each **D**:day **F**:if **G**:go **H**:he **HW**:why **J**:joy **K**:cow **KS**:ax **KWL**:equal **L**:all **M**:may **N**:in

PRJJ
prejudge
prejudged
prejudging
PRJJMNT
prejudgment
PRJKSHN
projection
PRJKT
project
PRJKTL
projectile
PRJKTR
projector
PRJKTV
projective
PRJN
progeny
progenies
PRJNTR
progenitor
PRJR
perjure(lie)
perjured
perjuring
perjury
perjuries
projeria(age)
purger(cleanser)
purge
PRJRR
perjurer
PRJTV
purgative
PRK
park
parka
parquet
perique(tobacco)
perk(slang)
perquisite
perk
perky
perkier
perkiest
perkiness
pork
prick
pyrrhic
PRKGNSHN
precognition
PRKGNTV
precognitive
PRKL
parochial
percale

prickle
prickled
prickling
prickly
pricklier
prickliest
prickliness
PRKLD
preclude
precluded
precluding
preclusion
PRKLM
proclaim
PRKLMSHN
proclamation
PRKLS
upper-class(adj)
upper class
upper classes
PRKLSHN
percolation
PRKLSMN
upperclassman
upperclassmen
PRKLSV
preclusive
PRKLT
percolate
percolated
percolating
percolation
PRKLTR
percolator
PRKLVT
proclivity
proclivities
PRKLZHN
preclusion
PRKMBNT
procumbent
PRKNS
Preakness
PRKNSHS
preconscious
PRKNSL
precancel
PRKNSNZL
Parkinson's law
PRKNSPSHN
preconception
PRKNSV
preconceive
preconceived
preconceiving
PRKPN

porcupine
PRKPT
per capita
PRKR
porker
PRKRNT
procreant
PRKRS
precarious
PRKRSHN
procreation
PRKRSR
precursor
precursory
PRKRSTNSHN
procrastination
PRKRSTNT
procrastinate
procrastinated
procrastinating
PRKRSTNTR
procrastinator
PRKRT
procreate
procreated
procreating
PRKRTR
procreator
PRKS
proxy
proxies
Pyrex
(trademark)
uppercase(n)(or)
upper case(n)
upper-case(v)
-cased,-casing
PRKSD
peroxide
peroxided
peroxiding
PRKSHN
precaution
percussion(music)
PRKSHNR
precautionary
PRKSHS
precautious
(caution)
precocious
PRKSLN
pyroxylin
PRKSLNS
par excellence
PRKSM
proximo

PRKSML
proximal
PRKSMSHN
approximation
PRKSMT
approximate
approximated
approximating
proximate
proximity
proximities
PRKSMTV
approximative
proximative
PRKSS
praxis
praxes
PRKSV
percussive
PRKSZ
praxes(pl)
praxis
PRKSZM
paroxysm
PRKSZML
paroxysmal
PRKT
apricot
parakeet
pricket(spike)
uppercut
PRKTKBL
practicable
practicably
PRKTKBLT
practicability
PRKTKL
practical
PRKTKLT
practicality
practicalities
PRKTKM
practicum
PRKTLJ
proctology
PRKTR
parquetry
precatory
proctor
PRKTS
practice
practise(B)
practiced
practised(B)
practicing
practising(B)

NGK:ink P:pie R:air S:ice SH:show T:toy THN:thin TH:the V:of W:we Y:you Z:is VZHN:vision

PRKTSHN
practition
PRKTSHNR
practitioner
PRKTSKP
proctoscope
PRKTSR
practicer
PRKW
parkway
PRKWZT
perquisite
PRKYP
preoccupy
  preoccupied
  preoccupies
PRKYPN
porcupine
PRKYPNS
preoccupancy
PRKYPSHN
preoccupation
PRKYR
procure
  procured
  procuring
PRKYRBL
procurable
PRKYRMNT
procurement
PRKYRR
procurer
PRKYRTR
procurator
PRL
 April
 apparel, (B)-lled
 parlay(bet)
 parley(confer)
 parole
  paroled
  paroling
 parolee
 payroll
 pearl(gem)
 pearly
  -lier, -liest
 peril(danger)
  (B)-lled, -lling
 purl(stitch)
PRLD
 prelude
PRLFK
 prolific
PRLFL
 April fool

PRLFLZD
 April Fools' Day
PRLFRT
 proliferate
  proliferated
  proliferating
  proliferation
PRLG
 prologue
PRLJST
 paralogist
PRLJSTK
 paralogistic
PRLJZM
 paralogism
PRLKS
 parallax
 prolix
PRLKST
 prolixity
PRLKYTR
 prolocutor
PRLL
 parallel
PRLLGRM
 parallelogram
PRLLZM
 parallelism
PRLMNR
 preliminary
  preliminaries
PRLMNT
 parliament
PRLMNTR
 parliamentary
PRLMNTRN
 parliamentarian
PRLN
 praline
 purlin(timber)
 purloin(to steal)
PRLNG
 prolong
PRLNGSHN
 prolongation
PRLNGT
 prolongate
  prolongated
  prolongating
PRLNS
 parlance
PRLPSS
 prolepsis
  prolepses
PRLR
 parlor, (B)parlour

 prowler
PRLS
 peerless
 perilous(danger)
 powerless
 prelacy
PRLSS
 paralysis
  paralyses
PRLT
 prelate
PRLTK
 paralytic
PRLTRN
 proletarian
PRLTRT
 proletariat
PRLZ
 paralyze
  paralyzed
  paralyzing
PRLZHN
 prolusion
PRM
 pram(boat)
 prim(neat)
  primmer
  primmest
 prime(first)
  primed
  priming
 primer(book)
 Purim(feast)
PRMBL
 permeable
 preamble
PRMBLT
 permeability
PRMBYLSHN
 perambulation
PRMBYLT
 perambulate
  perambulated
  perambulating
PRMBYLTR
 perambulator
PRMCHL
 pari-mutuel
PRMCHR
 premature
PRMD
 pyramid
PRMDK
 paramedic
PRMDKL
 paramedical

 premedical
PRMDL
 pyramidal
PRMDN
 prima donna
PRMDTSHN
 premeditation
PRMDTT
 premeditate
  premeditated
  premeditating
PRMFRST
 perma frost
PRMFSH
 prima facie
PRMJNCHR
 primogeniture
PRMJNTR
 primogenitor
PRML
 Permalloy
  (trademark)
 primal
PRMLGSHN
 promulgation
PRMLGT
 promulgate
  promulgated
  promulgating
PRMLGTR
 promulgator
PRMM
 premium
PRMN
 pyromania
PRMND
 promenade
  promenaded
  promenading
PRMNK
 pyromaniac
PRMNNS
 permanence
 preeminence
 prominence
PRMNNT
 permanent
 preeminent
 prominent
PRMNSHN
 premonition
PRMNT
 paramount
PRMNTR
 premonitory
 promontory

B:by CH:each D:day F:if G:go H:he HW:why J:joy K:cow KS:ax KWL:equal L:all M:may N:in

PRMNY
pyromania
PRMP
primp
PRMPLFR
preamplifier
PRMPSHN
preemption
PRMPT
preempt
prompt
PRMPTR
peremptory
peremptorily
peremptoriness
(no debate)
preemptor
(possession)
preemptory
prompter
PRMPTV
preemptive
PRMR
paramour
premier(chief)
premiere
(first showing)
premiered
premiering
primary(first)
primaries
primarily
primer(book)
primmer
primmest
prim
PRMRDL
primordial
PRMRL
primarily
PRMRT
prime rate
PRMRTL
premarital
PRMRZ
primaries
primary
primrose
PRMS
premise(land,
statement)
premised
premising
primacy(first)
primacies
promise(pledge)

promised
promising
PRMSBL
permissible
permissibly
PRMSBLT
permissibility
PRMSHM
paramecium
paramecia
PRMSHN
permeation
permission
promotion
PRMSKYS
promiscuous
PRMSKYT
promiscuity
promiscuities
PRMSN
puromycin
PRMSNG
promising
PRMSR
promissory
PRMSS
premises(area,
statements)
PRMST
uppermost
PRMSV
permissive
PRMSZ
premises(area,
statements)
PRMT
permeate
permeated
permeating
permit
permitted
permitting
primate(animal)
promote
promoted
promoting
prompt
PRMTBL
promotable
PRMTHS
Prometheus
PRMTL
promptly
PRMTR
parameter(math)
perimeter

(boundary)
premature
promoter
PRMTRK
pyrometric(adj)
pyrometer(n)
PRMTV
primitive
PRMTVZM
primitivism
PRMTYR
premature
PRMVL
primeval
PRMYCHL
pari-mutuel
PRMYM
premium
PRMYR
premier(chief)
premiere(first
showing)
premiered
premiering
PRMYT
permute
permuted
permuting
PRMYTBL
permutable
PRMYTSHN
permutation
PRN
apiarian
apron(garment)
epergne
paranoia
piranha
preen
prone
prune(fruit)
prune(cut)
pruned,pruning
PRND
paranoid
PRNG
prong
PRNGD
pronged
PRNGK
prank
PRNGKSH
prankish
PRNGKSTR
prankster
PRNGMNTS

praying mantis
PRNGRF
pornography
PRNGRFK
pornographic
PRNJR
porringer
PRNK
paranoiac
PRNL
perennial
PRNM
per annum
PRNMZH
paronomasia
PRNN
pronoun
PRNNS
pronounce
pronounced
pronouncing
PRNNSBL
pronounceable
PRNNSMNT
pronouncement
PRNNSSHN
pronunciation
PRNRML
paranormal
PRNS
appearance
prance
pranced
prancing
prancer
prince
PRNSHN
pronation
PRNSHS
pernicious
PRNSKNSRT
prince consort
PRNSL
princely
princelier
princeliest
PRNSLNG
princeling
PRNSPL
principal(chief)
principle
(basic rule)
principled
PRNSPLD
principled
PRNSPLT

NGK:ink P:pie R:air S:ice SH:show T:toy THN:thin TH:the V:of W:we Y:you Z:is VZHN:vision

principality
principalities
PRNSS
princess
princesses
PRNT
apparent
parent
print
pronate
pronated
pronating
pronation
pronto
PRNTBL
printable
PRNTHD
parenthood
PRNTHSS
parenthesis
parentheses
PRNTHSZ
parenthesize
parenthesized
parenthesizing
PRNTHTK
parenthetic
PRNTHTKL
parenthetical
PRNTJ
parentage
PRNTL
parental
prenatal
PRNTS
apprentice
PRNTSHP
apprenticeship
PRNTT
printout
PRNY
paranoia
piranha
PRNZ
Pyrenees
PRP
apropos
prepay
prepaid
prop
propped
propping
PRPCHL
perpetual
PRPCHSHN
perpetuation

PRPCHT
perpetuate
perpetuated
perpetuating
PRPCHTR
perpetuator
PRPD
prepaid
prepay
PRPGND
propaganda
PRPGNDZ
propagandize
propagandized
propagandizing
PRPGSHN
propagation
PRPGT
propagate
propagated
propagating
PRPGTR
propagator
PRPKJ
prepackage
prepackaged
prepackaging
PRPL
propel
propelled
propelling
propeller
purple
purplish
PRPLJ
paraplegia
PRPLJK
paraplegic
PRPLKS
perplex
perplexes
PRPLKST
perplexed
perplexity
perplexities
PRPLNT
propellant
PRPLR
propeller
PRPLSH
purplish
PRPLSHN
propulsion
PRPLSV
propulsive
PRPMNT

prepayment
PRPN
propane
PRPND
propound
PRPNDKYLR
perpendicular
PRPNDRNS
preponderance
PRPNDRNT
preponderant
PRPNDRT
preponderate
preponderated
preponderating
PRPNGKWT
propinquity
propinquities
PRPNNT
proponent
PRPNST
propensity
propensities
PRPR
prepare
prepared
preparing
proper
PRPRBL
appropriable
PRPRDNS
preparedness
PRPRFSHNL
paraprofessional
PRPRSHN
appropriation
preparation
proportion
PRPRSHNL
proportional
PRPRSHNT
proportionate
proportionated
proportionating
PRPRT
appropriate
appropriated
appropriating
property
propertied
properties
propriety
proprieties
purport
PRPRTR
appropriator

preparatory
proprietary
proprietaries
proprietor
PRPRTRS
proprietress
proprietresses
PRPRTV
appropriative
preparative
PRPS
porpoise
purpose
purposed
purposing
PRPSHS
propitious
PRPSHSHN
propitiation
PRPSHT
propitiate
propitiated
propitiating
PRPSHTR
propitiator
propitiatory
PRPSTRS
preposterous
PRPT
parapet
PRPTRSHN
perpetration
PRPTRT
perpetrate
perpetrated
perpetrating
PRPTRTR
perpetrator
PRPTT
perpetuity
perpetuities
PRPTTK
peripatetic
PRPTYT
perpetuity
perpetuities
PRPYS
prepuce
PRPZ
propose
proposed
proposing
PRPZL
proposal
PRPZM
priapism

PRPZS
prepossess
prepossesses
PRPZSHN
preposition
(relation)
proposition
(plan)
PRR
a priori
parure(jewelry)
prairie(land)
prayer
prier(pry)
prior(previous)
priory(monastery)
priories
uproar
PRRD
pro rata
PRRDN
preordain
PRRGSHN
prerogation
PRRGTV
prerogative
PRRJNS
pruriginous
PRRKRD
prerecord
PRRKWZT
prerequisite
(requirement)
PRRNJ
prearrange
prearranged
prearranging
PRRNJMNT
prearrangement
PRRNS
prurience
PRRNT
prurient
PRRS
prioress(nun)
uproarious
PRRSHN
peroration
PRRT
perorate
perorated
perorating
priority
priorities
pro rata
prorate

prorated
prorating
proration
PRRTBL
proratable
PRS
oppress
oppresses
Paris
parse
parsed
parsing
per se
pierce
pierced
piercing
piracy
piracies
porous
précis(abstract,
summary) -cis(pl)
press(news,push)
presses
price(cost)
priced
pricing
prowess
purse
pursed
pursing
pursue(chase)
pursued
pursuing
pursuer
PRSBKS
press box(news)
press boxes
PRSBP
presbyopia
presbyopic
PRSD
parricide
precede
(come before)
preceded
preceding
proceed(go on)
prosody
prosodies
PRSDL
parricidal
PRSDM
presidium
presidia(or)
presidiums
PRSDNG

preceding
PRSDNGZ
proceedings
PRSDNS
precedence
(priority)
precedents(rules)
PRSDNT
precedent
PRSDZ
proceeds(money)
PRSFLZH
persiflage
PRSGNF
presignify
presignified
presignifies
presignification
PRSH
parish(place)
parishes
perish(die)
perishes
PRSHBL
appreciable
appreciably
perishable
PRSHBLT
appreciability
perishability
PRSHL
partial
PRSHLT
partiality
partialities
PRSHN
apparition
apportion
operation
oppression
portion
PRSHNL
operational
portional
PRSHNMNT
apportionment
PRSHNR
parishioner
PRSHNS
prescience
PRSHPT
pear-shaped
PRSHR
pressure
pressured
pressuring

PRSHRNGK
preshrunk
PRSHRZ
pressurize
pressurized
pressurizing
pressurization
PRSHS
precious
PRSHSHN
appreciation
PRSHST
preciosity
PRSHT
appreciate
appreciated
appreciating
parachute
PRSHTR
appreciator
PRSHTST
parachutist
PRSHTV
appreciative
PRSJ
presage
presaged
presaging
PRSJR
procedure
PRSJRL
procedural
PRSK
parsec
PRSKL
preschool
PRSKLJ
parapsychology
PRSKP
periscope
PRSKPK
periscopic
PRSKRB
prescribe(order)
prescribed
prescribing
proscribe(forbid)
proscribed
proscribing
PRSKRPSHN
prescription
(order)
proscription
(forbid)
PRSKRPTV
prescriptive

NGK:ink **P**:pie **R**:air **S**:ice **SH**:show **T**:toy **THN**:thin **TH**:the **V**:of **W**:we **Y**:you **Z**:is **VZHN**:vision

proscriptive
PRSKT
Prescott
PRSKYSHN
persecution
(harass)
prosecution
(law)
PRSKYT
persecute(harass)
persecuted
persecuting
prosecute(law)
prosecuted
prosecuting
PRSKYTBL
prosecutable
PRSKYTR
persecutor(harass)
prosecutor
PRSL
parasol(umbrella)
parcel(quantity)
parsley(herb)
PRSLN
porcelain
PRSLT
proselyte
PRSLTZ
proselytize
proselytized
proselytizing
proselytizer
proselytization
PRSLTZM
proselytism
PRSMN
parsimony
persimmon(fruit)
pressman
pressmen
PRSMNS
parsimonious
PRSN
parson(preacher)
person
persona(character)
personae(drama)
personas
(psychology)
PRSNBL
personable
personably
PRSNF
personify
personified

personifies
personfier
PRSNFKSHN
personification
PRSNG
pressing
pricing
PRSNGKT
precinct
PRSNGRT
persona grata
PRSNGT
precinct
PRSNJ
parsonage(house)
personage
PRSNKT
persnickety
PRSNL
personal
(private)
personnel
(people)
PRSNLT
personality
personalities
PRSNLZ
personalize
personalized
personalizing
PRSNM
proscenium
proscenia(or)
prosceniums
PRSNNNGRT
persona non grata
PRSNP
parsnip
PRSNR
parcenary
PRSNS
pursuance
PRSNSHN
personation
PRSNSR
precensor
PRSNT
percent(%)
personate
personated
personating
pursuant
PRSNTJ
percentage
PRSNTL
percentile

PRSNTR
personator
PRSPCHL
perceptual
PRSPKS
perspicuous
PRSPKSHS
perspicacious
PRSPKST
perspicacity
PRSPKT
prospect
PRSPKTR
prospector
PRSPKTS
prospectus
PRSPKTV
perspective
(view)
prospective
(expected)
PRSPKYS
perspicuous
PRSPKYT
perspicuity
PRSPNT
percipient
PRSPR
perspire
perspired
perspiring
prosper
PRSPRS
prosperous
PRSPRSHN
perspiration
PRSPRT
prosperity
PRSPRTR
perspiratory
PRSPS
precipice
PRSPSHN
apperception
perception
PRSPT
percept(sight)
precept(rule)
PRSPTBL
perceptible
perceptibly
PRSPTR
preceptor
(teacher)
PRSPTS
precipitous

PRSPTSHN
precipitation
PRSPTT
precipitate
precipitated
precipitating
precipitator
precipitative
PRSPTV
perceptive
PRSPZ
presuppose
presupposed
presupposing
PRSPZSHN
presupposition
PRSR
oppressor
purser(money)
pursuer(chase)
PRSS
paresis
precise
(definite)
process
processes
PRSSHN
precession(a
going before)
procession
(parade)
PRSSHNL
precessional
(before)
processional(music,
parade,book)
PRSSR
processor(or)
processer
PRSST
persist
PRSSTNS
persistence
PRSSTNT
persistent
PRST
parasite
porosity
preset
priest(church)
pursuit
PRSTBLSH
preestablish
preestablishes
PRSTDJTTR
prestidigitator

B:by **CH**:each **D**:day **F**:if **G**:go **H**:he **HW**:why **J**:joy **K**:cow **KS**:ax **KWL**:equal **L**:all **M**:may **N**:in

PRSTHD
priesthood
PRSTHSS
prosthesis
prostheses
PRSTHTK
prosthetic
PRSTJ
prestige
PRSTJS
prestigious
PRSTK
parasitic
PRSTL
peristyle
priestly
priestlier
priestliest
PRSTLSS
peristalsis
peristalses
PRSTN
pristine
PRSTRS
prestress
prestresses
PRSTRSHN
prostration
PRSTRT
prostrate(prone)
prostrated
prostrating
PRSTS
priestess
priestesses
PRSTT
prostate(gland)
PRSTTSHN
prostitution
PRSTTT
prostitute
prostituted
prostituting
PRSTTYSHN
prostitution
PRSTTYT
prostitute
prostituted
prostituting
PRSTZH
prestige
prestigious
PRSV
oppressive
perceive
perceived

perceiving
PRSVBL
perceivable
perceivably
PRSVR
persevere
persevered
persevering
PRSVRNS
perseverance
PRSWD
persuade
persuaded
persuading
persuader
persuasion
PRSWDBL
persuadable
PRSWDR
persuader
PRSWRK
presswork
PRSWSBL
persuasible
PRSWSBLT
persuasibility
PRSWSV
persuasive
PRSWZBL
persuasible
PRSWZBLT
persuasibility
PRSWZHN
persuasion
PRSWZV
persuasive
PRSZHN
precision
PRT
apart
operate
operated
operating
operator
operetta
parity
parities
parrot(bird)
part
party
parties
pert
pirate
pirated
pirating
pirouette

pirouetted
pirouetting
port(wine,ship)
prate
prated
prating
pretty
prettied
pretties
prettier
prettiest
prettily
prettiness
upright
uproot
PRTBL
partible
portable
PRTBLT
portability
PRTBRNS
protuberance
PRTD
apartheid
parotid(gland)
parroted(repeat)
PRTF
aperitif
prettify
prettified
prettifies
PRTFL
portfolio
PRTGNST
protagonist
PRTHL
porthole
PRTHNJNSS
parthenogenesis
parthenogenetic
parthenology
PRTHNN
Parthenon
PRTHNTR
prothonotary
prothonotaries
PRTHT
apartheid
PRTJ
portage
PRTK
operatic
partake
partook
partaking
partaken

portico
pyretic
PRTKL
particle
protocol
PRTKLRD
parti-colored
PRTKLS
portcullis
PRTKNKS
pyrotechnics
PRTKSHN
protection
PRTKST
pretext
PRTKT
protect
PRTKTR
protector
PRTKTRT
protectorate
PRTKTV
protective
PRTKYLR
particular
PRTKYLRT
particularity
particularities
PRTKYLRZ
particularize
particularized
particularizing
PRTL
parietal
portal(door)
portly
portlier
portliest
portliness
prattle
prattled
prattling
PRTLND
Portland
PRTM
part-time(adj,adv)
part-timer
PRTMNT
apartment
portmanteau
PRTMPR
pro tempore
PRTN
appertain
opportune
pertain

protean(variable)
protein
proton
PRTNCHN
pretension
PRTNCHS
pretentious
PRTND
portend(omen)
pretend(act)
PRTNDR
pretender
PRTNNS
appurtenance
pertinence
PRTNNT
appurtenant
pertinent
PRTNR
partner
PRTNRSHP
partnership
PRTNS
pretense (B)pretence
PRTNSHN
pretension
PRTNSHS
pertinacious
pretentious
PRTNST
opportunist
pertinacity
PRTNT
opportunity
opportunities
portent
PRTNTS
peritonitis
portentous
PRTNZM
opportunism
PRTPLZM
protoplasm
PRTR
operator
parterre
porter
portray
Pretoria
PRTRB
perturb
PRTRBNS
perturbance
PRTRBSHN
perturbation
PRTRCHR

portraiture
PRTRD
protrude
protruded
protruding
PRTRHS
porterhouse
PRTRJ
partridge
PRTRK
Puerto Rico
PRTRKSHN
protraction
PRTRKT
protract
PRTRKTBL
protractible
PRTRKTL
protractile
PRTRKTR
protractor
PRTRL
portrayal
pretrial
PRTRNCHRL
preternatural
PRTRNT
parturient
PRTRPR
paratrooper
PRTRPS
paratroops
PRTRSHN
parturition
PRTRSL
protrusile
PRTRSV
protrusive
PRTRT
portrait
PRTRZHN
protrusion
PRTRZV
protrusive
PRTS
apparatus
Proteus(sea god)
PRTSHN
partition
PRTSL
pretzel
PRTSMTH
Portsmouth
PRSNM
proscenium(stage)
proscenia

PRTSPL
participial(adj)
participle(n)
PRTSPNT
participant
PRTSPSHN
participation
PRTSPT
participate
participated
participating
PRTSPTR
participator
PRTSS
pertussis
pertussal
PRTST
protest
PRTSTNT
Protestant
protestant
PRTSTR
protester
PRTSTSHN
protestation
PRTT
partite
PRTTP
prototype
PRTTPL
prototypal
PRTV
operative
PRTYBRNS
protuberance
PRTYN
opportune
PRTYNST
opportunist
PRTYNT
opportunity
opportunities
PRTYNZM
opportunism
PRTYR
portiere
PRTYRNT
parturient
PRTYRSHN
parturition
PRTZH
portage
portaged
portaging
protégé
(person)

PRTZL
pretzel
PRTZN
partisan
protozoan
PRV
approve
approved
approving
pareve(food)
privy
privies
prove
proved
proving
proven
purvey
PRVBL
approvable
provable
provably
PRVBLT
provability
PRVD
pervade
pervaded
pervading
provide(give)
provided
providing
provider
PRVDNCHL
providential
PRVDNS
Providence(God)
providence
PRVDNSHL
providential
PRVDNT
provident
PRVDR
pervader
provider
PRVK
provoke
provoked
provoking
PRVKSHN
provocation
PRVKSHS
pervicacious
PRVKTV
provocative
PRVL
approval
prevail

B:by **CH**:each **D**:day **F**:if **G**:go **H**:he **HW**:why **J**:joy **K**:cow **KS**:ax **KWL**:equal **L**:all **M**:may **N**:in

PRVLJ
privilege
privileged
privileging
PRVLN
provolone
PRVLNS
prevalence
PRVLNT
prevalent
PRVLT
Upper Volta
PRVN
parvenu
proven
prove
PRVNCHL
provincial
PRVNCHLZM
provincialism
PRVNCHN
prevention
PRVNDR
provender
PRVNS
province
purveyance
PRVNSHL
provincial
PRVNSHLZM
provincialism
PRVNSHN
prevention
PRVNT
prevent
PRVNTBL
preventable
PRVNTTV
preventative
PRVNTV
preventive
PRVNY
parvenu
PRVNYNT
prevenient
PRVR
approver
purveyor
upriver
PRVRB
proverb
PRVRBL
proverbial
PRVRKSHN
prevarication
PRVRKT

prevaricate
prevaricated
prevaricating
PRVRKTR
prevaricator
PRVRS
perverse
perversion
PRVRST
perversity
perversities
PRVRT
pervert
PRVRZHN
perversion
PRVS
pervious(open)
previous(before)
privacy
privacies
PRVSHN
privation
PRVST
provost
PRVSV
pervasive
PRVT
private
privet
PRVTR
privateer
PRVTSKTR
private sector
PRVY
preview
purview(range)
PRVZ
previse(foresee)
prevised
prevising
proviso
PRVZHN
pervasion(extent)
prevision(foresee)
provision(means)
PRVZHNL
provisional
PRVZR
provisory
PRVZV
pervasive
PRWR
prewar
PRYR
prayer
PRYRNS

prurience
PRYRNT
prurient
PRZ
appraise(estimate)
appraised
appraising
appraiser
appraisable
appraisement
apprise(inform)
apprised
apprising
peruse
perused
perusing
praise(glory)
praised
praising
prize(award)
prized
prizing
pros
pros and cons
professionals
prose(words)
prosy
prosier
prosiest
PRZBL
appraisable
PRZBP
presbyopia
presbyopic
PRZBTR
presbyter
PRZBTRN
Presbyterian
PRZD
preside
presided
presiding
PRZDNCHL
presidential
PRZDNS
presidency
presidencies
PRZDNSHL
presidential
PRZDNT
President,the
(title)
president
PRZDNTLKT
president-elect
PRZFT

prizefight
PRZFTR
prizefighter
PRZHN
Parisian
Paris
Persian
PRZHNGLF
Persian Gulf
PRZK
prosaic
PRZKL
prosaical
PRZL
appraisal
perusal
PRZM
presume
presumed
presuming
prism
PRZMBL
presumable
PRZMPCHS
presumptuous
PRZMPSHN
presumption
PRZMPTV
presumptive
PRZMTK
prismatic
PRZN
prison
PRZNG
uprising
PRZNR
prisoner
PRZNS
presence
presents(gifts)
PRZNT
present
PRZNTBL
presentable
PRZNTD
present-day
PRZNTMNT
presentiment
(premonition)
presentment
(presentation)
PRZNTSHN
presentation
PRZR
appraiser
PRZRV

preserve
  preserved
  preserving
PRZRVBL
  preservable
PRZRVSHN
  preservation
PRZRVTV
  preservative
PRZSTNT
  persistent
PRZWRTH
  praiseworthy
  praiseworthily
  praiseworthiness
PS
  apiece
  apse
  apsidal
  eyepiece
  oops(interj)
  opus
  opuses
  pace(stride)
  paced
  pacing
  pacer
  pass(move ahead)
  passes
  passé(aged)
  peace(harmony)
  peso(money)
  piece(part)
  pieced
  piecing
  pious(holy)
  posse(group)
  P.S.(postscript)
  pus(cellular
   debris)
  puss(cat,face)
  pusses
  pussy(pus)
  pussier
  pussiest
  pussy(cat)
  pussies
PSBK
  passbook
PSBL
  passable
  passably
  peaceable
  peaceably
  possible
  possibly

PSBLT
  possibility
  possibilities
PSCHL
  pustule
PSCHLNT
  postulant(request)
  pustulant(pus)
PSCHLR
  pustular(pus)
PSCHLSHN
  postulation
PSCHLT
  postulate
  postulated
  postulating
PSCHLTR
  postulator
PSCHMS
  posthumous
PSCHR
  pasture(land)
  pastured
  pasturing
  posture(position)
  postured
  posturing
PSCHRL
  postural
PSCHRZ
  pasteurize
  pasteurized
  pasteurizing
PSCHRZSHN
  pasteurization
PSD
  episode
  pesade
PSDK
  episodic
PSDKL
  episodical
PSDN
  upside-down(adj)
  upside down(adv)
PSF
  pacify
  pacified
  pacifies
  pacifier
PSFBL
  pacifiable
PSFK
  Pacific
  pacific
  pacifically

PSFKSHN
  pacification
  Pacific Ocean
PSFKT
  ipso facto
PSFL
  peaceful
PSFR
  pacifier
PSFZM
  pacifism
PSGDZ
  piece goods
PSGRF
  pasigraphy
PSH
  apache
  apish(imitative)
  posh(elegant)
  push
  pushes
  pushy
  pushier
  pushiest
  pushily
  pushiness
  uppish
PSHBT
  pushboat
PSHBTN
  push-button(n,adj)
PSHKRT
  pushcart
PSHN
  option
  passion
  potion
PSHNL
  optional
PSHNS
  patience
  patients(people)
PSHNT
  passionate
  patient
PSHP
  push-up
PSHPN
  push-pin
PSHR
  pusher
PSHT
  Pashto
  upshot
PSHVR
  pushover

PSJ
  passage
PSJW
  passageway
PSK
  passkey
  pesky
  peskier
  peskiest
  peskiness
  Pasch(passover)
PSKL
  paschal(Easter)
  PASCAL(computer)
PSKLCHR
  pisciculture
PSKPL
  episcopal
  episcopacy
PSKPLN
  Episcopalian
PSKPNG
  peacekeeping
PSKRPT
  postscript
  P.S.
PSKTRL
  piscatorial
PSKWND
  pasquinade
  pasquinaded
  pasquinading
  pasquinader
PSL
  apostle
  epistle(letter)
  pestle
  pestled
  pestling
PSLN
  epsilon
PSM
  opossum
  possum(playing)
PSMKR
  pacemaker
  peacemaker
  peacemaking
PSML
  piecemeal
PSMN
  postman
  postmen
PSMST
  pessimist
PSMSTK

B:by CH:each D:day F:if G:go H:he HW:why J:joy K:cow KS:ax KWL:equal L:all M:may N:in

pessimistic
PSMSTKL
pessimistically
PSMZM
pessimism
PSN
paisano
Pusan
PSNDNZ
ups and downs
PSNJR
passenger
PSNR
epicenter
PSNTR
epicenter
PSPN
postpone
postponed
postponing
PSPNBL
postponable
PSPNMNT
postponement
PSPP
peace pipe
PSPRT
passe-partout
passport
PSR
pacer
PSRB
passer-by
passers-by
PSRJ
upsurge
upsurged
upsurging
PSRZB
passers-by
PSS
piceous(pitch)
PST
opacity
opacities
passed(pass)
past(gone by,over)
paste(adhere)
pasted
pasting
pasty
pastier
pastiest
pastiness
pasties
paucity(few)

peseta
post
upset
upset
upsetting
PSTBKS
postbox
PSTBRD
pasteboard
PSTCH
pasticcio(music)
pasticci
PSTDT
postdate
postdated
postdating
PSTGRJT
postgraduate
PSTHL
pesthole
posthole
PSTHPNTK
posthypnotic
PSTHR
pass-through
PSTHST
posthaste
PSTJ
postage
upstage
upstaged
upstaging
PSTKRD
postcard
PSTL
pastel(color)
pastille(tablet)
pestle(tool)
pestled,-ling
pistil(plant part)
pistol(firearm)
pistole(coin)
postal(mail)
PSTLHWP
pistol-whip
-whipped,-pping
PSTLK
apostolic
PSTLNCHL
pestilential
PSTLNS
pestilence
PSTLNSHL
pestilential
PSTLNT
pestilent

PSTLR
epistolary
PSTLWP
pistol-whip
PSTLYN
postilion
PSTM
ipisteme
pastime
peacetime
PSTMN
postman
postmen
PSTMRK
postmark
PSTMRTM
post-mortem
PSTMSTR
past master
postmaster
PSTMSTRS
postmistress
postmistresses
PSTN
piston
PSTNDL
postnatal
PSTNDNG
upstanding
PSTNTL
postnatal
PSTPD
postpaid
PSTPN
postpone
postponed
postponing
PSTPNBL
postponable
PSTPNMNT
postponement
PSTR
pastor
pastry
pastries
pester
poster
PSTRF
apostrophe
PSTRL
pastoral
PSTRM
pastrami
upstream
PSTRR
a posteriori

posterior
PSTRT
pastorate
posterity
upstart
PSTRZ
pasteurize
pasteurized
pasteurizing
upstairs
PSTRZSHN
pasteurization
PSTS
apostasy
apostasies
PSTSD
pesticide
PSTSH
pastiche(or)
pisticcio(artistic)
pastichi
pistachio(tree)
postiche(fake)
PSTSKRPT
postscript
P.S.
PSTT
apostate
upstate
PSTWR
postwar
PSTYL
pustule
PSTYLNT
pustulant
PSTZ
pasties
pasty
PSV
passive
PSVR
Passover
PSVT
passivity
passivities
PSWNG
upswing
PSWP
upsweep
upswept
PSWRD
password
PSWRK
piecework
PSZ
Pisces

NGK:ink **P**:pie **R**:air **S**:ice **SH**:show **T**:toy **THN**:thin **TH**:the **V**:of **W**:we **Y**:you **Z**:is **VZHN**:vision

PT
apt
opiate
opt
pat(tap)
  patted
  patting
patio(place)
patty(cake)
  patties
pet(animal)
  petted
  petting
petty(trivial)
  pettier
  pettiest
  pettily
  pettiness
peyote
piety(devotion)
  pieties
  pietism
pit(hole)
  pitted
  pitting
pity(concern)
  pitied
  pities
  pitiless
  pitiable
poet(writer)
pot(vessel)
  potted
  potting
potty(toilet)
  potties
pout(sulk)
put(place)
  put
  putting
putt(golf)
puttee(cloth)
putty(cement)
  putties
uppity
PTBL
potable
potbelly
  potbellied
  potbellies
pitiable(pity)
PTBLR
potboiler
PTBT
PT boat
PTD

pitied
pity
pitted
pit
potato
  potatoes
PTDFWGR
paté de foie gras
PTDN
put-down(n)
put down(v)
PTDT
up-to-date
PTF
epitaph
PTFG
pettifog
  pettifogged
  pettifogging
PTFGR
pettifogger
PTFL
pitfall
pitiful
PTFR
petit four
  petit fours(or)
  petits fours
PTFSR
petty officer
PTGN
Patagonia
PTGNY
Patagonia
PTH
apathy
  apathies
path
pith
pithy
  pithier
  pithiest
  pithiness
PTHDK
apathetic
pathetic
PTHFNDR
pathfinder
PTHGRS
Pythagoras
PTHJNK
pathogenic
PTHK
pothook
PTHKR
apothecary

apothecaries
PTHL
pothole
PTHLDR
potholder
PTHLJ
pathology
  pathologies
PTHLJKL
pathological
PTHLM
epithelium
PTHLMLJ
ophthalmology
PTHLMLJST
ophthalmologist
PTHLMSKP
ophthalmoscope
PTHM
apothegm(maxim)
apothem(distance)
PTHN
python
PTHNK
pythonic
PTHR
pother
PTHRST
upthrust
PTHS
pathos
PTHT
epithet
PTHTK
apathetic
pathetic
PTHTKL
pathetical
PTJ
pottage
PTJR
petit jury
PTK
optic
poetic
uptake
PTKK
petcock
PTKL
optical
poetical
PTKRNLND
Pitcairn Island
PTKT
petticoat
PTL

petal(flower)
patella
  patellae(or)
  patellas
PTLCH
potlatch
PTLK
petallike
potluck
PTLS
pitiless(pity)
PTM
epitome
PTML
optimal
petit mal
PTMM
optimum
  optima(or)
  optimums
PTMRK
pockmark
PTMS
peat moss
PTMST
optimist
PTMSTK
optimistic
PTMSTKL
optimistical
PTMTR
optometry
PTMTRST
optometrist
PTMZ
epitomize
  epitomized
  epitomizing
optimize
  optimized
  optimizing
PTMZM
optimism
PTN
patina(or)
paten(plate)(or)
patin(or)
patine
piton
poteen(whiskey)
uptown
PTNCHL
potential
PTNG
petting
PTNS

appetency	patrolmen	potash	appetizer
patency(obvious)	**PTRLTM**	**PTSHN**	**PV**
pittance	petrolatum	optician	pave
potency	**PTRMN**	petition	paved
potencies	patrimony	potation	paving
PTNSHL	patrimonies	**PTSHNR**	peeve
potential	**PTRN**	petitioner	peeved
PTNSHLT	patron(person)	**PTSHRD**	peeving
potentiality	pattern(model)	potsherd	**PVLYN**
potentialities	upturn	**PTSHT**	pavilion
PTNT	**PTRNJ**	potshot	**PVMNT**
patent(right)	patronage	**PTSKD**	pavement
patentee(person)	**PTRNL**	pizzicato	**PVRT**
potent(strong)	paternal	**PTSKT**	poverty
PTNTT	petronel	pizzicato	poverties
potentate	**PTRNLSTK**	**PTSM**	**PVSH**
PTNY	paternalistic	potassium	peevish
petunia	**PTRNMK**	**PTSR**	**PVT**
PTPNT	patronymic	patisserie	pivot
petit point	**PTRNMKR**	pizzeria	**PVTL**
PTR	patternmaker	**PTSZM**	pivotal
patter(talk,tap)	**PTRNT**	poeticism	**PVYN**
peter(diminish)	paternity	**PTT**	pavilion
pottery	**PTRNZ**	appetite	**PW**
potteries	patronize	epitaph	peewee(or)pewee
poetry	patronized	petite	powwow
poetries	patronizing	potato	**PWBL**
putter(n)(golf)	patronizer	potatoes	pueblo
putter(v)(busy	**PTRPRNSPL**	putout(n)	**PWND**
about), (B)potter	Peter Principle	up tight	upwind
PTRDSH	**PTRRK**	**PTTD**	**PWNTLZM**
petri dish	patriarch	aptitude	pointillism
PTRDT	patriarchy	**PTTR**	pointillist
petered out	patriarchies	pituitary	pointillistic
PTRF	**PTRRKL**	**PTTYD**	**PWR**
petrify	patriarchal	aptitude	power
petrified	**PTRSD**	**PTW**	**PWRD**
petrifies	patricide	patois(language)	upward
PTRFKSHN	**PTRSHN**	patois(pl)	**PWRL**
petrifaction(or)	patrician	**PTWZ**	puerile
petrification	**PTRT**	patois(language)	**PWRTRK**
PTRGLF	patriot	patois(sing)	Puerto Rico
petroglyph	**PTRTK**	**PTYNY**	**PWSNT**
PTRKMSTR	patriotic	petunia	puissant
petrochemistry	**PTRTKL**	**PTYTR**	**PY**
PTRL	patriotically	pituitary	pew(bench)
patrol	**PTRTZM**	**PTZ**	**PYBK**
patrolled	patriotism	poetize	pubic
patrolling	**PTS**	poetized	**PYBRT**
petrol(gasoline)	patsy	poetizing	puberty
PTRLJ	patsies	pizza	**PYBS**
petrology	piteous	**PTZM**	pubis
PTRLM	pizza	pietism	pubes
petroleum(oil)	**PTSBRG**	**PTZNG**	**PYBSNS**
PTRLMN	Pittsburgh	appetizing	pubescense
patrolman	**PTSH**	**PTZR**	**PYBSNT**

pubescent
PYBZ
pubes
pubis(sing)
PYDNDM
pudendum
PYDNS
pudency
PYDR
pewter
PYFR
piaffer
PYJLST
pugilist
PYJLZM
pugilism
PYK
puke
puked
puking
PYL
pule(whine)
puled
puling
PYLNS
opulence
PYLNT
opulent
PYLTSRPRZ
Pulitzer Prize
PYM
puma
PYN
oppugn
puisne(law,
low rank)
puny
punier
puniest
punily
puniness
PYNTV
punitive
PYP
pupa
pupae(or)
pupas
PYPL
pupil
PYPSHN
pupation
PYPT
pupate
pupated
pupating
PYR

pure
purée
puréed
puréeing
PYRBRD
purebred
PYRF
purify
purified
purifies
PYRFKSHN
purification
PYRFR
purifier
PYRL
puerile
PYRLNS
purulence
PYRLNT
purulent
PYRMSN
puromycin
PYRNS
prurience
PYRNT
prurient
PYRT
purity
purities
PYRTN
puritan
PYRTNKL
puritanical
PYRYLNS
purulence
PYRYLNT
purulent
PYRZM
purism
PYSDRZSTNS
pièce de résistance
PYSLNMS
pusillanimous
PYSNT
puissant
PYT
peyote
PYTR
pewter
PYTRD
putrid
PYTRF
putrefy
putrefied
putrefies
PYTRFKSHN

putrefaction
PYTRFKTV
putrefactive
PYTRSNS
putrescence
PYTRSNT
putrescent
PYTS
piazza
PYTTV
putative
PZ
appease(satisfy)
appeased
appeasing
appeaser
appose(side by
side)
apposed
apposing
oppose(conflict)
opposed
opposing
pause(wait)
paused
pausing
piazza
poise(balance)
poised
poising
pose(position)
posed
posing
PZBL
appeasable
apposable(side by
side)
opposable
(conflict)
PZD
pesade
PZL
paisley
puzzle
puzzled
puzzling
PZLR
puzzler
PZMNT
appeasement
PZN
paisano
poison
PZNKYZ
p's and q's
PZNS

poisonous
PZNT
peasant
PZNTR
peasantry
PZR
appeaser
(satisfy)
opposer
(conflict)
PZS
possess
possesses
PZSHN
apposition
(side by side)
opposition
(conflict)
position(state,
area)
possession(own)
PZSR
possessor
PZSV
possessive
PZT
apposite(fitting)
opposite
(other side)
PZTV
appositive
(side by side)
positive(plus,
good)
PZTVZM
positivism
PZZ
pizzazz

R

aerie(nest)
air
airy
airier
airiest
airily
airiness
are
to be
am
is

B:by CH:each D:day F:if G:go H:he HW:why J:joy K:cow KS:ax KWL:equal L:all M:may N:in

was
area(space)
aria(music)
arietta
arioso
array(display)
arrow(weapon)
arroyo(place)
aura(light)
awry(wrong)
ear(hearing)
eerie
  (unsettling)
eerier
eeriest
eerily
eeriness
era(time)
err(go astray)
heir(inheritor)
hour(time)
ire(anger)
oar(boat)
or(choice)
ore(mineral)
Oreo(trademark)
our(possession)
Ra(sun god)
rah(interj)
  hurrah
raw(not cooked)
ray(light)
re(tone)
re(prep)
roe(fish eggs)
roué(lecher)
roux(food)
row(brawl,line)(n)
row(v) (boat)
rue(sorrow)
  rued
  ruing
rye(grain)
wry(twisted,
  humorous)
  wrier(or)
  wryer
  wriest(or)
  wryest
  wryly
  wryness

RB
Arab
Arabia
herb(plant)
herbal

orb(ball)
rib(bone)
  ribbed
  ribbing
rob(steal)
  robbed
  robbing
  robber
robe(clothes)
  robed
  robing
rub(touch)
  rubbed
  rubbing
ruby(gem)
  rubies

RBD
rabid
RBDN
rubdown
RBF
rebuff(refusal)
re-buff(buff again)
RBFKSHN
rubefaction
RBFLVN
riboflavin
RBK
Arabic
rebec
RBKND
rubicund
RBKNMRL
Arabic numeral
RBKSKYB
Rubic's Cube
  (trademark)
RBKYLR
orbicular
RBL
arable(land)
herbal(plant)
rabble(mob)
rabble(iron bar)
  rabbled
  rabbling
  rabbler
rebel(fight)
  rebelled
  rebelling
rouble(money)
rubble(stone)
rubella(disease)
RBLD
rebuild
  rebuilt

ribald
RBLDR
ribaldry
RBLT
rebuilt
  rebuild
RBLYN
rebellion
RBLYS
rebellious
RBN
Arabian
ribbon
robin(bird)
urban(of the city)
urbane
  (socially poised)
RBND
rawboned
rebound
RBNG
ribbing
RBNKL
rabbinical
RBNRNL
urban renewal
RBNS
Arabian Sea
RBNT
urbanite
urbanity
  urbanities
RBNZ
urbanize
  urbanized
  urbanizing
RBNZM
urbanism
RBNZSHN
urbanization
RBR
arbor, (B)arbour
robber
robbery
  robberies
rubber
rubbery
RBRB
rhubarb
RBRDKST
rebroadcast
RBRK
air brake
rubric
RBRL
arboreal

RBRN
airborne
reborn
RBRSH
airbrush
  airbrushes
RBRSTMP
rubber stamp(n)
rubber-stamp(v,adj)
RBRTH
rebirth
reborn
RBRTM
arboretum
RBRZ
rubberize
  rubberized
  rubberizing
RBS
air base
rebus
RBSH
rubbish
rubbishy
RBSK
arabesque
RBST
robust
RBT
air boat
orbit
rabbet(cut)
rabbit(animal)
rebate(money)
  rebated
  rebating
rebut(refute)
  rebutted
  rebutting
robot
rowboat
RBTK
aerobatic
RBTKS
aerobatics
RBTL
rebuttal
RBTPNCH
rabbit punch
  rabbit punches
RBTR
arbiter
rebutter
RBTRBL
arbitrable
RBTRMNT

arbitrament

RBTRR
arbitrary
 arbitrarily
 arbitrariness

RBTRSHN
arbitration

RBTRT
arbitrate
 arbitrated
 arbitrating

RBTRTR
arbitrator

RBTRZH
arbitrage

RBYK
rebuke
 rebuked
 rebuking

RBYTS
arbutus

RBZ
rabies
rebozo

RCH
arch
 arches
reach
 reaches
retch(strain to
 vomit)
 retches
Rh(factor)
rich
 riches
roach
 roaches
wretch(person)
 wretches

RCHBSHP
archbishop

RCHDK
archduke

RCHDKL
archducal

RCHDKN
archdeacon

RCHDSS
archdiocese

RCHFKTR
Rh factor
 Rh positive
 Rh negative

RCHL
ritual

RCHLSTK

ritualistic

RCHLSTKL
ritualistically

RCHLZM
ritualism

RCHMBR
air chamber

RCHMN
Richmond

RCHMND
Richmond

RCHN
richen
urchin

RCHNM
archenemy
 archenemies

RCHPLG
archipelago

RCHR
archer
archery

RCHRD
orchard

RCHRJ
recharge
 recharged
 recharging
 recharger

RCHRJBL
rechargeable

RCHS
righteous

RCHSTR
Rochester

RCHT
ratchet
rochet(vestment)

RCHW
archway

RCHZ
riches
rich

RD
air raid
aorta(blood)
 aortas(or)
 aortae
arid(dry)
erode
 eroded
 eroding
errata
rad(energy)
radio
raid(attack)

read(words)
read
 reading
ready(prepared)
 readied
 readies
 readier
 readiest
 readily
 readiness
Red(political)
red(color)
 redder
 reddest
 reddish
 redden
redeye(gravy)
redo(do again)
 redid
 redone
reed(stalk)
reedy
 reedier
 reediest
 reediness
rid(free from)
 ridded
 ridding
ride(travel)
 rode
 riding
 ridden
righty(person)
road(highway)
rode
ride
rodeo(event)
rood(cross)
rowdy(rough)
 rowdies
 rowdier
 rowdiest
 rowdiness
ruddy(color)
 ruddier
 ruddiest
 ruddily
 ruddiness
rude(crude)
 ruder
 rudest
rued(sorrow)
rue
 ruing
rutty(groove)
rut

RDBD
roadbed

RDBG
rutabaga

RDBL
readable
readably
redouble
 redoubled
 redoubling
rideable

RDBLDD
red-blooded

RDBLK
roadblock

RDBLT
readability
roadability

RDBT
redbait

RDDNDRN
rhododendron

RDF
ratify
 ratified
 ratifies
 ratification
 ratifier

RDFN
radiophone

RDFNGRF
radiophonograph

RDFT
radiophoto

RDG
red-dog
 red-dogged
 red-dogging

RDGRF
radiograph
radiography

RDGRM
radiogram

RDHD
redhead
 redheaded

RDHNDD
red-handed

RDHRD
red-haired

RDHT
red-hot

RDJNR
Rio de Janerio

RDK
erotic(sex)

B:by **CH**:each **D**:day **F**:if **G**:go **H**:he **HW**:why **J**:joy **K**:cow **KS**:ax **KWL**:equal **L**:all **M**:may **N**:in

erratic
RDKBL
eradicable
eradicably
RDKL
radical
RDKLZM
radicalism
RDKRS
Red Cross
RDKRSHN
redecoration
RDKRT
redecorate
redecorated
redecorating
redecorator
RDKS
radix
radixes(or)
radices
RDKSHN
eradication
redaction
reduction(reduce)
RDKT
eradicate
eradicated
eradicating
eradicator
redact
RDKTR
eradicator
redactor
RDKTV
radioactive
RDKTVT
radioactivity
RDKYL
ridicule
ridiculed
ridiculing
ridiculer
RDKYLS
ridiculous
RDL
Airedale(dog)
ordeal
radial
rattle(noise)
rattled
rattling
rattler
riddle(question)
riddled
riddling

ruddle(red dye)
ruddled
ruddling
RDLJ
radiology
RDLJST
radiologist
RDLN
Rhode Island
RDLND
Rhode Island
RDLNS
redolence
RDLNT
redolent
rutilant(glow)
RDLPLT
Rio de la Plata
RDLR
rattler
RDLSNK
rattlesnake
RDLTDSTRKT
red-light district
RDLTR
red-letter
RDLTRP
rattletrap
RDM
erratum
radium
redeem(save)
heirdom
RDMBL
irredeemable
irredeemably
redeemable
redeemably
RDMD
ready-made
RDMNT
rudiment
RDMNTD
rodomontade
rodomontaded
rodomontading
RDMNTR
rudimentary(basic)
rudiment
RDMPSHN
redemption
RDMR
redeemer
RDMTR
radiometer
RDN

aerodyne
ordain
radon
redound
RDND
redound
RDNDNS
redundancy
redundancies
RDNDNT
redundant
RDNG
reading(words)
reeding(reeds)
RDNK
redneck
RDNL
ordinal
RDNMK
aerodynamic
RDNMKS
aerodynamics
RDNNS
ordinance(law)
ordnance
(artillery)
RDNR
ordinary(plain)
ordinarily
ordinariness
RDNS
ardency
ardencies
radiance
riddance
RDNSHN
ordination
RDNT
ardent
irradiant
ordinate
ordinated
ordinating
radiant
rodent
RDPL
redeploy
RDPLKSHN
reduplication
RDPLKT
reduplicate
reduplicated
reduplicating
RDR
air-dry
air-dried

air-dries
ardor(emotion)
artery(blood)
arteries
order
radar(electric)
raider
(attacker)
ratter(cat,dog)
reader(words)
rider(traveler)
rotor(tool)
rudder(boat)
writer
RDRDM
Rotterdam
RDRKT
redirect
RDRL
orderly
orderlies
orderliness
RDRLS
riderless
RDRM
eardrum
RDRNR
roadrunner
RDRP
airdrop
airdropped
airdropping
RDRS
re-dress(dress
again)
re-dresses
redress(remedy)
redresses
RDRSHN
reiteration
RDRSHP
readership
RDRT
reiterate
reiterated
reiterating
reiteration
RDRV
hors d'oeuvre
RDRVZ
hors d'oeuvres
RDS
radius
radiuses(or)
radii
Red Sea

reduce(lessen)
reduced
reducing
reducer
RDSBL
irreducible
irreducibly
reducible
reducibly
RDSD
roadside
RDSH
radish(food)
reddish(color)
roadshow
RDSHFT
red shift
RDSHN
erudition
irradiation
radiation
RDSKP
radioscopy
RDSND
radiosonde
RDSNPR
red snapper
RDSNS
iridescence
reticence
RDSNT
iridescent
reticent
RDSTP
radioisotope
RDSTR
roadster
RDSTRBYSHN
redistribution
RDSTRBYT
redistribute
redistributed
redistributing
redistributor
RDSTRKT
redistrict
RDSTRNM
radio astronomy
radio astronomer
RDT
aridity(dry)
eradiate(radiate,
emanate)
eradiated
eradiating
erudite(learned)

irradiate(shine,
expose to
radiation)
irradiated
irradiating
radiate
radiated
radiating
read-out
redoubt(defense)
RDTBL
redoubtable
RDTHRP
radiotherapy
RDTLFN
radiotelephone
RDTLSKP
radio telescope
RDTP
red tape
RDTR
radiator
RDVLP
redevelop
RDVLPMNT
redevelopment
RDVRK
aardvark
RDW
roadway
RDWD
redwood
RDWLF
aardwolf
aardwolves
RDWRK
roadwork
RDWV
radio wave
RDYPLKSHN
reduplication
RDYPLKT
reduplicate
reduplicated
reduplicating
RDYR
ordure
RDYS
arduous
reduce
reduced
reducing
RDYSBL
irreducible
irreducibly
reducible

reducibly
RDZH
Rhodesia
RDZM
rowdyism
RDZNS
reticence
RDZNT
reticent
RF
raffia(palm)
reef(coral)
reify
reified
reifies
reifier
reification
rife(widespread)
rifer
rifest
riff(music,talk)
roof(top)
rough(not smooth,
tough)
ruff(collar,fish,
trump)
RFDR
roughdry
roughdried
roughdries
RFHS
roughhouse
roughhoused
roughhousing
RFHY
rough-hew
rough-hewn
RFHZ
roughhouse
roughhoused
roughhousing
RFJ
roughage
RFKSHN
reification
refection
RFKST
roughcast
RFKT
refect
RFKTR
refectory
refectories
RFL
airflow
airfoil, (B)aerofoil

air rifle
ireful
raffle(lottery)
raffled
raffling
refill
riffle(shoal,
shuffle)
riffled
riffling
rifle(firearm)
rifle(plunder,
search)
rifled
rifling
rueful(regret)
ruffle(disturb,
cloth decoration)
ruffled
ruffling
RFLBL
refillable
RFLD
airfield
RFLJNT
refulgent
RFLKS
reflex
reflexes
RFLKSHN
reflection (B)reflexion
RFLKSV
reflexive
RFLKT
reflect
RFLKTR
reflector
RFLKTV
reflective
RFLMN
rifleman
riflemen
RFLNT
refluent
RFLR
refiller
riflery
RFLSHN
reflation
RFN
earphone
orphan(child)
refine
refined
refining
roughen

B:by **CH**:each **D**:day **F**:if **G**:go **H**:he **HW**:why **J**:joy **K**:cow **KS**:ax **KWL**: equal **L**:all **M**:may **N**:in

ruffian(person)
RFND
  refined
  refund
RFNG
  roofing
RFNJ
  orphanage
RFNK
  roughneck
RFNMNT
  refinement
RFNR
  refiner
  refinery
   refineries
RFNSH
  refinish
   refinishes
RFR
  reefer
   (person,
   clothes,
   marijuana)
  refer
   referred
   referring
  referee(judge)
   refereed
   refereeing
  roofer
RFRBL
  referable
RFRBSH
  refurbish
   refurbishes
RFRF
  riffraff
RFRJRNT
  refrigerant
RFRJRSHN
  refrigeration
RFRJRT
  refrigerate
   refrigerated
   refrigerating
RFRJRTR
  refrigerator
RFRKSHN
  refraction
RFRKT
  refract
RFRKTR
  refractory
RFRL
  referral

RFRM
  airframe
  reaffirm
  re-form(make again)
  reform(make better)
RFRMSHN
  reformation
RFRMTR
  reformatory
   reformatories
RFRN
  refrain
RFRNDM
  referendum
   referenda(or)
   referendums
RFRNJBL
  irrefrangible
  refrangible
RFRNS
  reference
   referenced
   referencing
RFRNT
  referent
RFRR
  referrer
RFRS
  Air Force
   AF(or)USAF
  auriferous(gold)
RFRSH
  refresh
   refreshes
RFRSHMNT
  refreshment
RFRST
  reforest
RFRSTSHN
  reforestation
RFRSWN
  Air Force One
RFRT
  air freight
RFRZ
  rephrase
   rephrased
   rephrasing
RFS
  orifice
RFSHD
  roughshod
RFSNT
  rufescent
   rufescence
RFT

raft(boat,many)
  refit
   refitted
   refitting
  rift(separation)
RFTBL
  irrefutable
  irrefutably
  refutable
  refutably
RFTBLT
  irrefutability
  refutability
RFTR
  rafter(person,beam)
RFTSHN
  refutation
RFYJ
  refuge(safe place)
  refugee(person)
RFYL
  refuel
RFYN
  ruffian
RFYS
  refuse(trash)
RFYT
  refute
   refuted
   refuting
RFYTBL
  irrefutable
  irrefutably
  refutable
  refutably
RFYTBLT
  irrefutability
  refutability
RFYTSHN
  refutation
RFYZ
  refuse(reject)
   refused
   refusing
   refusal
RFYZL
  refusal
RG
  aerugo(color)
  argot
  erg
  ergo
  rag(cloth,tease)
   ragged
   ragging
  raga(music-Hindu)

ragout(soup)
  reggae(music-
   Caribbean)
  rig
   rigged
   rigging
   rigger
  rogue(person)
   rogued
   roguing
   roguery
  rug(floor)
RGB
  Rugby
RGBL
  irrigable(water)
  irrigate
RGD
  ragged(torn)
RGDN
  rigadoon
RGL
  argyle
  regal(adj)
  regale(v)
   regaled
   regaling
  regalia(n)
  Rogallo(kite)
   (trademark)
  wriggle(squirm)
   wriggled
   wriggling
   wriggler
RGLN
  raglan
RGLR
  irregular
  regular
RGLS
  hourglass
   hourglasses
RGLT
  regality
   regalities
RGLY
  regalia
RGM
  origami
RGMFN
  ragamuffin
RGMRL
  rigmarole(or)riga-
RGN
  air gun
  oregano

Oregon
organ
regain
RGND
organdy
  organdies
RGNG
rigging
RGNK
organic
RGNKL
organically
RGNMKS
ergonomics
Reaganomics
RGNS
arrogance
RGNST
organist
RGNT
Argonaut
arrogant
RGNZ
organza(cloth)
organize
  organized
  organizing
  organizer
RGNZBL
organizable
RGNZM
organism
RGNZR
organizer
RGNZSHN
organization
RGPKR
ragpicker
RGR
rigger(rig)
rigor(severity), (B)-
roguery   gour
RGRD
regard
RGRDLS
irregardless
regardless
RGRJTSHN
regurgitation
RGRJTT
regurgitate
  regurgitated
  regurgitating
RGRMRTS
rigor mortis
RGRN

Rio Grande
RGRND
Rio Grande
RGRS
regress
  regresses
rigorous
RGRSHN
regression
RGRSV
regressive
RGRT
regret
  regretted
  regretting
RGRTBL
regrettable
regrettably
RGS
argosy
  argosies
rugose(wrinkled)
RGSH
roguish
RGSHN
irrigation
RGSTRL
ergosterol
RGT
argot(jargon)
arrogate(take)
  arrogated
  arrogating
ergot(fungus)
irrigate
  irrigated
  irrigating
regatta
RGTM
ragtime
RGTN
rigatoni
RGW
Uruguay
RGWD
ragweed
RGY
argue
  argued
  arguing
  arguer
RGYBL
arguable
arguably
RGYF
argufy

argufied
argufies
argufier
RGYLR
irregular
regular
RGYLRT
irregularity
  irregularities
regularity
  regularities
RGYLSHN
regulation
RGYLT
regulate
  regulated
  regulating
RGYLTR
regulator
RGYMNT
argument
RGYMNTM
argumentum
  argumenta
RGYMNTSHN
argumentation
RGYMNTTV
argumentative
RGZBT
re-exhibit(show)
RGZM
orgasm
RGZMK
orgasmic
RGZMN
re-examine(look)
  re-examined
  re-examining
RGZMNSHN
reexamination
RHBLTSHN
rehabilitation
RHBLTT
rehabilitate
  rehabilitated
  rehabilitating
RHBLTTV
rehabilitative
RHD
arrowhead
rawhide
RHRS
rehearse
  rehearsed
  rehearsing
RHRSL

rehearsal
RHSH
rehash
  rehashes
RHZ
rehouse
  rehoused
  rehousing
RJ
orgy
  orgies
rage(anger)
  raged
  raging
raj(rule)
rajah(or)
raja
ridge
  ridged
  ridging
urge
  urged
  urging
RJD
rigid
RJDT
rigidity, (pl)-ties
RJKSHN
re-education
rejection
RJKT
re-educate(teach)
  re-educated
  re-educating
reject
RJMN
regimen
RJMNT
regiment
RJMNTL
regimental
RJMNTSHN
regimentation
RJN
origin
orogeny
  orogenic
  orogenesis
Regina
rejoin
region(area)
RJNDR
rejoinder
RJNG
ridging
RJNL

original
regional
RJNLT
originality
originalities
RJNRS
regeneracy
RJNRSHN
regeneration
RJNRT
regenerate
regenerated
regenerating
RJNRTR
regenerator
RJNRTV
regenerative
RJNS
erogenous
regency
regencies
urgency
urgencies
RJNSHN
origination
RJNSS
orogenesis
orogeny
RJNT
argent(silver)
originate
originated
originating
reagent(substance)
regent
urgent
RJNTN
Argentina
Argentine
argentine(silvery)
RJNTR
originator
RJPL
ridgepole
RJR
ordure
RJS
arduous
rejoice
rejoiced
rejoicing
RJSD
regicide
RJST
readjust
RJSTK

orgiastic
RJSTR
register
registry
registries
RJSTRNT
registrant
RJSTRR
registrar
RJSTRSHN
registration
RJVNSHN
rejuvenation
RJVNT
rejuvenate
rejuvenated
rejuvenating
RJVNTR
rejuvenator
RK
arc(curve)
arcked
arcking
ark(boat,chest)
earache
Iraq
Iraqi
irk(annoy)
rack
rake
raked
raking
rakish
reck(take heed)
re-echo
re-echoes
reek(smell)
Reich(German)
rickey(drink)
rock
rocky
rockier
rockiest
rockiness
rook(trick)
rookie(beginner)
roque(game)
ruck(fold,jumble)
wrack(ruin)
wreak(inflict,
    express)
wreck(destroy)
RKBND
rock-bound
RKCH
air coach

RKD
arcade
area code
orchid(flower)
RKFRT
Roquefort
RKGNSHN
recognition
RKGNZ
recognize
recognized
recognizing
RKGNZBL
recognizable
recognizably
RKGNZNS
recognizance
RKJ
wreckage
RKK
archaic
rococo
RKL
air-cool(v)
oracle(wise
    counsel)
recall
re-coil(coil again)
recoil(draw back)
RKLJ
archaeology
RKLJST
archaeologist
RKLKSHN
recollection
RKLKT
re-collect
    (collect again)
recollect
    (remember)
RKLM
re-claim
    (claim again)
reclaim(use)
RKLMBL
irreclaimable
reclaimable
RKLMSHN
reclamation
RKLN
recline
reclined
reclining
recliner
RKLS
recluse

RKLSNS
recalescence
RKLSTRNS
recalcitrance
RKLSTRNT
recalcitrant
RKLSV
reclusive
RKLZHN
reclusion
RKMBNS
recumbency
RKMBNT
recumbent
RKMJ
archimage
RKMND
recommend
RKMNDSHN
recommendation
RKMNTNZ
Rocky Mountains
RKMPNS
recompense
recompensed
recompensing
RKMPZ
recompose
recomposed
recomposing
RKMT
recommit
recommitted
recommitting
RKMTL
recommittal
RKMTMNT
recommitment
RKN
arcane
raccoon(animal)
reckon
RKND
iracund
RKNDRL
rock-and-roll
RKNDSHN
air-condition
recondition
RKNDSHNR
air conditioner
RKNDT
recondite
RKNGBR
wrecking bar
RKNJL

NGK:ink **P**:pie **R**:air **S**:ice **SH**:show **T**:toy **THN**:thin **TH**:the **V**:of **W**:we **Y**:you **Z**:is **VZHN**:vision

archangel
RKNNG
reckoning
RKNR
reckoner
RKNRL
rock 'n' roll
RKNS
Arkansas
RKNSDR
reconsider
RKNSL
reconcile
  reconciled
  reconciling
RKNSLBL
irreconcilable
irreconcilably
reconcilable
reconcilably
RKNSLMNT
reconcilement
RKNSLR
reconciler
RKNSLSHN
reconciliation
RKNSLTR
reconciliatory
RKNSNS
reconnaissance
RKNSTRKT
reconstruct
  reconstruction
RKNT
recant
re-count
  (count again)
recount(tell)
RKNTR
raconteur(person)
reconnoiter
RKNV
reconvey
RKNVRT
reconvert
RKNVRZHN
reconversion
RKNZNS
reconnaissance
RKP
recap
  recapped
  recapping
recoup
RKPBL
recappable

RKPCHLSHN
recapitulation
RKPCHLT
recapitulate
  recapitulated
  recapitulating
RKPCHR
recapture
  recaptured
  recapturing
RKPLG
archipelago
RKPRSHN
recuperation
RKPRT
recuperate
  recuperated
  recuperating
RKPTLZ
recapitalize
  recapitalized
  recapitalizing
RKR
aircrew
recur
  recurred
  recurring
rocker
rookery
  rookeries
wreaker
  (vent anger)
wrecker(vehicle,
  destroy)
RKRD
record
RKRDR
air corridor
recorder
RKRDS
recrudesce
  recrudesced
  recrudescing
RKRDSNS
recrudescence
RKRFT
aircraft
RKRK
rickrack
RKRMNSHN
recrimination
RKRMNT
recrement
recriminate
  recriminated
  recriminating

RKRNS
recreance
recurrence
RKRNT
rack-rent
recreant
recurrent
RKRS
recourse
RKRSHN
re-creation
  (create again)
recreation
RKRT
re-create
  (create again)
re-created
re-creating
recreate(play)
  recreated
  recreating
recruit
RKRV
recurve
  recurved
  recurving
RKRVSHN
recurvation
RKRVT
recurvate
RKRZHN
recursion
RKS
raucous
ricasso(rapier)
ruckus
RKSCHNJ
re-exchange(swap)
  re-exchanged
  re-exchanging
RKSH
rickshaw(or)
ricksha
ricochet
RKSHN
air cushion
erection
reaction
RKSHNR
reactionary
  reactionaries
RKSK
rucksack
RKSM
irksome
RKSPLN

re-explain(tell)
RKSPRNS
re-experience
  re-experienced
  re-experiencing
RKSPRS
air express
RKSPRT
re-export
RKST
recast
RKSTR
orchestra
RKSTRL
orchestral
RKSTRSHN
orchestration
RKSTRT
orchestrate
  orchestrated
  orchestrating
RKT
erect
eruct
racket
re-act(act again)
react(respond)
recto
rickety
  ricketier
  ricketiest
  ricketiness
ricotta(cheese)
rocket
RKTBL
racquetball
RKTF
rectify
  rectified
  rectifies, -fier
RKTFBL
rectifiable
rectifiably
RKTFKSHN
rectification
RKTFR
rectifier
RKTK
architect
Arctic
arctic
RKTKCHR
architecture
RKTKSHN
Arctic Ocean
RKTKSRKL

B:by **CH**:each **D**:day **F**:if **G**:go **H**:he **HW**:why **J**:joy **K**:cow **KS**:ax **KWL**:equal **L**:all **M**:may **N**:in

Arctic Circle
RKTKT
architect
RKTL
erectile
rectal
RKTLNR
rectilinear
RKTM
rectum
recta(or)
rectums
RKTNGL
rectangle
RKTNGLR
rectangular
RKTNGYLR
rectangular
RKTP
archetype
archetypal
archetypical
RKTR
erector
racketeer
reactor
rector
rectory
rectories
rocketeer
rocketry
RKTRSKL
Richter scale
RKTRV
architrave
(epistle)
RKTS
rickets
rickettsia
RKTSHN
eructation
RKTT
eructate
eructated
eructating
RKTTD
rectitude
RKTTYD
rectitude
RKTV
reactive
RKTVSHN
reactivation
RKTVT
reactivate
reactivated

reactivating
reactivation
RKV
archive
RKVL
archival
RKVR
air cover
re-cover(cover again)
recover(get back)
recovery
recoveries
RKVRBL
irrecoverable
recoverable
RKVST
archivist
RKWM
requiem
RKWP
re-equip
RKWR
require
required
requiring
RKWRMNT
requirement
RKWST
request
RKWT
requite
requited
requiting
RKWTL
requital
RKWZSHN
requisition
RKWZT
requisite
RKYLR
auricular
oracular
RKYPRSHN
recuperation
RKYPRT
recuperate
recuperated
recuperating
RKYVK
Reykjavik
RKYZNT
recusant
RKZM
archaism
RL

aerial(air)
areal(area)
arrayal(spread)
aural(hearing)
aureole(halo)
earl(rank)
early(time)
earlier
earliest
earliness
oral(mouth)
oriel(window)
oriole(bird)
rail(bar, language)
Raleigh
rally(revive)
rallied
rallies
rallier
real(actual)
reel(whirl)
re-lay(lay again)
relay(send)
rely(depend)
relied
relies
rile(anger)
riled
riling
riyal(money)
roil(stir up)
role(actor's part)
roll(round)
rouleau(small roll)
rouleaux(or)
rouleaus
rowel(tool)
royal(regal)
rule(control)
ruled
ruling
rulable
ruler
RLBK
rollback
RLBL
reliable
reliably
RLBLT
reliability
RLBRD
railbird
RLD
roulade
RLF

real-life
relief
RLFT
airlift
rail foot
RLGSHN
relegation
RLGT
relegate
relegated
relegating
RLHD
railhead
RLJN
religion
RLJS
irreligious
religious
RLK
air lock
oarlock
relic
rollick(romp)
rollicky
rollicksome
RLKL
roll call(n)
roll-call(adj)
RLKS
relax
relaxes
RLKSHN
re-election
RLKSN
relaxin(hormone)
RLKSNT
relaxant
RLKSSHN
relaxation
RLKT
re-elect
relocate
relocated
relocating
relocation
RLKTNS
reluctance
RLKTNT
reluctant
RLKWR
reliquary
reliquaries
RLM
realm
heirloom
RLN

NGK:ink P:pie R:air S:ice SH:show T:toy THN:thin TH:the V:of W:we Y:you Z:is VZHN:vision

air lane
airline
Ireland
Orlon(trademark)
RLND
Ireland
RLNG
railing
ruling(rule)
RLNGKWSH
relinquish
relinquishes
RLNR
airliner
RLNS
reliance
RLNT
relent
reliant
RLPL
roly-poly
RLPLTK
realpolitik
RLPS
relapse
relapsed
relapsing
RLR
raillery
railleries
roller
ruler
RLRD
railroad
RLS
airless
re-lease(lease
again)
release(set free)
released
releasing
RLSH
relish
relishes
RLSHN
relation
RLSHNSHP
relationship
RLSNT
relucent
RLSPLTR
rail-splitter
RLST
aerialist
realist
royalist

RLSTK
realistic
RLSTKL
realistical
RLSTT
real estate
RLZ
Rolls(car)
RLZRS
Rolls-Royce
(trademark)
RLT
reality(actual)
realities
realty(land)
realties
relate
related
relating
relation
roulette(game)
royalty
royalties
RLTBL
relatable
RLTP
roll-top
RLTR
Realtor(or)realtor
RLTV
irrelative
relative
RLTVT
relativity
relativities
RLTVZM
relativism
RLV
relieve(ease)
relieved
relieving
reliever
relive(live again)
relived
reliving
RLVBL
relievable
relievably
RLVNS
irrelevance
relevance
RLVNT
irrelevant
relevant
RLVR
reliever

RLW
railway
rollaway
RLZ
realize
realized
realizing
RLZBL
realizable
RLZM
realism
RLZSHN
realization
RM
army
armies
aroma
aurum(gold)
aurous
ram
rammed
ramming
ream
rheum(mucous)
rheumy
rheumier
rheumiest
rhumb(compass)
rhyme(verse)
rhymed
rhyming
rim(edge)
rimmed
rimming
rime(frost)
rimed
riming
roam
Rome(city)
room(area)
roomy
roomier
roomiest
roominess
rum(liquor)
rummy(game)
rummy(person)
rummies
RMB
rhumb(compass)
rumba
RMBD
re-embody
re-embodied
re-embodies
rhomboid

RMBL
ramble(roam,talk)
rambled
rambling
rambler
rumble(sound)
rumbled
rumbling
RMBLR
rambler
RMBND
armband
RMBNGKSHS
rambunctious
RMBRK
re-embark
re-embarkation
RMBRNT
Rembrandt
RMBRS
re-embrace
re-embraced
re-embracing
reimburse
reimbursed
reimbursing
RMBRSBL
reimbursable
RMBS
rhombus
rhombi(or)
rhombuses
RMCH
rematch
rematches
RMCHR
armature
armchair
RMD
armada
armed
armed forces
remade
remake
remedy
remedied
remedies
RMDBL
irremediable
remediable
RMDFRS
armed force
RMDK
aromatic
rheumatic
RMDL

armadillo
remedial
remodel
RMDSN
  aeromedicine
RMDY
  armadillo
RMDZH
  armadillo
RMF
  earmuff
  ramify
    ramified
    ramifies
RMFKSHN
  ramification
RMFL
  armful
  roomful
RMFSS
  re-emphasis
    re-emphases
RMFSZ
  re-emphasize
    re-emphasized
    re-emphasizing
RMHL
  armhole
RMJ
  rummage
    rummaged
    rummaging
RMJT
  ramjet
RMK
  remake
    remade
    remaking
RMKN
  ramekin
RMKNK
  aeromechanic
RMKNKS
  aeromechanics
RML
  air mail(n)
  airmail(v,adj)
RMLT
  armlet
RMMBR
  remember
RMMBRNS
  remembrance
RMMNT
  armament
RMN

airman
airmen
ermine
remain(continue)
romaine(lettuce)
Roman
roman
Romania
RMND
  remand(send back)
  remind(repeat)
RMNDR
  remainder
    (leftover)
  reminder(remember)
RMNK
  romantic
RMNKTHLSZM
  Roman Catholicism
RMNMRLS
  Roman numerals
RMNN
  Armenian
  Romanian
RMNNT
  remnant
  ruminant
RMNS
  reminisce
    reminisced
    reminiscing
  romance
    romanced
    romancing
RMNSNT
  reminiscent
RMNSR
  reminiscer
RMNSTRNS
  remonstrance
RMNSTRSHN
  remonstration
RMNSTRT
  remonstrate
    remonstrated
    remonstrating
RMNSTRTR
  remonstrator
RMNT
  army ant
  raiment
  remount
  ruminate
    ruminated
    ruminating
    rumination

RMNTK
  romantic
RMNTKL
  romantically
RMNTR
  ruminator
RMNTSZ
  romanticize
    romanticized
    romanticizing
RMNTSZM
  romanticism
RMNY
  Romania
RMNZ
  remains
RMP
  ramp
  rump
RMPJ
  rampage
    rampaged
    rampaging
RMPJS
  rampageous
RMPL
  re-employ(hire)
  rumple
    rumpled
    rumpling
RMPNT
  rampant
RMPRT
  rampart
RMPT
  armpit
RMR
  armoire(cabinet)
  armor, (B)-mour
  armory, (B)-mour
    armories
  reamer
  roamer
  roomer(lodger)
  rumor(words), (B)-
RMRD   mour
  ramrod
RMRJ
  re-emerge
    re-emerged
    re-emerging
    re-emergence
RMRK
  earmark
  remark
RMRKBL

remarkable
remarkably
RMRR
  armorer
RMRS
  remorse
RMRST
  armrest
RMS
  air mass
    air masses
  remiss
RMSBL
  irremissible
  remissible
RMSHKL
  ramshackle
RMSHKLD
  ramshackled
RMSHN
  remission
RMSK
  ransack
RMSTS
  armistice
RMT
  remit
    remitted
    remitting
  remote
    remoter
    remotest
  roomette
  roommate
RMTBL
  remittable
RMTD
  rheumatoid
RMTK
  aromatic
  rheumatic
RMTKNTRL
  remote control
RMTNS
  remittance
RMTNT
  remittent
RMTZM
  rheumatism
RMV
  remove
    removed
    removing
RMVBL
  irremovable
  removable

RMVL
removal
RMWR
armoire(cabinet)
RMWRM
army worm
RMYNRSHN
remuneration
RMYNRT
remunerate
remunerated
remunerating
RMYNRTR
remunerator
RMYNRTV
remunerative
RMYR
Réaumur
RMZ
arms
remise
remised
remising
RN
Aaron
arena(place)
Arian
Arianism
around
arraign(call)
earn
erne(eagle)
errand
Iran
iron(ore,press)
irony
ironies
Orion
rain(water)
rainy
rainier
rainiest
raininess
rand(shoes,money)
rayon
reign(rule)
rein(control)
renew
Reno
Rhine
roan(color)
round(circle)
ruin(destroy)
run
ran
running

runner
runny
runnier
runniest
runniness
urn(vase)
wren(bird)
RNB
rainbow
RNBL
ruinable
RNBND
ironbound
RNBT
runabout
RNCH
ranch
ranches
raunchy
raunchier
raunchiest
raunchiness
wrench(tool,twist)
wrenches
RNCHK
rain check
RNCHR
rancher
RND
around(near)
errand
rand(money,shoes)
randy
re-endow
rend
rondeau(poem)
rondeaux
rondo(music)
round
Rwanda
RNDBT
roundabout
RNDD
rounded
RNDHS
roundhouse
RNDL
roundelay
rundle(ladder)
RNDM
random
RNDMZ
randomize
randomized
randomizing
RNDN

run-down
RNDNG
rending
RNDP
roundup
RNDR
reindeer(animal)
render
RNDRBN
round robin
RNDRP
raindrop
RNDSHN
rendition
RNDTHKLK
round-the-clock
RNDV
rendezvous
rendezvous
RNDVZ
rendezvous
RNDWRM
roundworm
RNF
runoff
RNFL
rainfall
RNFRS
reinforce
reinforced
reinforcing
RNFRSMNT
reinforcement
RNG
earing(sail)
earring(ornament)
renege(fail to
follow through)
reneged
reneging
reneger
ring(circle)
ring(sound)
rang
rung
rung(crossbar)
wring(twist)
wrung
wringing
wrong(not right)
RNGD
renegade
ringed(circle)
RNGDNG
wrongdoing
RNGDR

wrongdoer
RNGJ
re-engage
re-engaged
re-engaging
RNGK
rank
rink
RNGKDNGK
rinkydink(slang)
RNGKL
rankle
rankled
rankling
wrinkle(crease)
wrinkled
wrinkling
wrinkly
wrinklier
wrinkliest
RNGKN
Rankine
RNGKNDFL
rank-and-file(adj)
RNGKR
rancor, (B)rancour
RNGKRS
rancorous
RNGKS
rhonchus(noise)
RNGL
wrangle
wrangled
wrangling
wrangler
RNGLDR
ringleader
RNGLR
wrangler
RNGLT
ringlet
RNGMSTR
ringmaster
RNGN
Rangoon
RNGNG
ringing
RNGR
reneger(fail to
follow)
ringer(ring)
ringer(not a legal
contestant)
wringer(squeezer)
RNGSD
ringside

RNGTN
  orangutan
RNHS
  roundhouse
RNJ
  arrange
    arranged
    arranging
  Orange
  orange(fruit)
  range
    ranged
    ranging
    ranger
  rangy
    rangier
    rangiest
    ranginess
RNJD
  orangeade
RNJMNT
  arrangement
RNJR
  arranger
  ranger
RNJWD
  orangewood
RNK
  Orinoco
  Roanoke
  irenic(place)(or)
    irenical
    irenics(n)
  ironic
RNKL
  ironical
RNKLD
  ironclad
RNKR
  reincur
    reincurred
    reincurring
RNKRNSHN
  reincarnation
RNKRNT
  reincarnate
    reincarnated
    reincarnating
RNKRTN
  Iron Curtain
RNKS
  irenics
RNKT
  re-enact
  raincoat
RNL

renewal
RNLST
  re-enlist
RNM
  aeronomy
RNMKR
  rainmaker
RNMNT
  arraignment
  ornament
RNMNTL
  ornamental
RNMNTSHN
  ornamentation
RNMSHN
  reanimation
RNMT
  reanimate
    reanimated
    reanimating
RNN
  Iranian
  renown
  run-in
  run-on
RNND
  renowned
RNNG
  ironing
  running
RNNGZ
  earnings
RNNS
  renounce
    renounced
    renouncing
RNNSSHN
  renunciation
RNPRF
  rainproof
RNR
  earner
  ornery
    ornerier
    orneriest
    orneriness
  runner
RNRP
  runner-up
RNRZP
  runners-up
RNS
  errancy
    errancies
  erroneous
  rawness

rinse
  rinsed
  rinsing
ruinous
Uranus
RNSD
  rancid
RNSHN
  ruination
RNSHR
  reinsure
    reinsured
    reinsuring
    reinsurer
RNSHS
  arenaceous
RNSK
  ransack
RNSM
  ransom
RNSMTH
  ironsmith
RNSNS
  Renaissance(time)
  renaissance
    (revival)
  renascence
    (new life)
RNSNT
  renascent
RNSRS
  rhinoceros
RNST
  earnest
RNSTN
  ironstone
  rhinestone
RNSTRM
  rainstorm
RNSTT
  reinstate
    reinstated
    reinstating
RNT
  aeronaut
  aren't
  are not
  arrant(out-and-out)
  errant(roving,
    erring)
  Orient(area)
    (Far East)
  orient(east,
    locate)
  ornate
  rant

rennet
rent(lease)
runt(small)
RNTFR
  rent-free
RNTGN
  roentgen
RNTHLJ
  ornithology
RNTK
  aeronautic
    aeronautical
RNTKS
  aeronautics
RNTL
  Oriental(area)
  oriental
  rental
RNTN
  rooten'-tooten'
    (slang)
RNTNT
  renitent
RNTR
  re-enter
  re-entry
    re-entries
RNTS
  rhinitis
RNTSHN
  orientation
RNTT
  orientate
    orientated
    orientating
RNVSHN
  renovation
RNVST
  reinvest
RNVT
  renovate
    renovated
    renovating
    renovator
RNW
  runaway
  runway
RNWR
  ironware
  Renoir
RNWRK
  ironwork
RNWRKS
  ironworks
RNY
  renew

RNYL
renewal
RNZNS
Renaissance(time)
renaissance(revival)
RP
rap(hit,prison,
talk)
rapped
rapping
rape
raped
raping
rapist
reap
repay(give back)
repaid
re-pay(pay again)
re-paid
rip
ripped
ripping
ripper
ripe(mature)
riper
ripest
ripen
rope(cord)
roped
roping
rupee
wrap(cover)
wrapped(or)
wrapt
wrapping
wrapper
RPBLK
republic
RPBLKN
republican
RPBLKSHN
republication
republish
republishes
RPCHR
rapture
raptured
rapturing
rupture(burst)
ruptured
rupturing
RPCHRS
rapturous
RPD
rapid
RPDFR

rapid-fire
RPDT
rapidity
RPF
rip off(v)
rip-off(n)
RPGNNS
repugnance
RPGNNT
repugnant
RPH
Arapaho
RPJ
arpeggio
RPKRD
ripcord
RPKT
air pocket
RPL
rappel(descend)
repeal(revoke)
repel(drive back)
repelled
repelling
reply
replied
replies
ripple
rippled
rippling
RPLG
earplug
RPLK
replica
RPLN
airplane (B)aeroplane
RPLNSH
replenish
replenishes
RPLNT
repellent
replant
RPLS
replace
replaced
replacing
replacer
repulse
repulsed
repulsing
repulser
RPLSBL
irreplaceable
replaceable
RPLSHN
repletion

repulsion
RPLSMNT
replacement
RPLSV
repulsive
RPLT
replete
RPLVN
replevin
RPM
rpm
revolutions
per minute
RPMP
air pump
RPN
rapine
ripen
RPNG
rapping(noise)
wrapping
RPNS
ripeness
RPNT
repent
RPNTNS
repentance
RPNTNT
repentant
RPP
wrap up(v)
wrap-up(n)
RPR
rapier(sword)
rapport(trust)
reaper
repair
reparable
reparably
ripper(rip)
wrapper(paper)
RPRBL
irreparable
irreparably
reparable
reparably
RPRBSHN
reprobation
RPRBT
reprobate
reprobated
reprobating
RPRCH
reproach
reproaches
RPRCHBL

irreproachable
irreproachably
reproachable
reproachably
RPRCHMN
rapprochement
RPRDKSHN
reproduction
RPRDKTV
reproductive
RPRDR
reporter
RPRDS
reproduce
reproduced
reproducing
RPRDSBL
reproducible
RPRDYS
reproduce
reproduced
reproducing
RPRDYSBL
reproducible
RPRF
airproof
reproof
RPRHND
reprehend
RPRHNSBL
reprehensible
RPRHNSHN
reprehension
RPRKSHN
repercussion
RPRMN
repairman
repairmen
RPRMND
reprimand
RPRN
riparian
RPRND
wraparound
RPRNT
reprint
RPRS
re-press(press
again)
re-presses
repress(restrain)
represses
RPRSBL
irrepressible
irrepressibly
repressible

B:by **CH**:each **D**:day **F**:if **G**:go **H**:he **HW**:why **J**:joy **K**:cow **KS**:ax **KWL**:equal **L**:all **M**:may **N**:in

repressibly
RPRSHN
reapportion
reparation
repression
RPRSHNMNT
reapportionment
RPRSS
reprocess
  reprocesses
  reprocessor
RPRT
airport
repartee
report
RPRTDL
reportedly
RPRTR
repertoire(or)
repertory
  repertories
reporter
RPRTRL
repertorial
RPRTWR
repertoire
RPRV
reprieve
  reprieved
  reprieving
re-prove(prove
  again)
  re-proved
  re-proving
reprove(rebuke)
  reproved
  reproving
RPRZ
reprise
RPRZL
reprisal
RPRZNT
re-present(present
  again)
represent
  (stand for)
RPRZNTSHN
representation
RPRZNTTV
representative
RPS
repass
  repasses
ripsaw
RPSD
rhapsody

rhapsodies
RPSDK
rhapsodic
RPSDKL
rhapsodical
RPSDZ
rhapsodize
  rhapsodized
  rhapsodizing
RPSHN
eruption(explode)
irruption(invasion)
RPSHS
rapacious
RPSKLYN
rapscallion
RPSNRTNG
ripsnorting
RPSNRTR
ripsnorter
RPST
rapacity
rapist
repast(food)
riposte(retort)
  riposted
  riposting
RPT
erupt(explode)
irrupt(invade)
rapt(enchant)
repeat
RPTBL
eruptible
RPTD
riptide
RPTL
reptile
RPTLN
reptilian
RPTLYN
reptilian
RPTRL
raptorial
RPTRSHN
repatriation
RPTRT
repatriate
  repatriated
  repatriating
RPTSHN
re-petition
  (petition again)
repetition(repeat)
RPTSHS
repetitious

RPTTV
repetitive
RPTV
eruptive(explode)
irruptive(invade)
RPWK
ropewalk
RPYDSHN
repudiation
RPYDT
repudiate
  repudiated
  repudiating
RPYN
repugn
RPYT
repute
  reputed
  reputing
RPYTBL
reputable
reputably
RPYTBLT
reputability
RPYTSHN
reputation
RPZ
re-pose(pose again)
  re-posed
  re-posing
repose(rest)
  reposed
  reposing
RPZHR
reposure
RPZS
repossess
  repossesses
RPZSHN
repossession
RPZTR
repository
  repositories
RR
arrear(debt)
aurora(sky lights)
error(mistake)
rah-rah(adj)
rare(scarce)
  rarer
  rarest
rear(behind)
roar(noise)
RRBK
roorback
RRBRLS

aurora borealis
RRBT
rarebit
RRDR
reorder
RRDS
reredos(screen)
RRF
rarefy(make thin)
  rarefied
  rarefies
  rarefiable
RRFL
air rifle
RRGNZ
reorganize
  reorganized
  reorganizing
RRGNZSHN
reorganization
RRGRD
rear guard
RRJ
arrearage
RRL
rural
RRM
rearm
RRMMNT
rearmament
RRN
rerun
  reran
  rerunning
RRNGTWNTS
Roaring '20s
RRNJ
rearrange
  rearranged
  rearranging
RRNJMNT
rearrangement
RRSHK
Rorschach
RRSHKTST
Rorschach test
RRT
arrowroot
rarity
  rarities
reroute
  rerouted
  rerouting
rewrite
  rewrote
  rewriting

NGK:ink **P**:pie **R**:air **S**:ice **SH**:show **T**:toy **THN**:thin **TH**:the **V**:of **W**:we **Y**:you **Z**:is **VZHN**:vision

rewritten
RRWRD
rearward
RRWRDZ
rearwards
RRZ
arrears(debt)
RS
arse(buttocks)
erase
erased
erasing
eraser
iris
irises(or)
irides
race
raced
racing
racer
racy
racier
raciest
racily
raciness
rice
ruse(n)(trick)
RSBL
erasable(rub out)
irascible
irascibly
RSBLT
irascibility
RSD
recede
receded
receding
RSDL
recital
RSDVST
recidivist(n)
RSDVSTK
recidivistic
RSDVZM
recidivism
RSF
Recife
RSFL
restful
RSFR
aerosphere
RSH
Irish
rash
rashes
ratio

reissue
reissued
reissuing
riche(rich)
ruche(fabric)
ruching
rush
rushes
RSHF
réchauffé
RSHFL
reshuffle
reshuffled
reshuffling
RSHFT
air shaft
RSHL
racial
RSHN
aeration(air)
oration
ration
Russian
RSHNG
ruching(fabric)
RSHNL
irrational
rational(adj)
rationale(n)
RSHNLT
irrationality
irrationalities
rationality
rationalities
RSHNLZ
rationalize
rationalized
rationalizing
RSHNLZM
rationalism
RSHNLZSHN
rationalization
RSHNRLT
Russian roulette
RSHPMNT
reshipment
RSHR
erasure
rasher(bacon)
reassure
reassured
reassuring
rush-hour(adj)
RSHRNS
reassurance
RSHRS

racehorse
RSHRSH
recherché
RSHSHN
Rosh Hashana
RSHSNT
ratiocinate
ratiocinated
ratiocinating
RSHT
earshot
RSHWR
rush-hour(adj)
RSK
air sac
airsick
risk
risky
riskier
riskiest
riskiness
risqué(sex)
RSKL
rascal
recycle
recycled
recycling
RSKLT
rascality
rascalities
RSKY
rescue
rescued
rescuing
rescuer
RSKYBL
rescuable
RSKYR
rescuer
RSL
aerosol
resale(n)
resell(v)
resold
resole(shoe)
resoled
resoling
rissole(food)
rustle(sound,
steal)
rustled
rustling
rustler
wrestle(grapple)
wrestled
wrestling

wrestler
RSLBL
resalable(resale)
RSLF
ourself
ourselves
RSLNG
wrestling
RSLR
rustler(steal)
wrestler(grapple)
RSLS
restless
RSLT
irresolute
resolute
RSLV
re-solve(solve
again)
re-solved
re-solving
RSLVZ
ourselves
ourself
RSN
arson
re-sign(sign again)
ursine
RSNCHN
recension
RSND
rescind(void)
re-send(send again)
re-sent
re-sound
(sound again)
RSNDBL
rescindable
RSNG
racing
RSNK
arsenic
RSNL
arsenal
RSNSHN
recension
RSNT
recent(time)
re-sent
re-send
(send again)
RSP
rasp
raspy
raspier
raspiest

B:by **CH**:each **D**:day **F**:if **G**:go **H**:he **HW**:why **J**:joy **K**:cow **KS**:ax **KWL**:equal **L**:all **M**:may **N**:in

raspiness
recipe(formula)
RSPD
airspeed(or)
air speed
RSPKT
respect
RSPKTBL
respectable
respectably
RSPKTBLT
respectability
RSPKTFL
respectful
RSPKTV
irrespective
respective
RSPLNDNS
resplendence
RSPLNDNT
resplendent
RSPND
respond
RSPNDNT
respondent
RSPNG
rasping
RSPNS
recipience
recipients(people)
response
RSPNSBL
irresponsible
irresponsibly
responsible
responsibly
RSPNSBLT
irresponsibility
irresponsibilities
responsibility
responsibilities
RSPNSV
responsive
RSPNT
recipient
RSPR
respire
respired
respiring
RSPRKL
reciprocal
RSPRKSHN
reciprocation
RSPRKT
reciprocate
reciprocated

reciprocating
RSPRKTR
reciprocator
RSPRSHN
respiration
RSPRST
reciprocity
reciprocities
RSPRTR
respirator
respiratory
RSPS
aerospace
airspace
RSPSHN
reception
RSPSHNST
receptionist
RSPT
recept(mental
  image)
respite
respited
respiting
RSPTBL
receptable
RSPTKL
receptacle
RSPTR
receptor
RSPTV
receptive
RSR
eraser
racer
RSRCH
research
researches
RSRCHR
researcher
RSRFS
resurface
resurfaced
resurfacing
RSRJ
resurge
resurged
resurging
RSRJNS
resurgence
RSRJNT
resurgent
RSRS
resource
RSRSFL
resourceful

RSRT
re-sort
  (sort again)
RSRV
re-serve
  (serve again)
RSS
reassess(think)
reassesses
recess
  recesses
rhesus
RSSHN
recession
RSSTBL
irresistible
irresistibly
resistible
resistibly
RSSTBLT
irresistibility
resistibility
RSSTSHN
resuscitation
RSSTT
resuscitate
resuscitated
resuscitating
RSSTTR
resuscitator
RSSV
recessive
RST
aorist(tense)
arrest
erst
receipt(receive)
recite(speak)
  recited
  reciting
reset(set again)
  reset
  resetting
rest
roast(heat)
roost(perch)
roust(action)
russet
rust
rusty
  rustier
  rustiest
  rustiness
wrest(pull)
wrist(hand)
RSTBLSH

re-establish
re-establishes
RSTBND
wristband
RSTBT
roustabout
RSTDL
Aristotle
RSTFL
restful
RSTHWL
erstwhile
RSTK
restock
rustic
RSTKL
rustical
RSTKRS
aristocracy
aristocracies
RSTKRT
aristocrat
RSTKT
rusticate
rusticated
rusticating
rustication
rusticator
RSTL
recital
RSTLK
wristlock
RSTLS
restless
RSTLT
wristlet
RSTNG
arresting
resting
RSTPN
wrist pin
RSTPRF
rustproof
RSTR
arrester
restore
  restored
  restoring
roaster(cooker)
roister
  (merrymaking)
rooster(chicken)
roster(list of
  names)
RSTRK
race track

NGK:ink **P**:pie **R**:air **S**:ice **SH**:show **T**:toy **THN**:thin **TH**:the **V**:of **W**:we **Y**:you **Z**:is **VZHN**:vision

RSTRKCHR
restructure
restructured
restructuring
RSTRKSHN
restriction
RSTRKT
restrict
RSTRKTV
restrictive
RSTRM
rostrum
rostra(or)
rostrums
restroom
RSTRN
re-strain(strain
again)
restrain(hold
back)
RSTRNT
restaurant
restraint
RSTRP
airstrip
RSTRR
roisterer
RSTRS
roisterous
RSTRSHN
restoration
RSTRTR
restaurateur
RSTRTV
restorative
RSTSHN
recitation
RSTST
rusticity
rustic
RSTT
aerostat
restate
restated
restating
rheostat
RSTTL
Aristotle
RSTTSHN
restitution
RSTTV
recitative
RSTTYSHN
restitution
RSTV
restive

RSTWCH
wrist watch
RSV
erosive
receive
received
receiving
RSVBL
receivable
RSVP
R.S.V.P.(or)r.s.v.p.
(please reply)
RSVR
receiver
RSVRSHP
receivership
RSW
raceway
RSZHN
recision
(cancellation)
rescission(void,
repeal)
RSZM
racism (B)(or)racialism
RT
aerate(air)
aerated
aerating
aorta(blood)
aortas(or)
aortae
aright(correctly)
art
arty
artier
artiest
artily
artiness
errata(errors)
erratum
irate(angry)
rat(rodent)
ratted
ratting
ratty
rattier
rattiest
rattiness
rate
rated
rating
right(correct)
righty(person)
righties
riot(disturbance)

rite(religious
act)
root(plant part,
cheer)
rot(decay)
rotted
rotting
rotten
rote(routine)
rout(defeat)
route(course)
routed
routing
rut(groove,sex)
rutted
rutting
rutty
ruttier
ruttiest
ruttiness
wright(skilled
person)
writ(court
order)
write(inscribe)
wrote
writing
written
wrote(write)
wrought(work)
RTBG
rutabaga
RTBL
irritable
irritably
ratable(rate)
ratably(rate)
retable(altar)
RTBLT
irritability
irritabilities
ratability(rate)
RTBR
root beer
RTCH
retouch
retouches
RTCHK
artichoke
RTF
ratify
ratified
ratifies
write off(v)
write-off(n)
RTFKSHN

ratification
RTFKT
artifact
RTFNGK
ratfink(slang)
RTFR
ratifier
RTFRM
retiform
RTFS
artifice(skill)
artificer
RTFSHL
artificial
RTFSR
artificer(worker)
RTGRVYR
rotogravure
RTH
Earth
earth
earthy
earthier
earthiest
earthiness
ruth(sorrow)
wraith(ghost)
wrath(anger)
wreath(flowers)
wreathe(flowering)
wreathed
wreathing
writhe(squirm)
writhed
writhing
RTHDKS
Orthodox
(religious title)
orthodox
orthodoxy
orthodoxies
RTHDNKS
orthodontics
RTHDNSH
orthodontia
RTHDNST
orthodontist
RTHDNTKS
orthodontics
RTHDNTST
orthodontist
RTHFL
ruthful(sorrow)
wrathful
RTHGRF
orthography

RTHKN
orthicon
RTHKWK
earthquake
RTHL
earthly
earthliness
rat-hole(store up)
rat-holed
rat-holing
RTHLNG
earthling
RTHLS
ruthless
RTHM
rhythm
RTHMK
arrhythmic
rhythmic
RTHMKL
rhythmical
RTHMTHD
rhythm method
RTHMTK
arithmetic
RTHMTSHN
arithmetician
RTHN
earthen
RTHNDD
right-handed
RTHNDR
right-hander
RTHNGK
rethink
rethought
RTHNWR
earthenware
RTHPDKS
orthopedics
RTHPDST
orthopedist
RTHR
rather
RTHRMSN
erythromycin
RTHRTK
arthritic
RTHRTS
arthritis
RTHSHKNG
earthshaking
RTHSKLR
rathskeller
RTHTKS
orthotics

RTHWRD
earthward
RTK
Arctic
arctic
erotic(sex)
erotica(sexual
art)
erratic
(not fixed)
retake
retook
retaking
retaken
RTKL
article
erotically(sexual)
erratically
(not fixed)
RTKSHN
Arctic Ocean
RTKSRKL
Arctic Circle
RTKT
urticate
urticated
urticating
RTKYL
reticule(purse)
ridicule(mock)
ridiculed
ridiculing
ridiculer
RTKYLR
articular
reticular
RTKYLSHN
articulation
RTKYLT
articulate
articulated
articulating
reticulate(network)
reticulated
reticulating
RTKYLTR
articulator
RTL
rattail(file)
rattle
rattled
rattling
rattly
retail(sell)
retool
RTLBRND

rattlebrained
RTLN
ratline
RTLNT
rutilant
RTLR
artillery
rattler
RTLS
rootless
RTLSHN
retaliation
RTLSNK
rattlesnake
RTLT
retaliate
retaliated
retaliating
rootlet
RTLTR
retaliatory
RTLTRP
rattletrap
RTM
erratum
errata
RTN
ratine(fabric)
rattan(palm)
ratoon
retain(keep)
retina(eye)
retinae(or)
retinas
retiné(fabric)
retinue(people who
accompany)
routine(pattern)
write in(v)
write-in(n,adj)
RTND
orotund
rotund
rotunda
RTNDT
rotundity
rotundities
RTNG
rating(rate)
writing
RTNGLD
right-angled
RTNGNT
rating nut
RTNR
retainer

RTNSHN
retention
RTNT
irritant
RTNTV
retentive
RTNTVT
retentivity
RTNV
retentive
RTNY
retinue
RTNZ
routinize
routinized
routinizing
RTP
write up(v)
write-up(n)
RTR
aerator
air-to-air(adj)
artery(blood)
arteries
orator
oratorio
oratory
oratories
ratter(dog,cat)
rater(person)
retire(stop)
retired
retiring
retiree
rhetor(orator)
rooter(root)
rotary
rotaries
rotor(mechanical)
writer(person)
RTRBYSHN
retribution
RTRD
retard(slow)
retread
RTRDM
Rotterdam
RTRDNT
retardant
RTRDSHN
retardation
RTRDT
retardate(person)
RTRFLKS
retroflex
retroflexion

RTRFR
retrofire
retrofired
retrofiring
RTRFT
retrofit
RTRGRD
retrograde
retrograded
retrograding
RTRGRS
retrogress
retrogresses
RTRGRSHN
retrogression
RTRK
rhetoric
RTRKL
oratorical
rhetorical
RTRKSHN
retraction
retroaction
RTRKT
retract
RTRKTBL
retractable
RTRKTL
retractile
RTRKTR
retractor
RTRKTV
retroactive
RTRL
arterial
retrial
RTRMNT
retirement
RTRN
return
returnee
wrought iron
RTRNBL
returnable
RTRNCH
retrench
retrenches
RTRP
rattrap
RTRRKT
retrorocket
RTRS
rat race
re-trace(trace
again)
re-traced

re-tracing
retrace(go back)
retraced
retracing
RTRSBL
retraceable
RTRSHN
reiteration
rhetorician
RTRSKLRSS
arteriosclerosis
RTRSPKSHN
retrospection
RTRSPKT
retrospect
RTRSSHN
retrocession
RTRT
reiterate
reiterated
reiterating
reiteration
retort
re-treat(treat
again)
retreat(go back)
RTRV
retrieve
retrieved
retrieving
RTRVBL
irretrievable
irretrievably
retrievable
retrievably
RTRVBLT
irretrievability
retrievability
RTRVL
retrieval
RTRVR
retriever
RTRVRND
Rt. Rev.
RTRZ
Reuters(news)
rooters
RTS
iritis
riotous
ritz(style)
ritzy(swanky)
ROTC
Reserve Officers
Training Corps
RTSHN

irritation
rotation
RTSHNL
irrotational
rotational
RTSNS
reticence
RTSNT
reticent
RTSR
rotisserie
RTSRFS
air-to-surface(adj)
RTST
artist
artiste(entertainer)
RTSTK
artistic
RTSTR
artistry
artistries
artistically
RTSZM
eroticism
RTT
airtight
irritate
irritated
irritating
irritation
rotate(turn)
rotated
rotating
rotation
RTTBL
rotatable
RTTR
irritator
rotator
RTTTT
rat-a-tat-tat
RTTV
irritative
RTTWRK
right-to-work(adj)
RTVW
right of way
rights of way
RTWNG
right wing(n)
right-winger
right-wing(adj)
RTWRK
right-to-work(adj)
RTZHN
artesian

RTZN
artisan
RTZNS
reticence
RTZNT
reticent
RV
arrive
arrived
arriving
rave(speak
wildly)
raved
raving
reeve(fasten,
officer)
rove(or)
reeved
reeving
rev(turn)
revved
revving
rive(tear apart)
rived
riving
riven
rove(roam)
roved
roving
rover
RVGT
ravigote
RVJ
ravage
ravaged
ravaging
RVK
revoke
revoked
revoking
RVKBL
irrevocable
irrevocably
revocable
revocably
RVKBLT
irrevocability
revocability
RVKSHN
revocation
RVL
arrival
ravel(tangle), (B)- lled,
ravioli(food)   (B)-lling
reveal(make
known)

reveille(bugle)
revel(delight)
revile(denounce)
  reviled
  reviling
rival(foe)
RVLMNT
ravelment
RVLNG
raveling
  (thread)
RVLR
revelry
  revelries
  (merrymaking)
rivalry(compete)
  rivalries
RVLSHN
revelation
  (reveal)
revolution
  (cycle)
revulsion
  (disgust)
RVLSHNR
revolutionary
  revolutionaries
RVLSHNZ
revolutionize
  revolutionized
  revolutionizing
RVLT
revolt(rebel)
RVLTNG
revolting
  (disgust)
RVLV
revolve
  revolved
  revolving
RVLVBL
revolvable
RVLVR
revolver
RVLYSHN
re-evaluation
RVLYT
re-evaluate
  re-evaluated
  re-evaluating
RVMP
revamp
RVN
raven(bird,
  devour)
ravine(ditch)

revenue(money)
RVNJ
revenge
  revenged
  revenging
RVNJFL
revengeful
RVNJR
revenger
RVNS
ravenous
RVNY
revenue
RVR
revere(venerate)
  revered
  revering
reverie(daydream)
river(water)
Riviera(resort)
rover(nomad)
RVRBRNT
reverberant
RVRBRSHN
reverberation
RVRBRT
reverberate
  reverberated
  reverberating
RVRBRTR
reverberator
  reverberatory
RVRNCHL
reverential
RVRND
reverend
RVRNS
irreverence
reverence
RVRNSHL
reverential
RVRNT
irreverent
reverent
RVRS
reverse
  reversed
  reversing
RVRSBL
irreversible
  irreversibly
reversible
  reversibly
RVRSBLT
irreversibility
reversibility

RVRSD
riverside
RVRSL
reversal
RVRT
revert
RVRZ
revers(part of
  garment)
RVRZHN
reversion
RVRZHNR
reversionary
RVSH
ravish
  ravishes
RVSHMNT
ravishment
RVSHNG
ravishing
RVST
revest
RVT
rivet
RVTLZ
revitalize
  revitalized
  revitalizing
  revitalization
RVTR
riveter
RVV
revive
  revived
  reviving
revolve
  revolved
  revolving
  revolver
RVVBL
revivable
RVVF
revivify
  revivified
  revivifies
  revivification
RVVL
revival
RVVLST
revivalist
RVVR
revolver
RVW
au revoir
RVWR
au revoir

RVY
review(look over)
revue(show)
RVYL
reviewal
RVYLT
rivulet
RVYR
reviewer(critic)
rivière
Riviera(resort)
RVZ
revise(edit)
  revised,-sing
RVZHN
revision
RVZR
reviser(or)revisor
revisory
RVZT
revisit
RW
areaway
airway
RWKS
earwax
RWND
rewind
  rewound
RWRD
reward
RWRTH
airworthy
  airworthiness
RWVZ
airwaves
RWZ
airways
RY
arroyo
RYD
Riyadh
RYDSHN
erudition
RYDT
erudite
RYL
royal
RYLST
royalist
RYLT
royalty
  royalties
RYNT
reunite
  reunited

NGK:ink **P**:pie **R**:air **S**:ice **SH**:show **T**:toy **THN**:thin **TH**:the **V**:of **W**:we **Y**:you **Z**:is **VZHN**:vision

reuniting
RYNYN
  Reunion
  reunion
RYZ
  reuse
  reused
  reusing
RYZBL
  reusable
  reusably
RYZBLT
  reusability
RZ
  Aries
  arise
    arose
    arising
    arisen
  arouse(excite,
    wake up)
    aroused
    arousing
  ours(not yours)
  raise(lift)
    raised
    raising
  rays(light)
  raze(demolish)
    razed
    razing
  razz(tease)
    razzes
  reseau(net,grid)
    reseaux(or)
    reseaus
  rise(move higher)
    rose
    rising
    risen
  rose(flower)
  rosy
    rosier
    rosiest
    rosily
    rosiness
  rouse(wake,spur)
    roused
    rousing
  ruse(n)(trick)
RZBD
  rosebud
RZBL
  risible(laughter)
RZBLT
  risibility

risibilities
RZBR
  raspberry
  raspberries
RZBSH
  rosebush
  rosebushes
RZD
  reside(live)
    resided
    residing
  residue(remainder)
RZDNCHL
  residential
RZDNS
  residence(place)
  residency
    residencies
  residents(people)
RZDNSHL
  residential
RZDNT
  resident
RZDSTN
  Rosetta stone
RZDY
  residue
RZGNSHN
  resignation
RZH
  rouge
    rouged
    rouging
RZHM
  regime
RZHN
  erasion(erase)
  erosion(earth)
RZHSR
  regisseur
RZJL
  residual
RZJM
  residuum
RZJR
  residuary
RZKLRD
  rose-colored
RZKRSHN
  Rosicrucian
RZL
  arousal
  resile(spring
    back)
    resiled
    resiling

roseola
RZLDZL
  razzle-dazzle
RZLSHN
  resolution
RZLT
  irresolute
  resolute
  result
RZLTNT
  resultant
RZLV
  resolve
    resolved
    resolving
RZLVBL
  resolvable
RZLVNT
  resolvent
RZLYBL
  irresoluble
  irresolubly
  resoluble
  resolubly
RZLYNS
  resilience
  resiliency
RZLYNT
  resilient
RZM
  resume(begin
    again)
    resumed
    resuming
  resumé(summary)
  rhizome
RZMBL
  resemble
  resumable
RZMBLNS
  resemblance
RZMN
  oarsman
  oarsmen
RZMPSHN
  resumption
RZMR
  rosemary
RZMSHN
  resumption
RZMTZ
  razzmatazz
RZN
  Arizona
  raisin(fruit)
  reason(think)

resign(give up)
resin(sap)
rezone(zone
  again)
  rezoned
  rezoning
rosin(pine resin)
RZNBL
  reasonable
  reasonably
RZNBLNS
  reasonableness
RZND
  resigned
  resound
RZNDTR
  raison d'etre
RZNNG
  reasoning
RZNNS
  resonance
RZNNT
  resonant
RZNS
  resinous
RZNT
  resent
  resonate
    resonated
    resonating
RZNTFL
  resentful
RZNTMNT
  resentment
RZNTR
  resonator
RZR
  razor
  riser(early)
  rosary
    rosaries
RZRBK
  razorback
RZRKSHN
  resurrection
RZRKT
  resurrect
RZRS
  resource
RZRSFL
  resourceful
RZRT
  resort
RZRV
  reserve
    reserved

reserving
RZRVDL
reservedly
RZRVR
reservoir
RZRVSHN
reservation
RZRVST
reservist
RZRVWR
reservoir
RZST
resist
RZSTBL
irresistible
irresistibly
resistible
resistibly
RZSTNS
resistance
RZSTNT
resistant
RZSTR
resister(one
who resists)
resistor
(electrical)
RZSTV
resistive
RZSTVT
resistivity
RZT
roseate(adj)
(rosy,bright)
rosette
(ornament)
RZTS
ersatz
RZTSTN
Rosetta stone
RZWD
rosewood

S

ace
aced
acing
ass, (B)arse
asses
assay(analysis)
Aussie

Australian
CIA
Central
Intelligence
Agency
essay(prose,try)
ice(water)
iced
icing
icy
icier
iciest
icily
iciness
say(speak)
said
saw(tool)
saw
see
sea(water)
see(eyes)
saw
seen
sew(stitch)
sewn
sigh(sound)
Sioux(Indian)
so(thus)
so(tone)(or)
sol
sow(reap)
sown
sow(hog)
sough(rustling
sound)
soy(bean)
sue(law)
sued
suing
us(pronoun)
SB
CB
citizens band
radio
sabot(shoe)
Seabee
sib(kinsman)
sob(cry)
sobbed
sobbing
sub(sandwich,
submarine)
sub(substitution)
subbed
subbing
substitution

SBCHSR
subchaser
SBD
subdue
subdued
subduing
SBDB
subdeb
SBDBL
subduable
SBDBYTNT
subdebutante
SBDKL
sabbatical
SBDMNNT
subdominant
SBDR
subduer
SBDSHN
subaudition
SBDVD
subdivide
subdivided
subdividing
SBDVDR
subdivider
SBDVZHN
subdivision
SBDY
subdue
subdued
subduing
SBDYBL
subduable
SBDYR
subduer
SBFML
subfamily
subfamilies
SBGRP
subgroup
SBHD
subhead
SBHYMN
subhuman
SBJDS
sub judice(law)
SBJGSHN
subjugation
SBJGT
subjugate
subjugated
subjugating
SBJGTR
subjugator
SBJKSHN

subjection
SBJKT
subject
SBJKTMTR
subject matter
SBJKTV
subjective
SBJKTVT
subjectivity
SBJKTVZM
subjectivism
SBJN
subjoin
SBJNDR
subjoinder
SBJNGKSHN
subjunction
SBJNGKTV
subjunctive
SBJNR
subgenera
SBJNS
subgenus
subgenera
SBJSNS
subjacency
SBJSNT
subjacent
SBK
sawbuck(slang)
($10 or $20)
SBKLBR
subcaliber, (B)-bre
SBKLCHR
subculture
SBKLS
subclass
subclasses
SBKMT
subcommittee
SBKNGDM
subkingdom
SBKNSHS
subconscious
SBKNTNNT
subcontinent
SBKNTRKT
subcontract
SBKNTRKTR
subcontractor
SBKS
icebox
iceboxes
SBKWS
subaqueous
SBKYT

subacute
SBKYTNS
subcutaneous
SBL
sable
sowbelly
sowbellies
suable(sue)
SBLM
sublime
sublimed
subliming
SBLMNL
subliminal
SBLMSHN
sublimation
SBLMT
sublimate
sublimated
sublimating
sublimity
sublimities
SBLNG
sibling
SBLNGGWL
sublingual
SBLNS
sibilance
SBLNT
sibilant
SBLS
sublease
subleased
subleasing
SBLT
suability
sue
sublet
sublet
subletting
SBLTRN
subaltern
SBMKRSKPK
submicroscopic
SBMLTPL
submultiple
SBMNCHR
subminiature
SBMNCHRZ
subminiaturize
subminiaturized
subminiaturizing
SBMNCHRZSHN
subminia-
turization
SBMNTN

submontane
SBMRJ
submerge
submerged
submerging
SBMRJBL
submergible
SBMRJNL
submarginal
SBMRJNS
submergence
SBMRN
submarine
SBMRNR
submariner
SBMRS
submerse
submersed
submersing
SBMRSBL
submersible
SBMRZHN
submersion
SBMSHN
submission
SBMSHNGN
submachine gun
SBMSV
submissive
SBMT
submit
submitted
submitting
SBMTL
submittal
SBMTR
submitter
SBN
C-band
S-band
soybean
SBND
C-band
S-band
icebound
SBNDKS
subindex
subindices
SBNRML
subnormal
SBNRMLT
subnormality
subnormalities
SBPKL
subapical
SBPLT

subplot
SBPRNSPL
subprincipal
SBR
isobar
saber, (B)sabre
seborrhea
sober
SBRB
suburb
suburbia
SBRBN
suburban
SBRBNT
suburbanite
SBRD
seaboard
subarid
SBRDK
subarctic
SBRDNSHN
subordination
SBRDNSHNST
subordinationist
SBRDNT
subordinate
subordinated
subordinating
SBRDNTV
subordinative
SBRDR
suborder
SBRG
iceberg
SBRGSHN
subrogation
SBRGT
subrogate
subrogated
subrogating
SBRJN
subregion
SBRJNL
subregional
SBRK
sobriquet
SBRKR
icebreaker
SBRKT
sobriquet
SBRMNDD
sober-minded
SBRN
seaborne
suborn
SBRNDKS

cybernetics
SBRNR
suborner
SBRNSHN
subornation
SBRNT
cybernate
cybernated
cybernating
SBRNTKS
cybernetics
SBRPSHN
subreption
SBRPTSHS
subreptitious
SBRT
sobriety
soubrette
sybarite
SBRTK
subarctic
sybaritic
SBRTKL
sybaritical
SBRZ
sea breeze
sub rosa
SBS
subbase
(molding)
subbass(music)
SBSD
subside
subsided
subsiding
subsidy
subsidies
SBSDNS
subsidence
SBSDR
subsidiary
subsidiaries
SBSDZ
subsidize
subsidized
subsidizing
SBSDZR
subsidizer
SBSDZSHN
subsidization
SBSHNK
suboceanic
SBSHS
sebaceous
SBSKRB
subscribe

B:by **CH**:each **D**:day **F**:if **G**:go **H**:he **HW**:why **J**:joy **K**:cow **KS**:ax **KWL**:equal **L**:all **M**:may **N**:in

subscribed
subscribing
SBSKRBR
subscriber
SBSKRPSHN
subscription
SBSKRPT
subscript
SBSKRPTV
subscriptive
SBSKWNS
subsequence
SBSKWNT
subsequent
SBSL
subsoil
SBSM
subsume
subsumed
subsuming
SBSMBL
subassembly
SBSMNT
subbasement
SBSNK
subsonic
SBSPSHZ
subspecies
SBSPSZ
subspecies
SBSRV
subserve
subserved
subserving
SBSRVNS
subservience
subserviency
SBSRVNT
subservient
SBSST
subsist
SBSSTNS
subsistence
SBSSTNT
subsistent
SBSSTR
sob sister
SBST
subset
SBSTNCHL
substantial
SBSTNCHLT
substantiality
substantialities
SBSTNCHT
substantiate

substantiated
substantiating
SBSTNDRD
substandard
SBSTNS
substance
SBSTNSHL
substantial
SBSTNSHLT
substantiality
substantialities
SBSTNSHSHN
substantiation
SBSTNSHT
substantiate
substantiated
substantiating
SBSTNTV
substantive
SBSTNTVL
substantival
SBSTR
sob story
sob stories
SBSTRKCHR
substructure
SBSTRKCHRL
substructural
SBSTRKSHN
substruction
SBSTRT
substrata
SBSTRTM
substratum
substrata(or)
substratums
SBSTS
asbestos
SBSTSHN
substation
SBSTTSHN
substitution
SBSTTSHNL
substitutional
SBSTTT
substitute
substituted
substituting
SBSTTTBL
substitutable
SBSTTTBLT
substitutability
SBSTTTV
substitutive
SBSTTYSHN
substitution

SBSTTYSHNL
substitutional
SBSTTYT
substitute
substituted
substituting
SBSTTYTBL
substitutable
SBSTTYTBLT
substitutability
SBSTTYTV
substitutive
SBSYM
subsume
subsumed
subsuming
SBT
sabot
subito
SBTDL
subtitle
subtotal
SBTH
Sabbath
SBTKL
sabbatical
SBTMK
subatomic
SBTND
subtend
SBTNK
subtonic
SBTNNS
subtenancy
SBTNNT
subtenant
SBTR
saboteur
SBTRFYJ
subterfuge
SBTRHND
subtrahend
SBTRKSHN
subtraction
SBTRKT
subtract
SBTRKTV
subtractive
SBTRNN
subterranean
SBTRPK
subtropic
SBTRPKL
subtropical
SBTTL
subtitle

subtotal
SBTZH
sabotage
sabotaged
sabotaging
SBVNSHN
subvention
SBVRSV
subversive
SBVRT
subvert
SBVRZHN
subversion
SBVRZHNR
subversionary
SBVRZV
subversive
SBW
subway
SBYDS
sub judice(law)
SCH
eschew
such
SCHL
eschewal
satchel
SCHNDSCH
such and such
SCHR
estuary
estuaries
oyster
suture
sutured
suturing
SCHRBL
saturable
SCHRL
estuarial
SCHRNT
saturant
SCHRSHN
saturation
SCHRT
saturate
saturated
saturating
SCHSHN
situation
SCHSHNL
situational
SCHT
escheat
situate
situated

situating
SCHWSHN
situation
SCHWT
situate
situated
situating
SD
acedia(apathy)
acid
cede(grant,
  give up)
ceded
ceding
city
cities
c.o.d.
cash on delivery
pseudo(false)
sad
sadder
saddest
sadden
said
say
seed(embryo,
  ranking)
seedy
seedier
seediest
seediness
side(edge)
sided
siding
sod(grass)
sodded
sodding
soda(water)
SDBD
seedbed
SDBL
suitable
suitability
SDBRD
sideboard
SDBRNS
sideburns
SDBSD
side-by-side(adj)
SDDL
citadel
SDF
acidify
acidified
acidifies
citify

citified
citifies
SDFNTN
soda fountain
SDJRK
soda jerk
SDK
acidic(like acid)
acid
acetic(an acid)
ascetic(person)
SDKK
sidekick
SDKR
sidecar
SDKRKR
soda cracker
SDKSHN
seduction
SDKTRS
seductress
seductresses
SDKTV
seductive
SDL
cedilla(mark)
saddle(seat)
saddled
saddling
seidel(mug)
sidle(movement)
sidled
sidling
sodal(brother-
  hood)
subtle(slight)
subtler
subtlest
subtly
SDLBG
saddlebag
SDLKLTH
saddlecloth
SDLN
acetylene(gas)
sideline
SDLNG
seedling
sidelong
SDLR
saddler
SDLSNS
sedulousness
SDLSR
saddle sore
SDLST

sodalist
SDLT
sedulity
  (diligent)
sidelight
sodality(brother-
  hood)
sodalities
subtlety(slight)
subtleties
SDM
sodium
sodomy
sodomies
SDMNT
sediment
SDMNTR
sedimentary
SDMNTSHN
sedimentation
SDMSKZM
sadomasochism
SDMT
sodomite
SDMVPRLMP
sodium-vapor lamp
SDMZ
sodomize
sodomized
sodomizing
SDN
sedan(car)
sodden(soggy)
Sudan, The
sudden(abrupt)
Sydney
SDNDTH
sudden death
SDNG
setting(place)
siding(side)
SDNM
pseudonym
SDNMS
pseudonymous
SDNMT
pseudonymity
SDNTR
sedentary
SDNZ
Sudanese
SDP
setup(n,adj)
SDR
cedar(wood)
cider(liquid)(B)cyder

seeder(tool)
siddur(book)
solder(weld,
  metal)
SDRB
Saudi Arabia
SDRFK
sudorific
SDRL
sidereal
SDRM
side arm
handgun
SDRN
sadiron
Saturn
SDRST
satirist
SDS
ac-dc(or)
ac/dc
ace-deuce
acey-deucy(game)
seduce
seduced
seducing
seducer
SDSBL
seducible
SDSDL
sidesaddle
SDSH
sideshow
SDSHN
sedation(soothe)
sedition(inciting
  rebellion)
SDSHS
seditious
SDSLP
sideslip
SDSN
citizen
SDSNS
pseudoscience
SDSPLTNG
sidesplitting
SDSR
seducer
SDSS
acidosis
SDST
sadist
sawdust
SDSTK
sadistic

SDSTKL
sadistically(pain)
SDSTP
sidestep(v)
sidestepped
sidestepping
sidestepper
SDSTRK
sidestroke
SDSWP
sideswipe
sideswiped
sideswiping
SDT
acidity
assiduity
assiduities
sedate
sedated
sedating
sedation
SDTRK
sidetrack
SDTV
sedative
SDWD
city-wide
SDWK
sidewalk
SDWNDR
sidewinder
SDWZ
sideways
sidewise
SDYLSNS
sedulousness
SDYLT
acidulate
acidulated
acidulating
acidulation
sedulity
SDYS
ace-deuce
acey-deucy(game)
seduce
seduced
seducing
SDYSBL
seducible
SDYSR
seducer
SDYT
assiduity
assiduities
SDZ

suds
sudsy
sudsier
sudsiest
sudsily
sudsiness
SDZM
sadism
SDZN
citizen
SF
ossify
ossified
ossifies
safe
safer
safest
sofa
Sofia
sough(noise)
SFBL
softball
SFBLD
soft-boiled
SFD
seafood
SFDPZT
safe-deposit
SFDRNGK
soft drink
SFGRD
safeguard
SFGS
esophagus
esophagi
SFKNDKT
safe-conduct
SFKPNG
safekeeping
SFKS
asphyxia
suffix
suffixes
SFKSHN
suffixion
suffocation
SFKSSHN
asphyxiation
SFKST
asphyxiate
asphyxiated
asphyxiating
SFKSTR
asphyxiator
SFKT
suffocate

suffocated
suffocating
SFKVR
soft-cover
SFL
icefall
soufflé
SFLD
ice field
syphiloid
SFLK
cephalic
cephalous
SFLR
safflower
SFLS
acephalous
cephalous
cephalic
Sioux Falls
syphilis
SFLT
asphalt
SFLTK
syphilitic
SFLTM
asphaltum
asphalt
SFLZ
Sioux Falls
SFMR
sophomore
SFMRK
sophomoric
SFMRKL
sophomorical
SFN
siphon
soften
SFND
sphenoid
SFNGKS
sphinx
sphinges(or)
sphinxes
SFNGKTR
sphincter
SFNGS
sphinx
sphinxes(or)
sphinges
SFNJZ
sphinges
sphinx
SFNK
sphenic(wedge)

SFNKS
sphinx
sphinges(or)
sphinxes
SFNKTR
sphincter
SFNKTRL
sphincteral
SFNR
softener
SFPDL
soft-pedal(v)
SFR
cipher(code,zero)
safari
sapphire(gem)
sphere
sphered
sphering
sphery
spherier
spheriest
suffer
SFRBL
sufferable
SFRD
spheroid
SFRJ
suffrage
SFRJST
suffragist
SFRJT
suffragette
SFRKL
spherical
SFRKS
spherics
SFRL
spheral
SFRN
saffron
SFRNG
seafaring
suffering
SFRNS
sufferance
SFRR
seafarer
SFRTSND
sforzando(music)
SFS
suffice
sufficed
sufficing
SFSH
soft-shoe

NGK:ink **P**:pie **R**:air **S**:ice **SH**:show **T**:toy **THN**:thin **TH**:the **V**:of **W**:we **Y**:you **Z**:is **VZHN**:vision

SFSHL
soft-shell
SFSHNS
sufficiency
SFSHNT
sufficient
SFSL
soft sell
SFSPKN
soft-spoken
SFSR
sufficer
SFST
sophist
SFSTKL
sophistical
SFSTKSHN
sophistication
SFSTKT
sophisticate
  sophisticated
  sophisticating
SFSTR
sophistry
  sophistries
SFSV
suffusive
SFT
safety
  safeties
sift
soffit
soft
softy
  softies
SFTBL
softball
SFTBLD
soft-boiled
SFTD
asafetida
SFTDRNGK
soft drink
SFTHRTD
softhearted
SFTKVR
soft-cover
SFTN
soften
SFTNGZ
siftings
SFTNR
softener
SFTPLD
soft-pedal(v)
SFTR

sifter
SFTSH
soft-shoe
SFTSHL
soft-shell
SFTSL
soft sell
SFTSPKN
soft-spoken
SFTWD
softwood
SFTWR
software
SFTWTR
soft water
SFWD
softwood
SFWR
software
SFYZ
suffuse
  suffused
  suffusing
SFYZHN
suffusion
SFZM
sophism
Sufism
SG
sag
  sagged
  sagging
saga(story)
saggy
  saggier
  saggiest
  sagginess
soggy(wet)
  soggier
  soggiest
  soggily
  sogginess
sago
SGJSCHN
suggestion
SGJST
suggest
SGJSTBL
suggestible
SGJSTBLT
suggestibility
SGJSTV
suggestive
SGL
sea gull
SGMNT

segment
SGMNTL
segmental
SGMNTSHN
segmentation
SGN
Saigon
SGNCHR
signature
SGNF
signify
  signified
  signifies
SGNFKNS
significance
SGNFKNT
significant
SGNFKSHN
signification
SGNG
seagoing
SGNL
signal
SGNLZ
signalize
  signalized
  signalizing
SGNSHN
assignation
SGNT
cygnet(swan)
signet
SGNTR
signatory
  signatories
SGR
cigar
SGRGSHN
segregation
SGRGSHNST
segregationist
SGRGT
segregate
  segregated
  segregating
SGRM
isogram
SGRT
cigarette
SGSHS
sagacious
SGST
sagacity
SH
ace-high
ash

ashes
issue
  issued
  issuing
  issuer
Shah(title)
shah(person)
she(pronoun)
shoe(foot)
shod
shoo(scare)
show
  shown
  showy
  showier
  showiest
  showily
  showiness
shy
  shied
  shies
  shyer
  shyest
SHB
shabby
  shabbier
  shabbiest
  shabbily
  shabbiness
SHBL
Chablis(wine)
issuable
SHBLTH
shibboleth
SHBNG
shebang
SHBT
showboat
SHBZ
show biz(slang)
SHBZNS
show business
SHD
eye shadow
shade
  shaded
  shading
shadow
  shadowy
shady
  shadier
  shadiest
  shadiness
shed
shed
  shedding

B:by **CH**:each **D**:day **F**:if **G**:go **H**:he **HW**:why **J**:joy **K**:cow **KS**:ax **KWL**:equal **L**:all **M**:may **N**:in

she'd
  she had
  she would
shod
  shoe
shoddy
  shoddier
  shoddiest
  shoddily
  shoddiness
should(shall)
shuteye
SHDF
shut-off(n)
SHDN
showdown
shut-in(person)
SHDNG
shading
shedding
SHDNT
shouldn't
should not
SHDR
shudder(movement)
shutter(cover)
SHDRBG
shutterbug
SHDT
shoot-out(battle)
shutout(no score)
SHDVR
chef-d'oeuvre
SHDYL
schedule, -led, -ling
SHF
chef(cook)
sheaf
  sheaves
showoff
SHFL
shoofly
shuffle
  shuffled
  shuffling
  shuffler
SHFLBRD
shuffleboard
SHFLS
shiftless
SHFN
chiffon
SHFNR
chiffonier
SHFR
chauffeur(driver)

shofar(trumpet)
  shofroth(or)
  shofars
SHFRW
chaudfroid
SHFT
shaft
shift
shifty
  shiftier
  shiftiest
  shiftily
  shiftiness
SHG
shag
  shagged
  shagging
shaggy
  shaggier
  shaggiest
  shagginess
SHGN
shogun(leader)
SHGR
sugar
sugary
  sugarier
  sugariest
  sugarily
  sugariness
SHGRBT
sugar beet
SHGRD
sugared
SHGRDD
sugar daddy
  (slang)
  sugar daddies
SHGRKN
sugar cane
SHGRKT
sugar-coat
SHGRKYRD
sugar-cured
SHGRL
showgirl
SHGRN
chagrin
SHGRND
chagrined
SHGRPLM
sugarplum
SHHRN
shoehorn
SHJ
shoji

SHK
chic(style)
  chicquer
  chicquest
shack(house)
shake(motion)
  shook
  shaking
  shaken
shaky
  shakier
  shakiest
  shakily
  shakiness
sheik(person)
shock
shuck
SHKBL
shakable
SHKDN
shakedown(n)
SHKG
Chicago
SHKL
shackle
  shackled
  shackling
shekel(money)
SHKN
ashcan
chicane(trick)
  chicaned
  chicaning
  chicaner
  chicanery
SHKNG
shocking
SHKNR
chicanery
  chicaneries
SHKP
shake-up(n)
shook-up(adj)
  (upset)(slang)
SHKPRF
shockproof
SHKR
chicquer
  chic
  shaker
  shikaree
  shocker(jolt)
SHKS
shucks(interj)
showcase
SHKSPR

Shakespeare
SHKSPRN
Shakespearean(or)
  Shakespearian
SHKST
chicquest
  chic
SHL
chalet(house)
challis(fabric)
shale(rock)
shall(will)
  should
shallow(not deep)
shawl(cape)
shell(cover)
shield(defense)
shill(decoy)
shoal(water)
shul(synagogue)
SHLD
shield
SHLDR
shoulder
SHLF
shelf
  shelves
SHLFSH
shellfish
SHLGM
shell game
SHLK
schlock(inferior
  merchandise)
shellac
  shellacked
  shellacking
shell-like
shylock(creditor)
SHLL
shillelagh
SHLM
shalom
SHLMZL
schlimazel
SHLN
echelon
SHLNG
schilling(Austrian
  money)
shilling(money)
SHLP
schlep
SHLPRF
shellproof
SHLS

NGK:ink P:pie R:air S:ice SH:show T:toy THN:thin TH:the V:of W:we Y:you Z:is VZHN:vision

shoelace
SHLSHKT
shell-shocked
SHLSHL
shilly-shally
shilly-shallied
shilly-shallies
SHLT
shallot
sheltie
SHLTR
shelter
SHLV
shelve
shelved
shelving
SHLVZ
shelves
shelf
SHM
chamois(mammal)
chamois
chamois(leather)
chamoises
schmo(person)
schmoes
sham(fake)
shammed
shamming
shame(emotion)
shamed
shaming
shim(wedge)
shimmed
shimming
shimmy(shake)
shimmied
shimmies
Shmoo(cartoon)
SHMBL
shamble
shambled
shambling
SHMBR
chambray
SHMD
ashamed
SHMFL
shameful
SHMFST
shamefaced
SHMK
schmuck
sumac(plant)
SHMKR
shoemaker

SHMLS
shameless
SHMLTS
schmaltz
SHMN
shaman
showman
showmen
SHMNDFR
chemin de fer
SHMP
shampoo
SHMPN
Champaign(city)
champaign(area)
champagne(wine)
SHMPNYN
champignon
(mushroom)
SHMR
schmeer
shimmer(shine)
shimmery
SHMRK
shamrock
SHMS
shamus
SHMZ
chemise
(undergarment)
schmoose(chat)
schmoosed
schmoosing
SHN
Cheyenne
(American Indian)
Cheyenne(or)
Cheyennes
Cheyenne
(city, river)
ocean
oceania
sheen(shiny)
shin(climb,leg)
shinned
shinning
shine(glisten)
shone(or)
shined
shining
shinny(game,climb)
shinnied
shinnies
shiny(glisten)
shinier
shiniest

shininess
shoe-in(sure thing)
shone(shine)
shown
show
shun(avoid)
shunned
shunning
SHNDG
shindig
SHNDL
chandelle
SHNDLR
chandelier
SHNGH
Shanghai
shanghai
SHNGK
shank
SHNGKR
chancre
SHNGL
shingle
shingled
shingling
SHNGLZ
shingles
SHNGNG
oceangoing
SHNGRF
oceanography
oceanographer
SHNGRFK
oceanographic
SHNGRL
Shangri-La
SHNK
oceanic
schnook
SHNKR
chancre
SHNL
chenille(cloth)
SHNLJ
oceanology
SHNNG
shining
shine
SHNNGN
shenanigan
SHNPS
schnapps
SHNR
shiner(black eye)
SHNRR
schnorrer

SHNS
issuance
shyness
SHNT
issuant
chantey(song)
shanty(house)
shanties
shunt(switch)
SHNTKLR
chanticleer
SHNTN
shantytown
SHNTNG
Shantung(China)
shantung(fabric)
SHNTSL
schnitzel
SHNTTN
shantytown
SHNTZ
chanteuse
SHNYN
chignon(hair)
SHNZL
schnozzle
SHNZR
schnauzer
SHP
chapeau(hat)
shape
shaped
shaping
sheep
sheep
ship(boat,send)
shipped
shipping
shipper
shop
shopped
shopping
SHPBL
shippable
SHPBLDNG
shipbuilding
SHPBLDR
shipbuilder
SHPBRD
shipboard
SHPHRDR
sheepherder
SHPKPR
shopkeeper
SHPL
shapely

B:by **CH**:each **D**:day **F**:if **G**:go **H**:he **HW**:why **J**:joy **K**:cow **KS**:ax **KWL**:equal **L**:all **M**:may **N**:in

shapelier
shapeliest
shapeliness
spiel
SHPLFTR
shoplifter
SHPLS
showplace
SHPMNT
shipment
SHPMT
shipmate
SHPNG
shipping
shopping
SHPNR
shipowner
SHPP
shape-up(n,adj)
SHPR
shipper
shopper(buyer)
SHPRD
shepherd
SHPRK
shipwreck
SHPRKHGFL
sprachgefuhl
SHPRL
chaparral
SHPRN
chaperon
SHPRT
shipwright
SHPS
chaps(leather)
showpiece
SHPSH
sheepish
SHPSHNGK
sheepshank
SHPSHP
shipshape
SHPSKN
sheepskin
SHPT
ashpit
SHPTK
shoptalk
SHPWRN
shopworn
SHPYRD
shipyard
SHR
assure
assured

assuring
Sahara
share(stock)
share(give part)
shared
sharing
shear(cut)
shorn
sheer(thin,
swerve)
sherry(wine)
sherries
shire(province)
shirr(cloth)
shirring
shoer(blacksmith)
shore(land)
shore(prop up)
shored
shoring
shower(water)
shrew(animal,
woman)
sure(certain)
surer
surest
usher
SHRB
shrub
SHRBNG
charabanc(bus)
SHRBR
shrubbery
shrubberies
SHRBRT
sherbet(ice cream)
SHRBT
sherbet(ice cream)
SHRD
charade(act)
shorty
shred(small part)
shredded
shredding
shrewd(smart)
shroud(cover)
SHRDZ
charades(game)
SHRF
sheriff
SHRFR
sure-fire
SHRFT
shrift(confession)
shrive(v)
SHRFTD

sure-footed
SHRG
shrug
shrugged
shrugging
SHRHLDR
shareholder
SHRK
shark(fish)
shirk(avoid)
shriek(screech)
SHRKR
shirker
SHRKRPR
sharecropper
SHRKSKN
sharkskin
SHRL
shrill(noise)
shrilly
surely(sure)
SHRLN
shoreline
SHRLNGK
Sri Lanka
SHRLT
Charlotte
charlotte(dessert)
SHRLTN
charlatan
SHRM
showroom
SHRMP
shrimp
SHRN
shrine(venerate)
shrined
shrining
Shrine
Shriner
shoran(navigation)
shorn
shear
SHRNG
shirring
shoring
shore
SHRNGK
shrink
shrank
shrunk(or)
shrunken
SHRNGKBL
shrinkable
SHRNGKJ
shrinkage

SHRNGKRP
shrink-wrap
shrink-wrapped
shrink-wrapping
SHRNS
assurance
SHRP
sharp
sharpie(boat,
person)
SHRPD
sharp-eyed
SHRPN
sharpen
SHRPNL
shrapnel
SHRPNR
sharpener
SHRPR
sharper
sharpest
SHRPSHTR
sharpshooter
SHRPSTD
sharp-sighted
SHRPTNGD
sharp-tongued
SHRPWTD
sharp-witted
SHRR
assurer
SHRS
sawhorse
seahorse
SHRT
charrette(effort)
cheroot(cigar)
shirt
short
shorty
surety
sureties
usherette
SHRTBRD
shortbread
SHRTCHNJ
shortchange
shortchanged
shortchanging
shortchanger
SHRTHND
shorthand
SHRTHNDD
short-handed
SHRTHRN
shorthorn

NGK:ink **P:**pie **R:**air **S:**ice **SH:**show **T:**toy **THN:**thin **TH:**the **V:**of **W:**we **Y:**you **Z:**is **VZHN:**vision

SHRTJ
shortage
SHRTKK
shortcake
SHRTKMNG
shortcoming
SHRTKT
short cut
SHRTLVD
short-lived
SHRTMPRD
short-tempered
SHRTN
shorten
SHRTNG
shirting
shortening
SHRTNNG
shortening
SHRTRM
short-term
SHRTRNJ
short-range
SHRTRS
chartreuse
SHRTRZ
chartreuse
SHRTSLV
shirt-sleeve(adj)
SHRTSRKT
short-circuit(v)
SHRTSTD
shortsighted
SHRTSTP
shortstop
SHRTSTR
short story
short stories
SHRTWNDD
short-winded
SHRTWST
shirtwaist
SHRTWSTD
short-waisted
SHRTWV
shortwave
SHRV
shrive
shrived(or)
shrove
shriving
shriven
SHRVL
shrivel
SHRVR
charivari

SHRWRD
shoreward
SHRZH
chargé(diplomat)
SHRZHDFR
chargé d'affaires
chargés d'affaires
SHS
chassis(frame)
chassis(pl)
chassé(dance)
chasséd
icehouse
otiose(indolent)
schuss(skiing)
schusses
SHSH
chichi
shush(interj)
shushes
SHSHKBB
shish kebab
SHSHN
shoeshine
SHSTR
shyster
SHSTRNG
shoestring
SHT
chateau(house)
chute(passage)
eyeshot
sheet(paper)
shit(excrement)
shit(or)
shitted
shitting
shoat(pig)
shoot(gun)
shot
shot(bullet,
broken)
shout(yell)
shut(close)
shut
shutting
shuteye(sleep)
SHTDN
shutdown
SHTF
shutoff(n)
SHTGN
shotgun
SHTH
sheath(case,
dress)

sheathe(v)
sheathed
sheathing
SHTHNG
sheathing
SHTK
shtick
SHTL
shuttle
shuttled
shuttling
SHTLKK
shuttlecock
SHTN
shut-in(n)
SHTNG
sheeting
shooting
SHTPT
shot put
SHTR
ashtray
shatter
shoetree
shutter
SHTRBG
shutterbug
SHTRK
Sheetrock
(trademark)
SHTRPRF
shatterproof
SHTS
stoss(direction)
SHTT
shoot-out
shutout
SHTTGRT
Stuttgart
SHV
Chevy
Chevrolet
(trademark)
schwa(sound
symbol)
shave
shaved
shaving
shaven
shaver
sheave(bind)
sheaved
sheaving
shiv(knife)
shove(push)

shoved
shoving
SHVL
Asheville
shovel
SHVLFL
shovelful
SHVLR
chevalier
chivalry
shoveler
SHVLRK
chivalric
SHVLRS
chivalrous
SHVN
chauvin
SHVNZM
chauvinism
SHVR
shaver
shiver(shake)
shover(pusher)
SHVRN
chevron
SHVS
Shavuot(feast)
SHVT
cheviot
SHVTH
Shavuot(feast)
SHVZ
sheaves
sheaf
SHW
schwa(sound)
SHWR
shower(water)
SHZ
chaise(carriage)
chose(property)
shoes(feet)
SHZLNJ
chaise longue
SJ
assauge(ease)
assauged
assauging
sage
sager
sagest
sewage
siege
SJBRSH
sagebrush
SJLS

acidulous
sedulous
SJLT
  acidulate
    acidulated
    acidulating
    acidulation
SJRN
  sojourn
SJS
  assiduous
SJSCHN
  suggestion
SJST
  suggest
SJSTBL
  suggestible
SJSTBLT
  suggestibility
SJSTV
  suggestive
SJTRS
  Sagittarius
SK
  acequia(canal)
  Osaka
  psych(v)
  psyche(n)
  psycho(slang)
  SAC
    Strategic Air
    Command
  sac(pouch)
  sack(bag)
  sake(purpose,wine)
  scow
  secco
  seek(look for)
    sought
  Seiko(trademark)
  sic(note mistake)
  sic(attack)
    sicced
    siccing
  sick(ill)
  Sikh(person)
  ski
    skied
    skiing
    skis
    skier
  sky
    skied
    skies
  soak(water)
  sock

suck
SKB
  scab
    scabbed
    scabbing
    scabby
    scabbier
    scabbiest
    scabbily
    scabbiness
  scuba
SKBD
  sickbed
SKBRD
  scabbard
SKBRS
  scabrous
SKBS
  scabious
SKBZ
  scabies
SKCH
  Scotch(people)
    Scot
    Scotland
  scotch
    scotches
  sketch
    sketches
    sketchy
    sketchier
    sketchiest
    sketchily
    sketchiness
SKCHBK
  sketchbook
SKCHN
  escutcheon
SKCHTP
  Scotch tape
    (trademark)
SKCHWSK
  Scotch whiskey
SKD
  cicada
  escudo
  scud(skin)
    scudded
    scudding
  skid
    skidded
    skidding
SKDL
  psychedelia
SKDLBT
  scuttlebutt

SKDLK
  psychedelic
SKDLKL
  psychedelically
SKDNMKS
  psychodynamics
SKDR
  skid row
SKDRL
  escadrille
SKDRM
  psychodrama
SKDSH
  Scottish
    Scot
SKDV
  skydive
    skydived
    skydiving
    skydiver
SKDZ
  scads(lots)
  skids
SKF
  scoff(mock)
  scuff(scrape)
  skiff(boat)
SKFD
  scaphoid
SKFL
  sackful
  scaffold
  scofflaw(person)
  scuffle(fight)
    scuffled
    scuffling
SKFLD
  scaffold
SKFLDNG
  scaffolding
SKFLNG
  scaffolding
SKFNS
  sycophancy
SKFNT
  sycophant
SKFNTK
  sycophantic
SKFNTKL
  sycophantical
SKFZLJ
  psychophysiology
SKG
  skeg(timber)
  skig(money)
SKH

sky-high
SKJ
  soakage
SKJK
  skyjack
SKJL
  schedule
    scheduled
    scheduling
SKJNK
  psychogenic
SKJRNG
  skijoring
SKK
  psychic
SKKL
  psychical
SKKLTH
  sackcloth
SKKNSS
  psychokinesis
SKKP
  skycap
SKL
  cycle
    cycled
    cycling
    cycler
  icicle(ice)
  scale(weigh,
    climb,fish)
    scaled
    scaling
  scall(skin sore)
  scaly(fish)
    scalier
    scaliest
    scaliness
  school
  scowl(frown)
  scull(oar,boat)
  sickle(tool)
  sickly
    sicklier
    sickliest
    sickliness
  skill(ability)
  skoal
  skull(bone)
  socle(pedestal)
  suckle(nurse)
    suckled
    suckling
SKLB
  schoolboy
SKLBL

NGK:ink **P:**pie **R:**air **S:**ice **SH:**show **T:**toy **THN:**thin **TH:**the **V:**of **W:**we **Y:**you **Z:**is **VZHN:**vision

scalable
SKLD
  cycloid
  escalade(climb)
  escaladed
  escalading
  scald(burn)
  scold(punish)
  seclude(private)
  secluded
  secluding
  so-called(adj)
SKLDGR
  skullduggery
SKLDNG
  scolding
SKLFL
  skillful
SKLFT
  ski lift
SKLGRL
  schoolgirl
SKLHS
  schoolhouse
SKLJ
  psychology
SKLJKL
  psychological
SKLJST
  psychologist
SKLJZ
  psychologize
  psychologized
  psychologizing
SKLK
  acyclic(not cyclic)
  cyclic
  skulk
SKLKL
  cyclical
SKLKP
  skullcap
SKLKT
  scilicet(namely)
SKLMN
  cyclamen
SKLMP
  C-clamp
SKLMRM
  schoolmarm
SKLMSTR
  schoolmaster
SKLMT
  cyclamate
  schoolmate
SKLMTR

cyclometer
SKLN
  cyclone(storm)
  scalone
    (equal sides)
  skyline
SKLNG
  suckling
SKLP
  escallop
    (scallop)
  scallop(mollusk,
    cook)
  scalp
SKLPCHR
  sculpture
  sculptured
  sculpturing
SKLPCHRL
  sculptural
SKLPCHRSK
  sculpturesque
SKLPD
  cyclopedia
  cyclopedic
  cyclopedist
SKLPL
  scalpel
SKLPN
  cyclopean
  scaloppine(or)-ini
SKLPR
  scalper
SKLPS
  Cyclops
SKLPT
  sculpt
SKLPTR
  sculptor
SKLR
  scalar(quantity)
  scholar(person)
  sclera(eye)
  scullery(room)
  sculleries
SKLRK
  skylark
SKLRL
  scholarly
  scholarliness
SKLRM
  cyclorama
  schoolroom
SKLRSHP
  scholarship
SKLRSS

sclerosis
SKLRST
  sclerosed
SKLSHN
  escalation
SKLSS
  scoliosis
SKLST
  cyclist(bicycle)
  scilicet(namely)
SKLSTK
  scholastic(school)
  scholastically
SKLSTSZM
  scholasticism
SKLSV
  seclusive
SKLT
  escalate
  escalated
  escalating
  escalator
  skillet
  skylight
SKLTCHR
  schoolteacher
SKLTHM
  cyclothyme
  cyclothymia
SKLTHMK
  cyclothymic
SKLTL
  skeletal
SKLTN
  skeleton
SKLTNK
  skeleton key
SKLTR
  escalator
SKLTRN
  cyclotron
SKLWG
  scalawag
SKLWRK
  schoolwork
SKLYL
  scagliola
SKLYN
  scallion(onion)
  scullion(servant)
SKLYR
  school year
SKLZHN
  seclusion
SKM
  cecum(cavity)

ceca(or)
  caecum
  Eskimo
  scam(swindle)
  schema(outline)
  schemata
  scheme(plan)
  schemed
  scheming
  schemer
  scum(dirty)
  scummy
  scummier
  scummiest
  skim
  skimmed
  skimming
  succumb
SKMDK
  schematic
SKMP
  scamp(rascal)
  scampi(shrimp)
  skimp
  skimpy
  skimpier
  skimpiest
  skimpily
  skimpiness
SKMPR
  scamper
    (run)
SKMR
  skimmer(hat,bird)
  sycamore
SKMT
  schemata
  schema
SKMTK
  schematic
SKMTR
  psychometry
SKMTZ
  schematize
SKN
  scan(look)
  scanned
  scanning
  scanner
  scone(pastry)
  second(time,two)
  sicken
  sick
  skean(dagger)
  skein(yarn)
  skin

---

skinned	**SKNKTD**	escaping	escrow
skinning	Schenectady	escapee(person)	Oscar(award)
skinner	**SKNLSS**	icecap	scar(mark)
skinny	psychoanalysis	scape(plant)	scarred
skinnier	**SKNLST**	scoop(tool)	scarring
skinniest	psychoanalyst	scope(range)	scare(frighten)
skinniness	**SKNLTK**	skip(omit)	scared
SKNBL	psychoanalytic	skipped	scaring
scannable	**SKNLTKL**	skipping	scary
SKND	psychoanalytical	skipper	scarier
second	**SKNLZ**	**SKPCHR**	scariest
SKNDGS	psychoanalyze	Scripture(Bible)	scariness
second-guess	psychoanalyzed	scripture	score(tally)
second-guesses	psychoanalyzing	**SKPD**	scored
SKNDHND	**SKNR**	escapade	scoring
secondhand(adj)	scanner	**SKPFL**	scorer
SKNDKLS	schooner(boat)	scoopful	scour(search)
second-class	skinner	**SKPGRS**	scree(rocks)
SKNDL	**SKNRSS**	scapegrace	screw
scandal	psychoneurosis	**SKPGT**	screwy
SKNDLMNGR	**SKNS**	scapegoat	screwier
scandalmonger	askance(sideways)	**SKPLN**	screwiest
SKNDLS	sconce(fort)	skiplane	scurry(hurry)
scandalous	**SKNSHN**	**SKPMNT**	scurried
SKNDLZ	scansion(verse)	escapement	scurries
scandalize	**SKNT**	**SKPR**	seeker(searcher)
scandalized	scant(small)	skipper	skier(ski)
scandalizing	scanty	**SKPRNNG**	soaker(water)
SKNDNV	scantier	scuppernong	soccer(game)
Scandinavia	scantiest	**SKPSHR**	succor(help), (B)-ccour
SKNDNVN	scantily	Scripture(Bible)	sucker(candy)
Scandinavian	scantiness	scripture	**SKRB**
SKNDP	secant(line)	**SKPST**	ascribe
skin-deep	second(time,	escapist	ascribed
SKNDR	place)	**SKPTH**	ascribing
secondary	**SKNTGS**	psychopath	scarab(beetle)
secondaries	second-guess(v)	**SKPTHK**	scribe(clerk)
secondarily	second-guesses	psychopathic	scribed
SKNDRL	second guess(n)	**SKPTHLJ**	scribing
scoundrel	second guesses	psychopathology	scrub(rub,tree)
secondarily	second-guesser	**SKPTK**	scrubber
SKNDRT	**SKNTHND**	skeptic	scrubby
second-rate	secondhand(adj,adv)	**SKPTKL**	scrubbier
SKNDV	**SKNTKLS**	skeptical	scrubbiest
skin-dive(v)	second-class(adj)	**SKPTSZM**	**SKRBBL**
-dived,-diving	**SKNTLNG**	skepticism	ascribable
skin diving(n)	scantling(wood)	**SKPYL**	scribable
skin diver	**SKNTRT**	scapula	**SKRBL**
SKNFLNT	second-rate(adj)	scapulas(or)	Scrabble(game)
skinflint	**SKNTSTRMN**	scapulae	(trademark)
SKNG	secondstory man	**SKPYLR**	scrabble(grope)
sacking	**SKNYRSS**	scapular	scrabbled
seeking	psychoneurosis	**SKPZM**	scrabbling
SKNGK	**SKP**	escapism	screwball
skink(lizard)	escape(flee)	**SKR**	scribble(write)
skunk	escaped	eschar	scribbled

NGK:ink **P**:pie **R**:air **S**:ice **SH**:show **T**:toy **THN**:thin **TH**:the **V**:of **W**:we **Y**:you **Z**:is **VZHN**:vision

scribbling
SKRBLR
scribbler(writer)
SKRBR
scrubber
SKRCH
scorch(burn)
scorches
scratch(scrape)
scratches
scratchy
scratchier
scratchiest
scratchiness
screech(noise)
screeches
screechy
screechier
screechiest
screechiness
SKRCHL
screech owl
SKRD
sacred(holy)
scared(fear)
screed(tool)
scrod(fish)
SKRDK
Socratic
SKRDRVR
screwdriver
SKRF
scarf(cloth)
scarfs(or)
scarves
scarify(mark)
scarified
scarifies
scruff(neck)
scruffy
scruffier
scruffiest
SKRFKSHN
scarification
SKRFS
sacrifice
sacrificed
sacrificing
SKRFSHL
sacrificial
SKRFYL
scrofula
SKRFYLS
scrofulous
SKRG
escargot(snail)

scrag
scraggy
scraggier
scraggiest
SKRGL
scraggly
scragglier
scraggliest
SKRJ
Scrooge
scourge
scourged
scourging
SKRKR
scarecrow
SKRKT
skyrocket
SKRL
escarole(food)
scrawl(write)
scroll(paper roll)
scurrile(low
  language)
skirl(tone)
SKRLJ
sacrilege
SKRLJS
sacrilegious
SKRLK
sacroiliac
SKRLS
scoreless
scurrilous
SKRLT
scarlet
scurrility
scurrilities
SKRLWRK
scrollwork
SKRM
ice cream
sacrum(bone)
sacrums(or)
sacra
scram(go at once)
scream(yell)
scrim(fabric)
sickroom
SKRMBL
scramble
scrambled
scrambling
scrambler
SKRMBLDGZ
scrambled eggs
SKRMBLR

scrambler
SKRMJ
scrimmage
scrimmaged
scrimmaging
SKRMNT
sacrament
Sacramento
SKRMNTL
sacramental
SKRMP
scrimp
scrimpy
scrimpier
scrimpiest
scrimpiness
SKRMPSHS
scrumptious
SKRMR
screamer
SKRMSH
Scaramouch
scrimshaw
skirmish
skirmishes
SKRMSHS
scrumptious
SKRN
saccharin(sweet
  powder)
saccharine(adj)
scorn(contempt)
scrawny(thin)
scrawnier
scrawniest
screen
SKRNCH
scrunch
scrunches
SKRNFL
scornful
SKRNJ
scrounge
scrounged
scrounging
scounger
scroungy
scroungier
scroungiest
SKRNPL
screenplay
SKRNRTR
screenwriter
SKRNTN
Scranton
SKRNTST

screen-test
SKRP
escarp(cliff)
scarp(cliff)
Scorpio
scrap(junk)
scrapped
scrapping
scrape(rub)
scraped
scraping
scrappy
  (quarrelsome)
scrappier
scrappiest
scrappily
scrappiness
scrip(money)
script(drama)
SKRPCHR
Scripture(Bible)
scripture
SKRPCHRL
scriptural
SKRPCHRLZM
scripturalism
SKRPHP
scrap heap(trash)
SKRPL
scrapple(food)
scruple(ethic)
scrupled
scrupling
SKRPMNT
escarpment
SKRPN
scorpion
SKRPNGZ
scrapings
SKRPR
scraper(scrape)
SKRPSHN
ascription
SKRPT
script(writing)
SKRPTRTR
scriptwriter
SKRPYLS
scrupulous
SKRS
isocracy
isocracies
scarce(not many)
secrecy(hidden)
secrecies
sucrose(sugar)

B:by **CH**:each **D**:day **F**:if **G**:go **H**:he **HW**:why **J**:joy **K**:cow **KS**:ax **KWL**:equal **L**:all **M**:may **N**:in

SKRSHN	scherzos	sexagenarian	sextuple
secretion	**SKRTSND**	**SKSKRPR**	sextupled
SKRSNGKT	scherzando	skyscraper	sextupling
sacrosanct	**SKRTSRVS**	**SKSKSHL**	**SKSTPLT**
SKRST	Secret Service	psychosexual	sextuplet
sacristy(room)	**SKRTV**	**SKSLJ**	**SKSTT**
sacristies	secretive	sexology	sextet
scarcity	**SKRTWR**	**SKSLS**	**SKSTTH**
scarcities	escritoire	sexless	sixtieth
SKRSTN	**SKRTZ**	**SKSMDK**	**SKSTYPL**
sacristan	Socrates	psychosomatic	sextuple
SKRT	**SKRV**	**SKSMN**	sextupled
escort(person)	scurvy	sockeye salmon	sextupling
secret(hidden)	scurvier	**SKSMTK**	**SKSTYPLT**
secrete(secret,	scurviest	psychosomatic	sextuplet
generate and	**SKRVZ**	**SKSN**	**SKSTZ**
push out)	scarves	Saxon	sixties
secreted	scarf	saxony	**SKSZ**
secreting	**SKS**	**SKSNGKT**	psychoses(pl)
secretion	scouse(food)	succinct	psychosis
secretor	sex	**SKSPK**	**SKSZM**
skirt	sexy	six-pack	sexism
skywrite	sexier	**SKSPN**	**SKT**
skywriting	sexiest	sixpenny	ascot
skywriter	sexily	**SKSS**	ice-skate
SKRTBL	sexiness	psychosis	ice-skated
scrutable	six(number)	psychoses	ice-skating
SKRTK	sixes	success	ice skater
escharotic	**SKSD**	successes	scat(leave)
Socratic	succeed	sycosis(hair)	scatted
SKRTM	**SKSFLD**	**SKSSFL**	scatting
scrotum	sixfold	successful	scoot(hurry)
scrota(or)	**SKSFN**	**SKSSHN**	Scot(person)
scrotums	saxophone	succession	scout(search)
SKRTN	**SKSFNST**	**SKSSHNL**	sect(group)
scrutiny	saxophonist	successional	skat(game)
SKRTNZ	**SKSGN**	**SKSSR**	skat(interj)
scrutinize	six-gun	successor	skate(glide)
scrutinized	**SKSHL**	**SKSSV**	skated
scrutinizing	sexual	successive	skating
scrutinization	**SKSHLT**	**SKST**	skater
SKRTNZR	sexuality	seacoast	skeet(target)
scrutinizer	**SKSHN**	sixty	skit(sketch)
SKRTR	section	sixties	socket(cavity)
secretary(person)	suction	**SKSTH**	Succoth(or)
secretaries	**SKSHNL**	sixth	Sukkot(or)Sukkos
secretory	sectional	**SKSTL**	**SKTFR**
secrete	**SKSHNLZ**	sextile	scot-free
skywriter	sectionalize	**SKSTN**	**SKTH**
SKRTRL	sectionalized	sexton	scathe
secretarial	sectionalizing	sixteen	scathed
SKRTRT	**SKSHNLZM**	**SKSTNT**	scathing
secretariat	sectionalism	sextant	**SKTHRP**
SKRTS	**SKSHRN**	**SKSTNTH**	psychotherapy
scherzo(music)	saxhorn	sixteenth	psychotherapies
scherzi(or)	**SKSJNRN**	**SKSTPL**	psychotherapist

NGK:ink **P:**pie **R:**air **S:**ice **SH:**show **T:**toy **THN:**thin **TH:**the **V:**of **W:**we **Y:**you **Z:**is **VZHN:**vision

psychotherapeutic
SKTK
psychotic
SKTL
scuttle(scrap)
scuttled
scuttling
sectile(cuttable)
SKTLBT
scuttlebutt
SKTLJ
eschatology
SKTLND
Scotland
SKTLNDYRD
Scotland Yard
SKTMSTR
scoutmaster
SKTN
socked in
SKTNG
scouting
SKTR
ice skater
psychiatry
psychiatrist
scatter
scooter(vehicle)
scutter(bustle)
sector(area)
skater(glider)
skitter(dart)
SKTRBRN
scatterbrain
SKTRK
psychiatric
SKTRKL
psychiatrical
SKTRKS
cicatrix
SKTRN
sectarian
SKTRST
psychiatrist
SKTSD
schizoid
SKTSFRN
schizophrenia
SKTSFRNK
schizophrenic
SKTSH
Scottish
skittish
succotash
SKV
skive(pare)

skived
skiving
skivvy(cloths)
skivvies
SKVNJ
scavenge
scavenged
scavenging
scavenger
SKVNJR
scavenger
SKVR
skiver
SKW
sequoia
squaw(Indian)
SKWB
squab(bird,
short & fat)
squabby
squabbier
squabbiest
squib(writing,
firecracker)
usquebaugh
SKWBL
squabble(quarrel)
squabbled
squabbling
SKWBLR
squabbler
SKWD
squad(group)
squid(mollusk)
SKWDKR
squad car
SKWDR
squatter
SKWDRN
squadron
SKWGL
squiggle
squiggled
squiggling
squiggly
squigglier
squiggliest
squigglily
squiggliness
SKWJ
squeegee
squeegeed
squeegeeing
squeegees
SKWK
squawk(loud

protest)
squeak(shrill cry)
squeaky
squeakier
squeakiest
squeakily
squeakiness
SKWL
sequel(follow)
squall(wind)
squally
squallier
squalliest
squeal(shrill cry)
SKWLCH
squelch(crush)
squelches
SKWLD
squalid
SKWLDT
squalidity
SKWLN
squall line
SKWLR
squalor(filth)
squealer
SKWM
squama(scale)
squamae
squamate(adj)
SKWMS
squamous(adj)
SKWMSH
squeamish
(nauseated)
SKWN
sequin
SKWNCHL
sequential
SKWNDR
squander
SKWNS
sequence
SKWNSHL
sequential
SKWNT
squint
SKWNTD
squint-eyed
SKWR
esquire(rank)
esquired
esquiring
square(shape)
squared
squaring

squarer
squarest
squire(rank)
squired
squiring
SKWRD
skyward
SKWRDNS
square-dance(v)
square-danced
square-dancing
square-dancer
SKWRGD
square-rigged
SKWRGR
square-rigger
SKWRL
squirrel
SKWRM
squirm
squirmy
squirmier
squirmiest
squirminess
SKWRRK
squirearchy
SKWRSH
squarish
SKWRT
square root
squirt
SKWSH
squash(crush)
squashes
squash(vegetable)
squash
squashy
squashier
squashiest
squashily
squashiness
squish(crush
noisily)
squishes
squishy
squishier
squishiest
squishiness
SKWSTR
sequester
SKWT
squat
squatted
squatting
squatter
SKWTR

squatter
SKWY
  sequoia
SKWZ
  skyways
  squeeze
    squeezed
    squeezing
    squeezings
    squeezer
SKWZBL
  squeezable
  squeezably
SKWZPL
  squeeze play
SKWZR
  squeezer
SKY
  askew
  skew
SKYBLD
  skewbald
SKYK
  sukiyaki
SKYLNS
  succulence
SKYLNT
  esculent
  succulent
SKYLR
  secular
SKYLRZ
  secularize
    secularized
    secularizing
    secularization
SKYLSHN
  osculation
SKYLT
  osculate
    osculated
    osculating
SKYR
  secure
    secured
    securing
  skewer
SKYRBL
  securable
SKYRCH
  skew arch
SKYRT
  security
    securities
SKZ
  scuzzo(slang)

SKZM
  schism
SKZMTK
  schismatic
SKZMTKL
  schismatical
SL
  acyl(chemistry)
  assail
  assoil(pardon)
  cell(unit)
  cilia(cell hairs)
  sail(boat)
  sale(n)
  sell(v)
  sallow(tree)
  sally(rush)
    sallied
    sallies
  seal(signet,
    animal)
  selah(rest)
  sell(v)
    sold
    sale(n)
  Seoul
  sill(window)
  silly(stupid)
    sillier
    silliest
    silliness
  silo(shelter)
  slaw(food)
  slay(kill)
    slew
    slain
  sleigh(snow)
  slew(many)
  slew(slay)
  sloe(fruit)
  slough(deep mud,
    marsh)
  slow(not fast)
  slue(turn)
    slued
    slueing
  sly(smart)
    slyer
    slyest
    slyly
    slyness
  soil(earth)
  Sol(the sun)
  sol(money,music)
  soles(money)
  sole(only,foot)

solo(single)
soul(spirit)
sully(mar)
  sullied
  sullies
Sulu
SLB
  slab(broad & flat)
    slabbed
    slabbing
  slob(person)
  slub(fiber)
    slubbed
    slubbing
SLBF
  syllabify
    syllabified
    syllabifies
SLBFKSHN
  syllabification
SLBK
  syllabic
SLBKT
  syllabicate
    syllabicated
    syllabicating
SLBL
  assailable
  assailably
  isolable
  salable(sale)
  syllable
SLBR
  isallobar
  slobber
  syllabary
    (syllable)
    syllabaries
SLBRD
  sailboard
SLBRNT
  celebrant
SLBRS
  salubrious
SLBRT
  celebrate
    celebrated
    celebrating
    celebration
    celebrity
    celebrities
SLBRTHR
  soul brother
SLBRTR
  celebrator
SLBS

celibacy
syllabus
  syllabi(or)
  syllabuses
SLBSDD
  slabsided
SLBT
  celibate(person)
  sailboat
SLCH
  slatch(waves)
    slatches
  slouch
  slouchy
    slouchier
    slouchiest
    slouchily
    slouchiness
SLD
  salad(food)
  sled(vehicle)
    sledded
    sledding
  slide(glide)
    slid
    sliding
  sloe-eyed
  sloyd(skill)
  sold
    sell
  solid(firm)
SLDF
  solidify
    solidified
    solidifies
SLDFKSHN
  solidification
SLDJ
  sledge
    sledged
    sledging
SLDJHMR
  sledgehammer
SLDM
  seldom
SLDN
  slowdown
SLDR
  slaughter
  slider(pitch)
SLDRL
  slide rule
SLDRLR
  slide ruler
SLDRT
  solidarity

SLDSTT
solid-state
SLDT
solidity
solidities
SLF
self, selves(pl)
sell-off
slough(skin)
sol-fa(scale)
sulfa(drug)
sylph(girl)
SLFBNGSHN
self-abnegation
SLFDFNS
self-defense
SLFDN
solifidian
SLFDNL
self-denial
SLFDNZM
solifidianism
SLFDRST
self-addressed
SLFDRVN
self-driven
SLFDSPLN
self-discipline
SLFDTRMNSHN
self-determination
SLFFSNG
self-effacing
SLFGVRNNG
self-governing
SLFJ
solfeggio
solfeggi
SLFJKTD
self-educated
SLFKNFDNS
self-confidence
self-confident
SLFKNFST
self-confessed
SLFKNSHS
self-conscious
SLFKNTND
self-contained
SLFKNTRL
self-control
SLFKNTRLD
self-controlled
SLFKSPLNTR
self-explanatory
SLFKSPRSHN
self-expression

SLFKTNG
self-acting
SLFL
soulful
SLFLDNG
self-loading
SLFLS
selfless
SLFLV
self-love
SLFMD
self-made
SLFMJ
self-image
SLFMPLD
self-employed
SLFMPRTNT
self-important
SLFMPRVMNT
self-improvement
SLFMPZ
self-impose
self-imposed
self-imposing
SLFMPZD
self-imposed
SLFN
cellophane
SLFNDLJNS
self-indulgence
SLFNDLJNT
self-indulgent
SLFNDST
self-induced
self-induce
self-inducing
SLFNDYS
self-induce
self-induced
self-inducing
SLFNFLKTD
self-inflicted
SLFNTRST
self-interest
SLFPRPL
self-propel
self-propelled
self-propelling
SLFPNTD
self-appointed
SLFPRTRT
self-portrait
SLFPRZRVSHN
self-preservation
SLFPT
self-pity

self-pitying(adj)
SLFPZSHN
self-possession
SLFPZST
self-possessed
SLFR
sulfur(element)
SLFRCHS
self-righteous
SLFRGYLT
self-regulate
self-regulated
self-regulating
self-regulation
SLFRLNS
self-reliance
SLFRLZSHN
self-realization
SLFRPRCH
self-reproach
SLFRSPKT
self-respect
SLFRSTRNT
self-restraint
SLFRT
sulfurate
sulfurated
sulfurating
SLFRZNG
self-rising
SLFSFSHNT
self-sufficient
SLFSH
sailfish(fish)
selfish(greed)
SLFSHRD
self-assured
SLFSHRNS
self-assurance
SLFSKNG
self-seeking
SLFSKRFS
self-sacrifice
self-sacrificed
self-sacrificing
SLFSLNG
self-sealing
SLFSM
selfsame
SLFSNTRD
self-centered
SLFSPRT
self-support
SLFSRVS
self-service
SLFSSTNNG

self-sustaining
SLFSTLD
self-styled
SLFSTM
self-esteem
SLFSTRTR
self-starter
SLFSTSFD
self-satisfied
SLFSTSFKSHN
self-satisfaction
SLFT
slewfoot
SLFTCH
self-teach
self-taught
self-teaching
SLFTR
solfatara
SLFTRCHR
self-torture
self-tortured
self-torturing
SLFTT
self-taught
SLFVDNT
self-evident
SLFWLD
self-willed
SLFWNDNG
self-winding
SLFYRK
sulfuric
SLFYRKSD
sulfuric acid
SLFZH
solfége
SLG
slag(residue)
slagged
slagging
slog(slow walk,
strike)
slogged
slogging
slug(bullet,hit)
slugged
slugging
slugger
SLGBD
slugabed
SLGFST
slugfest
SLGN
slogan
SLGR

slugger
SLGRD
sluggard
SLGSH
sluggish
SLJ
silage(fodder)
sledge(vehicle)
sledged
sledging
sludge(mud)
sludgy
sludgier
sludgiest
SLJHMR
sledgehammer
SLJN
sloe gin
SLJR
soldier(army)
SLJRZMDL
Soldier's Medal
SLJST
syllogist
SLJSTK
syllogistic
SLJSTKL
syllogistical
SLJZM
syllogism
SLK
Saluki(dog)
silica(sand)
silk(cloth)
silky, silkier
silkiest
silkiness
slack(slow)
slake(quench)
slaked
slaking
sleek(smooth)
slick(slippery)
sulk(mood)
sulky(vehicle)
sulkies
sulky(mood)
sulkier
sulkiest
sulkily
sulkiness
SLKLTH
sailcloth
SLKN
silicon
semiconductor

silicone
silken(cloth)
slacken(slow)
SLKR
slacker
slicker
SLKS
Silex(trademark)
silex
sulcus
SLKSHN
selection
SLKSKRN
silk-screen
SLKSN
siloxane
SLKSS
silicosis
SLKT
select(choose)
selectee
silicate
SLKTR
selector
SLKTV
selective
SLKTVT
selectivity
SLKWRM
silkworm
SLL
solely
SLLKW
soliloquy
soliloquies
SLLKWZ
soliloquize
soliloquized
soliloquizing
SLLM
slalom
SLM
asylum
Islam
psalm(song)
salaam(ceremonial)
salami(meat)
Salem
slam(hit)
slammed,-mming
slammer
slim(thin)
slimmed
slimming
slimmer
slimmest

slime(mud)
slimy
slimier
slimiest
sliminess
slum(area)
slummed
slumming
solemn(serious)
SLMBR
slumber
SLMBRS
slumberous
SLMGLYN
slumgullion
SLMGND
salmagundi
SLMLRD
slumlord
SLMN
salmon
SLMNDR
salamander
SLMNF
solemnify
solemnified
solemnifies
SLMNL
salmonella
salmonellae(or)
salmonellas
SLMNS
Solomon Sea
SLMNT
solemnity
solemnities
SLMNZ
solemnize
solemnized
solemnizing
SLMNZSHN
solemnization
SLMP
slump
SLMR
slammer(jail)
SLMSHN
slow-motion
SLMT
soul mate
SLN
Iceland
salina(salty
area)
saline(salt)
salon(gallery)

saloon(tavern)
sea lion
slain
slay
sullen
SLND
solenoid
Iceland
SLNDK
Icelandic
SLNDR
cylinder
slander(talk)
slender(thin)
solander
SLNDRKL
cylindrical
SLNDRS
slanderous
SLNDRZ
slenderize
slenderized
slenderizing
SLNG
ceiling(roof)
slang(words)
slangy
slangier
slangiest
slangily
slanginess
slaying
sling(throw)
slung
SLNGBK
slingback
SKNGK
slink
slunk
slinky
slinkier
slinkiest
slinkiness
SLNGSH
sling shoe
SLNGSHT
slingshot
SLNKPR
saloonkeeper
SLNM
selenium
SLNS
salience(highlight)
saliency
silence(no noise)
silenced

NGK:ink **P**:pie **R**:air **S**:ice **SH**:show **T**:toy **THN**:thin **TH**:the **V**:of **W**:we **Y**:you **Z**:is **VZHN**:vision

silencing
silencer
SLNSR
silencer
SLNT
assailant
salient(highlight)
salinity(salt)
sealant(sealing
agent)
silent(no noise)
slant(incline)
SLNTRT
coelenterate
SLNZ
Sea Islands
SLP
slap(hit)
slapped
slapping
sleep(rest)
slept
sleepy
sleepier
sleepiest
sleepily
sleepiness
slip(slide)
slipped
slipping
sloop(boat)
slop(liquid)
slopped
slopping
slope(incline)
sloped
sloping
sloppy(manner)
sloppier
sloppiest
sloppily
sloppiness
SLPDSH
slapdash
SLPHD
sleepyhead
SLPHP
slaphappy
SLPJ
slippage
SLPK
slowpoke
SLPKS
slipcase
SLPKVR
slipcover

SLPLT
soleplate
SLPN
slip-on
SLPNGBG
sleeping bag
SLPNGKR
sleeping car
SLPNT
slipknot
SLPP
slip-up
SLPR
sleeper
slipper(shoe)
slippery
slipperier
slipperiest
slipperiness
SLPSHD
slipshod
SLPSHT
slap shot
slip-sheet
SLPST
slip seat
SLPSTK
slapstick
SLPSTRM
slipstream
SLPSZM
solipsism
SLPWKNG
sleepwalking
SLPWKR
sleepwalker
SLR
assailer
celery(food)
cellar(place)
ostler(horse,
engine, worker)
sailer(boat)
sailor(person)
salary(money)
salaries
sealer(glue)
seller(person)
slur(speech)
slurred
slurring
slurry(liquid)
slurries
solar(sun)
solaria(place)
solarium

SLRD
salaried
SLRM
solarium
solaria
SLRP
slurp
SLRPLKSS
solar plexus
SLRSL
solar cell
SLRSSTM
Solar System
SLRT
celerity(speed)
cellaret(cabinet)
solleret(shoe)
SLRTS
saleratus
SLRZ
solarize
solarized
solarizing
SLRZSHN
solarization
SLS
cilice(hair shirt)
slice(cut)
sliced
slicing
sluice(trough)
sluiced
sluicing
solace(comfort)
solaced
solacing
solus(alone)
sola(f)
Sulu Sea
SLSCHL
celestial
SLSF
salsify
SLSH
slash(cut)
slashes
slosh(splash)
sloshes
slush(ice & water)
slushes
slushy
slushier
slushiest
solatia
solatium
SLSHFND

slush fund
SLSHM
solatium
solatia
SLSHN
isolation(solitude)
oscillation
(movement)
solution(answer,
liquid)
SLSHNST
isolationist
SLSHS
salacious(lust)
siliceous(silica)
SLSKN
sealskin
SLSKP
oscilloscope
SLSRCHNG
soul-searching
SLSS
Celsius
SLSST
solecist
solecism
solecistic
SLSSTR
soul sister
SLST
celesta(music)
scilicet(namely)
solicit(ask)
soloist(alone)
SLSTD
solicitude
SLSTR
solicitor
SLSTS
solicitous(ask)
solstice
SLSTSHN
solicitation(ask)
SLSTYD
solicitude
SLSZM
solecism
SLT
assault
celt(tool)
Celt(person)
isolate
isolated
isolating
isolation
ocelot(cat)

B:by **CH**:each **D**:day **F**:if **G**:go **H**:he **HW**:why **J**:joy **K**:cow **KS**:ax **KWL**:equal **L**:all **M**:may **N**:in

oscillate
  oscillated
  oscillating
  oscillation
SALT
  Strategic Arms
  Limitation Talks
salt(taste)
salty
  saltier
  saltiest
  saltily
  saltiness
salute(greet)
  saluted
  saluting
sellout
silhouette(outline)
  silhouetted
  silhouetting
silt(mud)
slat(wood)
  slatted
  slatting
slate(stone,list)
  slated
  slating
sleet(ice)
sleight(skill)
slight(frail)
slit(cut)
  slit
  slitting
slot(place)
  slotted
  slotting
slut(person)
solute(substance)
  solution
SLTBKS
saltbox
  saltboxes
SLTD
solitude
SLTH
sleuth
sloth(lazy)
SLTHFL
slothful
SLTHR
slither(move)
slather(lavish)
SLTK
Celtic
SLTLKST
Salt Lake City

SLTN
saltine(cracker)
sultan(ruler)
sultana(wife)
SLTNG
slating(stone)
SLTNPPR
salt-and-pepper
SLTPTR
saltpeter, (B)-tre
SLTR
oscillator
psaltery(music)
  psalteries
slater(slate
  worker)
slaughter(kill)
solitary(alone)
solitaire(gem,
  game)
sultry(torrid,
  sensual)
  sultrier
  sultriest
  sultrily
  sultriness
SLTRHS
slaughterhouse
SLTRN
slattern
SLTRR
slaughterer
SLTRS
slaughterous
SLTS
solstice
SLTSH
sluttish
SLTSHKR
saltshaker
SLTSLR
saltcellar
SLTST
slightest
SLTTR
salutatory
  salutatories
SLTTRN
salutatorian
SLTWRKS
saltworks
SLTWTR
saltwater
SLTYD
solitude
SLV

c'est la vie
  (French-such is life)
saliva(spittle)
salve(balm,save)
  salved
  salving
salvo(shots)
Slav(slavic)
slave(person,work)
  slaved,-ving,-ver
sleave(separate)
  sleaved
  sleaving
sleeve(shirt,shell)
  sleeved
  sleeving
solve(answer)
  solved
  solving
sylva(trees)
SLVBL
salvable(save)
solvable(answer)
SLVBLT
solvability
SLVDRVR
slave-driver
SLVJ
salvage(save)
  salvaged
  salvaging
selvage(fringe)
SLVJBL
salvageable
SLVK
Slavic(language)
Slovak
  (person)
Slovakian
SLVL
sea level
SLVLS
sleeveless
SLVN
sloven(careless)
sylvan(forest)
SLVNL
slovenly
  slovenlier
  slovenliest
  slovenliness
SLVNS
solvency
SLVNT
solvent
SLVR

salver(tray)
salivary(spittle)
silver(metal)
silvery
  silveriness
slaver(slobber,
  drivel)
slaver(person,ship)
slavery(bondage)
sliver(splinter)
SLVRFSH
silverfish
SLVRN
silvern
SLVRPLT
silver plate
  silver plated
  silver plating
SLVRSMTH
silversmith
SLVRTNGD
silver-tongued
SLVRWR
silverware
SLVSH
slavish
SLVSHN
salvation
SLVT
salivate
  salivated
  salivating
SLVVTS
slivovitz
SLVZ
selves
self
SLWT
silhouette
SLWTD
slow-witted
SLYBL
soluble
  solubly
SLYBLT
solubility
SLYBLZ
solubilize
  solubilized
  solubilizing
SLYL
cellule(cell)
SLYLD
celluloid
SLYLR
cellular

NGK:ink **P:**pie **R:**air **S:**ice **SH:**show **T:**toy **THN:**thin **TH:**the **V:**of **W:**we **Y:**you **Z:**is **VZHN:**vision

SLYLS
cellulose
SLYT
solute(substance)
solution
SLYTR
salutary
SLYTSHN
salutation
SLZ
sleazy
sleazier
sleaziest
sleazily
sleaziness
SLZBR
Salisbury
SLZKLRK
salesclerk
SLZM
sciolism
sciolist
SLZMN
salesman
salesmen
SLZMNSHP
salesmanship
SLZPPL
salespeople
SLZPRSN
salesperson
SLZWMN
saleswoman
saleswomen
SM
assume(think)
assumed
assuming
assumption
awesome(large)
cyma
cymae
cymatium
cyme(flower)
psalm(song)
SAM(missile)
SAMs
surface-to-air
same(like)
Samoa
seam(sew)
seamy(seam,sordid)
seamier
seamiest
seaminess
seem(appear)

some(part)
sum(all,add)
summed
summing
SMB
samba
SMBD
somebody
SMBDK
symbiotic
SMBL
assemble(build)
assembled
assembling
assembler
assembly
assemblies
assumable(assume)
cymbal(music)
symbol(mark)
SMBLJ
assemblage
symbology
symbologies
SMBLK
symbolic
symbolism
SMBLKL
symbolical
SMBLLN
assembly line
SMBLMN
assemblyman
assemblymen
SMBLNS
semblance
SMBLR
assembler
cymbaleer
SMBLST
cymbalist(music)
symbolist
SMBLSTK
symbolistic
SMBLZ
symbolize(mean)
symbolized
symbolizing
symbolizer
SMBLZM
symbolism
SMBNT
symbiont
SMBR
somber
SMBRR

sombrero
SMBSS
symbiosis
SMBTK
symbiotic
SMBTKL
symbiotical
SMCH
smooch
smooches
SMD
psalmody
psalmodies
someday
SMDK
Semitic
SMDRNL
semidiurnal
SMDTCHT
semidetached
SMFN
symphony
symphonies
SMFNK
symphonic
symphonically
SMFNL
semifinal
SMFR
semaphore
semaphored
semaphoring
SMFRML
semiformal
SMFSHL
semiofficial
SMG
smog(air)
smoggy
smoggier
smoggiest
smogginess
smug
smugger
smuggest
SMGL
smuggle
smuggled
smuggling
smuggler
SMGLR
smuggler
SMH
somehow
SMHWR
somewhere

SMHWT
somewhat
SMJ
smudge
smudged
smudging
smudgy
smudgier
smudgiest
smudgily
smudginess
SMJN
cymogene(gas)
smidgen
SMJPT
smudge pot
SMK
smack(hit)
smock(dress)
smoke(fire)
smoked
smoking
smoker
Smokey(bear)
smoky
smokier
smokiest
smokiness
sumac(plant)
SMKBL
smokable
SMKDB
smack-dab
SMKHS
smokehouse
SMKLN
semicolon
SMKMLD
summa cum laude
SMKMNTNZ
Smoky Mountains
SMKNCHS
semiconscious
SMKNDKTR
semiconductor
SMKNG
smocking(sewing)
SMKNSHS
semiconscious
SMKR
smacker
smoker
SMKSKRN
smoke screen
SMKSTK
smokestack

SML
sawmill
seemly(proper)
  seemlier
  seemliest
  seemliness
simile(figure of
  speech)
small(little)
smell(nose)
smelt(or)
  smelled
smelly
  smellier
  smelliest
  smelliness
smile(mouth)
  smiled
  smiling
Somalia
SMLBL
assimilable
SMLBZNS
small business
SMLDR
smolder
SMLFR
small fry
  small fries
SMLK
ice milk
SMLKST
simulcast
SMLMNDD
small-minded
SMLN
semolina
SMLNG
cymling(food)
SMLNTSTN
small intestine
SMLPKS
smallpox
SMLPTTZ
small potatoes
SMLR
smiler(person)
similar(like)
SMLRT
similarity
  similarities
SMLSKL
small-scale
SMLT
assimilate
  assimilated

assimilating
assimilation
assimilator
smalt(blue)
smelt(melt)
smelt(smell)
smolt(salmon)
SMLTD
similitude
SMLTK
small talk
SMLTM
smalltime
SMLTNS
simultaneous
SMLTNT
simultaneity
SMLTR
smelter
smeltery
SMLTYD
similitude
SMLY
Somalia
sommelier(wine)
SMM
simoom
SMMNTHL
semimonthly
  semimonthlies
SMN
cymene(resin)
iceman
icemen
salmon(fish)
  salmon
semen(sperm)
seaman(person)
seamen
simian(ape)
simony(money)
someone(person)
summon(call)
SMNFRS
somniferous
SMNFSHNT
somnifacient
SMNG
seeming
SMNKS
semantics
SMNL
seminal(semen)
Seminole(tribe)
SMNLNS
somnolence

SMNLNT
somnolent
SMNMBYLST
somnambulist
SMNMBYLT
somnambulate
  somnambulated
  somnambulating
SMNMBYLZM
somnambulism
SMNPYR
simon-pure
SMNR
seminar
seminary(school)
  seminaries
SMNRN
seminarian
SMNS
sameness
SMNSHP
seamanship
SMNT
cement
SMNTK
semantic
SMNTKL
semantical
SMNTKS
semantics
SMNYL
semiannual
SMNZ
Simonize
  (trademark)
simonize
  simonized
  simonizing
summons
  summonses
SMP
samp(food)
sump(low area)
SMPCHR
sumptuary
SMPCHS
sumptuous
SMPL
sample(try)
  sampled
  sampling
  sampler
simple(plain)
  simpler
  simplest
  simply

SMPLF
simplify
  simplified
  simplifies
SMPLFKSHN
simplification
SMPLFR
simplifier
SMPLMNDD
simple-minded
SMPLNG
sampling
SMPLR
sampler(try)
simpler(easier)
SMPLS
someplace
SMPLST
simplest
simplicity
  simplicities
SMPLTN
simpleton
SMPLZM
simplism
SMPN
sampan
SMPR
simper(smile)
SMPRFDLS
semper fidelis
SMPRFSHNL
semiprofessional
SMPRMBL
semipermeable
SMPRPRTS
semper paratus
SMPRSHS
semiprecious
SMPRVT
semiprivate
SMPSHN
assumption
SMPSHS
sumptuous
SMPTH
sympathy
  sympathies
SMPTHTK
sympathetic
SMPTHTKL
sympathetical
SMPTHZ
sympathize
  sympathized
  sympathizing

sympathizer

SMPTR
sumpter

SMPTRK
sympatric

SMPZM
symposium
symposia(or)
symposiums

SMR
isomer
Samaria
samurai(warrior)
simmer(cook)
smear(rub)
smeary
smearier
smeariest
smeariness
Sumer
Sumerian
summary(account)
summaries
summer(season)
summery

SMRCH
smirch
smirches

SMRGSBRD
smorgasbord

SMRHS
summerhouse

SMRJD
semirigid

SMRK
smirk

SMRKR
smirker

SMRL
summarily

SMRM
smarmy
smarmier
smarmiest

SMRSLT
somersault

SMRST
summarist(person)
somersault(flip)

SMRT
smart

SMRTLK
smart aleck
smart-alecky
smart-aleckiness

SMRTM

summertime

SMRTN
Samaritan
smarten

SMRZ
summarize
summarized
summarizing

SMRZR
summarizer

SMRZSHN
summarization

SMS
isthmus
isthmuses(or)
isthmi

SMSH
smash
smashes

SMSHM
cymatium
cymatia

SMSHN
assumption
summation

SMSHP
smashup

SMSHS
sumptuous

SMSKLD
semiskilled

SMSLD
semisolid

SMSN
samisen
Samson

SMSRKL
semicircle

SMSS
osmosis

SMSTR
semester

SMSTRS
seamstress
seamstresses

SMT
Semite
smite(hit)
smote
smiting
smitten
smut(filth)
smutty
smuttier
smuttiest
smuttiness

summit(top)

SMTH
smithy
smithies
smooth
smoothy
smoothies

SMTHBR
smoothbore

SMTHFST
smooth-faced

SMTHN
smoothen

SMTHNG
something

SMTHR
smother(air)

SMTHRNZ
smithereens

SMTHSHVN
smooth-shaven

SMTHSPKN
smooth-spoken

SMTK
Semitic

SMTL
summital

SMTM
sometime
symptom

SMTMTK
semiautomatic
symptomatic

SMTMZ
sometimes

SMTR
asymmetry(shape)
cemetery(grave)
cemeteries
scimitar(sword)
smatter(speak,
dabble)
symmetry(beauty)
symmetries

SMTRK
asymmetric(no
balance)
isometric(equal
measure)
symmetric(balance)

SMTRKL
asymmetrical
isometrical
symmetrical

SMTRKS
isometrics

symmetrics(verse)

SMTRLR
semitrailer

SMTRNG
smattering

SMTRPKL
semitropical

SMTRZ
symmetrize
symmetrized
symmetrizing

SMTRZSHN
symmetrization

SMTZM
Semitism

SMVR
samovar

SMW
someway

SMWKL
semiweekly
semiweeklies

SMWN
someone(person)

SMWR
somewhere(place)

SMWT
somewhat(partly)

SMYLNT
simulant

SMYLSHN
simulation

SMYLT
simulate
simulated
simulating
simulator

SMYLTR
simulator

SMYRL
semiyearly

SMZ
Psalms(book)
Siamese
smaze(air)

SN
assign(allot)
assignee
cion(twig)
cyan(blue-green)
sand(beach)
sandy
-dier,-diest
sandiness
sane(not crazy)
saner,sanest

B:by **CH**:each **D**:day **F**:if **G**:go **H**:he **HW**:why **J**:joy **K**:cow **KS**:ax **KWL**:equal **L**:all **M**:may **N**:in

Santa(Claus)
sauna(bath)
scene(view)
scion(heir)(or)
  cion(twig)
seen(see)
seine(net)
  seined
  seining
Seine(river)
sen(coin)
sewn(sew)
sienna(clay)
sign(poster)
sin(offense)
  sinned
  sinning
  sinner
sine(ratio)
snow(ice)
  snowy
  snowier
  snowiest
son(boy)
sonny(little boy)
soon(time)
sown(plant)
sow
sun(star)
  sunned
  sunning
  sunny
  sunnier
  sunniest
  sunnily
  sunniness
SNB
snib(latch)
  snibbed
  snibbing
snob(person)
snub(ignore)
  snubbed
  snubbing
SNBL
assignable
snowball
SNBLND
snow-blind
SNBLNDNS
snow blindness
SNBLT
Sun Belt
SNBM
sunbeam
SNBND

snowbound
SNBNT
sunbonnet
SNBNZD
snub-nosed
SNBR
snobbery
SNBRD
signboard
snowbird
SNBRN
sunburn
  sunburnt(or)
  sunburned
SNBRST
sunburst
SNBSH
snobbish
SNBTH
sun bath
sunbathe
  sunbathed
  sunbathing
  sunbather
SNBTHR
sunbather
SNBZM
snobbism
SNCH
cinch(girth,
  easy)
cinches
snatch(grab)
  snatches
  snatchy
  snatchier
  snatchiest
snitch(steal)
  snitches
SNCHL
essential(needed)
sensual(beauty)
SNCHLT
essentiality
sensuality
SNCHN
ascension
SNCHNS
sentience
SNCHNT
sentient
SNCHR
censure(blame)
  censured
  censuring
century(time)

centuries
snitcher(steal)
SND
ascend(rise)
cyanide(poison)
  cyanided
  cyaniding
sand(earth)
sandhi(sound)
sandy
  sandier
  sandiest
  sandiness
scend(heave
  upward)
scend(wave)
send(convey)
  sent
snide(sarcastic)
snood(cap)
snotty(snot)
  snottier
  snottiest
  snottiness
sound(noise)
sundae(ice cream)
Sunday
synod(council)
SNDBG
sandbag
SNDBKS
sandbox
  sandboxes
  sound box
  sound boxes
SNDBL
ascendable
SNDBLST
sandblast
SNDBR
sandbar
SNDBRR
sound barrier
SNDF
send-off(n)
SNDFKS
sound effects
SNDFKT
sound effect
SNDG
San Diego
SNDHG
sandhog
SNDK
syndic(agent)
synodic(synod)

SNDKL
syndical
SNDKLZM
syndicalism
SNDKMR
sound camera
SNDKS
sandix(lead)
SNDKSHN
syndication
SNDKT
syndicate
  syndicated
  syndicating
SNDL
sandal
sundial
SNDLT
sand-lot(adj)
SNDLWD
sandalwood
SNDMN
sandman
SNDN
sundown
SNDNG
sounding
SNDNGBRD
sounding board
SNDNR
sundowner
SNDNS
ascendance
ascendancy
  ascendancies
sun dance
SNDNT
ascendant
SNDPPR
sandpaper
sandpiper(bird)
SNDPRF
soundproof
SNDR
ascender(climber)
asunder(separate)
cinder(ash)
sander(machine)
sounder(one that
  sounds)
sunder(sever)
sundry(various)
  sundries
SNDRFT
snowdrift
SNDRM

syndrome
SNDRZ
sundries
SNDS
so-and-so
SNDSKL
Sunday school
SNDSTJ
sound stage
SNDSTN
sandstone
SNDSTRM
sandstorm
SNDTK
syndetic
SNDTRK
soundtrack
SNDWCH
sandwich
SNDWV
sound wave
SNF
snafu(confusion)
sniff(nose)
sniffy(haughty)
sniffier
sniffiest
snuff
SNFBKS
snuffbox
snuffboxes
SNFL
sinful(wrong)
snaffle(bit)
snaffled
snaffling
sniffle(nose)
sniffled
sniffling
snowfall(ice)
snuffle(noisy nose)
snuffled
snuffling
SNFLD
centerfold
SNFLK
snowflake
SNFLR
sunflower
SNFLWR
sunflower
SNFR
sniffer(nose)
snuffer(candle)
SNFRNSSK
San Francisco

SNFRW
sang-froid
SNFRZ
Sanforize
(trademark)
Sanforized
(trademark)
snuffers
SNFRZD
Sanforized
(trademark)
SNFTR
snifter
SNG
icing(cake)
saying(words)
seeing(eyes)
sewing(stitch)
sing(music)
sang
sung
snag(hinder)
snagged
snagging
snaggy
snaggier
snaggiest
snug(cozy)
snugger
snuggest
song(melody)
SNGFST
songfest
SNGG
synagogue
SNGGL
single
singled
singling
singly
SNGGLHNDD
single-handed
SNGGLR
singular
singularity
SNGGLSPS
single-space
single-spaced
single-spacing
SNGGLTN
singleton
SNGGLZ
Singhalese
SNGGPR
Singapore
SNGK

sink
sank
sunk
sunken
sync
synchronization
SNGKCHN
sanction
SNGKCHR
cincture(belt)
cinctured
cincturing
sanctuary(place)
sanctuaries
SNGKCHWR
sanctuary
sanctuaries
SNGKHL
sinkhole
SNGKN
sunken
SNGKP
syncope
SNGKPSHN
syncopation
SNGKPT
syncopate
syncopated
syncopating
SNGKR
sinker
SNGKRMSH
synchromesh
synchromeshes
SNGKRNK
synchronic
SNGKRNS
synchronous
SNGKRNZ
synchronize
synchronized
synchronizing
SNGKRNZM
synchronism
SNGKRNZSHN
synchronization
SNGKRTRN
synchrotron
SNGKRTZ
syncretize
syncretized
syncretizing
SNGKRTZM
syncretism
SNGKSHN
sanction

SNGKTF
sanctify
sanctified
sanctifies
SNGKTFKSHN
sanctification
SNGKTM
sanctum
sancta(or)
sanctums
SNGKTMN
sanctimony
SNGKTMNS
sanctimonious
SNGKTT
sanctity
sanctities
SNGL
Senegal
single
singled
singling
singly
snuggle
snuggled
snuggling
SNGLBRSTD
single-breasted
SNGLFZ
single-phase
SNGLHNDD
single-handed
SNGLSPS
single-space
SNGLSPST
single-spaced
SNGLSZ
sunglasses
SNGLTN
singleton
SNGLTTH
snaggletooth
SNGLTTHT
snaggletoothed
SNGLZ
Singhalese
SNGMSHN
sewing machine
SNGNDDNS
song and dance
SNGNG
singing
SNGPR
Singapore
SNGPRSTRT
Singapore Strait

B:by **CH**:each **D**:day **F**:if **G**:go **H**:he **HW**:why **J**:joy **K**:cow **KS**:ax **KWL**:equal **L**:all **M**:may **N**:in

SNGR
sangria(drink)
snuggery(place)
snuggeries
SNGRD
centigrade
Celsius
SNGSNG
singsong
SNGSTR
songster
SNGWN
sanguine
SNGWNR
sanguinary
SNGWNS
sanguineous
SNGYL
singular
SNGYLRT
singularity
singularities
SNGYLRZ
singularize
singularized
singularizing
singularization
SNHWT
snow-white
SNHZ
San Jose
SNJ
singe
singed
singeing
SNJB
snow job
SNJN
cyanogen(gas)
SNK
cyanic(color)
cynic(person)
scenic(beauty)
sink
sank
sunk
sunken
snack(food)
snake(animal)
snaked
snaking
snaky
snakier
snakiest
sneak(stealth)
snuck(or)

sneaked
sneaky
sneakier
sneakiest
sneakily
sneakiness
sonic(sound)
sync
synchronization
SNKBM
sonic boom
SNKBR
snack bar
SNKBRR
sonic barrier
SNKDK
synecdoche
synecdochic
SNKL
cenacle(room)
cynical(attitude)
snake oil(potion)
SNKLJ
synecology
SNKLZ
Santa Claus
SNKP
syncope
SNKPSHN
syncopation
SNKPT
snowcapped
syncopate
syncopated
syncopating
SNKR
sneaker(shoe)
snicker(laugh)
snooker(game)
SNKRMSH
synchromesh
synchromeshes
SNKRNK
synchronic
SNKRNS
synchronous
SNKRNZ
synchronize
synchronized
synchronizing
SNKRNZM
synchronism
SNKRNZSHN
synchronization
sync
SNKRTRN

synchrotron
SNKRTZ
syncretize
syncretized
syncretizing
SNKRTZM
syncretism
SNKRV
sine curve
SNKSKN
snakeskin
SNKTTD
senectitude
SNKTTYD
senectitude
SNKYR
sinecure
SNL
senile(old)
snail(mollusk)
snell(fishing line)
SNLMP
sunlamp
SNLN
snow line
SNLPRD
snow leopard
SNLPST
snail-paced
SNLS
sinless
SNLT
scintillate
scintillated
scintillating
scintillation
scintillator
senility
senilities
sunlight
sunlit(adj)
SNLZPS
snail's pace
SNM
cinema
SNMBL
snowmobile
snowmobiled
snowmobiling
SNMD
cyanamide
SNMDR
centimeter
SNMN
cinnamon
SNMNT

sentiment
SNMNTL
sentimental
SNMRN
San Marino
SNMTR
centimeter
SNN
asinine
cyanine(dye)
SNNG
signing
SNNL
son-in-law
sons-in-law
SNNM
synonym(same as)
synonymy, -mies
SNNMS
synonymous
SNNS
assonance(sound
alike)
sonance(sound)
SNNT
asininity(ass like)
asininities
sonant(voiced)
SNNTN
San Antonio
SNP
sannup
snap(break)
snapped
snapping
snappy(quick)
snappier
snappiest
snip(cut)
snipped
snipping
snippy
(impertinent)
snippier
snippiest
snipe(bird,shoot)
sniped
sniping
sniper
snoop(pry)
snoopy
snoopier
snoopiest
sunup
SNPBN
snap bean

NGK:ink **P:**pie **R:**air **S:**ice **SH:**show **T:**toy **THN:**thin **TH:**the **V:**of **W:**we **Y:**you **Z:**is **VZHN:**vision

SNPBRM snap-brim	snaring sneer(scorn)	essence(intrinsic) science(study)	Cincinnati senescent
SNPD centipede	snore(sleep) snored	séance(meeting) sense(feel,faculty)	**SNSPT** sunspot
SNPDRGN snapdragon	snoring snorer	sensed sensing	**SNSR** censer(incense)
SNPL Sao Paulo snowplow	sooner(time) Sooner(person) Oklahoma	sensory since(time) sinus(cavity)	censor(person) sensor(device) sensory(senses)
SNPR snapper(fish) snooper(prowler) sniper(rifleman)	sonar(radar) **SNRDRM** snare drum **SNRFL**	sinuses so-and-so **SNSBL** sensible	sincere(true) sincerer sincerest sincerely
SNPRSKP snooperscope	sneerful **SNRFLD**	sensibly **SNSBLT**	**SNSRL** sensorial
SNPS synapse(brain) (or) synapsis synapses	centerfold **SNRJSTK** synergistic synergistical **SNRJTK**	sensibility sensibilities **SNSDP** sunny-side up **SNSFKSHN**	sincerely **SNSRS** censorious **SNSRSHP** censorship
SNPSH snappish(bite)	synergetic synergetically	science fiction **SNSH**	**SNSRT** sincerity
SNPSHT snapshot	**SNRJZM** synergism(more)	snowshoe **SNSHD**	sincerities **SNSS**
SNPSS synapsis(or) synapse(sing) synapses synopsis(outline) synopses	**SNRKL** snorkel **SNRL** snarl snarly snarlier	sunshade **SNSHL** essential sensual **SNSHLT** essentiality	census cyanosis cyanosed **SNSSHN** sensation **SNSSHNL**
SNPST signpost	snarliest **SNRNT**	sensuality **SNSHN**	sensational **SNST**
SNPSZ synapses(pl)(brain) synapsis(or) synapse synopsize(outline) synopsized synopsizing	sonorant **SNRR** snarer snorer snore **SNRRM**	ascension sunshine **SNSHNT** sentient **SNSHP** sonship	snaste(wick) snowsuit sunset **SNSTHZH** synesthesia synesthetic
SNPT snippety snippetier snippetiest	cinerarium cineraria **SNRS** sonorous	**SNSHR** censure(blame) censured censuring	**SNSTR** sinister **SNSTRK** sunstroke
SNPTK synoptic	**SNRST** scenarist	cynosure(focal point)	**SNSTRM** snowstorm
SNR assigner assignor(law) center(middle) saunter(walk) scenario(plot) scenery(beauty) sceneries sinner(person) snare(trap) snared	**SNRT** snort sonority **SNRTR** cinerator **SNRZ** sunrise **SNS** cense(offer incense) censed censing	**SNSHRBL** censurable **SNSHS** sensuous(beauty) synoecious **SNSKRT** Sanskrit **SNSLS** senseless **SNSLVDR** San Salvador **SNSNT**	**SNSTRS** sinistrous **SNSTS** sinusitis **SNSTV** sensitive **SNSTVT** sensitivity sensitivities **SNSTZ** sensitize sensitized

B:by **CH**:each **D**:day **F**:if **G**:go **H**:he **HW**:why **J**:joy **K**:cow **KS**:ax **KWL**:equal **L**:all **M**:may **N**:in

sensitizing
SNSTZSHN
sensitization
SNSYT
snowsuit
SNSZM
cynicism
SNT
ascent(rise)
assent(agree)
cent(money)
saint(person)
Saint(title)
St.
sanity(sane)
Santa(Claus)
scent(odor)
senate(assembly)
sent
send
snit(irritation)
snooty(aloof)
snootier
snootiest
snot(nose)
snotty
snottier
snottiest
snottiness
snout(nose)
sonata(music)
sonnet(poetry)
suint(grease)
SNTDMNGG
Santo Domingo
SNTF
cenotaph
Santa Fe
SNTFK
scientific
SNTFKL
scientifically
SNTG
Santiago
SNTGRD
centigrade
Celsius
SNTGRM
centigram
SNTHD
sainthood
SNTHDK
synthetic
SNTHLN
St. Helena
SNTHSS

synthesis
syntheses
SNTHSZ
synthesize
synthesized
synthesizing
SNTHSZR
synthesizer
SNTHTK
synthetic
SNTHTKL
synthetical
SNTJNZ
St. John's
SNTKLZ
Santa Claus
SNTKR
St. Croix
SNTKS
syntax
SNTKTKL
syntactical
SNTKTKS
syntactics
SNTKTSNVS
St. Kitts-Nevis
SNTL
saintly
saintlier
saintliest
saintliness
scintilla
SNTLMTR
scintillometer
SNTLRNSRVR
St. Lawrence River
SNTLS
St. Louis
SNTLSH
St. Lucia
SNTLSHN
scintillation
SNTLT
scintillate
scintillated
scintillating
SNTLTR
scintillator
SNTM
Sao Tomé
SNTMNT
sentiment
SNTMNTL
sentimental
SNTMNTLT
sentimentality

sentimentalities
SNTMNTLZ
sentimentalize
sentimentalized
sentimentalizing
SNTMNTLZM
sentimentalism
SNTMPRNSP
Sao Tomé e Principe
SNTMRTS
St. Moritz
SNTMTR
centimeter(or)
cm
SNTN
sonatina
suntan
suntanned
suntanning
SNTNL
centennial
sentinel(guard)
SNTNR
centenary
SNTNRN
centenarian
SNTNS
sentence
sentenced
sentencing
sentience
(conscious)
SNTNSHS
sententious
(expressive)
SNTNT
sentient
(conscious)
SNTPD
centipede
SNTPR
Saint-Pierre
SNTR
assenter(agree)
centaur(monster)
center(middle), (B)- tre
sanitary(clean)
saunter(walk)
senator(lawmaker)
sentry(guard)
sentries
sonneteer(poet)
SNTRBRD
centerboard
SNTRFGL
centrifugal

SNTRFLD
center field
centerfold
SNTRFLDR
center fielder
SNTRFYGL
centrifugal
SNTRFYJ
centrifuge
SNTRFZH
centrifuge
SNTRK
acentric
acentrical
centric
centrical
SNTRL
central(main,
middle)
senatorial(senator)
SNTRLFRKN
RPBLK
Central African
Republic
SNTRLT
centrality
SNTRLZ
centralize
centralized
centralizing
centralization
SNTRLZM
centralism
SNTRM
sanatorium(disease)
sanatoria(or)
sanatoriums
sanitarium(health)
sanitaria(or)
sanitariums
SNTRPK
isentropic
SNTRPS
centerpiece
SNTRPTL
centripetal
SNTRST
acentricity
acentricities
centricity
centricities
centrist(person)
SNTSHN
assentation
sanitation
SNTST

scientist
SNTV
sanative
SNTVNSNT
St. Vincent
SNTZ
sanitize
  sanitized
  sanitizing
SNVBCH
son of a bitch
  sons of bitches
SNVL
snivel
SNWCH
sandwich
SNWN
San Juan
SNY
sinew
  sinewy
SNYR
signore
senior(top)
  Sr.(title)
señor(man)
  señores
señora(woman)
  señoras
SNYRS
coenurus(larval)
  coenuri
SNYRT
seniority
  seniorities
SNYS
sinuous
SNZ
sands(dirt)
sans(without)
signs(indications)
snazzy
  snazzier
  snazziest
sneeze(cough)
  sneezed
  sneezing
  sneezy
snooze(sleep)
  snoozed
  snoozing
SNZNL
sons-in-law
SNZSRF
sans serif
SNZVBCHZ

sons of bitches
SP
asp(snake)
espy(glimpse)
  espied
  espies
sap(plant juice)
  sapped
  sapping
sappy(juicy)
  sappier
  sappiest
seep(ooze)
sepia(brown)
sip(drink)
  sipped
  sipping
soap(clean)
  soapy
  soapier
  soapiest
  soapily
  soapiness
sop(soak)
  sopped
  sopping
  soppy
  soppier
  soppiest
  soppily
  soppiness
soup(food)
  soupy
  soupier
  soupiest
  soupiness
spay(cut)
spy(pry)
  spied
  spies
sup(eat)
  supped
  supping
SPBKS
soapbox
  soapboxes
SPCH
speech
  speeches
SPCHF
speechify
  speechified
  speechifies
SPCHJNRN
septuagenarian
SPCHKK

spitchcock
SPCHL
spatula
SPCHLT
spatulate
SPCHMKNG
speechmaking
SPCHMKR
speechmaker
SPD
sapid
spade
  spaded
  spading
speed
  sped(or)
  speeded
  speeding
  speedy
  speedier
  speediest
  speedily
  speediness
spode(porcelain)
  spoded
  spoding
spud(tool)
  spudded
  spudding
spud(potato)
SPDBL
speedball
SPDBT
speedboat
SPDKS
spadix
SPDL
spittle
SPDMTR
speedometer
SPDNG
speeding
SPDP
speedup
SPDR
speeder
spider
  spidery
SPDRL
espadrille
SPDSTR
aspidistra(plant)
speedster
SPDTRP
speed trap
SPDW

speedway
SPDWRK
spadework
SPF
spiffy
  spiffier
  spiffiest
  spiffiness
spoof
SPGD
spaghetti
SPGLS
spyglass
  spyglasses
SPGT
spaghetti
spigot
SPGTN
spaghettini
SPJ
seepage
SPK
aspic
speak(talk)
  spoke
  spoken
speck(small)
spic(slang)
spica(bandage)
spike(impale)
  spiked
  spiking
  spiky(pointed)
  spikier
  spikiest
spoke(wheel)
  spoked
  spoking
spook(scare)
  spooky(scary)
  spookier
  spookiest
  spookily
  spookiness
SPKBL
speakable
SPKL
Spackle(plastic
  paste)
  Spackled
  (trademark)
  Spackling
speckle(spotted)
  speckled
  speckling
SPKN

B:by **CH**:each **D**:day **F**:if **G**:go **H**:he **HW**:why **J**:joy **K**:cow **KS**:ax **KWL**:equal **L**:all **M**:may **N**:in

Spokane
SPKNDSPN
spick-and-span
SPKR
speaker
SPKS
specs
(eyeglasses,
specifications)
SPKSHV
spokeshave
SPKSMN
spokesman
spokesmen
SPKSWMN
spokeswoman
spokeswomen
SPKT
aspect
spiccato
spigot(water)
SPKTKL
spectacle
SPKTKLD
spectacled
SPKTKLZ
spectacles(eyes)
SPKTKYLR
spectacular
SPKTR
specter, (B)spectre
SPKTRGRF
spectrograph
SPKTRGRM
spectrogram
SPKTRL
spectral
SPKTRM
spectrum
spectra(or)
spectrums
SPKTRMTR
spectrometer
SPKTRSKP
spectroscope
spectroscopy
SPKTTR
spectator
SPKYLM
speculum
SPKYLR
specular
SPKYLSHN
speculation
SPKYLT
speculate

speculated
speculating
SPKYLTR
speculator
SPKYLTV
speculative
SPKZ
speakeasy
speakeasies
SPL
Sao Paulo
spall(stone)
spell(words)
spelt(or)
spelled
spell(time,trance)
spiel(talk)
spill(fall)
spilt(or)
spilled
splay(spread)
spoil(damage)
spoilt(or)
spoiled
spool(wind)
supple(pliant)
supply(provide)
supplied
supplies
SPLBND
spellbind
spellbound
SPLBNDR
spellbinder
SPLCH
splotch
splotches
splotchy
SPLDN
spelldown(n)
SPLDR
splatter
SPLFT
splayfoot
splayfeet
SPLFTD
splayfooted
SPLJ
spillage(fall)
spoilage(damage)
SPLKNT
supplicant
SPLKR
sepulcher, (B)-chre
SPLKRL
sepulchral

SPLKSHN
supplication
SPLKT
supplicate
supplicated
supplicating
SPLLJ
speleology
SPLLJKL
speleological
SPLLJST
speleologist
SPLMNT
supplement
SPLMNTL
supplemental
SPLMNTR
supplementary
SPLMNTSHN
supplementation
SPLN
seaplane
spleen
SPLND
esplanade
SPLNDD
splendid
SPLNDFRS
splendiferous
SPLNDNT
splendent
SPLNDR
splendor, (B)-dour
SPLNFL
spleenful
SPLNG
sapling(tree)
spelling
SPLNGKNG
spelunking
SPLNGKR
spelunker
SPLNR
splinter
SPLNT
splint
supplant(replace)
suppliant(asking)
SPLNTK
splenetic
SPLNTR
splinter
SPLR
speller
spoiler
supplier

SPLRJ
splurge
splurged
splurging
SPLS
splice
spliced
splicing
SPLSH
splash
splashes
splashy
splashier
splashiest
splashily
splashiness
SPLSHBRD
splashboard
SPLSHDN
splashdown
SPLSHN
spoliation
SPLSPRT
spoilsport
SPLT
spelt
spell
spilt
spill
splat(noise,wood)
split(divide)
split
splitting
SPLTH
isopleth
SPLTLVL
split-level
SPLTP
split up(divide)
SPLTR
splatter(liquid)
splutter(speak)
spoliator
SPLTS
splits(position)
SPLW
spillway
SPLYR
espalier
SPLZ
supplies
SPM
Spam(meat)
(trademark)
spume(foam)
spumed

NGK:ink P:pie R:air S:ice SH:show T:toy THN:thin TH:the V:of W:we Y:you Z:is VZHN:vision

spuming
spumy(foam)
spumier
spumiest
spumily
spuminess
SPMN
spumone(food)
SPMS
spumous
SPN
Aspen
aspen(tree)
Spain
span(cross)
spanned
spanning
spawn(birth)
spin(turn)
spun
spinning
spinner
spine(bone,thorn)
spiny
spinier
spiniest
spoon(utensil)
spoony(enamored)
spoonier
spooniest
subpoena(law)
supine(face up)
SPNBL
spoonbill
SPNCH
spinach
SPND
spend
spent
spending
spondee
SPNDFRS
splendiferous
SPNDKS
Spandex
(trademark)
SPNDL
spindle
spindled
spindling
spindly
spindlier
spindliest
SPNDLGZ
spindlelegs
SPNDNG

spending
SPNDNGMN
spending money
SPNDR
spender
SPNDRFT
spindrift
SPNDRL
spandrel
SPNDTHRFT
spendthrift
SPNF
saponify
saponified
saponifies
spinoff
SPNFD
spoon-feed
spoon-fed
SPNFL
spoonful
SPNFRS
spiniferous
SPNGGL
spangle
spangled
spangling
spangly
spanglier
spangliest
SPNGGLZ
spangles
SPNGK
spank(punish)
spunk
spunky
spunkier
spunkiest
spunkily
spunkiness
SPNGKNG
spanking
SPNGKR
spanker
spinnaker(sail)
SPNGL
spangle
spangled
spangling
spangly
spanglier
spangliest
SPNJ
espionage
sponge
sponged

sponging
spongy
spongier
spongiest
spongily
sponginess
SPNJBTH
sponge bath
SPNJKK
sponge cake
SPNJR
sponger
SPNKR
spinnaker
SPNL
spinal
SPNLKLM
spinal column
SPNLS
spineless
SPNNG
spinning
SPNR
spanner(tool,span)
spinner(spin)
SPNRT
spinneret(spider)
SPNRZM
spoonerism
SPNS
spinous
SPNSH
Spanish
SPNSHFL
Spanish fly
(beetle)
SPNSHMRKNWR
Spanish-American
War
SPNSHMS
Spanish moss
SPNSN
sponson
SPNSNT
spinescent
SPNSR
spencer
sponsor
SPNSRL
sponsorial
SPNSRSHP
sponsorship
SPNSTR
spinster
SPNT
sapient

spent
spend
spinet
SPNTHBTL
spin-the-bottle
SPNTNS
spontaneous
SPNTNT
spontaneity
spontaneities
SPNYL
spaniel
spinule
SPNYRD
Spaniard
SPNZH
espionage
SPR
aspire(desire)
aspired
aspiring
aspirer
esprit(spirit)
osprey
sapor(flavor)
Sapporo
sopor(stupor)
spar(fight)
sparred
sparring
spare(extra)
spared
sparing
sparrow(bird)
spear(weapon)
spier(spy)
spire(taper)
spired
spiring
spore
(microorganism)
spored
sporing
spoor(track)
spray(liquid)
spree(outing)
spry(active)
spryer
spryest
spryly
spryness
spur(spike,urge)
spurred
spurring
super(great)
supper(food)

B:by **CH**:each **D**:day **F**:if **G**:go **H**:he **HW**:why **J**:joy **K**:cow **KS**:ax **KWL**:equal **L**:all **M**:may **N**:in

SPRB	**SPRDPR**	sparker	sopranos
superb	superduper	**SPRKRG**	Spartan
SPRBL	**SPRDR**	supercargo	sporran(pouch)
separable(divide)	spreader	**SPRKT**	sprain(injury)
separably	**SPRFK**	sprocket	spurn(refuse)
superable(overcome)	soporific	**SPRL**	**SPRNCHRL**
Super Bowl	**SPRFLS**	spiral	supernatural, -ism
SPRBNDNS	superfluous	sprawl	**SPRNCHRLSTK**
superabundance	**SPRFLT**	**SPRLMNL**	supernaturalistic
SPRBNDNT	superfluity	supraliminal	**SPRNCHRLSTKL**
superabundant	superfluities	**SPRLNG**	supernaturalistical
SPRBZ	**SPRFN**	spiraling	**SPRNDS**
spareribs	superfine	**SPRLPSRN**	superinduce
SPRCHL	**SPRFRS**	supralapsarian	**SPRNDYS**
spiritual	spiriferous	**SPRLTV**	superinduce
SPRCHLST	**SPRFSHL**	superlative	**SPRNG**
spiritualist	superficial	**SPRM**	spring
SPRCHLSTK	**SPRFSHLT**	sperm	sprang
spiritualistic	superficiality	supreme	sprung
SPRCHLT	superficialities	**SPRMHWL**	Spring
spirituality	**SPRG**	sperm whale	(season)
spiritualities	sprag(wedge)	**SPRMKRT**	springy
SPRCHLZ	sprig(twig)	Supreme Court	springier
spiritualize	sprigged	**SPRML**	springiest
spiritualized	sprigging	supremely	springily
spiritualizing	superego	**SPRMN**	springiness
SPRCHLZM	**SPRGR**	Superman	**SPRNGBR**
spiritualism	sprigger	(trademark)	spring bar
SPRCHLZSHN	**SPRGS**	superman	**SPRNGBRD**
spiritualization	asparagus	supermen	springboard
SPRCHRJ	**SPRHD**	**SPRMNT**	**SPRNGFLD**
supercharge	spearhead	spearmint	Springfield
supercharged	**SPRHTRDN**	**SPRMPZ**	**SPRNGFVR**
supercharging	superheterodyne	superimpose	spring fever
supercharger	**SPRHW**	-posed,-posing	**SPRNGHD**
SPRCHRJR	superhighway	**SPRMRKT**	springhead
supercharger	**SPRHYMN**	supermarket	**SPRNGHS**
SPRCHS	superhuman	**SPRMS**	springhouse
spirituous	**SPRJ**	supremacy	**SPRNGKL**
SPRD	sparge	**SPRMSST**	sprinkle
spiroid	sparged	supremacist	sprinkled
spread	sparging	**SPRMST**	sprinkling
spread	**SPRJL**	spermaceti	**SPRNGKLR**
SPRDGL	aspergill	**SPRMSVT**	sprinkler
spread-eagle	**SPRK**	Supreme Soviet	**SPRNGL**
spread-eagled	spark	**SPRMTK**	sparingly
spread-eagling	**SPRKL**	spermatic	**SPRNGTD**
SPRDK	sparkle	**SPRMTZN**	spring tide
sporadic	sparkled	spermatozoon	**SPRNGTM**
SPRDKL	sparkling	-zoal,-zoan,-zoic	springtime
sporadical	sparkler	**SPRMWL**	**SPRNL**
SPRDKR	**SPRKLR**	sperm whale	supernal
esprit de corps	sparkler	**SPRN**	**SPRNMRR**
SPRDNG	**SPRKPLG**	aspirin	supernumerary
sporting	spark plug	soprano(person)	supernumeraries
spreading	**SPRKR**	soprani(or)	**SPRNR**

NGK:ink **P**:pie **R**:air **S**:ice **SH**:show **T**:toy **THN**:thin **TH**:the **V**:of **W**:we **Y**:you **Z**:is **VZHN**:vision

sprinter
SPRNT
aspirant(person)
Esperanto
spirant(sound)
sprint(run)
SPRNTND
superintend
SPRNTNDNS
superintendence
superintendents
SPRNTNDNT
superintendent
SPRNTR
sprinter
SPRNTRLSTK
supernaturalistic
SPRNYMRR
supernumerary
supernumeraries
SPRPR
superpower
SPRPWR
superpower
SPRPZ
superpose
superposed
superposing
SPRR
aspirer(aspire)
spurrier(makes
spurs)
superior
SPRRGSHN
supererogation
SPRRGT
supererogate
supererogated
supererogating
SPRRGTV
supererogative
SPRRT
superiority
superiorities
SPRS
asperse
aspersed
aspersing
asperser
aspersive
aspersion
cypress(tree)
cypresses
Cyprus(island)
espresso
sparse(scarce)

sparser
sparsest
spruce(tree,neat)
spruced
sprucing
sprucer
sprucest
suppress(crush)
suppresses
SPRSBL
suppressible
SPRSBLT
suppressibility
SPRSCHRSHN
supersaturation
SPRSCHRT
supersaturate
supersaturated
supersaturating
SPRSD
supersede
superseded
superseding
SPRSHN
aspiration(ambition)
separation(divide)
suppression(crush)
SPRSHS
sporaceous(spore)
SPRSJR
supersedure
SPRSKRB
superscribe
superscribed
superscribing
SPRSKRPSHN
superscription
SPRSKRPT
superscript
SPRSL
sparsely
SPRSLS
supercilious
SPRSNK
supersonic
SPRSNSBL
supersensible
SPRSNSTV
supersensitive
SPRSR
suppressor
SPRSSHN
supersession
SPRST
sparsity
sparsities

SPRSTRKCHR
superstructure
SPRSTSHN
superstition
SPRSTSHS
superstitious
SPRSV
suppressive
SPRT
asperity(severe)
aspirate(breathe)
aspirated
aspirating
seaport
separate(divide)
separated
separating
spirit
sport(game)
sporty
sportier
sportiest
sportiness
sprit(pole)
sprite(elf)
sprout(growth)
spurt(liquid)
support(sustain)
SPRTBL
supportable
SPRTDL
spiritedly
SPRTL
sprightly
sprightlier
sprightliest
sprightliness
SPRTN
Spartan
SPRTNG
sporting
SPRTNGCHNS
sporting chance
SPRTR
aspirator
separator
supporter(sustain)
SPRTS
spiritous
SPRTSKR
sports car
SPRTSMN
sportsman
sportsmen
SPRTSMNSHP
sportsmanship

SPRTST
separatist
spiritist
SPRTSWMN
sportswoman
sportswomen
SPRTSWR
sportswear
SPRTV
separative
sportive
supportive(sustain)
SPRTZM
separatism
spiritism
SPRV
Super-Vee
(trademark)
SPRVN
supervene
supervened
supervening
SPRVNCHN
supervention
SPRVNSHN
supervention
SPRVZ
supervise
supervised
supervising
SPRVZHN
supervision
SPRVZR
supervisor
supervisory
SPRZHN
aspersion
SPS
auspice
space(area)
spaced
spacing
spacer
speiss(metallic)
spice(flavor)
spiced
spicing
spicy
spicier
spiciest
spiciness
spouse
spoused
spousing
SPSDZ
soapsuds

SPSF
  specify
    specified
    specifies
SPSFBL
  specifiable
    specifiably
SPSFK
  specific
SPSFKL
  specifically
SPSFKSHN
  specification
SPSFLT
  space flight
SPSFST
  specificity
    specificities
SPSH
  specie(coin)
  species(category)
SPSHDL
  space shuttle
SPSHL
  especially
    (special emphasis)
  spatial(area)
  special(not usual)
SPSHLDLVR
  special delivery
SPSHLST
  specialist
SPSHLT
  spatiality(area)
    spatialities
  speciality(feature)
    specialities
  specialty
    (occupation)
    specialties
SPSHLZ
  specialize
    specialized
    specializing
SPSHLZM
  specialism
SPSHLZSHN
  specialization
SPSHP
  spaceship
SPSHS
  auspicious
  spacious(roomy)
  specious(deceptive)
SPSHTL
  space shuttle

SPSHZ
  species(kind)
SPSJ
  Space Age
SPSKPSL
  space capsule
SPSKR
  sapsucker
SPSKRFT
  spacecraft
    spacecraft
SPSL
  spousal
SPSMN
  spaceman
  spacemen
  spacewoman
  specimen
SPSN
  soupcon
SPSNG
  spacing
SPSPN
  soupspoon
SPSPRB
  space probe
SPSPRT
  spaceport
SPST
  space suit
SPSTK
  spastic
SPSTKL
  spastically
SPSTM
  space-time
SPSTN
  soapstone
SPSTSHN
  space station
SPSWK
  space walk
SPSZ
  auspices
    auspice
  species(kind)
SPT
  sippet
  spate(sudden rush)
  spit(saliva)
    spit(or)
    spat
    spitting
  spit(impale)
    spitted
    spitting

spite(ill will)
    spited
    spiting
spot
    spotted
    spotting
    spotter
    spotty
    spottier
    spottiest
    spottily
    spottiness
  spout(liquid)
SPTBL
  spitball
SPTCHK
  spot-check
SPTFL
  spiteful
SPTFR
  spitfire
SPTJNRN
  septuagenarian
SPTK
  aseptic
  septic
SPTL
  spittle
SPTLT
  spotlight
SPTM
  septum
SPTMBR
  September
SPTN
  spittoon
SPTNGMJ
  spitting image
SPTNK
  sputnik
SPTPL
  septuple
    septupled
    septupling
SPTR
  scepter, (B)-tre
  spatter(liquid)
  spitter(spit)
  spotter(spot)
  spouter(spout)
  sputter(sound)
SPTS
  spitz
SPTT
  septet
SPTYPL

septuple
    septupled
    septupling
SPV
  spiv(swindler)
SPY
  spew
    spewed
    spewing
SPYDM
  sputum
  sputa
SPYM
  spume
    spumed
    spuming
  spumy
SPYMS
  spumous
SPYRS
  spurious
SPYRSHN
  suppuration
SPYRT
  suppurate
    suppurated
    suppurating
SPYTM
  sputum
  sputa
SPZ
  espouse(adopt,
    marry)
    espoused
    espousing
  spies(spy)
  spouse(marry)
    spoused
    spousing
  suppose
    supposed
    supposing
SPZBL
  supposable
    supposably
SPZDL
  supposedly
SPZL
  espousal(support)
  spousal(marriage)
SPZM
  spasm
SPZMDK
  spasmodic
SPZMDKL
  spasmodically

SPZSHN
supposition
SPZTR
suppository
suppositories
SPZTSHS
supposititious
SR
assayer
cere(wrap)
cered
cering
cero(fish)
eyesore
sari(garment)
sear(burn)
seer(prophet)
sera
serum
serry(to crowd)
serried
serries
sewer(conduit, person)
sierra(mountains)
sir(man)
sire(father)
sired
siring
soar(fly)
sore(painful)
sorrow(emotion)
sorry
sorrier
sorriest
sorrily
sorriness
sour(flavor)
sower(planter)
surry(vehicle)
surrys
Syria
SRB
acerb(sour)
sorb
sorbed
sorbing
SRBKRSHN
Serbo-Croatian
SRBLM
cerebellum
SRBRL
cerebral
SRBRM
cerebrum
SRBRT

cerebrate(think)
cerebrated
cerebrating
SRBRTN
sauerbraten
SRBT
acerbate(vex)
acerbated
acerbating
acerbity(sour)
acerbities
SRCH
search
searches
SRCHLT
searchlight
SRCHN
sea urchin
SRCHR
searcher
SRCHRJ
surcharge
surcharged
surcharging
SRD
soared(fly)
soar
sord(flock)
sourdough
surd(sum, voiceless)
sword(weapon)
SRDD
assorted
sordid
SRDF
certify
certified
certifies
certification
SRDFSH
swordfish
SRDN
sardine
sordino
SRDNK
sardonic
SRDNKL
sardonically
SRDNKS
sardonyx
SRDPL
swordplay
SRDTD
certitude
SRDV

assertive
SRDZMN
swordsman
swordsmen
SRF
seraph(angel)
seraphim(pl)
seraphic
serf(slave)
serif(mark)
surf(waves)
SRFBRD
surfboard
SRFBT
surfboat
SRFKSTNG
surfcasting
SRFKSTR
surfcaster
SRFL
sorrowful
SRFM
seraphim(pl)
seraph
SRFN
seraphim(pl)
seraph
SRFNG
surfing
SRFNT
serpent
SRFR
surfer
SRFRZNBZ
surfer's knobs
SRFS
surface
surfaced
surfacing
SRFSHS
scire facias
SRFT
surfeit
SRGM
sorghum
SRGRF
serigraphy
SRGT
surrogate
surrogated
surrogating
SRHD
sorehead
SRJ
serge(fabric)
sewerage

surge(sudden rush)
surged
surging
SRJKL
surgical
SRJN
surgeon
SRJNT
sergeant
SRJR
surgery
surgeries
SRK
circa(about)
cirque(valley)
sirocco(wind)
SRKFGS
sarcophagus
sarcophagi
SRKFJ
sarcophagi
sarcophagus
SRKL
circle
circled
circling
circular
SRKLT
circlet
SRKM
sarcoma
sarcomas(or)
sarcomata
succumb
SRKMFRNS
circumference
SRKMK
seriocomic
SRKMLKYSHN
circumlocution
SRKMNVGT
circumnavigate
circumnavigated
circumnavigating
circumnavigation
SRKMSKRB
circumscribe
circumscribed
circumscribing
SRKMSKRPSHN
circumscription
SRKMSPKT
circumspect
SRKMSTNS
circumstance
SRKMSTNSHL

---

circumstantial
SRKMSZ
circumcise
circumcised
circumcising
SRKMSZHN
circumcision
SRKMVNT
circumvent
circumvention
SRKRM
sour cream
SRKRT
sauerkraut
SRKS
circus
circuses
SRKSTK
sarcastic
SRKSTKL
sarcastically
SRKT
circuit
SRKTBRKR
circuit breaker
SRKTR
circuitry
circuitries
SRKYLR
circular
SRKYLRZ
circularize
circularized
circularizing
SRKYLSHN
circulation
SRKYLT
circulate
circulated
circulating
SRKYLTR
circulatory
SRKYS
Syracuse
SRKYTS
circuitous
SRKYZ
Syracuse
SRKZM
sarcasm
SRL
cereal(grain)
serial(series)
sorrel(color)
sural(leg)
surly(rude)

surlier,-iest
surlily,-iness
surreal
(beyond real)
SRLK
Cyrillic(alphabet)
SRLN
Sierra Leone
sirloin
SRLNGK
Sri Lanka
SRLSTK
surrealistic
SRLZ
serialize
serialized
serializing
serialization
SRLZM
surrealism
SRM
cerium(element)
serum
serums(or)
sera
SRMK
ceramic
SRMN
ceremony
ceremonies
sermon
SRMNL
ceremonial
SRMNS
ceremonious
SRMNT
surmount
SRMSH
sour mash
sour mashes
SRMZ
surmise
surmised
surmising
SRN
saran(resin)
serene(peaceful)
siren(noise)
SRND
serenade
serenaded
serenading
surround
SRNDNGZ
surroundings
SRNDPT

serendipity
SRNDR
surrender
SRNG
sarong
SRNJ
syringe
SRNM
Surinam
surname
surnamed
surnaming
SRNT
serenity
serenities
SRP
serape(cloak)
syrup
SRPLS
surplice(cloak)
surplus(excess)
SRPLSJ
surplusage
SRPNT
serpent
SRPNTN
serpentine
SRPRZ
surprise
surprised
surprising
SRPRZL
surprisal
SRPRZNGL
surprisingly
SRPS
sourpuss
sourpusses
surpass
surpasses
SRPSHN
sorption
SRPTSHS
surreptitious
SRRL
sororal
SRRSD
sororicide
SRRT
sororate(custom)
sorority
sororities
SRS
cirrus(cloud)
cirri
cirrate

Cyrus
serious(not funny)
serous(serum)
source(origin)
SRSBK
sourcebook
SRSHN
assertion
SRSKR
seersucker
SRSL
seriously
SRSMKRD
sursum corda
SRSMNDD
serious-minded
SRSNGGL
surcingle
surcingled
surcingling
SRSNGL
surcingle
surcingled
surcingling
SRSNS
seriousness
SRSPRL
sarsaparilla
SRSR
sorcery
sorceries
SRSRR
sorcerer
SRSRS
sorceress
sorceresses
SRSS
cirrhosis(liver)
psoriasis(skin)
sorosis(club)
soroses
sources(origin)
source
surcease(stop)
surceased
surceasing
SRT
acerate(pointed)(or)
acerated
assert(affirm)
assort(classify)
cirrate(adj)
cirrus
serrate(notched)
serrated
serrating

NGK:ink **P**:pie **R**:air **S**:ice **SH**:show **T**:toy **THN**:thin **TH**:the **V**:of **W**:we **Y**:you **Z**:is **VZHN**:vision

serration
sort(arrange)
sortie(sally,
single flight)
SRTBL
assertible
assertibly
sortable
SRTD
acerated(pointed)
assorted
sordid
SRTF
certify
certified
certifies
SRTFBL
certifiable
certifiably
SRTFDCHK
certified check
SRTFDML
certified mail
SRTFKSHN
certification
SRTFKT
certificate
SRTK
cirrhotic(liver)
SRTKS
surtax
surtaxes
SRTMNT
assortment
SRTN
ascertain
certain
SRTNBL
ascertainable
SRTR
asserter(affirmer)
sorter(arranger)
SRTRL
sartorial
SRTTD
certitude
SRTTYD
certitude
SRTV
assertive
SRTZ
sorites(logic)
(pl,n)
sorties(pl)
sortie
SRV

serve
served
serving
server
survey
surveys
SRVKL
cervical
SRVKS
cervix
SRVL
servile
SRVLNS
surveillance
SRVLNT
surveillant
SRVLT
servility
SRVMKNZM
servomechanism
SRVNG
serving
SRVNMTK
servopneumatic
SRVNT
servant
SRVR
server
surveyor(land)
SRVS
service
serviced
servicing
SRVSBL
serviceable
serviceably
SRVSBLT
serviceability
SRVSMN
serviceman
servicemen
SRVSTS
cervicitis
SRVT
serviette
SRVTR
servitor
SRVTD
servitude
SRVTYD
servitude
SRVV
survive
survived
surviving
survivor

SRVVBL
survivable
SRVVL
survival
SRVVR
survivor
SRVVRSHP
survivorship
SRZ
series
SS
assess
assesses
cease(stop)
ceased
ceasing
Isis(goddess,
Oxford)
oasis(water)
oases
sass(talk)
sasses
sassy
sassier
sassiest
sassily
sassiness
sauce(food)
sauced
saucing
saucer
saucy
saucier
sauciest
sauciness
say-so
seesaw(activity)
sis(sister)
sissy(timid)
sissies
SOS(message)
S.O.S
(trademark)
so-so
souse(drench)
soused
sousing
sycee(silver)
SSBL
assessable
SSBR
sissy bar
SSBRDLZ
sauce bordelaise
SSBRNZ
sauce béarnaise

SSD
seaside
secede(pull out)
seceded
seceding
Sioux City
suicide(death)
SSDL
suicidal
SSFD
sissified
SSFN
sousaphone
SSFR
cease-fire(n,adj)
SSFRS
sassafras
SSGRM
sociogram
SSH
sachet(bag)
sash(ribbon,
frame)
sashes
sashay(strut)
seiche(wave)
SSHBL
satiable(satisfy)
sociable
(friendly)
sociably
SSHBLNS
sociableness
SSHBLT
sociability
SSHGRM
sociogram
SSHKLCHRL
sociocultural
SSHKNMK
socioeconomic
SSHL
seashell
Seychelles
social
SSHLJ
sociology
SSHLJKL
sociological
SSHLJST
sociologist
SSHLSKYRT
social security
Social Security
(title)
SSHLST

---

socialist
SSHLSTDZ
social studies
SSHLSTK
socialistic
SSHLSTKL
socialistically
SSHLT
socialite(person)
sociality
socialities
SSHLWRK
social work
SSHLZ
Seychelles
socialize
socialized
socializing
SSHLZM
socialism
SSHLZSHN
socialization
SSHN
cession(a yielding)
scission(cutting)
session(meeting)
SSHPLTKL
sociopolitical
SSHPTH
sociopath
SSHR
seashore
SSHSHN
association
satiation
SSHT
associate
associated
associating
satiate(satisfy)
satiated
satiating
SSHTV
associative
SSJ
sausage
SSK
seasick
SSKCHWN
Saskatchewan
SSKLCHRL
sociocultural
SSKNMK
socioeconomic
SSKNS
seasickness

SSKP
seascape
SSKWRT
sea squirt
SSKWSNTNL
sesquicentennial
SSL
scissile(cutable)
sisal(plant)
SSLJ
sociology
SSLJKL
sociological
SSLJST
sociologist
SSLN
Sicilian
SSLYN
Sicilian
SSLZ
isosceles
SSM
sesame
SSMNT
assessment
SSN
assasin
SSNGKT
succinct
SSNSHN
assassination
SSNT
assassinate
assassinated
assassinating
SSPKT
suspect
SSPL
cesspool
SSPLTKL
sociopolitical
SSPN
saucepan
suspend
SSPND
suspend
SSPNDDNMSHN
suspended
animation
SSPNDRZ
suspenders
SSPNS
suspense
SSPNSHN
suspension
SSPNSR

suspensor
suspensory
SSPNSV
suspensive
SSPR
suspire
suspired
suspiring
SSPRL
sarsaparilla
SSPRSHN
suspiration
SSPSHN
suspicion
SSPSHS
suspicious
SSPTBL
susceptible
susceptibly
SSPTBLT
susceptibility
susceptibilities
SSPTH
sociopath
SSPTV
susceptive
SSPTVT
susceptivity
susceptivities
SSR
accessory(adjunct)
assessor(value)
cicero(type)
Cicero
saucer
SSRDTL
sacerdotal
SSRN
Caesarean
cicerone(guide)
cicerones(or)-oni
SSRNSKSHN
Caesarean section
SSRNT
susurrant
SSRS
susurrus(or)
susurration
susurrous(adj)
SSRSHN
susurration
SSSHN
association
cessation(stop)
secession(pull out)
SST

assist(help)
cyst(sac)
essayist(writer)
siesta(nap)
Sioux City
society
societies
SST(supersonic
transport)
SSTD
cystoid
SSTK
cystic
SSTKFBRSS
cystic fibrosis
SSTKTM
cystectomy
cystectomies
SSTL
societal
SSTLTK
systaltic
SSTM
system
SSTMK
systemic
SSTMTK
systematic
SSTMTKL
systematical
SSTMTZ
systematize
systematized
systematizing
SSTMTZSHN
systematization
SSTMZSHN
systematization
SSTN
sustain
SSTNBL
sustainable
SSTNNS
sustenance
SSTNS
assistance(help)
assistants
SSTNT
assistant
sostenuto
SSTR
sister
SSTRHD
sisterhood
SSTRL
sisterly

NGK:ink **P**:pie **R**:air **S**:ice **SH**:show **T**:toy **THN**:thin **TH**:the **V**:of **W**:we **Y**:you **Z**:is **VZHN**:vision

sisterliness
SSTRLNS
sisterliness
SSTRN
cistern
SSTRNL
sister-in-law
sisters-in-law
SSTS
cestus(belt)
cestic
cestus(glove)
cestuses
cysts(sacs)
SSTSKP
cystoscope
SSTTS
cystitis
ST
asset(money)
cite(quote)
cited
citing
city
cities
East(region)
east
eyesight
oast(kiln)
oust(eject)
sate(indulge)
sated
sating
sauté(cook)
sautéed
sautéing
set(put,fix,group)
set
setting
settee(sofa)
set-to(contest)
sight(view)
sit(rest)
sat
sitting
site(place)
sited
siting
soot(carbon)
sooty
sootier
sootiest
sootiness
sot(drunkard)
sought
seek

stay(stop)
stew(food,cook)
stow(to store)
sty(sore)
sties(or)
styes
sty(pig pen)
stied
sties
stying
suet(fat)
suit(set, clothes)
suite(rooms,
furniture)
suttee(widow)
STB
stab(pierce)
stabbed
stabbing
stub(blunt)
stubbed
stubbing
stubby
stubbier
stubbiest
stubbily
stubbiness
STBK
setback
STBL
citable(quote)
stable(barn)
stabled
stabling
stable(firm)
stabler
stablest
stableness
stably(adv)
stubble(beard)
stubbly
stubblier
stubbliest
suitable(fit,
appropriate)
suitably
STBLNG
stabling
STBLSH
establish
establishes
STBLSHMNT
establishment
STBLT
seat belt
stability

stabilities
suitability(fit)
STBLZ
stabilize
stabilized
stabilizing
stabilizer
STBLZR
stabilizer
STBLZSHN
stabilization
STBNL
stub nail
STBRN
stubborn
STBRNS
stubbornness
STCH
statue(sculpture)
stitch(sew)
stitches
STCHNS
East China Sea
STCHR
stature
statuary
statuaries
stitcher
STCHSK
statuesque
STCHT
statute(law)
statuette(statue)
STCHTL
statute law
STCHTR
statutory
STCHTRRP
statutory rape
STCHTVLMTSHNS
statute of
limitations
STD
staid(sober)
stadia(pl)
stadium
stadia(survey)
stayed(stay)
stead(position)
steady(make firm)
steadied
steadies
steadier
steadiest
steadily
steadiness

steed(horse)
stud(post,breed,
game)
studded
studding
studio(workroom)
study(learn,room)
studied
studies
STDBK
studbook
STDD
studied
STDFSH
studfish
STDFST
steadfast
STDHL
study hall
STDHRS
studhorse
STDK
static
STDL
citadel(fort)
staddle(platform)
STDM
stadium
stadia(or)
stadiums
STDN
sit-down
STDNG
studding
STDNGSL
studdingsail
STDNT
student
STDNTCHR
student teacher
STDPKR
stud poker
STDR
stutter
STDRR
stutterer
STDS
studious
STDWRK
studwork
STDZ
studies
STF
acetify(convert to
vinegar)
acetifies

B:by **CH**:each **D**:day **F**:if **G**:go **H**:he **HW**:why **J**:joy **K**:cow **KS**:ax **KWL**:equal **L**:all **M**:may **N**:in

acetified
staff(rod,music,
  people)
staph(infection)
  staphylococcus
set off(v)(adorn)
setoff(n)(contrast)
stiff(rigid)
stuff(pack,things)
stuffy
  stuffier
  stuffiest
  stuffily
  stuffiness
STFD
citified
STFL
  stifle
  stifled
  stifling
STFLKKL
  staphylococcal
STFLKKS
  staphylococcus
  staphylococci
STFLKKSK
  staphylococcic
STFLNGL
  stiflingly
STFLR
  stifler
STFN
  stiffen
STFNG
  stuffing
STFNGBKS
  stuffing box
STFNKT
  stiff-necked
STFNR
  stiffener
STFR
  staffer(person)
STFSK
  stuffsack
STFSRJNT
  staff sergeant
STFT
  staffed
STFTSHRT
  stuffed shirt
STG
  stag(male)
    stagged
    stagging
  stogie(cigar)(or)

stogy
  stogies
STGFLSHN
  stagflation
STGM
  stigma
    stigmas(or)
    stigmata
STGMT
  stigmata
  stigma
STGMTK
  stigmatic
STGMTZ
  stigmatize
  stigmatized
  stigmatizing
STGMTZM
  astigmatism(eye)
  stigmatism
STGMTZR
  stigmatizer
STGMTZSHN
  stigmatization
STGMZ
  stigmas
  stigma
STGNNS
  stagnancy
STGNNT
  stagnant
STGNSHN
  stagnation
STGNT
  stagnate
    stagnated
    stagnating
STGR
  stagger
STGSR
  stegosaur
STH
  scythe(tool)
    scythed
    scything
  seethe(boil)
    seethed
    seething
  soothe(comfort)
    soothed
    soothing
  south(direction)
  South(region)
STHBND
  southbound
STHCHNS

South China Sea
STHDKT
  South Dakota
STHFRK
  South Africa
STHKR
  South Korea
STHKRLN
  South Carolina
STHMRK
  South America
STHNG
  seething(anger)
  soothing(comfort)
  southing
STHNK
  asthenic
STHP
  southpaw
STHPL
  South Pole
STHR
  cither
  souther
STHRL
  southerly
  southerlies
STHRM
  isotherm
STHRML
  isothermal
STHRN
  southern
STHRNLTS
  southern lights
STHRNMST
  southernmost
STHRNR
  southerner
STHS
  soothsay
    soothsaid
    soothsaying
STHSR
  soothsayer
STHST
  southeast
  Southeast(area)
STHSTHST
  south-southeast
STHSTHWST
  south-southwest
STHSTR
  southeaster
STHSTRL
  southeasterly

STHSTRN
  southeastern
STHSTWRD
  southeastward
STHT
  aesthete(person)
  (or)esthete
STHTK
  aesthetic(or)
  esthetic
STHTKL
  aesthetically(or)
  esthetically
STHTKS
  aesthetics(or)
  esthetics
STHTSZM
  aestheticism(or)
  estheticism
STHWRD
  southward
STHWST
  southwest
  Southwest(area)
STHWSTFRK
  South West Africa
STHWSTR
  southwester
STHWSTRL
  southwesterly
STHWSTRN
  southwestern
STHWSTWRD
  southwestward
STHZH
  esthesia
STJ
  stage(platform)
    staged
    staging
  stagy(theatrical)
    stagier
    stagiest
    stagily
    staginess
  stodgy(dull)
    stodgier
    stodgiest
    stodgily
    stodginess
  stooge(person)
    stooged
    stooging
  stowage(space)
STJHND
  stagehand

STJKCH
stagecoach
stagecoaches
STJKRFT
stagecraft
STJN
stygian
STJNG
staging
STJRMN
East Germany
STJSTRK
stage-struck
STK
acetic(acid)
ascetic(person)
sciatic(nerve)
sciatica
stack(on top of)
stake(share,post)
staked
staking
stalk(plant,track)
steak(meat)
stich(verse)
stichic(adj)
stiches
stick(wood,fixed)
stuck
sticking
sticky
stickier
stickiest
stickily
stickiness
stock(supply,share)
stocky(thick)
stockier
stockiest
stockily
stockiness
stoic(indifferent)
stoke(stir)
stoked
stoking
stoker
stucco(plaster)
stuccoed
stuccoing
stuck
stick
STKBL
stickball
STKBRDNG
stockbreeding
STKBRDR

stockbreeder
STKBRKNG
stockbroking
STKBRKR
stockbroker
STKBRKRJ
stockbrokerage
STKD
stockade
stockaded
stockading
STKHL
stokehole
STKHLD
stokehold(ship)
STKHLDR
stockholder(stocks)
stakeholder
STKHLM
Stockholm
STKHM
Stockholm
STKJBR
stockjobber
STKK
stichic(verse)(adj)
stich
STKKSCHNJ
stock exchange
STKL
stickle
stickled
stickling
stickler
stoical
STKLR
stickler
STKM
sitcom
STKMN
stockman
stockmen
STKMRKT
stock market
STKNG
stocking
STKNGHRS
stalking-horse
STKNT
stockinet
STKNTHMD
stick-in-the-mud
STKP
stackup(n)
stickup(n)(rob)
stuck-up(adj)

STKPL
stockpile
stockpiled
stockpiling
STKPN
stickpin
STKR
sticker
stockcar
stoker
STKRM
stockroom
STKS
suitcase
STKSS
psittacosis
STKSTK
stochastic
STKSTL
stock-still
STKT
staccato
stakeout
STKTRTR
steak tartare
STKTTVNS
stick-to-itiveness
STKYRD
stockyard
STL
Seattle
settle(fix)
settled
settling
sightly
sightlier
sightliest
stale(old)
staled
staling
staler
stalest
stall(barn,stop)
steal(rob)
stole
stolen
stealing
steel(metal)
steely(like steel)
steelier
steeliest
steeliness
stile(frame)
still(rest)
stilly(calm)
stole(scarf)

stole(rob)
steal
stool(chair)
stoolie(spy)
stull(prop)
style(way,mode)
styled
styling
stylist
subtle(elusive)
subtler
subtlest
STLBK
stylebook
STLBRN
stillborn
STLBRTH
stillbirth
STLD
stolid(impassive)
styloid
STLF
still life
still lifes
STLFD
stall-feed
stall-fed
stall-feeding
STLFS
still lifes
STLG
stalag
STLGMT
stalagmite(bottom)
stalactite(top)
STLHD
steelhead
STLJ
cytology
STLKTT
stalactite(top)
stalagmite
(bottom)
STLML
steel mill
STLMNT
settlement
STLMT
stalemate
stalemated
stalemating
STLN
acetylene(gas)
Stalin
stolen
steal

stollen(bread)
STLNZM
Stalinism
STLPJN
stool pigeon
STLR
settler(person)
stellar(star)
stylar(needle)
styler(style)
subtler(elusive)
subtle
sutler(person)
STLS
St. Lucia
stylus
styluses(or)
styli
STLSH
stylish
STLSNRNCH
Stillson wrench
(trademark)
STLST
stylist
STLSTK
stylistic
STLSTKL
stylistically
STLT
satellite(space)
stellate(star
shaped)
stellated
stellating
stiletto(dagger)
stilt(wood)
stylet(weapon)
subtlety(slight)
subtleties
STLTD
stilted
STLTDL
stiltedly
STLTF
stultify
stultified
stultifies
STLTFKSHN
stultification
STLTFR
stultifier
STLTH
stealth
stealthy
stealthier

stealthiest
stealthily
stealthiness
STLWL
steel wool
STLWRK
steelwork
STLWRKR
steelworker
STLWRT
stalwart
STLYLR
stellular
STLYN
stallion
STLYRD
steelyard
STLZ
stylize
stylized
stylizing
STLZSHN
stylization
STM
esteem(respect,
prize)
stem(branch)
stemmed
stemming
steam(hot)
steamy
steamier
steamiest
steamily
steaminess
stum(wine)
stummed
stumming
stymie(impasse)
stymied
stymieing
STMBL
estimable(estimate)
Istanbul
stumble
stumbled
stumbling
STMBLBM
stumblebum
STMBLNGBLK
stumbling block
STMBLR
stumbler
STMBT
steamboat
STMK

stomach
stomachs(pl)
STMKK
stomachache(pain)
stomachic(medicine)
stomachical
STMKR
stomacher
STMN
stamen(flower)
stamina
STMNL
staminal
STMP
stamp(postage,
foot)
stomp(foot)
stump(tree)
STMPD
stampede
stampeded
stampeding
stampeder
STMPJ
stumpage
STMPML
stamp mill
STMPNGGRND
stamping ground
STMR
stammer(speech)
steamer
STMRLR
steamroller
STMSHN
estimation
STMSHP
steamship
STMSHVL
steam shovel
STMSN
stemson
STMT
estimate
estimated
estimating
estimator
STMTLJ
stomatology
STMTR
estimator
STMWNDNG
stem-winding
STMWNDR
stem-winder
STMWR

stemware
STMYL
stimuli
stimulus
STMYLNT
stimulant
STMYLS
stimulus
stimuli
STMYLSHN
stimulation
STMYLT
stimulate
stimulated
stimulating
STMYLTR
stimulator
STMYLTV
stimulative
STN
acetone
Austin
Satan(devil)
sateen(cotton
fabric)
satin(fabric)
satiny(satin like)
sit-in(protest)
soutane(garment)
stain(mark)
stein(mug)
stone(rock)
stoned
stoning
stony(stone)
stonier
stoniest
stonily
stoniness
stun(daze)
stunned
stunning
STNBL
Istanbul
STNBLND
stone-blind
STNCH
stench(smell)
stenches
staunch(firm)
STNCHN
stanchion
STND
astound(wonder)
stand
stood

NGK:ink **P**:pie **R**:air **S**:ice **SH**:show **T**:toy **THN**:thin **TH**:the **V**:of **W**:we **Y**:you **Z**:is **VZHN**:vision

standing	stinging	stance	situp(n)(or)
standee(person)	suiting(cloth)	**STNSBL**	sit-up
stoned(state)	**STNGGR**	ostensible	steep(incline)
stound(time)	stinger	ostensibly	steepen
STNDB	**STNGK**	**STNSH**	step(foot)
stand by(v)	stink	astonish	stepped
standby(n)	stank(or)	astonishes	stepping
STNDBZ	stunk	astonishment	steppe(treeless
standbys	stinking	**STNSHN**	plain)
STNDF	**STNGKHRN**	stanchion	stoop(porch,bend)
stand off(v)	stinkhorn	**STNSL**	stop(block)
standoff(n)	**STNGKPT**	stencil	stopped
stone-deaf	stinkpot	**STNSLR**	stopping
STNDFSH	**STNGKR**	stenciler	stopper
standoffish	stinker	ostensive	stope(mining)
STNDGLS	**STNGKWD**	**STNSV**	stoped
stained glass	stinkweed	ostensive	stoping
STNDN	**STNGLS**	**STNT**	stoup(basin)
stand in(v)	stained glass	oscitant	stupa(shrine,hair)
stand-in(n,adj)	**STNGPWR**	stint(limit)	stupe(hot compress)
STNDNG	staying power	stunt(check,feat)	**STPBRTHR**
standing	**STNGR**	**STNTMN**	stepbrother
STNDP	stinger	stunt man	**STPCHLD**
stand up(v)	stingray	stunt men	stepchild
standup(adj)	**STNGRF**	**STNTNGL**	**STPCHLDRN**
STNDPNT	stenograph	stintingly	stepchildren
standpoint	stenography	**STNTP**	**STPD**
STNDPT	**STNGRFK**	Stenotype	stupid
standpat(adj)	stenographic	(trademark)	**STPDN**
stand pat(v)	**STNGRFKL**	stenotype	step down(v)
STNDRD	stenographical	stenotypy	step-down(adj)
standard	**STNGRFR**	**STNTPST**	**STPDT**
STNDRDBRR	stenographer	stenotypist	stupidity
standard-bearer	**STNJ**	**STNTR**	stupidities
STNDRDTM	stingy	stinter	**STPDTR**
standard time	stingier	**STNTRN**	stepdaughter
STNDRDZ	stingiest	stentorian	**STPF**
standardize(same)	stingily	**STNTSHN**	stupefy
-dized,-dizing	stinginess	ostentation	stupefied
STNDRDZSHN	Stone Age	**STNTSHS**	stupefies
standardization	**STNK**	ostentatious	**STPFKSHN**
STNDSTL	isotonic	**STNWD**	stupefaction
standstill	satanic	satinwood	**STPFKTV**
STNDT	**STNKL**	**STNWL**	stupefactive
stand out(v)	satanical	stonewall	**STPFSHNT**
standout(n,adj)	**STNKTR**	**STNWR**	stupefacient
STNFGS	stonecutter	stoneware	**STPFTHR**
stenophagous	**STNMSN**	**STNWRK**	stepfather
STNFSH	stonemason	stonework	**STPGP**
stonefish	**STNN**	**STNZ**	stopgap
STNG	Estonian	stanza	**STPJ**
seating(chairs)	**STNNG**	**STP**	stoppage
setting(place)	stunning	estop(prohibit)	**STPKK**
stang(pole)	**STNR**	estopped	stopcock
sting(bee)	stunner	estopping	**STPL**
stung	**STNS**	isotope(atomic)	estoppel(prohibit)
		setup(n,adj)	

staple(metal)
stapled
stapling
stapler
steeple(church)
stipple(paint)
stippled
stippling
stopple(plug)
stoppled
stoppling
STPLCHS
steeplechase
STPLCHSR
steeplechaser
STPLDR
stepladder
STPLJK
steeplejack
STPLR
stapler(machine)
stippler
STPLT
stoplight
STPMTHR
stepmother
STPN
steepen
step in(v)
step-in(adj)
STPND
stipend
STPNDR
stipendiary
stipendiaries
STPNDS
stupendous
STPNGSTN
steppingstone
STPP
step-up(adj)
STPR
steeper(steep)
steepest
stepper(dancer)
stopper(plug)
stupor(daze)
STPRNT
stepparent
STPSN
stepson
stop sign
STPSS
stypsis
STPSSTR
stepsister

STPTH
osteopath
osteopathy
STPTK
styptic
STPTKL
styptical
STPTP
stepped-up
STPVR
stopover
STPWCH
stopwatch
stopwatches
STPWZ
stepwise
STPYL
stipule
STPYLSHN
stipulation
STPYLT
stipulate
stipulated
stipulating
STPYLTR
stipulator
stipulatory
STPZ
stapes(bone)
stapes(or)
stapedez
stipes(stalklike)
stipites
STR
aster(plant)
astir(moving)
astray(lost)
austere(severe)
Austria
Easter
ouster(eject)
oyster(mollusk)
satire(literature)
satori(mental
state)
satyr(lecher)
setter(placer,dog)
sitar(music)
sitter(sit)
stair(step)
star(sun)
starred
starring
stare(look)
stared
staring

starry
starrier
starriest
starriness
steer(cow,guide)
stere(volume)
stereo(sound)
stir(mix)
stirred
stirring
store(market)
store(keep)
stored,storing
story(narrative)
storied
stories
straw(grain)
stray(wander)
strew(scatter)
strewn
stria(channel)
suitor(person)
sutra(scripture)
STRB
strobe
STRBK
storybook
STRBL
storable(store)
STRBLT
strobe light
STRBR
strawberry
strawberries
STRBRBLND
strawberry-blond
STRBRD
starboard
STRBS
straw boss
STRBSKP
stroboscope
STRBSKPK
stroboscopic
STRBT
store-bought
STRBZMS
strabismus
strabismal
strabismic
STRCH
ostrich
ostriches
starch(stiff)
starches
starchy

starchier
starchiest
starchily
starchiness
stretch
stretches
stretchy
stretchier
stretchiest
stretchiness
STRCHR
stretcher
STRD
astride(legs)
asteroid
Saturday
sight-read
sight-read
steroid(compound)
steward(person)
storied(famous)
strata(layers)
stratum(sing)
stride(step)
strode
striding
stridden
stroud(blanket)
sturdy(strong)
sturdier
sturdiest
sturdily
sturdiness
STRDJ
strategy
strategies
stratagem
strategic
STRDL
astraddle
(astride)
startle(surprise)
startled
startling
straddle
(both sides)
straddled
straddling
strudel(pastry)
STRDLR
straddler
STRDM
Astrodome
stardom
stratum
strata(or)

stratums
STRDNS
stridence
stridency
STRDNT
strident
STRDNTSPSHL
Saturday Night
Special
STRDR
stridor
STRDS
stewardess
stewardesses
STRDVRS
Stradivarius
STRF
strafe(attack)
strafed
strafing
strife(conflict)
strophe(stanza)
STRFM
Styrofoam
(trademark)
STRFN
stereophony
STRFNK
stereophonic
STRFNKL
stereophonically
STRFRNT
storefront
STRFSH
starfish
STRFYLS
strophulus
STRG
strega
STRGL
straggle
straggled
straggling
straggler
straggly
stragglier
straggliest
stragglily
straggliness
struggle(fight)
struggled
struggling
struggler
STRGLR
straggler
struggler

STRGNF
stroganoff
STRGRF
stereograph, -phy
STRGRFK
stereographic
STRGRFKL
stereographically
STRGRM
stereogram
STRGS
strigose
STRGZ
stargaze
stargazed
stargazing
stargazer
STRHS
storehouse
STRJ
steerage
storage(space)
STRJL
strigil
STRJLS
stridulous
STRJLSHN
stridulation
STRJLT
stridulate
stridulated
stridulating
STRJLTR
stridulatory
STRJN
estrogen
sturgeon
STRJW
steerageway
STRK
asterisk
awe-struck
citric
esoteric
steric(atomic)
stork(bird)
streak(mark)
streaky
streakier
streakiest
streakily
streakiness
strike(hit)
struck
striking
stricken(or)

struck
stroke(rub)
stroked
stroking
STRKBND
strikebound
STRKBRKNG
strikebreaking
STRKBRKR
strikebreaker
STRKCHR
stricture
structure(build)
structured
structuring
STRKCHRL
structural
STRKCHRLZ
structuralize
structuralized
structuralizing
STRKCHRLZSHN
structuralization
STRKJR
struck jury
STRKL
esoterical
satirical(poke fun)
sterical(atomic)
strickle(tool)
strickled
strickling
strictly(exact)
STRKN
astrakhan
awe-stricken
stricken
strike
STRKNG
striking
STRKNKD
stark naked
STRKNN
strychnine
STRKNS
strictness
STRKPR
storekeeper
STRKR
striker
STRKRZ
stir crazy
STRKS
staircase
styrax
STRKSBL

stork's-bill
STRKT
strict(exact)
strikeout(n)
STRKZN
strike zone
STRL
astral
austral(south)
Australia
easterly
sterile
stroll(walk)
STRLB
astrolabe
STRLJ
astrology
STRLJR
astrologer
STRLNG
starling
sterling(silver)
STRLNGSLVR
sterling silver
STRLR
stroller
STNLSSTL
stainless steel
STRLT
starlet(person)
starlight(n)
starlit(adj)
sterility
STRLY
Australia
STRLZ
sterilize
sterilized
sterilizing
STRLZR
sterilizer
STRLZSHN
sterilization
STRM
storm(weather)
stormy
stormier
stormiest
stormily
storminess
stream(water)
strum (play)
strummed
strumming
strummer
struma(goiter)

strumae(or)
strumas
STRMBND
stormbound
STRMDR
storm door
STRMLN
streamline
streamlined
streamlining
STRMLND
streamlined
STRMN
straw man
STRMPT
strumpet
STRMR
streamer
strummer
STRMSLR
storm cellar
STRN
astern(behind)
citron(tree)
eastern
eyestrain
Saturn
sauterne(wine)
stern(severe)
strain(breed,
stretch)
styrene(liquid)
STRNCHM
strontium
STRND
strand
STRNG
stirring
(exciting)
string(cord)
strung
stringy
stringier
stringiest
stringily
stringiness
strong(robust)
STRNGBKS
strongbox
strongboxes
STRNGBN
string bean
STRNGBRD
stringboard
STRNGBS
string base

STRNGGL
strangle
strangled
strangling
strangler
STRNGGYLT
strangulate
strangulated
strangulating
strangulation
STRNGHLD
stronghold
STRNGHLT
stringhalt
STRNGHWL
steering wheel
STRNGKTH
strength
STRNGKTHN
strengthen
STRNGKWRTT
string quartet
STRNGL
strangle
strangled
strangling
strangler
STRNGLHLD
strangle hold
STRNGLR
strangler
STRNGMNDD
strong-minded
STRNGR
stringer
STRNGRM
strong-arm(v,adj)
STRNGTH
strength
STRNGTHN
strengthen
STRNGWL
steering wheel
STRNGWLD
strong-willed
STRNGYLSHN
strangulation
STRNGYLT
strangulate(choke)
-lated,-lating
STRNHWLR
stern-wheeler
STRNJ
astringe(constrict)
astringed,-ging
astringent

estrange
estranged
estranging
strange
stranger
strangest
STRNJMNT
estrangement
STRNJND
stringendo
STRNJNS
astringency
astringencies
stringency
stringencies
STRNJNT
astringent
stringent
STRNJR
stranger
STRNL
saturnalia
sternal
STRNM
astronomy
sternum
STRNMKL
astronomical
STRNMR
astronomer
STRNMST
sternmost
STRNN
Saturnine
STRNR
strainer
STRNS
sternness
STRNT
astronaut
STRNTKS
astronautics
STRNTM
strontium
STRNYS
strenuous
STRNYST
strenuosity
STRNYTSHN
sternutation
STRP
satrap(ruler)
stirrup(saddle)
strap(belt)
strapped
strapping

strep
streptococcal
strep throat
strip(take off)
stripped
stripping
stripper
stripe(long mark)
striped
striping
stripy(stripe)
stripier
stripiest
strop(sharpener)
stropped
stropping
STRPD
strappado
STRPK
isotropic
STRPKP
stirrup-cup
STRPKRPNG
strip-cropping
STRPLNG
stripling
STRPMN
strip mine
strip mined
strip mining
strip miner
STRPNG
strapping
STRPR
strapper
stripper
STRPSS
stereopsis
STRPTHRT
strep throat
STRPTKKL
streptococcal
STRPTKKS
streptococci(pl)
streptococcus
STRPTKN
stereopticon
STRPTLSN
streptolysin
STRPTMSN
streptomycin
STRPTZ
striptease
STRPTZR
stripteaser
STRR

---

stirrer(stir)
strayer(wanderer)
STRRM
storeroom
STRS
citrus(tree)
estrous(adj)
estrus(n)(ovulate)
strass(glass)
stress(force)
stresses
STRSHN
striation
STRSK
asterisk
STRSKP
stereoscope
STRSKPK
stereoscopic
STRSKPKL
stereoscopical
STRSL
streusel
STRSPNGLD
star-spangled
STRSS
satyriasis
STRST
satirist
STRSZ
ostracize
ostracized
ostracizing
STRSZM
ostracism
STRT
austerity(severe)
austerities
start(begin)
straight(not bent)
strait(narrow way)
strata(layers)
stratum
street(roadway)
stretto(music)
strettos(or)
stretti
striate(ridged)
striated
striating
strut(walk)
strutted
strutting
strutter
STRTF
stratify

stratified
stratifies
STRTFKSHN
stratification
STRTFRM
stratiform
STRTFRWRD
straightforward
STRTFST
straight-faced
STRTGRF
stratigraphy
STRTJ
straightedge
strategy
strategies
STRTJK
strategic
STRTJKL
strategical
STRTJKS
strategics
STRTJKT
straitjacket(or)
strait jacket
STRTJM
stratagem
STRTJST
strategist
STRTKR
streetcar
STRTKRS
stratocracy
STRTKYLSHN
straticulation
STRTKYLT
straticulate
STRTL
startle
startled
startling
STRTLN
straight-line
STRTLR
storyteller
STRTLST
straight-laced
(moral)
strait-laced
(tight)
STRTM
stratum(layer)
stratums(or)
strata
STRTMN
straight man

STRTN
straighten
STRTNR
straightener
STRTP
stereotype
stereotyped
stereotyping
STRTPK
stereotypic
STRTPKL
stereotypical
STRTPR
stereotyper
STRTPT
stereotyped
STRTR
starter(begin)
strutter
STRTRF
Astroturf
(trademark)
STRTRM
straight-arm
STRTRZR
straight razor
STRTS
stratus
strati
STRTSFR
stratosphere
STRTTKT
straight ticket
STRTVJBRLTR
Strait of Gibralter
STRTW
straightaway(time)
straightway
STRTWKNG
streetwalking
STRTWKR
streetwalker
STRV
starve(no food)
starved
starving
strive(work)
strove(or)
strived
striving
striven(or)
strived
STRVLNG
starveling
STRVSHN
starvation

STRVT
straw vote
STRVZHN
stereovision
STRW
stairway
STRWL
stairwell
STRWRT
starwort
STRZ
satirize
satirized
satirizing
satirizer
satirist(writer)
STRZL
streusel
STRZMN
steersman
STS
stoss
STSBTH
sitz bath
STSF
satisfy
satisfied
satisfies
STSFKSHN
satisfaction
STSFKTR
satisfactory
STSFKTRL
satisfactorily
STSH
sottish(sot)
soutache
stash
stashes
STSHN
citation
station(place)
STSHNBRK
station break
STSHNHS
station house
STSHNR
stationer
stationary
(not moving)
stationery
(writing paper)
STSHNRFRNT
stationary front
STSHNWGN
station wagon

B:by CH:each D:day F:if G:go H:he HW:why J:joy K:cow KS:ax KWL:equal L:all M:may N:in

STSKR
setscrew
STSL
staysail
STSM
Satsuma
STSN
citizen
psittacine(parrots)
STSNG
sightseeing
STSNR
citizenry
citizenries
STSR
sightseer
STSS
stasis
stases
STSTT
city-state
STSZM
asceticism
stoicism
STT
acetate(material)
astute(smart)
estate(land)
satiety(satisfy)
stat(information)
stats
statistic
state(declare,
condition)
stated
stating
stet(nullify)
stetted
stetting
stoat(ermine)
stout(strong)
STTBL
statable(state)
STTGRT
Stuttgart
STTH
stithy
stithies
STTHD
statehood
STTHRTD
stouthearted
STTHS
Statehouse(title)
statehouse
STTHSKP

stethoscope
STTHT
saw-toothed
STTK
ecstatic
static
STTKL
ecstatically(joy)
statical
STTKS
statics
STTKSK
cytotoxic
STTL
stately
statelier
stateliest
stateliness
STTMNT
statement
STTR
stator(motor)
stutter
STTRM
stateroom
STTRR
stutterer
STTS
status
STTSD
stateside
STTSKW
status quo
STTSMN
statesman
statesmen
STTSRTS
States' rights
STTSTK
statistic
STTSTKL
statistical
STTSTSHN
statistician
STTSWMN
stateswoman
STTV
stative
STTWD
state-wide
STV
stave(puncture)
staved(or)
stove
staving
steeve(to pack)

steeved
steeving
stove(cook)
STVCH
sotto voce
STVDR
stevedore
stevedored
stevedoring
STVL
aestival
STVPP
stovepipe
STVSHN
aestivation
STVT
aestivate
aestivated
aestivating
STVZ
staves(wood,music)
staff
STVZKR
stavesacre
STW
stowaway(n)
stow away(v)
STWD
citywide
STWRD
eastward
STY
stew
STYD
studio
STYDNT
student
STYDNTCHR
student teacher
STYDS
studious
STYDZ
studios
STYP
stoop(bend,porch)
stupe(medical)
STYPD
stupid
STYPDT
stupidity
stupidities
STYPF
stupefy
stupefied
stupefies
STYPFKSHN

stupefaction
STYPFKTV
stupefactive
STYPFSHNT
stupefacient
STYPNDS
stupendous
STYPR
stupor
STYRD
steward
STYRDS
stewardess
stewardesses
STYT
astute
STZH
astasia
STZN
citizen
STZNR
citizenry
citizenries
SV
salve(soothe)
salved
salving
save(rescue)
saved
saving
Savoy
savvy(know)
savvied
savvies
sieve(sift)
sieved
sieving
soave(wine)
suave
SVBL
savable
SVJ
savage
SVJPN
Sea of Japan
SVJR
savagery
savageries
SVK
civic
SVKS
civics
SVL
civil
SVLDFNS
civil defense, (B)- fence

NGK:ink **P**:pie **R**:air **S**:ice **SH**:show **T**:toy **THN**:thin **TH**:the **V**:of **W**:we **Y**:you **Z**:is VZHN:vision

SVLL
civil law
SVLRTS
civil rights
SVLSRVS
civil service
SVLT
civility
civilities
svelte
SVLYN
civilian
SVLZ
civilize
civilized
civilizing
SVLZSHN
civilization
SVMRMR
Sea of Marmara
SVN
Savannah
savanna
(grassland)
savant(scholar)
seven(number)
SVNGZ
savings
SVNP
seven-up(game)
Seven-Up(or)
7-Up(trademark)
SVNR
souvenir
SVNSZ
seven seas
SVNT
savant(scholar)
seventy
seventies
SVNTH
seventh
SVNTN
seventeen
SVNTTH
seventieth
SVR
savor(taste), (B)-vour
savory. (B)savoury
savoriness,
(B)savouriness
sever(divide)
sever (divide)
severe(harsh)
severer
severest

soever(in any way)
SVRL
several
SVRN
sovereign
SVRNS
severance
SVRNT
sovereignty
sovereignties
SVRSHN
asseveration
SVRT
asseverate
asseverated
asseverating
severity
severities
SVT
civet(animal)
Soviet
soviet
SVTYNYN
Soviet Union
SVWRFR
savoir-faire
SVYR
savior, (B)saviour
SVYT
Soviet
soviet
SVZ
civvies(clothes)
SVZF
Sea of Azov
SW
seaway(water)
sway
SWB
swab
swabbed
swabbing
SWBK
swayback
swaybacked
zwieback
SWCH
swatch(cloth)
swatches
switch(change)
switches
SWCHBLD
switchblade
SWCHBRD
switchboard
SWCHHTR

switch hitter
SWCHMN
switchman
switchmen
SWD
seaweed(plant)
suede(leather)
Swede(person)
sweetie(name)
SWDL
swaddle
swaddled
swaddling
SWDN
Sweden
SWDR
swatter
SWDSH
Swedish
SWDZN
soi disant
SWFT
swift
SWG
swag
swig(drink)
swigged
swigging
SWGMN
swagman
SWGR
swagger
SWGRBG
swagger bag
SWJ
assuage(ease)
assuaged
assuaging
assuasive
swage(tool)
swaged
swaging
SWJMNT
assuagement
SWL
swale(land)
swallow(eat,bird)
swell(interj,good)
swell(expand)
swelled
swollen(or)
swelled
swill(drink)
SWLNG
swelling
SWLTLD

swallow-tailed
SWLTR
swelter
sweltry
sweltrier
sweltriest
SWLTRNG
sweltering
SWM
Swami(title)
swami(person)
swim(water)
swam
swum
swimming
SWMP
swamp
swampy
swampier
swampiest
swampiness
SWMPLND
swampland
SWMPR
swamper
SWMR
swimmer
SWMST
swimsuit
SWN
Suwannee(river)
swain(person)
swan(bird)
swine(pig)
swoon(faint)
SWNDL
swindle
swindled
swindling
swindler
SWNDV
swan dive
SWNG
swing
swung
swinging
SWNGBK
swing back(camera)
SWNGK
swank
swanky
swankier
swankiest
swankiness
SWNGR
swinger

B:by **CH**:each **D**:day **F**:if **G**:go **H**:he **HW**:why **J**:joy **K**:cow **KS**:ax **KWL**:equal **L**:all **M**:may **N**:in

SWNGSHFT
swing shift
SWNK
swank
swanky
swankier
swankiest
swankily
swankiness
SWNSH
swinish
SWNSNG
swan song
SWNT
suint
SWNY
soigné(elegant)
SWNZDN
swan's-down
SWP
swap(trade)
swapped
swapping
sweep(clean)
swept
swipe(hit)
swiped
swiping
swipe(steal)
swiped
swiping
swoop(fast action)
SWPR
swapper
SWPSTKS
sweepstakes
SWPTBK
sweptback
SWR
soiree
swear(oath)
swore
sworn
SWRD
seaward
sward(turf)
SWRL
swirl
SWRM
swarm
SWRR
swearer
SWRTH
seaworthy
seaworthiness
swarthy

swarthier
swarthiest
swarthily
swarthiness
SWRV
swerve
swerved
swerving
SWRWRD
swearword
SWS
Swiss
swiss(cloth)
SWSH
swash(liquid)
swashes
swish(noise)
swishes
SWSHBKLNG
swashbuckling
SWSHBKLR
swashbuckler
SWSTK
swastika
SWSTR
sou'wester
SWSV
assuasive
SWT
suite(rooms)
swat(hit)
swatted
swatting
sweat(liquid)
sweat(or)
sweated
sweating
sweaty
sweatier
sweatiest
sweatily
sweatiness
sweet(like sugar)
sweetie(person)
SWTBND
sweatband
SWTBRD
sweetbread
SWTH
swath(strip)
swathe(bandage)
swathed
swathing
SWTHRT
sweetheart
SWTKRN

sweet corn
SWTMT
sweetmeat
SWTN
sweeten
SWTNNG
sweetening
SWTNR
sweetener
SWTP
sweet pea
SWTPPR
sweet pepper
SWTPTT
sweet potato
SWTR
ice water
swatter(tool)
sweater(garment)
SWTSHP
sweatshop
SWTSHRT
sweat shirt
SWTSRLN
Switzerland
SWTSRLND
Switzerland
SWTST
sweat suit
SWTTTH
sweet tooth
SWV
suave
swive(copulate)
swived
swiving
SWVL
swivel
SWVT
suavity
SWZHN
suasion
SWZL
swizzle
SWZLND
Swaziland
SWZLSTK
swizzle stick
SWZV
assuasive
SY
sue(law)
sued
suing
SYNT
suint

SYR
assayer
sawyer
sewer(waste)
SYSD
suicide
SYSDL
suicidal
SYT
suit
SYTBL
suitable
suitably
SYTBLT
suitability
SYTKS
suitcase
SZ
assize(session)
oases(water)
oasis
seize(grasp)
seized
seizing
size(extent)
sized
sizing
SZBL
seizable(grab)
sizable
sizably
SZBTH
sitz bath
SZFN
sousaphone
SZHN
scission(cut)
SZHR
caesura(pause)
seizure(grasp)
SZJ
syzygy
SZL
sizzle
sizzled
sizzling
SZLR
sizzler
SZM
schism
SZMGRF
seismograph
SZMGRFR
seismographer
SZMK
seismic

T SZMKL / TBYLT

SZMKL
seismical
SZMLJ
seismology
SZMLJST
seismologist
SZMTK
schismatic
SZMTKL
schismatical
SZN
season
SZNBL
seasonable
seasonably
SZNG
sizing(size)
SZNL
seasonal
SZNNG
seasoning
SZR
Caesar
caesura(pause)
scissor(cut)
SZRNSKSHN
Caesarean section
SZRS
scissors
SZRZ
scissors
SZYR
caesura(pause)

T

at(prep)
aught(anything,
cipher-0)
auto
eat(food)
ate
eating
eaten
eight(number)
eighty
eighties
eye-to-eye(adj)
iota(letter)
it
oat(food)
ought(should)

out(not in)
Tao, the(the way)
tea(beverage)
tee(golf)
teed
Thai
ti(tone)
ti(tree)
tie(fasten)
tied
tying
to(prep)
toe(foot)
toed
toeing
too(also)
tow(pull)
toy(play)
two(2)
TB
tab(flap,bill)
tabby(silk,cat)
tabbies
taboo(ban)
tibia(bone)
toby(mug)
tub(vessel)
tubbed
tubbing
tuba(music)
tubas(or)
tubae
tubby(fat)
tubbier
tubbiest
tubbiness
tube(pipe)
tubed
tubing
TBBL
tubbable
TBD
outbid
outbid
outbidding
TBFR
two-by-four
TBG
tea bag
Tobago
TBGN
toboggan
TBGRF
autobiography
autobiographies
TBGRFKL

autobiographical
TBGRFR
autobiographer
TBK
tieback
tobacco
TBKNST
tobacconist
TBL
eatable(or)
edible
table
tabled
tabling
tableau
tableaux(or)
tableaus
tubal(tube)
TBLD
tabloid
TBLDNG
outbuilding
TBLDT
table d'hote
TBLHP
table-hop
table-hopped
table-hopping
TBLKLTH
tablecloth
TBLND
tableland
TBLSPN
tablespoon
TBLSPNFL
tablespoonful
TBLSTR
tubeless tire
TBLT
tablet
TBLTNS
table tennis
TBLVVN
tableau vivant
TBLWN
table wine
TBLWR
tableware
TBN
autobahn
T-bone
TBND
outbound
TBNG
tubing
TBR

T-bar
tabor
tuber(potato)
TBRD
outboard
tabard
TBRK
outbreak
TBRKL
tubercle
TBRKYLN
tuberculin
TBRKYLR
tubercular
TBRKYLS
tuberculous
TBRKYLSS
tuberculosis
TBRNKL
tabernacle
TBRS
tuberous
TBRST
outburst
TBRT
taboret
TBRZ
tuberose(plant)
TBSK
Tabasco(trademark)
TBT
towboat
two-bit
TBTN
Tibetan
TBTS
two bits
TBYL
tabula
TBYLR
tabular
tubular
TBYLRS
tabula rasa
TBYLRZ
tabula rasa
tabularize
tabularized
tabularizing
TBYLRZSHN
tabularization
TBYLS
tubulous
TBYLSHN
tabulation
TBYLT

B:by **CH**:each **D**:day **F**:if **G**:go **H**:he **HW**:why **J**:joy **K**:cow **KS**:ax **KWL**:equal **L**:all **M**:may **N**:in

tabulate
tabulated
tabulating
TBYLTR
tabulator
TBZ
tabs(keep track of)
TCH
attach
attaches
teach
teaches
taught
tetchy(peevish)
tetchier
tetchiest
tetchily
tetchiness
touch(feel)
touches
touchy
touchier
touchiest
touchily
touchiness
TCHBK
touchback
TCHBL
attachable
teachable
touchable
TCHBSHN
titubation
TCHDN
touchdown
TCHHL
touchhole
TCHLR
titular
TCHN
teach-in
TCHNG
teaching
touch-and-go(adj)
touch and go(n)
touching
TCHP
touch-up(n)
touch up(v)
TCHR
teacher
TCHSTN
touchstone
TCHT
touched
TCHTP

touch-type
-typed,-typing
TCHTPST
touch-typist
TD
outdo
outdid
outdone
tad(small)
TD(touchdown)
teddy(garment)
teddy(bear)
tide(water)
tidy(neat)
tidied
tidies
tidier
tidiest
tidily
tidiness
tie-dye
tie-dyed
tie-dyeing
toad(frog)
toady(flatter)
toadied
toadies
tod(weight)
today(time)
tody(bird)
todies
toddy(drink)
toddies
to-do(fuss)
TDBT
tidbit
TDBR
teddy bear
TDDR
toadeater
TDF
auto-da-fé(burn)
autos-da-fé
teed off
TDFRD
tutti-frutti
TDFSH
toadfish
TDL
tattle(gossip)
tattled
tattling
tattler
tidal(water)
title(name)
titled

titling
tittle(mark)
toddle
toddled
toddling
toddler
Toodle-oo(interj)
tootle(sound)
tootled
tootling
total(all)
TDLHLDR
titleholder
TDLND
tideland
TDLR
toddler
TDLTL
tattletale
TDLWNGKS
tiddlywinks
TDLWV
tidal wave
TDM
tedium
TDMNSHNL
two-dimensional
TDMPL
totem pole
TDMRK
tidemark
TDNG
tatting(knitting)
tiding
tidings
TDNS
toe dance
toe danced
toe dancing
toe dancer
TDPL
tadpole
TDR
outdoor
tawdry
tawdrier
tawdriest
teeter(unsteady)
totter(sway)
Tudor
tutor(teacher)
TDRBRD
teeterboard
TDRZ
outdoors
TDS

tedious
TDSTL
toadstool
TDSTN
toadstone
TDSTNS
outdistance
outdistanced
outdistancing
TDT
outdate
outdated
outdating
TDTR
toadeater
TDWTR
tidewaiter(person)
tidewater(water)
TDZ
to-dos(fuss)
TDZM
toadyism
TF
taffy(candy)
tafia(rum)
tee off
teed off
teeing off
tiff(fit)
toff(person)
tofu(food)
toffee(candy)
tough(strong)
tuff(rock)(or)
tufa
tuffaceous
tuft(material)
TFD
taffeta
typhoid
TFDL
typhoidal
TFDMR
Typhoid Mary
TFJNK
typhogenic
TFL
outflow
TFLD
twofold
TFLDR
outfielder
TFLN
Teflon
(trademark)
TFLNGK

NGK:ink **P**:pie **R**:air **S**:ice **SH**:show **T**:toy **THN**:thin **TH**:the **V**:of **W**:we **Y**:you **Z**:is **VZHN**:vision

outflank
TFMNDD
tough-minded
TFN
tiffany(cloth)
tiffin(eat)
toughen(strong)
typhoon(storm)
TFR
two-fer
TFRL
taffrail
TFS
outface
typhus
TFST
two-faced
TFSTD
two-fisted
TFT
outfit
taffeta(fabric)
toft(homestead)
tuffet(grass)
tuft(yarn)
TFTR
outfitter
TFZ
two-phase
TG
outgo
outgoes
outgoing
Taegu
tag(label)
tagged
tagging
tog(coat)
togged
togging
toga(garment)
Togo
tug(pull)
tugged
tugging
TGBT
tugboat
TGFWR
tug of war
TGL
toggle
toggled
toggling
TGLBLT
toggle bolt
TGLNT

topgallant
TGLSWCH
toggle switch
TGNG
outgoing
TGR
outgrow
outgrew
outgrown
tiger(animal)
tiger-eye(rock)
toggery(store)
TGRF
autograph
TGRLL
tiger lily
tiger lilies
TGRMTH
tiger moth
TGRP
out-group
TGRS
tigress(animal)
Tigris
TGRTH
outgrowth
TGRZ
tiger's-eye
TGS
outguess
outguesses
TGSGLP
Tegucigalpa
TGTHR
together
TGTHRNS
togetherness
TGYMNT
tegument
TGZ
togs(clothes)
TH
edh(letter)
eighth
oath
thaw(ice)
the
thee(you)
they(others)
thigh(leg)
thou(you)
though(while)
thy(your)
towhee(bird)
THBN
thighbone

THCH
thatch
thatches
THD
they'd
they had
they would
thud(sound)
thudded
thudding
towhead
THDLT
theodolite
THDR
theater
THF
thief
thieves
THFT
theft
THG
thug
THHG
The Hague
THK
ethic
thick
THKHD
thickhead
THKHDD
thickheaded
THKL
ethical
THKN
thicken
THKNNG
thickening
THKNS
thickness
THKRS
theocracy
theocracies
THKRTK
theocratic
THKS
ethics
THKSKND
thick-skinned
THKST
thickset
THKT
thicket
THKWTD
thick-witted
THL
ethyl

they'll
thill(wagon)
thole(endure)
tholed
tholing
THLD
toehold
THLDK
athletic
THLDMD
thalidomide
THLJ
theology
theologies
THLJKL
theological
THLJN
theologian
THLMS
thalamus
THLND
Thailand
THLPN
thole pin
THLSK
thalassic
THLT
athlete
THLTK
athletic
THLTKL
athletical
THM
at-home(n)
them
theme(topic)
thumb(finger)
THMBL
thimble
THMBLFL
thimbleful
THMDK
thematic
THMHL
thumbhole
THMK
thymic
THMN
thiamine
THMNDKS
thumb index(n)
thumb-index(v)
THMNL
thumbnail
THMNT
thumbnut

THMP
thump
THMPNG
thumping
THMS
thymus
THMSKR
thumbscrew
THMSLVZ
themselves
THMSNG
theme song
THMSTL
thumbstall
THMTK
thematic
thumbtack
THMTRJ
thaumaturge
thaumaturgy
THMTRJST
thaumaturgist
THMZ
Thames
THN
than
thane(freeman)
then(at a time)
thin(slim)
thinned
thinning
thinner
thinnest
THNDD
two-handed
THNDR
thunder
THNDRBLT
thunderbolt
THNDRBRD
thunderbird
THNDRHD
thunderhead
THNDRKLD
thundercloud
THNDRKLP
thunderclap
THNDRS
thunderous
THNDRSHR
thundershower
THNDRSHWR
thundershower
THNDRSKWL
thundersquall
THNDRSTRK

thunderstruck
THNDRSTRKN
thunderstricken
THNDRSTRM
thunderstorm
THNG
thing(object)
thong(leather)
THNGK
thank(gratitude)
think(mind)
thought
THNGKBL
thinkable
thinkably
THNGKNG
thinking
THNGKR
thinker
THNGKS
thanks
THNGKSGVNG
thanksgiving
Thanksgiving(Day)
THNGMBB
thingamabob
THNGMJG
thingamajig
THNGNTSLF
thing-in-itself
THNGRF
ethnography
THNK
authentic
chthonic(gods)
chthonian
ethnic
thionic
THNKL
ethnical
THNL
ethanol
THNLJ
ethnology
THNLJKL
ethnological
THNR
thenar(hand)
thinner(liquid)
THNS
thence
THNSFRTH
thenceforth
THNSKND
thin-skinned
THNSNTRK

ethnocentric
THNSNTRKL
ethnocentrical
THNSNTRZM
ethnocentrism
THNTHRP
ethnotherapy
THNTHRPK
theanthropic
THNTHRPZM
theanthropism
THNTK
authentic
THNTKSHN
authentication
THNTKT
authenticate
authenticated
authenticating
THNTKTR
authenticator
THNTST
authenticity
authenticities
THNZ
Athens
THP
Ethiopia
THPNSS
autohypnosis
THR
author(person)
either(alternative)
ether(compound)
other(different,
remaining)
their(belonging)
theory
theories
there(at that place)
they're(they are)
thorough(complete)
three(3)
threw(throw)
throe(pang)
through(from end
to end)(prep)
(finished)(adj)
throw(hurl)
threw
thrown
THRB
thereby
throb
throbbed
throbbing

THRBK
throwback(n)
THRBL
thurible
THRBRD
thoroughbred
THRBT
thereabout
THRBTS
thereabouts
THRD
third(3rd)
thirty, thirties(pl)
thread(sewing)
thready
threadier
threadiest
threadiness
three-D(or)3-D
thyroid(body)
THRDBR
threadbare
THRDBS
third base
THRDGLND
thyroid gland
THRDGR
third degree
THRDGRBRN
third-degree burn
THRDKLS
third class
third-class(adj,adv)
THRDKR
three-decker
THRDKTM
thyroidectomy
THRDMNCHNL
three-dimensional
THRDMNSHNL
three-dimensional
THRDPRSN
third person
THRDPRT
third party
THRDRKTD
other-directed
THRDRT
third-rate
THRDSKTR
Third Sector, the
foundations
THRDWRLD
Third World
THRFLD
threefold

THRFR
therefore
thoroughfare(road)
thurifer(alter boy)
THRFRM
therefrom
THRFT
thrift
thrifty
thriftier
thriftiest
thriftily
thriftiness
THRFTR
thereafter
THRGNG
thoroughgoing
THRHWLR
three-wheeler
THRK
thearchy
thearchies
THRKLR
three-color
THRKRDMNT
three-card monte
THRKS
thorax
thoraxes
thoraces
THRKSN
thyroxin
THRKWRTR
three-quarter
THRKWRTRZ
three-quarters
THRL
ethereal
thrall(bondage)
thrill(excite)
THRLDM
thralldom
THRLR
thriller
THRLZ
etherealize
etherealized
etherealizing
THRM
theorem(idea)
therm(heat unit)
thorium(metal)
thrum(play)
thrummed
thrumming
THRMBN

thrombin
THRMBS
thrombus
thrombi
THRMBSS
thrombosis
thromboses
THRMDNMK
thermodynamic
THRMDNMKS
thermodynamics
THRMGRF
thermography
THRML
thermal
THRMLKTRK
thermoelectric
THRMLKTRST
thermoelectricity
THRMMTR
thermometer
THRMNKLR
thermonuclear
THRMNKS
thermionics
THRMNYKLR
thermonuclear
THRMPL
thermopile
THRMPLSTK
thermoplastic
THRMS
thermos
THRMSBTL
thermos bottle
THRMSTR
thermistor
THRMSTT
thermostat
THRMSTTKL
thermostatical
THRMTHRP
thermotherapy
THRN
Tehran
therein
thorn(spine)
thorny(spiny)
thornier
thorniest
thorniness
throne(chair)
throned
throning
THRND
threnody

threnodies
THRNFTR
thereinafter
THRNG
throng
THRNN
threonine
THRNT
thereinto
THRP
therapy
therapies
THRPL
three-ply
THRPN
thereupon
THRPS
three-piece
THRPST
therapist
THRPYTK
therapeutic
THRPYTKL
therapeutical
THRPYTKS
therapeutics
THRR
either-or
THRRG
throw rug
THRRNGSRKS
three-ring circus
THRRZ
three R's
THRS
authoress
authoresses
thrice
THRSH
thrash(punish)
thrashes
thresh(beat grain)
threshes
thrush(bird)
thrushes
THRSHL
threshold
THRSHLD
threshold
THRSHNG
thrashing
THRSHR
thrasher(bird)
thresher
THRSK
thoracic

THRSKR
threescore
THRSM
threesome
THRST
theorist(person)
thirst(drink)
thirsty
thirstier
thirstiest
thirstily
thirstiness
thrust(push)
thrust
thrusting
THRSTKL
thersitical
THRT
authority
authorities
thereat(place,
time)
thirty(30)
thirties
threat(danger)
throat(body)
throaty
throatier
throatiest
throatily
throatiness
throughout
THRTFR
theretofore
THRTK
theoretic
THRTKL
theoretical
THRTL
throttle
throttled
throttling
THRTLCH
throatlatch
THRTN
thirteen(13)
threaten
THRTNTH
thirteenth
THRTRN
authoritarian
THRTSHN
theoretician
THRTTH
thirtieth
THRTTV

authoritative
THRV
  thrive
    thrived(or)
    throve
    thriving
    thriven(or)
    throve
THRW
  three-way
  throwaway(n,adj)
  throw away(v)
  thruway(highway)
THRWLR
  three-wheeler
THRWTH
  therewith
THRWZ
  otherwise
THRZ
  authorize
    -ized,-izing
  etherize
    (anesthetize)
    -ized,-izing
  theirs(not yours)
  theorize(reason)
    -ized,-izing
  there's(there is)
  throes(pang)
THRZD
  Thursday
THRZR
  authorizer
THRZSHN
  authorization
THS
  ethos
  outhouse
  teahouse
  this
    these
    thus
THSF
  theosophy
    theosophies
THSL
  thistle
  thusly
THSLDN
  thistledown
THSLF
  thyself(yourself)
THSPN
  Thespian(or)
  thespian

THSRS
  thesaurus
    thesauri(or)
    thesauruses
THSS
  thesis
    theses
THSTK
  theistic
THSTKL
  theistical
THT
  Tahiti
  that
    those
  thought
  think
THTFL
  thoughtful
THTFLNS
  thoughtfulness
THTHR
  thither
THTHRT
  thitherto
THTLS
  thoughtless
THTR
  theater
THTRKL
  theatrical
THV
  they've(they have)
  thieve
    thieved
    thieving
THVR
  thievery
    thieveries
THVSH
  thievish
THVZ
  thieves
THWK
  thwack
THWN
  Tijuana
THWRT
  athwart
  thwart
THY
  thew(muscle)
  thewy
THZ
  these(near)
  this

those(far)
  that
THZM
  atheism
  theism
THZND
  thousand
THZNDFLD
  thousandfold
THZNTH
  thousandth
TJ
  taj(cap)
  togae(pl)(toga)
  towage(tow)
TJD
  two-edged
TJMHL
  Taj Mahal
TJNS
  autogenous
TJNSS
  autogenesis
TJR
  autogiro
TK
  attack
  attic(roof)
  outtalk
  outtake
  tack(nail)
  tacky(shabby)
    tackier
    tackiest
    tackiness
  take(seize)
    took
    taking
    taken
  talk(speak)
  talky
    talkier
    talkiest
  teak(tree)
  Tech(or)
  tech
    technology
  tic(muscle spasm)
  tick(insect)
  tick(sound)
    ticktock
  toke(smoke)(slang)
    toked
    toking
  Tokyo
  toque(hat)

tuck(fold)
  tyke(child)
TKBL
  takeable(or)
  takable
TKCHL
  tactual
TKD
  toccata(music)
TKDN
  takedown(n)
TKF
  take off(v)
  takeoff(n,adj)
TKHMP
  take-home pay
TKL
  haute école
    (horsemanship)
  tackle(wrestle,
    rope)
    tackled
    tackling
    tackler
  tequila
  tickle(laugh)
    tickled
    tickling
TKLJ
  tocology
TKLR
  tickler
TKLS
  outclass
    outclasses
TKLSH
  ticklish
TKLV
  autoclave
TKM
  outcome
  Tacoma
TKMTR
  tachometer
TKN
  token
  tycoon(person)
TKNGRF
  technography
TKNK
  technic(rules,
    theory)
  technique(skill)
TKNKL
  technical
TKNKLR

NGK:ink **P:**pie **R:**air **S:**ice **SH:**show **T:**toy **THN:**thin **TH:**the **V:**of **W:**we **Y:**you **Z:**is **VZHN:**vision

Technicolor	taxable	Texarkana	tectonics
(trademark)	**TKSBLT**	**TKSS**	**TKTSHN**
TKNKLT	taxability	Texas	tactician
technicality	**TKSCHR**	**TKSSHN**	**TKTV**
technicalities	texture	taxation	talkative
TKNKRS	**TKSCHRD**	**TKSST**	**TKVR**
technocracy	textured	toxicity	takeover(n,adj)
technocracies	**TKSCHRL**	toxicities	**TKWKW**
TKNKRT	textural	**TKSSTND**	tu quoque
technocrat	**TKSD**	taxi stand	**TKWT**
TKNLJ	tuxedo	**TKST**	etiquette
technology	tux	outcast	**TKY**
technologies	**TKSDDKTBL**	text	Taegu
TKNLJKL	tax-deductible	**TKSTBK**	**TL**
technological	**TKSDRM**	textbook	atoll
TKNLJST	taxidermy	**TKSTCHL**	Italy
technologist	**TKSDRMST**	textual	outlaw(bandit)
TKNSHN	taxidermist	**TKSTL**	outlay(spend)
technician	**TKSGZMPT**	textile	outlaid
TKNZM	tax-exempt	**TKSTSKP**	tael(weight)
tokenism	**TKSHL**	tachistoscope	tail(hindmost,
TKP	tactual	**TKSTSRSPTS**	follow)
takeup(n,adj)	**TKSHLTR**	textus receptus	tale(story)
teacup	tax shelter	**TKSZ**	tall(high)
TKPFL	**TKSK**	taxes(money)	tallow(fat)
teacupful	toxic	tax	tally(count)
TKR	**TKSKB**	taxis(car)(or)	tallied
outcry	taxicab	taxies	tallies
outcries	**TKSKJNK**	**TKT**	teal(duck)
taker(seizer)	toxicogenic	etiquette(manner)	tell(speech)
talker(speaker)	**TKSKLJ**	tacet(silent)	told
ticker(device)	toxicology	tact(diplomacy)	telly(TV)
tucker(folder)	**TKSKLJST**	takeout(n,adj)	tellies
TKRP	toxicologist	ticket	tile(covering)
outcrop	**TKSKNT**	toccata(music)	tiled,tiling
TKRS	toxicant	**TKTFL**	till(plow,money,
autocracy	**TKSKSS**	tactful	time)
autocracies	toxicosis	**TKTK**	toil(work)
TKRTP	**TKSM**	tactic(maneuver)	tole(sheet metal)
ticker tape	toxemia	ticktack(sound)	toll(charge)
TKRTPRD	**TKSMTR**	(or)tictac	tool(instrument)
ticker-tape parade	taximeter	ticktock(clock)	towel(cloth)
TKS	**TKSN**	ticky-tacky(cheap)	tule(bulrush)
ataxia	tocsin(alarm)	**TKTKL**	tulle(net)
ataxic	toxin(poison)	tactical	**TLBK**
tax(levy)	**TKSNG**	**TKTKS**	tailback
taxes	taxing(adj)	tactics	**TLBKS**
taxi(car,plane)	**TKSNM**	**TKTKT**	toolbox
taxied	taxonomy	tic-tac-toe(or)	toolboxes
taxies(or)	**TKSNMK**	ticktacktoe(game)	**TLBL**
taxis	taxonomic	**TKTL**	tellable(speech)
taxying(or)	**TKSPR**	tactile(touch)	tillable(land)
taxiing	taxpayer	teakettle(pot)	**TLBRJ**
tux	**TKSR**	**TKTLS**	toll bridge(road)
tuxedo	taxer	tactless	**TLBRR**
TKSBL	**TKSRKN**	**TKTNKS**	talebearer

TLBTH
tollbooth
TLD
tilde
TLFN
tail fin
telephone
telephoned
telephoning
telephony
telephonies
TLFNK
telephonic
TLFR
telpher
TLFT
telephoto
TLFTGRF
telephotograph
telephotography
TLFTGRFK
telephotographic
TLGD
two-legged
TLGRF
telegraph
telegraphy
TLGRFK
telegraphic
TLGRFR
telegrapher
TLGRM
telegram
TLGT
tailgate
tailgated
tailgating
tollgate(money)
TLH
tallyho
TLHS
Tallahassee
tollhouse
TLHV
tail-heavy
TLJ
etiology
etiologies
etiologic
etiologist
tillage
TLJNK
telegenic
TLJST
etiologist
etiology

TLK
italic
outlook
talc(powder)
telic(goal)
TLKL
toll call
TLKM
talcum
TLKMYNKSHN
telecommunication
TLKNSS
telekinesis
TLKNTK
telekinetic
TLKPR
tollkeeper
TLKRS
telecourse
TLKS
italics
telex
TLKST
telecast
telecast(or)
telecasted
TLLJ
teleology
TLLJKL
teleological
TLLJST
teleologist
TLM
Ptolemy
TLMD
Talmud
TLMKR
toolmaker
TLMN
tallyman
TLMRK
telemark
TLMTR
telemeter(device)
telemetry(science)
telemetries
TLMTRKL
telemetrical
TLN
outline
outlined
outlining
talon
towline
TLND
tail end(last)

Thailand
TLNDR
outlander
uitlander
TLNDSH
outlandish
TLNG
outlaying(money)
outlying(area)
tiling(tile)
tilling(till)
tooling(tool)
TLNT
Atlanta
talent
TLNTD
talented
TLNTK
Atlantic
TLNTKSHN
Atlantic Ocean
TLNTKST
Atlantic City
TLP
tulip
TLPL
teleplay
TLPP
tail pipe
TLPRMPTR
TelePrompter
(trademark)
TLPS
tailpiece
TLPTH
telepathy
TLPTHK
telepathic
TLPTHKL
telepathically
TLPTR
tulip tree
TLR
outlawry(bandit)
outlawries
outlier(separate)
tailor(cloth)
teller(bank)
tiller(farmer)
tiller(lever)
TLRBL
tolerable
tolerably
TLRBLNS
tolerableness
TLRBLT

tolerability
TLRD
tailored
toll road
TLRM
tularemia
TLRMD
tailor-made
TLRN
Teleran
TLRNS
tolerance
TLRNT
tolerant
TLRS
tailrace
TLRSHN
toleration
TLRT
tolerate
tolerated
tolerating
TLRTR
tolerator
TLRTV
tolerative
TLS
tailless
toeless
Tulsa
TLSKD
tailskid
TLSKP
telescope
telescoped
telescoping
telescopy
TLSKPK
telescopic
TLSM
toilsome
TLSMN
talisman
TLSPN
tailspin
TLST
outlast
TLSTHTK
telesthetic
TLSTHZH
telesthesia
TLSTR
Telstar
TLSZ
italicize
italicized

NGK:ink **P:**pie **R:**air **S:**ice **SH:**show **T:**toy **THN:**thin **TH:**the **V:**of **W:**we **Y:**you **Z:**is **VZHN:**vision

italicizing
TLT
atilt(tilted)
etiolate(whiten)
etiolated
etiolating
etiolation
outlet
taillight
tilt
toilet
TLTGRF
telautograph
TLTHMR
tilt hammer
TLTHN
telethon
TLTL
telltale
TLTLNG
taletelling
TLTLR
taleteller
TLTP
Teletype
(trademark)
Teletyped
Teletyping
TLTPPR
toilet paper
TLTPRTR
teletypewriter
TLTR
toiletry
toiletries
TLTRZ
toiletries
TLTTP
tilt-top
TLTWTR
toilet water
TLV
outlive
outlived
outliving
TLVR
televiewer
TLVV
Tel Aviv
TLVWR
televiewer
TLVZ
televise
televised
televising
TLVZHN

television
TV
TLVZR
televisor
TLWND
tail wind
TLWRN
toilworn
TLY
atelier(studio)
TLYN
Italian
TLZ
tales
TLZMN
talesman(juryman)
talisman
TM
atom
autumn(season)
item
tame(gentle)
tamed
taming
tamer
tamest
team(group)
teem(abound)
thyme(herb)
time(duration)
timed
timing
timer
tomb(chamber)
tome(large book)
tommy(bread)
tummy(body)
tummies
TMB
tomboy
TMBKT
Timbuktu
TMBL
tameable(tame)
timbal(kettledrum)
timbale(food)
tumble(roll)
tumbled
tumbling
tumbler
TMBLDN
tumble-down
tumbled-down
TMBLNG
tumbling
TMBLNGBKS

tumbling box
TMBLR
tumbler
TMBLWD
tumbleweed
TMBM
atom bomb
A-bomb
time bomb
TMBR
tambour(drum)
timber(wood)
timbre(sound)
TMBRHCH
timber hitch
TMBRL
tumbrel
TMBRLN
timberline
TMBRLND
timberland
TMBRN
tambourine
TMBRT
timber right
TMBRWLF
timber wolf
TMBRWRK
timberwork
TMD
timid(shy)
tumid(swollen)
TMDD
outmoded
TMDL
timidly
TMDNS
timidness
TMDT
timidity
TMF
tumefy
tumefied
tumefies
TMFL
tomfool
TMFLR
tomfoolery
tomfooleries
TMGN
tommy gun(n)
tommy-gun(v)
(submachine gun)
TMHK
tomahawk
TMK

thymic
TMKBM
atomic bomb
A-bomb
TMKJ
Atomic Age
TMKLK
time clock
TMKNSMNG
time-consuming
TMKPR
timekeeper
TMKRD
timecard
TMKT
tomcat
TML
oatmeal
tamale(food)
timely
timelier
timeliest
timeliness
TMLCHS
tumultuous
TMLJ
etymology
etymologies
TMLJKL
etymological
TMLK
time lock
TMLPS
time-lapse
TMLS
timeless
TMLT
tumult
TMMMRL
time immemorial
TMN
atman(soul)
etymon
ottoman
ptomaine
time-in
TMNDHF
time and a half
TMNG
teeming(abound)
timing(time)
TMNL
autumnal
TMNPZNNG
ptomaine poisoning
TMNRD

time-honored
TMNVR
outmaneuver
TMP
tamp
tempo(time)
TMPL
temple
TMPLN
tumpline
TMPLT
template
TMPN
tampion(gun
  muzzle)
tampon(plug)
timpani(drum)
  (or)
tympani
tympan(padding)
tympany(bombast)
tympanies
TMPNK
tympanic(drum like)
TMPNL
tympanal
TMPNM
tympanum(ear)
TMPNST
tympanist(drummer)
TMPR
tamper(interfere)
temper(modify,mood)
tempera(painting)
tempura(food)
TMPRCHR
temperature
TMPRD
tempered
TMPRL
temporal
TMPRLT
temporality
  temporalities
TMPRMNT
temperament
TMPRMNTL
temperamental
TMPRNS
temperance
TMPRR
tamperer
temporary
  temporarily
  temporariness
TMPRRL

temporarily
TMPRT
temperate
TMPRTZN
Temperate Zone
TMPRZ
temporize
  temporized
  temporizing
TMPS
timepiece
TMPSCHS
tempestuous
TMPSFGT
tempus fugit
TMPST
tempest
TMPT
attempt
tempt
TMPTBL
attemptable
temptable
TMPTNG
tempting
TMPTR
tempter
TMPTRS
temptress
TMPTSHN
temptation
TMPZ
tempos
TMR
tamer(tame)
timer(time)
tomorrow
tumor(growth)
TMRRS
temerarious
TMRS
timorous(timid)
tumorous
TMRT
temerity(rashness)
tommy rot
TMSFR
atmosphere
TMSFRK
atmospheric
  atmospherical
  atmospherics
TMSHN
automation
TMSHNTR
tam-o-shanter

TMSNS
tumescence
TMSNT
tumescent
TMSRVNG
timeserving
TMSRVR
timeserver
TMSS
tmesis
TMST
outmost
utmost
TMSTN
tombstone
TMSTR
teamster
two-master
TMSTRZ
Teamsters
TMSVNG
timesaving
TMSVR
timesaver
TMT
automate
  automated
  automating
teammate
time-out
tomato
  tomatoes
TMTBL
timetable
TMTH
timothy
TMTK
automatic
TMTM
tom-tom
TMTN
automaton
TMTSTD
time-tested
TMTZ
tomatoes
  tomato
TMWRK
teamwork
timework
TMWRKR
timeworker
TMWRN
timeworn
TMYLS
tumulus(n), - lose(adj)

TMZ
atomize
  atomized
  atomizing
itemize
  itemized
  itemizing
Thames
times(multiply)
TMZN
time zone
TMZR
atomizer
TMZSHN
itemization
TMZSKWR
Times Square
TN
atone(make amends)
  atoned
  atoning
attain(gain)
attune(tune)
  attuned
  attuning
eighteen(18)
taenia(structure)
  taeniae
tain(thin tin)
tan(color)
  tanned
  tanning
tanner
tannest
tawny(brown)
  tawnier
  tawniest
  tawniness
teen(teenager)
teeny(tiny)
  teenier
  teeniest
  teeniness
ten(10)
tie in(v)
tie-in(n,adj)
tin(metal)
  tinned
  tinning
tine(prong)
tinny(tin)
  tinnier
  tinniest
  tinniness
tiny(small)
  tinier

NGK:ink **P**:pie **R**:air **S**:ice **SH**:show **T**:toy **THN**:thin **TH**:the **V**:of **W**:we **Y**:you **Z**:is **VZHN**:vision

tiniest
tininess
toe-in(direction)
ton(weight)
tone(sound)
toned
toning
tonneau(seating)
tonneaus(or)
tonneaux
town(city)
townie(person)
tun(cask)
tunned
tunning
tuna(fish)
tuna
tune(melody)
tuned
tuning
tuner

TNBL
attainable
tenable(logical)
tunable(tune)

TNBLT
attainability
tenability

TNBPR
teenybopper

TNBRS
tenebrous

TNBRST
tenebrosity

TNCHN
attention
tension

TND
attend
ctenoid
tend

TNDF
tone-deaf

TNDM
ctenidium
tandum

TNDN
tendon

TNDNCHS
tendentious

TNDNDS
tendinitis

TNDNS
attendance
attendants(people)
tendency

tendencies

TNDNSHS
tendentious

TNDNT
attendant

TNDNTS
tendinitis

TNDR
attainder(loss)
tender(soft)
tinder(dry twigs)
tundra(area)

TNDRBKS
tinderbox
tinderboxes

TNDRFT
tenderfoot
tenderfeet(or)
tenderfoots

TNDRHRTD
tenderhearted

TNDRL
tendril

TNDRLN
tenderloin

TNDRMNDD
tender-minded

TNDRNS
tenderness

TNDRZ
tenderize
tenderized
tenderizing
tenderizer

TNDRZR
tenderizer

TNDRZSHN
tenderization

TNFL
tenfold(10)
tinfoil(metal)
tuneful

TNFLD
tenfold

TNFR
ctenophore
to and fro
ut infra

TNG
outing
tang(taste)
tangy
tangier
tangiest
tanginess
tango(dance)

ting(sound)
tong(seize)
Tonga
tongue(organ)
tongued
tonguing

TNGG
tango
Tonga
tongue
tongued
tonguing

TNGGL
tangle
tangled
tangling
tingle
tingled
tingling
tingly
tinglier
tingliest
tingliness

TNGGRM
tangram

TNGKCHR
tincture
tinctured
tincturing

TNGKFL
tankful

TNGKJ
tankage

TNGKL
tinkle
tinkled
tinkling

TNGKR
tank car
tanker(boat)
tinker

TNGKRD
tankard

TNGKRR
tinkerer

TNGKT
tinct

TNGKTRL
tinctorial

TNGL
tangle(knots)
tangled
tangling
tingle
tingled
tingling

tingly
tinglier
tingliest
tingliness

TNGLNHT
ten-gallon hat

TNGLR
tingler

TNGLSHNG
tongue-lashing

TNGNCHK
tongue-in-cheek

TNGRM
tangram

TNGSTN
tungsten

TNGT
tongue-tie
tongue-tied
tongue-tying

TNGZ
tongs

TNHRN
tinhorn

TNHS
town house

TNJ
teen-age
tinge
tinged
tinging(or)
tingeing
tonnage(capacity)

TNJBL
tangible
tangibly

TNJBLT
tangibility
tangiblilties

TNJD
teen-aged

TNJL
tangelo

TNJNCHL
tangential

TNJNS
tangency

TNJNSHL
tangential

TNJNT
tangent

TNJR
teen-ager

TNJRN
tangerine

TNK

tannic(substance)
tonic(medicine)
tunic(garment)
TNKL
tentacle
TNKLR
tone color
TNKMNDMNTS
Ten Commandments
TNKN
tin can
TNKRZDM
tinker's damn
TNKSLF
tonic sol-fa
TNL
toenail(foot)
tonal(tone)
tunnel(hole)
TNLNGWJ
tone language
TNLT
tonality
tonalities
TNLZ
tin lizzie
TNM
autonomy
autonomies
two-name
TNMBR
outnumber
TNMK
autonomic
TNMNT
atonement(amends)
tantamount(equal)
tenement(place)
TNMS
autonomous
TNMTNG
town meeting
TNN
tannin(acid)
tenon(wood)
TNNG
tanning
TNNGFRK
tuning fork
TNNS
tenancy
tenancies
TNNT
tenant
TNNTR
tenantry

tenantries
TNP
tune up(v)
tune-up(n,adj)
TNPLT
tin plate(n)
tin-plate(v)
tin-plated
tin-plating
TNPN
tenpenny
TNPNS
tenpence
TNPNZ
tenpins
TNR
tanner(tans hides)
tannery(business)
tanneries
tenor(person,
meaning)
tinner(metal
worker)
tuner(person,
radio)
TNRM
tone arm
TNRNS
itinerancy
TNRNT
itinerant
TNRR
itinerary
itineraries
TNRT
itinerate
itinerated
itinerating
TNS
Tennessee
tennis(sport)
tense
tensed
tensing
tenser
tensest
Tunis
TNSD
teniacide
TNSH
Tunisia
TNSHN
attention
tension
TNSHP
township

TNSHR
tonsure
tonsured
tonsuring
TNSHS
tenacious
TNSHZ
tennis shoes
TNSL
tensile(tension)
tinsel(decorate)
tonsil(organ)
TNSLKTM
tonsillectomy
tonsillectomies
TNSLT
tensility
TNSLTS
tonsillitis
TNSMTH
tinsmith
TNSNTS
ten cents(dime)
TNSNTSTR
ten-cent store
TNSR
tensor(muscle)
TNSRL
tonsorial
TNST
tenacity
(persistent)
tensity(tense)
tensities
tonicity
(readiness)
TNSV
tensive
TNT
out-and-out
taint(stain)
taunt(deride)
tenet(doctrine)
tent(shelter)
tenuity(not firm)
tenuto(music)
tint(dye,shade)
TNT
trinitrotoluene
tonight(time)
TNTD
tainted
TNTH
tenth
TNTKL
tentacle

TNTLZ
tantalize
tantalized
tantalizing
TNTLZR
tantalizer
TNTLZSHN
tantalization
TNTMNT
tantamount
TNTN
tontine
TNTNBYLSHN
tintinnabulation
TNTP
tintype
TNTR
tantara(fanfare)
taunter(mocker)
tenter(framework)
TNTRHK
tenterhook
TNTRM
tantrum
TNTS
tinnitus
TNTTV
tentative
TNTV
tantivy
tentative
TNWR
tinware
TNWRK
tinwork
TNYR
tenure
TNYRL
tenurial
TNYS
tenuous
TNYSHN
attenuation
TNYT
attenuate
attenuated
attenuating
tenuity
TNYTR
attenuator
TNZ
teens
TNZH
Tunisia
TNZMS
tenesmus

TNZN
Tanzania
TNZPPL
townspeople
TP
atop(prep)
Taipei
tap(hit)
 tapped
 tapping
tape(fasten,
 record)
 taped
 taping
taupe(color)
teapoy(table)
tepee(tent)
tie up(v)
tie-up(n,adj)
tip(point)
 tipped
 tipping
top(uppermost)
 topped
 topping
tope(drink)
 toped
 toping
 toper
toupee(hair)
type(class)
 typed
 typing
typo(error)
TPBL
typable
TPD
tepid
TPDG
top dog
TPDK
tape deck
TPDNS
tap dance(n)
tap-dance(v)
 tap-danced
 tap-dancing
 tap dancer
TPDRR
top-drawer
TPDRS
top-dress
 top-dresses
TPDRSNG
top-dressing
TPDT

tepidity
TPF
tepefy(tepid)
 tepefied
 tepefies
tip-off(n)
typify(example)
 typified
 typifies
TPFKSHN
tepefaction
 (tepid)
typification
 (example)
TPFLT
topflight
TPFR
typifier
TPGLNT
topgallant
TPGRF
topography(map)
typography
 (printing)
TPGRFK
topographic(map)
typographic
 (printing)
TPGRFKL
topographical(map)
typographical
 (printing)
TPGRFR
topographer(map)
typographer
 (printer)
TPHMPR
top-hamper
TPHT
top hat
TPHV
top-heavy
 top-heavier
 top-heaviest
 top-heaviness
TPK
tapioca(food)
Topeka
topic
TPKL
atypical(not
 typical)
topical(topic)
typical(type)
TPKLT
topicality

topicalities
TPKRT
tipcart
TPKST
typecast(drama)
 typecast
 typecasting
type-cast(printing)
 type-cast
 type-casting
TPKT
topcoat
TPL
tipple(drink)
 tippled
 tippling
 tippler
topple(push over)
 toppled
 toppling
tupelo(tree)
two-ply
typal(type)
TPLFT
toplofty
 toploftier
 toploftiest
 toploftiness
TPLJ
topology
typology(type)
 typologies
TPLR
tippler
TPLS
topless
TPLVL
top-level
TPMST
topmast(mast)
topmost(highest)
TPN
tiepin
twopenny, (B)tuppenny
TPNCH
topnotch
TPNG
topping
TPNT
topknot
TPNTD
outpointed
TPR
taper(decrease,
 candle)
tapir(animal)

tapper(one that
 taps)
tipper(giver)
topiary(art)
topper(coat)
TPRKRD
tape-record
TPRKRDR
tape recorder
TPRM
taproom
TPRNG
outpouring
TPRT
taproot
typewrite
 typewrote
 typewriting
 typewritten
TPRTR
typewriter
TPS
autopsy
 autopsies
taps(signal)
tipsy(drunk)
 tipsier
 tipsiest
 tipsily
 tipsiness
tops(best)
two-piece
TPSHNT
outpatient
TPSKRPT
typescript
TPSKRT
top-secret
TPSL
topsail(boat)
topsoil(land)
TPST
outpost
typeset
 typeset
 typesetting
typist
TPSTR
tapestry(fabric)
 tapestries
tipster
typesetter
 (printing)
TPSTRV
topsy-turvy
TPT

B:by **CH**:each **D**:day **F**:if **G**:go **H**:he **HW**:why **J**:joy **K**:cow **KS**:ax **KWL**:equal **L**:all **M**:may **N**:in

output
tappet(lever)
teapot(tea)
tippet(garment)
tiptoe(walk)
tiptoed
tiptoeing
TPTH
towpath
TPTP
tiptop
TPWRM
tapeworm
TPZ
topaz
TR
attar(oil)
attire(dress)
attired
attiring
otter(mammal)
outer(external)
tahr(goatlike)
tar(oily)
tarred
tarring
tare(plant)
tare(weight)
tared,taring
taro(plant)
tarot(cards)
tarry(linger)
tarried
tarries
tarrier
tarry(tar)
tarrier
tarriest
tarriness
tear(rip)
tore
torn
tear(cry)
teared
tearing
teary(wet,cry)
tearier
teariest
tearily
teariness
terry(fabric)
terries
tiara(crown)
tier(row,level)
tier(one that ties)
tire(wheel)(B)tyre

tire(weary)
tired, tiring
Torah(Bible)
torah(tradition)
Tory(political)
Tories
Toryism
tour(trip)
tower(structure)
tray(holder)
tree(plant)
treed
treeing
trey(three)
trio(three)
troy(weight)
true(sure)
trued
truing(or)
trueing
truer
truest
truly
trueness
try(sample)
tried
tries
trying
tyro(beginner)
utter(speak)
TRB
tribe
TRBCHRJR
turbocharger
TRBD
turbid
TRBDR
troubadour
TRBJT
turbojet
TRBL
terrible(terror)
terribly
treble(triple,high)
trebled
trebling
tribal(tribe)
triable(try)
trouble(distress)
troubled
troubling
true-blue(loyal)
TRBLMKR
troublemaker
TRBLSHTR
troubleshooter

TRBLSM
troublesome
TRBLYN
tourbillion
TRBLZM
tribalism
TRBN
turban(headdress)
turbine(engine)
TRBNGKS
Outer Banks(NC)
TRBNT
turbinate
turbinated
turbinating
turbination
TRBPRP
turboprop
TRBRN
trueborn
TRBSH
tarboosh
TRBYLNS
turbulence
TRBYLNT
turbulent
TRBYLSHN
tribulation
TRBYN
tribune
TRBYNL
tribunal
TRBYNR
tribunary
TRBYSHN
attribution
TRBYT
attribute
attributed
attributing
tribute
TRBYTBL
attributable
TRBYTR
attributer
tributary
tributaries
tributarily
tributariness
TRBYTV
attributive
TRBZMN
tribesman
tribesmen
TRCH
outreach

outreaches
torch
torches
TRCHBRR
torchbearer
TRCHLT
torchlight
TRCHNT
trecento
TRCHR
torchier(lamp)
torture(pain)
tortured
torturing
torturer
treachery
treacheries
TRCHRS
torturous
(agonizing)
treacherous
TRCHRSHN
trituration
TRCHRT
triturate
triturated
triturating
TRCHS
tortuous(winding)
TRCHWD
torchwood
TRD
outride
outrode
outriding
outridden
outrider
tardy(late)
tardier
tardiest
tardily
tardiness
tirade(diatribe)
tired(fatigued)
toroid(shape)
torrid(parched)
toward(direction)
trade(skill)
trade(swap)
traded,trading
trader
tread(walk)
trod
treading
trodden(or)
trod

treaty(pact)
  treaties
triad(three)
triode(tube)
turd(dung)
TRDBL
  tradable(or)
  tradeable
TRDF
  tradeoff(n,adj)
TRDFRS
  tour de force
TRDKTL
  pterodactyl
TRDL
  towardly
    (favorable)
  towardliness
  treadle(pedal)
  treadled
  treadling
  tour-de-loup
    (trap)
  turtle(reptile)
TRDLFWG
  Tierra del Fuego
TRDLST
  trade-last
TRDML
  treadmill
TRDMNSHNL
  tridimensional
TRDMRK
  trademark
TRDN
  trade in(v)
  trade-in(n,adj)
  trodden
  tread
TRDNM
  trade name
TRDNT
  trident
TRDNYN
  trade union (B)trades
TRDR
  outrider
  toreador
  trader(dealer)
  traitor(treason)
  traitorous
  traitress(f)
  trotter(trot)
TRDRP
  teardrop
TRDS

traduce
traduced
traducing
TRDSBL
traducible
traducibly
TRDSHN
tradition
TRDSHNL
traditional
TRDSHNLST
traditionalist
TRDSHNLSTK
traditionalistic
TRDSHNLZ
traditionalize
traditionalized
traditionalizing
TRDSHNLZM
traditionalism
TRDSHNZM
traducianism
TRDSKRT
trade secret
TRDSMNT
traducement
TRDSR
traducer
TRDT
torridity
TRDWND
trade wind
TRDYNYN
trade union(B)trades
TRDYS
traduce
traduced
traducing
TRDYSBL
traducible
traducibly
TRDYSHNZM
traducianism
TRDYSMNT
traducement
TRDYSR
traducer
TRDZMN
tradesman
tradesmen
TRDZPPL
tradespeople
TRF
atrophy
atrophied
atrophies

tariff(charge)
terrify(terror)
  terrified
  terrifies
tref(unclean)
trophy(prize)
  trophies
trough(gutter)
turf(surface)
TRFK
traffic
  trafficked
  trafficking
  trafficker
terrific
TRFKL
terrifically
trifocal
TRFKLT
traffic light
TRFKR
trafficker
TRFKT
trifecta
TRFL
tearful
trefoil(plant)
trifle(slight)
  trifled
  trifling
truffle(fungi,food)
TRFLNG
trifling
TRFR
troffer
TRFRM
terra firma
TRG
trig
  trigged
  trigging
TRGLDT
troglodyte
TRGN
tarragon
TRGNMTR
trigonometry
TRGR
outrigger
trigger
TRGRHP
trigger-happy
TRGS
tear gas
TRGT
target

TRHDRN
trihedron
TRJ
outrage
outraged
outraging
trudge
trudged
trudging
TRJD
tragedy
tragedies
turgid
TRJDN
tragedian(actor)
tragedienne
  (actress)
TRJK
tragic
TRJKL
tragical
TRJKMD
tragicomedy
tragicomedies
TRJKMK
tragicomic
TRJKSHN
trajection
TRJKT
traject
TRJKTR
trajectory
trajectories
TRJN
Trojan
TRJNHRS
Trojan horse
TRJNS
terrigenous
TRJNWR
Trojan War
TRJRKR
tear-jerker
TRJS
outrageous
TRJSNS
turgescence
TRJVRSSHN
tergiversation
TRJVRST
tergiversate
tergiversated
tergiversating
TRJVRSTR
tergiversator
TRK

B:by **CH**:each **D**:day **F**:if **G**:go **H**:he **HW**:why **J**:joy **K**:cow **KS**:ax **KWL**:equal **L**:all **M**:may **N**:in

attract
autarky
  autarkies
  autarkic(or)
  autarkal
taroc(cards)(or)
tarok
toric(shape)
torque(force)
trachea(lung)
  tracheas(or)
  tracheae
track(mark,place)
trek(travel)
  trekked, trekking
trick(prank)
tricky
  trickier
  trickiest
  trickily
  trickiness
tricot(cloth)
troche(lozenge)
trochee(poetic
  meter)
truck(vehicle)
Turkey
turkey(animal)
TRKD
  terra cotta
TRKDM
  trichotomy
TRKFRM
  truck farm
TRKJ
  trackage
  truckage
TRKL
  treacle(syrup)
  trickle(flow)
    trickled
    trickling
  truckle(roller,
    yield)
    truckled
    truckling
TRKLD
  truckload
TRKLR
  tricolor
TRKLS
  terricolous
TRKM
  trachoma
TRKN
  trichina

trichinae
TRKNSS
  trichinosis
TRKR
  trickery
  trickeries
  trucker
TRKRMTK
  trichromatic
TRKRN
  tricorn
TRKSHBTH
  Turkish bath
TRKSHN
  attraction
  traction
TRKSL
  triaxial
TRKSTR
  trickster
TRKT
  attract
  terra cotta
  tract(land)
  tricot(cloth)
TRKTBL
  attractable
  attractably
  tractable
  tractably
TRKTBLT
  attractability
  tractability
TRKTL
  tractile
TRKTLT
  tractility
TRKTM
  tracheotomy
  tracheotomies
  trichotomy
  (division)
  trichotomies
TRKTR
  attractor
  tractor(vehicle)
TRKTV
  attractive
  tractive
TRKWS
  terraqueous
TRKWT
  torquat
TRKWZ
  torques(neck)
  turquoise(color)

TRKYLNS
  truculence
TRKYLNT
  truculent
TRKZ
  turkeys
  turquoise(color)
TRL
  trail(way,
    follow)
  trawl(net)
  trial(test)
  trill(sound)
  troll(fish)
  trolley(vehicle)
  trowel(tool)
  trull(harlot)
  truly(true)
  utterly(total)
TRLB
  terra alba
TRLBLZR
  trailblazer
TRLF
  true-life
TRLJ
  treillage(trellis)
  trilogy(three)
  trilogies
TRLM
  trillium
TRLNGGWL
  trilingual
TRLP
  trollop
TRLR
  trailer
  trawler(boat)
TRLS
  tireless
  trellis
TRLSWRK
  trelliswork
TRLTRL
  trilateral
TRLV
  truelove
TRLYN
  trillion
  trillionth
TRM
  atrium
    atria(or)
    atriums
  tearoom
  term(time)

tram(vehicle)
  trammed
  tramming
trauma(shock)
  traumas(or)
  traumata
trim(cut)
  trimmed
  trimming
  trimmer
  trimmest
triumph(win)
yttrium(element)
TRMBL
  tremble
  trembled
  trembling
TRMBN
  trombone
TRMBNST
  trombonist
TRMF
  triumph
TRMFL
  triumphal
TRMFNT
  triumphant
TRMGNS
  termagancy
TRMGNT
  termagant
TRML
  trammel(hinder)
  tremolo(music)
  trommel(sieve)
  turmoil(confusion)
TRMLN
  tourmaline
TRMLS
  termless
TRMN
  termini
  terminus
TRMNBL
  terminable
  terminably
TRMNDS
  tremendous
TRMNG
  trimming
TRMNL
  terminal
TRMNLJ
  terminology
  terminologies
TRMNLJST

---

terminologist
TRMNS
terminus
termini(or)
terminuses
TRMNSHN
termination
TRMNT
terminate
terminated
terminating
torment
TRMNTHL
trimonthly
TRMNTR
terminator
tormentor
TRMNTV
terminative
TRMP
tramp(hike,person)
triumph
tromp(heavy walk)
trump(cards)
TRMPL
trample
trampled
trampling
TRMPLN
trampoline
TRMPLNST
trampolinist
TRMPLT
tram plate(rail)
TRMPR
trumpery(showy)
trumperies
TRMPT
trumpet
TRMPTP
trumped-up
TRMPTR
trumpeter
TRMR
termer(term)
tremor(movement)
TRMRK
turmeric
TRMSN
Terramycin
(trademark)
TRMST
outermost(place)
uttermost
TRMSTR
trimester

TRMT
termite
TRMTK
traumatic
TRMTKL
traumatically
TRMTZM
traumatism
TRMVRT
triumvirate
TRMYLS
tremulous
TRN
attorney
outrun
outran
outrunning
tarn(lake)
tartan(fabric, ship)
Tehran
tern(bird)
terrain(ground)
terrane(rock)
terrene(earthly)
tourney(contest)
train(vehicle,
make fit)
trainee(person)
trine(three)
tureen(dish)
Turin
turn(rotate)
tyranny(power)
tyrannies
TRNBKL
turnbuckle
TRNBT
turnabout
TRNCH
trench
trenches
TRNCHKT
trench coat
TRNCHL
tarantula
torrential
TRNCHMTH
trench mouth
TRNCHN
truncheon
TRNCHNF
trench knife
TRNCHNS
trenchancy
TRNCHNT
trenchant

TRNCHR
trencher
TRND
tornado
trend
trendy
trendier
trendiest
trendily
trendiness
TRNDD
Trinidad
TRNDL
trundle
trundled
trundling
TRNDN
turndown
TRNDZ
tornados
TRNF
turn off(v)
turnoff(n)
TRNG
towering
trying
TRNGK
trunk
TRNGKLN
trunk line
TRNGKSHN
truncation
TRNGKT
trinket
truncate
truncated
truncating
TRNGL
triangle
TRNGYLR
triangular
TRNGYLSHN
triangulation
TRNGYLT
triangulate
triangulated
triangulating
TRNK
turnkey
tyrannic
TRNKL
tyrannical
TRNKT
tourniquet
turncoat
TRNKWL

tranquil
TRNKWLT
tranquility
tranquilities
TRNKWLZ
tranquilize
tranquilized
tranquilizing
TRNKWLZR
tranquilizer
TRNKWLZSHN
tranquilization
TRNL
eternal(time)
treenail(peg)
triennial(three
years)
trinal(triple)
TRNM
triennium
trienniums(or)
triennia
TRNML
trinomial
TRNMN
trainman
trainmen
TRNMNT
tournament
TRNN
Trenton
TRNNG
training
turning(rotate)
TRNNGPNT
turning point
TRNP
turnip
TRNPK
turnpike
TRNR
ternary
trainer
TRNRND
turnaround
TRNS
tarriance(tarry)
trance(state)
tranced, trancing
trounce(defeat)
trounced
trouncing
truancy(absent)
truancies
tyrannous(rule)
utterance(speech)

B:by **CH**:each **D**:day **F**:if **G**:go **H**:he **HW**:why **J**:joy **K**:cow **KS**:ax **KWL**:equal **L**:all **M**:may **N**:in

TRNSBSTNSHSHN
transubstantiation
TRNSBSTNSHT
transubstantiate
transubstantiated
transubstantiating
TRNSD
transude
transuded
transuding
TRNSDKSHN
transduction
TRNSDSR
transducer
TRNSDT
transudate(or)
transudation
TRNSDYSR
transducer
TRNSFGYR
transfigure
transfigured
transfiguring
TRNSFGYRMNT
transfigurement
TRNSFGYRSHN
transfiguration
TRNSFKS
transfix
transfixes
TRNSFKSHN
transfixion
TRNSFR
transfer
transferred
transferring
transferee
TRNSFRBL
transferable
TRNSFRBLT
transferability
TRNSFRL
transferal
TRNSFRM
transform
TRNSFRMR
transformer
TRNSFRMSHN
transformation
TRNSFRNS
transference
TRNSFRR
transferrer
TRNSFYSV
transfusive
TRNSFYZ

transfuse
transfused
transfusing
TRNSFYZBL
transfusible
TRNSFYZHN
transfusion
TRNSFYZV
transfusive
TRNSGRS
transgress
transgresses
TRNSGRSHN
transgression
TRNSGRSR
transgressor
TRNSH
tarnish
tarnishes
TRNSHBL
tarnishable
TRNSHL
tarantula
torrential
TRNSHN
tarnation
TRNSHNS
transience
TRNSHNT
transient
TRNSHP
transship
transshipped
transshipping
TRNSK
Transkei
TRNSKNTNNTL
transcontinental
TRNSKRB
TRNSKRBBL
TRNSKRBR
TRNSKRPSHN
TRNSKRPT
TRNSKSHL
transsexual
transsexuality
TRNSKSHN
transaction
TRNSKT

transact(to do)
transect(divide)
TRNSKTR
transactor
TRNSLKSHN
translocation
TRNSLKT
translocate
translocated
translocating
TRNSLSHN
translation
TRNSLSNS
translucence
translucency
TRNSLSNT
translucent
TRNSLT
translate
translated
translating
TRNSLTBL
translatable
TRNSLTR
translator
TRNSLTRSHN
transliteration
TRNSLTRT
transliterate
transliterated
transliterating
TRNSM
transom
TRNSMDL
transmittal
TRNSMGRSHN
transmigration
TRNSMGRT
transmigrate
transmigrated
transmigrating
TRNSMSBL
transmissible
TRNSMSHN
transmission
TRNSMT
transmit
transmitted
transmitting
TRNSMTL
transmittal
TRNSMTNS
transmittance
TRNSMTR
transmitter
TRNSMYT

transmute
transmuted
transmuting
transmuter
TRNSMYTBL
transmutable
transmutably
TRNSMYTBLT
transmutability
TRNSMYTSHN
transmutation
TRNSND
transcend
TRNSNDNS
transcendence
transcendency
TRNSNDNT
transcendent
TRNSNDNTL
transcendental
TRNSNDNTLZM
transcendentalism
TRNSNK
transonic
TRNSNS
transience
TRNSNT
transient
TRNSPLNT
transplant
TRNSPLNTSHN
transplantation
TRNSPNDR
transponder
TRNSPR
transpire
transpired
transpiring
TRNSPRNS
transparence
transparency
transparencies
TRNSPRNT
transparent
TRNSPRSHN
transpiration
TRNSPRT
transport
TRNSPRTBL
transportable
TRNSPRTBLT
transportability
TRNSPRTSHN
transportation
TRNSPRTV
transportive

NGK:ink P:pie R:air S:ice SH:show T:toy THN:thin TH:the V:of W:we Y:you Z:is VZHN:vision

TRNSPSFK
transpacific
TRNSPT
transept
TRNSPZ
transpose
transposed
transposing
TRNSPZBL
transposable
TRNSPZSHN
transposition
TRNSPZR
transposer
TRNSR
tyrannosaur
TRNSSHN
transition
TRNSSHNK
transoceanic
TRNSSHNL
transitional
TRNSSTR
transistor
TRNSSTRZ
transistorize
transistorized
transistorizing
TRNST
transit
TRNSTL
turnstile
TRNSTLNTK
transatlantic
TRNSTR
transitory
TRNSTV
transitive
TRNSVLY
transvalue
TRNSVR
transceiver
TRNSVRS
transverse
TRNSVRSL
transversal
TRNSVSTT
transvestite
TRNSVSTZM
transvestism
TRNSYD
transude
transuded
transuding
TRNSYDT
transudate

TRNT
eternity(time)
eternities
Toronto
torrent(water)
trinity(three)
trinities
truant(person)
turnout(number)
tyrant(ruler)
TRNTBL
turntable
TRNTFSR
truant officer
TRNTL
attorney at law
tarantella
TRNTN
Trenton
TRNVR
turn over(v)
turnover(n)
TRNYN
trunnion
TRNZ
tyrannize
tyrannized
tyrannizing
TRNZDKSHN
transduction
TRNZDSR
transducer
TRNZDYSR
transducer
TRNZFR
transfer
transferred
transferring
TRNZGRS
transgress
transgresses
TRNZGRSHN
transgression
TRNZGRSR
transgressor
TRNZHNS
transience
TRNZHNT
transient
TRNZKNTNNTL
transcontinental
TRNZKSHN
transaction
TRNZKT
transact
TRNZKTR

transactor
TRNZLKSHN
translocation
TRNZLKT
translocate
translocated
translocating
TRNZLSHN
translation
TRNZLSNS
translucence
translucency
TRNZLSNT
translucent
TRNZLT
translate
translated
translating
TRNZLTBL
translatable
TRNZLTR
translator
TRNZLTRSHN
transliteration
TRNZLTRT
transliterate
transliterated
transliterating
TRNZMGRSHN
transmigration
TRNZMGRT
transmigrate
transmigrated
transmigrating
TRNZMSBL
transmissible
TRNZMSHN
transmission
TRNZMT
transmit
transmitted
transmitting
TRNZMTL
transmittal
TRNZMTNS
transmittance
TRNZMTR
transmitter
TRNZMYT
transmute
transmuted
transmuting
transmuter
TRNZMYTBL
transmutable
transmutably

TRNZMYTBLT
transmutability
TRNZMYTSHN
transmutation
TRNZNS
transience
TRNZNT
transient
TRNZR
tyrannizer
TRNZSHN
transition
TRNZSHNK
transoceanic
TRNZSHNL
transitional
TRNZSKSHL
transsexual
TRNZSTR
transistor
TRNZSTRZ
transistorize
transistorized
transistorizing
TRNZSVR
transceiver
TRNZT
transit
TRNZTLNTK
transatlantic
TRNZTR
transitory
TRNZTV
transitive
TRNZVLY
transvalue
TRNZVRS
transverse
TRNZVRSL
transversal
TRNZVSTT
transvestite
TRNZVSTZM
transvestism
TRP
towrope(rope)
trap(device)
trapped
trapping
trapper
trip(journey)
tripped
tripping
tripe(food)
troop(soldiers)
trope(word)

B:by **CH**:each **D**:day **F**:if **G**:go **H**:he **HW**:why **J**:joy **K**:cow **KS**:ax **KWL**:equal **L**:all **M**:may **N**:in

troupe(actors)
trouped
trouping
TRPD
torpedo
torpedoes
torpid(dormant)
trepid(timid)
tripod(tool)
TRPDR
trap door
TRPDSHN
trepidation
TRPDT
torpidity
TRPHMR
trip hammer
TRPK
tropic
TRPKL
tropical
TRPKVKNSR
Tropic of Cancer
TRPKVKPRKRN
Tropic of Capricorn
TRPL
triple
tripled
tripling
triply
Tripoli
TRPLKS
triplex
TRPLKT
triplicate
triplicated
triplicating
TRPLN
tarpaulin
terreplein
(platform)
triplane
TRPLPL
triple play
TRPLSPS
triple-space
triple-spaced
triple-spacing
TRPLST
triplicity
TRPLT
triplet
TRPN
tarpon
terrapin
TRPNG

tripping
TRPNGZ
trappings
TRPNT
trapunto
TRPNTN
turpentine
TRPR
torpor(not active)
trapper(trap)
tripper(trip)
trooper
(policeman)
trouper(actor)
TRPRTT
tripartite
TRPS
traipse
traipsed
traipsing
TRPSFR
troposphere
TRPSHP
troopship
TRPSHTNG
trapshooting
TRPSHTR
trapshooter
TRPSKRN
terpsichorean
TRPT
trippet(cam)
TRPTD
turpitude
TRPTK
triptych
TRPTYD
turpitude
TRPZ
trapeze
TRPZD
trapezoid
TRPZM
trapezium
trapezia(or)
trapeziums
tropism
TRR
terrier(dog,law)
terror(fear)
TRRM
terrarium
terraria(or)
terrariums
TRRST
terrorist

terrorize
terrorism
TRRSTK
terroristic
TRRZ
terrorize
terrorized
terrorizing
TRRZM
terrorism
TRRZSHN
terrorization
TRS
Taurus
terrace(porch)
terraced
terracing
terse(short)
terser
tersest
tierce(time)
torse(math,wreath)
torso(body)
torus(bulging)
tori
trace(mark,copy)
traced
tracing
tress(hair)
tresses
trice(time)
trice(to lash)
triced,-cing
trousseau(clothes)
trousseaux(or)
trousseaus
truce(agreement)
truss(support)
trusses
TRSBL
traceable
traceably
TRSD
torsade
TRSH
trash
trashy
trashier
trashiest
trashily
trashiness
TRSHL
tertial
TRSHN
attrition(loss)
iteration(repeat)

tertian(time)
torsion(stress)
TRSHR
tertiary
TRSHS
atrocious
TRSKL
tricycle
TRSKT
trisect
TRSKWR
try square
TRSL
tercel(hawk)
trestle(beam)
trysail(sail)
TRSLWRK
trestlework
TRSM
tiresome
TRSNG
tracing
TRSNTNL
tricentennial
TRSNTNR
tercentenary
tercentenaries
TRSPS
outerspace
trespass
trespasses
triceps
TRSPSR
trespasser
TRSR
tracer
tracery
traceries
TRST
atrocity
atrocities
tercet(triplet)
tourist(traveler)
trist(trust)
triste(sad)
trussed
truss
trust(reliance)
trustee(agent)
trusteed
trusteeing
trusty(prison)
trusties
trusty
trustier
trustiest

trustily	tyrothricin	**TRTSSHL**	treillage
trustiness	**TRTHS**	tortoiseshell	**TRZ**
tryst(meeting)	truths	**TRTV**	terrazzo
TRSTBSTR	**TRTHZ**	iterative	trios
trustbuster	truths	**TRTY**	**TRZDFRS**
TRSTFL	**TRTHZM**	tortilla	tours de force
trustful	tritheism	**TRTZ**	**TRZH**
TRSTFND	**TRTL**	tortoise	triage
trust fund	turtle	**TRV**	**TRZHR**
TRSTKLS	**TRTLDV**	trave(wood)	treasure
tourist class	turtledove	travois(sledge)	treasured
TRSTRL	**TRTLJ**	travois	treasuring
terrestrial	teratology	trivia(trifles)	treasury
TRSTS	**TRTLN**	trove(a find)	treasuries
tristesse	trotline	**TRVL**	**TRZHRR**
TRSTSHP	**TRTLNK**	travail(hard work)	treasurer
trusteeship	turtleneck	travel(journey)	**TRZHRTRV**
TRSTWRTH	**TRTMNT**	trivial(trifle)	treasure-trove
trustworthy	treatment	**TRVLG**	**TRZM**
trustworthily	**TRTN**	travelogue	tourism(travel)
trustworthiness	tartan	**TRVLR**	truism(true)
TRT	tritone	traveler	**TRZMS**
iterate	**TRTP**	**TRVLRZCHK**	trismus
iterated	treetop	traveler's check	**TRZN**
iterating	**TRTR**	**TRVLT**	treason
outright	tartar	triviality	**TRZNS**
tart(taste,pie)	territory	trivialities	treasonous
terete(cylindrical)	territories	**TRVRS**	**TRZR**
terret(ring)	traitor	traverse	trouser
tort(act)	trotter(trot)	traversed	**TRZRS**
torte(cake)	**TRTRL**	traversing	trousers
trait(feature)	territorial	traverser	**TS**
treat(deal with)	**TRTRLT**	**TRVRSBL**	eighties
treaty(pact)	territoriality	traversable	its(of it)
treaties	**TRTRLZ**	**TRVRSL**	it's(it is,it has)
trite(overused)	territorialize	traversal	otiose
triter	territorialized	**TRVRTN**	Tass(USSR news)
tritest	territorializing	travertine	toss(throw)
trot(gait),-tted,	**TRTRS**	**TRVST**	tosses
-tting	tartarous	travesty	**TSD**
trout(fish)	traitorous	travestied	outside
try out(v)	traitress	travesties	**TSDD**
tryout(n)	(female)	**TRVT**	two-sided
turret(tower)	**TRTRSS**	trivet	**TSDR**
TRTBL	tartar sauce	**TRWKL**	et cetera(or)
treatable,-ably	**TRTS**	triweekly	etcetera
TRTD	terrazzo	triweeklies	(abbr. etc.)
teratoid	tortoise	**TRWL**	outsider
TRTH	treatise	trowel	**TSDRZ**
troth(marriage)	**TRTSHL**	**TRWMN**	etceteras
truth(true)	tortoiseshell	tirewoman	**TSH**
TRTHFL	**TRTSKZM**	**TRWR**	attaché(person)
truthful	Trotskyism	outerwear	tissue(paper)
TRTHLN	**TRTSRM**	**TRYN**	touché(interj)
triathlon	terza rima	triune	tusche(ink)
TRTHRSN	terze rime(pl)	**TRYZH**	tush(reproof)

B:by **CH**:each **D**:day **F**:if **G**:go **H**:he **HW**:why **J**:joy **K**:cow **KS**:ax **KWL**:equal **L**:all **M**:may **N**:in

tush(slang)
tushes
TSHKS
attaché case
TSHN
outshine
outshone
outshining
titian(brown)
tuition(charge)
TSHP
teashop
TSHPPR
tissue paper
TSHRT
T-shirt
TSK
task(job)
tusk
TSKFRS
task force
TSKMSTR
taskmaster
TSKNN
Toscanini
TSKPK
autoscopic
TSKRTS
outskirts
TSKT
zucchetto
TSKWR
T-square
TSL
outsell
outsold
outsole(shoe)
tassel
tussle(fight)
tussled
tussling
tussler
TSLF
itself
TSLSHN
tessellation
TSLT
tessellate
tessellated
tessellating
TSM
twosome
TSMRT
outsmart
TSMS
tsimmes

TSN
Tucson
TSNGR
zingaro
zingara(f)
TSNM
tsunami
TSP
toss up(v)
tossup(n)
TSPK
outspeak
outspoke
outspoken
TSPKN
outspoken
TSPN
teaspoon
TSPNFL
teaspoonful
TSPRD
outspread
TSPRDNG
outspreading
TSR
tessera
TSRKT
tesseract(four)
TSRS
tsuris
TSRVS
tea service
TST
attest
outset
outstay
tacet(music,
silent)
tacit(not spoken)
taste(tongue)
tasted
tasting
taster
tasty
tastier
tastiest
tastily
tastiness
test(try)
testy
testier
testiest
testily
testiness
toast(bread)
tossed(toss)

toss(throw)
tosses
TSTB
test tube
TSTBD
taste bud
TSTBL
testable
TSTF
testify
testified
testifies
TSTFL
tasteful
TSTFR
testifier
TSTGST
Zeitgeist
TSTKL
testicle
TSTKYLR
testicular
TSTLS
tasteless
TSTMN
testimony
testimonies
TSTMNL
testimonial
TSTMNT
testament
TSTMNTR
testamentary
TSTMSTR
toastmaster
TSTNDNG
outstanding
TSTP
two-step
TSTR
attester
et cetera(or)
etcetera(abbr. etc.)
outstare
outstared
outstaring
taster(tongue)
toaster(bread)
TSTRCH
outstretch
outstretches
TSTRN
taciturn
TSTRNT
taciturnity
TSTRP

outstrip
outstripped
outstripping
TSTRZ
etceteras
TSTS
testacy
testis
testes
TSTSFL
tsetse fly
tsetse flies
TSTSHN
attestation
outstation
TSTSTRN
testosterone
TSTT
testate
TSTTR
testator
TSTYB
test tube
TSZ
outsize
outsized
outsizing
TT
tattoo(skin)
taught(trained)
taut(tight)
teat(nipple)
tight(snug)
tit(bird)
titmouse
tit(teat,breast)
titi(monkey,shrub)
toot(sound)
tot(child)
tote(lug)
toted
toting
tout(praise)
tutti(music)
tutu(skirt)
TTBL
tea-table
TTBRD
tote board
TTD
attitude
TTDLR
teetotaler
TTDNZ
attitudinize
attitudinized

attitudinizing
TTFRT
tutti-frutti
TTFRTT
tit for tat
TTFSTD
tightfisted
TTFTNG
tightfitting
TTH
eightieth
eyetooth
teeth
tooth
teethe(chew)
teethed
teething
tithe(give)
tithed
tithing
tooth
teeth
toothy
toothier
toothiest
toothily
toothiness
TTHBRSH
toothbrush
toothbrushes
TTHK
toothache
TTHNG
tithing
TTHNGK
outthink
outthought
TTHNGRNG
teething ring
TTHPDR
toothpowder
TTHPK
toothpick
TTHPST
toothpaste
TTHR
tether
TTHRBL
tetherball
TTHSM
toothsome
TTHT
outthought
outthink
TTK
tie tack

TTL
tattle(gossip)
tattled
tattling
tattler
title(name)
titled
titling
tittle(mark)
tootle(sound)
tootled
tootling
total(sum)
TTLHLDR
titleholder
TTLJ
tautology
tutelage
TTLJZ
tautologize
tautologized
tautologizing
TTLPT
tight-lipped
TTLR
tattler
tutelary
TTLSHN
titillation
TTLT
titillate(arouse)
titillated
titillating
totality
totalities
TTLTL
tattletale
TTLTRN
totalitarian
TTLTRNZM
totalitarianism
TTLTTL
tittle-tattle
tittle-tattled
tittle-tattling
TTLTV
titillative
TTLZ
totalize
totalized
totalizing
TTLZSHN
totalization
TTLZTR
totalizator
TTM

teatime
tee time(golf)
totem(pole)
totemic
two-time
two-timed
two-timing
two-timer
TTMPL
totem pole
TTMR
two-timer
TTMS
titmouse
titmice
TTN
tauten(taut)
tighten(tight)
Titan(moon)
titan(gigantic)
TTNG
tatting
TTNK
teutonic
titanic
TTNM
titanium
TTNR
tightener
TTNS
tetanus
TTNT
tight knit
TTNZM
Titanism
TTR
tatter(cloth)
tattooer(skin)
teeter(unsteady)
titter(giggle)
totter(sway)
tutor(teacher)
TTRBRD
teeterboard
TTRD
tetrad
tattered(tatter)
TTRDMLN
tatterdemalion
TTRGN
tetragon
TTRHDRN
tetrahedron
tetrahedra(or)
tetrahedrons
TTRKRD

tetracord
TTRL
tetryl(explosive)
tutorial
TTRLJ
tetralogy
tetralogies
TTRP
tightrope
TTRPD
tetrapod
TTRR
titterer
TTRSHN
titration
TTRSKLN
tetracycline
TTRSL
tattersall
TTRT
titrate
titrated
titrating
TTRTTR
teeter-totter
TTS
tights(garment)
toots(person)
tootsy(foot)
tootsies
TTSFL
tsetse fly
tsetse flies
TTSTR
teataster
TTTLR
teetotaler
TTTLZM
teetotalism
TTTT
tête-à-tête
TTVT
titivate
titivated
titivating
TTWD
tightwad
TTZ
tattoos
TV
TV
television
TVs
TVA
Tennessee Valley
Authority

TVBNZ
  out-of-bounds(adj)
TVDNR
  TV dinner
TVDRZ
  out-of-doors
TVDT
  out-of-date
TVKRT
  out-of-court(adj)
TVL
  Tuvalu
TVPKT
  out-of-pocket
TVRN
  tavern
TVT
  outvote
    outvoted
    outvoting
TVTHW
  out-of-the-way
TVTNR
  out-of-towner
TVZM
  atavism
TW
  etui(case)(or)
  etwee
  Ottawa
  outweigh
  two-way
TWCH
  twitch
  twitches
TWD
  tweed
  tweedy
    tweedier
    tweediest
    tweediness
TWDL
  twaddle(talk)
    twaddled
    twaddling
  twiddle(fiddle)
    twiddled
    twiddling
TWDR
  tweeter(loud-
    speaker)
  twitter(chirp)
TWG
  twig(wood)
    twigged
    twigging

twiggy
  twiggier
  twiggiest
TWGN
  tea wagon
TWK
  tweak
TWKST
  twixt
TWL
  toile(linen)
  towel(dry)
  twill(weave)
TWLD
  twilled
TWLFTH
  twelfth
TWLNG
  toweling
TWLT
  toilette
  twilight
TWLV
  twelve
TWLVFLD
  twelvefold
TWN
  Taiwan
  Tijuana
  twain(set of two)
  twin(one of two)
    twinned
    twinning
  twine(cord,
    twist together)
    twined
    twining
TWNG
  twang
TWNGKL
  twinkle
    twinkled
    twinkling
TWNJ
  twinge
    twinged
    twinging
TWNNJND
  twin-engined
TWNSKR
  twin-screw
TWNT
  twenty
    twenties
  twi-night(adj)
TWNTFLD

  twentyfold
TWNTTH
  twentieth
TWNTWN
  twenty-one
TWR
  outwear
  outwore
  outworn
  tower
TWRD
  outward
  toward
TWRK
  outwork
TWRKR
  autoworker
TWRL
  twirl
TWRLR
  twirler
TWRP
  twerp
TWS
  twice
TWST
  twist
TWSTLD
  twice-told
TWSTR
  twister
TWT
  outwit
    outwitted
    outwitting
  tweet(chirp)
  twit(tease)
    twitted
    twitting
TWTR
  tweeter(loud-
    speaker)
  twitter(chirp)
TWTRR
  twitterer
TWZ
  'twas(it was)
  tweeze
    tweezed
    tweezing
  tweezer
TWZR
  tweezer(plucker)
TY
  chiao(China)
TYB

tube
  tubed
  tubing
TYBKYLN
  tuberculin
TYBL
  tubal(tube)
TYBLSTR
  tubeless tire
TYBNG
  tubing
TYBR
  tuber(potato)
TYBRKL
  tubercle
TYBRKYLR
  tubercular
TYBRKYLS
  tuberculous
TYBRKYLSS
  tuberculosis
TYBRS
  tuberous
TYBRZ
  tuberose
TYBYLR
  tubular(tube)
TYBYLS
  tubulous
TYDR
  tutor(teacher)
  Tudor
TYKWKW
  tu quoque
TYLP
  tulip
TYLPTR
  tulip tree
TYLRM
  tularemia
TYMD
  tumid
TYMF
  tumefy
    tumefied
    tumefies
TYMLCHS
  tumultuous
TYMLT
  tumult
TYMR
  tumor
TYMRS
  tumorous
TYMYLS
  tumulose

NGK:ink **P**:pie **R**:air **S**:ice **SH**:show **T**:toy **THN**:thin **TH**:the **V**:of **W**:we **Y**:you **Z**:is **VZHN**:vision

TYN
attune
attuned
attuning
tuna(fish)
tuna
tune
tuned
tuning
tuner
TYNBL
tunable
TYNFL
tuneful
TYNK
tunic
TYNLS
tuneless
TYNNGFRK
tuning fork
TYNP
tune up(v)
tune-up(n,adj)
TYNR
tuner
TYNS
Tunis
TYNSH
Tunisia
TYNZH
Tunisia
TYPL
tupelo
TYRN
tureen
Turin
TYSHN
tuition
TYTLJ
tutelage
TYTLR
tutelary
TYTNK
teutonic
TYTR
tutor
TYTRL
tutorial
TYZD
Tuesday
TZ
tease
teased
teasing
'tis(it is)
tizzy

tizzies
TZD
Tuesday
TZH
taj
TZHMHL
Taj Mahal
TZK
phthisic
TZKN
zucchini
TZL
teasel
tousle(rumple)
tousled
tousling
TZM
autism
Taoism
TZMN
Tasmania
TZMNS
Tasman Sea
TZMNY
Tasmania
TZN
ptisan(barley)
tisane(herb)
TZR
teaser
TZZ
tizzies
tizzy

V

avow(confess)
eave
(roof,edge)
eve(time)(or)
Eve
I've(I have)
ivy(plant)
ivies
of
ova
ovum
via(way)
vie(strive)
vied
vying
vow(oath)

VBL
viable
VBLT
viability
VBRD
vibrato
VBRFN
vibraphone
VBRNT
vibrant
VBRSHN
vibration
VBRT
vibrate(shake)
vibrated
vibrating
vibrato(music)
VBRTR
vibrator
vibratory
VBZ
vibes
VCH
vouch
vouches
VCHF
VHF
very high
frequency
VCHR
voucher
VCHSF
vouchsafe
vouchsafed
vouchsafing
VD
avid(eager)
avoid(shun)
avowed(confessed)
evade(escape)
evaded
evading
ivied(ivy)
ovoid(egg)
VD
veneral disease
Veda
V-E Day
vide(example)
vied(vie)
video(TV)
vita(outline)
vitae
void(empty)
voodoo
VDBL

avoidable
avoidably
voidable
voidably
VDK
Vedic
vodka
VDKN
vidicon
VDKNSD
Vatican City
VDKNST
Vatican City
VDKT
viaduct
VDL
avowedly
ovoidal(egg)
vital(essential)
VDNCHL
evidential
VDNS
avoidance
evidence(data,
prove)
evidenced
evidencing
VDNSHL
evidential
VDNT
evident
Vedanta
VDR
voter
vote
VDT
avidity
vedette
VDTP
video tape
videotape(v)
videotaped
videotaping
VDVL
vaudeville
VDVLYN
vaudevillian
VDZM
voodooism
VG
vague(not clear)
Vega
vogue(style)
VGBND
vagabond
VGL

vaguely
VGNR
Wagner
VGNRN
Wagnerian
VGR
vigor, (B)vigour
vagary
vagaries
VGRNS
vagrancy
vagrancies
VGRNT
vagrant
VGRS
vagarious
vigoroso
vigorous
VHKL
vehicle
VHKYLR
vehicular
VHMNT
vehement
VJ
voyage
voyaged
voyaging
voyager
VJD
V-J Day
VJL
vigil
VJLNS
vigilance
VJLNT
vigilant
vigilante(person)
VJLT
vagility
VJN
vagina
vaginas(or)
vaginae
VJNL
vaginal
VJR
voyager
VJTBL
vegetable
VJTL
vegetal
VJTRN
vegetarian
VJTSHN
vegetation

VJTT
vegetate
vegetated
vegetating
VJTTV
vegetative
VJZ
veggies(pl)(slang)
vegetables
VK
evoke
evoked
evoking
VKBL
evokable(inspire)
vocable(word)
VKBYLR
vocabulary
vocabularies
VKD
avocado
VKL
vehicle
vocal
VKLKRD
vocal cord
VKLST
vocalist
VKLZ
vocalize
vocalized
vocalizing
VKLZM
vocalism
VKLZSHN
vocalization
VKN
vicuña(animal)
VKNG
viking(or)
Viking
VKNS
vacancy
vacancies
VKNT
vacant
viscount
VKNTS
viscountess
VKNY
vicuña(animal)
VKR
vaquero
vicar
VKRJ
vicarage

VKRL
vicarial
VKRS
vicarious
VKS
vex
vexes
vexation
VKSHN
avocation(hobby)
eviction(expel)
evocation(calling)
vacation(time)
vocation(job)
VKSHNL
vocational
VKSN
vaccine
vixen
VKSNSHN
vaccination
VKSNT
vaccinate
vaccinated
vaccinating
VKSSHN
vexation
VKSSHS
vexatious
VKT
evict(kick out)
vacate(get out)
vacated
vacating
VKTM
victim
VKTMZ
victimize
victimized
victimizing
victimization
VKTR
victor(winner)
Victoria
victoria(car)
victory(win)
victories
VKTRL
vectorial
Victrola
(trademark)
VKTRN
Victorian
VKTRS
victorious
VKTV

evocative
VKY
evacuee
VKYM
vacuum
vacuums(or)
vacua
VKYN
vicuña(animal)
VKYS
vacuous
VKYSHN
evacuation
VKYT
evacuate
evacuated
evacuating
vacuity
vacuities
VL
avail(assist)
avowal(confess)
evil(bad)
evil eye
oval(shape)
vail(to lower)
vale(valley)
valet(person)
valley(place)
veal(meat)
veil(screen)
vial(bottle)
vile(evil)
viler
vilest
villa(house)
viol(instrument)
viola(violin)
voile(fabric)
vole(rodent)
vole(cards)
voled
voling
volley(shot)
vowel(sound)
VLBL
available
violable
volleyball
VLCHR
vulture
VLCHRN
vulturine
VLCHRS
vulturous
VLD

---

valid	volcanic	voluntary	volution
VLDKSHN	**VLKNLJ**	**VLNTRL**	**VLTJ**
valediction	volcanology	voluntarily	voltage
VLDKTR	**VLKNZ**	**VLNTRSTK**	**VLTK**
valedictory	vulcanize	voluntaristic	villatic(rural)
VLDKTRN	vulcanized	**VLPCHR**	voltaic
valedictorian	vulcanizing	voluptuary	**VLTL**
VLDR	**VLKNZSHN**	voluptuaries	volatile
evildoer	vulcanization	**VLPCHS**	**VLTLT**
VLDSHN	**VLM**	voluptuous	volatility
validation	Valium(trademark)	**VLPLN**	**VLTMPR**
VLDT	diazepam	volplane	volt-ampere
validate	vellum	**VLPN**	**VLTMTR**
validated	**VLMNDD**	vulpine	voltammeter
validating	evil-minded	**VLR**	(current)
validity	**VLMNS**	valor(bravery)(B)-lour	voltmeter(volts)
validities	voluminous	velour(cloth)	**VLTNS**
VLF	**VLMTR**	volar(foot,hand)	velutinous
vilify	volumeter	**VLRZ**	**VLTNT**
vilified	**VLN**	valorize	volitant
vilifies	villain(evil one)	valorized	**VLTR**
VLFKSHN	villainy	valorizing	violator
vilification	villainies	**VLRZSHN**	**VLTSHMRTS**
VLFR	villein(serf)	valorization	Weltschmerz
vilifier	violin(music)	**VLS**	**VLTV**
VLFS	**VLNCH**	valise	volitive
Oval Office	avalanche	**VLSHN**	**VLV**
VLG	**VLNCHL**	evolution(change)	evolve(change)
Ivy League	violoncello	violation	evolved
Volga	**VLNG**	(transgress)	evolving
VLGR	veiling	volition(will)	valve(device)
vulgar	**VLNRBL**	volution(turn)	vulva
VLGRN	vulnerable	**VLSHNR**	vulvae
vulgarian	vulnerably	evolutionary	**VLVL**
VLGRT	**VLNRBLT**	**VLSHNST**	vulval
vulgarity	vulnerability	evolutionist	**VLVN**
vulgarities	vulnerabilities	**VLSPD**	vol-au-vent(pastry)
VLGRZ	**VLNRR**	velocipede	**VLVT**
vulgarize	vulnerary	**VLST**	velvet(cloth)
vulgarized	**VLNS**	velocity(speed)	velvety
vulgarizing	valance(drapery)	velocities	velvetiness
VLGRZM	valence(chemistry)	violist(music)	**VLVTN**
vulgarism	valency	**VLT**	velveteen
VLGT	valencies	valet(person)	**VLVYL**
Vulgate(Bible)	villainous(evil)	vault(safe)	valvule
vulgate(vernacular)	violence(force)	velleity(wish)	**VLVYLR**
VLJ	**VLNST**	velleities	valvular
village	violinist	velouté(sauce)	**VLVYLS**
VLJR	**VLNT**	violate(transgress)	volvulus
villager	violent(force)	violated	**VLY**
VLKN	volant(agile,	violating	value
volcano	flying)	violator	valued
volcanoes(or)	**VLNTN**	violet(color)	valuing
volcanos	valentine	volt(unit)	**VLYBL**
vulcan	**VLNTR**	volute(spiral)	valuable(worth)
VLKNK	volunteer	(or)voluted	voluble(fluent)

volubly
VLYBLT
volubility
VLYLS
valueless
VLYM
Valium(trademark)
diazepam
volume
VLYMTRK
volumetric
VLYNT
valiant
VLYSHN
evaluation
valuation
VLYT
evaluate
evaluated
evaluating
evaluator
VLZ
vowelize
vowelized
vowelizing
VM
ovum
ova
vim
VMNS
vehemence
VMNT
vehement
VMP
vamp
VMPR
vampire
VMS
vamoose
vamoosed
vamoosing
VMT
vomit
VMTR
vomitory
VN
avenue(street)
avian(birds)
even(same)
oven(cook)
ovine(sheep)
vain(futile,
conceited)
van(vehicle)
vane(blade)
vein(blood,

streak)
Vienna
vina(music)
vine(plant)
vino(wine)
viny
vinier
viniest
VNCHL
eventual
VNCHLT
eventuality
eventualities
VNCHR
venture
ventured
venturing
VNCHRS
venturous
VNCHRSM
venturesome
VNCHT
eventuate
eventuated
eventuating
VND
vend(sell)
vendee(buyer)
vendor(seller)
vendue(auction)
viand(food)
VNDD
vendetta
VNDK
Vandyke
venatic(hunting)
VNDKSHN
vindication
VNDKT
vindicate
vindicated
vindicating
VNDKTR
vindicator
VNDKTV
vindictive
VNDL
vandal
VNDLZ
vandalize
vandalized
vandalizing
VNDLZM
vandalism
VNDR
vendor(seller)

VNDT
vendetta
VNDY
vendue
VNG
van Gogh
vying(vie)
VNGKWSH
vanquish
vanquishes
VNGKYLM
vinculum
vincula
VNGKYLR
avuncular
VNGLR
vainglory
vainglories
VNGLRS
vainglorious
VNGR
vinegar
VNGRD
vanguard
VNGRT
vinaigrette
VNHNDD
evenhanded
VNJ
avenge(pay back)
avenged
avenging
avenger
venge(avenge)
venged
venging
VNJFL
vengeful
VNJLK
evangelic
VNJLKL
evangelical
VNJLST
evangelist
VNJLSTK
evangelistic
evangelistically
VNJLZ
evangelize
evangelized
evangelizing
VNJLZM
evangelism
VNJLZSHN
evangelization
VNJNS

vengeance
VNJR
avenger
VNK
V-neck
VNKLCHR
viniculture
VNKS
avionics
VNKVR
Vancouver
VNKWSH
vanquish
vanquishes
VNKYLR
vernacular
VNL
vanilla(flavor)
venal(corrupt)
venial(easily
excused)
vinyl(material)
VNLDR
ventilator
VNLT
venality
venalities
VNLTR
ventilator
VNM
venom
VNMS
venomous
VNNG
evening
VNR
veneer(layer)
venery(hunt)
vinery(vines)
vineries
VNRBL
venerable
VNRDNR
vin ordinaire
VNRL
venereal
VNRLDZS
venereal disease
VD
VNRSHN
veneration
VNRT
venerate
venerated
venerating
VNS

evanesce(fade)
evanesced
evanescing
evenness(same)
evince(to show)
evinced
evincing
Venice
venous(vein)
Venus
vinasse(residue)
vinous(wine)
VNSBL
evincible(show)
vincible
(defeatable)
VNSH
vanish
vanishes
VNSHN
Venetian
VNSHNBLNZ
Venetian blinds
(trademark)
VNSN
venison
VNSNMSF
Vinson Massif
VNSNS
evanescence
VNSNT
evanescent
VNSTVN
even-steven
VNT
event
vanity
vanities
vaunt(brag)
vent(exit)
VNTD
eventide
VNTFL
eventful
VNTGRD
avant-garde
VNTJ
vantage(position)
ventage(vent)
vintage(wine)
VNTK
venatic(hunting)
VNTLSHN
ventilation
VNTLT
ventilate

ventilated
ventilating
VNTLTR
ventilator
VNTMPRD
even-tempered
VNTNR
vintner
VNTRKL
ventricle
VNTRLKWST
ventriloquist
VNTRLKWZM
ventriloquism
VNY
avenue(street)
venue
VNYRD
vineyard
VNYT
vignette
VNYTR
vignetter
VNYZHN
Venusian
VNZHN
Venusian
VNZWL
Venezuela
VP
veep(slang)
vice president
VIP
VIPs
VPD
vapid
VPR
vapor(gas), (B)-pour
viper(snake)
VPRLK
vapor lock
VPRS
oviparous
vaporous(gas)
viperous(snake)
VPRSH
vaporish
VPRSHN
evaporation
VPRT
evaporate
evaporated
evaporating
VPRZ
vaporize
vaporized

vaporizing
VPRZR
vaporizer
VPRZSHN
vaporization
VR
aver(affirm)
averred
averring
aviary(birds)
aviaries
ever(always)
every(each)
ivory(tusk)
ivories
ovary(gland)
ovaries
over(above)
overawe
overawed
overawing
vary(change)
varied
varies
veer(turn)
very(truly)
verier
veriest
verily
VRB
verb
VRBD
overbid
overbid
overbidding
everybody
VRBDM
verbatim
VRBJ
verbiage
VRBL
variable
variably
verbal
VRBLNS
overbalance
overbalanced
overbalancing
VRBLZ
overblouse
verbalize
verbalized
verbalizing
VRBLZM
verbalism
VRBLZSHN

verbalization
VRBN
verbena
VRBR
overbear
overbore
overborne
VRBRD
overboard
VRBRNG
overbearing
VRBS
verbose
VRBST
verbosity
VRBT
overbite
VRBTM
verbatim
VRBTN
verboten
VRCH
overreach
overreaches
virtue
VRCHL
virtual
VRCHR
overture
VRCHRJ
overcharge
overcharged
overcharging
VRCHS
virtuoso
virtuosos(or)
virtuosi
virtuous
VRCHST
virtuosity
VRD
everyday(daily,adj)
every day(n)
overdo
overdid
overdone
overdue(late)
override
overrode
overriding
overridden
VRDG
vertigo
VRDGRS
verdigris
VRDKT

B:by **CH**:each **D**:day **F**:if **G**:go **H**:he **HW**:why **J**:joy **K**:cow **KS**:ax **KWL**:equal **L**:all **M**:may **N**:in

verdict
VRDNT
verdant
VRDPZ
avoirdupois
VRDR
overdraw
overdrew
overdrawn
VRDRFT
overdraft
VRDRS
overdress
overdresses
VRDRV
overdrive
VRDS
overdose
overdosed
overdosing
VRDY
overdue
VRF
verify
verified
verifies
VRFBL
verifiable
verifiably
VRFKSHN
verification
VRFL
overflow
overfly
overflies
overflew
overflown
VRFLT
overflight
VRG
virago
Virgo
VRGLD
everglade
VRGLDZ
Everglades
VRGLZ
overglaze
VRGR
overgrow
overgrew
overgrown
VRGRMNT
overgarment
VRGRN
evergreen

overgrown
VRGSHN
variegation
VRGT
variegate
variegated
variegating
VRGYL
virgule
VRGZRSHN
overexertion
VRGZRT
overexert
VRHD
overhead
VRHL
overhaul
VRHND
overhand
VRHNG
overhang
overhung
VRHNGNG
overhanging
VRHR
overhear
overheard
VRHT
overheat
VRHWLM
overwhelm
VRHWR
everywhere
VRJ
average(normal)
averaged
averaging
overage
overjoy
verge
verged
verging
VRJN
virgin
VRJNL
virginal
VRJNLNDZ
Virgin Islands
VRJNT
virginity
VRJNY
Virginia
VRJR
verdure(green)
verger(person)
VRKLRD

varicolored
VRKM
overcome
overcame
overcoming
VRKMPNST
overcompensate
overcompensated
overcompensating
overcompensation
VRKNFDNT
overconfident
overconfidence
VRKPTLZ
overcapitalize
overcapitalized
overcapitalizing
overcapitali-
zation
VRKRZ
Veracruz
VRKS
varicose
varix
VRKSPZ
overexpose
overexposed
overexposing
VRKSPZHR
overexposure
VRKST
Ivory Coast
overcast
VRKSTND
overextend
VRKT
overcoat
VRKTM
varicotomy
VRL
overall
overlay
overlaid
(superimposing)
overlie(rest on)
overlay
overlain
overrule
overruled
overruling
verily(in truth)
viral(virus)
virile(vigor)
VRLD
overload
VRLDN

overladen
VRLJ
virology
VRLJST
virologist
VRLK
overlook
VRLP
overlap
overlapped
overlapping
overleap
VRLS
overalls
VRLSTNG
everlasting
VRLT
virility
VRLZ
overalls
VRM
vroom(interj)
VRMCHL
vermicelli
VRMFRM
vermiform
VRMFYJ
vermifuge
VRMKYLR
vermicular
VRMKYLT
vermiculite
VRMLYN
vermilion
VRMN
vermin
VRMNT
averment
varmint
Vermont
VRMR
evermore
VRMSD
vermicide
VRMT
varmint
VRMTH
vermouth
VRMTR
variometer
VRN
ovarian
overrun
overran
overrunning
VRND

veranda
VRNDLJ
  overindulge
    overindulged
    overindulging
VRNDLJNS
  overindulgence
VRNDLJNT
  overindulgent
VRNK
  veronica
VRNKYLR
  vernacular
VRNL
  vernal
VRNR
  vernier
VRNS
  overnice
  variance
VRNSH
  varnish
  varnishes
VRNT
  overnight
  variant
VRP
  overpay
  overpaid
VRPPYLT
  overpopulate
    overpopulated
    overpopulating
    overpopulation
VRPR
  overpower
VRPRDS
  overproduce
    overproduced
    overproducing
    overproduction
VRPRDYS
  overproduce
    overproduced
    overproducing
    overproduction
VRPRTKT
  overprotect
  overprotection
VRPS
  overpass
  overpasses
VRPWR
  overpower
VRRM
  variorum

VRS
  avarice(greed)
  averse(opposed)
  oversee
    oversaw
    overseen
    overseer
  various(several)
  Versailles
  verse(words)
    versed
    versing
  verso(page)
  virus(disease)
VRSBSKRB
  oversubscribe
    oversubscribed
    oversubscribing
VRSF
  versify
    versifies
    versified
VRSFKSHN
  versification
VRSH
  overissue
    overissued
    overissuing
  overshoe
VRSHD
  overshadow
VRSHLV
  Voroshilov
VRSHN
  aversion
  variation
  version
VRSHS
  avaricious(greedy)
  veracious(truthful)
  voracious(ravenous)
VRSHT
  overshoot
    overshot
VRSHZ
  overshoes
VRSKRT
  overskirt
VRSKST
  oversexed
VRSL
  oversell
    oversold
VRSLP
  oversleep
    overslept

VRSMLTD
  verisimilitude
VRSMLTYD
  verisimilitude
VRSMPLF
  oversimplify
    oversimplified
    oversimplifies
VRSMPLFKSHN
  oversimplification
VRSNG
  overseeing
VRSNS
  virescence
VRSPL
  oversupply
    oversupplied
    oversupplies
VRSPND
  overspend
    overspent
VRSPNDNG
  overspending
VRSPRD
  overspread
    overspread
VRSR
  overseer
VRSS
  verses(poetry)
  versus
  vs.
VRST
  oversight
  overstay
  varsity
    varsities
  veracity(truth)
    veracities
  voracity(ravenous)
VRSTF
  overstuff
VRSTK
  overstock
VRSTL
  versatile
VRSTLT
  versatility
    versatilities
VRSTMT
  overestimate
    overestimated
    overestimating
    overestimation
VRSTP
  overstep

    overstepped
    overstepping
VRSTRNG
  overstrung
VRSTT
  overstate
    overstated
    overstating
VRSTTMNT
  overstatement
VRSZ
  overseas
  oversize
    oversized
    oversizing
VRT
  avert(turn away)
  evert(turn inside
    out)
  overrate
    overrated
    overrating
  overt(open)
  overwrite
    overwrote
    overwriting
    overwritten
  overwrought(strain)
  variety(diverse)
    varieties
  verity(correct)
  virtu(arts)
VRTBL
  avertible
    avertedly(adv)
  veritable
  veritably
VRTBR
  vertebra
    vertebras(or)
    vertebrae
VRTBRL
  vertebral
VRTBRT
  vertebrate
VRTG
  vertigo
VRTHKNTR
  over-the-counter
VRTHNG
  everything
VRTHR
  overthrow
    overthrew
    overthrown
VRTJNS

---

vertiginous
(revolve)
vortiginous
(whirling)
VRTK
overtake
overtook
overtaking
overtaken
VRTKL
vertical
VRTKN
overtaken
overtake
VRTKS
overtax
overtaxes
vertex(apex)
vertexes(or)
vertices
vortex(whirlpool)
vortexes(or)
vortices
VRTL
varietal
VRTM
overtime
VRTN
overtone
VRTSZ
vortices
vortex
VRV
varve(layer)
verve(energy)
VRVLY
overvalue
overvalued
overvaluing
VRVY
overview
VRWLM
overwhelm
VRWN
everyone(each one)
every one(all)
overween
VRWND
overwind
overwound
VRWNNG
overweening
VRWR
everywhere
VRWRK
overwork

VRWT
overweight
VRYLNS
virulence
VRYLNT
virulent
VRYS
overuse(n)
VRYZ
overuse
-used,-using
VRZ
ivories
ivory
VRZHN
aversion
version
VRZM
verism
VS
vase(vessel)
vice(evil conduct)
visa(passport)
vise(clamp)
vised
vising
voice(utter)
voiced
voicing
VSBKS
voice box
VSCHNSLR
vice chancellor
VSCHRMN
vice chairman
VSD
viscid
VSDFRNZ
vas deferens
VSDRP
eavesdrop(listen)
-dropped,-dropping
VSFRS
vociferous
VSFRSHN
vociferation
VSFRT
vociferate
vociferated
vociferating
VSHBL
vitiable
VSHN
aviation
ovation
Vishnu

VSHS
vicious
VSHSHN
vitiation
VSHSRKL
vicious circle
VSHSWZ
vichyssoise
VSHT
vitiate
vitiated
vitiating
VSHTR
vitiator
VSKL
vesicle
VSKNSL
vice consul
VSKNT
vesicant
VSKS
viscous
VSKST
viscosity
viscosities
VSKT
vesicate
vesicated
vesicating
VSKTM
vasectomy
vasectomies
VSKWD
vice squad
VSKYLR
vascular
VSL
vassal(person)
vessel(ship,
container)
Vaseline
(trademark)
VSLS
voiceless
VSLSHN
vacillation
VSLT
vacillate
vacillated
vacillating
VSLTR
vacillator
VSNS
vastness
VSNT

vicinity
vicinities
VSPR
vesper
VSPRNT
voiceprint
VSPRZ
vespers
VSPRZDNT
vice president
VSR
viceroy
viscera
VSRGL
viceregal
VSRL
visceral
VSRN
vicereine
VSRSHN
evisceration
VSRT
eviscerate
eviscerated
eviscerating
VSSTD
vicissitude
VSSTYD
vicissitude
VST
avast(interj)
vast(big)
vest(garment)
vista(view)
voiced(speech)
VSTBYL
vestibule
VSTD
vested
VSTJ
vestige
VSTJL
vestigial
VSTL
vestal
VSTMNT
vestment
VSTNS
vastness
VSTPKT
vest-pocket
VSTR
vestry
vestries
VSV
evasive

vis-à-vis
VSVRS
  vice versa
VSWR
  voussoir
VT
  V-8(engine)
  vat(tub)
    vatted
    vatting
  vet
    veteran
  veto(reject)
    vetoes
    vetoed
    vetoing
  vette
    Corvette
    (trademark)
  vita(outline)
    vitae
  vote(ballot)
    voted
    voting
    voter
VTBL
  evitable
  votable
VTDD
  vat-dyed
VTGTR
  vote-getter
VTKN
  Vatican
VTKNST
  Vatican City
VTL
  vital
VTLT
  vitality
    vitalities
VTLZ
  vitalize
    vitalized
    vitalizing
    vitalization
VTMN
  vitamin
VTNM
  Vietnam
VTNMZ
  Vietnamese
VTNRN
  veterinarian
VTPRSHN
  vituperation

VTPRT
  vituperate
    vituperated
    vituperating
VTR
  avatar(archetype)
  aviator(pilot)
  votary(vow)
    votaries
VTRF
  vitrify
    vitrified
    vitrifies
VTRFBL
  vitrifiable
VTRFKSHN
  vitrification
VTRL
  vitriol
VTRLK
  vitriolic
VTRN
  veteran
VTRNR
  veterinary
VTRNRN
  veterinarian
VTRS
  vitreous
VTRST
  votarist
VTV
  votive
VTYPRSHN
  vituperation
VTYPRT
  vituperate
    vituperated
    vituperating
VV
  vive
VVCH
  vivace
VVD
  vivid
VVF
  vivify
    vivified
    vivifies
    vivifier
VVFKSHN
  vivification
VVFR
  vivifier
VVPRS
  viviparous

VVSHS
  vivacious
VVSKSHN
  vivisection
VVSKT
  vivisect
VVST
  vivacity
VVVS
  viva voce
VWL
  voilá(there it is)
  vowel(sound)
VWNS
  Walesa,Lech
VWRDPW
  avoirdupois
VWRDR
  voir dire
VWSLST
  voix céleste
VWYR
  voyeur
VWYRZM
  voyeurism
VWYZHR
  voyageur
VY
  view
  viewy
    viewier
    viewiest
  Villa(Pancho)
VYL
  ovule
VYLSHN
  ovulation
VYLT
  ovulate
    ovulated
    ovulating
VYNTYN
  Vientiane
VYPNT
  viewpoint
VYR
  viewer
  voyeur
VYRZM
  voyeurism
    voyeuristic
    voyeuristically
VZ
  eaves
  vase(vessel)
  visa(passport)

VZBL
  visible
  visibly
VZBLT
  visibility
VZDRP
  eavesdrop
    eavesdropped
    eavesdropping
    eavesdropper
VZHL
  visual
VZHLD
  visual aid
VZHLZ
  visualize
    visualized
    visualizing
    visualization
VZHN
  evasion(elude)
  vision
VZHNR
  visionary
    visionaries
VZJ
  visage
VZR
  visor
VZRD
  vizard
VZT
  visit
VZTNG
  visiting
VZTNT
  visitant
VZTR
  visitor
VZTSHN
  visitation
VZV
  vis-à-vis

W

away
aweigh (nautical)
Hawaii
Iowa
way(manner,route)
  ways

B:by **CH**:each **D**:day **F**:if **G**:go **H**:he **HW**:why **J**:joy **K**:cow **KS**:ax **KWL**:equal **L**:all **M**:may **N**:in

we(us)
wee(small)
weer
weest
weigh(weight)
whew(interj)
whey(milk)
whoa(stop)
why(cause)
woe(grief)
woo(seek)
wow(wonder)
wye(the
   letter y)
WB
web
   webbed
   webbing
WBFT
webfoot
webfeet
WBFTD
web-footed
WBGN
woebegone
WBL
waybill(document)
wobble(move)
   wobbled
   wobbling
wobbly(adj)
   wobblier
   wobbliest
WBNG
webbing
WBPRS
web press
WBR
weber
WCH
watch(time,look)
   watches
which(what one)
witch(person)
   witches
WCHBND
watchband
WCHDG
watchdog
WCHDKTR
witch doctor
WCHFL
watchful
WCHFR
watch fire
WCHHNT

witch hunt
WCHHZL
witch hazel
WCHKP
watch cap
WCHKRFT
witchcraft
WCHKS
watchcase
WCHMKLT
whatchamacallit
WCHMKR
watchmaker
WCHMN
watchman
watchmen
WCHNG
witching
WCHNT
watch night
WCHR
watcher(eyes)
witchery(magic)
   witcheries
WCHT
Wichita
WCHTR
watchtower
WCHTWR
watchtower
WCHVR
whichever
WCHWRD
watchword
WCHZBRM
witches'-broom
WD
wad(lump)
   wadded
   wadding
waddy(stick)
wade(walk in
   water)
   waded
   wading
   wader
wadi(gully)
   wadis
we'd(we
   would)
wed(marry)
   wedded(or)
   wed
   wedding
weed(plant)
weedy(adj)

weedier
weediest
weediness
weighty(heavy)
weightier
weightiest
weightily
weightiness
whitey(slang)
whydah(bird)
wide(broad)
wider
widest
widen
widow(woman)
witty(smart)
wittier
wittiest
wittily
wittiness
witticism
wood(tree)
woody
woodier
woodiest
would(will)
WDB
would-be
WDCHK
woodchuck
WDD
wide-eyed
wooded(trees)
WDKRFT
woodcraft
WDKRVNG
woodcarving
WDKT
woodcut
WDL
waddle(walk)
   waddled
   waddling
wheedle(persuade)
   wheedled
   wheedling
whittle(carve)
   whittled
   whittling
   whittler
WDLK
wedlock
WDLND
woodland
WDN
widen(wide)

wooden(wood)
WDNG
wadding(lump)
wedding(marry)
whiting
   (coloring, fish)
WDNGL
wide-angle
WDNNDN
wooden Indian
WDNT
wouldn't
   (would not)
WDPKR
woodpecker
WDPL
woodpile
WDPLP
wood pulp
WDPN
wide-open
WDR
wader(water)
wade
waiter(food)
water(liquid)
watery(adj)
   waterier
   wateriest
   wateriness
weeder(tool)
widower(man)
WDRB
water boy
WDRBFL
water buffalo
WDRBG
water bug
WDRBK
waterbuck
WDRBRN
waterborne
WDRCHSNT
water chestnut
WDRCHSTNT
water chestnut
WDRD
watered
water
WDRFL
waterfall(water)
waterfowl(bird)
WDRFRNT
waterfront
WDRGJ
water gauge

WDRGLS
water glass
  water glasses
WDRGT
  Watergate
WDRHL
  water hole
WDRHWL
  water wheel
WDRJ
  waterage
WDRKLD
  water-cooled
WDRKLR
  water color(paint)
  water cooler(thirst)
WDRKLZT
  water closet
WDRKRFT
  watercraft
WDRKRS
  watercourse
    (channel)
  watercress(food)
WDRL
  Waterloo
WDRLG
  waterlog
    waterlogged
    waterlogging
WDRLL
  water lily
    water lilies
WDRLN
  waterline
WDRLS
  waterless
WDRLVL
  water level
WDRMKSN
  water moccasin
WDRMLN
  watermelon
WDRMRK
  watermark
WDRMTR
  water meter
WDRNS
  wateriness
  watery
WDRPL
  water polo
WDRPLNT
  water-repellent
WDRPP
  water pipe

WDRPR
  water power
WDRPRF
  waterproof
WDRPRFNG
  waterproofing
WDRPRFT
  waterproofed
WDRPWR
  water power
WDRSD
  waterside
WDRSFR
  water sapphire
WDRSH
  waterish
WDRSHD
  watershed
WDRSK
  water-sick(illness)
  water-ski(sport)
    water-skied
    water-skiing
    water-skis
    water-skier
  water-soak
    (full of water)
WDRSKL
  water cycle
    (ecology)
WDRSKP
  waterscape
WDRSKR
  water-skier
WDRSKZ
  water-skis
WDRSLD
  waterslide
WDRSLYBL
  water-soluble
WDRSNK
  water snake
WDRSPNYL
  water spaniel
WDRSPT
  waterspout
WDRT
  water right
WDRTBL
  water table
WDRTNGK
  water tank
WDRTR
  water tower
WDRTT
  watertight

WDRTWR
  water tower
WDRVPR
  water vapor
WDRW
  waterway
WDRWCH
  water witch(finder)
WDRWL
  water wheel
WDRWNGZ
  water wings
WDRWRKS
  waterworks
WDRWRN
  waterworn
WDRZSTNT
  water-resistant
WDSHD
  woodshed
WDSPRD
  widespread
WDSZM
  witticism
WDTH
  width
WDWK
  wide-awake
WDWND
  woodwind
WDWR
  widower
WDWRK
  woodwork
WDZ
  woods(forest)
  woodsy(adj)
    woodsier
    woodsiest
WDZMN
  woodsman
    woodsmen(pl)
WDZPK
  widow's peak
WDZWK
  widow's walk
WF
  WAF(Woman's Air
    Force)
  waff(wave)
  waif(homeless)
  whiff(n,v)(air)
  wife(mate)
    wives
  wolf(animal)
  woof(fabric)

  warp
  weft
WFHND
  wolfhound
WFK
  wee folk(small)
WFL
  waffle(n,v)(words)
    waffled
    waffling
  whiffle(air)
    whiffled
    whiffling
  wifely(wife)
  woeful(full of woe)
WFLRN
  waffle iron
WFLTR
  whiffletree
WFPK
  wolf pack
WFR
  wafer(food)
  woofer(sound)
WFRNG
  wayfaring
WFRR
  wayfarer
WFT
  waft(n,v)(air)
  weft(thread)
WFTJ
  waftage
WG
  wag(swing)
    wagged
    wagging
  wig(hair)
    wigged
    wigging
WGD
  wigged
WGL
  waggle(move a
    part)
    waggled
    waggling
  wiggle(short
    motions)
    wiggled
    wiggling
    wiggler
  wiggly(adj)
    wigglier
    wiggliest
WGLR

wiggler(n)
WGLT
wiglet
WGN
wagon(vehicle)
wigan(fabric)
WGNLD
wagonload
WGNSTN
Wittgenstein
Ludwig
WGR
waggery
waggeries
WGSH
waggish
WGWG
wigwag
wigwagged
wigwagging
WGWM
wigwam
WH
Oahu(island)
wahoo(fish, plant)
WHN
wahine(woman)
WJ
Ouija(board)
(trademark)
wage(engage in)
waged
waging
wage(pay)
wedge(tool)
wedged
wedging
wedgie(shoe)
WJBRD
Ouija board
(trademark)
WJN
widgeon
WJR
wager
WJRNR
wage earner
WJT
widget
WJWD
Wedgwood
WK
awake(not asleep)
awoke
awaking
awaken

Wac(person)
WAC(Woman's
Army Corps)
wacky(crazy)
wackier
wackiest
wackily
wackiness
wake(sleep)
woke(or)
waked
waking
woken(or)
wake
walk(move)
weak(power)
week(time)
whack(strike)
wick(candle)
wok(pan)
WKD
weekday(time)
wicked(evil)
WKFL
wakeful
WKL
weakly(power)
weaklier
weakliest
weekly(time)
weeklies
WKLND
Wake Island
WKLNG
weakling
(strength)
week-long(adj)
WKLS
wakeless
WKLZ
weeklies
WKMNDD
weak-minded
WKN
awaken
awake
waken
wake
walk-in(n,adj)
walk-on(n,adj)
weaken(power)
WKND
weak-kneed
weekend(time)
WKNG
whacking

WKNGPPRZ
walking papers
WKNGSTK
walking stick
WKNNG
awakening
WKNS
eyewitness
eyewitnesses
weakness(power)
witness
witnesses
WKNSTND
witness stand
WKP
walkup(n,adj)
wickiup
WKR
weaker(power)
wicker
WKRMSM
Y-chromosome
WKRWRK
wickerwork
WKS
wax
waxes
waxy
waxier
waxiest
waxiness
WKSN
waxen
WKSSTR
weak sister
WKST
weakest
WKSWRKS
waxworks
WKT
walkout(n)
wicket
WKTHR
walk-through
WKTK
walkie-talkie
WKVR
walkover(n)
WKW
walkaway(victory)
walkway(area)
WL
awhile(adv)
vale(interj,a
good-by,valley)
voilà(interj,

there it is)
wail(cry)
wale(ridge)
waled
waling
wall(structure)
wallah(occupation)
walleye(eye)
wallow(roll)
waylay(ambush)
waylaid
we'll(we will)
weal(good,ridge)
well(water,fine)
whale (n,v)
(mammal)
whaled
whaling
whaler
whale(v)(strike)
whaled
whaling
wheal(pimple)
wheel(disk)
while(time)
whiled
whiling
wild(not tame)
wile(pass time,
trick)
wiled
wiling
will(future)
shall
would
will(volition,
choose,document)
willow(tree)
willowy(adj)
willowier
willowiest
wily(tricky)
wilier
wiliest
wilily
wiliness
wool(sheep)
woolly(wool)
woollier
woolliest
woolliness
WLB
wallaby
WLBHVD
well-behaved
WLBLNST

well-balanced
WLBN
whalebone
WLBNG
well-being
WLBR
wheelbarrow(tool)
wild boar(animal)
WLBRD
wallboard
well-bred
WLBRN
well-born
WLBS
wheelbase
WLBT
whaleboat
WLCH
Welsh
welsh(swindle)
welshes
WLCHR
welsher(person)
wheelchair(chair)
WLCHZN
well-chosen
WLD
walleyed(stare)
waylaid(ambush)
weald(area)
weld(join)
wheeled
whiled(time)
wield(handle)
wieldy(adj)
wieldier
wieldiest
wild(not tame)
wilds, the
willed(volition)
wold(plain)
WLDBL
wieldable
WLDBR
wild boar
WLDBST
wildebeest
WLDD
wild-eyed
WLDFLR
wildflower
WLDFLWR
wildflower
WLDFR
wildfire
WLDGSCHS

wild-goose chase
WLDKT
wildcat
wildcatted
wildcatting
WLDKTR
wildcatter
WLDLF
wildlife
WLDLNG
wildling
WLDMNT
weldment
WLDN
well-done(adj)
WLDPCH
wild pitch
wild pitches
WLDR
welder(joiner)
wielder(handler)
wilder(wild)
WLDRNS
wilderness
WLDSPZD
well-disposed
WLDVZD
well-advised
WLDWST
Wild West
WLF
well-off
  (prosperous)
wildlife(animals)
wolf(animal)
  wolves
WLFD
well-fed
WLFHND
wolfhound
WLFKST
well-fixed
WLFL
wailful(grief)
willful(force)
WLFLR
wallflower(person)
wildflower(plant)
WLFLWR
wallflower(person)
wildflower(plant)
WLFNDD
well-founded
WLFPK
wolf pack
WLFR

welfare(care)
wildfire(speed)
WLFVRD
well-favored
WLGRMD
well-groomed
WLGRNDD
well-grounded
WLGRR
woolgrower
WLGSCHS
wild-goose chase
WLGTHRNG
woolgathering
WLHD
wellhead
WLHLD
well-heeled
WLHNDLD
well-handled
WLHS
wheel house
WLKDR
wildcatter
WLKM
welcome
welcomed
welcoming
WLKMNG
welcoming
WLKMR
welcomer
WLKNTNT
well-content
WLKT
wildcat(cat)
wildcat(v)(search)
wildcatted
wildcatting
wildcatter(n)
WLKTR
wildcatter
WLM
whelm
WLMD
well-made
WLMNNG
well-meaning
WLMNRD
well-mannered
WLMNT
well-meant
WLN
well-nigh(near)
woolen(wool)
WLNFRMD

well-informed
WLNG
whaling(fishing)
willing(ready)
WLNGNS
willingness
WLNGTN
Wellington
WLNGWL
Wailing Wall
WLNL
willy-nilly
WLNN
well-known
WLNS
Walesa, Lech
woolliness
  woolly
  wool
WLNT
walnut(nut)
well-knit(strong)
WLNTNSHND
well-intentioned
WLP
wallop(hit)
whelp(young dog)
WLPCH
wild pitch
wild pitches
WLPNG
walloping
WLPNTD
well-appointed
WLPPR
wallpaper
WLPR
willpower
WLPRZRVD
well-preserved
WLPWR
willpower
WLR
whaler(person)
wheeler(wheel)
WLRD
well-read
WLRDLR
wheeler-dealer
WLRDRD
well-ordered
WLRNDD
well-rounded
WLRS
walrus
walruses(or)

B:by CH:each D:day F:if G:go H:he HW:why J:joy K:cow KS:ax KWL: equal L:all M:may N:in

walrus
WLRT
wheelwright
WLS
Walesa, Lech
Wallis
WLSH
Welsh(person)
welsh(swindle)
welshes
WLSHR
welsher
WLSHRBT
Welsh rabbit
WLSNFTN
Wallis and Futuna
WLSPKN
well-spoken
WLSPRNG
wellspring
WLSTPLR
wool-stapler
WLSTRT
Wall Street
WLT
wallet(money)
welt(seam,mark)
wilt(limp)
WLTD
well-to-do
WLTH
wealth
wealthy
wealthier
wealthiest
wealthiness
WLTHTV
well-thought-of
WLTHWSP
will-o'-the-wisp
WLTMBRD
well-timbered
WLTMD
well-timed
WLTNG
welting
WLTNT
wall tent
WLTR
welter
WLTRND
well-turned
WLTRWT
welterweight
(136-147 lbs)
WLTS

waltz
waltzes
waltzer
WLTWL
wall-to-wall
WLVRN
wolverine
WLVZ
wolves
wolf
WLW
williwaw(wind)
willowy(adj)(tree)
willowier
willowiest
WLWL
Walla Walla
WLWRN
well-worn
WLWSHR
well-wisher
WLWST
Wild West
WLZ
Wales(Britain)
wilds(area)
willies
(uneasiness)
woollies(fuzzy)
woolly
wool
WM
wham(sound, hit)
whammed
whamming
whammy(magic)
whammies
womb(birth)
WMBL
wamble(turn)
wambled
wambling
wimble(tool)
WMBLDN
Wimbledon
WMBLTN
Wimbledon
WMBT
wombat
WMN
woman
women
WMNFK
womenfolk
WMNG
Wyoming

WMNHD
womanhood
WMNKND
womankind
WMNL
womanly
womanlier
womanliest
womanliness
WMNSH
womanish
WMNZ
womanize
womanized
womanizing
womanizer
WMP
wimp
wimpy(adj)
WMPL
wimple
wimpled
wimpling
WMPM
wampum
WMPR
whimper
WMZ
whimsy
whimsies
WMZKL
whimsical
WMZKLT
whimsicality
whimsicalities
WN
one(number)
wain(wagon)
wan(pale)
wanned
wanning
wanner
wannest
wand(rod)
wane(decrease)
waned
waning
wean(detach)
weenie(food)(or)
wiener
when(time)
whine(complain)
whined
whining
whiner
whinny(neigh)

whinnied
whinnies
whiny(whine)
whinier
whiniest
whininess
win(victory)
won
winning
winner
wind(air)
wine(juice)
wined
wining
winnow(separate)
wino(person)
winy(wine)
winier
winiest
won(money)
won(v,past tense)
win
winning
winner
WNBBNG
winebibbing
WNBBR
winebibber
WNBG
windbag
WNBLN
wind-blown
WNBRK
windbreak
WNBRKR
windbreaker
WNBRN
windborn(in the
air)
windburn(painful)
WNCH
wench(woman)
wenches
winch(hoist)
winches
WNCHL
wind chill(n)
wind-chill
factor
WNCHSTR
Winchester
WND
wand(rod)
wind(air)
wind(wrap)
wound

NGK:ink **P**:pie **R**:air **S**:ice **SH**:show **T**:toy **THN**:thin **TH**:the **V**:of **W**:we **Y**:you **Z**:is **VZHN**:vision

W WNDBG / WNSKT

windy(air)
  windier
  windiest
  windily
  windiness
wound(v,past tense)
wind
WNDBG
  windbag
WNDBKS
  window box
WNDBLN
  wind-blown
WNDBRK
  windbreak
WNDBRKR
  windbreaker
WNDBRN
  windborn(in the
    air)
  windburn(painful)
WNDCHLFKTR
  wind-chill factor
  wind-chill index
WNDD
  winded
WNDDRSNG
  window-dressing
WNDFL
  windfall
WNDJ
  windage
WNDJMR
  windjammer
WNDKN
  wind cone
WNDLS
  windlass(winch)
  windlasses
  windless(no wind)
WNDML
  windmill
WNDP
  wind up(v)
  wound up
  wind-up(n,adj)
WNDPN
  windowpane
WNDR
  wander(stray)
  winder(tool)
  windrow(row)
  wonder(marvel)
WNDRFL
  wonderful

WNDRLND
  wonderland
WNDRLST
  wanderlust
WNDRMNT
  wonderment
WNDRR
  wanderer
WNDRS
  wondrous
WNDRWRK
  wonderwork
WNDRWRKNG
  wonderworking
WNDRWRKR
  wonderworker
WNDRZ
  wind rose
WNDSHD
  window shade
WNDSHLD
  windshield
WNDSHP
  window-shop
  window-shopped
  window-shopping
  window-shopper
WNDSK
  windsock
WNDSKR
  windsucker
WNDSL
  windowsill
WNDSPRNT
  wind sprint
WNDSRFR
  windsurfer
WNDSTRM
  windstorm
WNDSWPT
  windswept
WNDT
  wind tee(weather)
WNDTNL
  wind tunnel
WNDWRD
  windward
WNFL
  windfall
WNG
  whang(n,v)(chunk,
    beat, sound)
  wing(bird)
WNGBK
  wingback
WNGCHR

wing chair
WNGD
  winged
WNGDNG
  wingding
WNGFTD
  wing-footed
WNGGL
  wangle
  wangled
  wangling
WNGK
  eyewink
  wink
  wonky
  wonkier
  wonkiest
WNGKL
  Wankel
  (trademark)
WNGL
  wangle
  wangled
  wangling
WNGLS
  wineglass
  wineglasses
WNGNT
  wing nut
WNGRR
  winegrower
WNGSPN
  wingspan
WNGSPRD
  wingspread
WNGTP
  wing tip(shoe part)
WNHRS
  one-horse(adj)
WNJMR
  windjammer
WNKLRD
  wine-colored
WNKN
  wind cone
WNLNG
  weanling
WNLS
  windlass(winch)
  windlasses
  windless(no wind)
  winless
  (no victory)
WNML
  windmill
WNMNWNVT

one man, one vote
WNNG
  winning
WNNGPST
  winning post
WNP
  one-up
  one-upped
  one-upping
WNPG
  Winnipeg
WNPM
  wine palm
WNPMNSHP
  one-upmanship
WNPNG
  one-upping
WNPRS
  winepress
  winepresses
WNPT
  one-upped
WNR
  whiner(cry)
  wiener(food)
  weenie
  windrow(row)
  winery(wine)
  wineries
  winner(victor)
  winter(season)
WNRT
  wainwright
WNRTM
  wintertime
WNRZ
  wind rose
WNS
  once(one time)
  whence(direction)
  wince(recoil)
  winced
  wincing
  wincer
WNSDD
  one-sided
WNSHLD
  windshield
WNSK
  windsock
WNSKN
  wineskin
WNSKR
  windsucker
WNSKT
  wainscot

B:by **CH**:each **D**:day **F**:if **G**:go **H**:he **HW**:why **J**:joy **K**:cow **KS**:ax **KWL**: equal **L**:all **M**:may **N**:in

WNSLF
oneself
WNSLR
wine cellar
WNSM
winsome
WNSP
Winesap
WNSPRNT
wind sprint
WNSRFR
windsurfer
WNSTRM
windstorm
WNSVR
once-over
WNSWPT
windswept
WNT
want(desire)
went(v,past tense)
  go
  gone
wind tee
  (weather)
won't(will not)
wont(accustomed)
WNTD
want ad
WNTM
one-time(adj)
  (or)
onetime
WNTN
wanton(lewd)
won ton(food)
WNTNG
wanting
WNTNL
wind tunnel
WNTR
winter(season)
wintry(adj)
  wintrier
  wintriest
WNTRGRN
wintergreen
WNTRK
one-track
WNTRTM
wintertime
WNTRZ
winterize
  winterized
  winterizing
  winterization

WNTWN
one-to-one
WNVR
whenever
WNW
one-way
WNWRD
windward
WNZ
winze
WNZD
Wednesday
WP
weep(cry)
  wept
weepy(adj)(weep)
  weepier
  weepiest
  weepily
  weepiness
whip(strike)
  whipped(or)
  whipt
  whipping
whoop(yell)
whoopee(interj)
  (slang)
whop(hit hard)
  whopped
  whopping
wipe(rub)
  wiped
  wiping
  wiper
wop(slang)
WPDD
whoop-de-do
WPHL
weep hole
WPKRD
whipcord
WPLSH
whiplash
  whiplashes
WPN
weapon
WPNG
weeping(crying)
whipping
  (hitting)
whopping(large)
  whopper
WPNGB
whipping boy
WPNGWL
weeping willow

WPNR
weaponry
  weaponries
WPR
weeper(cry)
whooper(one that
  yells)
whopper(big)
  whopping
wiper(wipe)
WPRSNPR
whippersnapper
WPRWL
whippoorwill
WPS
whipsaw(tool)
whoops(interj)
WPSTCH
whipstitch
  whipstitches
WPSTK
whipstock
WPSTL
whipstall
WPT
wapiti(deer)
whipped(beaten)
whippet(dog)
WR
aware(conscious)
hour(time)
our(not yours)
war(fight)
  warred
  warring
ware(articles)
wary(cautious)
  warier
  wariest
  warily
  wariness
we're(we are)
wear(clothed)
  wore
  worn
weary(tired)
  wearied(v)
  wearies(v)
  wearier
  weariest
  wearily
  weariness
  weariless
weir(dam,fence)
were(v, past tense)
  to be

was
where(place)
wherry(boat)
  wherries
whir(revolve)
  whirred
  whirring
wire(metal)
  wired
  wiring
wiry(wire)
  wirier
  wiriest
  wiriness
worry(thoughts)
  worries
  worried
  worrying
  worrier(person)
WRB
whereby
WRBB
war baby
  war babies
WRBL
warble(sing)
  warbled
  warbling
  warbler
wearable(wear)
WRBLR
warbler(bird)
WRBLT
wearability
WRBTS
whereabouts
WRCHS
huaraches
WRD
award(prize)
ward(area)
weird(eerie)
weirdie(or)
weirdo(odd person)
  weirdoes
word(language)
wordy(adj)
  wordier
  wordiest
  wordily
  wordiness
WRDBK
wordbook
WRDD
worded
WRDJ

NGK:ink **P**:pie **R**:air **S**:ice **SH**:show **T**:toy **THN**:thin **TH**:the **V**:of **W**:we **Y**:you **Z**:is **VZHN**:vision

wordage
WRDLS
  wordless
WRDN
  warden
WRDNG
  wording
WRDNS
  war dance
WRDPL
  wordplay
WRDR
  warder(guard)
  wire-draw(stretch)
  wire-drew
  wire-drawn
WRDRB
  wardrobe
WRDRM
  wardroom
WRDVMTH
  word-of-mouth
WRF
  wharf
  wharfs(or)
  wharves
WRFJ
  wharfage
WRFNGR
  wharfinger
WRFR
  warfare(fight)
  wherefore
  (therefore)
WRFRT
  wharf rat
WRFT
  Wirephoto
WRGJ
  wire gauge
WRGMZ
  war games
WRGRS
  wiregrass
WRHD
  warhead
WRHR
  wirehair
WRHRD
  wire-haired
WRHRS
  war-horse
WRHS
  warehouse
WRHZ
  warehouse

warehoused
warehousing
warehouser
WRK
  work
WRKBK
  workbook
WRKBL
  workable(adj)
  workably(adv)
WRKBNCH
  workbench
  workbenches
WRKD
  workaday(adj)
  workday(time)
WRKFRS
  work force
WRKHRS
  workhorse
WRKHS
  workhouse
WRKLD
  workload
WRKMNLK
  workmanlike
WRKMNSHP
  workmanship
WRKNG
  working
WRKNGKLS
  working-class(adj)
WRKNGMN
  workingman
WRKP
  workup(n)(medical)
WRKR
  war cry(yell)
  war cries
  worker(person)
WRKRDR
  wire recorder
WRKRM
  workroom
WRKSHP
  workshop
WRKT
  workout
WRKTBL
  worktable
WRKWK
  workweek
WRL
  whirl(revolve)
  whorl(flywheel)
  world(earth)

WRLBNGK
  World Bank
WRLBRD
  whirlybird
WRLD
  world
WRLDBNGK
  World Bank
WRLDKLS
  world-class(adj)
WRLDL
  worldly
  worldlier
  worldliest
  worldliness
WRLDLWZ
  worldly-wise
WRLDPR
  world power
WRLDPWR
  world power
WRLDSHKNG
  world-shaking
WRLDSRZ
  World Series
WRLDWD
  worldwide
WRLDWR
  world-weary
WRLDWRT
  World War II
WRLDWRWN
  World War I
WRLGG
  whirligig
WRLK
  warlike
  (aggressive)
  warlock(person)
WRLKLS
  world-class(adj)
WRLPL
  whirlpool
WRLPR
  world power
WRLPWR
  world power
WRLRD
  warlord
WRLS
  wireless
WRLSHKNG
  world-shaking(adj)
WRLSRZ
  World Series
WRLWD

worldwide
WRLWR
  world-weary
WRLWRT
  World War II
WRLWRWN
  World War I
WRLWND
  whirlwind
WRM
  warm(heat)
  worm(animal)
  wormy(adj)
  wormier
  wormiest
  worminess
WRMBLDD
  warm-blooded
WRMDVR
  warmed-over
WRMFRNT
  warm front
WRMGR
  worm gear
WRMHL
  wormhole
WRMHRTD
  warmhearted
WRMHWL
  worm wheel
WRMNGGR
  warmonger
WRMNGPN
  warming pan
WRMNT
  worriment
WRMP
  warm up(v)
  warm-up(n)
WRMR
  warmer
  warmest
WRMTH
  warmth
WRMTN
  worm-eaten
WRMWD
  wormwood
WRMWL
  worm wheel
WRN
  warn(notify)
  warren(area)
  wherein(adv)
  worn(v,
    past tense)

B:by **CH**:each **D**:day **F**:if **G**:go **H**:he **HW**:why **J**:joy **K**:cow **KS**:ax **KWL**: equal **L**:all **M**:may **N**:in

wear	**WRST**	wares(articles	wash sale
WRNG	worst(bad)	to sell)	**WSHSTND**
wiring(wire)	worse	whereas(conj)	washstand
WRNNG	wurst(sausage)	worries(thoughts)	**WSHT**
warning	**WRSTD**	**WSBN**	washed
WRNS	worsted(fabric)	waistband(belt)	(v, past tense)
weariness(tired)	**WRT**	westbound(west)	wash
wiriness(wire)	wart(skin)	**WSBND**	wash out(v)
WRNT	warty(adj)	waistband(belt)	(clean, fade)
warrant(sanction)	wartier	westbound(west)	washout(n)
warrantee(person)	wartiest	**WSBSKT**	(failure)
warranty(guarantee)	whereat(conj)	wastebasket	**WSHTB**
warranties	**WRTH**	**WSD**	washtub
weren't(were not)	worth(value)	wayside	**WSHTP**
worn-out(adj)	worthy(adj)	**WSFL**	washed-up
WRNTFSR	worthier	wasteful	**WSHTT**
warrant officer	worthiest	wistful(wishful)	washed-out
WRNTR	worthily	**WSH**	**WSHWSH**
warrantor	worthiness	eyewash(liquid)	wishy-washy
WRP	**WRTHG**	eyewashes	wishy-washier
warp	warthog	wash(clean)	wishy-washiest
WRPLN	**WRTHHWL**	washes	wishy-washiness
warplane	worthwhile	whoosh(rush)	**WSK**
WRPLR	**WRTHLS**	whooshes	whisk(sweep)
wirepuller	worthless	wish(think)	whiskey(drink)
WRPN	**WRTHWL**	wishes	**WSKBRM**
whereupon	worthwhile	**WSHBL**	whisk broom
WRPNT	**WRTM**	washable	**WSKNSN**
war paint	wartime	(cleanable)	Wisconsin
WRPT	**WRTP**	washbowl(bowl)	**WSKR**
warped	wiretap	**WSHBN**	whisker
WRPTH	wiretapped	wishbone	**WSKT**
warpath	wiretapping	**WSHBRD**	waistcoat
WRR	wiretapper	washboard	**WSL**
warrior(fighter)	**WRTPR**	**WSHD**	wassail(hot drink)
wirer(wire)	wiretapper	washday	whistle(noise)
worrier(thinker)	**WRV**	**WSHFL**	whistled
WRS	whereof	wishful	whistling
Warsaw(city)	**WRVR**	**WSHKLTH**	whistler
worse(bad)	wherever	washcloth	**WSLN**
worst	**WRWLF**	**WSHNDWR**	waistline(body)
worsen	werewolf	wash-and-wear	wasteland(area)
WRSHP	werewolves	**WSHNG**	**WSLND**
warship(boat)	**WRWRK**	washing	wasteland(area)
worship(respect)	wirework	**WSHNGTN**	**WSLR**
WRSHPFL	**WRWRT**	Washington	whistler
worshipful	worrywart	**WSHNWR**	**WSLSTP**
WRSHPR	**WRWTH**	wash-and-wear	whistle
worshiper	wherewith	**WSHR**	stop(n)
WRSM	**WRWTHL**	washer	whistle-stop(v)
wearisome(tired)	wherewithal	**WSHRM**	whistle-stopped
worrisome	**WRYR**	washroom	whistle-stopping
(distress)	warrior(fight)	**WSHRWMN**	**WSP**
WRSN	worrier(thinker)	washerwoman	wasp(insect)
worsen	**WRZ**	washerwomen(pl)	Wasp(person)
worse	ours(not yours)	**WSHSL**	Waspy

NGK:ink P:pie R:air S:ice SH:show T:toy THN:thin TH:the V:of W:we Y:you Z:is VZHN:vision

Waspish
Wasp(person)
waspy(adj)
waspier
waspiest
wisp(frail)
WSPNT
West Point
WSPP
waste pipe
WSPPR
wastepaper
WSPR
whisper
WSPSH
waspish
WST
waist(body)
waste(squander)
wasted
wasting
west(direction)
West(region)
whist(n)(game)
whist(v,adj)
(quiet)
WSTBND
waistband(belt)
westbound (west)
WSTBSKT
wastebasket
WSTD
wasted
waste
WSTFL
wasteful
wistful(wishful)
WSTH
waist-high
WSTJ
wastage
WSTJRMN
West Germany
WSTKT
waistcoat
WSTLN
waistline
WSTLND
wasteland
WSTNG
wasting(declining)
westing(west)
WSTNRTHWST
west-northwest
WSTPNT
West Point

WSTPP
waste pipe
WSTPPR
wastepaper
WSTR
waster(person)
wester(west)
WSTRL
wastrel(person)
westerly(wind)
westerlies
WSTRN
western
WSTRNR
westerner
WSTRNSHR
Western Sahara
WSTRNSM
Western Samoa
WSTRNZ
westernize
westernized
westernizing
westernization
WSTSHN
way station
WSTSTHWST
west-southwest
WSTVRJNY
West Virginia
WSTWRD
westward
WT
await(wait)
wait(time)
watt(unit)
way-out(slang)
weight(load)
weighty(adj)
weightier
weightiest
weightily
weightiness
wet(water)
wet(or)
wetted
wetting
wetter
wettest
what(which one)
wheat(grain)
whet(sharpen)
whetted
whetting
whit(tiny bit)
white(color)

whited
whiting
whiten
whiter
whitest
wit(mind)
witted
witting
witty(wit)
wittier
wittiest
wittily
wittiness
WTBK
wetback
WTBL
wettable
WTBLNGKT
wet blanket
WTD
witted(wit)
WTFSD
white-faced(pale)
WTFSH
whitefish
WTGLD
white gold
WTGNSTN
Wittgenstein
Ludwig
WTH
width(distance)
with(beside)
withy(tree,tough)
WTHDD
white-headed
WTHDR
withdraw
withdrew
withdrawn
WTHDRL
withdrawal
WTHDRN
withdrawn
WTHDRWL
withdrawal
WTHHLD
withhold
withheld
withholding
WTHL
withal
WTHN
within
WTHR
weather(wind,

rain)
whether(conj)
whither(place)
wither(dry up)
WTHRBLN
weather balloon
WTHRBND
weather-bound
WTHRBRDNG
weatherboarding
WTHRBTN
weather-beaten
WTHRBYR
Weather Bureau
WTHRD
weathered
white-haired
WTHRKK
weathercock
WTHRMN
weatherman
weathermen
WTHRPRF
weatherproof
WTHRSTRP
weather-strip
weather-stripped
weather-stripping
WTHRSTRPNG
weather
stripping(n)
WTHRVN
weather vane
WTHRWRN
weatherworn
WTHRZ
withers(horse)
WTHS
White House
WTHSTND
withstand
withstood
WTHT
white-hot(hot)
with-it(slang)
without(outside,
unless)
WTJ
wattage
WTKLR
white-collar
WTKP
whitecap(wave)
WTL
wattle(build)
wattled

wattling
white lie
whitlow
whittle(carve)
   whittled
   whittling
   whittler
WTLDR
   white-tailed deer
WTLFNT
   white elephant
WTLFTNG
   weightlifting
WTLFTR
   weightlifter
WTLND
   wetland
WTLNGZ
   whittlings
WTLS
   weightless (light)
   witless(foolish)
WTLSNS
   weightlessness
WTMT
   white meat
WTMTR
   wattmeter
WTN
   whiten
WTNG
   whiting
   (coloring, fish)
WTNGL
   wittingly
WTNNG
   whitening
WTNR
   whitener
WTNRS
   wet nurse(n)
   wet-nurse(v)
   wet-nursed
   wet-nursing
WTNS
   eyewitness
   (witness)
   eyewitnesses
   whiteness(color)
   witness(see)
   witnesses
WTNSTND
   witness stand
WTNT
   whatnot
WTNZ

white noise
WTPPR
   white paper
WTR
   waiter(person)
   water(liquid)
   watery(adj)
   waterier
   wateriest
   wateriness
   watt-hour(unit)
WTRB
   water boy
WTRBFL
   water buffalo
WTRBG
   water bug
WTRBK
   waterbuck
WTRBRN
   waterborne
WTRCHSNT
   water chestnut
WTRCHSTNT
   water chestnut
WTRD
   watered
   water
WTRFL
   waterfall(water)
   waterfowl(bird)
WTRFRNT
   waterfront
WTRGJ
   water gauge
WTRGLS
   water glass
   water glasses
WTRGT
   Watergate
WTRHL
   water hole
WTRHWL
   water wheel
WTRJ
   waterage
WTRKLD
   water-cooled
WTRKLR
   water color(color)
   water cooler(thirst)
WTRKLZT
   water closet
WTRKRFT
   watercraft
WTRKRS

watercourse
   (channel)
   watercress(food)
WTRL
   Waterloo
WTRLG
   waterlog
   waterlogged
   waterlogging
WTRLL
   water lily
   water lilies
WTRLN
   waterline
WTRLS
   waterless
WTRLVL
   water level
WTRM
   white room
WTRMKSN
   water moccasin
WTRMLN
   watermelon
WTRMRK
   watermark
WTRMTR
   water meter
WTRNS
   wateriness
WTRPL
   water polo
WTRPLNT
   water-repellent
WTRPP
   water pipe
WTRPR
   water power
WTRPRF
   waterproof
WTRPRFNG
   waterproofing
WTRPRFT
   waterproofed
WTRPWR
   water power
WTRS
   waitress
   waitresses
WTRSD
   waterside
WTRSFR
   water sapphire
WTRSH
   waterish
   white trash

WTRSHD
   watershed
WTRSK
   water-sick(illness)
   water-ski(sport)
   water-skied
   water-skiing
   water-skis
   water-skier
   water-soak
   (full of water)
WTRSKL
   water cycle
   (ecology)
WTRSKP
   waterscape
WTRSKR
   water-skier
WTRSKZ
   water-skis
WTRSLD
   waterslide
WTRSLYBL
   water-soluble
WTRSNK
   water snake
WTRSPNYL
   water spaniel
WTRSPT
   waterspout
WTRT
   water right
WTRTBL
   water table
WTRTNGK
   water tank
WTRTR
   water tower
WTRTT
   watertight
WTRTWR
   water tower
WTRVPR
   water vapor
WTRW
   waterway
WTRWCH
   water witch(finder)
WTRWL
   water wheel
WTRWNGZ
   water wings
WTRWRKS
   waterworks
WTRWRN
   waterworn

WTRZSTNT
water-resistant
WTS
wits(wit)
WTSH
whitish
WTSTN
whetstone
WTSVR
whatsoever
WTSZM
witticism
WTT
white-tie(adj)
whiteout
(no shadows)
WTVR
whatever
WTWL
whitewall
WTWSH
whitewash
whitewashes
WTWTR
white water
WV
waive(give up)
waived
waiving
waiver
wave(curving
motion)
waved
waving
waver
Wave(Navy woman)
wavy(adj)(wave)
wavier
waviest
waviness
we've(we have)
weave(cloth)
wove
woven(or)wove
weaving
weave(in traffic)
weaved
weaving
wive(marry)
wived
wiving
WVBND
waveband
WVFRM
waveform
WVL

weevil
WVLNGTH
wavelength
WVR
waiver(give up)
waver(one that
waves)
waver(to sway)
weaver(cloth)
WVRBRD
weaverbird
WVZ
WAVES(Navy
women)
wives(wife)
WWRD
wayward
WWT
ahuehuete(tree)
WY
whew(interj)
WZ
was(v, past tense)
is
to be
ways(method)
wheeze(cough)
wheezed
wheezing
wheezy(adj)
wheezier
wheeziest
wheeziness
whiz(sound)
whizzes
whizzed
whizzing
wise(knowledge)
wiser
wisest
wise(way of doing)
wiz(skilled)
woozy(sick)
woozier
wooziest
woozily
wooziness
WZBNG
whiz-bang
WZDM
wisdom
WZDMTTH
wisdom tooth
wisdom teeth
WZG
wise guy

WZKR
wiseacre
WZKRK
wisecrack
WZKRKR
wisecracker
WZL
weasel(animal)
wisely(wise)
WZN
wizen
WZND
weasand
(windpipe)
wizened(wither)
WZNDMNZ
ways and means
WZNT
wasn't(was not)
WZRD
wizard
WZRDR
wizardry(magic)
wizardries

Y

ewe(sheep)
I.O.U.(or)
IOU
IOUs
(I owe you)
oyez(interj)
(court cry)
yaw(weave)
ye(poetic)
you
yea(yes)(interj)
yeah(yes)
yew(tree)
you(not me)
YBKWT
ubiquity
YBKWTS
ubiquitous
YBLT
U-bolt
YBT
U-boat
YCHF
UHF(ultrahigh
frequency)

YD
IUD(intrauterine
device)
yod(or)
yodh(letter)
you'd
(you would)
YDL
yodel(music)
yodeled
yodeling
YDLR
yodeler
YDLZ
utilize
utilized
utilizing
YDLZBL
utilizable
YDLZR
utilizer
YDLZSHN
utilization
YDRN
uterine
YDRS
uterus
YDSH
Yiddish
YF
UFO
UFOs
(unidentified
flying objects)
YFMSTK
euphemistic
YFMSTKL
euphemistically
YFMZ
euphemize
euphemized
euphemizing
YFMZM
euphemism
YFN
euphony
euphonies
YFNK
euphonic
YFNM
euphonium
YFNS
euphonious
YFR
euphoria
YFRK

B:by **CH**:each **D**:day **F**:if **G**:go **H**:he **HW**:why **J**:joy **K**:cow **KS**:ax **KWL**: equal **L**:all **M**:may **N**:in

euphoric
YFYSTK
euphuistic
YFYZM
euphuism
YG
yagi(antenna)
yoga(system)
yogi(person)
yogis
YGN
yogin(yogi)
YGND
Uganda
YGRT
yogurt
YGSLV
Yugoslav(adj,n)
Yugoslavia(country)
YGSLVY
Yugoslavia
YGZ
yogis
yogi
YH
yahoo(person)
yoo-hoo(hail)
YHMB
yohimbe(tree)
YHMBN
yohimbine(drug)
YHNSBRG
Johannesburg
YJN
Eugene
YJNKL
eugenical
YJNKS
eugenics
YK
yak(animal)
Yaqui(Indian)
yech(or)yecch
(interj)(disgust)
yoke(harness)
yoked
yoking
yolk(egg)
yucca(plant)
YKHM
Yokohama
YKL
yokel
YKLL
ukulele
YKLPT

eucalypti
eucalyptus
YKLPTS
eucalyptus
eucalypti(or)
eucalyptuses
YKN
Yukon
YKNTRTR
Yukon Territory
YKR
euchre
YKRST
Eucharist
YKS
ukase
YKTN
Yucatán
YKTYK
yackety-yak
YKZ
ukase
YL
y'all(slang)(you-all)
yawl(boat)
yell(noise)
yellow(color)
yellowy(adj)
you'll(you will)
you-all(you)
yowl(long cry)
Yule(Xmas)
YLBLD
yellow-bellied
YLD
yield
YLG
yule log
YLJ
eulogy
eulogies
YLJKT
yellow jacket
YLJZ
eulogize
eulogized
eulogizing
eulogizer
YLP
yelp
YLS
Yellow Sea
YLSH
yellowish
YLT
Yalta

YLTD
yuletide
YLYLSHN
ululation
YLYLT
ululate
ululated
ululating
YM
yam(food)
yum(interj)
(good taste)
yummy(taste)
yummier
yummiest
YMKPR
Yom Kipper
(Jewish holiday)
Day of Atonement
YMLK
yarmulke
YMN
Yemen(country)
yeoman(person)
yeomen
YMR
yammer
YN
ion(atom)
yawn(open)
yean(baby)
yen(money)
yen(desire)
yenned
yenning
yin(passive force)
yon(or)
yond(distance)
yuan(money,
China,Taiwan)
YND
yond
YNDR
yonder
YNF
unify
unified
unifies
unifier
YNFBL
unifiable
YNFKSHN
unification
YNFR
unifier
YNFRM

uniform
YNFRMT
uniformity
uniformities
YNG
yang(force)
young(age)
YNGK
Yank(person)
yank(pull)
Yankee
YNGSH
youngish
YNGSTR
youngster
YNGTS
Yangtze
YNJZ
Yangtze
YNK
eunuch(person)
eunuches
unique(only)
YNKMRL
unicameral
YNKRN
unicorn
YNKRZ
Yonkers
YNLTRL
unilateral
YNNG
yawning(open)
YNNMS
unanimous
YNNMT
unanimity
YNSF
UNICEF
United Nations
Children's Fund
YNSK
UNESCO
United Nations
Educational,
Scientific and
Cultural
Organization
YNSKCHL
unisexual
YNSKL
unicycle
unicycled
unicycling
unicyclist
YNSKS

NGK:ink **P**:pie **R**:air **S**:ice **SH**:show **T**:toy **THN**:thin **TH**:the **V**:of **W**:we **Y**:you **Z**:is **VZHN**:vision

unisex
YNSKSHL
unisexual
YNSLYLR
unicellular
YNSN
unison
YNSNL
unisonal
YNSNNT
unisonant
YNSNS
unisonous
YNT
unit(one)
unite(join)
united
uniting
unity(union)
unities
yenta(slang)
YNTCHRCH
Uniat Church
YNTDKNGDM
United Kingdom
U.K.(or)UK
YNTDNSHNS
United Nations
U.N.(or)UN
YNTDRBMRTS
United Arab
Emirates
YNTDSTTS
United States
U.S.(or)US
YNTR
unitary
YNTRN
Unitarian
YNTV
unitive
YNTZ
unitize
unitized
unitizing
YNVKL
univocal
YNVLNT
univalent
YNVLV
univalve
YNVRS
universe
YNVRSL
universal
YNVRSLT

universality
YNVRST
university
universities
YNYN
union
YNYNJK
union jack
YNYNZ
unionize
unionized
unionizing
unionization
YNYNZM
unionism
unionist
YNYSY
Yenisei
YNZ
ionize(atom)
YNZN
unison
YP
UPI(news)
United Press
International
yap(bark)
yapped
yapping
yawp(talk,cry)
yep(slang)(yes)
yippee(a shout)
yippie(person)
yuppie(person)
YPPS
eupepsia
YR
ewer(jug)
jura(law)
jus
year(time)
yore(long ago)
you're(you are)
your(possessive,
of you)
YRBK
yearbook
YRD
yard
YRDGDZ
yard goods
YRDJ
yardage
YRDLN
yard line
YRDLR

Eurodollar
YRDMSTR
yardmaster
YRDRM
yardarm
YRDSTK
yardstick
YRGW
Uruguay
YRK
eureka(find)
uric(adj)(urine)
YRLJ
urology
urologist
YRLJKL
urological
YRLNG
yearling(animal)
yearlong
YRM
uremia
YRN
urine(liquid)
yarn(lie,fabric)
year-end(adj)
yearn(desire)
year-round(adj)
(not seasonal)
YRND
year-end(adj)
(at year's end)
year-round(adj)
(not seasonal)
YRNDD
yarn-dyed
YRNK
uranic
YRNL
urinal
YRNLSS
urinalysis
urinalyses
YRNM
uranium
YRNNG
yearning
YRNR
urinary
YRNS
Uranus
YRNT
urinate
urinated
urinating
urination

YRP
Europe
YRPN
European
YRS
uraeus
YRSKP
uroscopy
YRSLF
yourself
yourselves
YRSLVZ
yourselves
YRT
yurt(tent)
yurta(pl)
YRTHM
eurythmy
YRTHMKS
eurythmics
YRTHR
urethra
urethras
(or)urethrae
YRTHRSKP
urethroscope
YRTK
uretic
YRTR
ureter(duct)
YRZ
yours
your
YRZHN
Eurasian
YS
jus(law)
oyez(interj)
(court cry)
U.S.(or)US
United States(n)
U.S.A.(or)USA
United States
of America
yes(consent)
yessed
yessing
YSFL
useful
YSHV
yeshiva
YSJ
usage
YSLS
useless
YSMT

B:by **CH**:each **D**:day **F**:if **G**:go **H**:he **HW**:why **J**:joy **K**:cow **KS**:ax **KWL**: equal **L**:all **M**:may **N**:in

Yosemite
YSR
usury
usuries
YSRP
usurp
usurper
usurpation
YSRPSHN
usurpation
YST
yeast(n)(fungus)
yeasty(adj)
yeastier
yeastiest
yeastiness
YSTKN
Eustachian(tube)
YSTRD
yesterday
YSTRYR
yesteryear
YSTSHN
Eustachian(tube)
YT
Utah(state)
yacht(boat)
yet(time)
YTH
youth
YTHFL
youthful
YTHNZH
euthanasia
YTK
Utica
YTL
ayatollah
YTLT
utility
utilities
YTLTRN
utilitarian
YTLZ
utilize
utilized
utilizing
YTLZBL
utilizable
YTLZR
utilizer
YTLZSHN
utilization
YTNSL
utensil
YTP

utopia
YTPN
utopian
YTRN
U-turn(movement)
uterine(body)
YTRS
uterus
uteri
YTSMN
yachtsman
yachtsmen
YV
you've(you have)
YVYL
uvula
YY
yo-yo
yo-yos
YZ
oyez(interj)
(court cry)
use(v)(utilize)
used
using
user
yaws(disease)
YZBL
usable
YZD
used(adj)
(secondhand)
YZFRKT
usufruct
YZHI
usual
YZHR
usury
usuries
YZHRR
usurer
YZHRS
usurious
YZNG
using(use)
YZNS
usance
YZR
user(use)
usury(money)
usuries
YZRP
usurp
usurper
YZRPSHN
usurpation

YZYFRKT
usufruct

Z

aahs(sound)
oohs
as(equally)
ease(no effort)
eased
easing
easy(adj)(ease)
easier
easiest
easily
easiness
is(v)(exist)
was
to be
am
are
oohs(sound)
aahs
ooze
(n)(lake bottom)
(v)(slow flow)
oozed
oozing
oozy(adj)(slimy)
oozier
ooziest
oozily
ooziness
zoo(animals)
ZB
zebu(animal)
ZBK
xebec
ZBLYN
zabaglione
ZBR
zebra
ZBSTS
asbestos
ZBTS
zaibatsu
ZBY
zebu
ZCHR
easy chair
ZDK
asdic(sonar)

zodiac(symbols)
ZDKL
zodiacal
ZDL
seidel
ZDRP
eavesdrop
eavesdropped
eavesdropping
eavesdropper
ZF
Azov
ZFD
xiphoid
ZFL
zoophile
ZFR
zephyr
ZFTG
zaftig(slang)
ZGNG
easygoing
ZGT
zygote
ZGZG
zigzag
zigzagged
zigzagging
ZGZGR
zigzagger
ZH
Asia
ZHDK
Asiatic
ZHG
gigue
ZHKR
Jacquard
ZHLYN
julienne
ZHLZ
jalousie
ZHNDRM
gendarme
ZHNR
genre
ZHNSDR
jeunesse dorée
ZHR
azure(sky blue)
osier(willow tree)
ZHRDNYR
jardiniere
ZHSN
jacana
ZHTK

NGK:ink **P**:pie **R**:air **S**:ice **SH**:show **T**:toy **THN**:thin **TH**:the **V**:of **W**:we **Y**:you **Z**:is **VZHN**:vision

Asiatic
ZHTZH
agiotage
ZHWDVVR
joie de vivre
ZJGRF
zoogeography
ZKN
zucchini
ZKS
zax
ZKT
zucchetto
ZL
azalea(flower)
easel(art)
Oslo(city)
zeal(eagerness)
ZLCH
zilch
ZLD
xyloid
ZLFN
xylophone
ZLFNST
xylophonist
ZLGRF
xylograph(wood
engraving)
xylography(art)
ZLJ
zoology
ZLJKL
zoological
ZLJST
zoologist
ZLM
Islam(religion)
Islamic
xylem(plant stem)
ZLMBD
Islamabad
ZLN
xylene
ZLS
zealous
ZLT
zealot(person)
zeolite(mineral)
zloty(money)
zloty(or)
zlotys
ZLTK
zeolitic
ZLY
azalea

ZLYN
zillion
ZM
asthma(illness)
ism(doctrine)
zoom(speed)
ZMB
Zambia(country)
zombie(person)
ZMBBW
Zimbabwe
ZMLJ
zymology
ZMLNZ
zoom lens
ZMND
osmund(or)
osmunda(fern)
ZMNT
easement
ZMRJ
zymurgy
ZMS
osmose(move)
osmosed
osmosing
ZMSS
osmosis(movement)
osmotic
osmotically
zymosis
zymotic
zymotically
ZMTH
azimuth
azimuthal
ZN
azan(prayer)
ozone(oxygen)
oxonic(adj)
zany(crazy)
zanies
zanier
zaniest
zaniness
Zen(meditation)
zinnia(plant)
Zion(Israel)
zone(area)
zoned
zoning
ZNBDZM
Zen Buddhism
ZND
Xanadu
ZNDZ

oohs and aahs
ZNFB
xenophobe
(person)
xenophobia(fear of
things foreign)
ZNFBK
xenophobic(adj)
ZNFL
xenophile(lover of
things foreign)
ZNFLS
xenophilous(adj)
ZNG
zing
zinger
ZNGGLS
isinglass
ZNGK
zinc(metal)
zincked (or)zinced
zincking
(or)zincing
zincky(like zinc)
zonk(strike)
ZNGKT
zonked
ZNGLS
isinglass
ZNGM
xenogamy
ZNK
zinc
zincked(or)
zinced
zincking(or)
zincing
ZNL
zonal
ZNNS
zaniness
zany
ZNT
isn't(is not)
ZNTH
zenith
ZNTHS
xanthous
ZNZ
oohs and aahs
(sound)
ozonize(v)
ozonized
ozonizing
ZNZM
Zionism

ZP
zap(hit)
zapped
zapping
zip(speed)
zipped
zipping
zipper
zippy(adj)(speed)
zippier
zippiest
ZPGN
zip gun
ZPKD
Zip Code(or)
ZIP Code
ZPLN
zeppelin
ZPR
zipper
ZR
czar(ruler)
Zaire(country)
zero(nothing)
zeroed
zeroing
zeros(or)
zeroes
zori(thong)
ZRDRM
xeroderma
ZRF
zarf
ZRFLS
xerophilous
ZRFT
xerophyte
ZRGRF
xerography
ZRK
xeric
ZRKN
zircon
ZRKS
Xerox
(trademark)
ZRL
Israel(country)
Israeli(person)
ZRZ
Azores
ZRZM
czarism
ZS
Zeus(mythology)
zoysia(grass)

ZSH
zoysia(grass)
ZST
zest
ZSTFL
zestful
ZSTRT
easy street(or)
Easy Street
ZT
ziti
ZTHR
zither
ZTHRN
zithern
ZTK
Aztec
ZTKN
zootechny
ZTST
zoot suit
ZVRKS
Zovirax(trademark)
ZVYR
Xavier
ZWBK
zwieback
ZYS
Zeus(mythology)
ZZ
zoysia(grass)
ZZH
zoysia(grass)

PUNCTUATION GUIDELINES

Punctuation marks are symbols used for making the meaning of a written sentence easily understood.

- The **PERIOD** is used:

(1) to end a sentence.
- The story is just beginning.

(2) to end an abbreviation.
- Mr. Reed is telling the story.

(3) to separate dollars from cents.
- $2.45

(4) as a decimal point.
- 2.5 lbs.

- The **EXCLAMATION POINT** is used to show strong feeling and emphasis.
  - Wow! She did it on the first try.
  - Now is the time to act!

NOTE: If you use the exclamation point a lot, the reader will soon learn to ignore it. When you want less emphasis or less emotion, use a comma or a period.
  - Now is the time to act.
  - Oh, I thought you wanted it today.

NOTE: Don't use a comma or period after an exclamation point.
  - "Stop!" screamed Tony.
  - Tony screamed, "Stop!"

- The **QUESTION MARK** is used after a direct question.
  - Do you know her name?
  - How many days are in a week?

NOTE: Indirect questions are not followed by question marks.
  - Timothy wondered if Margot knew the answer.

NOTE: Don't use a comma or period after a question mark.
  - "Why not?" he asked.
  - He asked, "Why not?"

? ? ? ? ? ? ? ? ? ?

- The **COMMA** is used:

(1) to separate independent clauses that are joined by conjunctions (and, but, or, nor, for, so, yet).
  - Alfred sings well and plays the piano, but he cannot read or write music.

NOTE: The comma *may* be left out if there is no possibility of confusing the reader. This is especially true with short and tightly connected clauses.
  - He ate the cookies and she ate the rice.
                    (or)
  - He ate the cookies, and she ate the rice.

(2) after an adverbial clause that begins a sentence.
  - Although all of the chicken had been eaten, there was plenty of dressing left to eat.
  - Before he could grab the plate of dressing, all of the lights went out.

(3) after an introductory phrase.
  - Having eaten the fish, Sally turned out the lights.
  - Pleased with the results, Frank stopped polishing his car.

NOTE: If a phrase or noun clause or a quote is the subject of a sentence, it is *not* separated from the verb by a comma.
  - Changing barbers in the middle of a haircut can be risky.
  - "I'll meet you in twenty minutes" were Sam's exact words.

(4) after introductory words and expressions.
- Yes, I believe she is correct.
- Still, there is room for doubt.
- No, I can't wait any longer.
- Fine, I'll see you later.
- By the way, have you seen Karen lately?
- On the other hand, have you not seen her?

(5) to set off a word, phrase or clause that is not necessary to the meaning of the sentence.
- Sally, the girl in the blue dress, was the one who saved the baby from drowning.
- Courage, then, is not the sole property of elders.
- Frank, who is a very good shot, made four baskets in a row.
- You may, if you want to, try again.
- Ms. Brown, a stamp collector, teaches math.
- Ms. Brown, they agreed, is an excellent teacher.

NOTE: Dashes, parentheses and commas may all be used to set off additional material: dashes set off sharply and give emphasis; parentheses are softer and do not emphasize; commas are the most common and mildest separators.
- The fishing — as Ivan said — is great.
- The fishing (as Ivan said) is great.
- The fishing, as Ivan said, is great.

(6) before a direct quotation.
- Frank said, "It's time to go."

(7) after a direct quotation.
* "It's time to go," Frank said.

NOTE: In the two examples above, the comma is *outside* the quotation marks when it comes before the quotation. The comma is *inside* the quotation marks when it's after the quotation.

NOTE: Don't use the comma after a quotation if the quote ends with a question mark or an exclamation point.
* "It's time to go!" Frank said.
* "It's time to go?" Frank said.

(8) to set off contrasting words and phrases.
* Tyrone has changed his style, not his music.
* The chicken, but not the dressing, was completely gone.

NOTE: When there is no contrast, the comma is not needed.
* Tyrone has changed his style and his music.
* The chicken as well as the dressing were completely gone.

(9) to separate words, phrases and clauses that make up a series of three or more items.
* Alice likes oranges, bananas, grapes and green apples. (or)
* Alice likes oranges, bananas, grapes, and green apples.

NOTE: When a conjunction is used before the last item in a series, the last comma *may* be omitted (but it doesn't have to be). If the absence of the last comma causes a lack of clarity in the meaning of the sentence, use the comma.
* Alice likes oranges, grapes, green apples, and bananas.
(If the final comma is omitted in this example, it might seem that Alice also likes green bananas.)

(10) to separate adjectives that share an *equal* relationship to the noun they modify.
- It was a beautiful, misty morning.
- He wants only strong, talented, dedicated players on his team.

NOTE: If you can substitute the word *and* for the comma (without having an odd sounding sentence), you can use the comma. If the sentence sounds odd when substituting the word *and* for the comma, do not use the comma.
- Juan picked six large ripe green apples from the tree.

The type of adjectives that cause odd sounding sentences when linked with the word *and* usually refer to:
    age (new, old, young, ripe, etc.)
    number (six, sixty-four, etc.)
    size (large, small, medium, etc.)
    location (southern, northern, etc.)
    color (red, green, etc.)

(11) to set off locations in addresses and geography.
- Dallas, Texas, is the home of the Cotton Bowl.
- Sally was born in Paris, France.
- Mr. Smith's address is 410 Main Street, Big Rock, Maryland 21212.

NOTE: The ZIP code is never separated from the name of a state with a comma. (It is separated from the state by two spaces.)
- San Diego, CA 92129

(12) to set off items in dates.

- Carlos is arriving Sunday, May 12, 1987.

NOTE: The comma *may* be omitted after the month—if
      (a) the day of the month is not given or
      (b) the day number comes before the month.
- Sally came to this country in August, 1986.
              (or)
- Sally came to this country in August 1986.
- Sally has to return to France on 19 August 1987.

(13) to separate thousands in numbers.

- 2,936,217

NOTE: The comma may be omitted in numbers that are less than 10,000.

- 7654 (or) 7,654

(14) to set off titles.

- Dr. Betty Couch, Dean of Students, will speak to the group.
- Billy Bob Shames, Jr., plays the violin.
- Harvey Nose, M.D.
- Betty Couch, Ph.D.

NOTE: Commas are not used to set off Arabic or Roman numerals that follow a name.

- John J. Brown III plays the flute.
- Alonso J. Brown 3d plays the flute.

(15) after the salutation in a personal letter.

- Dear Maria,

(16) after the closing in a letter.

- Love,
- Sincerely,

(17) to set off direct address.

- Do you deny, Ian, that you were blushing?
- I would like to talk to you, Herman.

- The **SEMICOLON** is used:

(1) to link independent clauses that are not joined by a conjunction.
- Osami ate the ice cream; his gerbil ate the lettuce.
- Some students work part-time; some work full-time; others do not work at all.

NOTE: A period should separate the independent clauses if the thoughts are not closely related.
- Some students work part-time. Some of the teachers are interested in astronomy.

(2) to link independent clauses that have commas in them.
- Miguel ate the ice cream; in fact, he ate all of it.
- Sally is now living in our country; however, she has to return to France next year.

(3) to separate items in a series when the items themselves contain commas.
- The class officers are Barbara Happerage, president; Max Pepper, vice president; Leo Soundly, secretary; and Joy Whitworth, treasurer.

NOTE: Items in a series may be separated by semicolons alone. This special use gives emphasis to the items. (Be careful not to overuse writing techniques that give emphasis. If you do, the emphasis is lost.)

(4) before a word, phrase or abbreviation that comes before material that explains.
- I am impressed with Amahl's work; for example, his use of vivid colors, his choice of subject matter and his attention to details.
- I was advised to buy the essentials; i.e., hiking shoes, backpack and compass.

- The **COLON** is used:

(1) to call attention to what is to follow.
- Rodney had only one desire: to breathe.

NOTE: When the colon is used in this manner, it serves like an equals (=) symbol: what has gone before is equal to what comes next.
- John finally told me the secret of his success: persistence.
- The items that you will need are as follows: the clothes on your back, a pillow, a toothbrush and a flashlight.
- Three people are expected to be present: Judy, Louis and Christine.

NOTE: The use of the colon brings emphasis to what follows, so don't use it needlessly. The examples above can be expressed in other ways.
- John finally told me that persistence was the secret to his success.

(2) to show that what follows explains or develops what has gone before.
- Rodney's only desire was to breathe: he was trapped underneath six feet of snow.

(3) after the greeting of a business letter.
- Dear Mr. Green: • Dear Ms. Burns:
- Gentlemen:

(4) to separate chapter and verse.
- Genesis 1:1

(5) to separate volume and page numbers in periodicals.
- 20:81 (refers to volume 20, page 81)

(6) to separate hours, minutes and seconds.
- 3:15 p.m. • 8:05 a.m. • 14:03:45

(7) after correspondence headings.
- To: • From: • Via: • Attention:

- The **APOSTROPHE** is used:

(1) to show possession.
  - Mary's hair • Carlo's robot

NOTE: Possession is usually formed by an apostrophe plus an *s*. Words that already end with an *s* usually just need the apostrophe to show possession.
  - the boys' team (the team the boys are on)
  - the boy's team (the team the boy is on)

NOTE: An exception is the word *it*. To show possession, do not use the apostrophe; just add *s*.
  - Its shape is hard to see in the dark.

NOTE: Don't confuse possession with description.
  - the cat's food (food belonging to the cat)
  - the cat food (describes the type of food)

(2) to show that parts of words or numbers are missing.
  - he's (he is) • you're (you are)
  - he'll (he will) • I'm (I am)
  - 'cause (because) • it's (it is)
  - the class of '87 (the class of 1987)

(3) to form plurals of letters, abbreviations and numbers.
  - Mr. Burns always says, "Cross your t's."
  - Some Ph.D.'s are also M.D.'s.
  - Her 8's look like two circles.

NOTE: The apostrophe is optional in forming plurals of numbers and capital letters that are not followed by a period.
  - the 1980s (or) the 1980's
  - her 8s (or) her 8's • his Bs (or) his B's
  - all PTAs (or) all PTA's
  - all P.T.A.'s

- **QUOTATION MARKS** are used:

(1) to set off direct quotations.
- Carl said, "I'll be glad to go."
- "Be home by 10 o'clock," Stella replied.

NOTE: Quotation marks set off the exact words of a speaker or writer. If you use an indirect quotation, quotation marks are not needed even if the words are exact.
- Carl said that he would be glad to go.
- Stella said to be home by 10 o'clock.

NOTE: You can set off a long quotation by:
> (a) writing it on a shorter line. (Indent on both sides and do not enclose with quotation marks.)

> (or)

> (b) beginning each paragraph of the quotation with a quotation mark and ending *only the last* paragraph with a quotation mark.

NOTE: Single quotation marks are used to set off a quotation within a quotation.
- Stella said, "I was glad to hear Carl say, 'I'll be glad to go.'"

(The British use single quotation marks to set off quotations and double quotation marks to set off a quotation within a quotation.)

(2) to set off fragments of quoted material.
- Carl made it clear that he was "glad to go."

NOTE: Emphasis is given to Carl's words when enclosed by quotation marks. If you don't want or need this emphasis, don't use the quotation marks.

(3) to emphasize a special word or to show that a word is used in a special way.

- When Olga said her frog had "croaked," she meant that her frog had died.
- When printed matter goes to the very edge of a page, it is called a "bleed."
- The word "moonshine" is another word for illegal liquor.

(4) to enclose titles of short stories; poems; chapters; lessons; reports; essays; articles; songs; radio and TV programs; and works of art such as paintings, sculptures, photographs and drawings when you mention them in your writing.

- "Mork and Mindy" is still being rerun.
- "Ode to Mario" is Sandra's best poem.
- "The Race" is the most exciting chapter.

NOTE: Titles of books, periodicals, epic poems, and major works of art and music are *not* enclosed with quotation marks when you write about them: they are written in capital letters or underlined. (Italics are used in printed matter.)

- Renoir's <u>Two Little Circus Girls</u> is a famous painting.
- TIME magazine's story on astronomy included many good photographs.
- Herman Melville's *Moby-Dick* is a great novel.

- **PARENTHESES** are used:

(1) to enclose additional comments and to set off material that explains or illustrates.
- Ronald is hoping (as we all are) that Judy will soon be well.
- Thomas Edison (1847-1931) invented the light bulb in 1879.
- The program will start at 3 p.m. MDT (mountain daylight time).
- The fee is five dollars ($5.00).

NOTE: Dashes, parentheses and commas may all be used to set off additional material: dashes set off sharply and give emphasis; parentheses are softer and do not emphasize; commas are the most common and mildest separators.
- The fishing — as Ivan said — is great.
- The fishing (as Ivan said) is great.
- The fishing, as Ivan said, is great.

(2) to enclose letters or numbers that make up a list when that list is in a sentence.
- Juanita's work will be judged on (a) creativity, (b) completeness and (c) correctness.
- Ginger said to (1) wash the dishes, (2) wash the clothes, (3) wash the car and (4) mow the lawn.

(3) to show alternatives.
- Please check the topic(s) you enjoy most.
                        (or)
- Please check the topic or topics you enjoy most.

- **BRACKETS** are used to set off the writer's comments, especially within quoted material.
  - Betty said, "It [the Fourth of July] was the best ever."

NOTE: An error, a questionable fact or a questionable expression in a quotation is followed by the Latin word *sic* (meaning "thus") enclosed in brackets. This shows the reader that you are quoting exactly and are aware of the questionable material or mistake.
  - The report stated, "Mr. Reed recieved [*sic*] only minor injuries."
  - "Thomas Edison invented the light bulb in 1889 [*sic*]." (or)
  - "Thomas Edison invented the light bulb in 1889 [actually in 1879]."

[ ]

[ ]

[ ]

[ ]

[ ]

[ ]

[ ]

[ ]

[ ]

[ ]

[ ]

- The **DASH** is used:

(1) to mark a sudden break in thought.
- Barry has a problem—but who doesn't.
- Ann moans and groans—laughing all the way to the bank—about what a bad job she has.

(2) to set off sharply and give special emphasis to added material.
- Mr. Olive is going to talk to Robert—in fact, he's going to talk to everyone—about the broken window.

NOTE: Dashes, parentheses and commas may all be used to set off additional material: dashes set off sharply and give emphasis; parentheses are softer and do not emphasize; commas are the most common and mildest separators.
- The fishing—as Ivan said—is great.
- The fishing (as Ivan said) is great.
- The fishing, as Ivan said, is great.

NOTE: To keep your writing expressive, don't use the dash as a substitute for commas or parentheses.

(3) to set off added material when the added material already has commas.
- Four people—Juan, Margaret, Sara and Kevin—have qualified for the finals.

(4) to set off an introductory series when the sentence explains or develops the series.
- Rugs, curtains, furniture—everything was clean and in its place.

(5) to show an interrupted or unfinished statement and hesitant or faltering speech.
- "Johnny, don't slam the—"
- "Well—er—ah—I thought I knew."

- The **ELLIPSIS** is used:

(1) to show that part of a quotation has been left out.
  - Harold said, "I'll be back . . . after I've cleaned up." (The original quote reads: "I'll be back in twenty minutes, after I've cleaned up.")

NOTE: If the missing words come at the end of a quoted sentence, four periods are used: one period to end the sentence and three periods for the missing words.
  - Harold said, "I'll be back . . . ."

NOTE: Four periods are also used if one or more sentences are left out of a quotation.

(2) to show an interrupted or unfinished statement and hesitant or faltering speech.
  - "Johnny, don't slam the . . ."
  - "Well . . . er . . . ah . . . I thought I knew."

- The **VIRGULE** or **SLASH** is used:

(1) to show alternatives.
  - Each student must have written permission from his/her parents.
  - You can buy a ticket to go to Denver and/or Dallas.

NOTE: Writing that has slashes in it is harder to comprehend. The slash can many times be avoided by rewriting the sentence.
  - All students must have written permission from their parents.

(2) to separate lines of verse when the verse is written with prose.
  - Leroy's poem goes like this: "Roses are red, violets are blue/Flowers are poetry, and so are you."

DIRECT PURCHASE

If *Word Finder* is not available through your bookstore, it can be purchased directly from Pilot Light by sending us your name, address, and a check or money order for $12.95 (per copy). If you purchase three or more copies, send $11.00 (per copy).

Send your orders to:

> Pilot Light
> PO Box 305
> Stone Mountain, GA 30086-0305

- The above prices include shipping and handling charges.
- Please allow three to four weeks for delivery.
- Georgia residents — please add sales tax.